African Studies and Research Forum Series

The African Studies and Research Forum Series invites monographs and contributed volumes on Africa and related topics written by authors from across the academic disciplines. The contributors will encompass the more than 400 active members of the African Studies and Research Forum (ASRF) across the globe and other non-members interested in the organization's broader and global conceptualization of Africa and, thus, topics dealing with Africa and its diaspora. Members of the AFSR hail from political science, economics, international relations, the humanities, social sciences, natural sciences, formal sciences, and applied sciences.

All titles in this series are peer-reviewed.

Abdul Karim Bangura • JP Afamefuna Ifedi
Editors

Conceptualizations of Africa

Perspectives from Sciences and Humanities

Springer

Editors
Abdul Karim Bangura
Center for Global Peace
American University
Washington, DC, USA

JP Afamefuna Ifedi
Department of Political Science
Howard University
Washington, DC, USA

ISSN 2948-2399 ISSN 2948-2402 (electronic)
African Studies and Research Forum Series
ISBN 978-3-031-74534-8 ISBN 978-3-031-74535-5 (eBook)
https://doi.org/10.1007/978-3-031-74535-5

This Springer imprint is published by the registered company Springer Nature Switzerland AG
The registered company address is: Gewerbestrasse 11, 6330 Cham, Switzerland

To Africans Everywhere!

Acknowledgments

We, and hopefully many readers, owe gratitude to the following:

The Creator, for providing us the analytical and rational reality to do this work.

The anonymous reviewers, for their substantive evaluations. Asking difficult questions leads to better answers and clarifications.

Our immediate and global families, for their prayers and support.

Contents

General Introduction

Abdul Karim Bangura and JP Afamefuna Ifedi

In 1988, what came to be Valentin-Yves Mudimbe's most celebrated book, *The Invention of Africa: Gnosis, Philosophy, and the Order of Knowledge*, was published by Indiana University Press. It was the first significant work that sought to examine multiple African and non-African scholarly discourses pertaining to the conceptualizations of Africa and being African. As a philosopher, Mudimbe tendered the following philosophical renderings of the meanings on the subject matter: (a) African genesis, (b) African conversion, (c) African gnosis, (d) Africanism/Africanity, (e) curse of Ham, (f) poor savage Africans, (g) Dark Continent, (h) primitives, (i) geography of monstrosity, (j) African authenticity, and (k) Blackness. It is quite obvious that these concepts are not exhaustive of the numerous ways Africa has been denoted in most of the academic disciplines.

A sequel to the preceding book written by Mudimbe and titled *The Idea of Africa* was also published by Indiana University Press in 1994. This book continues the discussion on the preceding conceptualizations, focusing on their constructions by the Western world.

The subsequent significant work on the subject matter did not come until 2018. It is titled *Doing Conceptual History in Africa* (2018) and edited by Axel Fleisch and Rhiannon Stephens. This book utilizes an array of novel methods to delineate a wider interdisciplinary approach to African historical studies. The foci of the chapters are on the multiplex function of language in Africa's historical development, paying specific attention to pragmatics and semantics. As Fleisch and Stephens put it, "From precolonial dynamics of wealth and poverty to the conceptual foundations of nationalist movements, each contribution strikes a balance between the local and

A. K. Bangura (✉)
Center for Global Peace, American University, Washington, DC, USA

J. A. Ifedi
Department of Political Science, Howard University, Washington, DC, USA
e-mail: Jifedi@howard.edu

A. K. Bangura, J. A. Ifedi (eds.), *Conceptualizations of Africa*, African Studies and Research Forum Series, https://doi.org/10.1007/978-3-031-74535-5_1

the global, engaging with a distinctively African intellectual tradition while analyzing the regional and global contexts in which categories like 'work,' 'marriage,' and 'land' take shape" (2018, p. 1). Since Fleisch is an Africanist focusing on language and linguistics and Stephens is an Africanist historian, it is therefore not accidental that the conceptualizations on Africa are limited to those two fields. In essence, while this book is a slight improvement over Mudimbe's books, it also falls short in exploring the very many ways Africa has been conceptualized in most of the academic disciplines.

The present book transcends the preceding limitation and offers a comprehensive range of disciplinary conceptualizations and analyses of what Africa is. In order to ensure balance, uniformity, cohesion, and coherence among the chapters, each chapter entails (a) an introduction section that encompasses what the chapter is about, a general definition of the selected discipline, the essence of investigating how Africa is conceptualized in the discipline, and what follows in the rest of the chapter; (b) a section on the conceptualization of the discipline that examines its key ideas, support for the ideas, critiques of the ideas, and a synthesis of the competing positions; (d) three analytical sections that provide a different example in each section on how Africa has been conceptualized and analyzed in the discipline by looking at competing views on the endeavor and synthesizing those views; and (d) a section on conclusion and recommendations that embodies a summary of the key points, implications of the points, and suggestions for future research.

Since the essence of this book hinges upon multidisciplinary conceptualizations and analyses of what Africa is, the rest of this chapter entails discussions of (a) what multidisciplinary denotes and (b) its importance. We present these aspects separately for lucidity. Before doing all this, however, we end this section with what seems as the most ascendant definition of Africa.

A Google search on January 15, 2023, of the question, "What is Africa?" in quotation marks so that only those entries which have the exact statement would emerge yielded about 1290.000 results in 0.92 seconds. The definition that came up first and most repeated by other sources is the following from the Idea Group Inc. (IGI) Global, i.e., Africa is "a term used in identifying all indigenous and migrant ethnicities living in the second biggest continent in the world" (IGI Global, 2022, p. 1). The organization then goes on to present 15 other geographical descriptors of the continent. It is the aforementioned general definition of Africa that is referred to whenever the continent is mentioned in this book.

Denotation of the Multidisciplinary Approach

The conceptualization of Africa from a multidisciplinary perspective requires an in-depth understanding of both the general and specific views of how Africa, a continent of profound interest to many, is viewed and understood by salient, if not all, disciplines. Africa is a geographical region steeped in misconceptions and discordant comprehension. It is, therefore, critical to present perspectives of Africa from the standpoint of respective disciplines in order to establish a heightened knowledge of the entity that we are analyzing.

We focus here on the denotation of the multidisciplinary approach to facilitate a better understanding of Africa by conceptualizing it through the lens of many distinct disciplines. Essentially, we seek to present in this section the meaning of the multidisciplinary approach, which is a method of research and/or analysis. The multidisciplinary approach involves drawing appropriately from multiple disciplines to redefine problems outside of normal boundaries and delineate solutions based on a new understanding of complex situations; it also enables a researcher to undertake the elucidation of a subject matter by borrowing concepts and techniques from other subject areas in a study.

It is necessary here to explain the approach relative to its general description, as well as its value as a research method. From an etiological standpoint, the word "multidisciplinary" is first recorded in the period of 1945–1950; and it connotes combining the disciplines of many different branches of learning or research. According to the *Webster's New World College Dictionary*, "multi means combining form, meaning 'many,' 'much,' multiple,' 'many times,' 'more than one,' 'more than two,' 'compound of many like parts,' 'in many respects,' used in the formation of compound words" (2023, p. 1). Multidisciplinary is also defined as bringing together the tools, viewpoints, and understandings of two or more disciplines (Dhadphale & Baughman, 2018).

Multidisciplinary thinking therefore centers primarily on different disciplines and the many and different perspectives and what they together bring to an illustration, conception, and understanding of an idea, issue, theme, or topic. Thus, a multidisciplinary approach can be employed to study a subject matter from the standpoint of multiple or more than one discipline. Essentially, the multidisciplinary approach involves the ability and leverage to study one topic from the vantage point of more than one discipline. In addition, it is evident that the multidisciplinary approach can be applied to the study of phenomena while still not overstepping their own disciplinary boundaries. Furthermore, the multidisciplinary approach entails drawing ideas from many distinct disciplines to define or redefine an issue or theme beyond the bounds and reach solutions based on a new understanding of an indefinite, complex, or indeterminate position. So, the multidisciplinary approach is a very effective way of elevating knowledge and sharpening an understanding of a phenomenon.

For linguists, the denotation of an expression, any expression for that matter, represents its literal meaning. So, generally, denotations are important elements of the meaning of a subject of discussion; accordingly, denotations are important in all fields as aspects of meaning. For example, the English word "warm" denotes the property of being warm. To contrast denotation with other aspects of meaning to include connotation would yield a word association such as described in the following manner of word meaning association: the word "warm" may evoke the feeling of calmness or coziness, but these associations are not part of the word's denotation. Similarly, an expression's denotation is separate from pragmatic or creative inferences which the word might trigger. For instance, describing something as "warm" often implies that it is "not hot," but this once again is not part of the word's denotation. Essentially then, denotation plays a major role in several fields; and, within the philosophy of language, denotation is studied as an important aspect of meaning. In natural language semantics, denotations are conceived as the outputs of the semantic component of grammar. For instance, the denotation of the word "blue" is the property of being blue and the denotation of the word (Afamefuna) is the person who goes by that name (Heim & Kratzer, 1998).

Based on the preceding viewpoint, it is evident that the concept of denotation is an important aspect of scholarship, as it enables a scholar and a learner to have clarity regarding the subject of discussion and/or examination. Without proper detonation of a subject matter, any scholarly exercise would be indeterminate, unclear, or nebulous, at best. Moreso, as a matter of further explanation, detonations can be extended to the nature of phrases. By way of example, the verb phrase "pass the class" denotes the property of having passed the class. Depending on one's theory of semantics, denotations may be identified either with terms, extensions, intensions, or other structures such as context change potentials (Nowen et al., 2016). Furthermore, when uttered in discourse, expressions may convey other associations which are not computed by the grammar and thus not part of its detonation. Hence, depending on the context, saying, "I ran five miles" may convey that you ran exactly five miles, and not more. This context is not part of the sentence's denotation, but it is a rather pragmatic inference arrived at by applying social cognition to its denotation (Kroger, 2019).

To further elucidate the nature, nuances, and character of denotation, it is important to clarify the difference between denotation and reference. In essence, denotation is distinctly different from reference, although they share a similarity. Linguistic discussion of the distinction between denotation, meaning, and reference is founded on the work of Ferdinand de Saussure, specifically in his theory of semiotics (Herbst, 2010). Other philosophers such as Gottlieb Frege and Bertrand Russel have also made important contributions to the understanding of the difference between "denotation" and "reference" (Makin, 2000). Essentially, the two terms should not be conflated. A reference is a specific place, thing, or person which a referrer, speaker, or writer identifies when gesturing, speaking, or writing. The explication of this idea is evident in John Searle's theory explained in his famous book titled *Speech Acts: An Essay in the Philosophy of Language* (1969). According to this theory, a speaker's action of identifying a person, place, or thing is called "referring." This specific person, place, or thing identified by the speaker is called the "referent." "Reference" itself captures the relationship between the referent in the word phrase used by the speaker. Before referring to expressions, the denotation of the phrase is most likely the phrase's referent. For content words, the denotation of the word can refer to any object, real or imagined, to which the word could be applied (Kroeger, 2019).

Additionally, many types of research can fit under the term multidisciplinary. They include the following: additive, non-disciplinary, integrated, synthetic, fusion of disciplines, and diffusion of disciplines. The subsequent paragraphs will elaborate on the meanings of these variants of the multidisciplinary approach.

In the case of the additive variance of the multidisciplinary approach, research entities are formed by various disciplines working separately. It means adding disparate things—studies, experience, interests, etc.—together to produce or alter the general quality of a research goal. In this case, generally, there are no linkages between the research groups and disciplines, and there is no concerted attempt to unify or synthesize their results, but often independent results could be included in the collective final work. And, usually, mutual respect among the disciplines is preserved.

Regarding the non-disciplinary form, no discipline can address the subject of study or research; hence, approaches derived from other or distant disciplines are applied. Also, even more to the point, this involves combining knowledge that is not emanating from a discipline of any sort at all; such knowledge can be culled from local knowledge, heuristic activity, or even native intelligence, meaning formally or informally acquired knowledge of everyday life, and knowledge that is embedded in the actions and reflections of the subjects that the researchers may also be involved or engaged in studying. Moreover, it may involve researchers independently addressing issues in their various disciplines. Essentially, the non-disciplinary variant of the multidisciplinary approach is fundamentally inclusive of self-direction, abolishing any divisions among the disciplines (Baldwin & Koh, 2012).

Vis-à-vis the integrative variant of the multidisciplinary approach, the word "integrated" means, basically to blend, form, or coordinate into a unified whole, perhaps into a larger unit of any issue or research; the subject matter is no longer a stand-alone issue but part of a whole. And, from a definitional standpoint, the integrated multidisciplinary approach entails making connections among concepts, studies, or experiences to enhance or enable the transfer of information, knowhow, and/or skills to be applied to a new research challenge or a complicated issue. In this case, many disciplines are utilized in the study, and a synthesis of disciplinary outcomes is developed. There is mutual harmony, respect, and understanding among the disciplines. Collaboration happens whenever it is necessary. It enables the researchers to understand, and perhaps recognize and articulate relationships among subject matters and apply learning from many areas to develop answers to a particular subject. In other words, through integrated studies one can bring together traditionally separate subjects to enhance the understanding of a subject matter of interest.

This form of multidisciplinary approach enables interaction, and such an interaction among disciplines can develop so intricately and extensively that it can turn into a new self-standing discipline, with its own principles, assumptions, and characteristics. Many disciplines are spin offs from other disciplines: examples include Political Economy, International Relations, etc. Therefore, it is a process of integrating support from more than one source for one idea or argument while also identifying how sources are related to one another and to a researcher's main idea. It is an acknowledgment of how the material from several sources may address the same question or research topic. When information is gathered from many sources and fashioned into a research project, the sources of the information are essentially synthesized and/or integrated information, basically putting things together and merging information from many sources to address a subject matter.

In the case of the diffusion of knowledge, this approach involves the flow of knowledge among disciplines and helps, at times, to determine disciplinary boundaries. It also concerns knowledge exchange which has cross-enriching properties for all the disciplines that might be involved in the knowledge diffusion process research model. Essentially, this method is characterized by the gathering of data about one subject matter by a researcher at a single point in time in a study following a widespread diffusion of knowledge from different disciplines. Diffusion concerns how knowledge moves from many individual disciplines or diverse subject areas. Essentially, the movement from one discipline to another can be attained and maximized for the benefit of all the disciplines involved in general and to other diverse subject matters and areas. It also pertains to the movement of ideas across academic or cognitive spaces. This concept succinctly explains how in the quest for discovery and production of knowledge, the idea of having a source of knowledge and to process it in such a way as to enable it to reach and enrich other disciplines is quite essential to the knowledge evolution and development effort. This process and method would deepen and broaden research by alloying the materials of study through having them intermingle and commingle for the benefit of knowledge enrichment.

The multidisciplinary aspect of fusion of disciplines also enables diffusion in the dissemination of tangible or intangible knowledge within a certain frame of reference. The fusion of disciplines entails the process of combining information from two or more input disciplines of study which would subsequently contain more information than the initial disciplines (Kaur & Kaur, 2012). As its name implies, the fusion of disciplines entails the mixing together of various subjects, thereby blurring the lines that distinguish various disciplines. Fusion of disciplines allows scholars to learn about or develop approaches that are similar in various disparate subject matter areas, as the various strands of knowledge that apply to the goal of interest are fused and blended into one study area, even if it takes place regarding different subject matter areas. So, in social studies, for instance, there is a distinct trend toward some type of fusion or merging, interweaving, or integrating of subjects (Preston, 2023).

The foregoing explication and analysis of the nature and forms, as well as the value of the multidisciplinary research approach, is meant to bring some clarity to the subject matter. It is also meant to advance the points of view to be adopted by the contributing scholars regarding the subject matter of this book.

Importance of the Multidisciplinary Approach

Having discussed in the preceding section what multidisciplinary is, we now turn our attention to the import of the approach. Numerous observers have pointed out many advantages of the multidisciplinary approach that make it important, a detailed discussion of which can take at least a book, if not more. Here, we present synopses of 23 suggestions for the sake of brevity. Some of the suggestions share certain characteristics and/or are labeled differently. So, we beg your indulgence in advance for the few overlaps in the ensuing review.

First, the multidisciplinary approach is important because it has emerged as "the most viable and efficacious approach" for solving multiplex problems. In an epoch of fast moving society, many types of socioeconomic problems, having relation to many disciplines, have arisen; this, of course, calls for a comprehensive approach to delineate solutions for the problems. For instance, "economists may focus on cost-effective mechanisms; sociologists on empowering the poor and addressing social inequity; anthropologists on acknowledging local customs, practices and social structures; psychologists on attributions of responsibility" (Choudhary, 2015, p. 1). Ignoring these variegated aspects, and the interactions of economic, sociological, and anthropological/cultural variables, etc., would lead to the increased probability of confirming bias (Choudhary, 2015).

Second, an important feature of the multidisciplinary approach is that it has been "adopted across the globe" because of its necessity. Ayush Choudhary provides the following reasons for this development:

(a) The "human being is the building block of society. All researches are directed to betterment of human being. Human life is regulated and determined by the knowledge of various disciplines. A number of researches are going on worldwide for human welfare. These researches cannot be conducted in isolation…" (Choudhary, 2015, p. 1).
(b) "Various types of incidents, natural and man-made, are taking place all around. It is not possible to study them in isolation. They can be studied, in the true sense of word, in an integral manner that is with the help of multidisciplinary research" (Choudhary, 2015, p. 1).
(c) "Objectivity and accuracy [constitute] the first and foremost goal of research. This purpose can be served by the help of multidisciplinary research. Actually this approach gives ample opportunity to study the problem with different viewpoints" (Choudhary, 2015, p. 1).
(d) "The most important feature of multidisciplinary research is that in this era of complicated life style it makes [a] study quite easy and comprehensive" (Choudhary, 2015, p. 1).
(e) "Multidisciplinary research helps in an overall study of the problem from various outlooks. It alleviates the chances of 'biasness' and 'monotonous' results" (Choudhary, 2015, p. 1).
(f) "Multidisciplinary research aims at avoiding the defects of incompleteness. Today's problems are of such a nature that their solution in isolation would give incomplete or no result" (Choudhary, 2015, p. 1).
(g) "No discipline can be sufficient or complete in itself. At the same time, it cannot assert about its capability to solve all the problems. Therefore, each and every discipline is bound to take the help of other discipline in order to reach at a suitable conclusion" (Choudhary, 2015, p. 1).

(h) "In the field of law, multidisciplinary research is of utmost significance, because law is not confined to one aspect of human being. It deals with all the aspects like social, political, economic, cultural, etc. of this day to day life" (Choudhary, 2015, p. 1).

Third, the multidisciplinary approach has been quite important in "providing an opportunity for the international development research community" vis-à-vis becoming more broadly consistent with the major postulates in development policy as a whole. By connecting development policies to the multidisciplinary approach, researchers from various disciplines working on these policies have been able to minimize the risk of "confirmation bias" (Choudhary, 2015).

Fourth, the amalgamation of different disciplines in the multidisciplinary approach is by itself important in that it facilitates the "employment of different disciplinary research methods" brought together to investigate a common issue or problem. This is vital because combining these various methods (a) "provides an understanding of complex social challenges and community responses to issues…that require a multifaceted approach to solve"; (b) "combines disciplinary breadth with the ability to collaborate and synthesize varying expertise"; (c) "enables researchers to reach a wider audience and communicate diverse viewpoints"; (d) "encourages researchers to confront questions that traditional disciplines do not ask while opening up new areas of research"; and (e) "promotes disciplinary self-awareness about methods and creative practices" (Global Arts and Society, 2013, p. 1).

Fifth, the multidisciplinary approach is important because its results provide "holistic understanding." For instance, when the approach is used to study an issue in the field of education, the whole world is examined. Instead of investigating individual academic institutions or departments, all of them are interrogated together. Rebekah Glebe (2020) cites the case of the Nijmegen School of Management with researchers from various disciplines that intertwine business administration and economic aspects, and look at business administration and political science as part of the geography, planning, and environment of those aspects.

Sixth, an important characteristic of the multidisciplinary approach is that it is a "real world methodology." Indeed, the multidisciplinary approach is not just a research perspective; it is a concrete way of comprehending the world. Most researchers are more likely to work with people from different disciplines. Thus, being capable of compiling information and collaborating with people from across the gamut of perspectives will help them to function more effectively in the professional world (Glebe, 2020).

Seventh, the development of "collaboration skills" has been noted as an important aspect of the multidisciplinary approach. It is coveted that any education research project, for instance, emphasizes the importance of collaboration, as it is advantageous for an educational idea to be anchored on "coming together to develop a better whole." This is mainly because being able to communicate effectively with people across disciplines is integral to multidisciplinary learning. People learn the same vocabulary, they understand their values, and they know what motivates them.

These skills will assist them to make linkages, generate answers to address big problems, and work cooperatively with their peers (Glebe, 2020).

Eighth, an important aspect about the multidisciplinary approach as it relates to users of research findings such as corporations is that the findings encompass a "rich view of the world developed by the researchers." This is possible because of the wide range of perspectives the researchers had encountered during their investigation and the combination of the subject matters they have investigated. The following are some of the transferable skills gained through such multidisciplinary explorations: (a) *critical thinking skills* "used and developed to look across disciplinary boundaries to consider other viewpoints and also begin to compare and contrast concepts across subject areas"; (b) *self-management* which "requires [researchers] to think carefully about how to identify their priorities and manage their study choices"; (c) *adaptability* which calls for "different subjects…to be viewed through different lenses which means an individual needs to be able to switch to the appropriate lens at the appropriate time for whichever subject [at which that person is] looking"; (d) *analysis and problem solving* which requires "studying across different subject boundaries, and by studying a wider range of subjects, [researchers] develop deeper skills of evaluation as they learn a number of different logical and methodical approaches and are able to select the best one to use for particular circumstances"; (e) *communication skills* are "well developed among multi-subject [researchers] as they learn to revert to the appropriate communication style for a particular subject area"; (f) *application of information technology* "across a range of subjects means that [researchers] can be more practiced in displaying and presenting information in a range of ways"; (g) *flexibility*, which "requires ability to adapt to different contexts and environments, is a strong skill gained from multi-subject study as [researchers] will be switching from one subject to another"; and (h) *synthesis of ideas* allows researchers to "begin to consolidate [findings] by combining ideas from many perspectives and consider an alternative way of acquiring knowledge" (The Open University, 2023, p. 1).

Ninth, "robustness" has been tendered as an important attribute of the multidisciplinary approach. The attribute is said to be connected to "local organization," which is interpreted as hinged upon the autonomy of an individual researcher Accordingly, "in a multidisciplinary research system, individual researchers remain semi-autonomously engaged in fulfilment of the research process, based on their perceptions of the meta-problem, and their chosen route of inquiry" (Dalton et al., 2021, p. 1). The individual researcher's autonomy is initially encouraged by the absence of a centralized organization, an arrangement that shelters the system from the introduction of a centralized directive. Amaris Dalton, Karin Wolff, and Bernard Bekker make the following illustration of the absence of a central directive to buttress the preceding point: "two researchers engaged in similar research problems but affiliated to different institutions and located in different geographic regions, though differing local restrictive parameters or incentive structures, may arise based on these researchers' academic affiliations, grant requirements and other associated externalities, these externalities are not centrally imposed on the multidisciplinary system, but only on the individual" (2021, p. 1).

Tenth, the "fostering of autonomy by disciplinary differences" is seen as an important facet of the multidisciplinary approach apropos "linguistic heterogeneity," particularly in situations where the "stigmergy" (i.e., an indirect, mediated mechanism of coordination between actions, in which the trace of an action left on a medium stimulates the performance of a subsequent action) between researchers is fragile at a systems level of analysis. This is due to the fact that local autonomy in ensuring that externalities impacting the individual researcher are unable to make large perturbations within a system is guaranteed, despite individual researchers being highly vulnerable to the influence of externalities due to the openness of a complex system. Besides, local autonomy and differentiation in relation to research objectives and selected methodologies are significantly "incentivized" by the significance that peer-reviewed scientific journals place on new discoveries. This reality discourages researchers from following in the veracious footsteps of their forerunners (The Open University, 2023).

Eleventh, "unconcealment" is proposed to be an important aspect of the multidisciplinary approach. The reason for this is that a group of goal-oriented researchers in multiple disciplines work on the same meta-problem while receiving "stigmergy" from different origins that may be portrayed as a multiplex arrangement displaying an "emergent form of swarm intelligence" in fulfilling its teleological, or research, objective. The suggestion on this matter is that this intelligence expresses itself in the "unconcealment" of the "form" of the meta-problem. In essence, "nnconcealment" is to be perceived more in terms of a process of revealing, or even discovery, and thereby concerned with the analysis of broad contexts (The Open University, 2023). Thus, as The Open University puts it,

> Indeed, propositional truth may to some extent be understood as being conditional to the broader context and scope of unconcealment…Therefore, the application of simple propositional truth within the context of resolving a meta-problem is deemed too narrow in describing the functionality of a multidisciplinary system. This is especially clear when considering conflicting disciplinary ontologies and epistemologies contained within a multidisciplinary system and in relation to areas of research where the correspondence theory of truth may not be suitable…Furthermore, error is as much a part of unconcealment, as error, in so far as it is the opposite of truth, is revealing as to the subject of inquiry…, or the form of the meta-problem. (2013, p. 1)

Twelfth, the "iterative quality of the research process" is mentioned as an important characteristic of the multidisciplinary approach. It is dubbed as the "unconcealment of the meta-problem" which is very much in close association with the energetic paths of inquiry. The notion of regarding research as an "iterative process" appears in different disciplines. The following are a few examples: (a) "phenomenological research as an unfolding phenomenon of 'seeing afresh'"; (b) "a model for the research process called the 'iterative theory-building process' whereby research questions are allowed to change over time"; and (c) "the iterative nature of falsification in science".

Thirteenth, it has been stated that the multidisciplinary approach permits a group of researchers to "learn more, at once." This means that by keeping best practices in mind, the researchers can interact among one another to transfer knowledge among disciplines. This also denotes that the breadth and depth of a research project will be significantly enhanced. In addition to exposing the researchers to novel and diverse disciplines, the concepts, thoughts or perspectives will also help them to discover what interests them and how to link their specialized areas to other variables. A team of researchers investigating, for example, public policy, while at the same time looking at that policy from the lenses of journalism, law, or environment, will be better informed for it (O. P. Jindal Global University, 2020).

Fourteenth, "strong mentorship" has been identified as an important trait of the multidisciplinary approach. A younger scholar fresh out of university with a doctoral degree does not always have a handle on life's choices ahead. After all, higher education is not only about gaining advanced knowledge of disciplines but also about learning more about oneself, discovering interests, nurturing passions, channeling talents, challenging oneself, and developing as a scholar, individual, and member of society. This leads to a peer-level, generational understanding, and senior researchers can better relate to younger researchers' circumstances, dilemmas, interests, thoughts, and ideas more easily, because they may have themselves been through similar aspects not too long ago (O. P. Jindal Global University, 2020).

Fifteenth, the multidisciplinary approach has been touted for helping researchers to develop and sustain their "critical thinking and problem-solving skills." This is made possible by the fact that the real world is complex. Thus, a researcher cannot simply understand it through one lens. It is important that the researcher has a "rounded, holistic perception." Accordingly, a major benefit of investigating a phenomenon via a multidisciplinary lens is the ability to approach problems with a broader perspective, since a researcher must begin to "think outside the box" and cull from a variety of concepts, disciplines, and points of view in order to pinpoint the best integrated solutions to today's problems that are themselves characterized by having many elements (O. P. Jindal Global University, 2020).

Sixteenth, "diversifying interests and opportunities" is said to be an important feature of the multidisciplinary approach. This potentiality pushes researchers to be "wild, free, adventurous" while at the same time encouraging them to "take responsibility" for their work. This aspect is reflected in their other scholarly activities as well. Therefore, even while specializing in one subject, researchers have the possibility to be involved in other areas that interest them and make use of the opportunity exhaustively. Put succinctly, the "sky is the limit" for researchers using the multidisciplinary approach (O. P. Jindal Global University, 2020).

Seventeenth, an important aspect of the multidisciplinary approach that has been identified in education entails "unique research experiences." This is manifested because research on educational issues can be "more interactive, engaging and intimate." In turn, this engaging approach allows researchers to have a lot of responsibility and bounce off ideas among themselves. Simultaneously, a great deal of discussion, debate, and dialogue takes place (O. P. Jindal Global University, 2020).

Eighteenth, "emerging new research opportunities" are noted to be an important attribute of the multidisciplinary approach. The O. P. Jindal Global University captures this aspect very well when it states the following:

> Even recruits are on the lookout for hiring multidisciplinary talent. Narrow training is giving way to transferrable and dynamic skills. Through a multidisciplinary approach, a [researcher] gains an arsenal of skills—problem-solving, critical thinking, time-management, self-management, communication and writing, analysis and research methodologies, team work, and much more—that are easily transferable across work environments. Youngsters can now find very interesting careers in new and emerging fields as a result of a vibrant multidisciplinary background. It gives them the exposure, education and experience to branch out into different directions and expands their avenues. (2020, p. 1)

Nineteenth, an important ingredient of the multidisciplinary approach is that "it caters for several clients with different and various needs." This is due to a number of factors pointed out by Michela Aquilina as follows: (a) "a multidisciplinary approach offers various services and resources to a range of clients with different backgrounds, experiences and issues"; (b) "professionals working within a multidisciplinary approach come from various disciplines, and [these] professionals may include psychologists, psychotherapists, counsellors, doctors, and psychiatrists"; (c) "through an intake process, an individualized care plan is drawn up for each client, in which the client's needs and goals are identified [and] the client is then referred to the corresponding professionals who will work together towards the specific established goals"; (d) "clients too may choose to receive particular services"; and (e) "some clients may have complex needs which may require the different skills of different professionals" (2021, p. 1). To support the assertion, Aquilina provides the following example:

> …the Willingness Team takes on a multidisciplinary approach and offers a variety of services including individual, couples and family therapy, sex and relationship therapy, integrative counselling, psychological assessments, cognitive behavioural therapy, child psychology, educational psychology, counselling for families going through illness, gestalt psychotherapy, career guidance, life coaching, parent coaching and consultations, psychosexual education sessions, physiotherapy, gynecological services and genito-urinary services, sexual health services through Sex Clinic Malta, Childminders by Willingness, and also other psycho-educational activities. (Aquilina, 2021, p. 1)

Twentieth, "the holistic approach" is an important method that underlies the multidisciplinary approach. This is because the multidisciplinary approach looks at and cares for the whole person, instead of just the symptoms of a situation or disease. The approach takes into consideration the cultural, emotional, intellectual, physical, psychological, social, and spiritual factors of a person. Consequently, professionals employing the multidisciplinary approach seek to alleviate symptoms, explore what is causing them, and address their root causes. The aspects that are taken into account by the professionals include (a) the individual's past experiences, (b) his/her interactions with the environment, and (c) the effects of family, school, work, peers, relationships, and community on him/her. After the client's needs and goals are first established, they can thereafter be addressed by the different professionals in the multidisciplinary team (Aquilina, 2021).

Twenty-first, indicated as an important feature of the multidisciplinary approach comprises "efficiency and continuity." This notion hinges on the fact that the approach can be perceived as efficient for clients since the first point of contact is most of the time a team or organization which offers a diversity of services. In essence, clients are already provided access to a variation of other services within a multidisciplinary team when those clients need to be referred to professionals for particular services. Thus, it is most likely that the professionals can refer the clients to other professionals or organizations which are trusted and which work alongside them should the team or organization not directly offer the service. The attendant results include (a) "a speedy referral process which leads to minimized delays"; (b) "less time searching for the right professionals, planning, scheduling and driving around"; and (c) "continuity of care, whereby care is offered and given from different perspectives, progress is monitored, access to needed services or professionals is facilitated, and any transitions needed can be facilitated too" (Aquilina, 2021, p. 1).

Twenty-second, the multidisciplinary approach is considered to be important because it "allows clients to create goals for themselves." By doing so, clients can be motivated to work toward achieving their desired results. The goals also assist the professionals to acquaint themselves with what the clients would like to achieve, which in turn provides the clients with the best possible services to achieve the goals. In addition, the process also gives the clients an opportunity to revisit the goals and, working with the professionals, the goals can be analyzed and revised if necessary (Aquilina, 2021).

Twenty-third, "better results and contentment" are reported to constitute an important trademark of the multidisciplinary approach. It has been demonstrated that different professionals who actively collaborate and work together with the goal of clearly addressing the needs of clients and a community strengthen health systems and also enhance clinical and health-related outcomes. To boot, with improved outcomes, clients gain increased satisfaction as they are being treated and cared for effectively and holistically (Aquilina, 2021).

In sum, the preceding review indicates that the cardinal importance of the multidisciplinary approach is that each aspect in a study can be analyzed by a particular specialty. This is frequently obligatory to generate answers for complex research problems.

Addenda

In light of the nature of this multidisciplinary book and the novelty of its subject matter, it behooves us to make three important points here. First, climate change is a new academic cross-discipline that studies ocean temperature, ocean salinity, sea level, glacial ice dynamics, sea ice extent, weather patterns, solar variability, radiative transfer, atmospheric physics and dynamics, paleoclimates, and a whole lot more related to climate on Earth, albeit from the social science perspective because the main focus is on how the phenomenon impacts the social lives of people and, thus, the need to develop climate solutions. Many universities now offer undergraduate and/or graduate degrees in the discipline. For example, the Massachusetts Institute of Technology offers an undergraduate degree that combines engineering, earth system science, and the social sciences (Massachusetts Institute of Technology, 2024). Also, the Climate Change Institute at the University of Maine offers a master's degree that focuses on the variability of the Earth's climate, ecosystems, and other environmental systems and on the interaction between humans and the natural world (University of Maine, 2024).

Second, there was a need to study climate science, which is a separate discipline from the preceding one, i.e., climate change. Climate science, also referred to as climatology, investigates the Earth's climate from a purely scientific point of view. Climate science focuses on a better understanding of our planet's atmosphere and how it affects various ecosystems. Many climate scientists equate climate with the weather (Pacific Northwest National Laboratory, 2024).

And, third, the academic fields represented by the chapters in this book include those in the humanities, social sciences, professions and applied sciences, and formal sciences. Thus, as to be expected, the analytical styles of the authors vary. To commence with, since the humanities have a strong connection to philosophy, their analytical style focuses significantly on the actual arguments and ideas. Next, as social sciences seek to look hard at information and sometimes be cautious, their analytical style tends to pay more attention to objective insights. Also, because professions and applied sciences use the scientific method and knowledge obtained via conclusions from the method to attain practical goals, their analytical style focuses more on applying existing scientific knowledge to develop more practical applications. In addition, since the formal sciences deal principally with mathematical and logical methods, their writing style tends to be geared toward the quest for basic information; it is the acquisition of knowledge without regard for usefulness but simply for the sake of knowing. In sum, due to the multidisciplinary nature of this book, there is something for most readers in it to understand and appreciate.

References

Aquilina, M. (March 15, 2021). 5 Benefits of a multidisciplinary approach. *Willingness.* Retrieved on January 12, 2023, from https://willingness.com.mt/5-benefits-of-a-multidisciplinary-approach/

Baldwin, A., & Koh. (2012). Enhancing student engagement in large, non-disciplinary first year survey courses. *Journal of Teaching and Learning in Higher Education, 24*(1), 113–121.

Choudhary, A. (2015). Multidisciplinary research. *academike.* Retrieved on January 12, 2023, from https://www.lawctopus.com/academike/multidisciplinary-research/

Dalton, A., Wolff, K., & Bekker, B. (August 16, 2021). Multidisciplinary research as a complex system. *International Journal of Qualitative Methods* 20. Retrieved on January 12, 2023, from https://journals.sagepub.com/doi/epub/10.1177/16094069211038400

Dhadphale, T., & Baughman, J. (September 6–7, 2018). Understanding characteristics of multidisciplinary collaboration using concept maps. *Proceedings of the International Conference on Engineering and Product Design Education* convened at the Dyson School of Design Engineering, Imperial College, London, UK. Retrieved on February 22, 2023, from https://www.designsociety.org/publication/40808/UNDERSTANDING+CHARACTERISTICS+OF+MULTIDISCIPLINARY+COLLABORATION+USING+CONCEPT+MAPS

Fleisch, A., & Stephens, R. (2018). *Doing conceptual history in Africa.* Berghahn Books.

Glebe, R. (October 1, 2020). Why pursue a degree program with a multidisciplinary approach? *GoAbroad Foundation*. Retrieved on January 12, 2023, from https://www.goabroad.com/articles/degree-abroad/advantages-of-multidisciplinary-curriculum

Global Arts and Society. (2013). Why cross-disciplinary research matters. *Discovery Theme: The Ohio State University*. Retrieved on January 12, 2023, from https://globalartsandhumanities.osu.edu/research/cross-disciplinary-research

Heim, I., & Kratzer, A. (1998). *Semantics in generative grammar*. Wiley-Blackwell Publishers.

Herbst, T. (2010). *English linguistics: A coursebook for students of English*. De Gruyter.

IGI Global. (2022). What is Africa. *Publisher of Timely Knowledge*. Retrieved on December 31, 2022, from https://www.igi-global.com/dictionary/concept-and-approach-to-land-management-interventions-for-rural-development-in-africa/38757

Kaur, S. and Kaur, K. (June 2012). Study and implementation of image fusion method. International Journal of Electronics and Computer Science Engineering 2(5):288–291. Retrieved on February 17, 2023, from https://citeseerx.ist.psu.edu/document?repid=rep1&type=pdf&doi=44a6687b4274f3b6fdd04808d1e4dbd7303f1f12

Kroger, P. (2019). *Analyzing meaning*. Language Science Press.

Makin, G. (2000). *The metaphysicians of meaning: Russell and Frege on sense and denotation*. Routledge.

Merriam Webster *New World College Dictionary*. (2023). *Multi*. Retrieved on February 22, 2023, from https://www.merriam-webster.com/dictionary/multi-.

MIT News. (April 16, 2024). *New major crosses disciplines to address climate change*. MIT News. Retrieved on July 1, 2024, from https://news.mit.edu/2024/new-major-crosses-disciplines-address-climate-change-0418

Mudimbe, V.-Y. (1988). *The invention of Africa: Gnosis, philosophy, and the order of knowledge*. Indiana University Press.

Mudimbe, V.-Y. (1994). *The idea of Africa*. Indiana University Press.

Nowen, R., Brasoveanu, A., Eijck, J. V., & Visser, A. (2016). *Dynamic semantics*. Stanford Encyclopedia of Philosophy Archive. Retrieved on February 18, 2023, from https://plato.Stanford.edu/archives/win2016/entries/dynamic-semantics/

O. P. Jindal Global University. (March 24, 2020). *The advantages of a multidisciplinary education*. The Blog. Retrieved on January 12, 2023, from https://jgu.edu.in/blog/the-advantages-of-a-multidisciplinary-education/

Pacific Northwest National Laboratory. (2024). *Climate science*. Retrieved on July 1, 2024, from https://www.pnnl.gov/explainer-articles/climate-science

Preston, R. C. (2023). An appraisal of fusion of social science in elementary school. *The Elementary School Journal, 44*(4), 202–207.

Searle, J. (1969). *Speech acts: An essay in the philosophy of language*. Cambridge University Press.

The Open University. (2023). *Multidisciplinary study: The value and benefits*. Open Learn. Retrieved on January 12, 2023, from https://www.open.edu/openlearn/education-development/multidisciplinary-study-the-value-and-benefits/content-section-7

University of Maine. (2024). *Climate change institute*. Retrieved on July 1, 2024, from https://climatechange.umaine.edu/graduate-program/

Abdul Karim Bangura holds five PhDs in Political Science, Development Economics, Linguistics, Computer Science, and Mathematics. He is a researcher-in-residence of Abrahamic Connections and Islamic Peace Studies at American University's Center for Global Peace. He is the author and editor of 106 books and the author of 709 scholarly articles. Many of these works have won eminent awards, in addition to more than 50 other distinguished national and international awards. He has served as president and then ambassador to the United Nations for the Association of Third World Studies. He is now the president of the African Studies and Research Forum and is fluent in a dozen African and six European languages.

JP Afamefuna Ifedi lectures in political science at Howard University in Washington, D.C. Ifedi has published in various scholarly peer-reviewed journals and participated in election monitoring and democracy development in Bosnia and Herzegovina under the auspices of the Organization for Security and Cooperation in Europe and the US Department of State. He directs the Council on African World Affairs, an organization dedicated to educating the public on African world issues. His PhD is from Howard University, and he completed a postdoctoral in political economy as an Institute for British and Irish Studies Summer Fellow at St. Anthony's College, Oxford, and Trinity College, Dublin.

Part I

Sciences

African Psychology

Pamela Anyango Oloo and Lilian Achieng Magonya

This chapter explores the concept of African psychology with a view to addressing the competing discourses on the existence or otherwise of a branch of psychology that is distinctly African. While in some literature African psychology is used interchangeably with Black psychology and African-centered psychology, this chapter adopts the term African psychology to refer to all elements of psychology centered on African people on the African continent. Notably, Black psychology focuses more on people of African descent, people of color, dispersed in the Diaspora. By African psychology, this chapter refers to Psychology as manifested and operationalized in African contexts by Africans. In defining the concept, the chapter draws from Jamison (2018) and echoes the questions he poses in reference to the concept of African psychology. Is it White psychology with a Black face? How does it differ from traditional (read Euro-American) psychology? Is there an indigenous African psychology rooted in the continent's own unique epistemologies, knowledge systems, and identities? Another question that is explored in this chapter is about the truth element regarding African psychology: Does African psychology exist? Is it a reality or is it a myth? What are its characteristics and subject matter? These are the key issues that this chapter addresses.

Some Definitions

By way of definition, African psychology is conceived as a branch of psychology that deviates or departs from the traditional Euro-American conceptualization of Psychology. There are as many definitions of African psychology as there are scholars. In the rest of this section, we explore the various definitions with a view to laying ground for the debates and contrasting stances on the concept. Jamison (2018)

P. A. Oloo (✉) · L. A. Magonya
Linguistics and Literary Studies, Maseno University, Kisumu, Kenya

A. K. Bangura, J. A. Ifedi (eds.), *Conceptualizations of Africa*, African Studies and Research Forum Series, https://doi.org/10.1007/978-3-031-74535-5_2

identifies a form of psychology that is distinct from traditional psychology and brands it as Black psychology. Nwoye (2020) avers that African psychology on the whole refers to a system of knowledge that concerns the nature of life from an African perspective. In essence, African psychology can be conceptualized from different standpoints, as shall be observed in the next section.

While Smith (1974) and Chrisman (1975) are in concurrence that African psychology refers to the study of Black behavioral patterns, dealing with the total behavior in all situations of Black people throughout the world, Smith (1974) extends the scope by identifying the social environment as one that is manifestly antagonistic and unhealthy, therefore calling for the development of appropriate methodologies and strategies for the exhaustive and valid analysis of the Black experience. This is in recognition of the traditional Western methodologies as being inappropriate and inadequate for the total encapsulation of the Black experience and situations. Baldwin (1986) avers that African psychology comprises a system of knowledge concerning the nature of the social universe from the perspective of African cosmology and entails the uncovering, articulation, operationalization, and application of the principles of the African reality structure to psychological phenomena. In a slight departure from the foregoing, Akbar (2004) conceives of African psychology as a place rather than a thing. He states that it is a perspective, a way of observing and conceptualizing experience, and that it does not claim to being an exclusive body of knowledge but rather situates itself as a perspective located in the historical view of Africa. Nobles (1980) contends that African psychology is more than the *darker dimension* of general psychology, with its unique status derived from the positive features of basic African philosophy rather than from the negative aspects of being Black. Wilson (1998) incorporates the power dimension in defining African psychology and states that it is a psychology of power that does not merely describe the traditional nature of African people or the orientations of African people based on traditional African culture, but it also captures the essence of power domiciled in the African way of life, power drawn from the intricate relation between the African and the other, comprising the supernatural and entire cosmos. Wilson's definition presents African psychology as both descriptive and prescriptive—a form of liberating consciousness raising that describes African worldviews and applies cultural constructs to psychological phenomena. In so doing, it seeks to provide solutions to Africans' contemporary conditions and prescribes directions for future engagements and activities. Grills (2006) defines Black or African-centered psychology as a dynamic manifestation of unifying African principles, values, and traditions that are reflected within broader Pan-African or transcultural communities. African psychology is therefore qualitative (rather than quantitative), contextual (not empirical), and focused on human science (not natural science). It is premised on the recognition of culture as highly relevant to people's everyday behavior. A people's values, shared history and experience, and language all affect how people see things, how they feel, and what matters to them. Most importantly, culture is motivational—it affects people's choice of goals and their level of commitment to them (Grills, 2006).

The perspectives offered by the preceding definitions of African psychology are at once unitary and diverse, capturing various aspects and essences of what constitutes African psychology. The point of convergence lies in the claim to the existence of the concept of African psychology as concerned with the behavior and lived experiences of the African self in different contexts. Notably, African psychology is the perceived antonym of traditional White Euro-American psychology, reflecting the knowledge, perceptions, and observations rooted in global historical perspectives. The definitions here clearly deconstruct the victimization basis of African psychology and seek a conceptual shift from simply reacting to reclaiming and revitalizing, seeking to locate African psychology back to the center from the peripheral position to which it had been relegated by Western conceptualizations. It therefore entails the deliberate and self-conscious location of psychological analyses and applications in African realities, cultures, and epistemologies. Being a system of thought and action, African psychology focuses on, examines, and is ultimately concerned with understanding the systems of meaning of human beingness, the features of human functioning, and the restoration of what is normal and natural to human development. As such, it is used to resolve personal and social problems and to promote optimal functioning.

In essence, the preceding viewpoints still leave unanswered the query apropos the nexus between psychology and African societies, especially vis-à-vis their renaissance and development. This question should lead scholars who confer about African Psychology, particularly those scholars in the developing world who profess to be socially compos mentis, to ponder its seriousness and provide careful and thoroughly considered answers. Until this is done, African Psychology as a discipline will remain stunted.

The rest of the chapter explores the contradictory stances adopted by scholars with reference to the existence or otherwise of a psychology that is distinctly African. Additionally, it seeks to examine the subject matter or content of African psychology as well as the Africanness of African psychology—i.e., Africanicity in African psychology.

African Psychology: Conceptual Orientations

As aforementioned, African psychology refers to the psychology or study of the behavior patterns of African people in their various contexts of existence, notably the conceptualization is unitary in nature despite the diversity of African people and regions (Nwoye, 2015). Thus, we have African psychology as we do African religion, African literature, African medicine, or African history. The concept of African psychology entails competing discourses and has variously been conceptualized as both reality and myth. As a myth, it is postulated that there is no domain of knowledge that is unique to a particular geographical region and its people; hence, the concept is nonexistent in the real world. Realistically, there is the existence of a substantive body of psychological literature that originates in the African context and is engaged with African issues and problems (Moll, 2022). The debate as to the existence of an African psychology is an ongoing one, with no consensus on the matter, a debate that rages on within and without Africa as well as among Africans and non-Africans. African psychology as a new field of study within the broad academic discipline of psychology in continental Africa can be defined as "the systematic and informed study of the complexities of human mental life, culture, and experience in the pre- and post-colonial African world" (Nwoye, 2020, p. 1).

According to Nwoye (2015, 2017), Puleng and Cakata (2017), and Ratele (2017), African psychology is premised on studying African experiences and societal behaviors using an African worldview lens. Thus, it is a psychology that examines research on African issues done in or on Africa by Africans (Ratele, 2017). Puleng and Cakata (2017), Ratele (2017), Murove (2018), and Oppong (2022) contend that African psychology is as old as humankind and all psychology is African because historically Africa is known to be the cradle of humankind and, by extension, the cradle of civilization. In other words, prior to the arrival of the colonialists, Africans had both indigenous mechanisms of solving their societal problems and vibrant civilizations like in the case of Kemet/Ancient Egypt whose ideologies have impacted various sectors such as education, religion, philosophy, and architecture (Nwoye, 2015; Puleng & Cakata, 2017; Owusu-Ansah & Mji, 2013; Murove, 2018). Therefore, African psychology emerges as a discipline that attempts to revitalize debates, thereby advancing African epistemologies, and as Puleng and Cakata (2017) package it, African psychology is an African platform designed for telling African stories and experiences in their worldview using their own voices and not be dependent on Western psychology which has muted their voices and by extension ideologies. Stated differently, African psychology defuses the negative imagery and stereotypes associated with the "dark continent." Apparently, the term "dark continent" was synonymous with the discourse of earlier Western explorers, anthropologists, and missionaries who struggled to comprehend the "mystery" and "primitiveness" of the African culture otherwise labeled "barbaric" or "savage" cultures (Murove, 2018). Obviously, this was a strategy to alienate Africans from their indigenous knowledge and distort their belief systems (Jaja, 2014; Puleng & Cakata, 2017; Murove, 2018). Furthermore, African psychology advocates for "pluriversality" in making sense of diverse worldviews, rather than imposing a *one-size-fits-all* subjective Eurocentric viewpoint on all world cultures. The reason for this as advanced by Puleng and Cakata (2017) is that knowledge is confined within geospatial dimensions whereby a society's history plays a role in generating a community's indigenous knowledge.

For Nwoye (2015, 2017), Puleng and Cakata (2017), and Owusu-Ansah and Mji (2013), Euro-American psychology largely downplayed African traditions which were bastardized and perceived as inferior. The same narrative was equally advanced by African elites who fully embraced Euro-American psychology in the curriculum of African universities while downplaying their own cultures; yet, African problems could not be effectively handled by Eurocentric theories developed from research experiences drawn from Western cultures. Moreover, such cultures advanced dissimilar ideologies that were unrelated to African culture. Nwoye (2015), Puleng and Cakata (2017), and Malherbe and Ratele (2021) seem to echo the Kenya prolific literary writer Ngugi wa Thiongo's "decolonizing the mind" thesis customized within the context of African psychology. In the sense that African psychology is a discipline that subscribes to the decolonization of the African mind thesis by advocating for Africans to present their psychology in a language that resonates with their cultural world under the umbrella of decolonial psychology. Besides this, Nwoye (2015, 2017) and Puleng and Cakata (2017) concur that African psychology is a sub-branch of psychology which conforms to scientific rigor whereby societal problems are researched using existing theories. Besides this, data analysis is undertaken and eventually the generated findings are disseminated so as to contribute to contemporary psychological debates. Hence, for Murove (2018) and Malherbe and Ratele (2021), decolonizing African Psychology demands rejecting oppressive Eurocentric ideologies in psychology, while embracing relevant transdisciplinary ideologies or inclusive ideologies that resonate with the African multicultural context.

Pertaining to the initial approaches to African psychology, Nwoye (2015) suggests dual positions. The first position holds that African psychology is enshrined in Black psychology, where Black scholars who were actually descendants of enslaved Africans in the United States developed the discipline following their racial and enslaved experiences in America and they were seeking an African solution to their problems in Diaspora. The latter position established the African Psychology Institute Association to focus on African culture, reality, and epistemologies. At this stage, it is noteworthy to state that Oppong (2022) makes the distinction that African American psychology focuses on experiences of Blacks in America, while African psychology is centered on African problems in Africa South of the Sahara. The second approach states that African psychology has its origins in Africa (Nwoye, 2015; Puleng & Cakata, 2017; Ratele, 2017) where it is visualized as protesting imperialistic Western psychological ideologies otherwise labeled by Puleng and Cakata (2017) as an "epistemic disobedience by reconstructing African epistemologies."

Nwoye (2015, 2017) contends that African psychology was initially not taught in African universities because after independence, colonial masters established offshore academic institutions such as Makerere University in Uganda and the University of Nairobi in Kenya, among others, which religiously conformed to Western psychology theories. Today, as observed by Oppong (2022), some Southern African universities such as the University of KwaZulu-Natal and Eswatini Medical Christian University offer bachelor's degree programs in indigenous psychology. Nwoye (2015, 2017) outlines three phases of the development of African psychology as follows:

1. Uncritical acceptance of Western psychology (1940–1960s): This stage, which is typical of the colonization period, is characterized by the dominance of Western approaches in psychology as Africans remained active listeners.
2. Selective appreciation of both African and Western psychology (1970–1980): The post-independence stage is marked by the introduction of African voices in psychological debates in the works of Aimė Césaire and Franz Fanon who both

examined and critiqued Eurocentric psychological debates while infusing African experiences in psychology literature.
3. Selective accommodation of African and Western psychological traditions (1970–1980): This stage is marked with appreciation of best practices in both Western and African psychology while being cognizant of the fact that not all European theories solve African problems.

Besides the classification, and more specifically in reference to the third phase, Puleng and Cakata (2017) contend that African psychology is far from being autonomous and there is still overdependence on Eurocentric principles when addressing African problems in psychology. A case in point is in South Africa where the State Department of Health compelled indigenous healers to subscribe to Western medical health regulations by subjecting them to scrutiny based on Western standards, albeit the two approaches are distinct. From the foregoing, this invites the call for Africans to be self-governing and reject Western ideologies when solving African problems. In the same vein, this raises the question about whether African psychology is a myth. We ask this against Puleng and Cakata's observation that where African healing systems are scrutinized using Western techniques, the vice versa is both unimaginable and an impossibility. Moreover, Puleng and Cakata (2017) argue that Africans will continue to be just receivers and replicators of Western knowledge and never become key role players in the production of their own knowledge. Indeed, such sentiments echo Karanja (2010), as cited in Ayuya et al. (2015), who states that African psychology occupies an outlier stand, and this disadvantageous position incapacitates the discipline, hence making it unable to generate its own psychology. In view of this postulate, the ensuing section examines some of the myths associated with African psychology.

Mythically Speaking

Questions abound as to the existence of a discipline of psychology that is distinctly African, leading to debates on whether there exists a local African psychology or psychology in Africa. One position holds that there is no such thing as a psychology that is distinctly African, but that there is psychology that is engaged with the issues and problems of Africa and Africans (Moll, 2022). Scholars in this school of thought argue that the fragmentation of psychology by identifying different shades or multiple variants of the discipline that is reflective of different people (Africans), different cultures, and different geographical locations (Africa) is an exercise in futility and self-defeatist, since it is at variance with the claim to psychology as a true science of humanity as a unitary whole rather than sectional and fragmentary; universal rather than local. The fragmentation is perceived as unconducive to the evolution and development of universally acceptable psychological principles that can be applied to the study of psychological issues (Nsamenang, 1990). Yet, as stated by Kim and Berry (1993), and Akotia and Olowu (2000), as cited in Nwoye (2007), an African psychology devoid of indigenous theories and conceptual tools for interrogating African-related issues and relating the meanings among Africans in African contexts is defeatist. These scholars all agree that there is a need for an Afrocentric perspective to explore the distinct African mind hitherto repressed by the application of Euro-American theories and standards in order to productively engage issues and problems of the continent—the underlying concern of any psychology.

This view is supported by Hountondji (1983) who asserts that African psychology remains a myth if it is conceived of as reflecting and studying the behavior patterns of specific people in specific geographical contexts. According to Hountondji, "African psychology is a myth if it is conceived of as the product of theories and epistemologies and correlates states of mind that are unique to a singular people, nation or continent" (Hountondji, 1983, p. 67).

The argument of Hountondji (1983) is hinged on the premise that there cannot be a coherent psychological theory that is particular to Africa, but only universal psychology engaged with the problems and issues of Africa since psychology functions across diverse cultures. Nonetheless, this is contestable if it is considered that the West's conceptualization of the universal is entirely peculiar to its own circumstances (Moll, 2007). That the West has, in its definition of universal, failed to acknowledge all that exists and instead located itself centrally as all that there needs to ever be. Thus, the following questions remain: Should psychologies be universal or locally situated? Is there a psychology that functions across diverse cultures?

The claim to the existence of an African psychology is at variance with the conception of psychology as a universal discipline with cross-cutting principles and tenets, concerned with different nations, peoples, regions, and cultures as a unitary whole. Questions are raised as to the existence of specific epistemological systems that are "relative to" and "constructed by" culture-specific forms of language and ways of live and living, of situatedness (Moll, 2007), casting doubts on the possibility of its existence. Furthermore, Nsamenang (1990) attests to the universality of basic characteristics of humans regardless of their geographical locations, thereby refuting the claim to an insular psychology that is in the interests of people of a specific culture and geographical location. Accordingly, Nsamenang asserts: "…the basic components of human personality—psychomotor, cognition and conation—can be identified in human beings everywhere" (1990, p. 3).

Psychology is a universal experience rather than a local enterprise; therefore, the notion of a distinct African psychology is unsustainable. Centering African psychology necessarily locates it within the larger global psychology. Glerce (1996) reinforces this position by stating that in the absence of a clear grasp of the epistemological variations and distinctions in Afrocentric and Eurocentric approaches, African psychology consists basically of replacements of African values and concepts in a Western framework "…replacing the values of x, y, and z in those universal equations with new African values" (1996, p. 122).

Based on the foregoing arguments, critics claim that the so-called African psychology is constructed in the shadow of dominant Euro-American psychology, essentially protest in nature but similar in content and theoretical underpinnings (Moll, 2007). Taking African culture into consideration, and given the unique conceptualization of the self in the African, Bodibe (1996) calls for the development and application of Afrocentric epistemology in order to Africanize psychology, without which the concept remains a wishful thinking. This is especially critical given that the African individual functions as a member of an intricate folk environment whose behavior reflects unique characteristics that can only be interpreted in context. Okpara (1998), as cited in Nwoye (2007), posits that these cannot be deconstructed within the confines of academic psychology. Indeed, Kottler (1990) concurs with Okpara (1998) and states that psychological phenomena, including those found among Africans, require appropriate theories and strategies concerned basically with how meanings and states of consciousness arise and are interpreted in different contexts and situations. This position exposes the necessary tension between culturally specific explanatory principles on the one hand and general explanations across contexts on the other, leading to the differences and similarities among discourses in relation to the existence of specific psychologies, including African psychology. Discourse of difference is hinged on the existence of particular and specific situated sociocultural contexts of indigenous experience. Hence, in the African context, is reference made to Africa in general or particularly to Africa South of the Sahara? Is Africa unitary in its sociocultural experiences to justify the existence of a psychology known as African psychology? The similarities discourse on the other hand presupposes the existence of a common similarities heritage as the basis of psychological experience.

Underlying the arguments branding African psychology a mythical creature are underlying tensions in the nexus of Afrocentrism and Universalism. Questions are raised as to the existence of a unique, distinctive, and exclusive African mind as the source of all behavior and experience which then calls for a special branch of psychology to account for, in context. Assertions are made as to the need for the development and application of specific psychological processes, methodologies, and structures that can account for and interpret appropriately the lives of people in Africa.

Africanicity in African Psychology

As a reality, evidence abounds as to the existence of distinct African psychological processes and procedures not found anywhere else in the world. Bodibe (1996) argues that only African epistemologies can account for the typical, manifest behavior patterns that distinguish African people from others around the world. In African thought, rather than dwell on one's own thoughts and feelings, one ideally projects oneself "outward" to establish relationships with the sky, the land, and one's kinship group. One school of thought postulates that African society is richly unique in its setup, philosophy, and cosmic reality that set it apart from Western society and, as such, there must be a worldview that explains and accounts for these variations. Given the distinctions, a Eurocentric approach or psychology would not sufficiently account for the African cosmology and worldview (Masolo, 1994; Moll, 2022; Bodibe, 1996). These debates manifest in the nascent tensions between a universal psychological theory and the distinctive, unique psychic experiences situated and located in African contexts (Moll, 2022). Bodibe (1996) argues that the existence of a distinct African psychology is an obvious reality, given that only African sets of knowledge can account for the distinct behavior patterns and thought processes that set African peoples apart from others around the world. The difference between African psychology and Eurocentric psychology therefore lies in the relation between self and the universe: that the African psyche is externalized rather than internalized and that rather than dwell on and focus internally on one's own thoughts, feelings, and perceptions, the individual projects the self outward to foster strong links and relations with the cosmos, notably kin. The African mind reveals itself through sociality or sociability (Moll, 2022) in an intricate relation between the self and kin.

Nwoye (2015) states that African psychology views African culture from a holistic perspective as a way of making sense of our experiences in terms of joys, sorrows, aspirations, life, marriage, ethics, morality, death, language, and so on. He points out the following aspects synonymous with the Africanicity or Africanness: the African concept of multiple realities, humanity, the notion of life and death, the theory of reality, theory of knowledge, theory of truth, theory of perception, capacity of synoptic time consciousness, concept of culture-bound rationality, African spirituality and condition, and mystery and African values.

First, on the question of multiple realities, Baloyi and Makobe-Rabothata (2014), Ayuya et al. (2015), Nwoye (2015), and Puleng and Cakata (2017) subscribe to the pluriversality thesis or multiple epistemologies of the African worldview whereby such realities are not a myth but a cultural reality. The African continent is predominantly multilingual, meaning that the pre-existing cultural diversities and experiences cannot be examined using one lens but multiple lenses because of dissimilar culture-specific realities. Furthermore, according to Baloyi and Makobe-Rabothata (2014), Owusu-Ansah and Mji (2013), and Nwoye (2015, 2017), the African worldview has essentially at most four components: (1) African cosmology, (2) ontology, (3) axiology, and (4) African epistemology. African cosmology is one that embraces collectivism and harmony in culture. Ontology explores the relations between the nature of being and African reality and extends to the domains of African spirituality. Axiology explores interpersonal relationships as a value system and, finally, African epistemology premised on truth and knowledge generation in African societies. For Nwoye (2015), the aforementioned aspects can be collapsed into three: (1) the physical, (2) the metaphysical, and (3) the spiritual realms of the African worldview.

Second, on the African concept of humanity, it is a truism in African culture that the universe is dynamic and there is independence between the individual and community, and even extends to the ancestors, which Baloyi and Makobe-Rabothata (2014) contend, would not only entail slaughtering animals to feed mourners during funerals but also performing rituals near the tomb of the departed and actually communicate with the dead by making pronouncements, such as "I am talking to my father or mother or grandparent and not the spirit or body of my dead mother." Put differently, Africans are socialized to value community-based associations and, by extension, value extended families (Ogbujah, 2014; Baloyi & Makobe-Rabothata, 2014; Nwoye, 2017; Murove, 2018). This resonates well with the popular adage that *no man is an island* and this apparently is the principle enshrined in the African philosophy of *Ubuntu* ("humanness") that draws from humanistic values whereby an individual depends on the society. Moreover, under the cultural philosophy of unity is strength, *Ubuntu* propagates the spirit of togetherness or communality in the society as expressed in the Kiswahili expression *mtu ni watu* ("a person derives his strength from others") or its semantic equivalent in the Nguni proverb *umuntu ngumuntu ngabantu* ("a person is a person through others") as cited in Nwoye (2017, p. 42). According to Jaja (2014), *Ubuntu* resonates with the *Ujamaa* ideology that was adapted by the late Julius Nyerere, a former president of Tanzania, who advocated for socialism where groups of families in villages worked together for the common good of the entire community. The same communality spirit extends even in the context of farming, hunting, and herding, or trade. In African societies communities would collectively participate in hunting, grazing and planting, weeding, harvesting of crops, selling produce in common markets, war, weddings, funerals, and so on (Ogbujah, 2014; Baloyi & Makobe-Rabothata, 2014). In fact, Baloyi and Makobe-Rabothata conceptualize *Ubuntu* as a "qualitative tapestry of connected systems which deal with issues collectively and collaboratively" (2014, p. 236). It is noteworthy to state that self-centeredness or individualism was un-African because it defied the *sharing is caring* humanistic principle. A case in point is among the Luo of Kenya, a person who ate alone is considered a glutton or reprimanded for being a witch doctor. This is because eating communally reinforced social ties and reinforced the spirit of unity.

Third, about the notion of life and death, Nwoye (2015, 2017) postulates that Africans subscribe to the belief that they are not controllers of their lives and that they are plagued by many misfortunes such as illnesses and natural calamities. For instance, in African societies, it is believed that unexplained death is caused by malevolent spirits and good happenings stem from good spirits. There is a popular African belief that natural death is a foreign concept whereby an African does not die and its occurrence is attributed to something or someone who is responsible for the death. Death was perceived as the transitional link between the living and the dead, and the departed had embarked on a journey to join their ancestors. For Nwoye (2017), there exists a two-way traffic in the life and death realities. The first holds that the living can access the ancestral world through death or can be facilitated to access the ancestral world through dreams, divinations, or rituals. The second way is the passage which ancestors use to indirectly communicate their emotions to the living, either through calamities or through bounty harvests. Belief in spirits is enshrined in African cosmology, and even in contemporary times, some Africans still believe in the omnipresent nature of ancestral spirits who are believed to be closely watching over the living. In most circumstances, the spirits are appeased by performing libations such as dropping some portion of food or pouring some drinks on the ground for the ancestors to consume. Moreover, during calamities, in some communities, such as the Ameru of Kenya and other communities, rituals were performed to appease ancestral spirits. Gordon (2012) cites the Batwa people of Central

Africa where spirits are said to manifest viscerally, they were felt by individuals, and are heard and seen through emotional phenomenon. Dreams, trance states, and glossolalia were all manifestations of the spiritual world (Baloyi & Makobe-Rabothata, 2014; Nwoye, 2017). Similarly, the Luo of Kenya have the concept of *nyawawa* (meaning "spirits from the lake") who in contemporary times are appeased by beating objects such as utensils, plates, and drums whenever their presence is felt. The fear of vengeful malevolent spirits is real in Africa. Nwoye (2017) adds that some African elites or politicians resort to soliciting protection services from witch doctors when they experience a series of misfortunes in their lives. Witch doctors are believed to possess powers to solve societal problems such as recovery of stolen property, ill luck, misfortunes, sudden illness, love-related problems, witch hunting, and job losses.

Fourth, concerning the theory of African reality, there are essentially two worlds: (1) the visible and (2) invisible worlds; and both worlds coexist in harmony, lest a calamity befalls on those in the land of the living (Gordon, 2012; Nwoye, 2015, 2017; Ayuya et al., 2015; Baloyi & Makobe-Rabothata, 2014). For Nwoye (2017), the visible world is the home of the living whereas the invisible world is the realm of divinities, ancestral spirits, ghosts, clan deities, and all unknown malevolent spirits.

Fifth, the theory of knowledge contends that in African culture, knowledge is not only historical but evolutionary. More so, in African society, there are multiple sources of knowledge where knowledge is cross-generationally transmitted orally, and a community's folklore comprising proverbs, narratives, riddles, songs, dances, recitations, dirges, puzzles, etc. were rich in knowledge. Additionally, the community had resource persons such as the council of elders, grandparents, parents, diviners, medicine women and men, village chiefs or kings, clan advisors, and oracles who would be consulted to explain phenomena in a community.

Sixth, in regard to the question of truth, there are multiple approaches and not a single way to approach truth. Seventh, vis-à-vis perception, a person's behavior is influenced by his/her psychological status, or even by a group. Moreover, with the advancement of age, one's perception enables him/her to rationally analyze situations. Eighth, apropos the notion of time consciousness, African society recognizes the past, present, and future, and that past actions have an effect on the future (Nwoye, 2017). Still related to the time concept, African societies are essentially "polychromic" (Jaja, 2014), whereby the approach to life is casual and time is not a constraining factor; hence, Africans unreservedly have expressions such as *African time* or *There is no hurry in Africa*. Finally, as it pertains to African values, Nwoye (2017) opines that children born and bred in the African context acquire the values of obedience, honesty, respect for elders, modesty, spirituality, and industriousness in the home environment.

Characteristics and Subject Matter of African Psychology

Having acknowledged the existence of a branch of psychology that is distinctly African, this section examines the distinct features and subject matter or concerns of African Psychology. In so doing, the chapter discusses the characteristics of African psychology that sets it apart from traditional Euro-American psychology.

To begin with, African psychology emerges as protest in nature, in response to the need to correct the misconceptions that abounded in the subjective and negative, self-serving discourse on and stereotypical images of Africa in Western literature and discourse. Key among the stereotypes are the beliefs that were held by European thinkers such as Georg Wilhelm, Friedrich Hegel, Immanuel Kant, and Joseph Conrad, among others, who questioned the humanity of the African people. One such position was advanced by British psychiatrist H. L. Gordon who served at the Mathari Mental (a psychiatric hospital) Hospital in Nairobi, Kenya, who carried out a study on the brain weight and mental capacities of dead bodies and concluded that "the brain of the adult African corresponded to that of a European child of seven or eight years of age" (McCulloch, 1995, as cited in Nwoye, 2017). Thus, African psychology emerged in response to such misrepresentations by the West and sought to present a more accurate and wholesome perspective of the lived experiences of Africans in their respective contexts of existence. In so doing, the rehabilitative aspect of African psychology emerged, as it sought to reorient the culture of Africans and place it at the center of research in African universities. Notably, this is with a view to locate African psychology as an independent entity, devoid of comparison with the Western worldview, cultures, and systems of knowledge. The argument is that evolution is not region or race specific to establish two distinct minds for Europeans and Africans, and that personality is not textured as African or European (Moll, 2007).

Next, African psychology is rehabilitative in intent, as it seeks to firmly anchor the experiences, perceptions, and culture of Africans in context. This is a sharp departure from the comparative stance adopted by Western Euro-American psychology that perceives the Western way as the standard against which all other forms of existence must be gauged. In the Western tradition, the accepted psychological canon comprises mainly European and/or White psychologists who analyze the human experience with their own cultural lenses, reflecting a disharmony between the dominant psychological theories and African reality and lived experiences. There was an obvious need to domesticate psychology in the African context through the establishment of a new canon of African psychology that accurately represents and captures the totality of African experiences and culture (Nwoye, 2022).

To iterate, the concerns of African psychology revolve around the lives and lived experiences of African people, both in the past and in the present. It embodies and brings to the fore the individual and collective experiences of Africans in terms of their hopes and impediments, joys and sorrows, gains and losses, frustrations and challenges, needs and preferences, life and death, spirituality and materiality (Nwoye, 2015)—i.e., the totality of human existence as encapsulated by Africans.

Dissenting Voices

In the previous sections, we unpacked the African psychology discipline, explored its Africanicity, defined its characteristics, and unveiled its myths. We now examine literature on some of the dissenting voices against African psychology or arguments downplaying its general development. The section begins by presenting the case study which describes experiences of Adelowo (2015) whose research area as a doctoral student of African psychology in New Zealand centered on the psychological adjustment of African women in New Zealand using African frameworks. Her three New Zealand supervisors were unfamiliar with African psychology, and throughout her research they remained receptive to her ideas. Nonetheless, they questioned the capacity for African psychology to scientifically handle the notion of structural adjustments in New Zealand. Subsequently, she was compelled to modify the title of her thesis by expunging the word "psychology" from it. In short, her experience unveiled the antagonism between African psychology and Western psychology.

First, from the foregoing, Adelowo's (2015) case presents certain truisms of attempts designed to muzzle African psychology. First and foremost, she highlights the overbearing dominance of Eurocentric psychological theories over African models and, by extension, other indigenous psychologies (Nsamenang, 2007; Narvaez, 2019; Oppong, 2022), which seemingly dwarf intellectual debates on indigenous psychologies by inculcating an inferiority complex aura within the realm of non-Euro-American psychology. Consequently, this leads to an overreliance on Western psychology because African psychology is marinated with stereotypes such as primitiveness, subjectiveness, mere superstition, and unscientific. Seemingly, the listed misconceptions reinforce the superiority of Western psychology. Moreover, Adelowo (2015) and Oppong (2022) add that apparently Western psychology is packaged as the universal truth and appears to be the vanguard that defines standards of scientific research. Hence, it is against such a framework that all other psychologies are measured. Ronald (2005), Narvaez (2019), and Serpell et al. (2022) argue that the Eurocentric framework conforms to the Western, European, Industrialized, Rich, and Democratic (WEIRD) paradigm, which ideally constitutes 12% of the world's population. In all fairness, such a small population cannot purport to be custodians of a universal psychological framework by downplaying research from other indigenous psychologies. Moreover, scholars such as Oppong (2022) contend that all psychologies are essentially indigenous, inclusive of Euro-American psychology which is premised on research from indigenous populations. In contemporary times, the field of psychology is striving toward accommodating all psychological models to comprehend humans' societal problems in diverse cultures.

Second, because of the dominance of Eurocentric psychology, Western psychologists remain unreceptive to African psychology, thereby compelling African scholars to modify their research areas or topics to conform to Euro-American models. The logic around this is that indigenous models are "handicapped" to address Western psychological problems. Indeed, Adelowo registers her frustrations that led her to expunge the word "psychology" from her thesis title to "please" her supervisors. Conversely, proponents of African psychology have argued that Euro-American theories developed in a Western environment are equally incapable of adequately articulating issues in African psychology. Furthermore, Ronald (2005) stresses that research in African psychology would benefit less from Western theories which are incapable of accounting for African social realities. It is important to note that rarely will a European scholar be intellectually "arm twisted" to customize Western models to conform to African realities since they host dissimilar worldviews. Likewise, African psychologists should remain assertive when advancing their psychology, lest they are swayed by the tides of Euro-American psychology.

Third, despite the push to embrace the African worldview in academia, African ideologies still remain scientifically unpalatable to Western scholars who are either ignorant about its philosophies or consider them unscientific and thus unworthy of scholarly attention. Ronald (2005) associates this indifference toward African psychology with racism by alluding that Africans are perceived as less intelligent than other races (Nwoye, 2015). Subsequently, their scholarly inputs are downplayed. In fact, this is echoed by Adelowo who contends that all her three New Zealand supervisors were unfamiliar with the field of African psychology since they were unaware of its existence. This brings to the fore the thesis of the invisibility of African psychology in the global arena; yet African psychologists are crying themselves hoarse for its recognition in the field of psychology. Seemingly, this takes African scholars back to the drawing board since a lot needs to be done in African psychology for it to respectfully claim its place in psychology. Ronald (2005) states that the omission of aspects touching on Africa is not only a problem of African psychology but even cascades to scientific articles touching on skin color or race, where Africa is largely ignored. In other words, race is either rarely discussed or is trivialized in Western psychology. Besides this, there are other pressing concerns about African psychology.

Fourth, some scholars have challenged the question of a common African worldview, although Africa is the epitome of multilingualism and, by extension, cultural diversity. Scholars such as Oppong (2022) have argued that despite the African diversity, there are commonalities as affirmed by ethnographic studies of various cultures from Eastern, Western, Northern, and Southern Africa, which lay the foundation of the African epistemologies in psychology.

Fifth, as it pertains to the negative attitudes of African scholars toward their own indigenous psychology, for instance, Serpell et al. (2022) were engaged in a project to collect research on diverse topics on African psychology. They used several professional networks such as obtaining contacts of African psychologists from their respective institutional websites and even going to the extent of establishing email lists. Of the 466 researchers contacted, 318 remained unresponsive and 56 declined their invitation. They eventually received 23 abstracts, rejected five for being substandard, and published the remaining articles. From the foregoing, the negative feedback on the call is what Oppong (2022) translates as lack of intellectual discourse among African scholars which frustrates efforts geared toward developing African psychology. In other words, a united front will be beneficial in raising the profile of African psychology which, if unchecked, might drown in the scholarly ocean of Euro-American psychology. According to Serpell et al. (2022), some of the issues raised by the responsive African scholars were the prohibitive costs of publishing manuscripts. In addition, they cited imposed restrictions by publishers in high-impact journals. To this list, Oppong (2022) adds that there is generally a low acceptance rate of manuscripts from Africa coupled with the fact that there are few African publishing houses. Therefore, sometimes, authors are literally compelled to distribute their own books. Serpell et al. (2022) contend that the negative response by African psychologists toward the mentioned academic initiative that would enhance their visibility in the global community by having an open access platform to showcase scholarly work on African psychology resonates with retarded advancement of African psychology that even postgraduate students are reluctant to study the discipline. This stems from the imperialistic ideology of Western psychology that made Africans cast doubts on their own epistemology and social realities (Nsamenang, 2007; Oppong, 2022).

Sixth, another school of thought posits that African psychology attempts to revive outdated traditions; for instance, consulting a *sangoma* ("traditional healer") which remains primitive in the eyes of Western psychologists. This line of thinking has since been dismissed in modern studies which are now exploring therapeutic benefits of indigenous healing practices. Undeniably, this has also been met by the overdependence on Western psychology; for instance, as previously observed in the earlier sections of the paper by Puleng and Cakata (2017) in South Africa, Nsamenang (2007) contends that in Malawi, citizens were receptive toward ethnomedicine healing systems. Nevertheless, the integration of traditional healing methods within the Malawian health sector remains a pipe dream since the Malawi Ministry of Health has generally ignored traditional healers and embraced Western health systems. This raises the question as to whether Africans lack confidence in their own indigenous health systems which they have reliably used for centuries to cure numerous ailments in their environment before the advent of Western medicine.

Seventh, in the context of psychology in academia, Nsamenang (2007) points out that from the onset, African universities had reservations about developing degree programs in psychology. By 1962, when some countries were obtaining independence, no African university had a psychology department. The first experimental laboratory in the continent was constructed in 1965 in Zambia and within 19 years after its establishment, Zambia began offering postgraduate programs in psychology. Moreover, not all African universities offer psychology degree programs; cases in point are universities in Chad, Cameroon, and Gabon which are yet to introduce the program. Elsewhere in Africa South of the Sahara, various institutions in Kenya, Liberia, and Namibia have departments of psychology offering degree programs in psychology. There are also institutions which do not have independent departments of psychology, but offer the course under the department of philosophy as is the case at the University of Cameroon. With few African institutions offering degree programs in psychology, this translates to a few African psychologists whose research are not well funded; hence, their scientific outputs in terms of publications will not be impactful for the discipline to cut its niche in academia. Issues raised about the retarded pace of the development of African psychology in the continent are consistent with the English proverb that states "Rome was not built in a day." In reality, the natural course of development is essentially systematic and time consuming. Likewise, steps taken by African psychology to spread its tentacles in the continent together with its share of challenges typify any academic growth.

Still on the question of psychology in African institutions, African psychologists can broadly be categorized into two groups: (1) those who are passionate about African psychology and (2) those who are ardent supporters of Euro-American ideologies. The former believes in the existence of an African psychology whereas the latter ignores its own psychology at the expense of Western psychology which is equally counterproductive for the development of African psychology. It cannot be overstated that in academia the popular adage is that "scholarship is a debate characterized by divergent views on any concept." From the foregoing, it is arguable that African psychologists should not shoot themselves in the foot by denying their own epistemology which is as old as humankind. More so, they should focus on highlighting their best practices and customize them to solve modern psychological problems in their respective societies.

Eighth, in addition to the highlighted challenges in academia, African psychology remains unsupported by most ruling elites and policy makers whose political interests are skewed toward science-oriented subjects as opposed to what they perceive to be art-based disciplines such as psychology. The lack of political will stifles the growth of the discipline within the continent. In sum, we concur that the highlighted cases reflect a true account of the challenges faced by African psychologists. Indeed, the same would transpire for any discipline struggling to establish itself in a polarized world that roughly dissects psychology into a favorable Euro-American model and devalued indigenous psychologies. For the raised issues, African institutions are striving to secure funds, build capacity, increase their scientific outputs, change mindsets of dissenting voices, and establish publishing houses so as to bridge the gap in academia. It cannot be overemphasized that these are teething problems which should not be construed as rubbishing the milestones African psychologists have made so far in affirming their position in psychology.

Despite the aforementioned shortcomings, what is equally obvious is that African psychology has its distinct disciplinary features that have been articulated by a circle of intellectuals and a history of academic exploration. This is the result of Black psychologists grounded in the African psychology convention have long challenged the hegemonic paradigms and racist perspectives immortalized by Eurocentric approaches to psychology. What is sorely needed now is the teaching of the significant contributions of African psychology to those who are unaware of both its historical and contemporary effects on the field of psychology in general.

Conclusion and Recommendations

From the foregoing and with all confidence, Baloyi and Makobe-Rabothale affirm that "…to the extent that there is such an animal as an African …there is an African epistemology, ways in which African use their knowledge systems to advance their development of course with variations, not all African subscribe to the same culture" (Baloyi & Makobe-Rabothata, 2014, p. 234). It is clear that Psychology has traditionally been polarized into African and Euro-American psychology which host dissimilar epistemologies. The former has been labeled inferior while the latter's superiority is manifested in its dominance in intellectual debates (Owusu-Ansah & Mji, 2013). To intellectually remedy the situation, African psychologists are now fighting for their space to safeguard their identity which essentially falls under cultural rights as enshrined in the UNESCO Universal Declaration on Cultural Diversity. As Murove (2018) asserts, any knowledge has some indigenous components and no knowledge system should be deemed more superior than another. More so, in the contemporary globalized multicultural world, there is a paradigmatic shift that is slowly erasing the monopoly of Euro-American ideologies by embracing cultural plurality. There is a consensus that multiculturalism cannot be wished away and inclusivity provides a rich platform for listening to previously muzzled alternative ideologies in the past intellectual debates in psychology. Indeed, what African psychologists are propagating is consistent with the *Ubuntu* philosophy in the sense that even in scholarship, we need one another to mutually enrich one another's intellectual knowledge, and no one culture can purport to monopolize knowledge in a world where cross-cultural experiences are transforming livelihoods.

The debates around the authenticity or otherwise of an African psychology are unlikely to find resolution in the near future given the inherent tensions between universality and variations in human existence. The danger in a designated African psychology lies in its indigenization and domestication of such an establishment. Indeed, Wiredu (1998) warns that a psychology that is considered the untouchable possession of Africans invites a touristic approach from foreign audiences where it becomes a mere cultural curiosity. This essentially makes the concept lose its intended utility value.

References

Adelowo, A. (2015). African psychology: The psychological adjustment of African women living in New Zealand. *Papers in Social Representations, 24*, 6–21.

Akbar, N. (Ed.). (2004). *Akbar papers in African psychology*. Mind Productions.

Akotia, C. S., & Olowu, A. (2000). Toward an African-centred psychology: Voices of continental African psychologist. *Psych Discourse, 31*(10), 7–12.

Ayuya, C., Niceta, I., Kimani, I., Mathenge, J., Murrithi, J., & Otieno, R. (2015). African worldview: An integrated psychological perspective. *International Journal of Humanities and Social Sciences and Education, 2*(5), 53–61.

Baldwin, J. A. (1986). African (Black) psychology: Issues and synthesis. *Journal of Black Studies, 16*, 235–249.

Baloyi, L., & Makobe-Rabothata. (2014). African concept of death: A cultural implication. In: Jackson, L. T. B., Meiring, D., Van de Vijver, F. J. R., Idemoudia, E. S., & Garbrenya, Jr., W. K. (Eds.). *Toward sustainable development through nurturing diversity: Proceedings from the 21st international congress of the international association for cross cultural psychology.* Retrieved on September 6, 2023, from https://scholarworks.gvs.edu/iaccp_papers/119

Bodibe, R. C. (1996). The responses of counselors to apartheid: An indigenous counselor enters the fray. *British Journal of Guidance and Counselling, 24*(2), 259–264.

Chrisman, R. (1975). Black psychology: The dual task. *The Black Scholar, 6*(10), 1.

Glerce, A. (1996). The transformational view of development and the African context. *Journal of Psychology in Africa, 1*(6), 100–119.

Gordon, D. (2012). *Invisible agents: Spirits in Central African History*. Ohio University Press.

Grills, C. T. (2006). *African-centered psychology: Strategies for psychological survival & wellness*. Retrieved on September 20, 2023, from https://www.baatn.org.uk/wp-content/uploads

Hountondji, P. J. (1983). *African philosophy: Myth and reality*. Hutchison University Library for Africa.

Jaja, J. (2014). Myths in African concept of reality. *International Journal of Educational Administration and Policy Studies, 6*(2), 9–14.

Jamison, D. F. (2018). Black psychology: A view from the bridge. *Journal of Black Psychology, 44*(8), 722–746.

Karanja, K. C. (2010). A genealogical analysis of the worldview framework in African-centered psychology. *The Journal of Pan African Studies, 3*(8), 109–134.

Kim, U., & Berry, J. W. (Eds.). (1993). *Indigenous psychologies: Research and experiences in cultural context*. Sage Publications..

Kottler, A. (1990). South African psychology's dilemma of multiple discourses. *Psychology in Society, 13*, 27–36.

Malherbe, N., & Ratele, K. (2021). What and from whom is a decolonizing African Psychology? *Theory & Psychology, 32*(1), 113–116.

Masolo, D. A. (1994). *African philosophy in search of identity*. Edinburgh University Press.

McCulloch, J. (1995). *Colonial psychiatry and the African mind*. Cambridge University Press.

Moll, I. (2007). *The paradox of "African psychology."* Retrieved on August 15, 2023, from https://www.wiredspace.wits.ac.za/server/api/core/bitstreams/4537a3c9-a0ba-428e-8c82-b5ec93b94b83/content.

Moll, I. (2022). African psychology: Myth and reality. *South Africa Journal of Psychology, 32*(1), 9–16.

Murove, F. M. (2018). Indigenous knowledge systems discourse and inclusionality: An Afrocentric quest for recognition in a globalized world. *Journal for the Study of Religion, 31*(1), 159–176.

Narvaez, D. (2019). *Indigenous psychologies contrast with Western psychology. Is it time to expand psychological theories?* Retrieved on October 20, 2023, from https://www.psychologytoday.com/za/blog/moral-landscapes/201910/indigenous-psychologies-contrast-western-psychology

Nobles, W. W. (1980). African philosophy: Foundations for Black psychology. In R. Jones (Ed.), *Black psychology*. Harper & Row.

Nsamenang, A. B. (1990). What's in a Name? *Journal of African Psychology, 1*(3), 1–5.

Nsamenang, A. B. (2007). Origins and developments of scientific psychology in Afrique Noire. In M. J. Stevens & D. Wedding (Eds.), *Psychology: IUPsyS*. Global resource Edition. Psych Press.

Nwoye, A. (2007). The practice of polygamy in two regions of Africa: Background, theory and technique. *Dialectical Anthropology, 31*, 383–421.

Nwoye, A. (2015). What is African psychology the psychology of? *Theory and Psychology, 25*(1), 96–116.

Nwoye, A. (2017). An Africentric theory of human personhood. *Psychology in Society, 54*, 44–66.

Nwoye, A. (2020). *From psychological humanities to African psychology: A review of sources and traditions*. Retrieved on August 15, 2023, from https://doi.org/10.1093/acrefore/9780190236557.013.659

Nwoye, A. (2022). *African psychology: The emergence of a tradition*. Oxford University Press.

Ogbujah, C. (2014). African cultural values and intercommunal relations: The case with Nigeria. *Developing County Studies, 4*(24), 208–217.
Oppong, S. (2022). Indigenous psychology in Africa: Centrality of culture, misunderstanding, and global positioning. *Theory & Psychology, 32*(6), 953–973.
Owusu-Ansah, F., & Mji, G. (2013). African indigenous knowledge and research. *African Journal of Disability, 2*(1), 1–5.
Puleng, S., & Cakata, Z. (2017). A psychology in our own language: Redefining psychology in an African context. *Psychology in Society, 47*, 29–41.
Ratele, K. (2017). Editorial: Six theses on African psychology for the world. *Psychology in Society, 54*, 1–9.
Ronald, H. (2005). From psychology to race to issue of skin color? Western trivialization and peoples of African descent. *International Journal of Psychology Therapy, 5*, 125–134.
Serpell, Z. N., Dzokoto, V. A. A., Anum, A., & Belgrave, F. Z. (2022). Editorial: African cultural models in psychology. *Frontiers in Psychology, 13*.
Smith, W. D. (1974). Editorial. *Journal of Black Psychology, 1*, 5–6.
Wilson, A. N. (1998). *Blueprint for Black power: A moral, political, and economic imperative for the twenty-first century*. Afrikan World.
Wiredu, K. (1998). Toward decolonizing African philosophy and religion. *African Studies Quarterly, 1*(4), 17–46.

Pamela Anyango Oloo holds a PhD in Linguistics. She is a senior lecturer and Chairperson in the Department of Linguistics and Literary Studies at Maseno University in Kenya. She is a DAAD scholar and author of one book, three book chapters, and over 20 scholarly articles in recognized peer-reviewed journals. She also holds various postgraduate professional development certificates. Her research interests include discourse analysis, language and gender, and health communication.

Lilian Achieng' Magonya is a lecturer in the Department of Linguistics at Maseno University in Kenya. She holds a PhD in Linguistics from the University of Geneva, a Master of Arts in Linguistics, and a Bachelor of Arts degree from Maseno University. Her research interests are in the fields of intercultural pragmatics, sociolinguistics, cognitive linguistics, and Africana studies. She has published over 13 articles in various subfields of linguistics.

Climate Change

Judith Irene Nagasha and Wilson Mugizi

The new academic discipline of "climate change" broaches the long-standing shifts in temperature (Rajak, 2021), precipitation patterns, and weather events caused by human activity such as the burning of fossil fuels and deforestation (Kumar et al., 2021). Greenhouse gases such as carbon dioxide (CO_2), methane (CH_4), and nitrous oxide (N_2O) are emitted into the atmosphere as a result of the combustion of fossil fuels, deforestation, and industrial activity. As a result of these gases trapping heat, the planet warms. Africa contributes to this through transportation and industrial endeavors (Hegerl et al., 2019). An example is the increasing emissions brought on by industrialization and the continent's expanding transportation industry.

Additionally, the cause of climate change is that the planet's capacity to absorb CO_2 is diminished by the removal of trees for logging, agriculture, and urban development, which raises atmospheric CO_2 levels that led to the destruction of tropical rainforests in West Africa and the Congo Basin. Through the process of photosynthesis, trees and forests serve as carbon sinks by absorbing and storing significant amounts of CO_2 from the atmosphere (Mordecai et al., 2020). When these trees are cut down or otherwise disturbed, the carbon that has been stored in them is released as CO_2 back into the atmosphere. As a result, the Earth's ability to absorb CO_2 from the atmosphere naturally is diminished, which raises atmospheric CO_2 levels.

Crop yields, water accessibility, and the presence of pests and diseases are all significantly impacted, and this has a great effect on agriculture and food security (Munaweera et al., 2022). Droughts, floods, and storms are examples of extreme weather that can harm crops, sabotage food supply lines, and cause food shortages

J. I. Nagasha (✉)
Department of Development Studies, Kyambogo University, Kampala, Uganda
e-mail: jnagasha@kyu.ac.ug

W. Mugizi
Department of Education Planning and Management, Kyambogo University, Kampala, Uganda
e-mail: wmugizi@kyu.ac.ug

A. K. Bangura, J. A. Ifedi (eds.), *Conceptualizations of Africa*, African Studies and Research Forum Series, https://doi.org/10.1007/978-3-031-74535-5_3

(Upadhyay, 2020). Adapting agricultural techniques such as switching crop kinds or planting seasons may be necessary in reaction to changes in rainfall and temperature patterns (Ponce, 2020). To mitigate the detrimental effects of climate change on food production, sustainable agriculture and climate-resilient farming techniques are crucial (Turyasingura et al., 2023).

Climate change also results in climate refugees, who are people or communities that have been compelled to abandon their homes because of the negative effects of climate change (Salem & Rosencranz, 2020). Increasing sea levels, droughts, severe weather, or other environmental problems that render their territories inhabitable compel people to flee their homes (Sakapaji, 2023). The necessity for international collaboration and legal structures to protect and help person affected by climate-induced displacement is highlighted by climate refugees. Therefore, the effects of climate change on food security, agriculture, health, and sociocultural dynamics are extensive. For the purpose of reducing the negative effects of climate change and guaranteeing a sustainable and fair future for all, it is crucial to recognize and solve these interconnected concerns (Praveen, 2022). For the sake of conciseness, the following three major conceptualizations are just briefly discussed here: (1) global climate change and food security, (2) African climate change and health, and (3) sociocultural impacts of climate change and climate refugees. Before doing all this, however, it behooves us to state a caveat based on the aforementioned negative aspects of climate change.

A Caveat

While our observations led us to some of the negative consequences of climate change, we do not, however, subscribe to the doomsday apocalypse or end-of-the-world proclamation being bandied around by radical climate change activists. This is because their postulate is not scientifically tenable. There are many mathematical models that have been tendered by various serious scholars that make the conjecture unacceptable. For the sake of brevity and ease to read, these models are very briefly described without the mathematical equations in the subsequent paragraph. The interested reader can learn more about the models in numerous sources that entail combinations of them. A good source that has relatively adequate coverage of the models is the work by David W. Pravica and Michael J. Spurr (2011).

The *Quarks and Groups* model denotes the tiny particles of leptons that easily travel through open space. The *Measuring Radioactivity* model is about radioactive atoms decaying into other material at a rate proportional to the sample size. The *Chemical Equilibrium and Reaction Rates* model deals with the fact that quantities of chemical reactions are controlled in the environment; thus, over time, a reaction will reach an equilibrium rate with the quantities present. The *Ising Model of Magnetism* pertains to the fact that the alignment of neighboring magnetic movements occur than an opposite alignment. The *Shape of DNA* model informs us about how the cellular mechanisms in biology exist in the nucleus of a cell as a double helix—i.e., an extended spiral chain of atoms in a protein, nucleic acid, or other polymeric molecule. The *Cellular Homeostasis Epidemics* model proffers that a cell is a large system of many processes of energy that keeps it alive. The *Species Population Models* indicate that when society approaches a resource crisis, it naturally structures itself to resolve the environmental stress. The *Intersecting Species* model relates to the fact that the environment is sustained because its components interact in a manner that ensures the survival of all constituent species. The *Thermodynamics of Oceans and Atmosphere* model is apropos the existence of intensive variables that do not depend on the size of the system. The *Climate and Tree Rings* model proffers that tree rings will be large enough to correspond to a good growth year and under moderate conditions, a positive linear relationship has been observed between the many species of trees and the size of a ring vis-à-vis yearly average precipitation. The *Motion of the Planets* model refers to the observation that on a clear night, stars appear to follow a well-defined path in the sky referred to as *luminaries*; these points of points of light, once considered the elements of a *celestial sphere*, have remained constant. The *Sky is Blue but the Universe Is Red* model tells us that light consists of only a small interval in the full width of the electromagnetic spectrum. Thus, we can observe the principle in large animals who utilize low frequencies to communicate over long distances, whereas small animals employ high frequencies to communicate over short distances. The *Quantum Cosmology and the Big-Bang Theory* model apprises us about the large-scale nature of the universe in terms of when events take place almost simultaneously, the physical length is an invariant to all observers moving with the same velocity or commoving (for more on these models, see Pravica & Spurr, 2011).

Climate Change and Food Security

Food security is the state in which every person, at any time, has physical and financial access to a sufficient supply of safe, nutritious food that corresponds with his/her dietary needs and personal food choices, enabling an active and healthy lifestyle (Molotoks et al., 2021). Food systems, which link the numerous stages of the food supply chain, including production, processing, distribution, and consumption, within a variety of social and environmental settings, form the basis of food security (Béné, 2020). Food security around the globe faces tremendous challenges as an outcome of urgent global climate change (Zsögön et al., 2022). Food insecurity is a regional issue in Africa South of the Sahara, exacerbated by severe drought, with disastrous consequences for households (Twongyirwe et al., 2019). The prevalence of susceptible and sensitive food production and distribution networks to economic and climate-related shocks is largely to blame for the insecurity.

Africa South of the Sahara is considered to be the area most vulnerable to the effects of climate change (Ofori et al., 2021). This is a result of the area's extremely poor capacity for adaptation, which is related to the severe poverty levels and the lack of available infrastructure for mitigating and or adapting to climate change (Ringler et al., 2010). The region's capability to meet its population's needs for water, food, and energy depends largely on precipitation. For instance, the region's food systems are extremely sensitive to changing precipitation patterns because most of the land uses rain-fed agriculture.

The region is also distinguished by its great climate variability (Ahmed, 2020). The interconnection between drought, climate change, and food security has become irrefutable. The occurrence of drought is a significant environmental issue that is particularly intense in specific sub-regions in Africa. Drought is a common climate variable that can have rather large intensities across the African continent on a monthly, annual, decadal, or century timescale. Drought mechanisms have been connected to variables like climate change, aerosol emissions, land use patterns, and subsequent interactions between the land and the atmosphere, according to some studies. Furthermore, El Niño Southern Oscillation (ENSO) and sea surface temperatures (SSTs) are substantial factors influencing dryness throughout Africa South of the Sahara. Nonetheless, Ahmed (2020) argues that it is imperative to remember that due to its overall complexity, drought prediction is a delayed and difficult procedure and, therefore, drought will certainly continue to put enormous strain on food security in fragile ecosystems in Africa South of the Sahara.

Climate change, caused by an increase in greenhouse gas emissions, causes weather patterns to change, temperatures to rise, and extreme weather events to occur more frequently. Agricultural systems may be disrupted by these changes, which could have an effect on crop yields the raising of livestock, along with overall food availability (Haile et al., 2020; Malhi et al., 2021). Crop yields are one of the main ways that climate change affects food security. A decrease in crop yield and an increase in the likelihood of crop failures owing to droughts, floods, and heat waves might result from changing patterns of precipitation and temperature in some places. Water scarcity problems are made worse by climate change, which has a negative influence on agriculture (Kogo et al., 2021; Vaughan et al., 2019). Changes in precipitation patterns and higher evaporation rates might result in a reduction in the amount of water available for irrigation, a crucial aspect of contemporary agriculture.

Increased funding and support for studies on food security and climate change are crucial to filling the knowledge and research gaps (Hasegawa et al., 2021). Research funding should be given top priority by governments, international organizations, and academic institutions in order to help vulnerable populations adapt to climate change and maintain food security for all. In order to construct a more resilient and sustainable global food system in the face of climate change, it will be essential to close this gap.

African Climate Change and Health

Health is described as a complete state of physical, mental, and social well-being and not simply the absence of disease or infirmity according to the World Health Organization (WHO). Global warming is a phenomenon that has an effect on all regions of the world in varying degrees (Zielinski, 2023). Additionally, it is linked to a broad variety of human health issues that place a strain on healthcare systems, particularly in places like Africa (Atwoli et al., 2023). In fact, public health services in the African continent are under tremendous strain in part because of their precarious socioeconomic situations. Temperature changes, extreme weather events, and patterns of rainfall are mostly to blame for the problem of waterborne, foodborne, and vector-borne infections, malnutrition, and its effects on mental well-being, constituting a health danger to the African continent. There is also evidence that climate change may have an impact on the quality and quantity of crops cultivated by smallholders, altering the nutritional value and variety of food offered (Thiede & Strube, 2020). Africa South of the Sahara accounts for one-third of all malnourished children worldwide, demonstrating that malnutrition among children under the age of five is still a serious health concern in the region. While the frequency has decreased since 2000, there has been an upsurge in undernourishment after 2015, which has been attributed in part to climate change and extreme weather occurrences (Niles et al., 2021). The impact of climate change on human health could take many different forms. Malaria, dengue fever, and cholera are examples of vector-borne illnesses whose geographic distribution and severity can shift as a result of climate change (Fouque & Reeder, 2019). The habitats of disease-carrying vectors like mosquitoes can grow as a result of rising temperatures and shifting patterns of rainfall which can boost transmission (Carlson et al., 2023).

Water supply and food production may be hampered by climate change (Saturday et al., 2021). Water scarcity and crop failures brought on by droughts and unpredictable rains can result in starvation and waterborne illnesses like diarrhea. Rainfall patterns may vary as a result of climate change, with some locations experiencing less rain and others experiencing more (Saturday et al., 2021). To address the demand for water, of towns, agriculture, and industry, this could disturb the availability of freshwater supplies. And, in order to adjust to shifting precipitation patterns, better regional water management systems are required. This comprises improved water storage facilities, a wide variety of water sources, and water-wise habits. Also, a reduction in the amount of water available for agriculture and human use can result from higher temperatures increasing the rate of evaporation from lakes, rivers, and reservoirs (Ofori et al., 2021). To lessen the consequences of rising temperatures, it is essential to develop and put into use cooling solutions for reservoirs and to increase agricultural water efficiency.

Conflicts and population displacement may result from resource scarcity and competition being exacerbated by climate change. Health concerns are frequently present among displaced persons as a result of their cramped and filthy living conditions. An all-encompassing strategy that combines mitigation tactics to lower greenhouse gas emissions with adaptation measures to improve healthcare infrastructure, bolster disease surveillance, and foster community resilience is needed in Africa to address the health implications of climate change (Marcus et al., 2023). To safeguard vulnerable communities from the escalating health hazards brought on by climate change in Africa, international cooperation and investments in public health infrastructure are also crucial.

Climate Change and Sociocultural-Climate Refugees

Climate refugees are defined as those people who have been forced to leave their traditional habitat, temporarily or permanently, because of a climate or environmental disruption (natural or triggered by people) that jeopardized their existence or seriously affected the quality of their lives Doyle and Chaturvedi (2011). The sociocultural impacts of climate change and the phenomenon of climate refugees have become increasingly significant in recent years, drawing the attention of scholars and policymakers (Yenigun et al., 2023). Climate change is not merely an environmental issue; it has profound social and cultural implications that are often overlooked. Communities being displaced as a result of climate change's rising sea levels, catastrophic weather events, and protracted droughts are among the main sociocultural effects of the change. As a result, those who are compelled to flee their homes and frequently their cultural heritage have come to be known as climate refugees. It is urgent to address the loss of social cohesion, cultural identity, and traditional traditions among these relocated groups (Ngcamu, 2023).

Climate-related migration affects impacted communities' social structures and cultural practices in addition to displacing people physically. According to some studies, it might be difficult for climate refugees to integrate into new communities, which can cause social unrest and cultural conflicts. Furthermore, these groups' resilience and sense of self can be significantly impacted by the loss of agricultural traditions and cultural knowledge. To address how climate change is affecting society and culture, it is crucial to preserve cultural heritage and adapt old behaviors to changing climatic circumstances (Tiwari et al., 2023).

Furthermore, the issue of climate refugees has broader implications for global society. As climate change intensifies, the number of displaced individuals and communities is expected to rise significantly. This will require coordinated international efforts to provide support and protection for climate refugees and to address the social and cultural challenges they face. In this context, the sociocultural impacts of climate change underscore the need for a holistic approach to climate adaptation and mitigation, one that considers not only environmental factors but also the intricate web of cultural and social dynamics that shape human experiences and identities. Overall, understanding and addressing the sociocultural impacts of climate change and climate refugees is crucial for building a more sustainable and resilient future for all (McAdam, 2020).

The rise of climate refugees is the greatest notable sociocultural effects of climate change. People or communities compelled to flee their homes because of the negative effects of climate change, such as rising sea levels, extreme weather, and protracted droughts, are referred to as climate refugees. Some communities are developing plans to modify their customary practices to the altered environmental circumstances as a result of climate change. Innovative farming practices, resource management, and cultural adaptation are all part of this effort to preserve their cultural legacy (Capisani, 2023). A multifaceted strategy is needed to address these sociocultural effects of climate change and relocation caused by it. This entails assisting marginalized groups in their efforts to adjust to a changing environment, respecting the rights of climate refugees, and safeguarding cultural assets. Additionally, to avoid the worst-case scenarios and reduce the number of climate refugees, worldwide measures to mitigate climate change through greenhouse gas reduction are crucial (Martínez, 2023).

Climate Change's Implications on Food Security, Health, and Climate Refugees

The connections between food security and global climate change are extensive. Climate change poses serious threats to global food production and access as it continues to alter weather patterns and boost the frequency of catastrophic occurrences. Millions of people might immediately experience food shortages, hunger, and possibly famine as a result of this. As food scarcity can lead to civil discontent and violence, the impact also extends to economic stability and geopolitical dynamics. To address these implications, a coordinated international effort is needed to advance sustainable agricultural methods, make investments in climate-resilient crops, and cut greenhouse gas emissions. By doing this, the detrimental effects of climate change on food security will be mitigated.

There are significant and varied effects of climate change on health in Africa. The health of the continent already faces many difficulties, and climate change poses a potential to make matters worse. Populations are at risk because of rising temperatures, harsh weather, and changed disease transmission patterns. The effects also affect healthcare systems, which could be overburdened by the spike in demand for medical care during climate-related emergencies. Additionally, the health hazards brought on by climate change might result in higher healthcare expenses, decreased labor productivity, and economic setbacks. Investments in healthcare infrastructure that is climate resilient, extreme event early warning systems, and public health education are necessary to address these concerns. Additionally, it should be emphasized just how crucial climate action is for lowering health risks and the overall load on healthcare systems.

For both affected communities and the larger global society, the sociocultural effects of climate change and the development of climate refugees have serious ramifications. The identity and resiliency of displaced groups suffer long-term effects from the loss of cultural customs and heritage. The ramifications go beyond climate change, as host communities and climate refugees may develop tensions that could spark violence. Globally, the dearth of international legal recognition of climate refugees emphasizes the demand for all-encompassing policy responses to safeguard the rights of persons uprooted by climate change. To preserve cultural diversity and legacy, it is essential to cultivate cultural resilience and adaptive techniques among impacted communities. These consequences highlight how human rights, cultural preservation, and climate change are all intertwined, and they advocate for a more comprehensive and all-encompassing strategy to mitigating and adapting to climate change.

Conclusion and Suggestions for Policy and Future Research

In conclusion, the association between food security and global climate change is a complicated and critical subject that needs immediate attention. The analysis in this study highlights how vulnerable food systems are to climate change, with effects ranging from decreased agricultural yields and higher food costs to supply chain disruptions. These issues not only put billions of people's lives in danger but also worsen already existing inequality. A multifaceted strategy incorporating climate-resilient crop types, sustainable agricultural methods, and international cooperation is necessary to reduce these effects and guarantee food security for everyone. Food security is not only a fundamental human right but also a cornerstone for general global stability, so the international community must prioritize climate action and invest in adaptation and mitigation techniques that protect the world's food supply.

The effect of climate change on health in Africa is a complicated and multifaceted issue that needs to be addressed right away. The literature evaluated for this study led to the uncovering of a variety of health hazards and vulnerabilities, including heat-related illnesses, vector-borne illnesses, hunger, and effects on mental health, all of which are aggravated by a changing environment. The disproportionate cost placed on vulnerable people and the possibility of expanding health inequities is particularly alarming. Governments, global organizations, and local communities must work together to address these concerns. To reduce health hazards, climate change policies must include adaptation measures, early warning systems, and public health initiatives.

The sociocultural effects of climate change and the rise in the number of climate refugees reflect intricate, interrelated problems that necessitate both awareness and action. The material examined here emphasizes the severe disruptions brought on by displacement triggered by climate change, including the loss of cultural legacy, difficulties integrating, and the possibility for social unrest. In order to address the human elements of climate change, it is essential to recognize the special vulnerabilities of climate refugees, especially those who belong to marginalized groups. To establish legal frameworks and assistance programs that protect the rights and welfare of climate refugees, international cooperation is crucial. Furthermore, maintaining cultural variety in the face of environmental change depends on encouraging cultural resilience and adaptability within impacted communities. In the end, a more inclusive and sustainable future for all, where human rights, cultural identities, and social cohesiveness are respected and maintained in the era of climate change, depends on recognizing and mitigating the sociocultural effects of climate change.

For future research, to start with, understanding food security's socioeconomic components in the context of climate change is essential. Since climate change affects both food security and livelihoods of communities, those engaged in production and value chains through multiple pathways that increase the number of food insecure people by shaping poverty, disasters recovery and migration patterns must be studied. Their study is required to develop and apply sustainable farming strategies that can successfully lessen the effects of climate change on food security.

Next, these studies should consider regional and indigenous knowledge systems and investigate how they can support food systems that are climate resilient. This is because there has never been a greater need to determine how indigenous and local knowledge may contribute to the development of resilient, sustainable, and healthy food systems than now. People from indigenous and local communities who contribute knowledge to climate change and food systems research must be involved from the start, take the lead on initiatives wherever possible, and profit from them in a sustainable way.

Also, more investigation is required to establish region-specific climate adaptation plans for Africa, with an emphasis on the health industry. This is because climate change is associated with a wide range of human health problems, which pose a burden to health systems, especially in Africa. Undoubtedly, the continent is witnessing these pressures and even surprises from climate disorder dimensions, especially human health and sustainability.

In addition, the establishment of comprehensive legal frameworks and global laws that explicitly handle climate refugees should be the main topic of future research. Therefore, academics, policy experts, and government representatives across Africa and beyond should join forces to focus on effective law and policy responses and, together, determine a research agenda that can aid climate-related refugees.

References

Ahmed, S. M. (2020). Impacts of drought, food security policy and climate change on performance of irrigation schemes in Sub-Saharan Africa: The case of Sudan. *Agricultural Water Management, 232*, 106064.

Atwoli, L., Erhabor, G. E., Gbakima, A. A., Haileamlak, A., Kayembe Ntumba, J. M., Kigera, J., Laybourn-Langton, L., Mash, B., Muhia, J., & Mulaudzi, F. M. (2023). COP27 Climate Change Conference: urgent action needed for Africa and the world: Wealthy nations must step up support for Africa and vulnerable countries in addressing past, present and future impacts of climate change. *Nutrition Reviews, 81*(7), 755–757.

Béné, C. (2020). Resilience of local food systems and links to food security: A review of some important concepts in the context of COVID-19 and other shocks. *Food Security, 12*(4), 805–822.

Capisani, S. (2023). Climate change and human mobilities. In G. Pellegrino & M. Di Paola (Eds.), *Handbook of philosophy of climate change*. Springer.

Carlson, C. J., Alam, M. S., North, M. A., Onyango, E., & Stewart-Ibarra, A. M. (2023). The health burden of climate change: A call for global scientific action. *PLOS Climate, 2*(1), e0000126.

Doyle, T., & Chaturvedi, S. (2011). Climate refugees and security: Conceptualizations, categories, and contestations. In J. S. Dryzek, R. S. Norgaard, & D. Schlosberg (Eds.), *The Oxford handbook of climate change and society*. Oxford University Press.

Fouque, F., & Reeder, J. C. (2019). Impact of past and on-going changes on climate and weather on vector-borne diseases transmission: A look at the evidence. *Infectious Diseases of Poverty, 8*(03), 1–9.

Haile, G. G., Tang, Q., Hosseini-Moghari, S. M., Liu, X., Gebremicael, T. G., Leng, G., & Yun, X. (2020). Projected impacts of climate change on drought patterns over East Africa. *Earth's Future, 8*(7), e2020EF001502.

Hasegawa, T., Sakurai, G., Fujimori, S., Takahashi, K., Hijioka, Y., & Masui, T. (2021). Extreme climate events increase risk of global food insecurity and adaptation needs. *Nature Food, 2*(8), 587–595.

Hegerl, G. C., Brönnimann, S., Cowan, T., Friedman, A. R., Hawkins, E., Iles, C., Müller, W., Schurer, A., & Undorf, S. (2019). Causes of climate change over the historical record. *Environmental Research Letters, 14*(12), 123006.

Kogo, B. K., Kumar, L., & Koech, R. (2021). Climate change and variability in Kenya: A review of impacts on agriculture and food security. *Environment, Development and Sustainability, 23*, 23–43.

Kumar, V., Ranjan, D., & Verma, K. (2021). Global climate change: The loop between cause and impact. *Global Climate Change*, 187–211.

Malhi, G. S., Kaur, M., & Kaushik, P. (2021). Impact of climate change on agriculture and its mitigation strategies: A review. *Journal of Sustainability, 13*(3), 1318.

Marcus, H., Hanna, L., Tait, P., Stone, S., & Wannous, C. (2023). Climate change and the public health imperative for supporting migration as adaptation. *Journal of Migration and Health, 7*, 100174.

Martínez, A. H. (2023). *Climate change on rural women in East Africa: Analysis of consequences and recommendations from a gendered approach* (Bachelors Dissertation, University of Alicante, Alacant, Spain). Retrieved on October 31, 2023 from https://rua.ua.es/dspace/handle/100 45/131612.

McAdam, J. (2020). Protecting people displaced by the impacts of climate change: The UN human rights committee and the principle of non-refoulement. *American Journal of International Law, 114*(4), 708–725.

Molotoks, A., Smith, P., & Dawson, T. P. (2021). Impacts of land use, population, and climate change on global food security. *Food and Energy Security, 10*(1), e261.

Mordecai, E. A., Ryan, S. J., Caldwell, J. M., Shah, M. M., & LaBeaud, A. D. (2020). Climate change could shift disease burden from malaria to arboviruses in Africa. *The Lancet Planetary Health, 4*(9), e416–e423.

Munaweera, T. I. K., Jayawardana, N. U., Rajaratnam, R., & Dissanayake, N. (2022). Modern plant biotechnology as a strategy in addressing climate change and attaining food security. *Agriculture & Food Security, 11*(1), 1–28.

Ngcamu, B. S. (2023). Climate change effects on vulnerable populations in the Global South: A systematic review. *Natural Hazards, 118*(2), 977–991.

Niles, M. T., Emery, B. F., Wiltshire, S., Brown, M. E., Fisher, B., & Ricketts, T. H. (2021). Climate impacts associated with reduced diet diversity in children across nineteen countries. *Environmental Research Letters, 16*(1), 015010.

Ofori, S. A., Cobbina, S. J., & Obiri, S. (2021). Climate change, land, water, and food security: Perspectives From Sub-Saharan Africa. *Frontiers in Sustainable Food Systems, 5*, 680924.

Ponce, C. (2020). Intra-seasonal climate variability and crop diversification strategies in the Peruvian Andes: A word of caution on the sustainability of adaptation to climate change. *World Development, 127*, 104740.

Praveen, N. (2022). Climate Refugees: A comprehensive and legal analysis to understanding climate change-induced migration and displacement. *Journal of Law and Emerging Technologies, 2*(2), 24–50.

Pravica, D. W., & Spurr, M. J. (2011). *Mathematical modelling for the scientific method*. Jones & Bartlett Learning.

Rajak, J. (2021). A preliminary review on impact of climate change and our environment with reference to Global Warming. *International Journal of Environmental Science, 10*, 11–14.

Ringler, C., Zhu, T., Cai, X., Koo, J., & Wang, D. (2010). *Climate change impacts on food security in sub-Saharan Africa: Insights from comprehensive climate change scenarios* (No. 1042). Washington, DC: International Food Policy Research Institute (IFPRI).

Sakapaji, S. C. (2023). Climate-induced migration a new normal? A systematic research analysis of the climate-induced migration crisis in Bangladesh. *European Journal of Theoretical and Applied Sciences, 1*(4), 463–489.

Salem, S., & Rosencranz, A. (2020). Climate refugees in the Pacific. *Environment Law Reporter, 50*, 10540.

Saturday, A., Lyimo, T. J., Machiwa, J., & Pamba, S. (2021). Spatio-temporal variations in physicochemical water quality parameters of Lake Bunyonyi, Southwestern Uganda. *SN Applied Sciences, 3*(7), 684.

Thiede, B. C., & Strube, J. (2020). Climate variability and child nutrition: Findings from sub-Saharan Africa. *Global Environmental Change, 65*, 102192.

Tiwari, P., Al Azzawi, N., & Amir, L. (2023). Sustainable refugee camp design in the Dalhamyie settlement (Bekaa, Lebanon) for climate change context. *City, Territory and Architecture, 10*(1), 1–14.

Turyasingura, B., Hannington, N., Kinyi, H. W., Mohammed, F. S., Ayiga, N., Bojago, E., Benzougagh, B., Banerjee, A., & Singh, S. K. (2023). A review of the effects of climate change on water resources in Sub-Saharan Africa. *African Journal of Climate Change and Resource Sustainability, 2*(1), 84–101.

Twongyirwe, R., Mfitumukiza, D., Barasa, B., Naggayi, B. R., Odongo, H., Nyakato, V., & Mutoni, G. (2019). Perceived effects of drought on household food security in South-western Uganda: Coping responses and determinants. *Weather and Climate Extremes, 24*, 100201.

Upadhyay, R. K. (2020). Markers for global climate change and its impact on social, biological and ecological systems: A review. *American Journal of Climate Change, 9*, 159–203.

Vaughan, C., Hansen, J., Roudier, P., Watkiss, P., & Carr, E. (2019). Evaluating agricultural weather and climate services in Africa: Evidence, methods, and a learning agenda. *Wiley Interdisciplinary Reviews: Climate Change, 10*(4), e586.

Yenigun, İ., Balcı, V., Yenigun, A., & Uyanik, S. (2023). Yesterday, today, tomorrow; environmental refugees. *Defense and Security Studies, 4*, 65–74.

Zielinski, C. (2023). COP27 climate change conference: Urgent action needed for Africa and the world. *Palliative Medicine, 37*(1), 7–9.

Zsögön, A., Peres, L. E. P., Xiao, Y., Yan, J., & Fernie, A. R. (2022). Enhancing crop diversity for food security in the face of climate uncertainty. *The Plant Journal, 109*(2), 402–414.

Climate Science

Chris Allan Shisanya, Jane Nyakecho Omalla Khayesi, and Meleckidzedeck Khayesi

This chapter examines what Africa is from the perspective of the academic discipline of Climate Science, i.e., the systematic inquiry of aspects of the Earth's climate—the weather conditions prevailing in an area in general or over a long period. The chapter addresses two research questions. The first question ponders over the kind of insights and possibilities that are generated when the study and management of climate in Africa is approached from an entrepreneurial perspective of opportunity identification and exploitation. There is limited research examining climate in Africa from this perspective. The general image of the climate of Africa is one characterized by droughts, floods, and tropical diseases like malaria, which could easily make one look at the climate of Africa as being problematic. Following sustainable entrepreneurship scholars who view such threats as opportunities for sustainable development (Patzelt & Shepherd, 2011), this chapter challenges this perspective and extends the approach to climate research and action by applying an entrepreneurial process model of opportunity identification and exploitation toward the development of Africa. It conceptualizes climate not merely as an analysis of trends and patterns of temperature, rainfall, wind, and air pressure that create hazards such as floods and droughts, but rather as an asset with opportunities to be discovered and exploited. The application of this framework leads to the second question addressed in this chapter: What is the role of scientists, decision makers,

C. A. Shisanya (✉)
Department of Geography, Kenyatta University, Nairobi, Kenya
e-mail: shisanya.christopher@ku.ac.ke

J. N. O. Khayesi
Department of Management, Leeds University Business School, Geneva, Switzerland
e-mail: j.khayesi@leeds.ac.uk

M. Khayesi
Geneva, Switzerland

A. K. Bangura, J. A. Ifedi (eds.), *Conceptualizations of Africa*, African Studies and Research Forum Series, https://doi.org/10.1007/978-3-031-74535-5_4

investors, and communities in identifying and exploiting opportunities offered by climate in Africa?

The climate of Africa means different things to different people. To some, it is the unbearable high temperature of the deserts (WMO, 2020). To others, it is the perennial destructive floods that they remember (Ramiaramanana & Teller, 2021). These two examples are in line with a prevailing view of the African crisis, a perspective that focuses on the environmental and developmental challenges facing the continent (Eze & Nwaiwu, 2012). Nonetheless, there are others who see the climate of Africa as a welcome asset that can be utilized for the development and benefit of society (AU, 2022). The conventional approach in climatology research is statistical modeling to determine trends and patterns in rainfall, temperature, wind, and air pressure. Although this approach does provide insights into changes in key climate elements, it does not offer the possibility of examining climate from the perspective of a sustainable development opportunity to be discovered and exploited. There is a general neglect of this perspective in climate research, even though the entrepreneurial process model has been in existence for over 20 years. We contribute to climatology research through extending the theoretical lens by specifically advancing an entrepreneurial process perspective as a way of conceptualizing the climate of Africa.

Conceptualizing the Climate of Africa from an Entrepreneurial Process Perspective

The conceptual model we utilize in this section is drawn from entrepreneurship research. Like most concepts in research, entrepreneurship is defined differently by different scholars. We build on three definitions toward our conceptual model. The first definition is from Schumpeter (1934) who considers entrepreneurship to be an innovative and creative activity that leads to the development of new products, services, and ways of managing organizations. The second definition comes from Gartner (1985) who focuses on new venture development as the core activity of entrepreneurship. The third definition is by Shane and Vankataraman (2000) who look at entrepreneurship as the discovery, evaluation, and exploitation of entrepreneurial opportunities. For long, entrepreneurship scholars focused on traits and characteristics of entrepreneurs such as persistence and creativity. In the 1980s, however, entrepreneurship scholars such as Gartner (1988) challenged the trait perspective, arguing that it did not provide insights into how entrepreneurs work to establish ventures.

Gartner (1988) set in motion a critical reflection, arguing that asking who an entrepreneur is was a wrong question. Instead, he argued that the behavioral approach of looking at entrepreneurship as new venture development was more productive. Shane (2003), while building on this behavioral approach, takes this perspective further by considering entrepreneurship as a process involving the interaction of an individual entrepreneur and the entrepreneurial opportunity in an entrepreneurial environment. Thus, individuals, organizations, and governments can be entrepreneurial in the different activities in which they are involved. Entrepreneurship has generally been associated with business. Whereas this view is correct, it is important to note that entrepreneurship can be applied to virtually every aspect of life, including politics, education, planning, and the environment.

Shane's framework offers an alternative approach that shifts the focus of entrepreneurship research from examining the profiles and traits of entrepreneurs to analyzing the interaction between enterprising individuals and valuable opportunities (Shane, 2003; Baron & Shane, 2008). The central thesis of the framework is that the entrepreneurship process begins with the discovery and perception of the existence of opportunities and moves through several actions of opportunity exploitation that involve opportunity evaluation, resource assembly, launch of a new venture and building success, and managing growth.

Entrepreneurial opportunities are defined as situations, circumstances, or problems that can generate business ideas for new products or services with profit potential (Baron & Shane, 2008; Barringer & Ireland, 2016). These opportunities arise from sources internal to a business (such as information possessed by entrepreneurs, their partners, and/or workers) or societal/social, technological, political/regulatory, and environmental changes that are external to a business (Baron & Shane, 2008; Barringer & Ireland, 2016). These opportunities may take the form of new products or services, new ways of organizing, new markets, new raw materials, or new methods or processes of production (Baron & Shane, 2008). Entrepreneurs, therefore, contribute toward resolving critical problems by exploiting opportunities through successful business development. Concomitantly, this chapter explores some of the climate situations, circumstances, or problems that generate business ideas for entrepreneurs in Africa. By exploiting such opportunities, entrepreneurs help to resolve what would have been viewed as climatic threats and challenges.

Discovering or recognizing opportunities is an important step but it does not necessarily lead to exploitation of these opportunities. An individual who discovers an opportunity may exploit it or someone else can do it. Closely related to opportunity discovery is opportunity evaluation, which involves assessing the potential in the opportunity and whether an individual or a group of individuals have the knowledge and skills to actually develop the potential recognized or discovered (Baron & Shane, 2008). Based on this evaluation, an individual or a group of individuals will decide to either proceed or stop. Thus, identifying an opportunity is distinct from exploiting or doing something about it (Baron & Shane, 2008). If a decision is made to proceed, an individual or a group of individuals will assemble resources, launch a new venture, build success and manage growth, and also harvest rewards of investing in the opportunity (Baron & Shane, 2008). While there is the discovery aspect in this process, it is the creative part that turns the potential opportunity or idea to a service or a product. Therefore, the entrepreneurship process consists of an opportunity being found and being made (Venkataraman, 2011); a process that Schumpeter (2008) has described as creative destruction that involves destroying and replacing old ways of doing things with new ones. The creative aspect of entrepreneurship contributes to innovation and socioeconomic change.

It is not enough to simply say there is an opportunity or to identify one. It is necessary to assess what the opportunity may offer, including risks and threats associated with an opportunity. Are they completely new opportunities or an expansion on existing ones? We provide illustrative examples from the climate of Africa to answer this question.

Examples of Climate Opportunity Identification and Exploitation in Africa

One of the ways of identifying entrepreneurial opportunities is looking for problems affecting people and then finding entrepreneurial solutions to those problems (Baringer & Ireland, 2016). In this section, we provide examples of how climate can be approached from an entrepreneurial opportunity identification and exploitation perspective by exploring problems related to three critical elements of climate; these are (1) rainfall, (2) wind, and (3) solar energy. They are discussed one by one in the ensuing subsections.

Rainfall and Its Value in Africa

Rainfall is a great asset and yet very little of the natural rainfall received in Africa is harvested, stored and utilized to supply water throughout the year. Rainfall is an essential climatic element that affects the livelihood of people living in Africa. It provides water resources for agriculture, human consumption, and industrial activities. Nonetheless, the distribution and amount of rainfall vary considerably across the continent, resulting in different ecological and social systems. The conceptualization of rainfall in Africa is multifaceted; therefore, this subsection explores different ways in which rainfall has been conceptualized, looking at its cultural, socioeconomic, and environmental significance. Rainfall has several cultural, socioeconomic, environmental, agricultural, and hydrological cycle values. These different types of significance are discussed.

Cultural Significance of Rainfall in Africa

In African culture, rainfall is often perceived as a sign of blessing, abundance, and prosperity. Many African communities have rain rituals and ceremonies that celebrate the onset of the rainy season or request for rain (Koster, 2011; Ouzman, 1994; Mbiti, 1988; Schapera, 1971). These rituals and ceremonies involve the use of traditional instruments, dances, and songs to invoke the spirits and gods believed to control rainfall. For instance, the Igbo people of Nigeria have a rain-making ceremony called the *Mmanwu* festival, whereby they dress up in elaborate costumes and perform rituals to appease the gods of the land to bring rain (Sabine, 2008).

Similarly, the people of Zimbabwe have a rain-making ceremony called the *Gule Wamkulu*, which is performed by masked dancers believed to have supernatural powers to bring rain (Matsuhira, 2013; Phibion, 2013). Rainfall is also associated with fertility and growth in African culture (Gumo, 2017). Many African societies believe that rainfall is essential for crop growth and fertility, and its absence results in famine, drought, and disease (Gumo, 2017). This belief is evident in the African oral literature, whereby rain is often associated with life and abundance (Phibion, 2013; Matsuhira, 2013). For instance, in the oral literature of the Shona people of Zimbabwe, rain is referred to as *Mvura* and is believed to be the source of life and fertility (Phibion, 2013).

By the same token, in the Yoruba culture of Nigeria, the goddess Oya is associated with rainfall, and her presence is believed to bring fertility and prosperity (Sabine, 2008). Rainfall is also associated with social cohesion in African culture (Gumo, 2017). The onset of the rainy season marks the beginning of planting and harvesting, which often involve communal work and sharing of resources (Mwale & Chita, 2015). Many African communities have traditional practices and customs that promote communal farming and resource sharing during the rainy season (Gumo, 2017). For instance, in the Igbo culture of Nigeria, the *Njala* festival is celebrated to mark the beginning of the planting season, and it involves communal farming and sharing of food and resources (Manus, 2007). Correspondingly, in the Bambara culture of Mali, communal work parties called *Sogo bo* are organized during the rainy season to clear the land for farming and share resources such as food and labor (Biodiversity International and IER, 2017). In some African cultures, however, excess rainfall and resultant flooding are seen as a curse or punishment from the gods (Gumo, 2017). This belief is often linked to certain societal practices such as witchcraft or immoral behavior. For instance, in Malawi, heavy rainfall and flooding are often associated with witchcraft, and those suspected of practicing it are sometimes blamed for the disasters (Mwafulirwa, 2019). In some cases, people are even killed or driven out of their homes as a result of such beliefs and suspicion.

Also, in some parts of Africa, rainfall is a source of conflict among different communities (Guariso & Rogall, 2017). This is especially true in areas where water resources are scarce. Communities may fight over access to water sources, leading to inter-communal conflicts that can be quite violent (Hendrix & Salehyan, 2012). For example, among the pastoralist communities of East Africa, disputes over grazing lands and water sources have been known to lead to clashes among different groups (Tafere, 2015). Consequently, in many African cultures, rainfall is seen as a predictor of events such as disease outbreaks, crop yields, and social changes (Gumo, 2017). For instance, in Zimbabwe, farmers believe that the first rain of the season can predict the success of the harvest (Matsuhira, 2013). If the rain is heavy, it is believed that the harvest will be good, while light rain is associated with poor harvests. Similarly, in some communities, the absence of rain is seen as a sign of impending disaster or social upheaval (Gumo, 2017).

Socioeconomic Significance of Rainfall in Africa

Rainfall patterns in Africa have significant socioeconomic implications, especially in the agricultural sector, which is the backbone of many African economies (Amare et al., 2018). Rainfall affects crop production, food security, and water resources, and its variability and unpredictability pose a significant challenge to farmers and policy makers. African countries have developed various strategies and policies to address the impacts of rainfall variability on agriculture, including rainwater harvesting, irrigation, drought-resistant crops, and early warning systems (Mwadzingeni et al., 2023; Usmail et al., 2023; Tamagnone et al., 2020; DEA, 2016).

Rainfall variability in Africa is a significant challenge to food security and poverty reduction efforts (DEA, 2016). Many African countries have experienced droughts, floods, and other extreme weather events that have resulted in crop failures, food shortages, and water scarcity. In 2022, East Africa experienced one of the worst droughts in decades, affecting over 23 million people and leading to widespread hunger and malnutrition (Kaplan, 2023). Similarly, floods in West Africa have led to loss of lives, destruction of property, and displacement of communities (WFP, 2022).

Environmental Significance of Rainfall in Africa

Rainfall plays a crucial role in shaping the environment in Africa (Fjelde & von Uexkull, 2012). The following are some of the ways in which rainfall impacts the ecology and natural systems in the African continent:

- *Rainfall as a Driver of Vegetation and Ecosystem Dynamics:* Rainfall is a critical factor in driving vegetation and ecosystem dynamics in Africa. In arid and semi-arid areas, vegetation growth is limited by the availability of water, and yet rainfall is the primary source of water for plant growth (Davis-Reddy, 2018). Rainfall variability affects vegetation growth patterns, which can have cascading effects on the ecosystem. For instance, a prolonged drought can lead to reduced vegetation cover, soil erosion, and the loss of biodiversity (Davis-Reddy, 2018). Conversely, heavy rainfall can lead to soil saturation, landslides, and flooding, which can have negative impacts on the ecosystem. Thus, rainfall is an essential driver of vegetation and ecosystem dynamics in Africa (Davis-Reddy, 2018).
- *Rainfall as a Driver of Agricultural Productivity:* Rainfall is also an essential driver of agricultural productivity in Africa (Amare et al., 2018). Agriculture is a significant source of livelihood for many people in Africa, and rainfall is the primary source of water for crop production (Amare et al., 2018). The timing, distribution, and amount of rainfall affect the growth and yield of crops. For instance, inadequate rainfall or prolonged dry spells can lead to crop failure, while heavy rainfall can lead to soil erosion, waterlogging, and the loss of nutrients. Thus, farmers in Africa rely heavily on rainfall to produce crops; thus, rainfall variability can have significant implications for food security (Amare et al., 2018).
- *Rainfall as a Driver of Hydrological Systems:* Rainfall is also a critical driver of hydrological systems in Africa (Banda et al., 2022). The amount and timing of rainfall affect the recharge of groundwater, the flow of rivers and streams, and the availability of surface water resources. In regions with limited water resources, rainfall is the primary source of water for human consumption and industrial activities. Thus, rainfall variability can have significant implications for water availability and management in Africa (Banda et al., 2022).

- *Rainfall Variability and Climate Change:* One conceptualization of rainfall in Africa is its variability and its link to climate change. Africa is highly vulnerable to the impacts of climate change, and rainfall variability is one of the most significant climate-related hazards facing the continent. The Intergovernmental Panel on Climate Change (IPCC) predicts that climate change will lead to increased frequency and intensity of extreme weather events such as droughts and floods (IPCC, 2014). Thus, the conceptualization of rainfall in Africa is often linked to climate change, and there is a growing awareness of the need to adapt to the impacts of climate change.
- *Rainfall and Food Security:* Another conceptualization of rainfall in Africa is its link to food insecurity (Affoh et al., 2022). As already stated, agriculture is the primary source of livelihood for many people in Africa, and rainfall is the primary source of water for crop production. Thus, rainfall variability has significant implications for food security in the region. In recent years, there has been a growing emphasis on climate-smart agriculture, which seeks to enhance agricultural productivity while reducing greenhouse gas emissions and building resilience to climate change (Affoh et al., 2022).
- *Rainfall and Water Resources Management:* Another conceptualization of rainfall in Africa is its link to water resources management. Rainfall is the primary source of water for human consumption, industrial activities, and ecosystems. Thus, the conceptualization of rainfall is often linked to the management and conservation of water resources (Banda et al., 2022).

We now present a few examples of exploiting rainfall as an opportunity in Africa (refer to Fig. 1). In Fig. 1, we note that A2, A3, and A4 are functions of A1. Given

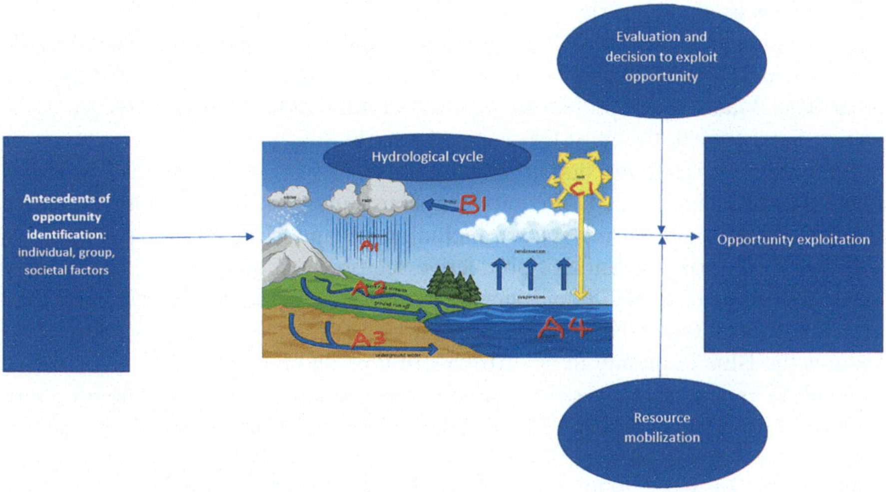

Fig. 1 Entrepreneurial opportunity identification and exploitation in the water cycle, wind, and solar energy systems. (Source: Self-generated by the authors)

this type of relationship, we proceed to illustrate how Africa has exploited the opportunities provided by A2. Africa has a chance to be the first continent to develop its economy using renewable and efficient energy opportunities availed by A2. The leader on the African continent in the production of energy in hydroelectric plants is Ethiopia, which produces over 4000 MW (Borowski, 2022). The construction of the 6350 MW Grand Ethiopian Renaissance Dam is currently underway; its construction began in 2011 on the Nile River. So far, the largest hydropower plant in Africa is Cahora Bassa with a capacity of 2075 MW in Mozambique (World Bank, 2018) and Lauca hydropower plant with a capacity of 2071 MW in Angola (GlobalData, 2022). Data presented by Borowski (2022) show the ten African countries with the largest installed hydroelectric power opportunities provided by A2 that is a function of A1 (refer to Fig. 1).

Let us now examine the opportunity offered by A3 in Fig. 1. Groundwater is the major source of drinking water in Africa and its use for irrigation is forecast to increase substantially to combat growing food insecurity (MacDonald et al., 2012). The total groundwater storage in Africa was estimated to be 0.66 million km^3 in 2012 (0.36–1.75 million km^3) (MacDonald et al., 2012). This is more than 100 times the annual renewable freshwater resources stored in dams and rivers, and 20 times the freshwater stored in Africa's lakes (UNEP, 2010).

Some African countries are already exploiting the opportunity provided by groundwater. South Africa has two massive aquifers. The largest one stretches from Cape Town to Gqeberha. This geological formation covers a surface area of 37,000 km^2 and ranges in thickness from 900 m to 4000 m (MacDonald et al., 2012). The other big one is the Cape Flats aquifer. It is estimated that by 2036, almost R5 billion (USD 274 million) will have been invested to tap these aquifers (Conversation, 2023). Another big aquifer in the continent, containing only ancient trapped water, is the Nubian Sandstone in North Africa. It covers about two million km^2, and spans the countries of Libya, Egypt, Sudan, and Chad (Conversation, 2023). It contains more than 150,000 km^3 of groundwater—more than what the Nile River discharges in 500 years (MacDonald et al., 2012). Libya has undertaken the Great Man-Made River project to pipe water hundreds of kilometers from the Nubian Sandstone to the coast by means of gravity flow.

We now interrogate the opportunities associated with component A4 in Fig. 1 within the African context. This component constitutes the Blue Economy in Africa covering aquatic and marine spaces, including oceans, seas, coasts, and lakes. In addition, it comprises a range of productive sectors such as fisheries, aquaculture, tourism, transport, shipbuilding, energy, bioprospecting, underwater mining, and related activities (see UNECA, 2016). Agenda 2063 of the African Union (AU) declares the Blue Economy to be "Africa's future" and recognizes the key role the ocean plays as a catalyst for socioeconomic transformation. This broad notion stemming from the African Union "Africa's 2050 Integrated Maritime Strategy" and the UNECA "Handbook on the Blue Economy" (UNECA, 2016) is in line with the requirements of the "2030 Agenda for Sustainable Development." The Blue Economy is interlinked with the 2030 Agenda in numerous ways. For instance, beyond Sustainable Development Goal 14 on conservation and sustainable use of oceans, seas and marine resources, the Blue Economy provides an array of opportunities to contribute to ending poverty (Goal 1), to improving food security and eliminating hunger (Goal 2), and to accessing clean water (Goal 6). We shall now illustrate four examples of the opportunities provided by Africa's Blue Economy in numbers, as depicted in UNECA (2016).

The first example is related to fisheries and aquaculture. In 2011, fisheries and aquaculture directly contributed $24 billion to the African economy, representing 1.3% of the total African GDP. A study (UNECA, 2016,) showed that Africa contributed to 9% of the global catch. The number one market for the top ten African exporters of fish products was Europe (70%), followed by Asia (15%), Africa (11%), and North America (2%). Oceania and South America are each estimated at 1%. In 2015, production had risen to 11 million tons, of which 5.5 million tons came from wild catch. The total African production thus represented 5% of global fish production. In 2017, it is estimated that total African imports of fishery products represented a value of $5.6 billion, while exports represented $6.5 billion.

The second example is from Ghana in terms of ocean energy development (UNECA, 2016). Ghana has adopted a scaled-up wave energy technology. The country signed a contract with Sea-based, contracted by TC's Energy, to develop 100 MW wave energy. The development is the first and largest in Africa, and among the few in the world, in commercially developing the emerging wave energy industry in the continent. Ghana has also negotiated for a 1000 MW plant with Yam Pro Energy under a long-term contract to generate wave energy-based electricity. The Ghanaian experience indicates that with resource endowment, engagement of the private sector for finance and technology, negotiation of long-term contracts and provision of the necessary incentives (power purchase agreement), ocean energy resources development in Africa at a large scale is possible (UNECA, 2016).

The third example is related to oil. African coastal States supply about 12% of the world's oil (UNECA, 2016). Algeria, Angola, Egypt, Libya, and Nigeria produce 81% of African oil. The Gulf of Guinea itself accounts for almost 50% of oil and gas production in Africa, or 10% of the world's total. Some statisticians estimate the reserves in this area at 24 billion barrels of oil. Africa has 7.6% of the world's total oil reserves, with Libya and Nigeria holding almost 79% of Africa's oil reserves.

And, the fourth example concerns Mauritius' exploitation of the ocean economy (UNECA, 2016). In recent years, the "Ocean Economy" in Mauritius has been dominated by three sectors: (1) the seaside tourism industry, which accounts for at least 60% of income generated in the national economy since 2012; (2) port activities, accounting for 18%; and (3) fishing industry, accounting for 14%. Figures relating to the ocean economy's contribution to Mauritia's GDP also speak volumes and are extremely encouraging; 11% of GDP in 2013, 14% in 2015, projections of 17% in 2020, and 20% in 2025. The same holds for job creation: 18,000 in 2013, while 21,000 in 2015, projections of 26,000 in 2020, and 35,000 in 2025.

Wind and Its Value in Africa

Africa is endowed with abundant wind resources. Research commissioned by the International Finance Corporation (IFC) in 2020 found that the continent's wind resources could supply its electricity 250 times over. The IFC's regional industry director for infrastructure Middle East and Africa Madam Linda Munyengeterwa and Sean Whittaker IFC Principal Industry Specialist observe the following: "In many areas of the continent, the wind tends to blow strongest at night and early morning. It is very complementary to solar which only generates during the day. Yet progress in harnessing power from winds has been limited. The Global Wind Energy Council notes that Africa is only using 0.01% of the 59,000 gigawatts (GW) that is available in the continent" (Munyengeterwa & Whittaker, 2012, p. 1).

Wind is an essential aspect of African culture and tradition. Throughout history, wind has played a significant role in African societies, impacting daily life and influencing cultural beliefs and practices. In the next subsections, we will look at its cultural, religious and social significance in different regions of the continent. Wind is a natural phenomenon that occurs when air moves from one place to another due to temperature and pressure differences.

Cultural Significance of Wind in Africa

In many African cultures, wind is believed to have spiritual and supernatural powers. For example, in the Yoruba culture of Nigeria, wind is associated with the god of the air, *Orunmila*, who is believed to control the direction of wind. In this culture, wind is believed to carry messages from the gods to the people, and its direction is used to interpret the will of the gods (Lewis, 1978). Similarly, in the Maasai culture of Kenya and Tanzania, wind is believed to have healing powers and is used in traditional medicine to treat various ailments (Casucci, 2015). In some African cultures, wind is also associated with specific seasons or events. For instance, in the Sahel region of West Africa, the Harmattan wind that blows from the Sahara Desert is associated with the dry season and is characterized by dusty and hazy conditions (Okeahialam, 2016). The Harmattan wind is often viewed as a time of reflection and introspection, with many people taking the opportunity to engage in spiritual practices and rituals (Adhvaryu et al., 2019).

Religious Significance of Wind in Africa

Wind is believed to be a manifestation of divine power in some African societies. For example, in the Akan religion of Ghana, wind is believed to be a messenger of the gods and is associated with the spirit world, carrying messages from the ancestors and is used in divination practices to communicate with the spirits (Agyarko, 2013). Similarly, in the traditional religion of the Wolof people of Senegal, wind is believed to be a manifestation of the supreme God, Roog (Venema, 1978). Wind is considered a powerful force that can both bless and curse individuals, depending on their behavior and actions (Venema, 1978).

Social Significance of Wind in Africa

Wind also has social significance in African societies, influencing daily life and shaping cultural practices. For example, in pastoral communities such as the Maasai of Kenya and Tanzania, wind is an essential factor in livestock management (Kereto et al., 2022). The direction and strength of wind can impact grazing patterns, and wind is also used as a signal for movement during migrations (Kereto et al., 2022). In farming communities, wind is also significant, influencing planting and harvesting seasons. For instance, in the coastal regions of West Africa, the Harmattan wind signals the end of the rainy season and the beginning of the planting season (Nicholson, 2013).

After discussing the cultural, religious, and social significance of wind, we now present a few examples where wind has been exploited as an opportunity in Africa. The wind industry in Africa is promising (Abbas et al., 2020). A growing number of African countries that have embraced wind energy and are taking steps to generate power from this renewable source. For example, Egypt, Morocco, South Africa, Kenya, Ethiopia, and Tunisia are the leading economies which are driving wind capacity installation in Africa. Senegal, Ghana, Gambia, Chad, and Algeria are steadily joining the wind power exploitation group in Africa.

There has been political acceptance of renewable energy sources in Africa and wind in general, with the establishment of the African Renewable Initiative 2015. The drivers of wind energy in Africa are South Africa with an estimated 6360 MW of power from wind by 2030; that is, 69% from the Independent Power Producers (IPPs), as part of the Renewable Energy Independent Power Procurement Program—REIPPP (Abbas et al., 2020). With 1.2 GW wind energy capacity, Morocco is another country which is a driver of wind energy in the African continent. The wind energy program which was launched in 2010 will enhance wind energy production capacity to over 2000 MW till 2020 (Abbas et al., 2020).

Egypt is blessed with superb wind speed, especially around the Suez Canal, and it is one of the best areas in the world for harnessing energy. The wind speed sometimes ranges between 8 and 10 m/s at height 100 M (IRENA, 2018). Egypt targets 40% of renewable energy sources (RES) to make its energy matrix by 2035 (Abbas et al., 2020). Under its distinctive feed-in tariff program that was launched in 2014, it seeks to encourage electricity generation from RES, targeting 4300 MW generation (IRENA, 2018). Ethiopia's current wind installed capacity is 324 MW (IRENA 2019). Furthermore, Kenya is a regional leader in the Eastern Africa Power Pool, with 335 MW installed capacity and another 350 MW expected to be procured by 2023 (GWEC, 2020; Abbas et al., 2020). Kenya has already awarded more than 1 GW of wind capacity under its prevailing feed-in tariff rate. Mauritania has a current installed capacity of 34 MW (Chen et al., 2017). However, the country is endowed with an excellent wind speed along its northern coastline between 8.3 and 8.7 m/s, which increases to 9 m/s in the Nouadhibou region (Mustapha et al., 2015).

Sunshine and Solar Energy and Its Value in Africa

Africa has 40% of the globe's potential for solar power, yet it only utilizes 1.48% of the total global capacity for electricity generation of solar energy (IRENA, 2021). While Africa as a continent generally faces major electricity issues, Africa South of the Sahara suffers most from these issues (Abdelrazik et al., 2022). The region is presently home to more than two-thirds of the world's population which does not have access to electricity (IEA, 2019). In comparison to other developing countries, inhabitants in the region have the lowest per capita access to modern energy (Brew-Hammond, 2010).

It is estimated that in Africa South of the Sahara, 0.6 billion people (out of the 1.14 billion) do not have access to electricity (Corfee, 2019); this represents about 53% of the total population (Abdelrazik et al., 2022). In addition, due to inadequate maintenance, around 15% of the installed capacity in the region is not functioning (Abdelrazik et al., 2022). Moreover, it is estimated that about 0.7 billion people of the entire African population still rely on traditional biomass for power generation since access to the national power grid can be costly (Adenle, 2020).

Solar energy has several benefits for Africa, which makes it an attractive option for meeting the continent's energy demands. The following are some of the benefits of solar energy for Africa:

- *Energy security*: Solar energy can reduce Africa's dependence on fossil fuels and imported energy. The continent has vast reserves of coal, oil, and gas, but these resources are often located in remote areas, making them expensive to extract and transport. Solar energy, on the other hand, can be generated in any location with access to sunlight, providing a decentralized source of energy.
- *Job generation*: The adoption of solar energy can generate thousands of jobs in Africa. Solar energy projects require a range of skills, from engineering and installation to maintenance and operation. A study by the International Renewable Energy Agency (IRENA) found that the solar energy sector in Africa could create up to four million jobs by 2030 (IRENA, 2020).
- *Improved access to electricity*: Solar energy can provide access to electricity to millions of people in Africa who currently lack it. According to the World Bank, more than 600 million people in Africa South of the Sahara lack access to electricity (IRENA, 2021). Solar energy can provide a clean, affordable and reliable source of electricity to these communities, particularly in rural areas.
- *Environmental benefits*: Solar energy is a clean and renewable source of energy, which can help reduce greenhouse gas emissions and mitigate climate change. The adoption of solar energy in Africa can help the continent to meet its commitments under the Paris Agreement and contribute to global efforts to reduce emissions.

Despite the apparent huge potential of solar energy and solar photovoltaic (PV) in Africa, there are still significant challenges to the widespread adoption of the technologies which are linked to a scarcity of resources (Dagnachew et al., 2020). Financial, human resource, environmental and technology challenges are all prevalent. As a result, a thorough understanding of the challenges associated with solar technology adoption is crucial (see Abdelrazik et al., 2022).

We finally present examples where solar has been exploited as an opportunity in Africa. The data presented in Table 1 show the solar energy capacity in selected countries in Africa in the year 2022.

Taking Kenya as an example, it has introduced a range of policies that have bolstered renewable generation at both the utility scale and at a micro-grid level. Having an energy policy that encourages scale at both ends of this spectrum has led to impressive penetration rates for an array of renewable technologies, and across urban and rural populations. Solar energy is almost ubiquitous across Kenya, both at utility scale and through solar home systems (SHS). SHS have provided an affordable route to energy access for millions of people across Kenya—especially amongst rural communities—as it allows them to bypass central grid connection, which can often be prohibitively expensive. Approximately 200,000 rural homes in Kenya have SHS and the country sells between 25,000 and 30,000 PV modules each year, making it the second most dynamic commercial solar energy marketplace in the world after India (Gogla, 2019).

A variety of innovative business ventures have also emerged from this solar energy ecosystem (Gogla, 2019). M-KOPA, which helps low-income communities get access to energy, provides affordable solutions whereby people can gradually increase their ownership through flexible micro-payments, enabled by smartphone technology. Once a customer has paid off the installments, s/he can use this asset as well as his/her credit history with M-KOPA to gain access to further products and services that will enable the person to develop in his/her life more quickly. M-KOPA has been instrumental in scaling up pay-as-you-go (PAYG) solar across Kenya. By the end of 2021, M-KOPA had unlocked $600 million in credit for its customers;

Table 1 Solar energy capacity in selected countries in Africa in the year 2022

Country	Solar energy capacity (MW)
South Africa	6326
Egypt	1724
Morocco	858
Algeria	460
Senegal	263
Reunion	224
Kenya	307
Namibia	176

Source: Self-generated by the authors based on data gleaned from Abdelrazik et al. (2022), IRENA (2019), and IEA (2019)

brought energy to 4.5 million Kenyans; and installed one million SHS that prevents around two million tons of CO_2e from being emitted. M-KOPA is just one actor within a vibrant and dynamic energy market in which all stakeholders are pushing clean energy generation throughout Kenya (Gogla, 2019).

The preceding discussion has unearthed a number of entrepreneurial opportunities generated by climate in Africa. Analyzing these climate-induced sources in Africa reveals varied forms of opportunities for entrepreneurs in Africa (refer to Table 2).

Table 2 Examples of climate-induced entrepreneurial opportunities in Africa

Climate as a source of opportunity	Opportunity identified	Form of opportunity
Rainfall	Hydroelectric power plants	• Energy is generated and sold as a *new product* • Energy is used as a *new raw material* to power devices such as refrigerators, processing machines, and computers used for different businesses • Energy makes it possible for processing to occur; hence, it facilitates *new production methods* • Energy facilitates the operation of computers and the internet thus enabling entrepreneurs to use a *new method of organization*, i.e., selling their products online. Online selling, in turn, enables entrepreneurs to reach *new markets*
	Fisheries	• Sea foods as *new products*
	Agribusinesses	• Rainfall facilitates crop cultivation, yielding *new products* • Crop cultivation is facilitated by irrigation and thus a *new production process*
	Aquifers	• Water is piped and sold as a *new product*
	Water transport	• *New service* of water transportation, e.g., transporting goods and people by ship or boat • Water transport enables entrepreneurs to supply their products to *new markets*
Wind	Wind energy power plants	• Wind energy is generated and sold as a *new product* for individual, household and commercial use
Solar	Solar energy/ electricity	• Solar energy is generated and sold as a *new product* for individual, household and commercial use • Solar energy is used as a *new raw material* to recharge gadgets such as phones, radios, TVs, lights, and machines like posho mills

Source: Self-generated by the authors

The Role of Scientists, Decision Makers, Investors, and Communities in Identifying and Exploiting Opportunities Offered by Climate in Africa

We have identified two key areas for action by scientists, decision makers, investors, and communities. The first is cultivating an entrepreneurial approach to analyzing and managing the climate of Africa. While we recognize that not everyone is born with an entrepreneurial mind-set or can attain mastery of it, we have learnt from research that an entrepreneurial approach can be cultivated through learning and training. It is with this understanding that we draw upon the work of Carol Dwek (2006) pertaining to the growth and fixed mind-set model to point out that an entrepreneurial mind-set needs to be cultivated among scientists, decision makers, investors, and communities working on climate in Africa. We see this undertaking as a vital approach to incorporate in the lifelong learning of this group of people to enable them to constantly look for opportunities in the climate of Africa and find sustainable ways of exploiting them.

In practical terms, an entrepreneurial approach to analyzing and managing the climate of Africa means that the training of the scientists and decision makers should go beyond the existing statistical modeling and a strong focus on characteristics of the climate to incorporate skills and techniques in entrepreneurial opportunity identification and exploitation. Courses and practices in entrepreneurship need to be made available to climate scientists and decision makers through tailored programs developed specifically for this group of learners in their regular climate courses or by encouraging this group of learners to take a course on entrepreneurship in departments of management or entrepreneurship.

Furthermore, research on the entrepreneurial approach to climate needs to be explored. More importantly, institutions such as universities could, for example, start thinking of offering professional training courses in Climate Science via the Massive Open Online Courses (MOOC) platform in the following areas: Climate Change—Transforming Your Organization for Sustainability; Building Sustainable Future with Technology; Communicating Climate Change for Effective Climate Action; Environmental Entrepreneurs—Strategies for Green Business in Africa; and Tackling Climate Change—Sustainable Business Models for a Circular Economy.

The second area of action is for these stakeholders to take practical steps to assess and invest in the existing potential of the climate of Africa. Although there is some investment in solar energy, wind energy, and rainfall in Africa, the extensive potential presented in the preceding sections is yet to be fully exploited. A "Blue Ocean" strategy needs to be adopted by investors to go beyond the existing areas of investment in order to identify and exploit opportunities in the climate of Africa. The "Blue Ocean" strategy advances the view that instead of staying and operating in the overcrowded and extremely competitive zones of red oceans, a prudent solution is to invent and capture new demand, representing uncontested market spaces where the competition is irrelevant (Kim & Mauborgne, 2011). There are several actions that can be taken, and we highlight the following three examples:

(1) Organizations, communities, and individuals need to undertake basic water harvesting such as roof water and runoff harvesting to build a reasonable reservoir of water. Most of the rainfall and its surface runoff in high-rainfall regions of Africa is rarely meaningfully harvested by individuals, businesses, educational institutions, industrial and commercial establishments, and households. The water is largely left to run by, although these institutions are in need of water for their operations.
(2) Extensive and intensive investment in diverse technology for harvesting water, wind energy and solar energy.
(3) Address administrative, procedural and financial barriers to exploiting water, solar and wind resources in Africa.

The agenda of the recently concluded Africa Climate Summit in Nairobi highlighted the importance of investing in key aspects of Africa's climate. An insightful description of this possibility is reflected in one of the sessions indicated in a document produced by the Africa Climate Summit Programme (2023). It is stated in the document that the existing and potential investors can explore investment in renewable energy in Africa. It is also mentioned that the growing sustainable investment portfolios offer an opportunity that can be utilized to generate funds, human resources and technology for growing the untapped climate potential in Africa.

Conclusion and Recommendation

Based on the analyses in the foregoing sections, we conclude that the climate of Africa offers an entrepreneurial opportunity that has been inadequately exploited with respect to assessing and investing in specific aspects. We therefore recommend that the potential of the three examples of (1) rainfall, (2) wind energy, and (3) solar energy should be fully exploited for the development of the African continent.

References

Abbas, Q., Khan, A. R., Bashir, A., Alemzero, D. A., Sun, H., Iram, R., & Iqbal, N. (2020). Scaling up renewable energy in Africa: Measuring wind energy through an econometric approach. *Environmental Science and Pollution Research, 27*, 36282–36294.

Abdelrazik, M. K., Abdelaziz, S. E., Hassan, M. F., & Hatem, T. M. (2022). Climate action: Prospects of solar energy in Africa. *Energy Reports, 8*, 11363–11377.

Adenle, A. A. (2020). Assessment of solar energy technologies in Africa opportunities and challenges in meeting the 2030 agenda and sustainable development goals. *Energy Policy, 137*, 111180.

Adhvaryu, A., Bharadwaj, P., Fenske, J., Nyshadham, A., & Stanley, R. (2019). *Dust and death: Evidence from the West African Harmattan*. Working Paper 25937. Boston, MA: National Bureau of Economic Research.

Affoh, R., Zheng, H., Dangui, K., & Dissani, B. M. (2022). The impact of climate variability and change on food security in sub-Saharan Africa: Perspective from panel data analysis. *Sustainability, 14*(2), 759.

Africa Climate Summit Programme. (2023). *Event programs*. Retrieved on September 26, 2023, from https://africaclimatesummit.org/side-events/

African Union—AU. (2022). *Climate change strategy and action plan*. African Union.

Agyarko, R. O. (2013). God of life: Rethinking the Akan Christian concept of God in the light of ecological crisis. *The Ecumenical Review, 65*(1), 51–66.

Amare, M., Jensen, N. D., Shiferaw, B., & Cisse, J. D. (2018). Rainfall shocks and agricultural productivity: Implication for rural household consumption. *Agricultural Systems, 166*, 79–89.

Banda, V. D., Dzwairo, R. B., Singh, S. K., & Kanyerere, T. (2022). Hydrological modelling and climate adaptation under changing climate: A review with a focus in Sub-Saharan Africa. *Water, 14*, 4031.

Baron, R. A., & Shane, S. A. (2008). *Entrepreneurship: A process perspective*. South-Western Cengage Learning.

Barringer, B. R., & Ireland, R. D. (2016). *Entrepreneurship: Successfully launching new ventures* (5th ed.). Pearson.

Biodiversity International and IER. (2017). *Underutilised crops in the livelihoods, diets and adaptation practices of smallholders in Sikasso and Segou, Mali: Baseline results from the programme "Linking Agrobiodiversity Value Chains, Climate Adaptation and Nutrition: Empowering the Poor to Manage Risk."* Rome, Italy.

Borowski, P. F. (2022). Water and hydropower – Challenges for the economy and enterprises in times of climate change in Africa and Europe. *Water, 14*, 3631.

Brew-Hammond, A. (2010). Energy access in Africa: Challenges ahead. *Energy Policy, 38*(5), 2291–2301.

Casucci, B. A. (2015). *A cold wind: Local Maasai perceptions of the common health landscape in Narok South*. Unpublished PhD Dissertation, Department of Anthropology, Case Western Reserve University, Cleveland, Ohio.

Chen, L., Xu, L., & Yang, Z. (2017). Accounting carbon emission changes under regional industrial transfer in an urban agglomeration in China's Pearl River Delta. *Journal of Clean Production, 167*, 110–119.

Conversation. (2023). *Africa's aquifers hold more than 20 times the water stored in the continent's lakes, but they aren't the answer to water scarcity*. Published March 21, 2023.

Corfee, J. (2019). *Achieving clean energy access in Sub-Saharan Africa: A case study for the OECD, UN Environment, World Bank Project*. Financing Climate Futures: Rethinking Infrastructure.

Dagnachew, A. G., Hof, A. F., Roelfsema, M. R., & van Vuuren, D. P. (2020). Actors and governance in the transition toward universal electricity access in Sub-Saharan Africa. *Energy Policy, 143*, 111572.

Davis-Reddy, C. (2018). *Assessing vegetation dynamics in response to climate variability and change across Sub-Saharan Africa*. Unpublished PhD Thesis, Faculty of Sciences, Stellenbosch University, South Africa.

DEA—Department of Environmental Affairs. (2016). Climate information and early warning systems for supporting the disaster risk reduction and management sector in South Africa under future climates. In S. M. Munzhedzi, V. P. Khavhagali, G. M. Midgley, P. de Abreu, S. Scorgie, M. Braun, & Z. Abdul (Eds.), *Long-term adaptation scenarios flagship research programme*. DEA.

Eze, C., & Nwaiwu, I. U. (2012). Africa in the 21st century: The challenges of environmental degradation. *International Journal of Environmental Sciences, 1*(4), 263–273.

Fjelde, H., & von Uexkull, N. (2012). Climate triggers: Rainfall anomalies, vulnerability and communal conflict in Sub-Saharan Africa. *Political Geography, 31*(7), 444–453.

Gartner, W. B. (1985). A conceptual framework for describing the phenomenon of new venture creation. *The Academy of Management Review, 10*(4), 696–706.

Gartner, W. B. (1988). Who is an entrepreneur is the wrong question. *American Journal of Small Business, 12*(4), 11–32.

Global Wind Energy Council—GWEC. (2020). *Global Wind Report 2019*. GWEC.

GlobalData. (2022). *Hydropower to continue to dominate Angola power generation through 2035*. Retrieved on August 20, 2023, from https://www.power-technology.com/comment/hydropower-dominate-angola-power/

Gogla. (2019). *Powering opportunity in East Africa: Proving off-grid solar is a power tool for change*. UK Aid.

Guariso, A., & Rogall, T. (2017). Rainfall inequality, political power and ethnic conflict in Africa. *LICOS Discussion Paper* 391/2017.

Gumo, S. (2017). Praying for rain: Indigenous systems of rainmaking in Kenya. *The Ecumenical Review, 69*(3), 386–397.

Hendrix, C. S., & Salehyan, I. (2012). Climate change, rainfall, and social conflict in Africa. *Journal of Peace Research, 49*(1), 16–25.

IEA. (2019). *Africa energy outlook 2019*. IEA. Retrieved on May 25, 2023, from https://www.iea.org/reports/africa-energy-outlook-2019

IPCC. (2014). *Climate change: Impacts, adaptation and vulnerability: Contribution of working group II to the fifth assessment report*. Cambridge University Press.

IRENA. (2018). *Renewable Energy outlook: Egypt*. Abu Dhabi, United Arab Emirates: International Renewable Energy Agency (IRENA).

IRENA. (2019). *Renewable Capacity Statistics 2019*. Abu Dhabi, United Arab Emirates: International Renewable Energy Agency (IRENA).

IRENA. (2020). *Renewable Energy and Jobs – Annual Review 2020*. Abu Dhabi, United Arab Emirates: International Renewable Energy Agency (IRENA).

IRENA. (2021). *Renewable Capacity Statistics 2021*. Abu Dhabi, United Arab Emirates: International Renewable Energy Agency (IRENA).

Kaplan, S. (2023). *Climate change caused catastrophic East Africa drought, scientists say*. Retrieved on September 27, 2023, from https://www.washingtonpost.com/climate-environment/2023/04/27/climate-change-drought-east-africa/

Kereto, J., Nkurumwa, A. O., Obara, J., & Mango, N. (2022). Livestock management and protection using indigenous technical knowledge among the Maasai of Narok county, Kenya. *Cogent Social Sciences, 8*(1), 2040793.

Kim, W. C., & Mauborgne, R. (2011). *Blue ocean strategy. HBR's 10 Must Reads on Strategy*. Harvard Business Review Press.

Koster, M. M. (2011). The Kilumi rain dance in modern Kenya. *The Journal of Pan African Studies, 4*(6), 171–193.

Lewis, M. W. (1978). Yoruba religion in Trinidad-transfer and reinterpretation. *Caribbean Quarterly, 24*(3/4), 18–32.

MacDonald, A. M., Bonsor, H. C., Dochartaigh, B. E. O., & Taylor, R. G. (2012). Quantitative maps of groundwater resources in Africa. *Environmental Research Letters, 7*, 024009.

Manus, U. C. (2007). The sacred festival of Iri Ji Ohuru in Igboland, Nigeria. *Nordic Journal of African Studies, 16*(2), 244–260.

Matsuhira, Y. (2013). Rain making ceremony in the Nyandoro region Zimbabwe. *African Religions Dynamics, 1*, 165–182.

Mbiti, J. S. (1988). *African religions and philosophy*. Heinemann.

Munyengeterwa, L., & Whittaker, S. (2012). *Powering Africa's sustainable development through wind*. Retrieved on September 27, 2023, from https://blogs.worldbank.org/climatechange/powering-africas-sustainable-development-through-wind

Mustapha, T., Gauri, S., & Gürbüz, G. (2015). Mauritania: Renewables readiness assessment. *Energia, 1*, 192.

Mwadzingeni, L., Mugandani, R., & Mafongoya, P. L. (2023). Perception of climate change and coping strategies among smallholder irrigators in Zimbabwe. *Frontiers in Sustainable Food Systems, 2023*, 7.

Mwafulirwa, J. (2019). Characterising local knowledge across the flood management cycle: A case study of Southern Malawi. *Sustainability, 11*(6), 1681.

Mwale, N., & Chita, J. (2015). African traditional religion harvest festivals in the context of climate change in Eastern Zambia: The experiences of women. *International Journal of Multidisciplinary Research and Development, 2*, 9–30.

Nicholson, S. E. (2013). The West African Sahel: A review of recent studies on the rainfall regime and its inter-annual variability. *International Research Notices 2013*. Retrieved on June 01, 2023, from https://doi.org/10.1155/2013/453521

Okeahialam, B. N. (2016). The cold dusty Harmattan: A season of anguish for cardiologists and patients. *Environmental Health Insights, 10*, 143–146.

Ouzman, S. (1994). Rain from the mountain of Zion. *The Digging Stick, 11*(4), 2–4.

Patzelt, H., & Shepherd, D. A. (2011). Recognizing opportunities for sustainable development. *Entrepreneurship Theory and Practice, 35*(4), 631–652.

Phibion, O. S. (2013). The rain praying music of the Bakalanga of Botswana and Zimbabwe. *Case Studies Journal, 2*(5), 8–17.

Ramiaramanana, F. N., & Teller, J. (2021). Urbanization and floods in Sub-Saharan Africa: Spatiotemporal study and analysis of vulnerability factors-case of Antanarivo Agglomeration (Madagascar). *Water, 2012*(13), 149.

Sabine, J. B. (2008). *The Water Goddes in Igbo Cosmology*. Africa World Press.

Schapera, I. (1971). *Rainmaking Rites of Tswana Tribes*. Afrika-Studienzentrum.

Schumpeter, J. A. (1934). The theory of economic development: An inquiry into profits, capital, credit, interest and the business cycle. *Harvard Economic Studies 46*. Cambridge, MA: Harvard College.

Schumpeter, J. A. (2008). *Capitalism, socialism and democracy*. Harper Perennial.

Shane, S. (2003). *A general theory of entrepreneurship: The individual-opportunity nexus*. Edward Elgar.

Shane, S., & Vankataraman, S. (2000). The promise of entrepreneurship as a field of research. *The Academy of Management Review, 25*(1), 217–226.

Tafere, K. (2015). Natural resource degradation and conflict in the East African pastoral drylands. *African Security Review, 24*(3), 1–9.

Tamagnone, P., Cea, L., Comino, E., & Rosso, M. (2020). Rainwater harvesting techniques to face water scarcity in African drylands: Hydrological efficiency assessment. *Water, 12*(9), 2646.

UNEP. (2010). *Africa Water Atlas*. Division of Early Warning and Assessment (DEWA), United Nations Environment Programme.

United Nations Economic Commission for Africa—UNECA. (2016). *Africa's blue economy: A policy handbook*. UNECA.

Usmail, A. J., Maja, M. M., & Lakew, A. A. (2023). Farmers' perceptions of climate variability and adaptation strategies in the rural areas of Dire Dawa administration, eastern Ethiopia. *Heliyon, 9*(5), e15868.

Vankataraman, S. (2011). Entrepreneurship and entrepreneurial opportunity: Made as well as found. In R. K. Mitchell & R. N. Dino (Eds.), *Search of research excellence: Exemplars in entrepreneurship*. Edward Elgar.

Venema, L. B. (1978). *The Wolof of Saloum: Social structure and rural development in Senegal*. Centre for Agricultural Publishing and Documentation.

WMO. (2020). *State of the Climate in Africa: WMO-No. 1275*. World Meteorological Organization.

World Bank. (2018). *Zambezi hydropower sustainability protocol assessment: The Cahora Bassa North Bank Power Project*. Washington, DC: World Bank. Retrieved on September 27, 2023, from http://documents.wworldbank.org/curated/en/home

World Food Programme—WFP. (2022). *West Africa hard-hit by climate crisis as deadly floods decimate lives and livelihoods*. Retrieved on September 27, 2023, from https://www.wfp.org/news/west-africa-hard-hit-climate-crisis-deadly-floods-decimate-lives-and-livelihoods/

Chris A. Shisanya is an agroclimatologist by training. He is a full professor in the Department of Geography at Kenyatta University in Kenya. He has won over 60 national and international competitive research grants over the last 25 years, with over 110 peer-reviewed journal articles and 10 book titles to his credit. He serves on various editorial boards of high-impact scientific journals. His recent ongoing multidisciplinary and multi-institutional research projects include Women's Economic Empowerment funded by BMGF and GECRES funded by IDRC/UKaid under the theme "Advancing Gender Equality in Fragile Food Systems in African Sahel."

Jane Nyakecho Omalla Khayesi is an experienced higher education teacher, researcher, and consultant in management and entrepreneurship. She is Fellow of the Higher Education Academy and currently holds the position of Lecturer in Enterprise and Entrepreneurship at Leeds University Business School in the UK. She also holds the position of Director of the Master of Science in Enterprise and Entrepreneurship program at Leeds University Business School. She presents regularly at international conferences and publishes in leading journals such as *Entrepreneurship Theory and Practice*, the *Academy of Management Journal*, and the *Journal of Occupational and Organizational Psychology*.

Meleckidzedeck Khayesi is a teacher by profession. He holds a PhD degree in Transport Geography. He was born in Vihiga District, Kenya. Over the years, he has honed his competences in knowledge synthesis, scientific and normative guidance writing, listening, training, mentoring, leading project teams, networking, resource mobilization, and delivery of products. He loves transformative pedagogy and local level-led development change. He greatly supports individuals to nurture their skills and talents to become the best they can be.

Computer Science

Alie Kunda

Probed in this chapter is the conceptualization of Africa in relation to computer science, commonly defined as the systematic study of the principles and use of computers—i.e., electronic devices for storing and processing data, typically in binary form, according to instructions given to it in a variable program; also, persons who make calculations, especially with a calculating machine. Thus, in order to narrow the focus of the chapter, the key question investigated here is the following: What are some of the ways Africa has been conceptualized apropos the academic discipline of computer science?

Given that the preceding question is a "What is?" type, the fitting methodology used to ground the analysis in this chapter is a *descriptive case study* approach, which is defined as "a qualitative approach that illustrates facts focusing on a single or specific nature of a phenomenon…one that is focused and detailed on propositions and questions about a phenomenon that is carefully scrutinized and articulated at the outset (and one that is employed as) a means to provide tools for researchers to study complex phenomena within their contexts" (Bangura et al., 2019, p. 63).

Concomitantly, three among the most investigated facets of the link between Africa and the field of computer science are examined in this chapter. The first is the African binary code, the second deals with Africa as the origin of algorithm, and the third concerns African universities rankings in the computer science academic discipline. But before interrogating these facets, a general conceptualization of computer science is presented. Thereafter, a conclusion is reached and recommendations are provided.

A. Kunda (✉)
Department of Research, The African Institution, Washington, D.C., USA

A. K. Bangura, J. A. Ifedi (eds.), *Conceptualizations of Africa*, African Studies and Research Forum Series, https://doi.org/10.1007/978-3-031-74535-5_5

Computer Science: A Conceptualization

With a focus on the conceptions of "automation," "computation," and "information," the general conceptualization of the academic discipline of computer science has traversed the following two strands: (1) *theoretical disciplines* such as algorithms, information theory, and theory of computation; and (2) *applied disciplines* like the design and implementation of hardware and software. I broach these strands one at a time in the ensuing subsections for intelligibility.

Theoretical Disciplines

To begin with, individuals working in the subfield of *theoretical computer science* utilize a conglomeration of concepts from both computer science and mathematics fields to examine the abstract mathematical concepts involved in computing. The subfield is the genesis of the theory of computation, it can be a bit complex, and it is at the same time fascinating to those who are interested in the ways in which Mathematics, technology and science intersect. Accordingly, the subfield is quite broad and comprises concepts from many other disciplines. Examples of the subject matters that are breached by individuals who study the subfield include (a) "distributed computation," (b) "algorithms," (c) "cryptography," (d) "algebra," (e) "Computational Number Theory," (f) "data structures," (g) "quantum computation," (h) "machine learning," and (i) "computational neology." This listing is, of course, not exhaustive, as there are many more topics that intersect to make up this diverse subfield of computer science (Computer Science Degree Hub, 2023). Nonetheless, as it will become abundantly clear in the next subsection, the demarcation between theoretical disciplines and the applied disciplines in computer science is not totally irrevocable, since the theoretical component of the field and the applied aspects all come together with regard to computing.

Next, theoretical computer science is generally divided into four disciplines. I discuss each one of these disciplines in the remainder of this section separately for clarity.

First, the discipline of *Language Theory* deals with the manner information and computation are expressed. The discipline commences with the question "What is information?" and addresses this question by hypothesizing that any piece of "human-usable information" can be represented as a string of symbols. Thus, in this discipline, individuals seek to explicate how to express these functions, in addition to the data upon which they operate and the modules, objects, and control structures which host these functions. They also investigate how *syntax* (i.e., the arrangement of words and phrases to create well-formed sentences in a language) definitions can be written to denote which strings belong to the language and how *semantic* (i.e., relating to meaning in language or logic) notations can give meaning to these strings. In addition, they interrogate how these languages are employed by human beings—i.e., *pragmatics* (or language in use and the contexts) (Loyola Marymount University, 2023).

Second, the discipline of *Automata Theory* involves the study of the construction and examination of formal models of computational devices (i.e., computers). Individuals utilizing this discipline begin by generating a theory by thinking about how it is they expect their functions to be formally denoted and, in some sense, how they operate. In essence, Automata Theory allows these individuals to actually compute—or "carry out," or "evaluate"—these functions (Loyola Marymount University, 2023). Thus, Automata Theory has been commonly defined as "the study of abstract machines called automata, which computer scientists use to describe and analyze the behavior of computer systems" (Indeed, 2023, p. 1).

Third, the discipline of *Computability Theory* is predicated on the following major question: "Can every function be represented as a string of symbols that we can process with a machine?" Put differently, "Is there a program for every function?" The obvious answer is no. The explanation for this answer is that "Programs are just strings, so we can list them in increasing alphabetic order" (Loyola Marymount University, 2023, p. 1).

Also, Computability Theory is referred to as "Recursion Theory" because it is used to investigate decision problems a computer program can and cannot solve. Decision problems are characterized as "yes or no questions" that can possess an infinite number of factors. For instance, if a computer can determine whether numbers in a set are even or odd, no matter what the numbers are, that would constitute a decision problem the computer is capable of solving (Indeed, 2023).

And fourth, the discipline of *Complexity Theory* sets theoretical limits on what individuals can and cannot compute, but it does not tell them what is "practically computable." Essentially, it is not worth running a problem that will take thousands of years to complete. The theory arises when individuals encounter a question such as, "What resources are required to perform certain computations?" or stated differently "How much time and memory is needed to solve this problem?" Accordingly the theory yields results such as "This function requires ___________ to compute: only a single step, only a fixed number of steps, logarithmic time, linear time, quadratic time, polynomial time, exponential time, no more than a single cell of scratch memory, scratch memory in the form of a stack (which is very efficient), logarithmic space, linear space, polynomial space, exponential space" (Loyola Marymount University, 2023, p. 1). In addition, since the focus of computational complexity is on how much time and memory different algorithms require, the more resources an algorithm requires, the more complex it is (Indeed, 2023).

Applied Disciplines

For starters, *applied computer science* is commonly conceptualized as an area of computer science in which those who specialize in it study the following core aspects: (a) programming fundamentals—object-oriented, event-driven, and algorithms; (b) information management—database systems, data modeling, data warehousing, relational databases, and query languages; (c) software engineering—software requirements and design, software process, and software project management; (d) operating systems and net-centric computing—Internet programming, networks, and security; (e) human-computer interaction—graphical user interface design and programming; and (f) intelligent systems—machine learning. Individuals who specialize in this area are instructed on how to strengthen their communication skills, encounter group dynamics, and promote self-confidence (The University of Winnipeg, 2023). Accordingly, these individuals learn a broad set of computer science skills that are useful in any industry such as programming (python, object-oriented, and system-level), web development, mobile applications, graphics, networks, communications, database design and programming, and linear algebra (University of South Carolina, 2023).

Next, since computer science is now applied in every field, and each of these fields has many subfields, it is only to be expected that there are numerous *applied computer science* disciplines. A detailed coverage of these disciplines will require several volumes. Thus, only 13 among the most popular of these disciplines are briefly described one at a time in the rest of this subsection for conciseness and lucidness.

First, the discipline of *Artificial Intelligence* deals with the brainpower of machines as opposed to that of human beings or other animals. The discipline's objective is to amalgamate goal-orientated processes such as problem-solving, decision-making, and environmental adaptation. It has emerged as a crucial component of every technology-driven industry. Individuals specializing in this discipline study automated reasoning, Prolog, automated theorem provers, mathematical theorems, computer vision, soft computing, and natural language, etc. (From Sources across the Web, 2023).

Second, the *Computer Programming* discipline focuses on the procedures of implementing certain computational tasks that usually require designing and building executable computer programs. The discipline involves functions like (a) investigation, (b) producing algorithms, (c) depicting the preciseness of algorithms and utilization of resources, and (d) executing algorithms. Via computer graphics and computational geometry, it addresses the generation of images; and through Programming Language Theory, it considers different ways to describe computational techniques. Specialists in the discipline study formal methods, software engineering, algorithm design, computer programming, human-computer interaction, reverse engineering, and theory of computation (From Sources across the Web, 2023).

Third, specialists in the discipline of *Human-computer Interaction* pay particular attention to the design and utilization of computer technology that deals with the interfaces between people and computers. These specialists observe the manners humans interact with computers and design technologies that allow them (i.e., humans) to interact with computers in new ways. Among their subject matters are formal methods, software engineering, algorithm design, computer programming, human–computer interactions, reverse engineering, theory of computation, information systems analysis, mobile application development, network architecture, and operating systems (From Sources across the Web, 2023).

Fourth, in their investigations, specialists in the discipline of *Data Science* employ a mixture of statistics, scientific computing, scientific methods, processes, algorithms and systems to extract or extrapolate knowledge and insights from noisy, structured and unstructured data. They work with large data sets to delineate meaningful insights. They also engage in software development, game development, data analytics, etc. (From Sources across the Web, 2023).

Fifth, *Computer Network* as a discipline deals with a collection of computers sharing resources situated on or furnished by "network nodes." The discipline's import hinges on the fact that computers employ basic communication protocols over digital interconnections to communicate with one another (From Sources across the Web, 2023).

Sixth, the discipline of *Cybersecurity* (also referred to as "Computer Security," "Digital Security," "Information Technology Security," or "Internet Security") is about the protection of computer systems and networks from attacks by malicious actors. Specialists in this discipline engage in the study of a hybrid of computer science subjects, cybersecurity, data science, information systems, etc. (From Sources across the Web, 2023).

Seventh, *Software Engineering* is a discipline that deals with the utilization of an "engineering-based approach" to develop computer software. Specialists in this discipline apply the engineering design procedure to devise, develop, maintain, test, and evaluate computer software (From Sources across the Web, 2023).

Eighth, in the discipline of *Computer Architecture*, individuals learn how to describe the structure of a computer system designed from component parts. These individuals' tasks include ensuring that all the components of a complex system work together so that the system can operate as expected. It has been observed, however, that these individuals can occasionally focus too much on high-level descriptions that lead them to ignore the details of the implementation process. Their foci include databases, algorithms and data structures, information security, computer architecture, wireless networking, operating systems, and cybersecurity (From Sources across the Web, 2023).

Ninth, as a discipline, *scientific computing*, also dubbed "Computational Science" or "Technical Computing," tackles advanced computing capabilities in order to comprehend and resolve complex physical problems. Experts in this discipline construct mathematical models and quantitative analytical techniques to address these problems. Since these experts also employ tools from numerical analysis, symbolic computation, computational physics, computational chemistry and bioinformatics, they have been characterized as scientific, practical, and theoretical problem solvers (From Sources across the Web, 2023).

Tenth, in the discipline of *computer vision*, the focus is on techniques of how to obtain, perform a series of mechanical operations, explore and comprehend "digital depictions," and produce "high-dimensional information" from the real world in order to generate numerical or symbolic data. The other areas from which the discipline draws techniques for its inquiry include image processing, computational geometry, parallel programming, animation for computer games, advanced game development, etc. (From Sources across the Web, 2023).

Eleventh, the *computer graphics* discipline probes how art and images are generated be utilizing computers. The focus of the discipline is on the core technology in digital photography, film, video games, digital art, cellular phones and computer displays, and many specialized applications. With the aid of computational geometry, specialists in the discipline examine the generation of images by using programming language theory, image processing, information visualization, concurrent parallel and distributed systems, databases, and compilers (From Sources across the Web, 2023).

Twelfth, in the *data mining* discipline, emphasis is placed on the procedures for discovering and extracting patterns in large data sets by employing techniques at the intersection of machine learning, statistics, and database systems. The main goal is to organize, store, and retrieve large amounts of data easily. Thus, the relevant subject matters for the discipline are computer networks, Internet programming, data mining, computer graphics, formal languages and automata, and algorithms and complexity (From Sources across the Web, 2023).

And thirteenth, specialists in the *bioinformatics* discipline combine techniques from the fields of biology, computer science, mathematics, statistics, augmented with information theory, to analyze biological data for interpretation and prediction. With the aim of solving problems in biological and medical science, these specialists utilize methods from machine learning, data mining, artificial intelligence, optimization, visualization, and simulation, and also develop novel techniques as required. Their areas of specialization include precision medicine, regenerative medicine, metabolomics; machine learning, mass spectrometry, phenotyping, multiomics, and mass spectrometry imaging (From Sources across the Web, 2023).

African Binary Code

To commence with, Abdul Karim Bangura (2020a, b) provides ample evidence to show that it was the people of Kemet/Ancient Egypt and other Africans who invented the number zero (0) and the binary code upon which modern computing is based. And from Ron Eglash (1999), one learns that it is not improbable to envision the genesis of base-2 calculation to be traced to African divination that found its way to the geomancy of European alchemists and subsequently translated into binary calculation, where it is today applied in every digital circuit from alarm clocks to supercomputers. Eglash provides the following examples of the pseudorandom number generation from shift register circuits to support his assertion:

> (a) If we think of the two-strokes as zero and single stroke as one, the Bamana divination, system is almost identical to the process of pseudorandom number generation used by digital circuits called "shift registers." Here the circuit cakes mod 2 of die last two bits in the register and places the result in the first position. The other bits are shifted to the right, with the last discarded. This four-bit shift register will only produce 15 binary words before the cycle starts over, but the period of the cycle increases with more bits (2^n-1). For the entire 16 bits (four symbols of four bits each) that begin the Bamana divination, 65,535 binary words can be produced before repeating the cycle. (b) Electrical circuit representation of a

> four-bit shift register combined with exclusive-or to perform the mod 2 operation. While schoolteachers are making increasing use of African culture, in the mathematics classroom, few have explored the potential applications to technology education (1999, p. 98).

Next, according to Paulette Brown-Hinds, in about 20,000 BC, the Ifà of Nigeria's Yoruba emerged as "concept originators of today's computers." She points out that the Yoruba believed in the existence of a depository of "Knowledge containing Universal Forms–Idea-Forces as patterns, expressing itself in Numbers" ((2014, p. 1). For the Ifáà, these "Cosmic Numbers" represented concealed orderly and balanced systems that are made up of two digits: 0 and 1, each of which is now referred to as a "bit." These numbers, she says, were derived from the

> Amenta—and therefore being a 'Divine Archetype' (i.e. Seed)—each by itself reproduces itself and become the "Thing" it makes, called a "Divine Paradigm." They symbolized and called this Binary System the Dafa—using them for forecasting. By applying this same principle more broadly into two parts, situated on the extremes of the same pole, is what formed the Principle of Polarity basis–that the Universe is founded upon multiple contradictions. A later Chinese renaming and symbolizing of these African Laws of Opposites are Yin (negative principles of the Cosmos) and Yang (positive Principles). Symbolized as fishes, Yin/Yang are positioned in opposition to each other and go round and round, like night and day. Though Yin and Yang are not in conflict, as in trying to eat each other, each can only be there because of the other. This Yin/Yang concept essentially translates into the positive and negative duality as the ultimate reality of all existence and all that permeates the Material universe. It is based on the primordial binary (i.e. something consists of two parts) elements of dark and light (Brown-Hinds, 2014, p. 1).

More instructive is that as Brown-Hinds adds, the aforementioned binary system display

> ...was accessible to the specially trained Very Ancient African Shaman via Trance—a Possession upon contact. Very Ancient Africans taught that all Dualities (pairs of natural opposites like light/dark) must obey Binary Laws. With respect to numerics, binary signifies any mathematical system having two at its base—e.g. black/white, hot/cold, inside/outside. Yes/no, on/off, and positive/negative are all encounters of a binary nature. These polar opposites are like two sides of a coin—each side joined to the other—meaning one is void without the other—the entire coin being composed of Vibrations (2014, p. 1).

Brown-Hinds continues by pointing out that given that vibrations are pulsations, the existence of an electrical pulse = 1 and its nonexistence = 0. Accordingly, she says, early African thinkers believed in the existence of a type of "energy-knowledge field" that encompasses the life and soul of the human that binds people together with their families and own destinies from life to life—thus, there exists a need for a process using a binary system to unravel the distinct patterns (Brown-Hinds, 2014).

Also, Omoniyi Osadare (2019), tracing the origin of "binary counting" to the West African traditional system, recounts from his elementary school days how students learnt about number systems: integers, base-2, and base-10. He notes that they were taught how base-2 is the binary system of counting that reflects 0 and 1, and that in Mathematics and digital electronics the base-2 number system (the binary number system) is utilized for their operations. He also recalls that they were instructed that the binary number system reflects the duality of Nature. He further points out that "Western scientists and mathematicians have admitted that the binary system existed in the African divination system which, in Yorùbá, is known as Ifá, prior to the works of (Gottfried Wilhelm) Leibniz and his contemporaries. The historical path for base-2 calculation begins with African divination, runs through the geomancy of European alchemists, and is finally transformed into binary calculation, where it is now applied in every digital circuit" (Osadare, 2019, p. 1).

To buttress his preceding rendering, Osadare provides the following example he titled "COMPUTER PROGRAMMER and the BABALÁWO" with accompanying explanations:

> "Bí Ifáà mi bá hù kan, màá tẹ méjì; bí Ifáà mi bá hù méjì màá tẹ kan."
>
> (Ifá my Ifá brings up one, I will mark two; If my Ifá brings up two, I will mark one)
>
> For computer programmers, making the connection between Ifá binary notation and programming is a relatively straight-forward notion. The parallel between a babaláwo and a computer programmer is striking.
>
> Programmers
>
> Babaláwo
>
> Write codes/instructions the codes are on the CPU (Central Processing Unit) the processor
>
> Incantations (ohùn or ọfọ̀)
>
> Chant/write binary codes
>
> Recites Odù Ifá!
>
> Write on sand (Silicon/CPU),
>
> writes on Ìyẹ̀rẹ̀osùn (Ìrosùn powder) (Osadare, 2019, p. 1).

Thus, according to Osadare, a computer code is essentially an "Àfọ̀ṣẹ (oun tí a fọ̀ tí ó sì ṣẹ)!—i.e., a command which invokes action." Concomitantly, he points out, computer codes, like incantations, have the ability to animate the entities in the CPU (sand) and make them become whatever users want, e.g., a game console, financial trading systems, air traffic controls, and social media operations. He adds that the "ohùn of the Babaláwo invoked from the Odù of Ifá brings about a result" from his preceding query (Osadare, 2019, p. 1). It behooves me to explain here for those readers who may not be familiar with the acronym CPU that it refers to the "central processing unit," which is the basic component of a computer that acts as its "control center." The CPU, also called the "central" or "main" processor, is a complex set of electronic circuitry that runs the machine's operating system and applications.

Osadare adds that the Yoruba notion of binary system vis-à-vis Ifáà employs various systems to generate a binary pattern from the 256 corpuses of "Ifá. Ọpẹ̀lẹ̀," a divining chain that contains eight seeds strung together and held at the middle, thereby creating equal distances between the seeds. He also mentions that the seeds have "convex and concave sides" which represent the 0 and 1 values in the binary coding. The major aspect here, he states, is that the Yoruba system of denoting a problem and generating solutions is deeply implanted in a binary coding system used before Leibniz and Boolean (i.e., George Boole) found this numbering system. Osadare further posits that "the power of this binary system has been harnessed in the electronics and computing industry since the dawn of the Information age because of its simplicity and efficiency" (2019, p. 1).

To boot, like the other aforementioned authors, Osadare similarly mentions that Ifáà is the "African Information Retrieval system" utilized across the African continent. He also repeats the observation that Europe modified the system and named it "Geomancy." He likewise adds that it is this same system which was practiced in Kemet that spread to Asia where the Chinese call it "I Ching" and the Japanese call it "Shinto" (Osadare, 2019).

In addition, Bangura (2014) mentions that the Lebombo Bone demonstrates the existence of a quite sophisticated accounting system which enabled Africans to master time, and it is the first visible evidence of the emergence of calculation in human history. He describes the bone as having up to six phases, thereby suggesting that it represents a binary calendar. He then cites the mathematical analysis offered by Franz Gnaedinger for the bone as follows:

> The pattern consists of 14 by 14 dots, linked by two more dots. The 29 dots of the top line can be read as a lunar calendar. There are 30 spaces between and next to the 29 dots. Read the spaces and dots as follows: 30 spaces plus 29 dots plus 30 spaces plus 29 dots plus 30 spaces …, yielding 30 29 30 29 30 29 30 29 30 29 30 29 30 29 30 … nights or 30 59 89 118 148 177 207 236 266 295 325 354 384 413 443 472 502 … nights for 1 2 3 4 5 6 7 8 9 10 11 12 13 14 15 16 17 … lunations. There are 2 × 13 × 14 dots below the top line, yielding 364 days; add the dot in the middle of the bottom line and you obtain 365 days for a year (Gnaedinger, 2005, p. 1; quoted in Bangura, 2014, p. 21; Bangura, 2020b, p. 128).

Furthermore, Angel Brown (2021) in her analysis of the African binary code begins by stating her comprehension of "binary" as a notion employed to portray all instructions and data in a digital computer system, in addition to all communications among digital systems. Next, she points out that almost all of the data and instructions she expresses in programs that she develops are eventually converted into and/or represented in binary form. Thereafter, she mentions that most of the history of the binary code with which she is familiar traces back to Leibniz with the invention of the system in 1689. Nonetheless, she, just like the preceding authors discussed in this section, says that it is also known that Leibnitz acquired his knowledge of the system from ancient Chinese teachings of I Ching. Thus, according to her, there are notable examples of binary systems that predate Leibniz's system (Brown, 2021).

Nonetheless, as Brown goes on to reveal, she was quite surprised to learn about the existence of the system called Ifáà in West Africa and is common across various groups of people and cultures in the region. She notes that Ifáà remains in use in West Africa and throughout the African Diaspora and that in 2005 it was officially added to the list of "intangible cultural heritage of humanity" by the United Nations Educational, Scientific and Cultural Organization (UNESCO). She mentions that the Ifáà corpus is comprised of 256 components similar to modern computing one is likely to see in hardware such as random-access memory (RAM), flash drives, and memory cards divided into increments of 256. This is because, as she states, each decimal number is represented by eight integers and various combinations of ones and zeros when converted into binary form (Brown, 2021).

Brown adds that the Ifáà corpus is a 16-bit system utilized to communicate with the "Yoruba Gods" (i.e., *Orishas*). She describes the religious ceremony as involving a number of steps. First, a priest holds six sacred palm nuts in his left hand. Second, he tries to grab all of the six palm nuts at the same time with his right hand. Third, if one nut remains in his left hand, he makes a mark on the divination board to represent a zero; if two nuts remain, he makes two marks to represent one; if none or more than two nuts remain, he makes no marks at all. Fourth, he continues the procedure until four pairs of unique marks are left on the board, which generate an 8-bit binary code. This code is equivalent to one of the 256 corpuses or Odù—and, thus, the existence of a divining chain that is a similar process (Brown, 2021).

Brown concludes by stating that it is quite impressive to know that there exists a religious divination that relies on Mathematics, rather than faith alone. For her personally, she adds, this knowledge is even more impressive because she originates from a Nigerian ancestry that has a part in what makes technology function today (Brown, 2021).

Africa as the Origin of Algorithm

Among the many authors who have written about the genesis of "algorithm" are Ron Eglash (1999) and Joseph Pyram (2020). Beginning with Eglash, one learns that the term "algorithm" can be traced to a Persian Arab mathematician named Abu Abdullah Muhammad ibn Musa Al-Khawarizmi, who lived from about 780 to about 850 AD. Through his book titled *Hisabal'jabrw' al-muqabalci* (translated into English as *Calculation by Restoration and Reduction*), Al-Khawarizmi is also said to have given us the term "algebra" (and, thus, he is called by many "the Father of Algebra"). Eglash points out that while the focus of Al-Khawarizmi was on "numeric procedures for solving equations," the contemporary term "algorithm" is applicable to any formally specified procedure. Eglash also notes that a geometric algorithm provides explicit steps for producing a specific set of spatial patterns. He adds that it has been demonstrated that the iterations of such "pattern-generating procedures" yield fractals on a computer screen. He then proceeds to show how iterations of these procedures are utilized to produce scaling designs for two indigenous African algorithms: (1) the 45-degree–angle constructions of the Mangbetu ivory sculpture and (2) the lusona drawings of the Chokwe (Eglash, 1999).

Next, according to Pyram, customary names like "Abdullah," "Muhammad," "Musa," etc. were given to Arabs, and so they would, and still to this day, distinguish one another by their location—cities, states, etc. In this context, if "John Doe were an American," he would be called "John Doe al-Amriki"—i.e., "John Doe the American"—to distinguish him from say "John Doe the Canadian." Likewise, Muhammad ibn (i.e., "son of") Musa became known as "al-Khwarizmi," meaning "the native of Khwarizm" (in Arabic, the letter "ya," from which the "i/ee" sound is derived, is added to the end of a word to denote "belonging to"). Pyram adds that

Al-Khwarizmi penned many important mathematical books that were later translated into Latin. It was his book on Arabic-Hindu numerals and arithmetic titled *Al-Khwārizmī on the Hindu Art of Reckoning*, later Latinized as *Algoritmi de numero Indorum*, from which the Western world got the term "algorithm" (Pyram, 2020).

Nonetheless, as Pyram goes on to point out, from the denotation of an "algorithm" as a "series of step-by-step instructions that aim to solve a particular problem" (2020, p. 1), it is therefore only true that algorithms have existed for as long as humans have been striving to solve problems on earth. Accordingly, he proffers, things like "recipes," "mathematics," and "physics" are all forms of algorithms. He therefore contends that the making of the first artificial fire in the Wonderwerk Cave of South Africa millions of years ago by Homo Erectus constitutes the first evidence of the use of algorithms (Pyram, 2020).

So, an immediate question that arises here is the following: What is the evidence of the first artificial fire made by Homo Erectus in the Wonderwerk Cave of South Africa millions of years ago all about? In the article on the subject written by Kim Luke, one gleans that an international team led by the University of Toronto in Canada and Hebrew University in Israel identified the earliest known evidence of the use of fire by human ancestors based on microscopic traces of wood ash, alongside animal bones and stone tools found in a layer at the cave. The research was funded by three organizations: (1) the Social Sciences and Humanities Research Council of Canada, (2) the National Science Foundation, and (3) the Wenner Gren Foundation. The other research team members include (a) James Brink and Sharon Holt of the National Museum, Bloemfontein; (b) Marion Bamford of the University of Witswatersrand; and (c) Ari Matmon and Hagai Ron, colleagues at Hebrew University. In addition, the research at Wonderwerk Cave is carried out in collaboration with the McGregor Museum, Kimberley and under permit for the South African Heritage Resources Agency (Luke, 2012).

Luke goes on to cite Michael Chazan, anthropologist and co-director of the project and director of University of Toronto's Archaeology Centre, as stating that their analysis "pushes the timing for the human use of fire back by 300,000 years, suggesting that human ancestors as early as Homo erectus may have begun using fire as part of their way of life" (quoted by Luke 2012, p. 1). Luke mentions that the research findings were published in the *Proceedings of the National Academy of Sciences* on April 2, 2012. He adds that "Wonderwerk is a massive cave located near the edge of the Kalahari where earlier excavations by Peter Beaumont of the McGregor Museum in Kimberley, South Africa, had uncovered an extensive record of human occupation. A research project, co-directed by University of Toronto's Chazan and Liora Kolska Horwitz of Hebrew University, has been doing detailed analysis of the material from Beaumont's excavation along with renewed field work on the Wonderwerk site" (quoted by Luke, 2012, p. 1).

Also, Luke states that according to the analysis of the sediments found by lead authors Francesco Berna and Paul Goldberg of Boston University, the "ashed" plant residues and burned bone particles seem to have been burned locally instead of having been carried into the cave by water or wind. He adds that these researchers also found extensive evidence of surface discoloration that is typical of burning. He then quotes Chazan as asserting that "The control of fire would have been a major turning point in human evolution…The impact of cooking food is well documented, but the impact of control over fire would have touched all elements of human society…Socializing around a camp fire might actually be an essential aspect of what makes us human" (cited by Luke, 2012, p. 1).

Another profitable question that is worth probing here is this one: What other evidence of early African algorithms exist? Indeed, there are many authors who have provided evidence for early African algorithms. For the sake of brevity, I discuss two examples from Eglash (1999) and one from Bangura (2014).

First, Eglash indicates that thousands of years ago, "lusona figures" were traditionally drawn in the sand by the Chokwe people of Angola. He also shows "successive iterations of the same algorithm were sometimes used to produce similar patterns of increasing size" and "the first and third iterations of another lusona algorithm carved into a wooden box lid" (Eglash, 1999, p. 69).

Second, according to Eglash, the Yoruba "adire" cloth (a "tie and dye" cloth first produced and worn by the Egbaland people in the Southwestern city of Abeokuta in Nigeria dating back to the nineteenth century) is veritably two separate pieces attached along the horizontal midline. The dye pattern is established by sewing along folds before dye is applied and then removing the threads so that the white lines are left where the dye did not penetrate. He points out that the folding method is based on "reflection symmetry across a diagonal" and is easiest to understand by malting a paper model. He adds that "adire" artisans have not only developed an algorithm for generating this nonlinear scaling series, but have done so in a way that maximizes efficient production, i.e., all folds fall along the same two edges, so only two edges need to be sewn. He also mentions that a paper model can imitate this effect by running a heavy felt marker along the two edges, so that the ink bleeds through all the layers, and that one can cheat by inking each fold as s/he unfolds it. He further notes that the white lines in the "adire" are triple; and that this, too, is made by a reflection symmetry, sewing next to the fold to yield the two outer lines—one on each side of the fold—and sewing right on the edge of the fold to make the center line (Eglash, 1999).

Third, from Bangura, one learns that Paulus Gerdes in his book titled *Geometry from Africa: Mathematical and Educational Explorations* (1999) demonstrates that while the sona sand tradition was cultivated primarily by the Chokwe, related peoples such as the Ngangela and Luchazi also did so. Bangura notes that these peoples inhabit eastern Angola, neighboring zones of Congo/Zaire, and northwest Zambia. He adds that among the many excellent examples of how culture is transmitted through the sona sand tradition that is undergirded by mathematics dating back to thousands of years mentioned by Gerdes is this monolinear one: the "chased chicken design of dimensions 5×6, 9×10, and 3×8, respectively. When the same algorithm is applied to a grid of dimension 10×5, the three chased chicken lines are needed to embrace all points on the grid" (Gerdes, 1999, p. 182; Bangura, 2014, p. 24).

African Universities Rankings in Computer Science

In addition to the subject matter examined in this section being among the most investigated facets of the link between Africa and the field of computer science, it is also important for understanding how the descendants of the earliest inventors of the phenomenon have capitalized on its contemporary developments. To start with, the SCImago Institutions Rankings (SIR) has the most authoritative and cited, and up-to-date rankings of universities in the field of computer science across the globe. Thus, the discussion in this section is based on the organization's work. For the sake of clarity, the remainder of this section is divided into two subsections. The first subsection is about the methodology utilized by the organization, so that the reader can understand the system of techniques used to rank the universities; the second subsection deals with the rankings themselves.

The SIR Methodology

The SIR methodology is anchored on three key facets: (1) general considerations, (2) inclusion criteria, and (3) score indicators. These facets are discussed separately in the rest of this subsection for coherence.

First, as it concerns *general considerations*, to commence with, the SIR classifies academic and research-related institutions according to a composite indicator that amalgamates three different sets of indicators based on (1) research performance, (2) innovation outputs and (3) societal impact measured by their web visibility. The organization provides what it refers to as "a friendly interface" that permits one to visualize a customized ranking from the amalgamation of the abovementioned three sets of indicators. It also allows one to compare the trends for individual indicators of up to six institutions. In addition, for each large sector, it allows one to generate distribution charts of the different indicators. Furthermore, if one wants to engage in comparative analysis, the value of the composite indicator has been set on a scale that ranges from 0 to 100. Nonetheless, the line graphs and bar graphs always represent ranks—lower is better, so the highest values are the worst (SIR, 2023).

Next, in the new (2023) version of the methodology, the manner of "numbering the ranks" of the institutions was amended. The novel approach of numbering employs the same numerical ranks when the institutions are matched in terms of the values of their indicators, and "jumps" as many ranks as institutions are tied. This technique allows the number of ranks to correspond roughly with the number of institutions. The change has been applied to previous versions in order to allow one to observe the realistic comparisons and observations of the developments of institutions over time (SIR, 2023).

Thereafter, for standardization, the methodology requires an extensive manual process of disambiguation of the institutions' names so that the highest level of precision for the different indicators can be achieved. A gigantic data processing task related to the identification and disambiguation of institutions through the institutional affiliation of documents included in Scopus is required for the development of an assessment tool for bibliometric analysis aimed to characterize research institutions. In this respect, the goal of the methodology is twofold: (1) in order to define and generate unique identifications for institutions, a list of research institutions whereby every institution is correctly identified and defined has be drawn up; the common issues on this task include institution's merge or segregation and denomination changes; and (2) attribution of publications and citations to each institution is taken into account vis-a-vis the institutional affiliation of each author in the field "affiliation" of the database; a mixed system—"manual and automatic"—for the assignment of affiliations to one or more institutions, as applicable, is utilized; as well, an identification of multiple documents with the same Digital Object Identifier (DOI) and/or title is employed (SIR, 2023).

Also, one of the major characteristics of the assured standardization process, which is the highest possible level of disambiguation, is the great care and detail exercised in the identification of institutional affiliations. Institutions can be categorized by the countries to which they belong. Institutions which operate in different countries and, thus, cannot be subsumed under any one country, have likewise been included. An institution marked with an asterisk comprises a group of sub-institutions, identified by the abbreviated name of the parent institutions, which in turn indicates the results of all of its sub-institutions. To boot, institutions are also grouped by sectors such as "Universities," "Health," and "Government" (SIR, 2023).

In addition, in order to rank the institutions, the calculation is generated each year from the results obtained over a period of five years ending two years before the edition of the ranking. For example, when the selected year of publication is 2021, the results used are those from the five-year period of 2015–2019. The only exception is the case of web indicators that have only been calculated for the last year (SIR, 2023).

Second, in terms of *inclusion criteria*, to begin with, an institution must have published at least 100 works included in the SCOPUS database during the last year of the selected time period. Next, the citable documents, which include articles, book chapters, conference papers, and review and short surveys, must represent at least 75% of the total documents published by the institution. Also, (a) the information source utilized for the indicators for innovation is the PATSTAT database; (b) the sources of information used for the indicators for website visibility are Google and Ahrefs; (c) the Unpaywall database is used to identify Open Access documents; and (d) Altmetrics from PlumX metrics and Mendeley are used for societal factors (SIR, 2023).

In addition, the methodology is now treated as a "LEAGUE TABLE" with the objective of providing a useful metric tool for institutions, policymakers and research managers for the analysis, evaluation and improvement of their activities, outputs, and outcomes. Furthermore, the methodology's "best quartile" is generated by the institution in its country comparing the quartiles based on the overall indicator, research factor, innovation factor, and societal factor. Moreover, the indicators are categorized into three groups intended to reflect the (1) scientific, (2) economic and (3) social characteristics of institutions. The methodology includes both size-dependent and size-independent indicators that are indicators-influenced rather than by the size of the institutions. Accordingly, the methodology delineates overall statistics of the scientific publications and other outputs of institutions, while facilitating comparisons among institutions of different sizes. It is emphasized that once the final indicator has been calculated out of the combination of the different indicators, to which a different weigh is assigned, the resulting values are normalized on a scale that ranges from 0 to 100 (SIR, 2023).

Third, vis-à-vis *score indicators*, the following factor indicators and weights are utilized for the three categories: (1) Research (50%)—Normalized Impact (NI) 13%, Excellence with Leadership (EwL) 8%, Output (O) 8%, Scientific Leadership (L) 5%, Not Own Journals (NotOJ) 3%, Own Journals (OJ) 3%, Excellence (Exc) 2%, High Quality Publications (Q1) 2%, International Collaboration (IC) 2%, Open Access (OA) 2%, and Scientific Talent Pool (STP) 2%; (2) Innovation (30%)—Innovative Knowledge (IK) 10%, Patents (PT) 10%, and Technological Impact (TI) 10%; and (3) Societal (20%)—Altmetrics (AM) 10%, Inbound Links (BN) 5%, and Web Size (WS) 5% (SIR, 2023).

The SIR Rankings

As displayed in Table 1, a total of 143 African academic institutions were ranked in the SIR 2023 rankings. Of these institutions, the majority (94 or about 66%) are in North Africa. South Africa has the highest representation (17 or about 35%),

Table 1 SIR rankings of African academic institutions by country for 2023

Country's name	Number of institutions
Egypt	33
Algeria	25
Morocco	21
South Africa	17
Nigeria	15
Tunisia	14
Ethiopia	5
Ghana	3
Cameroon	2
Botswana	1
Mauritius	1
Uganda	1
Rwanda	1
Tanzania	1
Senegal	1
Libya	1
Namibia	1
Total	143

Source: Self-generated by the author using data from SIR (2023)

Table 2 Top 20 of the SIR rankings of African academic institutions by country for 2023

Country's name	Number of institutions
Egypt	11
South Africa	4
Morocco	2
Tunisia	2
Ethiopia	1
Total	20

Source: Self-generated by the author using data from SIR (2023)

followed by Nigeria at a close second (15 or about 31%), among the remaining 49 (approximately 34%) academic institutions which are in Africa South of the Sahara.

From Table 2, it can be gleaned that among the top 20 ranked academic institutions, the majority (15 or 75%) are also in North Africa. Of the remaining five (25%), four (80%) are in South Africa and one (20%) is in Ethiopia.

Conclusion and Recommendation

It is quite evident from the preceding sections that the designs of what is referred to today as computer science were birthed by the progenitors of Africans. Equally evident, however, is that the contemporary descendants of these African ancestors have not harnessed the principles and use of computers to their full potential in the African continent. The second part of this assertion is supported by the fact that, as the preceding results indicate, only 143 African academic institutions engaging in computer science were ranked by SIR in 2023. The number represents only about 11% of the 1279 "officially recognized higher-education institutions in Africa" (see the database of uniRank, 2023). The import of the uniRank database hinges on the following question and response:

> What are the most popular Universities in each African country? uniRank answers this question by publishing a list of African countries and providing a ranking of their higher-education institutions meeting the following uniRank selection standards: being chartered, licensed or accredited by the appropriate higher education-related organization in each country; offering at least three-year bachelor's degrees or postgraduate master's or doctoral degrees; delivering courses predominantly in a traditional, non-distance education format (uniRank, 2023, p. 1).

Thus, I recommend that every university in Africa should launch a computer science program: certificate, diploma, or degree. This is because computer technology plays a major role in today's digital epoch. The technology has not only impacted every aspect of our personal lives, it has also revolutionized industries such as commerce, communication, education, entertainment, healthcare, and scientific research. Indeed, as Krati Joshi, for example, points out,

> Computing and computer technology has infiltrated every aspect of our lives. For instance, we can work, shop, and play at the click of a button, because computer science has made it possible. So what is computer science? Why is it important? And is it a promising career? According to the U.S. Bureau of Labor Statistics (BLS), overall employment in computer and information technology occupations will grow by 15% between 2021 and 2031. That makes it even more important for you to understand 'what is computer science' so that you can decide whether you want to pursue a career in that field (2022, p. 1).

Besides, Africans harnessing the full potential of computer science will be part and parcel of the endeavor to reclaim their heritage.

References

Bangura, A. K. (2014). Domesticating mathematics in the African mother tongue. *The Journal of Pan African Studies, 6*(7), 12–58.

Bangura, A. K. (2020a). *Seshu nu per ānkh*: The ancient Kemetian genesis of digital communication. In K. Langmia (Ed.), *Digital communications at crossroads in Africa*. Springer.

Bangura, A. K. (2020b). *The African mother tongue and mathematical ideas: A diopian pluridisciplinary approach*. Vernon Press.

Bangura, A. K., Obando, J., Munene, I. I., & Shisanya, C. (2019). *Conducting research and mentoring students in Africa: CODESRIA college of mentors handbook*. CODESRIA Publications.

Brown, A. (September 2, 2021). *African binary code*. Medium.com. Retrieved on August 8, 2023, from https://arbrown110.medium.com/african-binary-code-70de3076e395

Brown-Hinds, P. (September 27, 2014). African binary system. *Black Voice News*. Retrieved on August 8, 2023, from https://blackvoicenews.com/2014/09/27/african-binary-system/

Computer Science Degree Hub. (2023). *What is theoretical computer science?* Retrieved on July 30, 2023, from https://www.computersciencedegreehub.com/faq/what-is-theoretical-computer-science/

Eglash, R. (1999). *African fractals: Modern computing and indigenous design*. Rutgers University Press.

From Sources across the Web. (2023). *Applied computer science disciplines*. Retrieved on August 5, 2023, from https://www.google.com/search?q=%22applied+computer+science…

Gerdes, P. (1999). *Geometry from Africa: Mathematical and educational explorations*. American Mathematical Association.

Gnaedinger, F. (2005). *Very early calendars*. Retrieved on August 11, 2023, from https://www.seshat.ch/home/calendar.htm

Indeed. (2023). 15 computer science fields. *Career Guide*. Retrieved on July 30, 2023, from https://www.indeed.com/career-advice/finding-a-job/computer-science-fields

Joshi, K. (October 12, 2022). What is computer science? Why does it matter? *Emeritus Blog Technology*. Retrieved on August 23, 2023, from https://emeritus.org/blog/technology-what-is-computer-science/

Loyola Marymount University. (2023). *Theories in computer science*. Retrieved on July 30, 2023, from https://cs.lmu.edu/~ray/notes/cstheories/

Luke, K. (April 2, 2012). Evidence that human ancestors used fire one million years ago. University of Toronto. *Science Daily*. Retrieved on August 12, 2023, from https://www.sciencedaily.com/releases/2012/04/120402162548.htm

Osadare, O. (April 13, 2019). Binary counting: Is its origin in West African traditional system? *Jimi Disu's Blog*. Retrieved on August 8, 2023, from https://jimidisu.com/binary-counting-is-its-origin-in-west-african-traditional-system/

Pyram, J. (July 17, 2020). A brief history of algorithms and their impact on the world. *Level Up Coding*. Retrieved on August 12, 2023, from https://levelup.gitconnected.com/a-brief-look-at-algorithms-and-their-impact-on-the-world-2794f8dd70aa

SCImago Institutions Rankings—SIR. (2023). *University overall rankings in computer science: Africa 2023*. Retrieved on August 14, 2023, from https://www.scimagoir.com/rankings.php?sector=Higher+educ.&country=Africa&area=1700

The University of Winnipeg. (2023). *Applied computer science*. Retrieved on August 5, 2023, from https://www.uwinnipeg.ca/applied-computer-science/

uniRank. (2023). African universities world representation. *Universities in Africa: Higher Education in Africa*. Retrieved on August 23, 2023, from https://www.4icu.org/Africa/

University of South Carolina. (2023). Applied computer science. *Aiken*. Retrieved on August 5, 2023, from https://www.usca.edu/mathematical-sciences/majors-minors/applied-computer-science

Alie Kunda holds a PhD in Political Science. He is a research associate at The African Institution in Washington, D.C., USA. He is the author of six book chapters and more than 25 scholarly articles. He is the recipient of more than ten prestigious national and international scholarly and community service awards. He has lectured and done television and newspaper interviews in many countries across the globe. He is also fluent in many African and several European languages, and enjoys computer programming.

Criminology

Omosefe Oyekanmi

This chapter focuses on conceptualizing Africa from the prism of criminology as an academic discipline. Its core objective is to understand crime, criminal behavior, and the criminal justice system from the perspective of African philosophy. To achieve this, it examines the state of being criminal, the legal system for managing criminals, crime prevention and control mechanisms from the classical, positivist, and conflict/radical/critical schools of thoughts in criminology. The rationale for this objective is hinged on the fact that the field of criminology has developed with more Western and liberal thoughts, thereby excluding a greater part of a section of the world's view on crime and its management. In essence, this chapter elucidates what Africa is in criminology in order to provide a globally inclusive and holistic understanding of the discipline.

Based on a qualitative method of data collection and analysis, the chapter utilizes secondary sources of data. Thus, the particular context of experiences and perspectives of individuals or groups on the complex phenomena of criminology as a discipline is interpreted and analyzed. It is the most appropriate method of inquiry given that when studying fields in social behavior, such as criminology, a qualitative method helps to explain the philosophical and contextual meanings of inquiry. This chapter therefore employs a wide range of historical and anthropological sources, as well as legal and academic scholarship. By understanding the historical context and the interplay between traditional African and Western influences, insights into the challenges and adaptations faced by African nations in their pursuit of justice and the management of crime in contemporary times can be gained. To this end, this chapter is divided into six sections: (1) conceptualization of criminology from an African perspective; (2) the three basic schools of thoughts in criminology—i.e.,

O. Oyekanmi (✉)
Institute for Pan African Thoughts and Conversations, University of Johannesburg, Johannesburg, South Africa
e-mail: ooyekanmi@uj.ac.za

A. K. Bangura, J. A. Ifedi (eds.), *Conceptualizations of Africa*, African Studies and Research Forum Series, https://doi.org/10.1007/978-3-031-74535-5_6

classical, positivist, and conflict/radical/critical; (3) Africa and criminology; (4) contemporary challenges of African criminology; (5) criminal justice system in Africa; and (6) conclusion and recommendations.

Conceptualizing Criminology: An African Perspective

This section explicates criminology based on "What it is" and "What it ought to be" within its African historical and cultural development. Criminology generally focuses on the scientific study of criminal activities. It is a systematic process involving both collective and individual criminal behavior. Despite the fact that modern criminology is multidisciplinary and draws from a wide range of disciplines, including anthropology, biology, economics, political science, psychiatry, and law, the sociological approach to criminology is particularly prevalent (Erickson, 2013). Thus, conceptualizing criminology stems from its Western orientation and intellectual foundation.

According to Moosavi (2019), criminology is dominated by Western academic literature and perspectives, just like the rest of the social sciences. Factored on this Western-centric nature of the discipline, non-Western criminological work has mainly been disregarded or marginalized. As a discipline, criminology developed between the late 1700s and the early 1800s in Europe but excelled in the United States (Wellford, 2015). The discipline developed through the contributions of Cesare Beccaria and Jeremy Bentham, with more thinkers building ideas around their philosophies of crime. In other words, the development of criminology as applied globally has its bearing from Western scholars. This negates African ideas of crime, criminal behavior and criminal justice system before Western influence in the continent. According to Odili (2021), African perceptions of criminology are regarded wrongly as new ideas both by Western and some African scholars to the point that African perspectives of the discipline are regarded as inferior to Western ideas of crime and its management. Although little research has been done within African criminology, it has prospects of becoming a promising field of study globally, which is factored in the movement to decolonize and democratize the discipline (Chan & Adjorlolo, 2021).

The Western approach to criminology (i.e., crime, criminal behavior, and criminal justice system) conflicts with African ideology of same. For instance, Cesare Beccaria, often referred to as the "father of criminology," propounded the following three ideologies: (1) every person has the right to exercise his/her free will and should not be constrained; (2) every person behaves rationally in pursuit of his/her wants and benefits and, as a result, the law should be protective of an individual; and (3) because every person's conduct is predictable, it may be anticipated and managed (Corner, 2022). On the other hand, Africa provides a unique perspective on a variety of facets of human life. This worldview is a result of the traditions and culture that have developed inside it over time and have taken the form of sayings, myths, tales, religion, and ideologies. For instance, the African proverb "No two people can be friends and not fight occasionally and no two people can fight and not be friends again" captures reconciliation as a criminal justice theory.

Basically, from the prism of Africa, criminology considers how tradition, culture, and beliefs have an impact on the African environment. This is evident in the fight for reparation and the *Ubuntu* ideology in South Africa that underestimates the place of absolutism and relativism in the identification of crime and the application of punishment (Ovens, 2003; Agozino, 2017). While there were presumably offensive types of punishment like burying/burning a criminal alive and death by hanging within the African criminal system, conceptualizing criminology ideally is however factored on the existing belief and value system of any society. This explains the reason behind some barbaric criminal justice acts practiced before the classical approach to criminology.

Three Schools of Thoughts in Criminology

There are three major schools of thoughts in the development of criminology as a discipline. These schools have shaped the entire discipline and the criminal justice system globally. They include the (1) classical; (2) positivist; and (3) conflict, radical or critical schools of thought. To understand "What is Africa" from the angle of criminology as a discipline, for the clarity, these schools of thoughts are analyzed one at a time using the African conceptualization of crime and the legal system for managing crime.

Classical School

The classical school is the first modern phase of philosophy in the discipline of criminology founded by Cesare Beccaria and Jeremy Bentham. It was a reaction to the brutal and capricious legal system that existed in Europe, particularly in France and England in the Middle Ages (from the late fifth to the late fifteenth centuries). During this time, France, and England in particular, experienced a corrupt and capricious legal system, whereby the judges essentially had absolute control over those who appeared before them and ruled arbitrarily. This was the era when "quartering" (a penalty for treason in England which involved hauling the condemned to the gallows, often on a horse, hanging criminals until they are nearly dead, dismembering and castrating them, then beheading them) was a way of punishing treasonable felons (Slabbert, 1987).

These classical thinkers who were concerned about these penal codes agitated for legal reforms rather than studying the causes of deviant behavior or crime. Hence, the classical school focused more on restructuring laws binding criminal behavior by promoting the rights of those charged with crimes to fairness, equity, and due process. This is premised on the thinking that people should make the decision to do things that provide them joy or enjoyment and refrain from doing things that harm them or other people. Thus, in accordance with the utilitarian principles,

Beccaria promoted just and certain punishments to deter crime which, according to him, results in laws that benefit the community they are designed to serve (Ikhenoba, 2023). Punishment, according to these philosophers, is intrinsically harmful and can only be defended if it can prevent more evil than it will inflict. Beccaria's major contribution to the discipline centered on presenting a consistent and logically constructed penological system.

Bentham's contribution was also based on his utilitarian philosophy that prioritizes the happiness and well-being of the general population. He advocated that punishment in the form of suffering should always be justified in terms of a greater good. The pleasure–pain principle, which is at the core of Bentham's work, holds that human behavior is geared toward maximizing pleasure and minimizing pain. To him, people who want to experience thrill, money, sex, or anything else that is valuable to them initially commit crimes (Ikhenoba, 2023).

Unequivocally, criminal justice practice and criminological theory both benefited much from classical criminology. Altering the nature of punishment and the appropriateness of the punishment for the crime decreased the usage of death penalty along with the use of torture and corporal punishment, following the classical view of criminology (Edubirdie, 2023). As proponents argued, social control and order, rather than moral and religious principles, should be the main focus of the discipline of criminology. This was founded on Beccaria's belief that the severity of the punishment should be commensurate with the offense.

In essence, the classical philosophers in criminology emphasized that people have the capacity for free will and that punishment must be equitable and appropriate for the offense committed. This is premised under the assumption that people naturally make logical decisions based on a cost–benefit calculation before engaging in unlawful behavior. They suggest that people consider the advantages and disadvantages of their choices before taking action.

Positivist School

By the late nineteenth century, the positivist school emerged as the second phase in the evolution of criminology. Associated with Italian thinkers like Cesare Lombroso, Enrico Ferri, and Raffaele Garofalo, it was a detour from the major idea of the classical school that people have free will. The positivist school's main impression was centered on behavior as a predetermined agenda, whereby the individual and his pathology is the core emphasis (Slabbert, 1987). The view of these thinkers is that crime is not a product of rational calculation, suggesting that patterns and causal mechanisms for crime could be found through a deeper scientific study of observable phenomena (Dulisse, 2022).

Some theorists have concentrated on biological and psychological aspects, attributing the majority of the responsibility for crime to the individual and raising issues with individual pathology. Contrarily, other theorists have maintained that greater understanding can be acquired by examining the social framework outside of individuals since they view crime as a result of social factors rather than individual inadequacies.

According to the Chicago School (2021), the positivist view connects criminal behavior to the external or internal pressures that people experience and explains why criminal behavior occurs as a result of these circumstances. This thought suggests that criminal behavior is correlated with the psychological or sociological characteristics of the perpetrator, with a focus on personality formation, mental diseases, and unconscious impulses and drives.

Over the years, this therapy model has examined a number of hypotheses regarding the symptoms that underlie criminal behavior. The theory supports the notion that biological traits like the shape of a person's head, nose, or lips, or psychological elements and others economic disadvantages account for the reasons behind a crime, i.e., a person and his/her pathology are the main points of attention (McLennan, 1980). Hence, for the positivist school of criminology, the offender is the subject of research. For this school, the response to crime is providing an unknown amount of treatment, depending on the specifics of each case. Thus, criminal behavior is seen as irrational and may be the result of a condition that an individual has (biological, physical, or psychological), thereby making perpetrators of crimes partially absolved of the crimes committed. Nevertheless, the positivist views, mainly Lombroso's biological theories, have received criticisms and outright rejections in some quarters of the criminology discipline, mainly due to issues of methodology and the absence of control groups in his experiment (Siegel, 2003).

Critical, Radical, or Conflict School

British criminologists Ian Taylor, Paul Walton, and Jock Young made the earliest contributions in this area of inquiry. According to them, crime is a behavior that is outlined by the dominant political group in a society, and this process is connected to social development (Taylor et al., 2013). This view of criminology grew as a result of many social and historical events, such as the women's movements, student protest, the rise of countercultures, and the dissatisfaction with governments due to the Vietnam War, Watergate, etc. These authors and their supporters were devoted to decreasing disparities in wealth, power, and inequality, especially those that affected social, economic and vocational mobility. Critical, conflict, and radical criminology, although slightly different from one another, share a focus on class conflict and the Marxist foundation. These criminologists consider crime to be a tool used by the ruling class. They argue that upper classes enact laws, which are subsequently used to further their goals at the expense of the lower classes.

To these thinkers, the current criminal justice system solely works to uphold the interests of the ruling class, which serves to maintain social injustice. The legal system excludes oppressed minorities from the employment market while producing white collar, high class jobs. The justice system's obsession with repeat offenders and punishment reveals a reliance on personal conceptions of blame that downplay the responsibility of those in positions of authority. This is demonstrated by the emphasis on street crime as different to white collar crime (Shantz, 2012).

As opposed to challenging the fundamental definition of crime, this criminological methods departed from the positivist roots of mainstream criminology, which had centered primarily on the search for reasons of crime. Rather than concentrating on the laws themselves, these critical perspectives concentrate on the procedures that lead to the criminalization of people and groups.

Slabbert (1987) suggests that the radical, critical, and conflict perspectives of criminology challenge the political institutions using criminology. As such, the illusion that the state is a beneficent and caring father protecting the good and punishing the delinquent with the introduction of state architectures like public police is spread by every ruling class. This perspective explains the majority of conventional criminology in Africa concerned with crimes that are only investigated and tried against the poor. The objective of this school of thought is to show that crime control was not the original objective of colonial and neocolonial policing in the continent.

From the preceding three schools of thoughts, the classical school focuses on the offender as the main object of crime and societal control as a mechanism for crime management. The African philosophy of criminology rather stems from the value culture and belief system in the particular environmental setting, thereby making any approach to crime context-specific.

As Saleh-Hanna (2023) points out, the rise of classical criminology was as a result of European systems of colonialism, chattel slavery, and hundreds of years of witch hunts. In addition, the rise of the positivist school was a key reform that brought the power of chattel slavery into the criminal justice system and the transition into sociological positivism as an abstraction and expansion of racial violence and capitalist expansion. A notable reference is the colonial style of administration, reflective in oppression, subjugation, and human rights violation, as a way of sustaining its hegemony over African resources and culture. This mode of administration was inherited by African elites and has continued till this day. In this view, neocolonial governments in Africa are portrayed as the most lawless of all states. This is due to the fact that all neocolonial states implement policies that threaten the independence of their communities, making them potentially guilty of treasonable felonies (Ikhenoba, 2023).

Even though the classical school of thought has demonstrated marginal success in lowering crime rates and acting as a deterrent, it appears more as a means of containing those who rebel against the system. Its major drawback within the African context has been its detachment to sociopolitical structures like family life, employment, and social relationships in conceptualizing criminology. More so, because it assumes that all criminals are rational and make decisions out of free will, it is limited in explaining African criminology. Considering that rationality is relative to individual experiences, not all humans are rational, and not all of their behaviors are voluntary. The colonial conquest and balkanization of Africa by Europeans was rational to them, as the domination of Africa was strategic to expanding European markets and territories. Likewise, the positivist school, which centers on external and internal reasons for committing crime, somewhat legitimizes crime, as it provides justification for criminal acts within the law.

Hence, these views in criminology were reactions to subtly accommodate crimes not conceptualized as crime under Western penal codes. Since there is no common understanding of what constitutes a crime or what constitutes a just punishment (Ikhenoba, 2023), the approaches of these schools of thoughts are counterproductive to Africa's concept of criminology. Similarly, when compared to other schools of thoughts, the critical/radical/conflict school reflects more on Africa's view of criminology. This is evident in the agenda of this school of thought in addressing inequality and the radical detour from the Western approach that focuses on legal processes rather than how the laws are made.

What constitutes a crime and what constitutes an appropriate punishment are concepts that are not universally agreed upon. The classical and positivist views are particularly contentious in nations like those in Africa where the criminal code is developed and applied by individuals with ideological and financial motivations conflicting with the legitimate interests of the great majority of citizens. Flowing from these schools of thoughts, the current criminal justice system as seen do little to discourage breaking the law, especially from the manipulations by Western influence.

Africa and Criminology

Crime and the pursuit of justice have been integral aspects of human society throughout history, and the African continent is no exception. Traditional African societies developed their own unique perspectives on what constitutes crime, how to address its causes, methods for preventing it, and mechanisms for punishment. These indigenous approaches were deeply rooted in communal values, restorative justice, and cultural norms. For centuries, these systems served as effective means of maintaining order, resolving conflicts, and preserving harmony within African communities. Remarkably, in trying to examine the superiority of the Western criminal justice system over the criminal justice system in Africa, the Songhai study by Dalgleish (2005) indicates that the latter shared several similarities with the British criminal justice system at the time. In precolonial West Africa, a distinguishing feature was that of a local police chief and a two-tiered system of justice with common law/Sharia law cases being handled by the Cadi and treason cases handled by royal justice under the control of the King. This suggests that African criminology developed to the extent of controlling its society outside external influence.

The emergence of Western colonial powers in Africa, beginning in the late nineteenth century, brought profound changes to the continent's social, political, and legal landscape. With colonialism came the imposition of Western legal frameworks and definitions of crime, which often clashed with traditional African approaches. This transformative encounter between African and Western perspectives on crime has left an enduring impact on the continent's criminal justice systems. Abdi (2000) argues that the issue of crime in Africa was exacerbated by the establishment of new models cum institutions of government by the European colonialists. These structures were alien and thus posed a new issue of mistrust between the power brokers which emerged.

It is crucial to acknowledge the diversity of African societies and legal traditions. Each region and culture in Africa has contributed to the complex tapestry of perspectives on crime and justice as evident in the ensuing subsections.

African Perspective of Crime Before Westernization

A fundamental aspect of the African perspective on crime was the strong emphasis on communal values and cohesion. Traditional African societies often viewed crime as an offense not just against an individual but against the entire community. The concept of crime extended beyond individual actions to include any act that disrupted the harmony of the community. Such acts were seen as offenses against the collective and were often linked to violations of social norms, taboos, or customs (Nader, 2008). For instance, among the Igbo people of Nigeria, crimes included offenses against the gods or ancestors, theft, adultery, and disputes that undermined the community's cohesion (Mbiti, 1969).

Causes of crime in traditional African societies were multifaceted and rooted in both individual and societal factors. These factors included poverty, jealousy, land disputes, or perceived violations of taboos and customs (Nader, 2008). For example, among the Akan people of Ghana, disputes over property and inheritance often led to conflicts and acts of crime (Gyekye, 1997). The custodians of justice in these African communities understood the motivations for committing crime and sought out ways to prevent the reoccurrence of it through punitive and restorative measures.

Preventing crime in traditional African societies involved collective efforts and a strong focus on mediation, reconciliation, and restitution rather than punitive measures. Elders, chiefs, or councils often played the role of mediators (Mbiti, 1969). Restitution was a common practice, whereby offenders were required to compensate victims or the community as a whole. This approach aimed to restore harmony rather than exact retribution (Nader, 2008). According to Odili (2021), traditional African criminal proceedings were quite similar to contemporary civil proceedings in that they established a debtor–creditor relationship between the victim and the offender. The goal was to ensure that the victim received compensation and that the offender was accepted back into society.

Based on the preceding rationale, the death sentence was despised as a way to punish criminal behavior. Punishment in traditional African societies was primarily focused on restoring balance and harmony within the community. Punishments ranged from fines, public humiliation, or exclusion from community activities to rituals aimed at cleansing the offender's wrongdoing (Gyekye, 1997). Among the Yoruba of Nigeria, a common punishment was the *afe*, which involved public acknowledgment of the offense and payment of restitution to the victim or the victim's family (Mbiti, 1969). Traditional African perspectives on crime prior to

Westernization emphasized communal values, restorative justice, and reconciliation.

Additionally, the African concept of crime weighed heavily on "intention over act," thereby influencing the gravity of punishment accorded for each crime and criminal. The Yoruba proverb *Aniyan ni siwaju ise*, which literally translates as "intention precedes the act," captures the importance of intention in determining whether or not an accused person will be held accountable for a crime (Odili, 2021). Using this as a foundation, it is acknowledged that some people, such as children and the mentally unstable, lack the mental capacity to commit a crime. To execute rites for a juvenile offender, the community's elders are required to perform them. Such a ceremony is known as *Atukhiuki* among the Esan of Nigeria's Edo state. After the elders have inquired about the behavior that has been criticized, the ritual includes specific objects that the child's parents must donate. The youngster is brought to a remote area toward the outskirts of town where the sacrifice is made, and the child must stay inside his house for seven days without interacting with other kids.

The ritual's main purpose is to emphasize the parent's responsibility for raising the child and denotes the youngster's reintegration into society. Additionally, it gives the youngster a chance to consider the seriousness of his actions and acts as a deterrent to prevent him/her and other kids from engaging in similar behavior (Odili, 2021).

About insane persons, Okafor (1992) states that an insane person's family is held criminally accountable for the crime committed by the member, with the justification that had they been vigilant and responsible enough, they would have identified the offender's mental condition and sought the necessary medical attention. Aside from these exceptional conditions, crime was also perceived as committed by one or more individuals rather than a group (including family members), who were held criminally responsible. The Yoruba proverb *Ika t'oba se l'oba n'ge* captures this and means that the King amputates the finger that offends.

Traditional Africa also acknowledged defenses that may be invoked by the accused based on compulsion or need. For instance, a man or traveler who took crops from a nearby farm out of necessity in Yoruba society was not considered to have stolen anything, as long as he did not consume more than what he needed to satiate his current hunger. The emphasis here is that criminality focuses on greed as a crime and this crime can be punished through instant death or instant deformity or insanity by mystical powers. This idea was premised on taking only what was needed in order to promote collective ownership.

Accordingly, before the arrival of the Westerners, different African civilizations had quite different approaches to categorizing and managing crime. There was no consistent system of crime classification or management throughout the diverse continent of Africa, which has a rich history of indigenous legal and social institutions. Based on the religious and traditional practices of individual communities, crime was conceptualized and managed accordingly. In essence, these systems were heavily localized and tailored to the unique cultural, social and economic settings of each African society. With the imposition of European legal systems on African communities following Western colonialism, these traditional systems underwent significant alterations, which frequently resulted in a complicated blend of indigenous and colonial legal approaches to the field of criminology. This historical setting has had a long-lasting influence on how crime is defined and handled in modern-day Africa, where many nations are attempting to harmonize traditional justice systems with cutting-edge legal frameworks.

Western Approach on African Criminology

Since the beginning of Africa's appearance in contemporary international relations, it has been characterized as having one of the worst criminal justice systems globally. This is anchored on several essays full of disparaging remarks about Africa by revered luminaries in the philosophical and academic world (Dalgleish, 2005). Specifically, the idea that Africa needs law and order as a common neocolonialist discourse was put forward by the British government itself. According to the body, "For many indigenous peoples in Africa and elsewhere the British Empire often brought more regular, acceptable and impartial systems of law and order than many had experienced under their own rulers…The spread of the English language helped unite disparate tribal areas that gradually came to see themselves as nations" (Home Office, 2004, p. 1).

African opposition to the International Criminal Court (ICC) has grown over time from initial support to more recent animosity, sparking concerns about African legal systems that could replace the ICC. This is also in view of the fact that the court is yet to bring to trial non-Africans for crimes against humanity (Kaledzi, 2023). Although there are issues with Africa's criminal justice system, it is important to acknowledge that most of what it is today's criminal justice practice is a product of the Western approach. Like many other fields of study, the development of criminology as a discipline in Africa has emerged out of these biased and unverified claims void of an African truth.

With the onset of Western colonialism, Africa underwent significant transformations in its legal and justice systems, leading to a notable shift in how crime was perceived, managed, and punished. This transition had a profound impact on traditional African perspectives on crime and justice. As Western powers asserted their control over African territories, they brought with them their legal systems and concepts, influenced by Enlightenment-era thought and European jurisprudence. One of the key elements of this Western approach was the introduction of formal legal codes, often modeled after European legal systems which began to replace or marginalize the existing customary laws and practices within African communities (Mamdani, 1996).

A fundamental distinction in the Western approach was its emphasis on individual accountability for criminal actions. Western legal systems, unlike traditional African perspectives, focused on the offender as a distinct entity, separate from the collective responsibility that was characteristic of many indigenous African societies. This shift from communal to individual accountability was a defining feature of the Western approach to crime (Mamdani, 1996). Furthermore, Western legal systems prioritized punitive measures as the primary means of addressing crime. Imprisonment, fines, and other forms of retribution became prevalent, diverging from the traditional African emphasis on restoration, reconciliation, and communal healing. This shift in punitive measures had significant consequences for how justice was perceived and enacted (Mamdani, 1996).

In addition to these changes in the definition and punishment of crime, the Western approach also redefined the causes of crime in Africa. Rather than attributing crime to societal factors, as was common in traditional African perspectives, Western influences tended to focus on individual moral failings. Furthermore, economic changes under colonialism, including land dispossession and labor exploitation, contributed to the emergence of new forms of crime within African societies (Mamdani, 1996). With the Western approach came the introduction of formal policing systems, which placed a greater emphasis on law enforcement over community-based prevention.

Traditional conflict resolution mechanisms, often guided by elders, chiefs, or councils, were sometimes replaced by Western-style courts, thereby diminishing the role of community mediation and reconciliation (Mamdani, 1996). Perhaps one of the most visible and enduring legacies of the Western approach was the establishment of prisons as institutions for punishment and rehabilitation. These institutions transformed the African penal landscape, representing a stark departure from the traditional African focus on restoration and reconciliation as the primary goals of justice (Mamdani, 1996). The actual operations of a culture's judicial system at any given period will serve as a foundation for both the crime itself and its narrative ramifications.

Hence, one of the challenges African nations grapple with today is the complexities of integrating traditional and Western approaches to crime and justice. The challenge lies in finding a balance between individual rights and community interests within legal systems, thereby addressing the overrepresentation of certain groups in the criminal justice system and adapting to contemporary issues such as cybercrime, corruption, and transnational organized crime. The influence of the West has left a lasting legacy that continues to shape the criminal justice systems in many African nations and remains a subject of debate and adaptation in contemporary times.

African Criminal Justice System

The criminal justice system, which is a branch of the discipline of criminology, specifically deals with the arrest, prosecution, defense, sentencing, and punishment of individuals who are suspected or found guilty of crimes. It involves punishing criminal activities through a complicated web of authorities and procedures. Like every other continent and region, the criminal justice system in Africa encompasses a multitude of actors, including judges, attorneys, police officers, and penitentiary staff.

The composition of Africa in terms of her historical, cultural, and colonial origin further makes the continent's criminal justice system more complicated. As such, numerous African countries share certain characteristics and obstacles in common, resulting in a diversified and complicated criminal justice system that differs from nation to nation throughout the continent. Thus, the police, court, and correction systems are among the basic components of the criminal justice system. These components are critical to the discipline of criminology.

For instance, the police is the primary component of the criminal justice system, considering that it represents the first contact with the law for offenders. Although the African policing system varies from nation to nation, it has however not changed in major ways from its colonial creation. According to Alemika et al. (2018), African police forces and services face a number of critical challenges and constraints that have an impact on rights-based policing. This policing structure which stems from the authoritarianism's political legacy of colonial policing culture is characterized by repression and impunity; violent conflicts and crimes, insurgency and terrorism; widespread disrespect for the law; and distrust of law enforcement officials. Prior to Western incursion, traditional African police, court, and correctional tactics were deeply ingrained in the community and intricately intertwined with social and religious systems.

Community structures such as age grades (formal groups whose membership is based on a predetermined age range), secret societies, or vocational guilds (e.g., of hunters, farmers, or fishermen) enforced ancient norms and beliefs. Law and order was maintained largely without the use of violence through these dispersed systems of criminal control (Akin, 1994). With colonialism, however, the established police structure was essentially to solidify non-recognition of marginalized entities by keeping the natives in their place. This essentially was instrumental to both the colonial African rulers and the colonizers in expanding their wealth, influence and power over the masses through the collection of heavy taxes and transporting them back to the original state (Adebisi, 2018). Essentially, the impact of colonialism introduced foreign legal systems to the continent which were largely not consistent with African realities and human rights commitments. In particular, the British legal system for the police is founded on the fact that "The police are primarily responsible for the maintenance of public order, prevention and detection of crimes in the state. It also protects the life, liberty and property of the people" (Adebisi, 2018, para 9). While this pronouncement entirely resonates with British culture and history, this is not entirely the same for Africa where several crime control mechanisms engraved in spiritual and cultural belief systems proved more effective.

Without discountenancing the Western criminal justice system, African criminal justice structures must be indigenous to the people so as to achieve their desired aim. Again, in most African countries, the style of policing is centralized. This policing structure was adopted during colonialism in order to exert the powerful influence of Western police over the people. This sadly remains the policing culture to this day in most African countries, even where federalism is purportedly practiced. Prior to the Western incursion, the police, court, and correction systems were decentralized and effective in curbing crime. In Nigeria, for example, following independence, the Africanization of the police resulted in very minor modifications. The Nigerian police has adopted a violent, exploitative, repressive, and oppressive culture. It appears that the only method to sustain the stability of a state that is not yet formed is by persistent and repeated displays of brute force.

Furthermore, the criminal justice system in Africa presents a system that isolates crime from the process of labeling a crime, prosecution, and correction. This was captured by Van Dijk's analysis of correlating non-formal crime to weak governance, which remains the bane of Africa's continued underdevelopment. According to the author, issues such as organized crime, corruption, and weak legal systems account for the 80% of the variance in gross domestic product (GDP_scores of countries) (cited in Marenin, 2014). The author suggests that a significant portion (80%) of the differences in countries' economic performance, as measured by GDP, can be attributed to the presence of organized crime, high-level corruption, and weak legal systems. In essence, Van Dijk concludes that the combined impact of organized crime, grand corruption, and weak rule of law accounts for 80% of the variation in countries' GDP scores. In essence, organized crime, corruption, and fragile governance are detrimental to development. In other words, while the criminal justice system in most African states focuses on isolating crime and establishing the process for the furtherance of the political elites, the real issue of crime rests on corruption and weak government institutions.

Bowd (2009) points out that the legal systems in Sierra Leone, Tanzania, and Zambia are based on, at least in part, obsolete the British judicial system, which has consequences on how well justice can be accessed, considering that most African states face enormous obstacles in accessing and understanding formal justice systems. Hence, formal judicial systems tend to play a more dominant role in the provision of justice in urban regions. Although customary courts are in place in these societies to close the legal gap for traditional laws and rites, these laws are, however, not recognized by international treaties and protocols, which in most cases invalidates customary practices and places international laws over them.

It is evident that the processes, institutions, and actors of African criminal justice specifically define what Africa is in the field of criminology. Despite the Western idea backed policing, court and correctional structures, which has its gains, has not reduced crime in Africa; instead, it has complicated it. As such, decolonization of criminology and criminal justice in Africa has become a given.

Contemporary Challenges of African Criminology

The Western influence on African perspectives of criminology has left a lasting legacy that continues to shape the criminal justice landscape in contemporary times. This influence has not only redefined the conceptualization of crime but has also introduced challenges and complexities to African societies' management of criminal behavior and the discipline of criminology. Two major challenges are highlighted here:

1. *Balancing Individual Rights and Community Interests*: One of the enduring challenges in the wake of Western influence is the need to strike a balance between individual rights and the broader interests of the community. Western legal systems emphasize the protection of individual rights and liberties, which sometimes conflict with traditional African notions of communal harmony and collective responsibility (Bohler-Muller, 2007). According to Nafukho (2006),

Ubuntu, an African philosophy, stands for the moral code and/or social ethic in traditional Africa since it acknowledges that people are social beings who need to interact with others. In effect, contrary to Western individualistic ideology, the African philosophy hinges on collective responsibility captioned in "I am because we exist" (De Liefde, 2005, p. 52).

In contemporary African legal systems, this tension often plays out in debates over issues such as freedom of speech, political dissent, and the rights of accused individuals. Striking a harmonious balance between these competing interests remains a challenge. In recent times, we have seen a clash of interests between the United States and African nations over the Gay Rights Bill and the LGBTQ trend. The question of what constitutes crime therefore always resurfaces.

2. *Overrepresentation of Certain Groups*: The Western approach to crime in Africa has also contributed to the overrepresentation of certain groups within the criminal justice system. For example, marginalized communities and minority groups often face disproportionate rates of arrest, prosecution, and incarceration (Okolie, 2018). This overrepresentation raises questions about equity, access to justice, and the potential perpetuation of social inequalities within the criminal justice system. It underscores the need for reforms that address these disparities and ensure a more equitable application of the law (Okolie, 2018). As Ikhenoba (2023) notes, neocolonial regimes are portrayed as being particularly criminal not only because they criminally disregard the needs of their citizens for basic social services, but also because they encourage and support the capital accumulation process, which is prone to organized crime and is based on the prehistoric accumulation of wealth, which in turn is also portrayed as being particularly criminal. This is premised on the fact that the precolonial approach of justice placed more emphasis on greed as more criminal than an act of crime not based on greed. In essence, Western criminology has influenced inequality within the application of justice in Africa. This form of encouragement, which takes the form of light punishment, pardon, or non-prosecution of political and economic criminals, amnesty, and immunity clauses for political elites, is inversely proportional to the justice system for some other offenders. Thus, harsh punishment for pickpockets and victimization-as-punishment for the defenseless poor exposes the overt and covert partisanship of the legal system.

Conclusion and Recommendations

This chapter has analyzed criminology from African thinking by conceptualizing what is crime, criminal behavior and the legal system for addressing crime before and after Western influence in Africa. It examined the three significant theoretical foundations of the discipline: (1) classical, (2) positivist, and (3) critical/radical and conflict schools. It submits that in Europe and America, the idea of punishments being appropriate to the nature of the crime has become a foundation for modern criminal justice systems across continents, despite its incompatibility. It is revealed that culture, tradition, religion, and the African belief system shaped the definition and management of crime before Western influence.

Emphasizing the development of Western criminal laws as a colonial contraption to impoverish Africa and Africans, the chapter reveals that these laws were inherited by neocolonial governments to further impoverish their citizenry. Thus, it accounted for the establishment of public institutions like the police mainly for protecting members of the ruling class in their quest for wealth accumulation. Based on dissimilar ideologies between Western and African philosophy of crime, the issue of appropriate and acceptable legal structures across different societal foundations have remained a quagmire in the development of criminology as a discipline. Hence, Western influence on African criminology presents contemporary challenges that African nations, especially their scholars, must address.

It is recommended, therefore, that theories on African criminology should entail an integrated assessment and implementation to numerous experiencing realms as opposed to a conventional method promoted by perspectives in Western criminology. This can be achieved by advancing ongoing reforms in the discipline through adopting context-specific and innovative approaches within African criminal justice systems.

References

Abdi, A. A. (2000). Review of *the Criminalization of the State in Africa. Canadian Journal of African Studies, 34*(2), 454–456.

Adebisi, F. (2018). The colonial origins of the Nigerian police. *Africanskies*. Retrieved on October 29, 2023 from https://folukeafrica.com/the-colonial-origins-of-the-nigerian-police/

Agozino, B. (2017). Reparative justice: A pan-African criminology primer. In B. Agozino & A. Kalunta-Crumpton (Eds.), *Pan-African issues in crime and justice*. Routledge.

Akin, O. (1994). Police brutality: Dimensions and control in Nigeria. *Civil Liberties Organisation, Law Enforcement and Human Rights in Nigeria, HRW, 17*(11), 1–76.

Alemika, E. E., Ruteere, M., & Howell, S. (Eds.). (2018). *Policing reform in Africa: Moving towards a rights-based approach in a climate of terrorism, insurgency and serious violent crime*. African Policing Civilian Oversight Forum (APCOF).

Bohler-Muller, N. (2007). Western liberal legalism and its discontents: A perspective from post-apartheid South Africa. *Socio-Legal Review, 3*, 1.

Bowd, R. (2009). *Access to justice in Africa comparisons between Sierra Leone, Tanzania and Zambia*. Institute for Security Studies. Retrieved October on 30, 2023 from https://www.files.ethz.ch/isn/112459/NO13OCT09.pdf

Chan, H. C., & Adjorlolo, S. (2021). Introduction: Exploring crime, mental health, and criminal justice in Africa from a psycho-criminological perspective. In: *Crime, mental health and the criminal justice system in Africa: A psycho-criminological perspective* (pp. 1–10).

Corner, L. (November 24, 2022). *Schools of criminology*. Retrieved on September 21, 2023 from https://lawcorner.in/schools-of-criminology/

Dalgleish, D. (2005). Pre-colonial criminal justice in West Africa: Eurocentric thought versus Africentric evidence. *African Journal of Criminology and Justice Studies: AJCJS, 1*(1), 55–69.

De Liefde, W. H. J. (2005). *Lekgotla: The art of leadership through dialogue*. Jacana.

Dulisse, B. (2022). *Positivist criminology*. Oxford Bibliography. Retrieved on September 23, 2023 from https://www.oxfordbibliographies.com/display/document/obo-9780195396607/obo-9780195396607-0324.xml

Edubirdie. (January 31, 2023). *Classical vs. positivist school of criminology*. Retrieved on September 25, 2023 from https://edubirdie.com/examples/classical-vs-positivist-school-of-criminology/

Erickson, P. E. (2013). Criminology. In: Runehov, A. L. C., & Oviedo, L. (eds.). *Encyclopedia of sciences and religions*. Dordrecht: Springer. Retrieved September 25, 2023 from https://doi.org/10.1007/978-1-4020-8265-8_1298.

Gyekye, K. (1997). *An essay on African philosophical thought: The Akan conceptual scheme*. Temple University Press.

Home Office. (2004). *Life in the United Kingdom: A journey to citizenship*. Home Office.

Ikhenoba, J. (2023). Criminology and African literature: A didactic approach. *Humanities Commons*. Retrieved on September 25, 2023 from https://hcommons.org/deposits/item/hc:52789/

Kaledzi, I. (July 17, 2023). *Africa's fractured relationship with the ICC*. Retrieved on September 26, 2023 from https://www.dw.com/en/africas-fractured-relationship-with-the-icc/a-66257611

Mamdani, M. (1996). *Citizen and subject: Contemporary Africa and the legacy of late colonialism*. Princeton University Press.

Marenin, O. (2014). Styles of policing and economic development in African states. *Public Administration and Development, 34*(3), 149–161.

Mbiti, J. S. (1969). *African religions and philosophy* (1st ed.). Heinemann Educational Publishers.

McLennan, G. (1980). *Crime and society: Readings in history and theory*. Routledge.

Moosavi, L. (2019). Decolonising criminology: Syed Hussein Alatas on crimes of the powerful. *Critical Criminology, 27*, 229–242.

Nader, L. (2008). *Harmony ideology: Justice and control in a Zapotec Mountain Village*. Stanford University Press.

Nafukho, F. M. (2006). Ubuntu worldview: A traditional African view of adult learning in the workplace. *Advances in Developing Human Resources, 8*(3), 408–415.

Odili, J. (2021). Criminological thoughts and the African contribution to its development. *GRIN*. Retrieved on September 24, 2023 from https://www.grin.com/document/1031366

Okafor, F. U. (1992). *Igbo philosophy of law*. Fourth Dimension Publishers.

Okolie, A. (2018). Criminal justice in Africa: Issues, challenges, and prospects. *Journal of Contemporary African Studies, 36*(1), 17–30.

Ovens, M. (2003). A criminological approach to crime in South Africa. *Acta Criminologica: African Journal of Criminology & Victimology, 16*(3), 67–80.

Saleh-Hanna, V. (2023). The history of criminology is a history of white supremacy. In V. Saleh-Hanna, J. Williams, & M. J. Coyle (Eds.), *Abolish criminology*. Routledge.

Shantz, J. (2012). Radical criminology: A manifesto. *Radical Criminology, 1*, 7–17.

Siegel, L. J. (2003). *Criminology: The core*. Pocket Books.

Slabbert, M. (1987). The development of criminology: From traditional to contemporary views on crime and crime causation. *Kronos: Journal of Cape History, 12*(1), 3–7.

Taylor, I., Walton, P., & Young, J. (2013). *The new criminology for a social theory of deviance*. Routledge.

The Chicago School. (July 2, 2021). *Insight*. Retrieved on September 23, 2023 from https://www.thechicagoschool.edu/insight/psychology/what-is-positivism-in-criminology/#:~:text=Positivism%20in%20criminology%2C%20on%20the,sociological%20traits%20of%20the%20offender

Wellford, C. F. (2015). Criminology: Development and current status of the discipline. In J. D. White (Ed.), *International encyclopedia of the social & behavioral sciences* (2nd ed.). Elsevier.

Omosefe Oyekanmi holds a PhD in Political Science. She is a postdoctoral fellow at the Pan African Women Studies Unit, Institute of Pan African Thought and Conversation, University of Johannesburg, South Africa. She is also a research fellow at the Nigerian Institute of Social and Economic Research in Ibadan, Nigeria. She is a recipient of the British Academy funded program, Writing and Researching the Political Economy of Inequality in Africa, cohorts 2021 and 2023, and a prestigious scholar of CODESRIA College of Mentors (2019). She has over 30 published articles on humanitarianism, development, public policy, gender issues, and international peace building.

Economics

Abdul Karim Bangura

In this chapter, I broach conceptualizations of what Africa is in the field of Economics, i.e., the sphere of erudition that deals with the production, consumption, and transfer of wealth. Concomitantly, African economies are investigated in terms of their condition as regards material prosperity. Thus, the major research question probed in the chapter is logically the following: What conceptualizations have been offered about what Africa is in the academic discipline of Economics? The immediate answer to this question is that many conceptualizations have been tendered vis-à-vis what Africa is in the field of Economics that range from the positive to the negative, albeit the latter are more preponderant. Obviously, it is beyond the scope of this chapter to deal with all of these conceptualizations. Therefore, for the sake of brevity, the following three major conceptualizations are examined here: (1) Africa as an economic periphery, (2) African countries as mono economies, and (3) Africa as an important source to the world economy.

Since the focus of the chapter is on economic conceptualizations, the ensuing analyses are decidedly qualitative, i.e., words are emphasized as opposed to numerical values. Nonetheless, numerical data are noted to augment certain qualitative analyses where and when necessary. Secondary data are mostly utilized and they are analyzed in terms of descriptive case studies, which means that the "What is?" question underlies the analyses. Before engaging in the review of the three aforementioned conceptualizations, that of Economics is first provided as a backdrop, as it is the discipline upon which the investigation here is pegged. The time frames covered by the data are variable in line with the nature of the conceptualizations.

The immediate question that arises here, therefore, is this one: What is the essence of investigating how Africa is conceptualized in the field of Economics? The answer to this query is quite straightforward because it is fundamental to any investigation in the Economics discipline, i.e., it allows an analyst to engage in "a

A. K. Bangura (✉)
Center for Global Peace, American University, Washington, DC, USA

A. K. Bangura, J. A. Ifedi (eds.), *Conceptualizations of Africa*, African Studies and Research Forum Series, https://doi.org/10.1007/978-3-031-74535-5_7

systematic process for examining alternative uses of resources, focusing on assessment of needs, objectives, options, costs, benefits, risks, funding, affordability and other factors relevant to decisions" (Airgeadais, 2022, p. 1). In essence, the interrogation in this chapter makes it possible to explicate how these factors are relevant in the analyses of what Africa is in the field of Economics.

Economics: A Conceptualization

The academic discipline of Economics has been conceptualized in several ways, which include (a) history of economic thought, (b) methodology, and (c) branches of economics. In this chapter, I focus on two of the time-tested branches of economics—i.e., (1) microeconomics and (2) macroeconomics—for conciseness. I discuss them one at a time in the following subsections for perspicuity.

Microeconomics

Microeconomics is generally conceptualized as the component of Economics that deals with single factors and the effects of individual decisions. Seven aspects have been tendered in the conceptualization of microeconomics. First, economists who study "production, cost, and efficiency" characterize *production* as the conversion of inputs into outputs and, thus, it is an economic process that employs inputs to make a commodity or a service for exchange or direct use. The economic *cost* of production then is referred to as *opportunity cost*, i.e., the value of the next best opportunity that must be given up in order to produce a particular good or service. Economic *efficiency* is gauged in terms of how well a system generates desired outputs with a given set of inputs and available technology. A commonly accepted standard of measuring economic efficiency is *Pareto optimality*, which is achieved when no further change can make someone better off without making someone else worse off (McConnell et al., 2020).

Second, those who investigate "specialization" assert that, based on empirical and theoretical reflections, the factor is pivotal for ensuring economic efficiency. This is because, according to these economists, different individuals or countries may have different real opportunity costs of production. Accordingly, this situation may endow a comparative advantage in production of goods or services that make more intensive utilization of the relatively more abundant, thus relatively cheaper, inputs. Therefore, even if an individual or a country possesses an absolute advantage apropos the ratio of outputs to inputs in every type of output, the person or country may still specialize in the output in which the person or the country has a comparative advantage and thereby gain from trading with those that lack any absolute advantage but have a comparative advantage in producing different things (McConnell et al., 2020).

Third, specialists who study "supply and demand" postulate that *price* and *quantity* are the two most directly observable facets of goods and services produced and exchanged in a market economy. They use demand and supply theory as an organizing principle to explain how prices determine the coordination of the amounts of goods and services produced and consumed. *Demand* is the relation of the quantity that all buyers would be prepared to purchase at each unit price of the good or service for a given market. Demand theory is employed to describe why individual consumers rationally choose the most preferred quantity of each good or service, given income, prices, tastes, and so on. This outcome is called "constrained utility maximization," which means that with income and wealth as the constraints on demand, *utility* is the hypothesized relation of each individual consumer for ranking different commodity bundles as more or less preferred. Also, the law of demand signifies that price and quantity demanded in a given market are generally inversely related; this means that the higher the price of a product, the less of it people would be prepared to buy, ceteris paribus—i.e., other conditions remaining the same. In addition, *supply* is the relation between the price of a good or service and the quantity available for sale at that price. In essence, *supply* is generally represented as a function relating price and quantity, ceteris paribus (McConnell et al., 2020).

Fourth, enthusiasts of "firms" are interested in the fact that while people most of the time do not trade directly on markets, they instead, on the supply side, may work in and produce through firms—the most obvious of which are corporations, partnerships, and trusts. A firm amalgamates capital and labor in order to attain a far greater *economy of scale* as the average cost per unit declines as more units are produced compared to individual market trading. According to demand and supply theory, in what is referred to as "perfectly competitive markets," there exist many producers, and none of them is capable of significantly affecting price. Thus, by utilizing quantitative methods, scholars of managerial economics apply microeconomic analysis to specific decisions in business firms or other management units. An underlying notion of their analyses is the optimization of business decisions, which include unit-cost minimization and profit maximization, vis-à-vis a firm's goals and limitations dictated by market conditions and technology (McConnell et al., 2020).

Fifth, economists who focus on "uncertainty and game theory" begin by pointing out that whether quantifiable as a "risk" or not, "uncertainty" in economics indicates the likelihood of loss or gain that is undetermined. The absence of "uncertainty," they say, would mean that (a) household behavior would not be impacted by uncertain employment and income possibilities, (b) capital and financial markets would be reduced to the exchange of a single commodity during each market era, and (c) the communications industry would not exist. Next, these economists apprise us that game theory is a branch of Applied Mathematics that takes into account strategic interactions among agents—a situation that represents one type of "uncertainty." The theory is therefore used as a mathematical tool for analyzing industrial organization. Traced back to the mid-1940s, the theory has also been employed to analyze such diverse topics as "ethics," "evolutionary biology," "formulation of nuclear strategies," and "public choice" (McConnell et al., 2020).

Sixth, those who assess "market failure" inform us that the idea entails several challenges that appear to erode fundamental economic suppositions. Observers who are critical of the field of Economics are inclined to dismiss the notion of "market failure" as a red herring utilized by some economists when they fail to link their theories to real-world circumstances. While the lack of information equality and incomplete markets may lead to economic inefficiency and subsequent failure, so also does the possibility of improving efficiency through legal, market, and regulatory correctives (McConnell et al., 2020).

Seventh, and finally, evaluators of "welfare" demonstrate how well-being emerges from the allocation of productive factors due to the desirability and economic efficiency within an economy that is frequently relative to "competitive general equilibrium," i.e., a situation whereby "profit-maximizing producers" and "utility-maximizing consumers" in competitive markets with freely determined prices arrive at an equilibrium price. These scholars assess social welfare, no matter how it is calculated, in relation to the economic activities of the individuals that make up the considered theoretical society. In short, the individual is the unit of analysis in "welfare" evaluations (McConnell et al., 2020).

Macroeconomics

Macroeconomics is commonly conceptualized as the constituent of Economics that investigates large-scale or general economic factors such as interest rates and national productivity. In the conceptualization of Macroeconomics, many features have been emphasized. To begin with, proponents of "growth" interrogate economic factors that can be used to explicate the increase in output per capita of a country over a long time span. These factors are utilized to show disparities of the levels of output per capita among countries, with a particular focus on why some countries grow faster than others and whether countries cross at the same rates of growth. The most frequently investigated factors are (a) population growth, (b) rate of investment, and (c) technological change (Mankiw, 2018).

Next, economists who study "business cycles" engage in the analyses of different research initiatives that are either related to or contrastive to "Keynesianism," i.e., the economic theory or practice based on the ideas of the English economist John Maynard Keynes, which contends that since prices are to a moderate extent inflexible, fluctuations in any component of spending—consumption, investment, or government expenditures—cause output to change; thus, if a government's spending increases, for instance, and all other spending components remain unchanged, then output will also increase. While the neoclassical synthesis argues that Keynesianism is correct in the short term, albeit it must be qualified by neoclassical-like considerations in the intermediate and long term, the new classical macroeconomic perspective postulates that prices and wages are "sticky," meaning that they do not adapt immediately to changes in economic conditions (Mankiw, 2018).

Also, those who broach "unemployment" do so by assessing the percentage of workers without jobs in the labor market. These workers are those who are actively looking for jobs, not those who are retired, pursuing education, or discouraged from seeking work because of the absence of job opportunities. Unemployment is generally classified into the following types relative to their causes: (a) "classical models of unemployment" such as "frictional unemployment" refer to when wages are too high for employers to be willing to hire more workers; (b) "structural unemployment" encompasses a number of possible causes of unemployment including a mismatch between workers' skills and the skills required for available jobs; and (c) "cyclical unemployment" is an outcome of stagnated economic growth (Mankiw, 2018).

In addition, economists who look at "inflation and monetary policy" are interested in how money is a medium of final payment for goods and services in most price system economies and is the unit of account in which prices are quintessentially represented. The many attributes of money that have made it universally acceptable include "divisibility," "durability," "elasticity in supply," "longevity with mass public confidence," "portability," and "relative consistency in value." Thus, as a medium of exchange, money makes trade possible. It has also become a measure of value and a basis for establishing credit. Money is therefore used to determine and control "inflation," which is a general increase in prices and fall in the purchasing value of money (Mankiw, 2018).

Finally, scholars of "fiscal policy" discuss how governments implement such policy in order to influence macroeconomic conditions by modifying their spending and taxation policies to adjust aggregate demand. If aggregate demand falls below the likely output of an economy, an output gap emerges that leaves certain productive capacity to be unutilized. In order to increase aggregate demand, a government will be compelled to increase its spending and cut taxes. This will allow the government to use resources that have been idled. Nonetheless, cynics of fiscal policy maintain that an increase in debt will have to be paid for with future tax increases, which will force people to reduce their consumption and save money in order to pay for the future tax increases (Mankiw, 2018).

Africa as an Economic Periphery

The conceptualization of Africa as an "economic periphery" can be traced back to Immanuel Wallerstein's brand of dependency theory. Before discussing his postulates, it makes sense to first provide a very brief general description of the theory.

Dependency Theory is an approach employed to explain economic underdevelopment by focusing on the presumptive restrictions imposed by the world economic and political order. The theory was initially tendered by Argentinian economist and statesman Raúl Prebisch in the late 1950s. It subsequently achieved intellectual notability in the 1960s and 1970s due to the works of other eminent dependency theorists such as Brazilian sociologist and later president Fernando Henrique Cardoso and German American economic historian Andre Gunder Frank (Munro, 2018). André Munro describes the propositions of the theory as follows:

> underdevelopment is mainly caused by the peripheral position of affected countries in the world economy. Typically, underdeveloped countries offer cheap labour and raw materials on the world market. These resources are sold to advanced economies, which have the means to transform them into finished goods. Underdeveloped countries end up purchasing

> the finished products at high prices, depleting the capital they might otherwise devote to upgrading their own productive capacity. The result is a vicious cycle that perpetuates the division of the world economy between a rich core and a poor periphery. (Munro, 2018, p. 1)

Turning my attention now to Immanuel Wallerstein, in his first (1974) and second (1979) of a series of books dealing with the "Modern World-System," followed up in many subsequent books and years later, he articulates his version of Dependency Theory apropos the concepts of "Core," "Periphery," and "Semi-periphery." According to him, countries classified as periphery are those that are dependent on core countries for capital and have underdeveloped industries; the core countries are comprised of the dominant capitalist countries that exploit the countries in the periphery for labor and raw materials; and, the countries in the semi-periphery constitute those that share features of both core and periphery countries (Wallerstein, 1974, 1979).

Wallerstein delineates five features of the modern world-system that distinguish it from the earlier ones, as John Agnew (2020) correctly points out. The first feature has to do with the notion that at the center of the world-system is a "single world market" within which the production of goods and services is mostly done for exchange, not necessarily for use. Accordingly, competition among producers dictates the prices for goods and services. As it is inevitable in capitalist exchange, by forcing out the less efficient producers, the efficient ones can gain monopoly in the global market. Accordingly, a genuine single world-system resulted from the development of trading exchanges and the commodification (i.e., the action or process of treating something as a mere commodity) of labor (Wallerstein, 1974, 1979; see also Agnew, 2020).

The second feature concerns the spatiality of the divisions among countries in the modern-world economy, which existed and developed at the same time with its spread. The occurrence permitted the capitalists to place the world market to their advantage and also protect their interests, both legally and politically. Another aspect of this development is that it made it impossible for any one country to convert the world economy into a world empire, even though some countries did attempt to do so. Since not all countries are equal in terms of economic and/or political power, a country's standing in the world system hinges upon its likelihood within the world economy (Wallerstein, 1974, 1979; see also Agnew, 2020).

The third feature relates to how the modern world-system spread steadily to encompass the entire world, denoted by an international division of labor vis-à-vis its different phases of expansion. The first world economy comprised Europe and parts of Central and South America colonized by Portugal and Spain, and the remainder of the world treated as an "external arena." Over time, much of the rest of the world was transformed from an external arena into a periphery, an outcome facilitated by pillage, European occupation, and the forced changes in focus of local economies to the world economy (Wallerstein, 1974, 1979; see also Agnew).

The fourth feature deals with the modern world-system's pro-tem recurrent sequence of economic growth and recession (Wallerstein, 1974, 1979). As Agnew describes this development so well,

> This is not the short-term business cycle but long cycles of 50 years or so in patterns of commodity prices produced by overinvestment and overproduction in novel technologies and, in the absence of any central regulation, followed by stagnation and decline. Since the late eighteenth century, it is possible to identify four such cycles and link them to new technological clusters and their subsequent exhaustion. The technology cycles are highly correlated with interstate competition such that the geographical distribution of cyclical effects empowers those states invested in new technologies and leads to the declining status of those overinvested in the old ones. (2020, p. 21)

And the fifth feature is in reference to the modern world-system being connected together both by the presiding political ideologies and their opponents—a situation Wallerstein dubs "geoculture"—and materially. Based on this perspective, the ascendant discernments about how the world operates led to competing ideologies like conservatism, liberalism, and radicalism. While in the nineteenth century these ideologies were also amalgamated with nationalism that later birthed a paragon for anti-system movements in Asia and Africa, by the early twentieth century "centrist liberalism" emerged prevalent in Britain and the United States, which constituted the deteriorating and the rising dominant powers, respectively (Wallerstein, 1974, 1979; see also Agnew, 2020).

The question that arises here then is the following: Why is Africa classified as an economic periphery in the modern world-system? Many authors have provided answers to this question. Here, I present only a handful of these writers' offerings for the sake of brevity, especially since they propound similar responses.

For starters, Geography (2022) categorizes Africa as a periphery. The rationale provided for this is that most African countries are characterized as "technologically simple," "labor-intensive," "low skill," and "low-wage occupations." The only exception to the categorization is South Africa which is designated as a semi-periphery country in that core processes are present in certain cities where high technology businesses are located. Nonetheless, in other parts of South Africa, there are millions of people who work in subsistence agriculture and earn less than one dollar a day.

Next, investigating Chinese-African economic relations within the context of core and periphery, Jean-Claude Maswana (2009) assesses the validity of dependency theories apropos those relations. The argument proffered is that while advocates of dependency theories contend that economic domination runs across north–south geo-economic arrangements, Chinese-African economic relations represent a distinct south–south dialectic taking place in an emerging new global economic configuration marked by a technology gap. Nevertheless, Maswana concedes that while synergies can be established by taking into account the legitimate interests of each party, no matter how well-intentioned China is, Africa must still develop its own technological capacities and free itself of its socioeconomic constraints. He concludes that the only way for Africa and China to gain long-run benefits is that they both contribute to a new economic framework that is deeply established on common or joint interests.

Also, studying Canadian-African economic relations as a dynamics of core-periphery nexus, Elizabeth Cobbett (2017) tells us that Canada's Department of

Foreign Affairs sees the dynamism occurring across the African continent as "calling out for Canadian engagement." Since in the twenty-first century Africa is no longer the continent emerging from colonial rule, it is looking for new forms of relationships with international partners. Cobbett cites the African Development Bank (AfDB) as an example of an entity that has identified certain priorities for inclusive growth in Africa. Nonetheless, according to her, the obstacles for Africa are quite significant akin to the continent's possibilities for transformative change. On the one hand, as the conditions for international collaboration in achieving the AfDB's objectives have metamorphosed, African leaders are looking for new modes of alliances and collaborations. On the other hand, Canada is poised to "come back" differently if it could look beyond its narrow mining interests and become an active partner working with public authorities in need of new and bold international partnerships. Cobbett, however, is not optimistic about Prime Minister Justin Trudeau's "Canada is back" agenda being ready to change the status quo. She adds that in a world where political-economic power is moving East, African countries do not have much justification to listen to Canada (Cobbett, 2017).

In addition, considering whether Africa belongs to the periphery or core during the current globalization era, Caroline Roussy (2021) commences by pointing out the following two observable developments that have occurred in Africa since the end of the Cold War and the emergence of the "global village": (1) Africa's scanty level of integration into the globalization process which is characterized as establishing the conditions for "interconnectedness" and "interdependence" within a restricted space-time, given its low participation in global trade; and (2) Africa's desire to play a significant role in international relations in accordance with its demography, the capacity projections of its market, etc. as potential new economic and financial partners line up to "pay court." Thereafter, Roussy points out that Africa's relationship to globalization can be understood only through the core–periphery framework, which highlights both the diversity of Africans and the challenges of the mechanisms they inherited from colonization. This situation, according to her, suggests that there exists the necessity for a "cross-cutting analysis" that pays particular attention to the complicated nexuses among the forces at play and to the significant importance of context.

Furthermore, in its argument that Africa should be moved from the global periphery to the core, the World Economic Forum on Africa (2010) at the end of its 20th annual meeting on the theme "Rethinking Africa's Growth Strategy" convened in Dar es Salaam, Tanzania and attended by 13 African heads of state/government and more than 1000 participants from 85 countries conceded that despite its huge potential, the continent suffers from a lack of integration in the global economy. The host of the meeting, former President Jakaya M. Kikwete of Tanzania, is quoted as stating the following: "If there is any predicament to African development, it is this state of affairs. [It is time] to move Africa from the periphery to the centre of the global economy" (World Economic Forum on Africa, 2010, p. 1). He is also noted to have pointed out that "the smallest share of global exports comes from Africa—just 3.5%. Just a trickle of global foreign direct investment (FDI) goes to Africa at 0.96% and the continent is not integrated into international financial markets"

(World Economic Forum on Africa, 2010, p. 1). He is further cited as saying that "Africa remains predominantly a primary producer and importer for industrial use. We produce what we don't consume and we consume what we don't produce. This cannot continue" (World Economic Forum on Africa, 2010, p. 1). Also quoted is former President Jacob Zuma of South Africa who noted that the 2010 World Cup would show the world that Africa is ready to do anything and indicated that "There were a lot of doubts and skepticism. But people who come to Africa will see that we are not just bushes and mountains. They will see how Africa is ready to do anything that can be done anywhere else in the world" (World Economic Forum on Africa, 2010, p. 1).

African Countries as Mono Economies

The question probed in this section is this: Why are African countries characterized as mono economies? Before providing an answer, I first offer a general overview of the concept "mono economy" as a background.

To begin with, a "mono economy" has been generally defined as an economic system which relies principally on a single product for its exports (see, for example, Semenya, 2022). Also, quoting Igwe (2005), Akinkuolie Akeem Akinlolu and colleagues apprise us that he has suggested that a better comprehension of the concept mono economy would be gained by considering an economy as denoting a "system of production and production relations peculiar to a society characterized in each epoch by identifiable means and modes of production" (Akinlolu et al., 2018, p. 263, quoting Igwe, 2005). Accordingly, these scholars also point out that an economy denotes a chain of economic activities that keep the economic life of the members of a particular society revolving. They add that over time, the economies of various countries have moved from one economic type or relationship to another. Based on this perspective, they further note that a mono economy infers an economic system that is primarily based on the existence of only one major economic product upon which it is dependent for its economic sustenance. Accordingly, they say, the economic life and existence of that economy "revolve around the existence, relevance and currency of that product" and would remain "buoyant only if such product does fine in the international market. The reverse though would be the case, if its showing at that level is poor" (Akinlolu et al., 2018, p. 263).

Next, we can glean from Nick Mullins (2017) that in a mono economy, the certainty of no other job alternatives exists that can provide a living wage within the areas of the product, families with generational ties to the land, or those who are financially incapable of moving away, are compelled to do what they can to survive. This circumstance leads younger adults, their fathers, and grandfathers to work in the industry. When moving away is not an option financially, they opt to remain close to home in order to raise their children in the same areas that their ancestors settled for centuries. Without enough land to farm and few if any good paying jobs outside of the industry, they had little choice for a profession (Mullins, 2017).

Also, according to Mullins, a mono economy is characteristic of an important aspect that is shared among a majority of the workers in an industry, i.e., if jobs existed that offered similar wages without the dangers and long-term health issues in that industry, those workers would jump on them instantly. This is the reason there is great competition for the few well-paying careers that do exist outside an industry in a mono economy (Mullins, 2017).

In addition, the concept "mono economy" has been slightly renamed by some writers as "mono-cultural economy." For example, Victor Nwaoba Itumo (2016) states that the term mono-cultural economy denotes an economy that is mostly reliant on one product or resource for economic development and growth. He adds that the term could also be applied to a case where a country depends on a single product sales or exports for its budget funding, especially to the tune of 70% of revenue. He also says that a mono-cultural economy could be further related to a circumstance whereby a country depends on a primary product for an overall higher percentage of national earnings and contribution to its gross domestic product (GDP). Itumo cites Uwafiokun Idemudia for describing the mono-cultural economy concept very well when he states the following in relation to the case of Nigeria: "The discovery of oil in 1956, and its subsequent extraction since 1958, over the past 50 years, has transformed the Nigerian economy from an agricultural based economy to an economy essentially dependent on petroleum" (Idemudia, 2012, p. 1, quoted by Itumo, 2016, p. 21).

Furthermore, a mono economy is said to have advantages and disadvantages. The advantages include (a) spurring specialization in production, (b) enlarging real income due to a country's earnings from its product; and (c) stimulating the development of manpower and employment. The disadvantages are (a) facilitating stagnation of other sectors of the economy, (b) giving rise to unemployment due to lack of diversification, and (c).fostering economic instability and poor leadership (Semenya, 2022).

I will now address the question of this section: Why are African countries characterized as mono economies? For conciseness, I look at five randomly selected sources among the many that have investigated the topic. First, we are informed by Paul Ezeoke (2020) that most African countries are endowed with plenty of human and other natural resources; yet these countries possess the highest poverty ratings. The reason provided for this circumstance is that African economies are structured around a "mono" or "near mono" export commodity. He cites Nigeria as an example of an African country which, since the 1970s, operated on a mono-cultural economic framework by depending significantly on oil as its major income earner. This means that the dynamics of the economy is at the mercy of the impulses of the oil market. Ezeoke adds that this situation signifies "the truth and reality" of African countries that sustainable economic growth depends on the diversification of the economies in order to escape the burden that underlies a mono economy. He also mentions that diversification will assist African economies to protect themselves from the vagaries of external macroeconomic shocks, ensure that trade volumes grow, and sustain higher productivity in the economies. He further suggests that the most effective way to diversify African economies is to encourage and build private sector-driven economies that will help reactivate income-generating activities in underdeveloped sectors through effective public-private sector collaborations (Ezeoke, 2020).

Second, as pointed out by Wale-Oshinowo et al. (2022), Africa is still "the most underdeveloped" among the continents across the globe. They note that the continent has more than 70% of the least developed countries (LDCs) in the world. They also mention that the continent depends mostly on foreign aid, with most countries in Africa still running as mono-product economies, and a larger percentage affected by corruption, ethnoreligious conflicts, and civil wars. They further mention that what additionally complicates this African conundrum is that "out of the 47 countries that make up the global list of least developed countries, 33 of them are found on the African continent..." (Wale-Oshinowo et al., 2022, p. 1). They add that the situation exacerbates the problem of inadequate access to basic livelihood needs such as shelter, health, education, food, water, and transportation (Wale-Oshinowo et al., 2022).

Third, we are apprised by Olaniyi Felix Olayinka (2021) that Africa's participation in the current globalization era hinges upon the strength of its "mono economy status" which, he says, comprises different unrefined products that attract very little prices on the world market. Added to this situation is Africa's lack of control of the pricing of its products and that of the imported goods that it consumes in very large quantities. The result, according to Olayinka, is a continent with a large number of poor countries and people who suffer from malnutrition, diseases, and short life span, all of which stymie productivity. He goes on to make the following observations about the consequences of the present globalization as it relates to Africa's "mono culture economy" that are worthy of direct quotation:

> Globalization and the prospect of attainment of poverty alleviation on the basis of mono culture economy appear as contradiction in terms. The dearth of infrastructure, absence of political will and endemic corruption in the public sector hinder diversification of the economy in Africa. The acquiescence of the Continent on mono-culture economy manifests in the education sector, which remains inadequately funded, with education policies and programmes running without meeting the immediate or future needs of the various states in Africa. (Olayinka, 2021, p. 1)

Olayinka adds:

> Globalization applies in Africa as a marriage of nations of unequal influence and strength of which the developed economies continue to grow at the expense of the poor and developing Africa. The Continent may attain poverty alleviation and sustainable development where equality and mutual respect are accorded nations and when all the internal and external policies that operate in perpetuating mono-culture economies in Africa are stopped. Within the nations of Africa, the just and equitable access of everyone to land and communal resource of the pre-colonial administration should be revived with a view of curbing endemic public sector corruption, which has been hindering the attainment of a diversified economy, poverty alleviation and sustainable development. (Olayinka, 2021, p. 1)

Fourth, according to Samuel Onyenaezchi Odoh (2022), a major obstacle to Africa's economic development is the lack of diversification as most African countries still practice a "single-economy" or "mono-economy" whereby a country's revenue is generated mostly from a particular mineral resource to the disadvantage of the other sectors of the economy. Odoh cites the case of Nigeria where the discovery of crude oil and its successive prosperity in the world market in the 1970s propelled crude oil to become the dominant source of revenue to the federal and state governments. He notes that beginning in the early 1970s on to the second decade of this twenty-first century, oil and gas have invariably represented between 95% and 98% of Nigeria's export earnings. Consequently, the large revenue from oil and gas has led Nigeria to neglect its agricultural sector, both in terms of funding and provision of basic social infrastructure and modern inputs (Odoh, 2022).

Also, Odoh indicates that another difficulty with mono-economy in Africa is that almost all African countries such as Angola, Ghana, Kenya, and Nigeria still export a single product in a raw form instead of refining it in Africa to establish job opportunities for the growing population. He adds that even though most African mono-economies are still in their developing stage in relation to the available resources for export, African countries still compare their economies with those of the industrialized countries—a comparison Odoh thinks is preposterous (Odoh, 2022).

Fifth, focusing on Nigeria as a case study of the challenges of Africa's mono economies, Samuel S. Idowu (2020) shows that the country faces enormous challenges from its "mono-culture economy" because of its overreliance on oil and the possibility of being left high and dry as a result of the global campaign and signed Paris Agreement in 2015—an economic risk that could jeopardize its economic development. Idowu points out that due to these developments, Nigeria's manufacturing sector plays a peripheral role in the country's economic development hankering. In addition to this quandary, according to him, is that the measures and policies that have been launched to invert the inclination have produced minimal effects. He is optimistic, however, that the manufacturing sector "is imbued with a huge capacity for an enduring sustainable diversified economy [that will] generate employment and foreign income" (Idowu, 2020, p. 77). This is because, according to him, manufacturing has a long-term significant impact on economic growth, albeit the Nigerian government's selective intervention and the poor political environment are responsible for the economy's underperformance (Idowu, 2020).

Africa as an Important Source to the World Economy

Investigated here is the following question: Why is Africa an important source to the world economy? The answer to this question is preceded by a synopsis of the "world economy" as a backdrop.

It is no exaggeration to assert that a full discussion of the "world economy" would require at least a volume, if not more. Thus, for succinctness, I limit my review here to the meaning and three major types of world economies—more accurately, the three major types of economies that operate in the world-system.

To commence with, "world economy," also called "global economy" or "worldwide economy," is commonly defined as "the system of industry and trade around the world that has developed as the result of globalization: i.e. the way in which economies have been developing to operate together as one system" (Cambridge Dictionary, 2023, p. 1). An example of this is the United States whose financial structure and stability are based on trust. When it comes to debt payments, the country has displayed an exemplary financial record for many years. Accordingly, the United States' debt is graded "AAA," meaning that the country can get the lowest interest rates on all its financial instruments. Currently under the administration of President Joseph Robinette Biden, issues such as large budget deficits and a negative trade balance have raised doubts about the long-term stability of the country's finances. Thus, the global economy is anxious about any possible loss of the US financial instruments. Such a development will lead to an increase in the country's financial costs, which will cause even bigger budget deficits. The occurrence will precipitate the necessity to compute "budget costs that will have a global impact, since a 1% budget cost on the United States budget can have considerable effects worldwide. This is an example of how the global economy works, where one country's decisions might have a big impact in the overall worldwide economy" (Accounting Dictionary, 2022, p. 1).

Next, stated more simply, "world economy" refers to all the economies of the countries of the world considered together as a single economic system or one giant entity. In essence, it is the way in which all of the countries' economies have been developing to operate collectively as one system. Two other denotations associated with "world economy" are the following: (1) the economy of the whole planet expressed in terms of a global domestic product (GDP—i.e., the total value of goods and services produced in a country); and (2) the way the world is today, with countries' economies so intertwined and interdependent that they all seem like parts of one whole. Therefore, the world economy is measured separately from national economies, as the former is simply an aggregate of all the separate countries' measurements. Nonetheless, it has been observed that this distinction is not fixed in place as many people employ both terms interchangeably (Market Business News, 2022).

Also, many economists have identified and analyzed three types of world economies. Phil Holleran (2007), for example, describes them as follows:

1. *Command Economy*: "In a command economy, what goods and services are produced, how they are produced, and for whom they are produced are all questions answered by government planning. The government makes economic decisions for the good of society. In a pure command economy, all resources are owned by the government, so the government can direct them to produce what is best for society as a whole, rather than what might be in the interests of private individuals...The Soviet Union until its breakup in the late 1980s was an excellent example of a command economy. Cuba and North Korea are good examples in today's world of command economies" (Holleran, 2007, p. 1).
2. *Market Economy*: "In a market economy, resources are owned by private individuals. The goods and services that are produced are not determined by the government. Rather, production is determined by businesses responding to the

wants and desires of consumers…Consumers determine what will be produced…" (Holleran, 2007, p. 1).
3. *Mixed Economy*: "A mixed economy is a blend of market and command economies. In a mixed economy some parts or sectors of the economy are left to private ownership (market) while in other sectors there is substantial government ownership or government-directed production (command). In a mixed economy, government intervenes in those sectors where private ownership is believed to be not in the best interests of society as a whole. For example, in a mixed economy the government might control the production and distribution of health care (as in Great Britain and Sweden)" (Holleran, 2007, p. 1).

So, why is Africa an important source to the world economy? The discussion in the rest of this section is devoted to providing an answer to this question. A Google search on the question on January 7, 2023, yielded about 527,000,000 results in 0.49 s. It is therefore neither possible nor is it necessary to examine all of these sources here. Thus, I restrict myself to a small number of randomly selected sources from some of the major organizations that specialize on the subject matter.

First, the National Geographic (2023) focuses on (a) "the climate and agriculture," (b) "forestry and fishing," (c) "mining and drilling," and (d) "the built environment" as factors that underlie Africa's importance to the world economy. To start off, the National Geographic points out that the climate greatly affects Africa's agriculture, which is acknowledged to be the continent's single most important economic activity. It notes that agriculture employs two-thirds of Africa's working population and contributes between 20% and 60% of every country's gross domestic product (GDP). It adds that the continent's important climatic regions of agriculture include tropical wet, savanna, desert, Mediterranean, and highland. It then goes on to provide detailed descriptions of these climatic conditions (National Geographic, 2023).

Next, concerning forestry and fishing, we learn from the National Geographic that forestry, which involves "the management of trees and other vegetation in forests," is a vital economic pursuit in Africa. It states that on average, forest products account for 6% of the continent's GDP, which is greater than that of any other continent. This, it says, is due to the fact that "Africa's abundant forest cover, with 0.8 hectares (2 acres) per person, [is greater] compared with 0.6 hectares (1.5 acres) globally. In central and western Africa, where forest cover is heaviest, the forest sector contributes more than 60 percent of GDP" (National Geographic, 2023, p. 1). It continues with overviews of forest and marine products that are exported by Africa.

Thereafter, as it pertains to mining and drilling, we glean from the National Geographic that Africa is a key producer of important metals and minerals. It identifies the metals exported by African countries to include (a) uranium, used to produce nuclear energy; (b) platinum, used in jewelry and industrial applications; (c) nickel, used in stainless steel, magnets, coins, and rechargeable batteries; (d) bauxite, a main aluminum ore; and (e) cobalt, used in color pigments. Nonetheless, according to the organization, Africa's two most profitable mineral resources are (1) gold and (2) diamonds. It also draws attention to the following important statistics pertaining to these two products for 2008: "Africa produced about 483 tons of gold, or 22 percent of the world's total production. South Africa accounts for almost half of Africa's gold production. Ghana, Guinea, Mali, and Tanzania are other major producers of gold. Africa dominates the global diamond market…the continent produced 55 percent of the world's diamonds. Botswana, Angola, South Africa, the Democratic Republic of the Congo, and Namibia are Africa's largest producers of diamonds" (National Geographic, 2023, p. 1).

Finally, vis-à-vis Africa's built environment (i.e., "human-made buildings and structures."), the National Geographic points out that the continent's natural resource economy contributes significantly to it. The organization observes that the largest engineering projects and urban areas in Africa are directly linked to the production and trade of resources such as minerals, oil, and water. An example of the many engineering marvels in Africa cited is the Aswan Dam, which is described as "a complex of two dams in Aswan, Egypt [that] captures the world's longest river, the Nile, in the world's third-largest reservoir, Lake Nasser. The Aswan High Dam, the newer and larger of the two dams, produces more than 10 billion kilowatt-hours of electricity every year, enough power for about 15 percent of the country" (National Geographic, 2023, p. 1). Other major engineering feats with similar economic impacts mentioned are (a) the Driefontein Gold Mine outside of Johannesburg, South Africa; (b) Lagos as Africa's second most-populous city, with a population of about 10.2 million people, and is the commercial and industrial hub of Nigeria, which has a GDP that is triple that of any other West African country; and (c) Johannesburg as the largest city in South Africa, with a metropolitan population of more than seven million, and is also the world's largest city not situated on a river, lake, or coastline; instead, it developed around the gold and diamond industry situated on a mineral-rich mountain range (National Geographic, 2023).

Second, the United Nations Environment Programme (2023) probes the following question: "What resources make Africa important to the world economy?" The organization mentions a number of factors in its answer to the question. One factor is that Africa is endowed with "abundant natural resources" that include (a) fertile land, (b) forests, (c) minerals, (d) natural gas, (e) oil, (f) water, (g) minerals, and (h) wildlife. To boot, the continent holds a huge proportion of the world's renewable and nonrenewable natural resources (United Nations Environment Programme, 2023).

The other factor is that Africa possesses "roughly 30 percent of the world's mineral reserves," which entail 8% of the world's natural gas and 12% of the world's oil reserves. What's more, the continent owns 40% of the world's gold and up to 90% of its chromium and platinum. As well, Africa is home to the largest reserves of cobalt, diamonds, platinum, and uranium in the world. Besides, Africa enjoys 65% of the world's arable land and 10% of the globe's internal renewable fresh water source (United Nations Environment Programme, 2023).

Another factor is that "natural capital" (i.e., the natural resources and environmental features in a given area, regarded as having economic value or providing a service to humankind) constitutes between 30% and 50% of aggregate finance in the majority of the African countries. Add to that the fact that more than 70% of the people living in Africa South of the Sahara rely on forests and woodlands for their livelihoods. Therefore, land is a vital asset for economic development as well as a sociocultural resource (United Nations Environment Programme, 2023).

An additional factor is the recognition of the "African Ministerial Conference on the Environment (AMCEN) that natural capital underpins the Africa's economy, affirming that using natural capital as a getaway to wealth creation and investments will allow for actions towards achievement of the United Nations' 2030 Agenda on Sustainable Development Goals (SDGs)" (United Nations Environment Programme, 2023, p. 1). It is also noted that the African Union's Agenda 2063 makes the same recognition via financial, economic, social, and environmental contributions (United Nations Environment Programme, 2023).

Third, Landry Signé and Ameenah Gurib-Fakim, writing on behalf of the Brookings Institution, make the point that "while narratives over the past few decades have painted a wide range of views of Africa—as a child in need of development, a rising economic power, an imminent threat, a tinderbox of terrorism, poverty, forced migration, and disease—the truth is, as always, more nuanced" (2019, p. 1). They instead insist that what is obvious is that the transformation that Africa has undergone in recent decades has been remarkable, as the continent is shaping its own destiny and should be referred to as the "African opportunity," not the "African threat" (Signé & Gurib-Fakim, 2019).

And fourth, the company Ernst & Young Americas explicates how "a surplus of workers, more stability and technology" are metamorphosing Africa's economies, making the continent less dependent on extractive industries. The company begins by pointing out that for over 100 years, foreign direct investment (FDI) in Africa was almost exclusively focused on the extraction and export of natural resources, but that since the turn of the millennium the momentum has shifted—and in the past few years the trend has finally inverted. As a result, investors now come to Africa more frequently for the promise of its people than for its physical properties (Ernst & Young Americas, 2020).

Next, the company points out that petroleum and mining now represent a minority of long-term capital inflows, with more investors focused on retailing, services, and telecommunications. It notes that the extractive industries have represented more than half of FDI just once in the past 7 years. It adds that the trend is even more evident in the 46 "jurisdictions" of Africa South of the Sahara in that from 2005 to 2011, extractives in the region accounted for more than half of investments in all but 1 year. The opposite was the case during the subsequent 7 years ending in 2018, which is the most recent year for which full and final data were available (Ernst & Young Americas, 2020). The company states a number of reasons for this development which I present in the ensuing paragraphs.

One reason is that the current investment evolution mirrors the improvement in governance and stability that began in the 1990s, with the end of the Cold War. Democratic institutions are established and recognized, and fewer people live in extreme poverty. Nonetheless, these democratic transitions continue to be callow and tenuous, with countries developing at different paces (Ernst & Young Americas, 2020).

Another reason is that long-term trends measured over decades in lieu of years reveal that African countries are now more attractive investment destinations. This development is taking place in the last continent of the world providing a "demographic dividend." Consequently, Africa South of the Sahara is poised to be the only place in the world with birth rates at replacement level or higher (Ernst & Young Americas, 2020).

An additional reason is that the new "value chains" (i.e., the processes or activities by which companies add value to a product or service, including production, marketing, and the provision of after-sales service) which are emerging in Africa are rooted in agribusiness, energy, and telecommunications platforms. Nonetheless, the transformation away from the extractive industries is both a response to improved investment climates in Africa (for instance, extractives make up a smaller share of total investment) and the rate rising and falling in response to oil prices (Ernst & Young Americas, 2020).

Conclusion and Recommendations

The general conclusion in this chapter is that while the preceding conceptualizations of African economies reveal many challenges for the continent, they also show some positive attributes. Thus, the ultimate question of the chapter is this one: What can be done to address the challenges to African economies? I end here by making some policy recommendations in response to the question and a suggestion for future research on the subject matter.

First, while the movement toward democratic rule across Africa has been touted by many observers, the recent developments of military interventions into politics in countries such as Burkina Faso, Chad, Guinea, Mali, and Sudan have upended the trend. But even in the democratic dispensations, the regime types include pluralist, administrative hegemonic, party mobilizing, and ambiguous. These regime types reflect the many constraints and the variegated options open to Africans since independence. Thus, a close analysis of these regime forms and their mutations will assist in linking a government with its purpose, the political process and the dominant modes of social organization, and the tenets of politics with the African setting in which they unfold. Indeed, the analysis of political processes in Africa through the lenses of these relatively fluid regime forms calls for the unraveling of the ways decisions are made and implemented and what responses these actions evoke. It also will force us to pay attention to (a) how centers are constructed and legitimated, (b) how their political visions are crystalized and authority conceived, (c) how civil societies form and break down, and (d) how and why transformations take root.

Second, due to its failure to develop a Union of African States to date, it is obvious that the strengthening of sub-regionalism is the next best alternative for economic development strategies in Africa. Sub-regionalism means African countries working together as neighbors on common development efforts and problems. Within this sub-regional approach, various types of disagreements are likely to hamper increasing cooperation from time to time, providing sub-regional groups or other countries with the occasion to mediate and restore harmony. None of these characteristics is likely to be changed by any state fusions that may occur.

Third, the several economic models African countries have employed since independence (simple growth, redistribution with growth, and regional integration/collective self-reliance) indicates that successful policy reforms and economic development in Africa require substantial political will on the part of the African governments. In light of the fact that the international community has failed to provide the requisite external support needed to promote substantive economic development in Africa, the continent's leaders must shoulder this responsibility by being willing to make the painful policy decisions.

Fourth and finally, I suggest that future research on the conceptualizations of Africa's economic standing be based on *public choice theory*, which postulates that individual behavior in the political arena will be motivated by considerations similar to those that influence market behavior. In essence, the theory advances the notion that the number of saints and sinners in both the economic and public sectors will be comparable. Thus, the public choice approach has significantly advanced our understanding of the collective decision-making process and how it applies the principles and methodology of economics to collective choices. Through theory and empirical testing, a public choice analyst can explain various economic, political, and social actions of decision makers and, in general, how African societies operate.

References

Accounting Dictionary. (2022). What is a global economy? *My Accounting Course*. Retrieved on January 7, 2023 from https://www.myaccountingcourse.com/accounting-dictionary/global-economy

Agnew, J. (2020, December 8). Immanuel Wallerstein, the "modern world-system," and radical human geography. *Human Geography, 14*(1):17–30. Retrieved on January 3, 2023 from https://journals.sagepub.com/doi/10.1177/1942778620974056.

Airgeadais, A. R. (2022). *What is economic appraisal and when is it required?* United Kingdom Department of Finance. Retrieved on December 30, 2022 from https://www.finance-ni.gov.uk/articles/what-economic-appraisal-and-when-it-required

Akinlolu, A. A., Gbemiga, F. L., Ayodeji, O. E., & Emmanuel, A. O. (2018). Business education and economic diversification: Antidote to a mono-sector economy. *Nigerian Journal of Business Education (NIGJBED), 5*(1), 263–273. Retrieved on January 5, 2023 from http://www.nigjbed.com.ng/index.php/nigjbed/article/view/223

Cambridge Dictionary. (2023). The global economy. Retrieved on January 7, 2023 from https://dictionary.cambridge.org/us/dictionary/english/global-economy

Cobbett, E. (2017). Canada-Africa relations in changing core-periphery dynamics: A chance to "come back" differently. *International Journal of Canadian Studies, 55*, 31–41.

Ernst & Young Americas. (2020, September 11). Why Africa is becoming a bigger player in the global economy. Retrieved on January 7, 2023 from https://www.ey.com/en_us/tax/why-africa-is-becoming-a-bigger-player-in-the-global-economy

Ezeoke, P. (2020). Commentary: Africa and bitter lessons of mono economy. *Anambra Broadcasting Service*. Retrieved on January 6, 2023 from http://www.absradiotv.com/2020/06/17/commentaryafrica-and-bitter-lessons-of-mono-economy/

Geography. (2022). Core and periphery. Retrieved on January 4, 2023 from https://geography.name/core-and-periphery/

Holleran, P. (2007). *Economic systems: Command, market, and mixed*. Radford University, a public university in Radford. Retrieved on January 7, 2023 from http://pholleran.asp.radford.edu/505_fall06_notes_week01_systems2.html

Idemudia, U. (2012). The resource curse and the decentralization of oil revenue: The case of Nigeria. *Journal of Cleaner Production, 35*, 183–193.

Idowu, S. S. (2020, May). Mono economy syndrome of Nigeria: Reposition of manufacturing sector for sustainable diversification and development. *Research Nepal Journal of Development Studies, 3*(1), 77–90.

Igwe, O. (2005). *Politics and globe dictionary*. Eagle Publishers.

Itumo, V. N. (2016). Nigeria's mono-cultural economy: Impact assessment and prospects. *European Journal of Interdisciplinary Studies, 8*(2), 20–35.

Mankiw, N. G. (2018). *Principles of macroeconomics* (8th ed.). Cengage Learning.

Market Business News. (2022). Global economy—Definition and meaning. Retrieved on January 7, 2023 from https://marketbusinessnews.com/financial-glossary/global-economy/

Maswana, J.-C. (2009). A center-periphery perspective on Africa-China's emerging economic links. *African and Asian Studies, 8*, 67–88.

McConnell, C., Brue, S., & Flynn, S. (2020). *Microeconomics* (22nd ed.). McGraw Hill.

Mullins, N. (2017, August 22). The mono-economy of coal. *Huffpost*. Retrieved on January 5, 2023 from https://www.huffpost.com/entry/the-mono-economy-of-coal-or-how-to-maintain-a-captive_b_599c53a1e4b09dbe86ea374b

Munro, A. (2018). Dependency theory. *Encyclopaedia Britannica*. Retrieved on January 1, 2023 from https://www.britannica.com/topic/dependency-theory

National Geographic. (2023), Africa: Resources. *Resource Library*. Retrieved on January 7, 2023 from https://education.nationalgeographic.org/resource/africa-resources

Odoh, S. O. (2022). The challenges to Africa's economic development since the 1960s. *Iconic Research and Engineering Journals, 5*(9), 359–365. Retrieved on January 6, 2023 from https://www.irejournals.com/formatedpaper/1703283.pdf

Olayinka, O. F. (2021, January). Mono-culture economy, globalization and the prospect of Africa attaining poverty alleviation. *ResearchGate*. Retrieved on January 6, 2023 from https://www.researchgate.net/publication/348117089_Mono_-_culture_Economy_Globalization_and_the_Prospect_of_Africa_Attaining_Poverty_Alleviation

Roussy, C. (2021). Africa: Periphery or new centre of globalization? *Revue internationale et stratégique, 123*(3), 97–106.

Semenya, M. (2022). Nature of Nigerian economy. *Academia.edu*. Retrieved on January 5, 2023 from https://www.academia.edu/32028454/NATURE_OF_NIGERIAN_ECONOMY

Signé, L., & Gurib-Fakim, A. (2019). Africa is an opportunity for the world: Overlooked progress in governance and human development. *Brookings Africa in Focus*. Retrieved on January 7, 2023 from https://www.brookings.edu/blog/africa-in-focus/2019/01/25/africa-is-an-opportunity-for-the-world-overlooked-progress-in-governance-and-human-development/

United Nations Environment Programme. (2023). Our work in Africa. Retrieved on January 7, 2023 from https://www.unep.org/regions/africa/our-work-africa

Wale-Oshinowo, B. A., Omobowale, A. O., Adeyeye, M. M., & Lebura, S. (2022). Least developed countries in Africa. In S. Romaniuk (Ed.), *The Palgrave encyclopedia of global security studies*. Palgrave Macmillan.

Wallerstein, I. (1974). *The modern world-system I: Capitalist agriculture and the origins of the European world economy in the sixteenth century*. Academic Press.

Wallerstein, I. (1979). *The capitalist world-economy*. Cambridge University Press.

World Economic Forum on Africa. (2010, May 7). Time to move Africa from the periphery to the centre of the global economy. Retrieved on January 4, 2023 from https://www.weforum.org/agenda/2010/05/time-to-move-africa-from-the-periphery-to-the-centre-of-the-global-economy/

Abdul Karim Bangura has five PhDs in political science, development economics, linguistics, computer science, and mathematics. He is a researcher-in-residence of Abrahamic Connections and Islamic Peace Studies at American University's Center for Global Peace. He is the author and editor of 106 books and the author of 709 scholarly articles. Many of these works have won eminent awards, in addition to more than 50 other distinguished national and international awards. He has served as president and then ambassador to the United Nations for the Association of Third World Studies. He is now the president of the African Studies and Research Forum, and is fluent in a dozen African and six European languages.

Education

Azeez Babatunde Adebakin

This chapter conceptualizes Africa within the lens of Education—a field of study that focuses on the theory, practice, and methods of teaching and learning. Generally, education encompasses how individuals learn and how knowledge is transmitted. Specifically, African education is investigated in terms of its unique challenges and opportunities. The duo are evolving through transmission of culture, customs, and traditions from one generation to another. Thus, this chapter majorly probes the conceptualizations of Africa within the context of education as a field of study.

Although impracticable to explore all of the conceptualizations, however, readers of this chapter may be curious as to why the investigation on how Africa is conceptualized in the field of education. The curiosity is satisfied given the vital roles of education on the continent—promotes cultural pride, critical thinking, and a balanced understanding of Africa (Mwamidi et al., 2018). In essence, this chapter gives an explanation of how these roles are significant to Africa and Africans. As a result, the following conceptualizations were explored thematically: (1) Africa and evolution of education, (2) African pedagogical practices, and (3) decolonizing African education.

Given that the chapter emphasizes education conceptualizations, the analyses are distinctly qualitative through the use of published journal articles, conference papers, and reports on outcomes from education related interventions in Africa. However, relevant quantitative data are noted to supplement certain qualitative analyses as may be required. Secondary data are mostly used, and they are analyzed in terms of descriptive case studies. Before delving into the thematic breakdown, Education as a field of study is provided as a backdrop upon which the investigation is based.

A. B. Adebakin (✉)
Department of Educational Management, Obafemi Awolowo University, Ile-Ife, Nigeria
e-mail: adebakinazeez@oauife.edu.ng

A. K. Bangura, J. A. Ifedi (eds.), *Conceptualizations of Africa*, African Studies and Research Forum Series, https://doi.org/10.1007/978-3-031-74535-5_8

Education: A Conceptualization

Despite the various viewpoints to education, the concept seems vague. However, to comprehend it, one must explain its meaning or nature in terms of the functions it performs and/or the contexts in which it is used. While economists would regard education as a commodity in which the community should profitably invest, Sociologists described it as a socializing force where teachers are the community's socializing agency. From the role context, psychiatrists opined that education ensures children's mental health. Meanwhile, education is what it is, not how it is interpreted. It is present in all the viewpoints, and each is linked to the educational process, but in its real sense, it is above all of them.

The term education is etymologically derived from the Latin words *educare* and *educere*. The earlier refers to *bring up* or *nourish*, while the later means to *bring forth* or *drag out*. Juxtaposing these words, one will notice that education aims at providing learners a nourishing environment that will bring out and develop their latent innate potentialities. Education is the process of acquiring knowledge, skills, values, and attitudes that enable individuals to develop their full potential and lead to successful and fulfilling lives. It is an essential aspect of human life giving its roles in personal, social, and economic developments. Education is the process of bringing desirable change into the behavior of learners. It can also be defined as the process of imparting or acquiring knowledge or habits through instruction or study (Adelabu, 2019). The behavioral changes must be directed toward a desirable end. They should be acceptable socially, culturally, and comically and result in a change in knowledge, skill, attitude, and understanding.

Education as a discipline refers to the systematic study of various aspects of education, including its theories, practices, policies, and processes. It involves a critical examination and analysis of educational systems, institutions, and practices, aiming to understand how individuals learn, how knowledge is transmitted, and how education can be improved. As a discipline, education encompasses a wide range of subdisciplines and areas of study, such as educational psychology, curriculum development, assessment and evaluation, instructional design, educational leadership and management, sociology of education, philosophy of education, and more. Each of these subdisciplines focuses on different aspects of education and contributes to a comprehensive understanding of the field. The discipline is concerned with exploring and applying research-based knowledge to improve educational practices and policies. Scholars and researchers in this discipline conduct empirical studies, engage in theoretical analysis, and develop evidence-based interventions to enhance teaching and learning processes. They also critically examine societal factors that influence education—cultural, political, and economic contexts, and address issues related to equity, inclusivity, and social justice in education.

Education as a discipline aims at deepening individual understanding of complex and multifaceted phenomena, with the ultimate goal of fostering effective learning environments, promoting educational equity, and contributing to the development of informed and knowledgeable individuals and societies. Thus, it is a systematic study of examining educational theories, practices, and policies toward teaching–learning and their implications for individuals, communities, and societies. The conceptualization of education as a discipline draws from various fields such as psychology, sociology, philosophy, and history.

Overall, education attracts various conceptions emanating from its functional and etymological grounds. However, this chapter encapsulates it from its widest sense around the forms of education—informal (self-improvement), nonformal (inculcation and sustenance of basic and post-basic life skills), and formal (awakening and continuous development of the human potential). While each of these forms is detailed one at a time in the following subsections for clarity, it must be noted that the forms are unremarkably coiffured through the goals and objectives of teaching–learning, the level of flexibility of subject matter in focus, the period and time of learning, resources required, level of control, process of knowledge dissemination and ultimately, the beneficiaries.

Informal Education

Informal education refers to any kind of education that does not use a formal learning and teaching method. It covers everything from a parent teaching a child how to read or count in the home to being taught a skill by a friend. Informal education occurs when the learners are not confined within a four-walled classroom of a school and do not use any particular learning strategy or method. This type of education precludes conscious efforts that are not necessarily involved in scientifically planned outcomes. Informal education may be a parent teaching a child how to prepare a meal or ride a bicycle. This could also be by reading many books from a library or educational websites. It is neither preplanned nor deliberate. Often, it may be learned at some public spaces or at home. Sometimes, it is referred to as individual or cultural education, and it has little or no anticipated goal. For example, the son of a farmer acquired knowledge about farming from the father. In informal education, experiences are unstructured and indefinite.

Its purpose is to cultivate communities, associations, and relationships that make for human flourishing. Informal education can be said to encompass learners' interest within a curriculum in a regular classroom. Some see informal education as learning that goes on daily in life or as the learning projects that we undertake for ourselves. This type of education allows us to satisfy our curiosity and, in the process, helps to improve our knowledge base and pick up a new technique or an existing skill. It is spontaneous and can happen anytime the learners see something that piques their curiosity or will add value to their job. For many centuries education was informally given. Yet a lot of values were transmitted through this informal educational system.

Unlike formal education, informal education is not imparted by an institution such as school or college. This is not given according to any fixed timetable and there is no curriculum set out or required. However, it consists of experiences and are actually found living in the family or community. Some of the examples of informal education are found in teaching the child some basics such as numeric characters and someone learning his/her mother tongue. Basically, informal education features independent learning boundaries, no definite syllabus, no preplanned timetable, and no fees stipulated required.

In Medieval times informal education was transmitted orally using conversational methods that are simple, rational, and direct. Some were given in songs and allegories. The informal system of education could also have a framework that may be adopted in any community. It is not preplanned or deliberate. It is incidental and takes place consciously as well as unconsciously. The child learns many habits, manners, and patterns while with others or moving in different spheres like home, society, and groups, etc. In an informal way, the child imitates the older members of the community and, thus, imbibes certain virtues most essential for life. There is no prescribed course, no fixed timetable and no formal means of education. The transmission of cultural heritage and life experiences takes place in a natural way. In informal education, you are not taught how to do things but you know what to do because learning is by correction and observation. Such education becomes a lifelong process.

There is no gain saying that the literature on informal learning is enormous, growing and expanding. Informal learning is experiential, unstructured, and non-institutional learning. It is the construction, co-construction or acquisition of new knowledge, understanding, skills or attitude which people undertake whether consciously or unconsciously (Hrimech, 2005; Livingstone, 2001). Furthermore, informal education is a conscious process when the control of what, how, where and when to learn rests with the learner. It is an unconscious process if it does not involve teaching by persons designated as facilitators, instructors, or teachers. Consequently, informal education becomes pervasive. This is not in any way different from traditional African education, where everyone teaches at some point and learns at other times.

A cursory look at the literature reveals some forms of informal education include self-directed learning, autodidactic learning, tacit and explicit informal learning and the informal learning which occurs within formal nonformal teaching–learning interaction that is not a part of the curriculum but thus called the hidden curriculum.

Nonformal Education

It must first be placed on record that nonformal education is not synonymous to formal education. However, there is a need for complementary efforts of both formal and nonformal education systems. The nonformal form of education is planned, structured, and organized outside the curriculum of the formal school system. It is similar to formal education in the sense that it involves instruction from a teacher. The focus of the nonformal education is targeted toward some specific needs of selected persons or groups. Hence, its curriculum is flexible and does not have certification as a goal. It does not rely on a syllabus or any other set structure. If there is a structure in place, it is malleable by the teacher and can be customized to meet learners' needs.

Similarly, it can take place in workplaces, community settings, homes, religious places, formal school settings, town halls, and other cultural institutions. Education, here, is given via training, seminars, and workshops where ideas are shared among people of similar professions as colleagues. Some examples of nonformal education include job training, adult education courses, fitness courses, and any one-on-one tutoring session that can be customized with the learners in mind where ideas are shared among people of similar professions as colleagues.

This conception of nonformal education depicts an education that serves an additional, alternative, or education meant to compliment the formal education within the process of the lifelong learning of individuals. This also because it is often provided to guarantee the right to access to education for all hence, it caters for people of all ages but does not necessarily apply in continuous pathway-structure. This is why its duration may be short with low intensity and mostly provided in the form of short courses with life skills, work skills, social and cultural development, and literacy as its focus (UNESCO-UIS, 2012).

Formal Education

Formal education or formal learning is a Western form of education which usually occurs in the premises of the school, where a person may learn basic, academic, or trade skills. Learners often begin in elementary school and continue with secondary and, later, higher education. This form of education involves the process in which the teacher trains or develops the skills and knowledge of the learners facing each other in a classroom situation on a regular and continuous basis and predetermined timetable according to syllabus, source of promotion to next class after passing the previous one. It is the type of education regulated by the state and which activities are constitutionally based, legitimately supported, internationally recognized with a policy document leading to awards of certificates, diplomas, and degrees. This is why every formal education has mostly served young people in basic and secondary schools as well as young adults in higher education institutions.

Additionally, formal education is the process whereby persons intentionally guide the development of other individuals. It is the process of learning to live as a useful and acceptable member of the community. It is highly structured, organized, rigid, and classroom based with a curriculum and always delivered by trained teachers. It uses age, and other criteria for admission into the system. It is systematic but does not give consideration to individual ability to learn. It is the government or its accredited agencies that determines what is enough for learning. It is certificate and examination oriented. Education is considered formal when it is consciously planned, when instruction is graded and when definite infrastructures exist for its promotion. It is a structured and systemic form of learning. This is the education of a certain standard delivered to learners by trained teachers. This type of education usually takes place in school and within a classroom setting. It usually begins in elementary school and continues through secondary school and higher institutions. In formal education, learners are usually grouped by age or education level and are taught by professional teachers in a structured environment. The curriculum is planned, deliberate and often follows a strict syllabus.

Some of the characteristics of formal education in Africa include planned, deliberate and hierarchical structure, payment of scheduled fees (paid by beneficiaries or state), chronological grading system, syllabus and subject-oriented with specific coverage and time frame.

Educational Foundations

Education as a discipline refers to the systematic study of various aspects of education, including its theories, practices, policies, and processes. It encompasses a wide range of subdisciplines and draws from various fields such as philosophy, psychology, and sociology. Each of these subdisciplines focuses on different aspects of education and contributes to a comprehensive understanding of the field.

Philosophical Foundation of Education

Philosophical foundation of education refers to the underlying principles, beliefs, and theories that guide the practice and development of education. It encompasses various perspectives on education, including the purpose of education, the role of teachers and students, and the methods and approaches used in teaching and learning. The word "philosophy," coined by the Greek philosopher Pythagoras (c. 570–495 BCE), comes into being from original Greek via Latin to English. The Greek word *philos* meaning "love" and *sophia* meaning wisdom. So, etymologically, "philosophy" means "love of wisdom."

Initially, the term referred to any body of knowledge. In this sense, philosophy is closely related to education, religion, mathematics, natural science, and politics. Njoroge and Bennaars (2016), as well as Hountondji (2022), summarize views of earliest philosophers as follows. To Plato, philosophy is knowledge about everything that exists, philosophy is knowledge that can fulfill the desires of those who are interested in advancing the real truth. To Karl Marx, philosophy is the interpretation of the world in order to change it. Bertrand Russel called philosophy the science of the possible. By this, Wiredu (2014) suggests that any philosophical proposition should have two distinctive characteristics: it must be general and/or a priori, knowledge that comes from the power of reasoning based on self-evident truths, not from experience or personal observation. This therefore means that Philosophy is an activity people undertake when they seek to understand fundamental truths about themselves, the world in which they live, and their relationship to the world and each other.

Philosophy of education thus examines the goals, forms, methods, and meaning of education. The term is used to describe both fundamental philosophical analysis of these themes and the description and analysis of pedagogical approaches (Waghid, 2014). It explores fundamental ideas, moral standards, religious convictions, and ethical issues in education, focusing on teaching and learning (Noddings, 2013). Considerations of how education relates to broader philosophical contexts may be included. The philosophy of education overlaps with the field of education and applied philosophy. For example, philosophers of education study what constitutes upbringing and education, the values and norms revealed through upbringing and educational practices, the limits and legitimization of education as an academic discipline, and the relation between educational theory and practice. In universities, the philosophy of education usually forms part of departments or colleges of education.

Psychological Foundation of Education

Educational psychology, as described by Schwartz et al. (2022), is a field that straddles two large domains: education and psychology. Reaching far back into antiquity, the field was borne from philosophies and theories that weaved back and forth between each domain all with the intent of understanding the way learners learn, teachers teach, and educational settings should be effectively designed. Educational psychology examines human learning and development, including cognitive ability, emotional status, social interactions, and moral dispositions. It explores theories of learning, motivation, intelligence, and educational assessment. Educational psychology, as a field of study, is devoted to the application of a wide variety of theories to understand the way humans learn so that the most effective practices of instruction can be implemented.

While educational psychology seems rather simple to describe, its application to education is complex. After all, when examining the two words separately, education exists in a myriad of contexts, formal, nonformal, and informal, over the course of one's life. Psychology, on the other hand, is an ocean of concepts, principles, and processes across layers of dynamic human-environmental transactions. Ormrod and Anderman (2020), Santrock (2021), Slavin (2021), Snowman and McCown (2015), and Woolfolk (2019) compose a wide collection of vectors pointing to the target of the field; that is, the subsection of learning and instruction within educational psychology traditionally includes multiple theoretical and conceptual domains.

The common domains of educational psychology include "developmental theories, learning and motivation, student heterogeneity, classroom instruction and assessment and evaluation. The first domain, developmental theories, addresses the development of cognition and language, as well as social, emotional, and moral development. The second domain, learning and motivation, encompasses behavioral and social learning theory, motivation, and cognitive views of learning. Given that learners are very different across a wide swath of the student landscape. The third domain, student heterogeneity, is addressed with a focus on culture and diversity as well as students' special needs. Fourth, classroom instruction focuses on: how instruction may be organized, models for managing the learning environment, use of technology for teaching and how to think about instructional strategies given what we know about how students actively construct knowledge. Finally, the fifth domain, assessment and evaluation, underscores the importance of evidence-based practices and making educational decisions empirically. Thus, the field of educational psychology has, over the decades, embraced and continues to embrace the need for the measurement of learners' summative and formative performance" (Schwartz et al., 2022).

Tracing its origin to some six generations of thinkers ago, the educational psychology emerged from a combination of convergent and divergent ideas (Schwartz et al., 2022). For example, Democritus in the fifth century BC, Plato and Aristotle a century later, Quintilian was around AD and Vives during the early years of the sixteenth century. Thus, from those beginnings in antiquity, Santrock (2021) traced the agreed-upon ideas at the time that can be considered precursory thinking of the field today. Those ideas were: "getting to know and leveraging the unique characteristics of learners; developing criteria for selecting teachers; making teaching engaging within an interesting curriculum to circumvent behavior problems of learners; using visual material to enhance learning; focusing on understanding rather than rote learning; ordering instruction and deploying it from higher-order ideas to specific details; making certain all material to be taught is vetted in experience; recognizing that students teaching other students is the best way to learn; and involving parents in the education of their children" (Schwartz et al., 2022).

Sociological Foundation of Education

The word Sociology is derived from the combination of the Latin *socius*—meaning companion and the Greek *logos*, meaning the study of. So, the word literally means the study of companionship, or social relations. It is the science or study of the origin, development, organization, and functioning of human society. It is the science of fundamental laws of social behavior, relations, institutions, etc. Emile Durkheim was the first person who indicated the need for a sociological approach to education. He considered education to be essentially social in character and in its functions. As a result, he relates education more clearly to sociology than any other science. He emphasized that education is not a static phenomenon but a dynamic and ever-changing process.

Educational sociology, by the description of the earliest sociologist, examines social structures, institutions, processes influencing education, addressing inequality, power dynamics, and societal impact (Durkheim, 1956). It is a discipline which studies education sociologically, with the premise that it recognizes education as a social fact, a process and an institution, having a social function and being determined socially (Akínsolá, 2019). Educational sociology could appear only when it accepted the social nature of education. The sociology of education investigates how social institutions and structures influence education. It examines issues of equity, socialization, social stratification, and the relationship between education and society. Briefly, sociology of education is defined as a study of the relations between education and society. It is an investigation of the sociological processes involved in an educational institution. To Fadipe (2010), Sociology is a scientific branch of social science that focuses on the study of educational aims, methods, institutions, administration, and curricula. It examines these aspects in relation to the economic, political, religious, social, and cultural forces of the society in which they operate.

The sociology of education focuses on the impact of social life and social relationships on the formation of an individual's personality. It emphasizes the sociological aspects of educational phenomena and institutions. The challenges faced in this field are considered to be primarily sociological problems rather than issues related to educational practice (Fadipe, 2010).

Africa and Evolution of Education

In this section, the following three perspectives of the evolution of education vis-à-vis Africa are presented: (1) historical, (2) cultural, and (3) sociopolitical. They are discussed one at a time for the sake of clarity.

Historical Perspectives

Historically, Africa's conceptualization within the education discipline has been marked by colonial influences. Education in Africa started through long-standing traditions beginning historically from Black colleges and universities having erudite African American scholars and professionals. The emergence of education in Africa initially started with policy-based means after World War II and metamorphosed into more academic initiative in the postwar era. The colonial era had a profound impact on education in Africa, primarily serving the Western interests and perpetuating colonial control. European colonial powers imposed their educational systems, which often prioritized European languages, history, and culture, effectively erasing indigenous knowledge and traditions. Altbach (2018) explained that education was introduced with the aim of facilitating colonial administration and advancing the agenda of the West. The limited access to education for the majority of Africans, the Eurocentric curriculum, and the marginalization of African cultures and languages were significant consequences of colonial education policies.

The continent's educational landscape has been shaped by various factors, including colonialism, the introduction of Western education systems, and subsequent efforts to decolonize education. The Pan-African movement emphasized the importance of education in liberating African nations from colonial rule (Abdi, 2018). The decolonization period witnessed significant efforts to reclaim and transform education in Africa. Nationalist movements emerged, advocating for the decolonization of education and the promotion of indigenous cultures, languages, and knowledge systems. African countries implemented policy reforms to establish national education systems that emphasized local values and languages. Challenges such as limited resources, capacity building, and resistance to change were encountered during this process (Asante & Abarry, 2016). Consequently, many academic programs witnessed an upsurge in the introduction of African education with waves of independence in many African countries (De Ycaza, 2015).

Understanding this history is crucial for envisioning an inclusive and culturally relevant education system in Africa through the examination of the impact of colonialism, the introduction of Western education systems, and the subsequent decolonization efforts. It therefore becomes evident that education in Africa has been a battleground for reclaiming cultural identity, promoting inclusivity, and fostering national, regional and continental development.

Cultural Perspective

Africa is a continent with rich culture from a multitude of ethnic groups, diverse languages, customary patterns, and traditions. Education in Africa is not merely about imparting knowledge but also about preserving and celebrating cultural heritage. The cultural dimension is pivotal to understanding how indigenous knowledge and traditions can be integrated into formal education. African culture is diverse, encompassing numerous languages, belief systems, and practices. Acknowledging this diversity and incorporating it into the education system can create a more inclusive and culturally relevant approach. Cultural relevance in education is crucial for recognizing the diverse identities, experiences, and aspirations of African societies. Asante and Abarry (2016) concluded that cultural relevance in education acknowledges its diversity by integrating cultural elements, practices, and values into the curriculum. Several African countries have embraced cultural relevance and contextualization in education. For instance, South Africa's Curriculum and Assessment Policy Statement (CAPS) prioritizes the inclusion of local knowledge, languages, and histories. Uganda's Universal Primary Education (UPE) program integrates local cultural practices and values into the curriculum. These examples demonstrate the positive outcomes of cultural relevance and contextualization in education (Abdi, 2018).

Africa witnessed the introduction of formal education through European, Arabian colonists and imperialists. While the west and central African countries still practice both African and Western education in the form of teaching and schooling systems, the North African countries co-opted Arabic education with the Western education in their nations. However, the emergence of Western education systems in Africa relegated the African indigenous education system rapidly (Techomite & Wirdze, 2018). The indigenous African education systems, rooted in African cultures, offer valuable insights into various fields such as agriculture, medicine, and traditional arts.

Cultural factors have been the primary determinants of education in Africa. Since the primary function of education is enculturation, all traditional African societies sustained themselves through that form of education that seeks to inculcate social norms in the young ones. They equally embarked on language policy reforms, recognizing the importance of using indigenous languages as mediums of instruction. This approach was aimed at enhancing cultural relevance, improving learning outcomes, and fostering language diversity (Mgqwashu & Makhathini, 2017). Language is intimately tied to culture and identity. By incorporating local languages in education, African societies can preserve their cultural heritage, traditions, and knowledge systems. Baker and Sunal (2017) explained that using mother tongue-based education, learners can develop a stronger foundation in their own language while acquiring additional languages. This is to improve learning outcomes and cognitive development.

Culturally, African indigenous education seeks to prepare each person for his or her future role in society. The indigenous knowledge systems are valuable resources that can be leveraged to enhance educational content and pedagogy. It inculcates the skills needed for survival in the immediate environment and mobilizes all available human energies and talents for holistic societal development. This is corroborated by Mwamidi et al. (2018) who demonstrated that culturally responsive and inclusive education promotes cross-cultural understanding.

Sociopolitical Perspective

Education in Africa has evolved over the past few decades with efforts made through propaganda, lobbying, demonstration, positivity, and boycott geared toward attracting political decisions concerning the educational system. These sociopolitical contexts are directed at recognizing political factors influencing issues and challenges that militate against education processes.

Mkwananzi (2020) provided a new understanding of the current institutional positions of education disciplines and pointed to the theoretical, practical, and methodological achievements of each discipline as well as to their potential ability to contribute to educational research in the twenty-first century. As a result, Mkwananzi (2020) resolved that to further develop the professional element of education, it should be closely connected with attempts to strengthen the educational knowledge base. These were initially forthcoming in the 1960s and 1970s as part of reforms and expansion in all aspects of the education system. However, these attempts were met with considerable contestation from conservative voices and traditionalists seeking to defend what they considered to be under threat in terms of the school curriculum and the culture of schooling. Therefore, the different disciplines in the education field, namely, educational sociology, psychology, history, and philosophy, present central pillars of this area of knowledge in the twenty-first century.

African Pedagogical Practices

The African pedagogical systems and practices are very crucial to the discourse of education in the continent. Many African countries have witnessed shifts from traditional pedagogical methods to more student-centered and experiential learning approaches. The incorporation of African perspectives and contexts into curricula can make education more relevant and engaging for African learners. Additionally, recognizing the role of storytelling, oral traditions, and community-based education in African societies is essential for a holistic approach to education (Mamdani, 2007).

The African pedagogy involves examining the methods, practices, and approaches to teaching and learning employed across the continent. This focuses on how education is delivered and how it can be improved to better meet the needs of African learners and society. African educational systems have undergone a transition from traditional pedagogical methods to more contemporary approaches. Traditional methods often involved rote memorization, teacher-centered instruction, and an emphasis on examinations. In contrast, modern pedagogy in Africa places a greater emphasis on student-centered and experiential learning, critical thinking, and problem-solving skills (Mamdani, 2007).

Multilingualism is a significant consideration in African education. Many African countries are linguistically diverse, with numerous indigenous languages spoken alongside official languages. The pedagogical perspective calls for policies that promote multilingual education, allowing students to learn in their mother tongue while gradually transitioning to other languages, including international ones (Brock-Utne, 2007). Also, experiential learning is gaining prominence in African education. This approach encourages students to actively engage with real-world problems and scenarios, fostering critical thinking and problem-solving skills. Field trips, internships, and practical projects are increasingly integrated into the curriculum to enhance the educational experience (Mamdani, 2007).

Traditionally, storytelling and oral traditions are integral to many African societies. In the pedagogical considerations, there is recognition of the value of these traditions as teaching tools. Incorporating storytelling and oral history into the curriculum can help preserve cultural heritage and make learning more engaging and interactive (Nyerere, 1968). In involving the local communities in the education process, community-based education is pedagogically relevant. This approach recognizes the importance of community knowledge and values and aims to create a strong connection between education and the local context (Mamdani, 2007). To effectively implement modern pedagogical methods, there is a growing emphasis on teacher training and professional development. Teachers need to be equipped with the necessary skills and knowledge to adopt student-centered and inclusive teaching approaches (Brock-Utne, 2007).

Generally, the African pedagogical systems and practices highlight the transformation of teaching and learning methods, focusing on inclusivity, cultural relevance, multilingualism, experiential learning, and community engagement. By adapting pedagogy to the unique needs and characteristics of African learners, education can become a more powerful tool for personal and societal development across the continent.

Decolonizing African Education

Decolonizing African education is a critical concept within the field of education that seeks to address the historical legacy of colonialism and reimagine educational systems on the continent. The movement aims to address the legacy of colonialism; promote a more equitable and culturally sensitive approach; and reevaluate curricula, language of instruction, and pedagogical approaches to reflect African perspectives and values. It is not only about removing colonial vestiges but also recognizing the diversity of knowledge systems and epistemologies within Africa. It is a multifaceted and transformative process aimed at creating a more inclusive, culturally sensitive, and equitable educational environment.

Decolonizing African education acknowledges the historical impact of colonialism on the continent's educational systems. During the colonial period, European powers imposed their languages, curricula, and value systems on African societies. This led to the marginalization of indigenous knowledge and traditions, which are fundamental to African cultures (Mbembe, 2001). Therefore, decolonizing African education requires acknowledging the colonial legacies that persist within African educational institutions. This includes recognizing the Eurocentric biases present in curricula, pedagogical methods, and assessment criteria. The response to reforming African curriculum to be more inclusive and culturally relevant includes incorporating African history, literature, and perspectives into the curriculum. It also involves recognizing and respecting indigenous knowledge systems and traditions (Sleeter, 2017). Multilingual education is also an essential aspect of decolonizing African education. Many African countries are linguistically diverse, and students often speak indigenous languages. Supporting mother tongue instruction while gradually introducing other languages, including official and international languages, is a key component of this approach.

Decolonization emphasizes the importance of promoting and integrating indigenous knowledge systems into the educational process. This can involve recognizing traditional African medicine, agricultural practices, storytelling, and oral history as valuable sources of knowledge and learning. Equally, teacher training and professional development programs that equip educators with the skills and knowledge to implement culturally sensitive and inclusive pedagogical approaches is important. Teachers need to understand the significance of indigenous knowledge and cultural diversity (Mamdani, 2007). This will aid the emphasis on student-centered learning, critical thinking, and problem-solving. It moves from rote memorization to experiential learning and inquiry-based methods.

Decolonizing education is not limited to Africa but also has global implications. It calls for a broader rethinking of how knowledge and education are structured on a global scale, moving away from Western-dominated perspectives and valuing diverse worldviews and contributions (Maldonado-Torres, 2007). To successfully achieve this, there is a need for active involvement from local communities and stakeholders. Communities can contribute to shaping the education process and ensuring that it remains culturally relevant and responsive to local needs.

In summary, decolonizing African education is a complex and vital process that seeks to address the historical imbalances and inequities present in educational systems on the continent. It aims to create educational environments that reflect African cultures, values, and knowledge while preparing students for a rapidly changing world. Decolonizing education is not only a local endeavor but also a global one, with implications for reshaping the broader discourse on knowledge and learning.

Conclusion and Recommendations

In conclusion, understanding African education is crucial for the development and progress of the continent. Despite the challenges, there are several gains and initiatives that highlight the importance and potential of education in Africa. Supporting education in Africa requires sustained investment, policy reforms, and collaboration between governments, civil society, and international partners. The preceding conceptualizations of African education as presented in this chapter reveal many challenges and also show some promising potentials for the continent. Thus, the ultimate question of the chapter is: What can be done to address the challenges to African education? To address the question, some policy recommendations and suggestions for future research are made on the subject matter.

By addressing the challenges and building on the strengths of the education system, Africa can unlock its full potential, promote inclusive development, and create a brighter future for its people. Beyond the general budgetary allocation and financial investment in education, African countries are to work out sustainable policy reforms capable of strengthening teacher training programs, investing in infrastructure development, promoting public-private partnerships, and mobilizing international support. Regional organizations such as the African Union (AU) and the African Development Bank (AfDB) would also play a significant role in coordinating efforts and promoting cooperation in education across the continent.

While progress has been made, there is still much work to be done to ensure universal access to quality education in Africa. Decolonizing education is central to this process, as it seeks to rectify past injustices and promote the use of indigenous knowledge in a way that empowers African learners. By engaging with African perspectives, languages, and traditions, education in Africa can become a more relevant and transformative force for the continent's development and progress. Collaborative efforts and innovative approaches are crucial to overcoming the existing barriers and unlocking the transformative potential for quality education nationally, regionally, and continentally.

Future research on African education could focus on several key areas to address the unique challenges and opportunities on the continent. Some of these areas are as follows: (1) Research effort toward strategic improvement in the quality of education in Africa. This may involve investigating effective teaching methods, curriculum development, teacher training, and the use of technology in education. Additionally, understanding the factors that contribute to successful educational outcomes, such as parental involvement and community engagement, can also be explored; (2) research can focus on identifying barriers to education, such as poverty, gender inequality, and geographic remoteness. Strategies to increase access, such as inclusive policies, infrastructure development, and innovative approaches like distance learning and mobile technology, can be studied; (3) research can delve into the factors contributing to these disparities, including socioeconomic status, gender, ethnicity, and disability. Exploring interventions and policies that promote equity, such as targeted scholarships, affirmative action, and inclusive classrooms, can help bridge these gaps; (4) with the changing nature of work, research can explore how education in Africa can better prepare students for the future job market. This includes identifying key skills and competencies needed for economic growth, entrepreneurship, and innovation. Additionally, investigating effective models of vocational and technical education can contribute to developing a skilled workforce; and (5) research can examine education policies and governance structures across different African countries to identify effective practices. Comparative studies can provide insights into the impact of policy decisions, decentralization of education systems, and the role of stakeholders such as governments, NGOs, and communities in improving education outcomes.

References

Abdi, A. A. (2018). *Decolonizing African education: African development and the future of African minds*. Routledge.

Adelabu, M. A. (2019). As it was in the beginning so it is now: Politics and education policies in Nigeria. In *The 334th inaugural lecture series, Obafemi Awolowo University*. OAU Press.

Akínsolá, A. (2019). Indigenous sociologies: Extending the scope of the argument. *International Sociology, 14*, 115–138.

Altbach, P. G. (2018). *Comparative higher education: Knowledge, the university, and development*. Comparative Education Research Centre.

Asante, M. K., & Abarry, A. S. (2016). *African intellectual heritage: A book of sources*. Temple University Press.

Baker, D. B., & Sunal, C. S. (2017). *Education in Africa: A comparative survey*. Bloomsbury Publishing.

Brock-Utne, B. (2007). Language of instruction and student performance: New insights from research in Tanzania and South Africa. *International Review of Education, 53*(5/6), 509–530.

De Ycaza, C. (2015). Competing methods for teaching and researching Africa: Inter-disciplinarity and the field of African Studies. *Journal of African Studies, 38*(3), 63–79.

Durkheim, E. (1956). *Education and sociology*. Free Press.

Fadipe, N. A. (2010). *The sociology of the Yoruba*. Ibadan University Press.

Hountondji, P. (2022). *The struggle for meaning: Reflections on philosophy, culture, and democracy in Africa*. Ohio University Centre for International Studies.

Hrimech, M. (2005). Informal learning. In L. M. English (Ed.), *International encyclopedia of adult education*. Palgrave Macmillan.

Livingstone, D. W. (2001). *Adults' informal learning: Definitions, findings, gaps and future research*. Centre for the Study of Education and Work, OISE/UT.

Maldonado-Torres, N. (2007). On the coloniality of being. *Cultural Studies, 21*(2–3), 240–270.

Mamdani, M. (2007). *Scholars in the marketplace. The dilemmas of neo-liberal reform at Makerere University, 1989–2005*. CODESRIA Publications.

Mbembe, A. (2001). *On the postcolony*. University of California Press.

Mgqwashu, E., & Makhathini, B. (2017). Transforming primary school teachers' perceptions of the 'place' of teaching reading: The role of reading to learn methodology. *The Independent Journal of Teaching and Learning, 12*(1), 30–49.

Mkwananzi, F. (2020). Equality in education: Insights from the African context. *Journal of Education, 75*(1), 7–25.

Mwamidi, D. M., Burgas, D., Llamazares, A. F., & Domínguez, P. (2018). Contemporary pastoral commons in East Africa as OECMs: A case study from the Daasanach community. *PARKS, 24*, 49–58.

Njoroge, R. J., & Bennaars, G. (2016). *Philosophy and education in Africa: An introductory text for students of education*. Transafrica Press.

Noddings, N. (2013). *Philosophy of education* (3rd ed.). Westview Press.

Nyerere, J. K. (1968). *Education for self-reliance*. Oxford University Press.

Ormrod, J. E., & Anderman, L. H. (2020). *Educational psychology: Developing learners*. Pearson.

Santrock, J. W. (2021). *Educational psychology*. McGraw-Hill.

Schwartz, N., Click, K., & Barte, A. (2022). Educational psychology: Learning and instruction. In J. Zumbach, D. A. Bernstein, S. Narciss, & G. Marcico (Eds.), *International handbook of psychology learning and teaching*. Springer.

Slavin, R. E. (2021). *Educational psychology: Theory and practice*. Pearson.

Sleeter, C. E. (2017). Critical race theory and the whiteness of teacher education. *Urban Education, 52*(2), 155–169.

Snowman, J., & McCown, R. R. (2015). *Educational psychology*. Wadsworth/Cengage Learning.

Techomite, J. M. S., & Wirdze, L. (2018). *Harnessing cultures to advance education in sub-Saharan Africa: A desk review of education policy and practice*. Report submitted to United Nations Educational Scientific and Cultural Organisation (UNESCO).

UNESCO-UIS. (2012). *International standard classification of education [ISCED-2011]*. UNESCO Institute for Statistics.

Waghid, Y. (2014). African philosophy of education: Implications for teaching and learning process. *Journal of Higher Education, 18*(3), 56–64.

Wiredu, K. (2014, June). Prolegomena to an African philosophy of education. Paper presented at the Faculty of Education Seminar Series, Stellenbosch University, South Africa.

Woolfolk, H. A. (2019). *Educational psychology in teacher education*. Pearson.

Azeez Babatunde Adebakin is in the Department of Educational Management at Obafemi Awolowo University, Ile-Ife, Nigeria. His research areas are educational planning, economics of education, and entrepreneurship education. He has considerable experience in conducting mixed-methods research and has published scholarly articles in national and international reputable outlets. He has attended and presented papers at various national and international academic conferences. He is a DAAD scholar, a fellow of the CODESRIA College of Academic Mentors, and a recipient of TETFund research and development grants. He holds memberships in various national and international professional associations and research organizations.

E-Learning

Wilson Mugizi and Judith Irene Nagasha

In this chapter, we elucidate the state of E-learning and the way forward in higher education in Africa. We look at E-learning as an emerging discipline, the progress achieved in education through the use of information and communication technologies (ICTs) and specifically the Internet, the multiple definitions that have emerged during the past few decades, and the advance in the uptake in African institutions of higher education to suggest a way forward. Since this chapter is an exploration of the state of the field, it is a critical review. The chapter familiarizes stakeholders in education with current knowledge and trends in E-learning in higher education in Africa. This offers an understanding of the progress, the steps taken to implement E-learning, and the way forward. The pertinent question that emerges is: Why evaluate E-learning in African higher education? The answer to this question is a simple one. Basically, since the education landscape worldwide has changed following the outbreak of the coronavirus disease 2019 (COVID-19) which made E-learning a requirement, and is no longer a peculiar way providing education by specific institutions and departments, mainly those offering distance education (Masalimova et al., 2022), stakeholders in higher education in Africa have to take steps to fully integrate E-learning in teaching and learning. This chapter provides insights for the implementation of E-learning in higher institutions of education in Africa. But, in order to do this effectively, it is very important to show how E-learning has conceptualized the continent.

W. Mugizi (✉)
Department of Education Planning and Management, Kyambogo University, Kampala, Uganda
e-mail: wmugizi@kyu.ac.ug

J. I. Nagasha
Department of Development Studies, Kyambogo University, Kampala, Uganda
e-mail: jnagasha@kyu.ac.ug

A. K. Bangura, J. A. Ifedi (eds.), *Conceptualizations of Africa*, African Studies and Research Forum Series, https://doi.org/10.1007/978-3-031-74535-5_9

It should be noted that today technology has become a vital part of our everyday lives and thus educators and other professionals have had to change their primary beliefs towards technology in order to use it to redesign or reengineer the education system. Technological devices perform an essential role that enables learners and instructors to obtain more benefits from educational technologies (Basak et al., 2018). E-learning makes learning possible, irrespective of the learner's physical location and time (Kimura et al., 2023). E-learning using ICTs has emerged as a recent educational paradigm in an era of information technology. Today, worldwide, virtually all universities regard E-learning as an essential tool for making education available to every interested individual (Smyrnova-Trybulska, 2019). Especially following the COVID-2019 pandemic, the education landscape has changed due to the intermittent closure of educational institutions with E-learning becoming part and parcel of education delivery. Educational institutions have changed the mode of delivering education from face-to-face on-campus to using technologies in the online teaching and learning mode (Mugizi & Nagasha, 2023). During COVID-19, online learning provided an emergency solution. Instructors were compelled to completely shift from face-to-face instruction to using online platforms, irrespective of technical know-how of use (Singh et al., 2022).

Increase of E-learning has attracted a bigger audience of learners especially since COVID-19. E-learning electronic modes include the Internet, intranet, computer-based web or mobile applications and interactive television (TV), among others. E-books, journals, live or pre-recorded lectures, discussion boards, live question and answer sessions, assessment elements (quizzes and assignments) and other electronic materials are examples of E-learning resources (Ahmed et al., 2021). Due to advances in E-learning technologies, several E-learning platforms cater for a broader range of learners. Their setups provide a variety of features, interaction approaches and customization to meet needs of the user (Liu & Yu, 2023). E-learning platforms fall into two main learning categories: (1) synchronous and (2) asynchronous. With synchronous learning, instructors and learners come together in one place in a real-time situation. The instructor is available and the learning occurs in real time at a specific time. Learners generally have the chance of interacting with the instructor and peers (Kimura et al., 2023). Learning is restricted to real-time interaction, in a collaborative way. Learning is also provided through a virtual platform that allows interactive learning. Interaction between instructors and learners takes place through live chat, video conferencing, teleconferencing and streaming, among others (Fernandez et al., 2022). Asynchronous learning is the type of E-learning that does not require availability of the instructor or facilitator because it is self-directed and learning can take place at the convenience of the learner at the time and place of their own choice (Kimura et al., 2023). With asynchronous E-learning, students access learning resources and complete the assignments using audio or videos, hand-outs, articles, power points presentations, and other materials that have already been provided by the instructor and can be accessed whenever the students want (Maghdalena et al., 2022).

With online learning taking root, instructors' require expertise in course content management, using technology devices, and planning and delivering content in an entirely online instructional mode (Singh et al., 2022). Instructors need E-learning implementation competences that include technical, course design, communication, and time management (Mugizi et al., 2023). Technical competences are specific to using technological devices and involve technical knowledge and aptitude in using prevailing technologies and the efficacy to effectively facilitate learners (Reichert et al., 2020). Course design concerns having the skill to choose content, determine the most appropriate pedagogical strategies, work to improve a course, and implement revisions, refining instruction and learning (Kasule et al., 2023). Course communication is the efficacy to deliver information to learners through effective and suitably available interactive platforms (Kiessling & Fabry, 2021). For time management competence, it is about the instructor's ability to plan, work within and adjust time to changing situations (Humpherys & Lazrig, 2021). Mugizi et al. (2023) expound that instructors with high time management competence are able to ensure that their ability to deliver a course is not hampered by their other engagements. Accordingly, higher-level time management is essential for the E-learning teaching mode because designing course objectives, creating content, planning activities and evaluation appropriate for online formats require a lot of time.

E-Learning: A Conceptualization

The term *E-learning* is a short form for "Electronic learning" and denotes improvements in education made possible by the use of ICTs, particularly the Internet (Tibaná-Herrera et al., 2018). The concepts E-learning, digital learning (D-learning) and mobile learning (M-learning) are used interchangeably to imply learning using technologies. Other terms include E-education, virtual learning, and online learning (Alqahtani & Rajkhan, 2020; Basak et al., 2018; Valverde-Berrocoso et al., 2020). Alqahtani and Rajkhan (2020) indicate that E-learning involves utilizing a variety of applications and procedures that make use of readily available electronic media and tools to deliver knowledge. Rodrigues et al. (2019) contend that E-learning is an inventive web-based system built on digital technologies and other educational resources to give students access to a customized, learner-centred, open, engaging, and interactive learning environment that support and improve their learning processes. Wheeler (2012) describes it as a collection of technology-mediated techniques used to enhance student learning and incorporate components of instruction, tutoring and assessment. According to Tsai and Machado (2002), E-learning involves using computers and interactive networks at the same time. Pham et al. (2019) indicate that E-learning is a cutting-edge method of providing educational services by using electronic information to improve students' knowledge, abilities, and other learning outcomes. Furthermore, they expound that E-learning involves the use of current ICTs and computers linked to the Internet to deliver instruction.

The term *E-education* is much broader than E-learning. E-education embodies making learning resources accessible to learners electronically, teaching and supporting them online, and providing them on-line administrative services such as enrolment, billing, information and advice (Rumble, 2001). Lee et al. (2022)

indicate that E-education encompasses using the Internet and electronic devices to extend a broad range of solutions that improve the quality of instructional activities. E-education extends beyond teaching and learning to include administrative services. A concept that is part of E-learning is M-learning or mobile learning and is a macro concept denoting being able to learn from anywhere in online environments. While E-learning is a substitute of traditional teaching and learning and might also be supplementary to it, M-learning supplements both traditional and E-learning (Basak et al. (2018). M-learning has been defined variously by different scholars. Adzifome and Agyei (2023) indicate that it is the practice of learning while in transit by using wireless or mobile devices. Crompton et al. (2017) contend that M-learning is the process of learning via social and content interactions with personal electronic devices in a variety of contexts. Pedro et al. (2018) posit that M-learning is the use of mobile devices to participate in learning anytime and anywhere. Talan (2020) suggests that M-learning involves using portable devices like laptops, mobile phones and tablets to learn while moving. These definitions are consistent with the assertion by Pedro et al. (2018) that most definitions of M-learning highlight positive attributes such as convenience, flexibility, accessibility, ubiquity, locatability and contextuality.

A term encompassing E-learning and M-learning is digital learning (D-learning). D-learning denotes instructional strategies that make use of technology to enhance students' learning opportunities by offering communication channels, interactive learning materials, content and learning assessments (Pratiwi, 2020). D-learning is about using ICTs in both open and distance learning (Basak et al., 2018). Sujan and Eswari (2021) indicate that digital learning is any form of learning that is supported by technology or that occurs across all subject areas using instructional strategies that effectively leverage technology. Verma (2017) points out that digital learning describes the procedure of learning involving digital content or platform, or even facilitators. Pratiwi (2020) explains that three basic elements inherent in D-learning are (1) technology, (2) digital content, and (3) learning itself. "Technology" refers to the applications or ICT platforms that can be utilized to conduct educational activities. "Digital content" is learning material organized in digital form, either by the instructors for direct delivery or as content available to be utilized as a learning resource. For learning, it is connected to a teacher's function as a mentor who guides students' learning.

Another subset of E-learning is *online learning*, which refers to an educational programme via which a course is deliberately planned prior to delivery fully online and asynchronously. With online learning, courses are specifically developed to provide a learning experience independent of the instructor's face-to-face presence (Swenson, 2020). Maddison et al. (2017) define it as teaching offered electronically via different media, Internet platforms and applications. Tsai and Machado (2002) indicate that online learning is linked to easily accessible computer-based content. The content might be accessible on the Web or the Internet, or just loaded on a Compact Disc Read-Only Memory (CD-ROM) or the computer hard disk. Singh and Thurman (2019) provide two definitions that affirm the preceding definitions. First, they define online learning as the learning practice involving interacting with teachers and fellow students in asynchronous classroom setting via the Internet and online computers. Students can participate in this type of learning regardless of where they are physically located. Second, they indicate that it is asynchronous learning that takes place over the Internet, allowing students to interact with teachers and other learners whenever it is convenient for them to do so. It eliminates the need for students to be present in person or virtually at all.

A concept closely related to digital learning is *virtual education*, which is teaching and learning in a learning context where the teacher and learner are detached by time or space, or both (Dung, 2020). Broadly, Parlakkilic (2014) defines it as instruction in a setting where the instructor and the student are not physically present in the same place at the same time, and the instructor uses course management software, multimedia resources, the Internet, and videoconferencing to deliver course material, among others. Three basic types of virtual education are (1) asynchronous, (2) synchronous and (3) hybrid (Dung, 2020). *Asynchronous* learning refers to a kind of online learning involving learners being engaged on their own without requiring to be online simultaneously (Cahyani et al., 2021). Asynchronous online courses are not bound by time; hence, students direct themselves, doing study activities within a timeframe with interaction taking place through discussion boards, blogs, e-mail, etc. (Perveen, 2016). Synchronous online learning is a method that offers a chance for instructors to link with learners at a specific time only separated by location (Martin et al., 2021).

With *synchronous* online learning, students receive instruction from their instructor while interacting with him/her and their fellow students in a virtual classroom through texts, voice chats, and video chats (Belt & Lowenthal, 2023). *Hybrid online courses*, also known as blended courses, provide both face to face and online interaction. In hybrid courses, in-person meetings are required throughout the semester with computer-based communication taking place in between. Therefore, hybrid virtual learning can involve both synchronous and asynchronous open communication (Dung, 2020). The preceding definitions show that E-learning is an emerging discipline because the concept has not been clearly distinguished from other related or complementary learning concepts of M-learning, D-learning, E-education, virtual learning, and online learning. Different writers and technology users employ the concepts interchangeably.

Pros and Cons of E-Learning

E-learning is associated with several pros or advantages. It is associated with high peer communication and, with the wider institution, easy access to the teacher, access to the curricula by students, reduced administrative burden for the instructor, and is cost effective (Abed, 2019). With peer communication, E-learning enables student–student interaction (Aldulaimi et al., 2021). Also, students acquire knowledge by reading the comments made by other students on platforms, comment on posts of one another on E-learning platforms, and ask one another questions through online chats (Mugizi & Rwothumio, 2023). Besides the increased possibility of communication among students, they are also able to communicate with different parties in the institution because of the ease of communication using different channels like discussion boards, E-mail, and dialogue rooms (Abed, 2019). In addition, E-learning offers students the chance to instantly interact with the teacher electronically. E-learning breaks the barrier of fear and anxiety students possess in front of instructors and peers enabling them to speak their ideas in more effective means than what is used in traditional classrooms (Aldulaimi et al., 2021). This is particularly for those students who feel fear and anxiety. Such students are motivated to express their thoughts easily because they can easily send their opinions and even their voices via social networks like E-mail, discussion boards and chat rooms (Al-Kayed, 2020). Furthermore, teachers are also accessible to the learners even outside formal working hours (Aldulaimi et al., 2021).

Another advantage of E-learning is that the curricula are available to the learners at any time. Learners have the possibility to select the time and place appropriate for learning. Therefore, it provides flexible learning opportunities to students and they can effectively engage in the E-learning process at their convenience. This is important for learners who want to learn at a time that suits them (Kokoç, 2019). Besides, educational institutions and students with flexibility can send and receive learning information (Al-Kayed, 2020). Moreover, as hinted earlier, E-learning reduces the administrative burden for the instructor because it provides online enabled administration. This includes assessment, preserving of library functions, and making of reports. Instructors can easily maintain assessment records, compile examinations data banks; carryout online inspections; and keep records, chronicles, and archives with fast retrieval and easy entry. The technologies solve the challenges of obtaining, storing and retrieving essential data at any time (Mugizi & Amwine, 2020). There is also the added advantage of E-learning being a cost effective way of accessing education especially by working students. It is cheaper to study online compared to physical classes that demand transport fares, accommodation, and feeding while at a university; yet one can study from the comfort of his/her home away from the university (Dhawan, 2020). Therefore, E-learning technologies make life relatively easy, especially for working and distant students.

In terms of the cons, there are also a number of them. To note, it is a truism that learning can be expensive for some learners and even instructors. Some learners' economic capacity might impose restrictions on the ability to access the necessary equipment to attend E-learning classes. Besides, the cost of Internet connectivity and the requirements of ancillary appliances such as audio and camera devices might be prohibitive for certain learners (Aldulaimi et al., 2021). Poor or lack of Internet, especially because of connectivity coverage, can greatly hamper E-learning. Learners in areas of poor Internet connection can fail to join classes and a weak Internet network can cause connectivity challenges, thereby interrupting the flow of lessons (Clarin & Baluyos, 2022; Cullinan et al., 2021). Unreliable electricity that goes off can also hamper E-learning (Mugizi & Nagasha, 2023). Unreliable electricity power supply contributes to the difficulties of accessing the Internet and engaging in interrupted classes (Adarkwah, 2021).

The lack of technical know-how or the ability to use E-learning devices can also be a challenge (Mailizar & Fan, 2020). Limited knowledge of how to use the technologies by both instructors and learners can affect E-learning implementation. Instructors with limited knowledge of ICTs fear technology integration. This is normally as a result of a skills gap in conducting E-learning classes. The challenge can also be associated with resistance to change and negative attitudes. Some instructors are quite conservative and like to stick to the old pedagogy. Learners can also resist participation in E-learning because of lack of technical knowledge and fear of change (Bada et al., 2020). Besides, there are those teachers and students that lack access to the required digital devices and the Internet. Non-access to appropriate digital devices and lack of or poor Internet connections can be troublesome with many students losing out on learning opportunities. Therefore, E-learning demands a lot of time and investment in devices and equipment, maintaining them, training the human resources, and developing the online content (Dhawan, 2020). Also, E-learning results in isolation because students interact with computers rather than with one another, thus lacking the opportunity of exchanging experiences, which makes them feel lonely and isolated (Al-Kayed, 2020).

Furthermore, the sudden digital transformation has increased the work burden for instructors and learners. This is because of the nature of the educational material that has to keep pace with the educational platforms and the soft material suitable for E-learning. Preparing educational material which students have to study and then work on assignments they have to upload is an added burden for all and takes a long time because of the complexity of technology. Besides, online learning is more compatible with humanities in general but poses great challenges for scientific specializations such as engineering, chemistry, and physics. This is because of the higher correlation between teaching science subjects and the need for laboratories to conduct scientific experiments (Aldulaimi et al., 2021). Precisely, the disadvantages of E-learning include being expensive, the challenge of poor Internet connectivity and unreliable electricity, low technical know-how of use, reduced interaction, high work burden, and activities incompatibility.

Digital Divide and E-Learning in Universities in Africa

E-learning has been a part of teaching and learning for quite some time. In 1966, International Business Machines (IBM) introduced the IBM 1500 to implement computer-assisted instruction. Instructors used the system to remotely access learners' course materials and assess assignments (Fernández-Manjón et al., 2007). E-learning consistently continued to grow, albeit in the Western World. For instance, the British government in 1969 launched the Open University, specifically to provide distance education (Pregowska et al., 2021). In 1982, the Western Behavioural Sciences Institute in the United States used computer conferencing to offer a distance education programme for business executives while in 1983 the defunct Electronic University Network made online courses accessible to individuals on personal computers (Thompson, 2023). In 1984, the University of Toronto was the first to begin a completely online course. Thereafter, in 1986, the Electronic University Network was launched (Harasim, 2000). Nevertheless, the concept of E-learning was first used in November of 1999 by Elliott Masie in his presentation at the TechLearn Conference at Disneyworld. The term in use before was "online learning" that basically pointed to the same concept. Since the emergence of E-learning, there has been a sustained increase in the use of its platforms and evolving functionalities (Yusif & Hafeez-Baig, 2023).

In spite of the long history of E-learning, its development in Africa has been very slow because of the so-called digital divide (linguistically and grammatically correct, digital division, as "divide" is a verb), which describes inequalities in access to and use of ICT facilities. Digital division is in three domains: (1) social resources, (2) cognitive and (3) material. Social resources are the relationships that a person has with other members of their social circles who either regularly use or own digital devices (Lembani et al., 2020). Cognitive resources concern the ability to read, process, handle, and interpret information obtained via ICT while material access refers to a person's financial capacity to purchase a computer, use the Internet at home, or access public ICT resources at work, such as Internet cafés and information kiosks (Masalimova et al., 2022; Mugizi & Nagasha, 2023).

Initial steps to E-learning can be traced to 1976 when the National Teachers' Institute at Kaduna in Nigeria was founded to offer open and distance learning (ODL). Nonetheless, the instruction was offered predominantly through print media. Later, it was carried out using an FM radio station courtesy of the Commonwealth of Learning (Ojo & Olakulehin, 2006). In Africa, web-based E-learning is a recent phenomenon. The World Bank was the first to introduce it in 1996 to improve cyber education in the continent. Based at Kenyatta University in Kenya, it served as the centre for Ethiopia, Ghana, Kenya, Uganda and Zimbabwe. The project was intended for those from the working class and recent high school graduates unable to enrol in universities due to a shortage of vacancies. Science, engineering, and business courses were the first to be considered, later other courses such as vocational courses, were added. Instruction involved use of satellite broadcast that comprised videos, MPEG 4 involving Internet video and compact disc (CD) distribution, voice and broadcast television applications, and E-mail interaction between instructors and learners (Kotoua et al., 2015).

While in Africa the first decade of the twenty-first century saw increasing popularity for off-campus education, it still depended on printed materials and only a few institutions were starting to explore Internet use through platforms such as Massive Open Online Courses (MOOCs) and videoconferencing. Technology remained the main challenge to the delivery of off-campus education, especially in Africa South of the Sahara (Nyerere, 2016). An important development in the continent towards E-learning was the implementation of the African Virtual University (AVU) Project in 1997 by the World Bank. The project implemented Internet and satellite linked distance education programmes in the field of Science and Engineering (Rumajogee, 2002). AVU worked with more than 53 partner institutions in 27 countries in Africa to increase access to quality higher education and training through the innovative use of ICTs (Diallo et al., 2010). Programmes were delivered through ICTs (degree programmes, certificate and diploma programmes); developed African-based residential and E-learning materials for partner institutions; established state-of-the-art E-learning centres in partner institutions; trained partner institution staff in E-learning methodologies; developed and implemented education resources (OER) strategy; and managed a digital library (Nyerere, 2016).

Another milestone to the implementation of E-learning in Africa was the introduction of the World Wide Web (WWW) MOOCs in 2008, providing free online courses for anyone interested in enrolling (Jouicha et al., 2020). The platform provided open access course materials through the web and was an interactive user forum supporting interaction between students and their teachers (Wong, 2021). Unfortunately, Africa was not ready for MOOCs due to a lack of locally produced electronic content, low bandwidth Internet connectivity, limited computer access, low computer literacy among college entrants, and frequent power outages (Oyo & Kalema, 2014). Even a large number of students in different institutions of higher learning in Africa had a negative attitude towards E-learning and complained about E-learning being ineffective, low access to the Internet because of cost, web systems being extremely slow and not able to accommodate many users at a go (Mugula, 2023).

Nonetheless, over time, African higher education institutions have worked to improve their E-learning. For example, by 2020, approximately 55% of African universities had established E-learning policies, although a big chunk of 45% of the universities lacked them. In addition, 89% were connected to the fiber optic backbone while 11% were not. Furthermore, 47% of the institutions had a total bandwidth of at least 100 Mbps, 37% had between 10 Mbps and 100 Mbps, and 16% had between one and 10 Mbps (RUFORUM, 2020). Despite this progress, reports that came out following the lockdowns as a result of COVID-19 in 2020 showed that E-learning was still an upcoming mode of instruction in Africa considered a peculiar way of providing education by specific institutions and departments, mainly those offering distance education. Most instructors lacked the competency to integrate E-learning digital devices and platforms into education (Masalimova et al., 2022; Mugizi & Nagasha, 2023). Therefore, E-learning uptake in Africa was still low.

E-Learning Surge and Challenges in Universities in Africa

In December of 2019, COVID-19 that was identified in Wuhan, China, spread fast to various parts of the world, making it a global pandemic (Lai et al., 2020). With COVID-19 spreading quickly across the globe and very many people dying, most countries declared lockdowns as a mechanism to thwart the fast spread of the virus and protect their people (Mugizi et al., 2021). While countries had anticipated that the lockdowns would come to an end fast, it was realized that this was a farfetched dream necessitating new strategies to ensure continuous provision of education leading to the adoption of E-learning. The education landscape changed with E-learning taking the centre stage (Watermeyer et al., 2022). While before COVID-19 E-learning was deemed a peculiar way of providing education by specific institutions and departments, mainly those offering distance education (Masalimova et al., 2022), university teachers everywhere had to be adaptive and reorganize themselves and their instructional methodologies by designing innovative lessons for online involvement of learners and adopting alternative procedures for virtual evaluation of learners' achievements (Baroudi & Shaya, 2022).

The challenge for African universities, especially those South of the Sahara, was that while universities in many Western countries and Asia had already progressed highly in using E-learning for instruction purposes, few African educational institutions had adopted it to reasonable levels (Mugizi et al., 2023). Most African universities were not ready for E-learning but had to secure some forms of digital or self-study solutions. The universities had insufficient preparedness, prior knowledge, and/or capacity to fast establish E-learning or maximally use accessible learning platforms. The majority of universities came to the broad consensus that integrating E-learning would enable them to continue operations until normalcy was restored. Nevertheless, their efforts were hampered by the digital divide in access to technology and connectivity between learners from wealthy and low socioeconomic backgrounds. While largely universities adopted E-learning following COVID-19 lockdowns, success was hampered by limited access to reliable technological infrastructure, unstable Internet connections, instructors and students' limited technology knowhow, and use of instructional methods not suitable for E-learning environments (Bekele, 2021). Learners suffered greatly when learning shifted to the online mode, not only because they were not ready cognitively but also socially and economically. It is imperative to note that, especially in Africa South of the Sahara, there are high levels of poverty. Still, the students lacked the training for engaging in E-learning. Generally, most students had never used digital devices such as smartphones to engage in learning (Osabwa, 2022).

Among the critical obstacles to the adoption of E-learning was the lack of frameworks for its implementation, except for South Africa, which had a clearly stipulated E-education policy. Even so, in South Africa, gaps existed in policy comprehension among those involved in delivering education, which consequently affected E-learning implementation. Many instructors did not understand the policy and how E-learning could be implemented in the classrooms and did not promote it (Skhephe, 2022). The practice of instruction and learning remained unchanged, despite the presence of the E-learning policy (Chikuni et al., 2021). Still, the country did not have meaningful investments in ICT infrastructure; hence, many university students had to fend for themselves during the COVID-19 lockdown. In both urban and rural locations, the majority of Black learners from vulnerable families lacked access to the Internet networks needed for E-learning. Many academics and students in South Africa struggled with insufficient access to E-infrastructure. Besides, Internet access in homes and educational institutions was affected by high levels of electricity load shedding, which have plagued the country for a long time and compromising the quality of E-learning (Hlatshwayo, 2022).

In Namibia, unlike universities in rural areas where Internet access was inconsistent and limited, universities in the country's capital, Windhoek, had access to the Internet. Still, when the universities tried to implement E-learning, many students were unable to participate because they lacked laptops or computers (Bekele, 2021). In Nigeria, successful implementation of E-learning was hampered by a number of factors, including limited financial resources, poor Internet access, unstable or slow Internet, a lack of mobile data, poor communication between instructors and students due to low proficiency with E-learning technologies, and a lack of access to technological devices (Ogolodom et al., 2023). Similar problems were encountered in other countries. For instance, in Ghana, the National Union of Ghana Students (NUGS) protested the implementation of E-learning and appealed to the government to stop its implementation. Issues included inexistence of a well laid framework, vulnerability of some learners who could not easily access devices necessary for E-learning, poor Internet connectivity, and inability to pay for Internet data. Students from low-income or rural households, in particular, found it difficult or impossible to engage in the E-learning initiatives because they lacked the necessary devices, had trouble connecting to the Internet, or did not have access to electricity. Educational institutions, especially the public ones, faced challenges that included limited funding; thus, they were unable to procure the needed equipment. Some educational institutions lacked the needed well-resourced computer laboratories (Amankwa & Asiedu, 2022).

In Kenya, a majority of the universities implemented E-learning, but thousands of students particularly those from underprivileged areas experiencing sporadic electricity blackouts, bad Internet, and lack of digital devices were unable to participate in online courses. In addition, instructors encountered several difficulties, especially low digital literacy and lack of strong Internet connectivity (Bekele, 2021). The readiness of Kenya to implement E-learning was very low because of inadequate Internet access and inadequate electrical infrastructure. Several areas of the country experienced low mobile network coverage, and where it was available, the signal was weak. In addition, erratic electricity in areas connected to the national grid exacerbated the already dire situation. Teachers who were located in underprivileged areas were unable to access the Internet, leaving them powerless and unable to assist students (Osabwa, 2022). The challenge of poor electrical infrastructure was worsened by the lack of alternative sources of power, such as standby generators. With no electricity, E-learning could not be implemented. In one of Kenya's universities, online examinations were postponed for an entire examination session because of a prolonged power blackout (Gaceri, 2021).

In Uganda, some universities attempted to offer online teaching and learning to ensure that the students' learning cycle was not disrupted by the COVID-19, but the Ministry of Education blocked those universities from going ahead, citing the low preparedness of the universities. The Parliament of Uganda declared that by the closure of educational institutions, the government meant that every educational activity was supposed to shut down, including the running of any online activity. Later on, when the government allowed universities to introduce E-learning, students protested by complaining about poor Internet connectivity, lack of money to purchase mobile data to participate in E-learning, and some lecturers' lack of competence to teach online (Mugizi & Nagasha, 2023). At one of the Ugandan public universities, a study reported that some instructors were conservative and, thus, were resistant to change in the way of education delivery, and many had limited teaching and assessment of E-learning skills which impeded its uptake. A number of instructors had a negative attitude about E-learning and were inclined to the traditional face-to-face pedagogical strategies (Bada et al., 2020; Mugizi & Nagasha, 2023). In sum, Bwire et al. (2020) reported that most instructors in public universities in Uganda did not have the required skills to design online courses.

The Future of E-Learning in African Universities

The COVID-19 pandemic changed the mindset of many education stakeholders to the effect that students can take courses and complete their programmes using online platforms without on-campus physical attendance (Dos Santos, 2022). For the first time, learning via the Internet became a significant part of teaching and learning in Africa (Faturoti, 2022). While the transition to online learning was made without adequate preparation and, hence, the effort did not consider whether the study materials and teaching methods used were suitable for the mode of delivery, it became an eye opener. E-learning has expanded and has become a mode of instruction with which everyone in the education arena has to live. It provides a flexible way of delivering education (Aristovnik et al., 2023). Since the COVID-19 pandemic, E-learning in Africa has become and remains an unavoidable option for the provision of education. It is now essential that African governments invest in digital learning by strengthening Internet connectivity and improving ICT infrastructure (Matete et al., 2023). According to Osabwa (2022), while in Africa during COVID-19 universities quickly assembled digital curricula whose quality could not be guaranteed and not all students could be brought on board because of digital division, lessons were learnt. Various stakeholders, including university management, faculty, and governments, have been prompted to rethink their modes of education delivery with quality and access in mind. In retrospect, the pandemic has served as a catalyst for digitalization in Africa's higher education systems.

There is evidence that gives hope for E-learning's increased uptake in Africa. Since COVID-19, governments of countries such as South Africa, Nigeria, Kenya and Uganda, among others, have designed strategic plans and guidelines to support E-learning. In the same vein, universities have also developed clear policy directions on the integration of ICT solutions in teaching and learning (Mpirirwe et al., 2021; Ngqulu & Nomnga, 2023). In South Africa, although lecturers had mixed feelings about using E-learning platforms such as Zoom at the outbreak of COVID-19, they became acquainted with online teaching strategies through critical reflection. Lecturers used different online teaching strategies to engage students for social construction of knowledge that included case studies, slide presentations, class discussions, and short videos related to the content (Mpungose, 2023). While in South Africa prior COVID-19 most students and academics had hardly used E-learning, despite higher education institutions already having made efforts to adopt E-learning at least at the policy level, the situation changed. COVID-19 was a necessary catalyst for E-learning adoption and implementation as the government and higher learning institutions became more committed to technological integration in teaching and learning than before. The pandemic availed a great opportunity for higher learning institutions to adopt E-learning both at the policy level and adapting new E-learning methodologies and practices to prepare universities for times of uncertainty. Strides taken include universities providing students devices for accessing E-learning services and Internet data. Students were also provided technical support through short training and support to students during submissions and access to learning material (Ngqulu & Nomnga, 2023).

In Nigeria, about 73% of the population comprised Internet users before COVID-19. Therefore, there were higher chances that universities had the capacity to transit to E-learning. Nonetheless, even with the presence of technologies in the different universities in the country, instructors lacked the skills, interest, and/or willingness to provide online instruction. There were, however, some cases that exhibited success. For instance, when the Pan-Atlantic University transitioned to E-learning, there were minimal interruptions. Students were provided with rechargeable data credit which ensured continued learning. E-learning was provided with sufficient access, demonstrated sufficient human capacity, and an understanding that it was a valid learning modality (Akpan-Obong, 2023). In Ghana, Adzovie and Jibril (2022) found that the COVID-19 outbreak had a positive and significant impact on the adoption of E-learning strategies in the nation's higher education institutions. Higher education institutions' use of E-learning platforms as their primary means of delivering lectures to students during the pandemic spurred rapid advancements in academic innovation and infrastructure, leading to a rise in the use of E-learning methodologies.

In East Africa, empirical evidence study done in Uganda indicated that since the COVID-2019 pandemic, lecturers' E-learning teaching competences in terms of course design, technical communication and time management are high (Mugizi et al., 2023). In addition, E-learning classroom self-efficacy of lecturers in terms of instructional methods, classroom management and student engagement have become high since the pandemic (Rwothumio et al., 2023). During COVID-19, lecturers in Uganda were using E-learning technologies that included Zoom and Google Meet to deliver interactive virtual lectures, and Google Classroom to forward assignments and receive feedback. Nevertheless, the challenge was that few lecturers were involved in E-learning and some students missed out. Another challenge in Uganda was the low attitude of students towards E-learning (Mugizi & Nagasha, 2023). Mugula (2023) established that university students perceived usefulness, effectiveness, E-learning system satisfaction and self-efficacy was moderate. Mugizi and Nagasha (2023) suggested that universities should support lecturers and students to enhance their efficacy for an increased uptake of E-learning. Lecturers and students should also be trained in using E-learning technologies, and more ICT infrastructure such as computer laboratories should be established. They also recommended that more proactive measures should be taken, such as lobbying government and telecommunication companies, to reduce the cost of access to the Internet, establish more WiFi hotspots, and work to change the mindset of lecturers and students through workshops.

E-Learning Conceptualizations of Africa

There are several ways E-learning has conceptualized Africa. One way is the continent as *part of a global technological network*. In this regard, African E-learning experts are characterized as members of a world system of professionals working in the field of information and communications technology (ICT) to support education and training. These individuals include educators, investors, policy makers, technology specialists, and trainers. They have been sharing their knowledge and experience of technologically enhanced learning, which has led their network to now be the largest professional community promoting African expertise and talent in education within Africa and to certain other parts of the world (eLearning Africa, 2024).

Another way E-learning has conceptualized Africa is as *an environment of many socioeconomic challenges*. Utilizing data from the United Nations Educational, Scientific and Cultural Organization (UNESCO), the following six socioeconomic challenges are noted as hampering E-learning in Africa: (1) "low electricity access rate," (2) "no Internet access," (3) "slow Internet speed," (4) "conventional teacher training programs," (5) "unavailability of localized learning materials," and (6) "economic condition and financial situation." It is therefore argued that until policymakers and educational organizations improve the state and standard education in Africa, the aforementioned challenges will continue to stifle efforts to implement E-learning in Africa. It is also maintained that while the challenges differ across basic educational and higher educational institutions, no educational institution can improve education quality without eliminating some of these challenges (Mintbook., 2021, p. 1).

The other way E-learning has conceptualized Africa is as a prime example of the "digital divide." For this conceptualization, it is shown how significant disparities of access to digital technology (computers and smartphones) within and between African countries mirror the uneven access to other resources such as electricity. The call is therefore made for government officials to rectify the widespread inequalities in order to ameliorate, if not completely eliminate, the widening education gaps among their citizens. It is also suggested that these officials should quickly begin by providing smartphones and computers to those who currently do not have access to the devices (Krönke, 2020).

Conclusions and Recommendations

E-learning is an emerging discipline and the concept has not been clearly distinguished from other related or complementary concepts such as mobile learning (M-learning), digital learning (D-learning), E-education, virtual learning, and online learning. Different writers and technology users use the concepts interchangeably. The advantages of E-learning include high peer communication and, with the wider institution, easy access to the teacher, access to the curricula by students, reduced administrative burden for the instructor, and cost effectiveness. The disadvantages of E-learning include being expensive for both instructors and learners because of the cost of Internet connection and devices necessary for learning. Its adoption is also affected by poor or absence of the Internet, unreliable electricity, low technical know-how or the ability to use E-learning devices. In addition, there is the issue of reduced interaction among users, thereby increasing the work burden and activities incompatibility.

In Africa, the implementation of E-learning has been an uphill task. This has been because of insufficient readiness, experience, and the capacity to quickly establish E-learning environments or optimally use available learning platforms. There is also the challenge of the digital divide between students from low and high socioeconomic backgrounds regarding access to technology, limited access to dependable facilities and equipment, unreliable Internet connections, faculty and students' limited technology skills, and use of pedagogies not relevant for E-learning environments. Instructors and learners also lack the training necessary for engaging in E-learning. Furthermore, some countries lack frameworks for the implementation of E-learning. Even so, where policies exist, comprehension among those charged with delivering education is low which, consequently, affects E-learning implementation. Many instructors do not understand the policies and how E-learning can be implemented. Many countries also lack meaningful investments in ICT infrastructure and electricity, which impede E-learning implementation.

Africa has an opportunity for expanding the implementation of E-learning in higher education institutions. This is because since the COVID-19 pandemic, there has been a change in the mindset of many education stakeholders to the effect that students can take courses and complete their programmes using online platforms. In retrospect, the pandemic has served as a catalyst for digitalization in Africa's higher education systems. A number of governments have designed strategic plans and guidelines to support E-learning. Universities have also developed clear policy directions on the integration of ICT solutions in teaching and learning. Some universities have taken strides in providing students devices for accessing E-learning services and Internet data. Students have also been provided technical support through short-term training. The COVID-19 pandemic ignited swift academic innovativeness and infrastructural change which has triggered the increased adoption of E-learning strategies. There has also been an improvement in lecturers' E-learning teaching competences in terms of course design, technical communication and time management, and E-learning classroom self-efficacy in terms of instructional methods, classroom management and student engagement.

In lieu of the preceding conclusions, we recommend that, first, universities in Africa improve their readiness to effectively implement E-learning by acquiring the necessary technologies and training instructors and students in E-learning. Instructors need to be equipped with pedagogies for effective E-learning implementation and students be trained in the use of ICTs. Second, effort should be made to establish a mindset change among instructors and students so that they develop positive dispositions towards E-learning. Third, universities should partner with governments, banks, ICT companies and stakeholders supporting university education in order to reduce the digital divide between poor and rich students. Poor students can be helped to access ICT devices necessary for participation in E-learning at low cost. Fourth, governments should remove taxes on E-learning devices in order to reduce their cost, banks can offer soft loans to needy students, ICT companies can supply students and instructors E-learning devices at low cost and enable them to pay on friendly terms. Fifth, governments in Africa should also increase their investments in infrastructure in order to enhance E-learning implementation. The investment should focus on increasing Internet connectivity and electricity supply to reduce load shedding such that E-learning can take place uninterrupted. Finally, African countries that lack frameworks and policies for the implementation of E-learning should develop and enact them, and also sensitize those involved in implementing E-learning about them.

References

Abed, E. K. (2019). Electronic learning and its benefits in education. *Eurasia Journal of Mathematics, Science and Technology Education, 15*(3), em1672.

Adarkwah, M. A. (2021). I'm not against online teaching, but what about us? ICT in Ghana post COVID-2019. *Education and Information Technologies, 26*(2), 1665–1685.

Adzifome, N. S., & Agyei, D. D. (2023). Learning with mobile devices-insights from a university setting in Ghana. *Education and Information Technologies, 28*(3), 3381–3399.

Adzovie, D. E., & Jibril, A. B. (2022). Assessment of the effects of COVID-2019 pandemic on the prospects of E-learning in higher learning institutions: The mediating role of academic innovativeness and technological growth. *Cogent Education, 9*(1), 2041222.

Ahmed, S. U., Ahmad, T., Ahmad, N., & Ahamad, M. (2021, November). Current trends and future perspectives of E-learning in India. In *2021 sustainable leadership and academic excellence international conference* (*SLAE*) (pp. 1–6).

Akpan-Obong, P. (2023). COVID-19 and African e-learning systems: structural and institutional strategies for resilience and antifragility. *Journal of Information Policy, 13*, 1–33.

Aldulaimi, S. H., Abdeldayem, M. M., Keir, M. A., & Al-Sanjary, O. (2021). E-learning in higher education and COVID-2019 outbreak: Challenges and opportunities. *Psychology and Education Journal, 58*(2), 38–43.

Al-Kayed, R. I. (2020). Advantages and disadvantages of e learning in basic private schools in Al Jama'a District in Jordan from teacher perspective. *Ilkogretim Online, 19*(4), 920–927.

Alqahtani, A. Y., & Rajkhan, A. A. (2020). E-learning critical success factors during the COVID-2019 pandemic: A comprehensive analysis of E-learning managerial perspectives. *Education Sciences, 10*(9), 216.

Amankwa, E., & Asiedu, E. K. (2022). Emergency E-learning acceptance in second-cycle institutions in Ghana: A conditional mediation analysis. *SN Social Sciences, 2*, 42. https://doi.org/10.1007/s43545-022-00338-3

Aristovnik, A., Karampelas, K., Umek, L., & Ravšelj, D. (2023). Impact of the COVID-2019 pandemic on online learning in higher education: A bibliometric analysis. *Frontiers in Education, 8*, 225834.

Bada, J. K., Asianzu, E., Lugemwa, B., Namataba, J., & Milburga, A. (2020). An empirical study on E-learning uptake by teaching staff at Makerere University Business School. *International Journal of Education and Development using Information and Communication Technology, 16*(2), 188–206.

Baroudi, S., & Shaya, N. (2022). Exploring predictors of teachers' self-efficacy for online teaching in the Arab world amid COVID-2019. *Education and Information Technologies, 27*, 8093–8110.

Basak, S. K., Wotto, M., & Belanger, P. (2018). E-learning, M-learning and D-learning: Conceptual definition and comparative analysis. *E-Learning and Digital Media, 15*(4), 191–216.

Bekele, T. A. (2021). COVID-2019 and prospect of online learning in higher education in Africa. *Journal of Comparative & International Higher Education, 13*(5), 243–253.

Belt, E. S., & Lowenthal, P. R. (2023). Synchronous video-based communication and online learning: An exploration of instructors' perceptions and experiences. *Education and Information Technologies, 28*(5), 4941–4964.

Bwire, F., Bagarukayo, E., & Muyinda, P. B. (2020). Online learning challenges in academia: The case of Uganda. *CSEDU, 2*, 484–489.

Cahyani, N. M. W. S., Suwastini, N. K. A., Dantes, G. R., Jayantini, I. G. A. S. R., & Susanthi, I. G. A. A. D. (2021). Blended online learning: Combining the strengths of synchronous and asynchronous online learning in EFL context. *Jurnal Pendidikan Teknologi Dan Kejuruan, 18*(2), 174–184.

Chikuni, P. R., Makwambeni, B., & Chigona, W. (2021). Dominant discourses informing E-learning policies in higher education institutions in South Africa. *International Journal of Education and Development using Information and Communication Technology (IJEDICT), 17*(4), 5–21.

Clarin, A. S., & Baluyos, E. L. (2022). Challenges encountered in the implementation of online distance learning. *EduLine: Journal of Education and Learning Innovation, 2*(1), 33–46.

Crompton, H., Burke, D., & Gregory, K. H. (2017). The use of mobile learning in PK-12 education: A systematic review. *Computers & Education, 110*, 51–63.

Cullinan, J., Flannery, D., Harold, J., Lyons, S., & Palcic, D. (2021). The disconnected: COVID-2019 and disparities in access to quality broadband for higher education students. *International Journal of Educational Technology in Higher Education, 18*, 1–21.

Dhawan, S. (2020). Online learning: A panacea in the time of COVID-2019 crisis. *Journal of Educational Technology Systems, 49*(1), 5–22.

Diallo, B., Traoré, S., & Fernandes, T. (2010). AVU's experience in increasing access to quality higher education through E-learning in Sub-Saharan Africa. In *Multiple literacy and science education: ICTs in formal and informal learning environments* (pp. 165–179). IGI Global.

Dos Santos, L. M. (2022, September). Online learning after the COVID-2019 pandemic: Learners' motivations. *Frontiers in Education* 7. Frontiers Media SA. Retrieved on October 2, 2023 from https://doi.org/10.3389/feduc.2022.879091

Dung, D. T. H. (2020). The advantages and disadvantages of virtual learning. *IOSR Journal of Research & Method in Education, 10*(3), 45–48.

eLearning Africa. (2024). Welcome to eLearning Africa. Retrieved on July 1, 2024 from https://www.elearning-africa.com/

Faturoti, B. (2022). Online learning during COVID19 and beyond: A human right based approach to internet access in Africa. *International Review of Law, Computers & Technology, 36*(1), 68–90.

Fernandez, C. J., Ramesh, R., & Manivannan, A. S. R. (2022). Synchronous learning and asynchronous learning during COVID-2019 pandemic: A case study in India. *Asian Association of Open Universities Journal, 17*(1), 1–14.

Fernández-Manjón, B., Sánchez-Pérez, J. M., Gómez-Pulido, J. A., Vega-Rodríguez, M. A., & Bravo-Rodríguez, J. (Eds.). (2007). *Computers and education: E-learning, from theory to practice*. Springer.

Gaceri, M. (2021). The readiness, acceptance, success and challenges for online learning in universities during the pandemic. *International Academic Journal of Information Sciences and Project Management, 3*(6), 499–507.

Harasim, L. (2000). Shift happens: Online education as a new paradigm in learning. *The Internet and Higher Education, 3*(1–2), 41–61.

Hlatshwayo, M. (2022). Online learning during the South African COVID-2019 lockdown: University students left to their own devices. *Education as Change, 26*(1), 1–23.

Humpherys, S. L., & Lazrig, I. (2021). Effects of teaching and practice of time management skills on academic performance in computer information systems courses. *Information Systems Education Journal, 19*(2), 45–51.

Jouicha, A. I., Berrada, K., Bendaoud, R., Machwate, S., Miraoui, A., & Burgos, D. (2020). Starting MOOCs in African university: The experience of Cadi Ayyad University, process, review, recommendations, and prospects. *IEEE Access, 8*, 17477–17488.

Kasule, G. W., Mugizi, W., & Rwothumio, J. (2023). Digital teaching competence and lecturers' self-efficacy in online classes: Insights from public universities in Uganda. *Journal of the National Council for Higher Education, 10*(2), 26–47.
Kiessling, C., & Fabry, G. (2021). What is communicative competence and how can it be acquired? *GMS Journal for Medical Education, 38*(3), 1–8.
Kimura, R., Matsunaga, M., Barroga, E., & Hayashi, N. (2023). Asynchronous E-learning with technology-enabled and enhanced training for continuing education of nurses: A scoping review. *BMC Medical Education, 23*(1), 505.
Kokoç, M. (2019). Flexibility in E-learning: Modelling its relation to behavioural engagement and academic performance. *Themes in E-learning, 12*(12), 1–16.
Kotoua, S., Ilkan, M., & Kilic, H. (2015). The growing of online education in Sub Saharan Africa: Case study Ghana. *Procedia-Social and Behavioral Sciences, 191*, 2406–2411.
Krönke, M. (2020, June). Africa's digital divide and the promise of e-learning. *Afrobarometer Policy Paper No. 66*. Retrieved on July 1, 2024 from https://www.afrobarometer.org/wp-content/uploads/2022/02/pp66-africas_digital_divide_and_the_promise_of_e-learning-afrobarometer_policy_paper-14june20.pdf
Lai, C. C., Shih, T. P., Ko, W. C., Tang, H. J., & Hsueh, P. R. (2020). Severe acute respiratory syndrome coronavirus 2 (SARS-CoV-2) and coronavirus disease-2019 (COVID-19): The epidemic and the challenges. *International Journal Of Antimicrobial Agents, 55*(3), 105924.
Lee, V. H., Hew, J. J., Leong, L. Y., Tan, G. W. H., & Ooi, K. B. (2022). The dark side of compulsory e-education: Are students really happy and learning during the COVID-2019 pandemic? *International Journal of Human–Computer Interaction, 38*(12), 1168–1118.
Lembani, R., Gunter, A., Breines, M., & Dalu, M. T. B. (2020). The same course, different access: The digital divide between urban and rural distance education students in South Africa. *Journal of Geography in Higher Education, 44*(1), 70–84.
Liu, M., & Yu, D. (2023). Towards intelligent E-learning systems. *Education and Information Technologies, 28*, 7845–7876.
Maddison, T., Doi, C., Lucky, S., & Kumaran, M. (2017). Literature review of online learning in academic libraries. In T. Maddison & M. Kumaran (Eds.), *Distributed learning: Pedagogy and technology in online information literacy instruction* (1st ed.). Chandos Publishing.
Maghdalena, A. H., Faridi, A., & Hartono, R. (2022). The effectiveness of synchronous and asynchronous E-learning environments in teaching writing to different personalities. *English Education Journal, 12*(3), 333–346.
Mailizar, M., & Fan, L. (2020). Indonesian teachers' knowledge of ICT and the use of ICT in secondary mathematics teaching. *Eurasia Journal of Mathematics, Science and Technology Education, 16*(1), 1–13.
Martin, F., Sun, T., Turk, M., & Ritzhaupt, A. D. (2021). A meta-analysis on the effects of synchronous online learning on cognitive and affective educational outcomes. *The International Review of Research in Open and Distance Learning, 22*(3), 205–242.
Masalimova, A. R., Khvatova, M. A., Chikileva, L. S., Zvyagintseva, E. P., Stepanova, V. V., & Melnik, M. V. (2022). Distance learning in higher education during COVID-2019. *Frontiers in Education, 7*, 822958.
Matete, R. E., Kimario, A. E., & Behera, N. P. (2023). Review on the use of eLearning in teacher education during the corona virus disease (COVID-2019) pandemic in Africa. *Heliyon, 9*(2), e13308.
Mintbook. (2021, July 8). Key Challenges in implementing eLearning in Africa. *Mintbook*. Retrieved on July 1, 2024 from https://mintbook.com/blog/challenges-implementing-elearning-africa/
Mpirirwe, H., Mirembe, D. P., Lubega, J., & Agaba, J. E. (2021). E-learning platforms and security mechanisms used by educational institutions in Kampala, Uganda. *International Journal of Information Technology, Communications and Convergence, 4*(1), 47–62.
Mpungose, C. B. (2023). Lecturers' reflections on use of Zoom video conferencing technology for E-learning at a South African university in the context of coronavirus. *African Identities, 21*(2), 266–282.

Mugizi, W., & Amwine, C. M. (2020). Information communication technology use and job performance of teachers at a private international school in Uganda. *Creative Education, 11*, 166–181.
Mugizi, W., & Nagasha, J. I. (2023). Students' experiences using online learning during the COVID-2019 pandemic: The case of Kyambogo University, Uganda. In L. Namatende-Sakwa, S. Lewinger, & C. Langsford (Eds.), *COVID-2019 and education in Africa*. Routledge.
Mugizi, W., & Rwothumio, R. (2023). Universities' capabilities and effective implementation of E-learning in public universities in Kampala City, Uganda. *The Uganda Higher Education Review, 10*(2), 68–86.
Mugizi, W., Rwothumio, J., & Amwine, C. M. (2021). Compensation management and employee wellbeing of academic staff in Ugandan private universities during COVID-2019 lockdown. *Interdisciplinary Journal of Education Research, 3*(1), 1–12.
Mugizi, W., Rwothumio, J., & Kasule, G. W. (2023). Measuring digital teaching competence of academic staff in public universities in Uganda. *African Journal of Education, Science and Technology, 7*(3), 736–745.
Mugula, O. (2023). Adult learners' attitudes as correlates of E-learning uptake during the COVID-2019 era at Makerere University, Uganda. *Makerere Journal of Higher Education, 12*(1), 119–131.
Ngqulu, N., & Nomnga, P. (2023). COVID-2019 pandemic: A necessary catalyst for E-learning adoption and application. *South African Computer Journal, 35*(1), 115–130.
Nyerere, J. (2016). Open and distance learning in Kenya. *A baseline survey report commissioned by the commonwealth of learning*. Retrieved on October 31, 2023 from https://oasis.col.org/bitstream/handle/11599/2491/2016Nyerere_ODL-Kenya.pdf
Ogolodom, M. P., Mbaba, A. N., Okpaleke, M. S., Chukwueze, I. O., Okankwu, E. A., Joseph, D. Z., & Brownson, E. E. (2023). Online learning in Nigerian universities during COVID-19 pandemic: The experiences of nursing and radiography undergraduate students. *Journal of Radiology Nursing, 42*(1), 128–135.
Ojo, D. O., & Olakulehin, F. K. (2006). Attitudes and perceptions of students to open and distance learning in Nigeria. *The International Review of Research in Open and Distance Learning, 7*(1), 1–10.
Osabwa, W. (2022, February). Coming to terms with COVID-2019 reality in the context of Africa's higher education: Challenges, insights, and prospects. *Frontiers in Education, 7*, 643162.
Oyo, B., & Kalema, B. M. (2014). Massive open online courses for Africa by Africa. *The International Review of Research in Open and Distance Learning, 15*(6), 1–13.
Parlakkilic, A. (2014). Bridging the gap with distance education students: Telepresence. In T. V. Yuzer & G. Kurubacak (Eds.), *Handbook of research on emerging priorities and trends in distance education: Communication, pedagogy, and technology*. IGI Global.
Pedro, L. F. M. G., Barbosa, C. M. M. D. O., & Santos, C. M. D. N. (2018). A critical review of mobile learning integration in formal educational contexts. *International Journal of Educational Technology in Higher Education, 15*(1), 1–15.
Perveen, A. (2016). Synchronous and asynchronous e-language learning: A case study of virtual university of Pakistan. *Open Praxis, 8*(1), 21–39.
Pham, L., Limbu, Y. B., Bui, T. K., Nguyen, H. T., & Pham, H. T. (2019). Does E-learning service quality influence E-learning student satisfaction and loyalty? Evidence from Vietnam. *International Journal of Educational Technology in Higher Education, 16*(1), 1–26.
Pratiwi, W. R. (2020). The practice of digital learning (D-learning) in the study from home (SFH) policy: Teachers' perceptions. *Journal of Southwest Jiaotong University, 55*(4), 1–12.
Pregowska, A., Masztalerz, K., Garlińska, M., & Osial, M. (2021). A worldwide journey through distance education—From the post office to virtual, augmented and mixed realities, and education during the COVID-2019 pandemic. *Education Sciences, 11*(3), 118.
Reichert, F., Zhang, D. J., Law, N. W., Wong, G. K., & de la Torre, J. (2020). Exploring the structure of digital literacy competence assessed using authentic software applications. *Educational Technology Research and Development, 68*(6), 2991–3013.

Rodrigues, H., Almeida, F., Figueiredo, V., & Lopes, S. L. (2019). Tracking E-learning through published papers: A systematic review. *Computers & Education, 136*, 87–98.

RUFORUM. (2020, September). Status analysis of E-learning in African universities. Retrieved on October 30, 2023 from https://www.ruforum.org/sites/default/files/Reports

Rumajogee, A. R. (2002). *Distance education and open learning in sub-Saharan Africa: A literature survey on policy and practice*. ADEA Working Group on Distance Education and Open Learning. Retrieved on November 1, 2023 from http://www.adeanet.org

Rumble, G. (2001). Just how relevant is e-education to global educational needs? *Open Learning: The Journal of Open, Distance and E-learning, 16*(3), 223–232.

Rwothumio, J., Mugizi, W., & Kasule, G. W. (2023). Measuring online classroom self-efficacy of lecturers in public universities in Uganda. *African Journal of Education, Science and Technology, 7*(3), 766–775.

Singh, J., Evans, E., Reed, A., Karch, L., Qualey, K., Singh, L., & Wiersma, H. (2022). Online, hybrid, and face-to-face learning through the eyes of faculty, students, administrators, and instructional designers: Lessons learned and directions for the post-vaccine and post-pandemic/COVID-2019 world. *Journal of Educational Technology Systems, 50*(3), 301–326.

Singh, V., & Thurman, A. (2019). How many ways can we define online learning? A systematic literature review of definitions of online learning (1988-2018). *American Journal of Distance Education, 33*(4), 289–306.

Skhephe, M. (2022). Teachers' readiness for E-learning during the COVID-2019 pandemic, South Africa. In E. Cvetković (Ed.), *MOOC (massive open online courses)*. BoD—Books on Demand.

Smyrnova-Trybulska, E. (2019). E-learning-evolution, trends, methods, examples, experience. *International Conference E-learning*, 155–162.

Sujan, S. V., & Eswari, M. (2021). A study of impact of digital learning among students. *Journal of the Maharaja Sayajirao University of Baroda, 55*(3), 105–109.

Swenson, B. (2020, April 15). Remote teaching vs. online learning in higher education today. Retrieved on August 15, 2023 from https://www.uagrantham.edu/blog/remote-teaching-vs-onlinE-learning-in-higher-education-today/

Talan, T. (2020). The effect of mobile learning on learning performance: A meta-analysis study. *Educational Sciences: Theory and Practice, 20*(1), 79–103.

Thompson, E. (2023, October 17). A history of online education. *The Best Schools*. Retrieved on October 28, 2023 from https://thebestschools.org/magazine/online-education

Tibaná-Herrera, G., Fernández-Bajón, M. T., & Moya-Anegón, D. (2018). Categorization of E-learning as an emerging discipline in the world publication system: A bibliometric study in SCOPUS. *International Journal of Educational Technology in Higher Education, 15*(1), 1–23.

Tsai, S., & Machado, P. (2002). E-learning, online learning, language learning, or distance learning: Unveiling the ambiguity in current terminology. *Association for Computer Machinery eLearn Magazine, 2002*(7), 3–5.

Valverde-Berrocoso, J., Garrido-Arroyo, M. D. C., Burgos-Videla, C., & Morales-Cevallos, M. B. (2020). Trends in educational research about E-learning: A systematic literature review (2009–2018). *Sustainability, 12*(12), 51–53.

Verma, S. (2017). *Corporate cocktail*. Notion Press.

Watermeyer, R., Chen, Z., & Ang, B. J. (2022). 'Education without limits': The digital resettlement of post-secondary education and training in Singapore in the COVID-2019 era. *Journal of Education Policy, 37*(6), 861–882.

Wheeler, S. (2012). E-learning and digital learning. In N. M. Seel (Ed.), *Encyclopedia of the sciences of learning*. Springer.

Wong, B. T. M. (2021). A survey on the pedagogical features of language massive open online courses. *Asian Association of Open Universities Journal, 16*(1), 116–128.

Yusif, S., & Hafeez-Baig, A. (2023). Cybersecurity policy compliance in higher education: A theoretical framework. *Journal of Applied Security Research, 18*(2), 267–288.

Wilson Mugizi holds a PhD in Educational Management. He is a lecturer at Kyambogo University in Uganda where he is the PhD programme coordinator in the School of Education. He was formerly the deputy director of Postgraduate Studies and Research Directorate at Kampala International University-Western Campus. He is the author of a book chapter and more than 50 scholarly articles. His research focus includes, but is not limited to, human behaviour and its antecedents in educational institutions, curriculum implementation, pedagogy, the role of higher education in national development, and the use of technology in education.

Judith Irene Nagasha holds a PhD in gender and climate change. She is a lecturer at Kyambogo University in Uganda. She is the author of a book chapter and ten scholarly articles. She is spearheading the milk and fisheries value chain and marketing systems projects in Uganda. She is the lead collaborator for translating science into policy and practice AgriFoSe2030 project for young researchers in Africa, which is supported by the Swedish International Development Cooperation Agency. Her research focus is on the gender perspective in food security, climate change, and indigenous knowledge.

International Political Economy

Julius Niringiyimana

In this chapter, I examine conceptualizations of what Africa is in the field of International Political Economy: that is, the study of the interplay of economics and politics in the world arena. Understandably, African political economies are examined in respect to their material wealth and the nature of institutions to harness that wealth. Thus, the major research question investigated in the chapter is logically the following: What conceptualizations have been offered about Africa in the academic discipline of International Political Economy? The immediate answer to this question is that many conceptualizations have been offered vis-à-vis what Africa is in the field of International Political Economy. Moreover, these conceptualizations range from the positive to the negative, albeit the latter are more preponderant. It needs to be noted from the onset that it is beyond the scope of this chapter to deal with all of these conceptualizations. Therefore, for the sake of conciseness, the following three major conceptualizations are analyzed here: (1) Africa as a poor economy, (2) Africa as a continent dependent on foreign aid, and (3) Africa as aspiring for greater global agency.

This chapter employs the qualitative approach and, therefore, words are emphasized as opposed to numerical values because the study focuses on international political economic conceptualizations. Nonetheless, numerical data are noted to supplement certain qualitative analyses where and when necessary. Secondary data are mostly utilized and they are analyzed in terms of descriptive case studies, which means that the "What is?" question underlies the analyses (Bangura, 2019; Bangura et al., 2014). Before engaging in the analyses of the three aforementioned conceptualizations of Africa, that of International Political Economy is first provided as a backdrop. This is because it is the discipline upon which the investigation here is

J. Niringiyimana (✉)
Political Science and Public Administration, Makerere University, Kampala, Uganda
e-mail: julius.niringiyimana@mak.ac.ug

A. K. Bangura, J. A. Ifedi (eds.), *Conceptualizations of Africa*, African Studies and Research Forum Series, https://doi.org/10.1007/978-3-031-74535-5_10

anchored. The timeframes covered by the data are variable in line with the nature of the conceptualizations.

Based on the preceding backdrop, the main question here is the following: What is the essence of investigating how Africa is conceptualized in the field of International Political Economy? The answer to this question is that it allows an analyst to engage in a systematic process for examining methods of producing, distributing, and consuming wealth and the social, political, and economic interactions of these wealth at the international arena. It enables the analyst to examine the political basis of economic actions: that is, the ways in which government policies affect market operations at the global level. Conversely, it also enables the analyst to investigate the economic basis of political actions and the ways in which economic forces mold government policies at the global level. Generally, the chapter aims to reveal how politics and economics are in a constant state of mutual interaction. By implication, the interrogation in this chapter makes it possible to explain how these political and economic forces are relevant in the analyses of what Africa is in the field of International Political Economy.

International Political Economy: A Conceptualization

The academic discipline of International Political Economy has been conceptualized in several ways, which include (a) history of International Political Economy, (b) methodology of International Political Economy, and (c) approaches of International Political Economy. In this chapter, I focus on three of the time-tested approaches of International Political Economy—i.e., (1) liberalism, (2) Marxism, and (3) realism—for brevity. I discuss them one at a time in the following subsections for lucidity.

Liberalism

Liberalism is generally understood as a theoretical strand that advocates for free trade and free markets in the global economy. Five aspects have been proffered in the conceptualization of liberalism. First, political economists who study the relationship between the state and the market emphasize how both the market and politics are environments in which all parties can benefit by entering into voluntary exchanges with others. These political economists reason that if there are no impediments to trade among individuals, everyone can be made well off through voluntary exchanges. They explain how this is possible as long as there are enough existing stocks of goods and services. That is to say, all participants in the market are able to be at their highest possible level of utility. Nonetheless, the neoclassical economists believe strongly that the market is a superior mechanism for allocating scarce resources (Frieden & Lake, 2003; Balaam & Dillman, 2019).

Second, those who strongly believe in the market as a mechanism for allocating scare resources reason that the economic role of government should be reasonably limited. They note that many forms of government intervention in the economy, intentionally or unintentionally, restrict the market and thereby prevent potentially rewarding trades from occurring. In this respect, they believe that market mechanisms should be determined by the powers of demand and supply in the economy (Frieden & Lake, 2003; Balaam & Dillman, 2019).

Third, political economists who believe in "social welfare" do generally support the idea that the state may get involved in social services provisioning of certain "public goods." These are goods and services that benefit society and that would hardly be provided by private markets. They note that while the state plays an important role in supplying the conditions necessary for the maintenance of a free and competitive market, it should also ensure that the poor and vulnerable people are protected. These scholars, for example, note that states must provide for the defense of the country, protect the property rights of the vulnerable, and prevent any unfair collusion or concentration of power within the market. It is also the role of the state to educate its citizens, build infrastructure, and provide and regulate a common currency. These roles of the state, in other words, provide the necessary foundation for the market (Frieden & Lake, 2003; Balaam & Dillman, 2019).

Fourth, liberals who conduct research on interests and actors in the field of International Political Economy assert that a fundamental harmony of interests exists between, as well as within, countries. They argue that all countries are best off when goods and services move freely across national borders in mutually rewarding exchanges. If universal free trade were to exist, they posit, all countries would enjoy the highest level of utility and there would be no economic basis for international conflict or war.

Fifth, liberals also believe that states should manage the international economy in much the same way as they manage their domestic economies. They note that states should establish rules and regulations, often referred to as "international regimes," to govern exchanges among different national currencies and ensure that no country or domestic group is damaged by "unfair" international competition (Frieden & Lake, 2003; Balaam & Dillman, 2019).

Marxism

Marxism originated from the ideas of Karl Marx, a nineteenth-century political economist and perhaps the strongest critic of capitalism and its liberal enthusiasts. Marxist scholars saw capitalism and the market as accumulating excesses of wealth for capitalists and poverty for workers. Consequently, the population was drowning in hardcore poverty amidst plenty and hard work. There are different ways how Marxism explains International Political Economy. Marxist scholars reject the assertion that "exchange between individuals necessarily maximizes the welfare of the whole society." This denunciation is based on the argument that there is no "free exchange" since capitalists exploit the workers and constantly alienate labor. According to Marxism, labor is reduced to being a mere commodity (product for sale) in three ways. First, workers are alienated from the products of their labor because products are put on the market on the higher prices than what workers can afford. Second, workers are alienated from their fellow workers. This is because in capitalism, everyone is busy struggling to get a job and therefore little attention is paid to social solidarity. Consequently, and therefore the third point, workers are alienated from themselves as creative social beings (Frieden & Lake, 2003; Balaam & Dillman, 2019).

Moreover, Marxists and their supports believe that classes are the dominant actors in the International Political Economy. Specifically, classes are determined in two aspects: (1) capital, or the owners of the means of production; and (2) labor, or the workers. Marxist theorists assume that classes act in their economic interests: that is, "to maximize the economic well-being of the class as a whole" (Frieden & Lake, 2003, p. 11). Therefore, the basis of the capitalist economy is the exploitation of labor by capital. This is because capitalism, by its very nature, denies workers the full return for their efforts (Frieden & Lake, 2003).

Also, Marxists view International Political Economy as conflictual because the relationship between the owners of capital (capitalists) and workers is essentially antagonistic. Marxists and other proponents of this view explain how the means of production are controlled by a minority within society—the capitalists. They also document how a worker does not receive its full return, as a laborer. This condition is perceived to be exploitation which leads to conflict between the classes. The workers will rise up against the capitalists and believe to win because (a) they are the majority, (b) they have nothing to lose but their chains, and (c) they are concentrated at their places of work. Marxists believe that periodic exploitation and class struggle between capitalists and workers cause economic crises. Accordingly, these crises ultimately lead to the overthrow of capitalism by labor and the establishment of a socialist society. In the socialist society, Marxists assert that the means of production will be owned equally by all members of society and exploitation will cease (Frieden & Lake, 2003; Balaam & Dillman, 2019).

In addition, some scholars such as Lenin have expanded Marxist ideas to explain imperialism and war. Lenin argues that imperialism was endemic to modern capitalism because of the exploitative means for capitalists to solve their problems. For example, Lenin illustrates how capitalists would solve their problems by exporting capital abroad when capitalism faced a crisis in the developed countries. Lenin further shows how the developed countries would colonize the weaker states to acquire protection of their capital and to safeguard the interests of their foreign investors. Consequently, capitalist countries have continued to compete for control over these areas and intra-capitalist wars have followed (Frieden & Lake, 2003).

Indeed Africa is at the center stage of capitalism because of its natural resource endowments. Africa possesses "almost 30 percent of the world's mineral reserves," which entail 8 percent of the world's natural gas and 12 percent of the world's oil reserves (Alao, 2007; Niringiyimana, 2022). The continent also owns 40 percent of the world's gold and up to 90 percent of chromium and platinum. Besides, Africa enjoys 65 percent of the world's arable land and 10 percent of the globe's internal renewable fresh water source (United Nations Environment Programme, 2023). It is these natural resources that have attracted multinational corporations (MNCs) and the consequential rise of globally integrated financial markets in Africa. One of the concerns for Marxists, however, is how these MNCs have weakened the economic and political power of labor. If workers in a particular country raise up their arms and demand higher wages, for example, the MNCs can simply transfer production to another country where labor is more compliant. This nature of capitalism therefore creates worries for Marxists that the conditions of workers may continue to deteriorate because their ability to negotiate with capital for a more equitable compensation is constantly being diluted (Frieden & Lake, 2003).

Furthermore, the continued manifestations of poverty and underdevelopment in Africa raise more worries for the enthusiasts of Marxism. Frieden and Lake observe that "development is blocked by domestic ruling classes, which pursue their own, narrow interests at the expense of national economic progress" (2003, p. 11). Moreover, "dependency" theorists apply Marxist ideas of class analysis to explain how the global system is stratified into a wealthy area (First World) and a region of oppression and poverty (Third World). The implication for this is that global capitalism exploits the Third World and benefits the First World, just like capitalists exploit workers within a country (Frieden & Lake, 2003).

Realism

The intellectual background of Realism can be traced from the writings of Niccoló Machiavelli, Thomas Hobbes, Jean-Baptiste Colbert, and Friedrich List. These forerunners and other supporters of Realism raise arguments that unequivocally relate realism to International Political Economy. The first argument of Realism is that it focuses on "nation-states" which pursue power and shape an economy to this end. Those who believe in Realism further note that nation-states are the dominant actors within the International Political Economy. Realists believe that the international system is characterized by anarchy and this explains why "nation-states are sovereign, the sole judges of their own behaviors, and subject to no higher authority" (Frieden & Lake, 2003, p. 12). The theoretical implication for this postulate is that since no authority is higher than the nation-state, then all actors must be subordinate to it. It further implies, at least conceptually, that citizens may interact with their counterparts in other countries, but the nation-state must formulate legislations and laws to regulate their interactions. The epistemological value for this submission is that Liberals focus on individuals, Marxists on classes, and Realists on nation-states.

Also, Realists who study power echo that nation-states are fundamentally concerned about international power relations. The basis of this belief is that "since the international system is based on anarchy, the use of force or coercion by other nation-states is always a possibility" (Frieden & Lake, 2003). Moreover, Realists assert that in such conditions, no higher authority is obliged to rescue a nation-state under attack. This implies that the nation-states are ultimately dependent on their own resources for protection. This explains why Realists aver that each nation-state must always be prepared to defend itself to the best of its ability. For Realists, politics is largely a zero-sum game and by necessity actors have to engage in conflict. As such, for one nation-state to win, another must lose (Frieden & Lake, 2003).

Moreover, power gives Realism idiosyncratic methodology to International Political Economy. One of the lenses of understanding power is through decision-making. This view of power is important in understanding the discipline because actors in the global arena deploy different technologies of power to acquire what they need in the system. These include (a) those actors who dominate power may use force or intimidation (the stick) to access resources or punish those that may undermine the global order; (b) they may also use productive exchanges involving mutual gain (the deal), especially if the power hegemon has an interest to achieve; and (c) actors in the international system may decide to create obligations, loyalty, and commitment (the kiss). Therefore, despite the fact that economic considerations oftentimes supplement power concerns, in the Realist view, power is more superior to economic considerations. This is because Realists believe that once there is power, for example, military power, then economic power may easily be attained. As such, they comprehend that nation-states may sacrifice economic gains in some situations to weaken their rivals or strengthen themselves in military or diplomatic power. This demonstrates why some countries may impose trade protection, which might reduce the overall income of the nation by restricting the market for reasons of national political power.

Equally important, Realist political economy is primarily concerned with "how changes in the distribution of international power affect the form and type of international economy" (Frieden & Lake, 2003). The understanding of this question of political economy is best explained in the "Hegemonic Stability Theory." This theory pinpoints how an open global economy characterized by the free exchange of goods, capital, and services is most likely to exist when a single dominant or hegemonic power is present to stabilize the system and construct a strong regime. In addition, Hegemonic Stability Theory explains that the presence of a dominant state can create a sense of predictability and stability in the international system. In other words, the international system is more likely to remain stable when a single state is the dominant world power hegemon because the hegemonic state provides stability and cooperation in the international system through leadership and setting rules and norms that govern the system. Nevertheless, it is prudent to note that a hegemonic state may use its power to exploit other states to further its own interests, rather than acting in the best interests of the international system. At the end of it, grievances may arise, thereby creating resentment among other states. This may lead to conflicts and instability as other emerging powers may wish to take over. These observations are important to help us reflect on why there are constant instabilities in the global system. It also helps us to ponder why China is the second global power and why Africa has continued to demand equal space at all global economic and political fora.

Lastly, Realists who believe in rationality are certain of the fact that nation-states are rational actors in the International Political Economy. These scholars submit that nation-states are thought of as rational actors in the same sense like individuals are thought to be rational. As such, cost–benefit analysis is assumed to be one of the guiding principles of the nation-states. In other words, states have to choose the option that yields the greatest value, especially on issues of international geopolitical and power positions such as securing petroleum concessions in other states.

From the foregoing analyses, I proffer that the three dominant approaches may help one to conceptualize International Political Economy. I also submit that each of these approaches has different assumptions about International Political Economy. For example, Liberals accept that individuals are the proper unit of analysis, while Marxists consider classes, and Realists view nation-states as critically important points of analyses. The standpoints for these approaches also differ on the basis of irrevocability of conflict within the International Political Economy. Liberals consider economics and politics as largely independent domains, Marxists maintain that economics determines politics, and Realists claim that politics determines economics. While these perspectives are critical in explaining International Political Economy, especially with regard to economic efficiency (Liberals), class conflict (Marxists), and geo-strategic and geo-political considerations (Realists), some of their theoretical arguments are blurry. This is because some Marxists agree with the Realist focus on inter-state conflict and others on the Liberal emphasis on economic interests. Moreover, some Liberals employ neoclassical apparatuses to analyze inter-state strategic and political questions. In the same vein, Realists examine the conflicts in classes as do the Marxists. Despite these theoretical and conceptual overlaps, these perspectives are credited for clarifying the conceptualization of International Political Economy, which is the main focus of the section.

Africa as a Poor Economy

The conceptualization of Africa as a "poor economy" can be traced back to Modernization Theory as stipulated by scholars such as Walt Whitman Rostow, Samuel Huntington, Morris Janowitz, Goran Hyden, and Robert Bates. These scholars came up with the discourse that was founded on the tenets of the colonial social sciences. This discourse was urging Africa (and other "underdeveloped" countries) to flee their primitiveness, backwardness, violence and be like the Europeans. As such, it was premised on the colonial social sciences to introduce new words such as backwardness, lazy, lack of acumen, thrift, lack of saving culture, and lack of entrepreneurship to describe the causes of poverty and to blame Africans for their poverty problems. Based on these assumptions of poverty in Africa, modernization scholars noted that the African continent was pre-capitalist, pre-modern, traditional, and backward. The solution for these poverty-related problems was in Western modernity, which required Africa to follow the path of Europe in form of capitalism. In order to develop, Rostow (1960) suggests an "analytic bone-structure" of the five stages of development which underdeveloped societies must follow to achieve development. These include (1) traditional stage, (2) pre-take off stage, (3) take off stage, (4) drive to maturity stage, and (5) stage of high mass consumption. These stages of development are explained in the ensuing paragraphs.

The first is the "traditional stage." It needs to be argued that the developers of modernization discourse tended to be very persuasive as the proponents constructed solutions that were seemingly rational. One of their main argumentations was that poor countries were poor because they were poor; and that these countries were trapped in a vicious cycle of poverty. These scholars noted that African economies were poor because people were trapped in traditions and superstitions, subsistence production, use of rudimentary tools in production, averse to work, and no saving culture. As such, they saw the only way for these poor countries to get out of poverty was found in embracing capitalism and allowing foreign capital in their continent in order to harness their natural resources. In this way, capitalism would be developed locally and local capitalists created (Rostow, 1960).

The second stage is "preconditions for takeoff stage" which is developed under the influence of scientific progress: scientific innovations are applied, for instance to agriculture, thereby increasing the funds available for investment. This is manifested through importing capital and improved seeds such as genetically modified seeds (GMOs) to improve agricultural production, constructing dams, and encouraging foreign direct investments (FDIs). According to the supporters of modernization discourse, accessing foreign loans and aid would help finance their agricultural projects and reform African public service. These donor-funded programs would enable African states to become efficient and thereby turn to the higher stage. They argue that attracting FDIs would also help the poor African continent to harness its natural resources by fully exploiting them and increase their exported products. This is because foreign investors would be equipped with technology, finance, and expertise necessary to exploit natural resources. Areas of investments would include oil exploration and development, gold mining and refinery, and agricultural mechanization and modernization.

These conditions would transform Africa into the third stage of development known as the "take off stage." This stage is triggered by a particular stimulus, often from outside the national society that leads to self-sustained growth: investment levels that are higher than before—especially transport and strategic manufacturing sectors that experience high rates of growth and in turn stimulate the whole economy. For this to happen, an entrepreneurial elite must have developed in terms of education and knowledge economy, international trade, improved infrastructure and communication. The argument here is that the "take off stage" would drive the African continental economy into economic transformation and growth because strategic industries and high-tech schools would be established. The supporters of this paradigm used an example from developed countries to explain how an educated population with specialized knowledge was essential for their socioeconomic and political transformation. For Africa, Huntington uses the example of military elites as agency to explain how African countries would ensure security in order for modernization project to take place. It is not surprising, therefore, that many African countries are investing heavily in military training to improve their knowledge economy and promote national and regional security in Africa. As a result, the Uganda People's Defence Forces (UPDF), for instance, has been actively involved in different security missions in Africa such as "Operation Shuja" in the Democratic

Republic of Congo (DRC) to eliminate the Allied Democratic Forces (ADF), a rebel group in the DRC.

The fourth stage, "the drive to maturity," is characterized by the growth of new economic sectors displacing the leading sectors of the takeoff stage. Rostow (1960) gives the example of Europe where new activity was mainly concentrated in heavy industry. He avers that heavy industries replaced agriculture as an important part of the economy from the eighteenth to the nineteenth century. In this respect, African countries would be directly involved in heavy industries and exporting manufactured goods. These manufactured goods would not only be diversified but also fetching high dollar value. In addition, such trade would be characterized by free exchange whereby African capitalists and investors have equal powers of negotiation with those of the West. These conditions would enable the continent to have most of its population employed in productive jobs and expand its tax base and the national treasury. More investments would then be made and multiplied to other direct and indirect sectors.

The aforementioned achievements would finally drive Africa to the last stage of "high mass consumption" whereby Africa would be among the "first" countries or developed countries. The main emphasis in this stage of development is consumption instead of production (Rostow, 1960). Rostow (1960) sees three possible developments in this phase: the pursuit of power through investment in military strength, the emphasis on the welfare state, and the expansion of consumption. Based on the supporters of the modernization paradigm, this is the highest stage of capitalism whereby investors have satisfied all avenues of investments and profits. At this stage, African countries would be able to finance their national budgets and give international loans and grants to other needy countries. Investors would be many and some would be in the paradise enjoying the profits. Everybody in the world would be happy and able to meet their basic needs.

Despite the preceding descriptions, it is important to communicate that Modernization Theory has some weaknesses that would not enable it to fully explain poverty and underdevelopment in Africa. For brevity, five weaknesses have been presented. First, the theory failed to unravel imperialism in Africa. It is impossible to understand the realities in Africa without identifying the locus and roles of imperialism, how it facilitates the siphoning of African resources, and how it facilitates the internal accumulation processes—i.e., "internal exploitation."

Also, the theory is characterized by a history of analogy because it failed to grasp African people's history and the nature of suffering they were going through before suggesting the path of development. To understand any people's history requires an approach that will focus on their society dialectically with an interest to examine their activities, relations, modes of production and their different forms of struggles. For example, it failed to reflect on many crucial processes taking place in Africa that had as much or more influence on economic development than many of those suggested processes of modernization (Frank, 1967, pp. 20–73).

In addition, the theory suggested a unilinear presentation of human history. Yet, not all countries were fated to take the same developmental path through the same stages, and neither Europe nor America had reached the end of history as Fukuyama would like us to believe. Thus, first, I argue that Europe and America were different from Africa. For instance, Africa had lost its resources, both human and natural, to the West. On its part, Europe transformed these resources to develop itself. Second, European countries did not take the same capitalist path. Neither did they have a homogenous type of capitalism, nor were they all at the same level of development. Third, Africa was not homogenous in the way the modernization discourse enthusiastically projected it. While some societies were highly differentiated, other peoples were at lower levels of social differentiation. Their point of commonality was that they were not static the way the modernization paradigm projected them to be. Fourth, many societies were dynamic. Fifth, there were examples of countries which had developed without following the European capitalist modular. These included China, the Soviet Union, Cuba and other East Asian countries. Even the United States itself had not followed the European type of development. And sixth, the emphasis on social change and education, important subjects as these may be, unfortunately resulted in the ignoring of traditional institutions and norms, which still play a major role in the economic life of many Africans.

Finally, and critically important, the theory externally conceived inappropriate solutions for completely different problems. That is, the modernization paradigm formulated the solution of modernity to a problem that it had not studied because its prescription was not based on any concrete diagnosis of the problems in Africa. It had come up with the problem of poverty. Yet, this was not organically developed from any concrete and committed studies following V. I. Lenin's methodological approach of concrete analysis of concrete conditions. This methodological flaw led this discourse to formulate idealistic, utopian, and externalized solutions instead of analyzing the internal dynamics, contradictions, and possible solutions. Contrary to the law of dialectics which underlines how solutions to any problem have to be sought from within the problem itself, the modernization paradigm underlined the role of imports in the form of technology: capital, machinery, loans, aid, and episteme/knowledge, among others. The consequence of full implementation of this externalized solution without examining the internal capacities to provide solutions to their problems or even the local capacities to internalize and absorb the externalized solutions ended up with tied aid, expensive, sophisticated inappropriate or obsolete technologies. All these led African countries to incur heavy debts for scattered white elephant industries/projects. African countries were through this advice surrounded by the debt trap and this debt entrapment has been on the increase. What needs to be underlined is that technology and knowledge are always area and problem specific.

The question that arises here then is the following: Why is Africa classified as a poor economy in the field of International Political Economy? Many scholars have provided answers to this question. Here, for the sake of brevity, I present only a handful of these writers' offerings, especially since they advocate for similar responses.

Following the modernization submissions, one can argue that economic stagnation is one of the causes of poverty in Africa. Various authors submit that Africa is still "the most underdeveloped and poor" among the continents across the globe

(Wale-Oshinowo et al., 2022). These authors remind us that the continent has more than 70 percent of the least developed countries (LDCs) in the world. They also mention that the continent depends mostly on foreign aid to finance most of its development programs. These scholars are not shy to demonstrate how most of the countries in the continent are affected by corruption, ethno-cultural conflicts and civil wars. They eloquently declare that "out of the 47 countries that make up the global list of least developed countries, 33 of them are found in the African continent" (Wale-Oshinowo et al., 2022, p. 1). More so, according to them, inadequate access to basic livelihood needs such as shelter, health, education, food, water, and transportation characterizes poverty in Africa.

In addition, poor economic growth and poverty in Africa are considered to be caused by bad governance such as poor accountability mechanisms, corruption, lack of transparency and low local participation in the implementation of government programs. Saidi, Labidi, and Ochi (2023) suggest that good governance is essential to combating poverty. These scholars are concerned that despite the fact that Africa has experienced rapid growth at an average rate of 5 percent since the 1990s, this acceleration in Africa has not been accompanied by a significant reduction in poverty compared to other regions of the world. As such, Africa has continued to experience high levels of poverty (Kouadio & Gakpa, 2022; Saidi et al., 2023). One of the explanations for the continued poverty is "the degree to which the poor participate in the growth process and share in its proceeds. As such, both the pace and pattern of growth matter for reducing poverty" (DFID, 2008, p. 1).

Furthermore, Africa is dubbed as a poor economy because it has limited diversified resources for exports to the international market that can improve its economic growth. Various scholars such as Paul Ezeoke (2020) inform us that most African countries are endowed with plenty of natural resources but they possess the highest poverty rates. These resources include gold, petroleum, copper, timber, and tourism services. Nonetheless, the challenge is that most African countries have put much of their efforts to agricultural production and recently in petroleum exploration and production with limited diversification and low value addition. With respect to diversification, Ezeoke (2020) uses Nigeria as an example to enlighten how the country has depended significantly on oil as its major income earner since the 1970s. Ezeoke (2020) also observes that low diversification of economies reveals "the truth and reality" of African countries. Nevertheless, it needs to be noted that countries that have limited diversification of export products are vulnerable to changes in prices at the international market. It is therefore necessary for African countries to embrace innovations, especially with regard to value addition on their agricultural products to protect themselves from the vagaries of external economic shocks. Since the continent has also become the center stage for petroleum exploitation, oil revenues need to be invested in other sectors of the economy such as agriculture. This will also enable the continent to avoid the "resource curse" and instead improve its productivity in the economies and compete favorably in the global market.

Moreover, political violence and conflicts have contributed to Africa's poor economy. For many years, Africa has been characterized by violent conflicts and wars that have led to the stagnation of the development process in the continent.

While the list is long, cases such as Somalia, the Democratic Republic of Congo, and South Sudan can serve as evidence. Samuel Huntington argues that stability or political order is a key goal during the processes of modernization. He identifies the "political gap" similar to the "economic gap" identified by economists as the main challenge for the African continent. He believes that political violence and instability that characterize societies with a political gap "is the product of slow development of political institutions" (Huntington, 1968, p. 4). There is a need for African governments to embrace good governance and democratic and strong institutions that are resistant to political instabilities. These political institutions need to embrace an increased level of participation and inclusivity in order to achieve political and economic stability. This proposition is in reflection to Huntington that "If political institutionalization fails to keep pace with participation, instability will result" (1968, p. 78).

Africa as Foreign Aid Dependent

The question probed in this section is this: Why are African countries characterized as foreign aid dependent? Before providing an answer, I first offer a general overview of the concept "foreign aid" as a background.

To begin with, "foreign aid" has been generally understood as a financial support, technical assistance, and other non-financial assistance (food, military equipment, and medicine), designed primarily for developing countries to promote their development and social welfare (Izobo, 2020). Those scholars who investigate the nature of foreign aid disbursed in developing countries apprise us that foreign aid in Africa comes in two broad forms: (1) grants and (2) subsidized loans (Radelet, 2006). They explain how foreign aid can flow in the form of "official development assistance," such as government aid that targets the economic development and welfare of developing countries. These scholars also observe that foreign aid may be in the form of "official assistance" and "private voluntary assistance" (Radelet, 2006).

Categorically, foreign aid has been given as bilateral assistance directly from one state to another and indirectly through multilateral assistance organizations such as the World Bank, International Monetary Fund, and United Nations Development Programme (Radelet, 2006). Generally, the proportion of foreign aid to Africa is currently about 70 percent bilateral and 30 percent multilateral. It has also been noted that about 80–85 percent of foreign aid comes from government sources as official development assistance (ODA) and the remaining 15–20 percent comes from private organizations such as "non-governmental organizations" (NGOs), foundations, and other development charities such as Oxfam. In addition, remittances received from migrant workers living in the Diaspora form a significant amount of international transfer (Izobo, 2020; Radelet, 2006).

We can glean that foreign aid in Africa serves several reasons. Some realist scholars have argued that foreign aid may be given as a signal of diplomatic approval and strengthening a military ally. Others have observed that it is given to reward a government for behaviors desired by the donor and to extend the cultural influence of the donor. Neo-liberalists have tendered their own claim that foreign aid is provided to establish infrastructure in the recipient states to enable the donor states to effectively extract resources and gain other kinds of commercial access from the recipient countries.

I will now address the question of this section: Why are African countries characterized as foreign aid dependent? For curtness, I look at four randomly selected sources among the many that have investigated the topic. First, Resnick (2018) and Bermeo (2016) inform us that African governments are not democratic and have bad governance. They note that foreign aid plays a significant role in facilitating democratic transitions and encouraging good governance in African states. These scholars give examples of African states that experienced multiparty politics in the 1990s, leading to the improvement of civil liberties and independence of the media. Examples gleaned here include President Hastings Banda of Malawi who was convinced by the donor community to allow a referendum on multiparty politics in 1993. Another example provided is the withholding of budget support to the Mozambique government from mid-2009 to early-2010 to protest violations in the 2009 elections and perceived increase in government corruption. Resnick (2018) and Bermeo (2016) ascertain that this feat was achieved through the direct coercion by donor states through withholding aid in response to military coups and severe human rights violations.

Second, those who believe in external support to stimulate local development argue that foreign aid plays an important and positive role in the economic development of African states through good governance, effective economic management, a stable political system and establishing anti-corruption institutions (Izobo, 2020; Calleja & Prizzon, 2019). These scholars provide the example of Botswana to illustrate how it was the first state to graduate from the group of LDCs in 1994 because of foreign aid; thus

> The state of Botswana is one of the good governance stories of Africa as it has a politically stable, people-serving, effective economic system, and incorruptible leaders. With an enabling environment that enables development initiatives to thrive, the aid dependency of Botswana declined from 100 percent in 1970 to less than 5 percent in 1997, leading to the state graduating from the league of Least Developed Countries in 1994. (Izobo, 2020, p. 1)

Indeed, Global Economy (2022) points out that the planned allocation to Botswana between 2014 and 2020 declined to €33 million from €73 million. To boot, between 2012 and 2019, the total aid to Botswana was summed up to $692.66 million. The authors also point out that few donors such as the European Union, Germany, and Japan remain in Botswana and that these donors focus on specific priorities. These include supporting economic development aspects like increased competitiveness, economic diversification, and supporting inclusive and sustainable growth and skills development. The aim for specific focus, the authors indicate, is to avoid duplication of government programs and supporting rural development.

Third, those who believe that agriculture is essential for the political economy of development proffer how foreign aid in Africa has been instrumental in promoting agricultural development. Agriculture in Africa is an important engine in economic development and it contributes more than 10 percent of the gross domestic product (GDP) of most African countries (Olofin et al., 2017; Djokoto et al., 2014). For example, in Uganda, agriculture accounted for about 24.1 percent of GDP and 33 percent of export earnings for the 2021/2022 financial year. Overall, more than 70 percent of Uganda's working population is employed in agriculture and 78 percent of its population lives in rural areas, with farming being the main economic activity. For Ivory Coast, Paul-Alfred (2020) explains how the agricultural sector contributes about 40 percent of the total export earnings and about 30 percent of the tax revenues to the state. He demonstrates how foreign aid has been needed in boosting major technology transfer, agricultural extension and mechanization, as well as agribusiness. He also shows how foreign investment predominantly funds agribusiness in Ivory Coast through foreign companies such as Olam Group, SIFCA, SAF Cacao, Outspan Ivoire, and Nestlé Côte d'Ivoire. He documents that the International Fund for Agricultural Development (IFAD), a specialized agency of the United Nations, has since 1984 supported Ivory Coast in 12 projects to the tune of US$171.19 million benefitting 585,500 households. He adds that IFAD offers loans aimed at promoting food security and reducing household poverty. He further shows that IFAD also undertakes activities that help local organizations for farmers to improve the marketing of agricultural products with a focus on rural finance, technology development and transfer, and rural infrastructure. Paul-Alfred (2020) further illustrates how IFAD supports farmers by partnering with the Directorate for Programming in the Ministry of Agriculture. It is these evidences from agricultural aid that confirm why Africa is designated as being foreign aid dependent.

Fourth, some scholars aver that foreign aid has been important in improving health standards of people in Africa (Morrison, 2018, p. 3). Nonetheless, Morrison (2018) claims that between 2012 and 2017, donor supports in fighting HIV/AIDS in Africa declined by US$3 billion with eight of the 14 major donors decreasing their commitment in 2017 because of the growing global economic hardships and corruption scandals of African governments. Despite the decrease, it is on record that Africa has been relying heavily on foreign aid to help in fighting against epidemic diseases such as HIV/AIDS and the Coronavirus Disease (COVID)-2019. For example, many African countries got foreign aid during the COVID-2019 pandemic, either financially or through drugs. Using HIV/AIDS in Namibia as an example, Morrison (2018) explains, albeit a generalization, how Africa has made tremendous progress in preventing and reducing the spread of HIV/AIDS through the use of foreign aid. It is estimated that Namibia received US$1550.6 million between 2012 and 2019 in the form of foreign aid. A quick look at the Namibian government's expenditure on health and general medical clinics and public health services reveals that all health indicators improved in the period from 1990 and 2013 with an increase in foreign aid (Namandje, 2015). United States through its United States Agency for International Development (USAID) is one of the main health donors in Africa. It mainly focuses on the fight against HIV/AIDS by encouraging sustainable national ownership and leadership of HIV/AIDS programs. It also encourages evidence-based HIV prevention efforts such as biomedical and structural interventions and behavioral change.

Despite those who propose that Africa is defined on the basis of its dependent syndrome on foreign aid, critics argue that the money that comes to Africa in the form of aid is actually African money that was looted through imperialism (Burgis, 2015). In a shocking revelation, Burgis (2015) explains how in 2010, fuel and mineral exports from Africa were worth $333 billion, more than seven times the value of the aid that went in the opposite direction. This resonates well with how United Nations Economic Commission for Africa (2023) talks about financial flows from Africa. In 2015, profit shifting and tax evasion led to an estimated $240 billion annual revenue loss for countries around the world in all sectors. The impact of profit shifting as a percentage of tax revenues is higher in developing countries than in developed countries (Ndikumana et al., 2020; Ngono, 2022). In 2013, profit shifting cost Africa an estimated 2.7 percent of GDP in lost revenues. With regard to repatriation, in Uganda, the daily monitor reported that 528 billion Uganda shillings in the banking sector alone have been exposed to profit repatriation. This money accounts to 72 percent of the total profits after tax has been made by banks in Uganda in 2019. This capital flight is high and it stifles Africa in terms of economic transformation.

Moreover, field experts like Milton Friedman and William Easterly opine that foreign aid has been very detrimental to recipient states because it enlarges bureaucracies of state governments and perpetuates bad governments (Easterly, 2006; Radelet, 2006; Moyo, 2009). They cite widespread poverty in African countries such as Somalia and the Democratic Republic of Congo that have benefited from foreign aid yet this aid has failed to bring the needed economic development and eradication of poverty, with Moyo stating the following:

> Aid to Africa has made the poor poorer, and the growth slower. The treacherous aid culture has left African countries more debt-laden, more inflation prone, more vulnerable to the vagaries of the currency markets and more unattractive to higher quality investment. It has increased the risk of civil conflict and unrest. Aid is an unmitigated political, economic and humanitarian disaster. Aid flows destined to help the average African end up supporting bloated bureaucracies in the form of the poor-country governments and donor-funded non-governmental organizations. (Moyo, 2009, p. 2)

As illustrated in the preceding paragraphs, the presence of numerous donors lead to transaction costs being high within recipient African states, thereby decreasing aid values. A direct cost of aid is linked to the attention and energies of top state officials which are absorbed, "in establishing and maintaining relationships with a multiplicity of donor agencies and adjusting to their differing procedural requirements, languages, and forms of expression, policy idioms, and financial periods" (Djankov et al., 2006, p. 23). This is because where there are many aid donors, they are frequently unclear and sometimes visible, competition with one another–for attractive projects and attention of senior policymakers or influence over the policies of the recipient government. This competition can spill over into their relationship and lead to the "hoarding" of information, which may affect "donor coordination." Moreover, those who disfavor foreign aid argue that aid is insignificant in improving economic development as poverty is not caused by capital shortage; instead, it makes politicians to embrace distortionary policies when they receive aid flows. As such, foreign aid distorts development and causes aid dependency (Moyo, 2009).

Africa as Aspiring Global Agency

Broached here is the following question: How is Africa aspiring to greater global agency? The answer to this question is preceded by a synopsis of why the continent is aspiring as global agency in the international political economy.

It is no exaggeration to assert that Africa was treated as a "peripheral actor" and mostly considered as a "taker rather than a maker" of policies in the international system, with little or no exertion of influence because of its lack of agency power in the international economy. Nevertheless, Chipaike and Knowledge (2018) are quick to assert that the notion that African states were always on the margins of the international political economy has been problematized. Taylor asserts that "Africa has never existed separately from the world but rather has been inextricably entwined in the world political economy and has continually exercised its agency" (2010, p. 2). I draw from the preceding submission to argue that Africa's agency has grown over the last decade because the institutions that the continent established in the twenty-first century have become more effective at coordinating Africa's voice in multilateral fora.

While various reasons can explain why Africa is turning to be a greater global agency, I point out three aspects for brevity before explaining how the continent has exercised its agency in the international political economy. First, Africa is proud of having the youngest population with a median age of 20 years. Indeed, 60 percent of the African population is under the age of 25 which is a potentially important source of labor and market (if well managed in terms of education) in the international political economy. Second, the impact of the Ukrainian-Russian war has made the world to turn its eyes toward Africa as a possible solution for not only commodities like food and energy resources, but also for African leaders to mediate the two countries on war. In June of 2023, for example, a delegation of African leaders and officials from six countries—namely South Africa, Uganda, Comoros, Egypt, Senegal, and Zambia—arrived in Kyiv to begin separate peace talks with the Ukrainian and Russian Presidents on the war (Nzuki, 2023). While the impact of this peace talk has not yet been fully realized, African involvement in such strategic security issues signals Africa's great aspiration for global agency. Third, Africa is endowed with plenty of most profitable natural resources that enable the continent to aspire for agency in the international political economy. For instance, "about 30 percent of mineral reserves in the world, 40 percent of gold in the world and 90 percent of chromium and platinum in the world are found in Africa" (United Nations Environment Programme, 2023, p. 1). Also, Niringiyimana (2022) indicates that since 1990, the petroleum industry alone has attracted more than 70 billion United States dollars investments in Africa, which accounts for the largest investment in the continent's history. These reasons, among others, are enabling the African continent to aspire for global agency, despite the competing positions of not only the two major powers—the United States and China—but also actors such as the European Union (EU). As such, Africa has navigated in the international political economy through pushing for its own concerns to be heard at the global level. Africa has aspired for global agency in different ways; but for the sake of brevity, three areas are explained in the ensuing paragraphs.

First, Africa has demonstrated its agency in the international trade system. Africa as a continent has long decried some of the rules of the World Trade Organization (WTO) such as the perceived inequitable sharing of benefits from tariff liberalization under the WTO. For example, Africa's share of global trade declined from 4.4 percent in 1970 to 2.7 percent in 2020, when others such as China's accession to the organization was accelerating the country's economic growth (Opinion, 2020). These challenges triggered the African Union (AU) to request observer status at the WTO in November of 2019. The Africa Union argued that "the status would allow the Union to formulate common African positions on various policies, as mandated by its member states" (Sidiropoulos, 2022, p. 100).

Relatedly, African agency was manifested in February of 2021 when the election of the first African WTO director general, Ngozi Okonjo-Iweala, was done. While it is clear that her position requires her to seek consensus among member states rather than push for particular positions, she can use the same position to call attention to the plight of African economies. For example, during the Global Health Summit which was convened by the European Commission and the Group of Twenty (G20) Presidency in May of 2021, Okonjo-Iweala argued for greater equity in the global distribution of vaccines. She argued that lowering supply chain barriers, maximizing existing production capacity, and tackling obstacles over intellectual property, access, and innovation would ease African access to COVID-2019 vaccines (WTO, 2021).

Also, Africa has continuously agitated for the principle of special and differential treatment at the WTO, which gives the continent particular rights. The African Group at the WTO secretariat has always reasoned that special and differential treatment "shall be an integral part of all WTO agreements" to "enable African countries, to effectively address their development needs in line with Africa's industrial development priorities" (World Trade Organization, 2019, p. 1). In fact, the African Group in its June 2020 statement on the implications of the pandemic noted that "a clear articulation of special and differential treatment across various WTO agreements has to remain an integral part of trade agreements and negotiations" (World Trade Organization, 2020, p. 1). The main focus of the statement was on provisions that would strengthen promoting public health, industrialization, technology transfer, and closing the digital division (World Trade Organization, 2020).

Moreover, in 2018, Africa launched the African Continental Free Trade Area (AfCFTA), which became operational on January 1, 2021. The objective of AfCFTA is to deepen trade relations among African countries by building regional value chains. While the area is still a work in progress, as African states are negotiating agreements on different sectors incrementally, AfCFTA is an opportunity for African states to exploit continental competitive advantages. This will be important to jumpstart strategic areas of production value chains and accurate industrialization. Since the AfCFTA has been launched, the next main issue for the secretariat is to establish harmonized industrial policies across African countries. These policies need to focus on major products such as agricultural goods, pharmaceuticals, textiles, and clothing where the continent has comparative advantage.

Second, African agency in the international political economy has been observed in global financial systems such as the International Monetary Fund (IMF). It is no exaggeration that Africa has had limited voice in the Bretton Woods Institutions such as the World Bank and IMF. Moreover, most African states have not been adequately represented in many global financial regulations on the pretext that African financial institutions are not systemically important, despite the fact that the rules made would impact their operations. Nevertheless, African countries and institutions such as the United Nations Economic Commission for Africa (UNECA) have argued for both an issuance of new special drawing rights (SDRs) and a more coordinated reallocation of SDRs for the African continent (Songwe, 2021). Following the concerted demand from Africa, the IMF's board approved a new SDR allocation of $650 billion in August of 2021. From this, Africa received about $33.6 billion (Danny, 2021). This was more than what the continent would directly receive from the IMF or multilateral development banks. In addition, as a result of African agency, the IMF revealed how it would explore viable options for "voluntary channeling of SDRs from developed to underdeveloped and more vulnerable member countries to support their pandemic recovery and achieve resilient and sustainable growth" (Danny & Kring, 2019; IMF, 2021, p. 1).

Furthermore, it is hoped that African aspiration for greater agency will even be higher because of its interests in launching alternative global financial institutions. The African Monetary Fund (AMF) that African countries established in 2014 is raising more hopes for African agency in the field of International Political Economy. It needs to be noted, however, that only 12 African countries have signed and, thus, has not been ratified because it is short of the required 15 ratifications (African Union, 2014). It has also been projected that the capital subscription for AMF will be $22.6 billion. In its objectives, the fund stresses that countries can take out loans equal to twice their contributions. Therefore, while AMF has not yet been operationalized, it has been argued that with the AfCFTA now in effect, the AMF should receive renewed impetus. If this argument merits sense, it could enable more African regional trade by providing countries with financial support to mitigate balance-of-payment challenges caused by expanded intraregional trade.

Third, the international tax regime is being reformed to accommodate the interests of the African continent. One of the biggest challenges facing African countries is their limited ability to generate domestic revenues. For example, low industrialization and the high informality in the economy make the tax base very low and reliant on a few major taxpayers. According to the African Tax Administration Forum (2019), on average, 6.3 percent of large taxpayers generate 77.7 percent of tax receipts. It needs to be mentioned that the large taxpayers generally belong to multinational corporations (MNCs). The challenge with MNCs is that they are aggressive tax planners and, therefore, can take advantage of tax loopholes in the countries of their operations to minimize their tax burdens. Moreover, African states often lack the capacity to deal with aggressive tax planning; yet, the international tax regime also disadvantages Africa. Moreover, the prevalence of illicit financial flows (IFFs) compounds this problem. A 2015 UNECA report indicated that Africa was a net creditor to the rest of the world in terms of IFFs. Commercial flows, including tax evasion, trade and services mispricing, and abuses of transfer pricing by multinationals comprised the largest proportion of IFFs, followed by proceeds from planning criminal activities and corruption. A 2020 UNCTAD report on IFFs estimated that "$88.6 billion—the equivalent of 3.7 percent of Africa's GDP—leaves the continent annually as illicit capital flight" (United Nations Conference on Trade and Development, 2020, p. 1). This is compared with "annual official development assistance of $48 billion and investment flows of $54 billion, on average, between 2013 and 2015" (United Nations Conference on Trade and Development, 2020).

Following the aforementioned hitches, UNECA established a high-level panel on IFFs from Africa in 2012. One of the objectives of the panel was to mobilize support for putting in place rules and regulations at all levels to tackle illicit outflows from the continent. The panel also sought to impress on the G20 the need for improved transparency and tighter oversight of international banks and offshore financial centers that absorb these flows (United Nations Economic Commission for Africa, 2023). Accordingly, in 2009, the G20 called upon the Organization for Economic Cooperation and Development (OECD) Global Forum on Transparency and Exchange of Information for Tax Purposes. This aimed at ensuring a rapid implementation of the exchange of information for tax on request. Furthermore, the G20 adopted a new automatic exchange of information in 2014. This was intended to further bridge the informational gap between taxpayers and tax authorities. These moves were potentially positive developments for African tax authorities because it increases transparency and reduces tax evasion.

Nevertheless, while these systems have addressed the supply side of the exchange of information to reduce tax evasion from Africa, the demand side in Africa remains weak. This is because the processes required are burdensome to implement. For example, the exchange of information on request requires a legal basis or mechanism in each authority and the Global Forum assesses each authority's framework and implementation in practice. Sidiropoulos (2022) explains how few African countries have made requests through the exchange. She explains that this was partly because of a lack of domestic capacity or technical expertise and associated costs. Moreover, African countries were not consulted when the Global Forum developed these standards. In the case of the automatic exchange of information, Sidiropoulos (2022) shows how authorities provide such information on a reciprocal basis. Therefore, the OECD and the G20 should adopt a more flexible approach to standards, with reference to the capacities and concerns of African countries. Waiving full reciprocity in exchanging information, at least for Africa, would remove the burden from these countries of having to collect and compile financial information before receiving information from other jurisdictions.

Conclusion and Recommendations

The general conclusion in this chapter is that while the preceding conceptualizations of Africa in the field of International Political Economy expose many challenges for the continent, they also show some positive attributes. Thus, the ultimate question of the chapter is this one: What can be done to address the challenges to Africa in the international political economy? I end here by making some policy recommendations in response to the question.

First, Africa needs to embrace development ideologies such as Pan-Africanism and *Ubuntuism* that are African based instead of adapting foreign imposed ones. Pan-Africanism is a movement that expresses two fundamental facts: (1) the desire for African unity, as well as (2) a sense of unity between all peoples whose ancestors originally came from Africa. *Ubuntuism*, on the other hand, denotes the ideology or logical model that is undergirded by Ubuntu and constructed to defend African values in areas such as education, social justice, and social commitment. Metaphorically, *Ubuntuism* emerges from *Ubuntu* which expresses itself in *umuntu ngumuntu ngabantu*. This demonstrates the significance of group solidarity on survival issues and how communities are developed by linking the individual through "brotherhood" or "sisterhood" (Nkhukhu-Orlando et al., 2021). These ideologies need to be embraced in all African countries to encourage unity, solidarity, and inclusive institutions. Embraced with these African-based ideologies, Africans can work together, promote regional industries, and trade together, which can stimulate development.

Second, strengthening regional integration would be a good alternative for economic development strategies in Africa. Regional integration would imply African countries working together as neighbors on common development efforts and problems, as seen in the East African Community (EAC) and the Economic Community of West African States (ECOWAS), among others. These regional blocs are very important for promoting regional development; but for them to be successful, they should operate on two principles: (1) having the mindset of Pan-Africanism and *Ubuntuism* and (2) ensuring that country boarders are open to all African people who wish to trade in another country.

Third, African states need to embrace inclusive and developmental institutions that deliver quality services. These institutions need to have strong, small, and educated cadres, recruited on merit rather than neo-patrimonial principles. They should also be autonomous and insulated from the demands of special interests. These institutions should embrace innovations, participation, accountability, and adaptability to changes, instead of emphasizing institutional mono-cropping and monotasking. Above all, only strategic and important institutions need to be established for efficient policy performance, better coordination, and avoidance of institutional shopping.

Fourth and lastly, African governments need to embrace innovations and creativity to be self-reliant. This can be achieved through promoting education and technology (knowledge economy) and industrialization, and supporting innovative research and value addition on agricultural production. If well embraced, this would enable the African continent to reduce its foreign aid burden that has caused more problems than it has solved.

References

Africa Tax Administration Forum. (2019). *African Tax Outlook, African Tax Administration Forum*. Retrieved May 23, 2023, from https://events.ataftax.org/index.php?page=documents&func=view&document_id=49

African Union—AU. (2014). *Protocol on the Establishment of the African Monetary Fund, African Union, June 27, 2014*. Retrieved June 20, 2023, from https://au.int/en/treaties/protocol-establishment-african-monetary-fund

Alao, A. (2007). *Natural resources and conflict in Africa: The tragedy of endowment*. University of Rochester Press, Rochester.

Balaam, D., & Dillman, B. (2019). *Introduction to international political economy* (7th ed.). Routledge.

Bangura, A. K. (2019). Revisiting the basics. In A. K. Bangura, J. A. Obando, I. I. Munene, & C. Shisanya (Eds.), *Conducting research and mentoring students in Africa: CODESRIA College of mentors handbook*. CODESRIA Publications.

Bangura, A. K., Thomas, A., & Hopwood, J. (2014). *A comprehensive introduction to research methods, Volume 2: Qualitative methods*. Cognella Press.

Bermeo, S. B. (2016). Aid is not oil: Donor utility, heterogeneous aid, and the aid democratization relationship. *International Organization, 70*(1), 1–32.

Burgis, T. (2015). *The looting machine: Warlords, oligarchs, corporations, smugglers and the theft of Africa's wealth*. Public Affairs.

Calleja, R., & Prizzon, A. (2019). *Moving away from aid: The experience of Botswana*. ODI Report.

Chipaike, R., & Knowledge, M. (2018). The question of African agency in international relations. *Cogent Social Sciences, 4*(1), 1487257.

Danny, B. (2021). How Africa can seize the moment and start resetting its relationship with the IMF. The Conversation. Retrieved September 10, 2023, from https://theconversation.com/how-africa-can-seize-the-moment-and-start-resetting-itsrelationship-with-the-imf-166302

Danny, B., & Kring, W. N. (2019). Why the African monetary fund is a good idea and what can be done to get it going. The Conversation. Retrieved September 12, 2023, from https://theconversation.com/why-the-african-monetary-fund-is-a-good-ideaand-what-can-be-done-to-get-it-going-119827

Dfid, G. B. (2008). *Growth: Building jobs and prosperity in developing countries*. Department for International Development. Retrieved June 13, 2023, from www.oecd.org/derec/unitedkingdom/40700982.pdf

Djankov, S., Montalvo, J. G., & Reynal-Querol, M. (2006). Does foreign aid help? *SSRN e-Learning*. Retrieved June 13, 2023, from https://papers.ssrn.com/sol3/papers.cfm?abstract_id=896550

Djokoto, J. G., Srofenyoh, F. Y., & Gidiglo, K. (2014). Domestic and foreign direct investment in Ghanaian agriculture. *Agricultural Finance Review, 74*(3), 427–440.

Easterly, W. (2006). Planners vs. searchers in foreign aid. *Asian Development Review, 23*(2), 1–35.

Ezeoke, P. (2020). Commentary: Africa and bitter lessons of mono economy. Anambra Broadcasting Service. Retrieved June 13, 2023, from http://www.absradiotv.com/2020/06/17/commentaryafrica-and-bitter-lessons-of-mono-economy/

Frank, A. G. (1967). *Capitalism and underdevelopment in Latin America*. Monthly Review Press.

Frieden, J., & Lake, D. (2003). *International political economy: Perspectives on global power and wealth* (4th ed.). Routledge.

Huntington, S. P. (1968). *Political order in changing societies*. Yale University Press.

International Monetary Fund. (2021). IMF managing director announces the US$650 billion SDR allocation comes into effect. Retrieved July 23, 2023, from https://www.imf.org/en/

News/Articles/2021/08/23/pr21248-imf-managing-director-announces-the-us-650-billion-sdr-allocation-comes-into-effect

Izobo, M. (2020). The impact of foreign aid in Africa: A case study of Botswana and Somalia. *Journal on Rule of Law, 5*, 1–13.

Kouadio, H. K., & Gakpa, L. L. (2022). Do economic growth and institutional quality reduce poverty and inequality in West Africa? *Journal of Policy Modeling, 44*(1), 41–63.

Morrison, J. S. (2018). *The new realism. An uncomfortable middle* (Vol. 17). Center for Strategic and International Studies.

Moyo, D. (2009). *Dead aid: Why aid is not working and how there is another way for Africa*. Farrar, Straus and Giroux.

Namandje, T. N. (2015). *Health foreign aid and health outcomes in Namibia. Doctoral dissertation*. Stellenbosch: Stellenbosch University, South Africa.

Ndikumana, L., Naidoo, K., & Aboobaker, A. (2020). Capital flight from South Africa: A case study.

Ngono, J. F. L. (2022). Capital flight, quality of institutions and domestic investment in Africa. *Economics Bulletin, 42*(1), 193–202.

Niringiyimana, J. (2022). *Oil politics and land conflicts in the Albertine region, Uganda. PhD Thesis*. Makerere University, Kampala, Uganda.

Nkhukhu-Orlando, E., et al. (2021). Ubuntuism. In A. K. Bagura (Ed.), *African isms: Africa and the globalized world*. Peter Lang.

Nzuki, C. (2023). Africa's peace delegation: A new chapter for Africa and the Ukraine war. Retrieved September 16, 2023, from https://www.csis.org/analysis/africas-peace-delegation-new-chapter-africa-and-ukraine-war

Olofin, O. P., Aiyegbusi, O., Arawomo, O., & Olofin, O. J. (2017). Foreign direct investment, social factors & poverty Reduction in West Africa (1980–2015).

Opinion. (2020). Making the WTO work for Africa. African Business. Retrieved July 16, 2023, from https://african.business/2020/09/trade-investment/opinion-making-the-wto-work-for-africa/

Paul-Alfred, K. K. (2020). Agricultural production and its implications on economic growth in Ivory Coast: The use of the econometric approach. *Applied Economics and Finance, 7*(4), 126–137.

Radelet, S. (2006). A primer on foreign aid. Center for Global Development Working Paper (92).

Resnick, D. (2018). Foreign aid and democratization in developing countries. In *The Oxford handbook of the politics of development* (pp. 409–430).

Rostow, W. W. (1960). *The stages of economic growth: A non-communist manifesto*. Cambridge University Press.

Saidi, Y., Labidi, M. A., & Ochi, A. (2023). Economic growth and extreme poverty in sub-Saharan African countries: Non-linearity and governance threshold effect. *Journal of the Knowledge Economy, 15*(2), 7819–7851. Retrieved August 30, 2023, from. https://doi.org/10.1007/s13132-023-01421-7

Sidiropoulos, E. (2022). Africa: Aspiring to greater global agency. In S. Ülgen et al. (Eds.), *Rewiring globalization* (pp. 99–115).

Songwe, V. (2021). Rich countries should reassign funds to Africa as the path out of COVID. *Financial Times*. Retrieved September 10, 2023, from https://www.ft.com/content/71c9644b-ba39-458d-9649-e48b6a95dc7a

Taylor, I. (2010). *The international relations of sub-Sahara Africa*. Bloomsbury Publishing.

The Global Economy.com. (2022). Namibia: Foreign aid. Retrieved July 16, 2023, from https://www.theglobaleconomy.com/Namibia/foreignaid/

United Nations Conference on Trade and Development. (2020). Tackling illicit financial flows for sustainable development in Africa. Retrieved September 04, 2023, from https://unctad.org/system/files/official-document/aldcafrica2020_en.pdf

United Nations Economic Commission for Africa. (2023). High level panel (HLP) on illicit financial flows (IFF) from Africa. Retrieved August 10, 2023, from http://www.regionalcommissions.org/hlpiffnote.pdf

United Nations Environment Programme. (2023). Our work in Africa. Retrieved May 20, 2023, from https://www.unep.org/regions/africa/our-work-africa

Wale-Oshinowo, B. A., Omobowale, A. O., Adeyeye, M. M., & Lebura, S. (2022). Least developed countries in Africa. In S. Romaniuk (Ed.), *The Palgrave encyclopedia of global security studies*. Palgrave Macmillan.
World Trade Organization. (2019). African Group declaration on WTO issues. Retrieved July 21, 2023, from https://docs.wto.org/dol2fe/Pages/SS/directdoc.aspx?filename=q:/WT/L/1054.pdf&Open=True
World Trade Organization. (2020). African Group statement on COVID-19. Retrieved July 21, 2023, from https://www.tralac.org/news/article/14697-wto-african-group-statement-on-the-implications-of-covid-1
World Trade Organization. (2021). DG Okonjo-Iweala calls on WTO members to tackle vaccine inequity. Retrieved July 21, 2023, from https://www.wto.org/english/news_e/news21_e/dgno_21may21_e.htm

Julius Niringiyimana holds a PhD in Political Science. He is a lecturer and undergraduate program coordinator in the Department of Political Science and Public Administration at Makerere University in Uganda. He is a CODESRIA laureate and mentee under the College of Mentors. He has published three journal articles in internationally recognized journals and ten book chapters. He has received three national and international awards and several travel grants to attend international academic conferences. He has attended and presented papers at several national and international conferences. His research interest is in the political economy of development.

International Relations

Omosefe Oyekanmi

This chapter conceptualizes Africa in the field of International Relations (IR), particularly as it relates to corrupt practices on power distance, national interest, and international politics between nation-states and non-state actors. While the next section will be devoted to conceptualizing corruption in IR, an understanding of corruption from the stance of the discipline is quite fitting in unraveling what Africa is in global politics. With emerging trends and issues on globalization, climate change, military, economy, health, etc., this chapter explores the philosophy of Africa in an interdisciplinary field and its effect in constructing the gap between Africa and the West. Thus, this chapter is devoted to unpacking corruption in IR from the purview of Africa's position.

In order to adequately identify and assess corruption in the field of IR, this chapter is divided into seven sections: (1) a conceptualization of IR, (2) the origin and development of IR as a discipline, (3) Africa and corruption in the field of IR, (4) Africa and corruption in the conceptual taxonomy in the IR discipline, (5) issues on global polarities and corruption in the IR system, (6) a new world order and what is next for Africa, and (7) international law and Africa's development. The chapter ends with a conclusion and recommendations.

International Relations: A Conceptualization

Originally domiciled in the field of Political Science, but largely an interdisciplinary area by design, IR is the study and practice of the relationships among nation-states and other entities within the international system. It entails understudying

O. Oyekanmi (✉)
Institute for Pan-African Thoughts and Conversations, University of Johannesburg, Johannesburg, South Africa
e-mail: ooyekanmi@uj.ac.za

A. K. Bangura, J. A. Ifedi (eds.), *Conceptualizations of Africa*, African Studies and Research Forum Series, https://doi.org/10.1007/978-3-031-74535-5_11

cross-national conduct such as psychological and social-psychological factors, as well as institutional and political dynamics that influence foreign officials' behaviors and the actions and inactions of nation-states. Considering that modern global interactions transcend nation-states, IR now encompasses a wider spectrum of issues and challenges that are more complex and comprehensive.

Traditionally, the discipline of IR has been dominated by an analysis of "what is" (positivism) compared to the normative view of "what ought to be." This positivist view explicates IR through a central view of science by dedicating basic ideas in the field to natural science approaches so as to describe the social world and establish theories. Consequently, ideas and perceptions shaping IR discourse and the international system have resonated around theories like realism, liberalism, constructivism, etc. These IR theories had been developed and expanded by European and American thinkers like Hobbes, Rousseau, Morgenthau, Marx, and so on. These socially constructed theories emanated from the perceptions of pioneering philosophers, ranging from Plato, Aristotle, Kant, and Locke. In effect, flowing from the word itself and its conceptual meaning, IR in the modern world is a deviation from its original meaning. According to Jones, "the idea of a discipline called 'International Relations' conveys a notion of a field of knowledge whose scope and constituency is international and constructed by peoples all over the world. To date, however, the majority of literature in the discipline of IR is written by and about only some of the peoples of the world, predominately Americans and Europeans" (2005, p. 1).

As an aside, some of these IR theories have been characterized as *positivist* and others as *non-positivist*. Proponents of the former theories (i.e., *positivist*) depend on measurement and reason in the belief that knowledge is disclosed from neutral and measurable (quantifiable) observations of activities, actions, or reactions. The underlying proposition is that if something is not measurable in this way, it cannot be known for certain. The latter theories (i.e., *non-positivist*) purport that humans are free-thinking individuals with the capacity to affect society. Accordingly, advocates of these theories reject the over-socialized notion of humans. They therefore attempt to understand the inner thoughts of humans and their impact on society. For example, of the three aforementioned theories, (1) realist theories are essentially predicated on a positivist conception of law; (2) liberalist theories, like realist theories, highlight how power is exercised, just like in positivism; and (3) constructivist theories proffer that reality is socially constructed and that knowledge is derived from interactions and interpretations.

Debates on IR as a social discipline therefore have been dominated by European and American scholars' empirical observations of global politics. Nonetheless, in view of how states interact and how they are expected to interact, there is a conflicting role between the positivist and normative approach of IR in Africa. On the one hand, the positivist view explains the role and action of states in foreign policy decisions, particularly in the course of projecting their national interests. On the other hand, the normative view of IR describes the role of the state and the international system in public policy engineering. In this case, the normative view guides policy makers toward framing ideas and actions that can change the world for the better: i.e., what the world ought to be (Steinmetz, 2021). Although some African scholars

(Mphahlele, Mafeje, Asante, Zerbo and Nabudere, Nolutshungu, Chinweizu, etc.) have contributed to the Afrocentric scholarship of IR, their contributions, however, have been largely downgraded and classified loosely as an appendage in conventional Eurocentric theories (Mvulane-Moloi, 2012).

From the African perspective, the diverse historical, cultural, political, and economic background of the African continent has an impact on the views and methodologies that African researchers employ to study and analyze IR. African scholars make a contribution to the field by providing analyses, criticisms, and different viewpoints that take into account the various experiences of African countries and their interactions with the rest of the world (Morumbasi, 2021; Smith, 2018; Van Wyk, 2015). Issues such as colonial legacy postcolonial challenges, global economic inequality, peacebuilding interventions, human rights, and social justice define the core variables of African's philosophy of IR. Several conceptualizations of IR frequently focus on the influence and function of exogenous actors on the continent, rather than the distinct political, economic, and cultural environment of Africa.

Origin and Development of International Relations Discipline

The relations among states date back to the establishment of territories and provinces, particularly with the development of the Treaty of Westphalia in 1648. Although as a discipline IR is a recent field in the social sciences, beginning in the twentieth century after the First World War, IR began in most universities in Western Europe and America by launching separate courses in the 1920s. Prior to the War, IR as a subject focused on the historical analyses of international political system which could not progress the discipline into building theories. With the devastating effects of the war, conversations on the relations among nation-states were emboldened to take on research and teaching in IR (McClelland & Pfaltzgraff, 2022).

The second phase of the development of IR focused heavily on contemporary issues with little attention on historical accounts. Emphasis was on current policy issues such as diplomacy, arm stocking, balance of power, etc., that informed the First World War and subsequently led to the formation of the League of Nations in 1920. The discipline was tactically designed by the West to understand the causes of the war and prevent a relapse. Basically, IR as a distinct study was taught and researched in institutions that designed their scope and content along annual academic International Studies Conferences (ISCs) linked to the League of Nations (LON). Hence, the framework of IR as an academic field was rooted and crafted largely to Western international relations ideology (Acharya & Buzan, 2019).

Soon after the Second World War in 1945, the third phase of IR as a discipline began. As a field of inquiry, it moved from an idealist conceptualization of international events to a realist school. Ideas on the subject resonated around power and real politics. Factors such as decolonization, the emergence of new states, and the Cold War characterized research and teaching in the IR field. At this level, the discipline progressed significantly to accommodate broader issues on globalization, terrorism, and climate change. Thus, from the 1960s until the 1990s when the Cold War ended, neo-liberal thoughts emerged adding to the study of IR concepts like international organization, transnational institutions, and multinational corporations. Concomitantly, as an academic discipline, the development of IR along the three phases were largely characterized by Western nuances and nativity which in the long run influenced not just scholarships in IR but the dynamics in interpreting global politics between the Global South and the Global North.

Africa and Corruption in the Field of International Relations

Having identified the central idea of what Africa is within the context of this book (see Chap. "General Introduction") and conceptualized IR in the previous section of this chapter, it is now important to highlight elements of corruption within the IR discipline which influence Africa's position before proceeding. Importantly, at the time the IR discipline was being conceived and developed, most African and other Third World states were still under colonization. Although African scholars have made laudable contributions to the body of IR scholarship (Gondwe, 2022; Mvulane-Moloi, 2012), the field however remains largely dominated by Western scholars and ideology. Several African IR experts have contributed to the discipline in refining the conceptual differentiations among terms like isolation, alienation, obscurity, seclusion, and isolationism (Acharya & Buzan, 2019). Most of these contributions have not been considered in shaping the structures of international institutions and the dynamics of world politics. For instance, the contributions of theorists like Robert Keohane and Joseph Nye were instrumental in framing a somewhat negative effect of interdependence. Corroborating this, Coate et al. (2015) submit that due to the nature of unequal exchange and relative dependency, inequality among the parties is bred and maintained by the system of interdependence.

As such, the emergence of transnational economic cooperation, security networks, regional organizations, and political alliances have resulted in unbalanced relations between poor and rich countries. Even so, the relationship has yielded more intervention into the affairs of Africa by the West; in which case, this relationship favors Western economic and political interests. This is evident in the establishment of artificial concepts like First, Second, Third, and Fourth World; Global South and Global North; Developed, Developing, and Underdeveloped countries. These categorizations from the mid-1940s have led to artificial gaps that have strengthened the perpetual domination of the South by the North.

According to Gbadamosi (2020), the definitions of these concepts apply to the rules of multilateral or bilateral agencies that influence a country's right to receive aid from these agencies. The difference in terms like "North/South vs. Developed/Developing Countries" also highlights the dominance of international financial institutions (IFIs) like the World Bank, the International Monetary Fund, and other lenders that maintain imperialist and neocolonial practices under the watchful eyes of the main powers in the North. For instance, as Haug, Braveboy-Wagner, and Maihold (2021) infer, Africa, Latin America and the Caribbean, and parts of Asia and Oceania have all been referred to as the "Global South," with the boundaries among these regions frequently appearing obscure. As commonly used in social science literature, the nomenclature "South" and terminology related to it do not reflect any geographical inclination but rather refer to decolonized countries that are roughly, but not exclusively, South of the former colonial centers of power.

Africa and Corruption in the Conceptual Taxonomy in the International Relations Discipline

Be it Developed/Underdeveloped, Global-South/Global-North, First-World/Third-World, Low-income/High-income countries, etc., these concepts and the way they are operationalized emanate from academic fields for guidance and understanding. In so far as they guide the operations of an academic field, the originators of these concepts sometimes present dishonest and fraudulent processes and interpretations that have an impact on African and other states. These concepts and the institutions they birth, as in the case of relations among states and real politics, change from their original ideas and expressions. Hence, an analysis of Africa's view on corruption in the IR discipline must discuss the taxonomy of concepts in the discipline.

Originally, the United States, Western Europe, and their allies made up the First World, while the alleged Communist bloc, which included the Soviet Union, China, Cuba, and allies, was referred to the Second World. The Third World was given to the remaining countries that sided with neither group (Silver, 2015). The conceptualization, which is largely credited to the French demographer Alfred Sauvy in his 1952 article titled "Three Worlds, One Planet," has undergone changes since the end of the Cold War. This model of geopolitics in the mid-twentieth century has taken different interpretations to confer the intended meaning of the writer. Nonetheless, the First World is now largely assumed as a group of powerful economies of the West. The Second World is now obsolete with the end of the Cold War. The Third World, which originally included almost all non-aligned nations of Africa, the Middle East, Latin America and Asia, has now assumed a contraption for poverty and underdevelopment.

Howbeit, with the end of the Cold War, conceptualizing countries and their economies has remained a global debate, particularly with the effect of these categorizations on African and other developing economies. The World Bank categorizes developing countries into three categories based on their incomes as follows (CADTM, 2020):

- There are 60 "upper-middle-income economies" (countries with GDP per capita between $3996 and $12,375 per year).
- There are 47 "lower middle income economies" (countries with GDP per capita between $1026 and $3995).
- There are 31 "low income economies" (countries with GDP per capita less than or equal to $1025 per year).

Similarly, the Global North as identified by the World Bank is made of 80 countries having high-income economies (those with GDP per capita of over $12,375 annually). In the same vein, as the First World, the Global North is made up of countries in West Europe; countries in Central and Eastern Europe that are also members of the European Union (EU), aside from Bulgaria and Romania; as well as the United States, Canada, Japan, South Korea, Australia, and New Zealand, along with about 40 other nations at various latitudes (CADTM, 2020). Likewise, the Global South, just like the Third World, according to a generalized map, is made up of Latin America, the Caribbean, the Middle East, North Africa, Africa South of the Sahara, South Asia, South-East Asia, the Pacific, Central Asia, Turkey, and countries in Central and Eastern Europe that are not EU members, as well as EU members Bulgaria and Romania.

In the views of Haug et al. (2021), the constant usage of the term Global South has not led to a more methodical approach of the idea or contributed to analytical framing by its many users. Similarly, Hickel et al. (2021) argue that most academic and policy institutions when presenting their classifications rely heavily on indices such as North–South when grouping countries outside the "high-income," "advanced economies," or "very high human development." The categorization systems established by these bureaucracies have a substantial impact on how powerful countries in the global economy treat classified countries. As such, the classification of a country as developing has significant impact on critical choices like aid, investment, credit, and democratic ratings accorded to them by the West. In essence, a country that transits to medium income status loses help but gains higher ratings for its credit worthiness and democracy (Dolan, 2018).

On the flip side, despite their significance, IR concepts and categorizations launched by Africans and scholars from the other Third World countries have not received academic fame like those of Western nativity. Notable amongst them are Thomas Tieku's African worldview of *Ubuntu* which suggests the re-conceptualization of states in a collectivist, societal way (Smith, 2018); Mohammed Ayoob's notion of "subaltern realism" which explains the origin and existence of state conflict (Ferencik, 2020); and Eduard Jordaan's 2003 schema on the "middle power" concept to include states in "the new middle." So many novel theories and conceptual elucidations from Africa sufficient to unravel complexities in IR have either been debunked or left on the fringes. Although modifications made by scholars in the West are accepted as genuine and added to the canon of theory, this is not necessarily the case for adaptations made by researchers in Africa.

Consequently, in a skewed distribution, accumulated wealth is concentrated in the North, while accumulated natural resources are domiciled in the South. This opposite reality reveals the continued exploitation of Africa and other countries in their category by the North. Virtually all the countries in the Northern Hemisphere have developed economies that benefit from international policies and IFI conditionalities. The implication of this is that the South is perpetually impoverished by the North. This is evident in the many loans, grants, aids, and bail-out funds given to countries in the Third World. According to Niyonkuru (2016), assistance in the form of economic bailouts appears as a way of exploiting these developing economies, as they tend to worsen their economic status in comparison to the budgetary aims set by the International Monetary Fund (IMF), which always compels the receiver to take actions that have negative implications in the long run.

Furthermore, in the global economy approach, countries are categorized differently as a result of the classification systems designed by international institutions and Western scholars in the IR field. Basically, on the area of development, a country's classification as a developing country has a significant impact on high-stakes decisions like aid, investment, and credit and democratic ratings. Whatever name is given to them, these countries are those that have high rates of child mortality, extreme poverty, inadequate economic and educational advancement, and poor natural resource self-consumption. These countries are susceptible to being exploited by powerful corporations and industrialized countries.

Thus, the essentiality of international organizations like the World Trade Organization (WTO) and IMF is not clearly representing the idea of liberal economic internationalism. More profound is the negative effect some of these organizations have on developing countries in Africa. For WTO, its free trade policy and lack of transparency give more leverage to multinational corporations (MNCs) and industrialized countries over African countries which export more of raw materials than finished goods. Hence, the construction of IR concepts further exacerbates inequalities that buttress the rich countries' continuous access to international policies to become richer and limit access to poor countries and make them poorer.

Issues of Global Polarities and Corruption in the International Relations System

Having identified elements of corruption in the previous sections, an analysis of corrupt practices within the different polars in the IR system is imperative for an in-depth analysis of what Africa is. In the field of IR, the concept of polarity refers to the dominance of one or more great powers over the international system. At different eras, powers are distributed across polars (powerful states) which control the affairs of IR within the international system. The world has transited among unipolar, bipolar, and multipolar world order in the IR system. At each phase, one or more states may exhibit hegemony over international affairs which largely shapes global politics and reveals corruption in the IR field. Since the development of the modern state, IR has also been dominated by one or more hegemons that influence the interpretations of theories and paradigms in world politics. The following subsections discuss these polars.

Multipolar World Order (1815–1945)

Following the end of the 30-year war, solidified with the Peace of Westphalia in 1648 and the subsequent Congress of Vienna in 1815, a new phase of international system began with multi power blocs. As Lebow points out, before the Treaty of

Westphalia, the great powers were at war for the most part and only experienced an almost ideal situation of peace between 1815 and 1914. Thus, the Congress of Vienna marked the development of the modern state, with rapid development and industrialization in Great Britain, Germany, France, the United States, Japan, and Italy.

The advancement in steel technology and industrialization accorded these countries' economic, military, and political influence in and around Europe. Most of these great powers formed alliances for fear of other power blocs usurping their powers. In 1894, the fear of Germany motivated the alliance between France and Russia, which in turn inspired the alliance between Germany and the Austro-Hungarian Empire (IWM, 2023). Bearing in mind that this was the era of slavery and colonialism, Africa was one of the major instruments for actualizing Western expansionist policy. According to Russo (2018), through direct conflict, colonization, and basic relations in the international system, the influence and acceptance of the great powers of Europe, especially those who participated in the systems rise and creation, was established.

This preceding situation infers that the corrupt practices in contemporary IR were derived from the foundations of European interpretation of the nation-state. The divide-and-rule policy that has left Africa as a war-ridden continent with gross underdevelopment was fashioned out of the multipolar system that zeroed in on a state's rise, leading to another state's fall. This necessitated the introduction of the "balance of power" doctrine in other to avoid mass destruction.

Similarly, the multipolar nature of the IR system in the early eighteenth century led to imperial and colonialist conquests in Africa, Asia, and Latin America by competing European powers seeking influence and power. The conquests of African and other nations were significant in boosting European military arsenals and trade markets. Again, the scramble and partition of Africa between 1881 and 1914, to a large extent, contributed to the peaceful century in Europe. In essence, given the availability of raw materials and cheap labor in Africa, imperialism was a convenient strategy for managing the myriads of problems ravaging Europeans' economies and their peaceful coexistence. Consequent on this, new states like Belgium, Germany and Italy entered into the trade of imperialism. The seeming value of Africa in Europe informed the much heated Berlin Conference in the winter of 1884–1885 where demarcation lines on the African map was subject to colonial possessions. Alluding to this, Evans (2011) suggests that the expansionist policy by the West was to cater for the changes in the European economy due to the increase of European nationalism. Nonetheless, the growing concern of Germany's unification and the opposing alliances in Europe did not only invalidate the balance of power system but made the two World Wars inevitable. In addition, with the Allied powers (Britain, France, Russia, Belgium, Serbia, Italy, and the United States), on the one hand, and the Central power (Germany, Austria-Hungary, and Turkey), on the other hand, competitions and battles were fought at the expense of Africa's natural and human resources.

These wars were fought despite the establishment of the LON which had a principal objective to maintain world peace through collective security. Even though

African colonies were not members of the LON at the time, but considering that its formation was premised on liberal thinking, the IR system was a misgiving. Africans were forced to support their colonizers and recruited as combatants to fight for Europeans against their wish. Over 1 million Africans comprising soldiers, porters, and laborers were active in World War I (Meldrum, 2018). For the European Allies, more than 2 million individuals throughout Africa made significant sacrifices during World Wars I & II. About 100,000 soldiers lost their lives in East Africa, 65,000 in French North and West Africa, and the remaining troops were left crippled by conflict, sickness, devastation, and infrastructure damage (Joseph, 2011). One of the most devastating events of this era for Africans was the sinking of the SS Mendi when Black South Africans were traveling by ship from England to France to deliver supplies to the front lines. A considerably larger British mail ship attacked the Mendi on a foggy night in February of 1917; the Mendi swiftly sank, killing 607 men. It was the single-largest death toll for Black South African civilians during the conflict (Meldrum, 2018).

Notwithstanding the multipolar system with the World Wars that manifested, it was significant in changing the tide of Africa's enslavement and colonialism. There was intense political and intellectual re-awakening, which led to demands for emancipation, freedom, and decolonization campaigns all over Africa (Joseph, 2011). Having fought in the World Wars, Africans believed that they were ready for freedom and this was instrumental to the nationalist struggles that led to the independence of most African states in the late 1950s and early 1960s. More profound was the outcome of the Second World War in 1945 which gave rise to a bipolar world order in the IR system.

Bipolar World Order (1945–1991)

By the end of the Second World War in 1945, the United Nations was formed and two super powers had emerged (the Soviet Union and the United States of America). The stealth battle between these two emerging global powers shaped the IR system in the next four decades (Lupitu, 2014). The bipolar world order was a function of the ambition of the United States to advance capitalism and democracy and the Soviet Union's desire to promote communist principles. Even though the conflicts were mostly covert, they heated steady pressure on the rest of the world, particularly Africa.

The Cold War era, as popularly known, was significant in revealing corrupt practices in the practicality of IR as a field. The era witnessed the political conflict that arose after World War II between the Soviet Union and the United States with their respective allies. The political conflict was devoid of military confrontations, but was however an exposition of intelligence gathering, arms stocking, and nuclear weapon threats. Several times, these tensions nearly erupted into full-fledged war, particularly with the Cuban missile crisis of 1962. Africa was made to choose between two brides and faced the consequences of rejecting a choice. Appearing more as a reward and sanction relationship, proxy wars like the Nigeria-Biafra War in 1967, Apartheid in South Africa, etc. (Jackson, 2010; Heitz, 2016) were sponsored by either the East or the West ideological camp.

Likewise, scholarships were given to many African nationals based on where their loyalty lies. International institutions like the World Bank and IMF were very instructive during this era in sabotaging Africa's development. In all, the resultant effect of the bipolar system was a reflection of oppression and aggression on Africa and Africans. During the nationalist struggles for independence in Africa, the two superpowers, the United States and the Soviet Union, used arms and financial resources as convenient tools to deepen divisions within African colonies and sustain their economic dominance on the continent. This influenced the many military coups and civil wars that occurred shortly after independence in most African states.

In another vein, the bipolar system revived African consciousness toward cooperation and the need for self-reliance, which the East-West rivalry could not guarantee. Organizations, such as the Organization of African Unity (OAU), Non-Alignment Movement (NAM), G-77, etc., were remarkable in providing a balance for Third World states. Although the actual reality of these institutions in projecting Africa's interest remains debatable, they were however a viable response to oppressive tendencies from the two power blocs at the time. According to Polet (2016), the disdain for this idea was a mirror of the West's more or less open antagonism toward the Global South, which was growing more politically organized and confrontational within the United Nations. In retaliation, the United States destabilized the Southern nations allied with the Soviet bloc, halted investment in the most militant United Nations organizations, and liberalized international development organizations.

Despite the application of double standards in a globalized world, the bipolar system contributed to the independence of African colonies, the development of African-centered institutions, and the spread of capitalism and democratization. Dolorously, the effect of bipolar world order continues to destabilize the continent (Atomic Heritage Foundation, 2018). Since its take off, there have been intra-ethnic wars, genocide, and highly dysfunctional economies that are still evident today.

Unipolar World Order: What Next?

Following the end of the Cold War, propelled by the collapse of the Soviet Union in 1991, the United States emerged as a single powerful nation globally. This was the beginning of the unipolar era that saw the global dominance of the United States combined in economic, cultural, military, and political spheres. It was a turning point in IR, mainly because the hegemonic dominance of one global power was foreseen to activate economic development and progress across the world (Wohlforth, 1999; Kagan, 2000). Even though general assumptions were of the opinion that a multipolar system after the Cold War was eminent, scholars like Krauthammer (1991) opposed this standpoint, stating that the center of world power (the United States) is the unchallenged superpower (Rourke, 2007). The American hegemony accelerated by globalization spread the ideology of capitalism and democratization across Africa (Kiely & Marfleet, 1998). To this end, Western democracy and democratization became the prerequisite for African states seeking access to international aid and loans from the IMF and the World Bank.

Yet again, as observed during the bipolar world order, elements of corruption in the application of IR principles, especially as it relates to Africa, were evident. International institutions were used by American hegemon to perpetrate its interest globally. As Ipinyomi (2016) asserts, Africa is left out of the international community's vision or formulation due to its imperfect state structures, which causes conflict between their governments' allegiances to the people and the international community. In effect, the targeted crusade on democracy in Africa was to dominate African economies through American market-oriented policies and not necessarily to better the lives of the African populace.

With extreme hardship and incessant conflicts, and the reoccurrence of military incursions, most African states were pressured into embracing the Western principles of capitalism and democracy. Even so, there has been economic retrogression, increasing poverty and underdevelopment since the end of the bipolar world order. Considerably, the neo-liberal obsession and confidence that the United States hegemonic control will bring about unipolar peace therefore became a distant reality for the African continent. For instance, Africa fought more wars under the unipolar system, with less or inadequate intervention to quell crisis of devastating consequence. Precisely, the conflict in the Democratic Republic of Congo—DRC (formerly Zaire) that began in 1994 was not resolved by the United Nations until its Observer Mission in the DRC was established in 1999 (Ngara, 2017). Likewise, the United States did not take any immediate action on the civil wars in Sierra Leone and Liberia. The Rwandan genocide may not have claimed as many lives to the tune of about 800,000 persons (Bhalla, 2019) had the international community waded in promptly. Without any intention of encouraging impunity among African leaders, the partial and unfair approach of the International Criminal Court (ICC) and the United Nations held sway.

The United Nations Security Council (UNSC) intervention in Africa is noteworthy. Bearing in mind that similar requests from other organizations were accepted favorably, despite their contentious circumstances, the refusal to attend to repeated requests by the African Union over the past 7 years suggests the application of double standards (Usman, 2013).

A New World Order? What Next for Africa in International Relations?

For over three decades since the United States emerged as the single hegemon in the IR system, there has been several debates on the future of the world order, especially within the context of Africa. No doubt, events such as the September 11, 2001 terrorist attack in the United States, economic recessions, diffusion of technology, the rise of China, the growth of nationalism, issues on climate change, the Coronavirus Disease (COVID)-2019 pandemic, and the Russian-Ukrainian War have consistently established Africa's indispensability in IR. Hence, any new world order must redirect thoughts toward an IR discipline which embraces the African ideology of IR.

While the United States may not appear as powerful as it was after the Second World War, its military and political might which are major factors for determining global powers remains unparalleled. However, this dynamic is likely to shift in the near future, with the growing development various states globally. For instance, most underdeveloped states have become developed and seeking new rules of the game. In a meeting of economic partnership of the heads of Brazil, Russia, India, China, and South Africa (BRICS), the idea to launch a new single currency from a "basket" of the currencies of all the BRICS member states was key (Lesseraux, 2022). More so, with the organization's membership list continuing to grow, countries like Argentina and Iran have submitted membership applications to BRICS. Be that as it may, the world has unequivocally moved toward cooperation and collectiveness facilitated by global connectedness. Undoubtedly, Africa is at the center of any new world order and must not be ignored in the field of IR.

The COVID-2019 pandemic and the Russia-Ukraine War, among other calamities, bring to the fore the increasing need for not only applying international rules without fear or favor, but also engaging new models from Africa which have proven successful. In particular, even though Africa was initially claimed by the World Health Organization (WHO) to be severely hit by COVID-2019, the pandemic was least devastating in Africa compared to other continents. This remarkable success made possible by several scientific and unorthodox procedures are yet to be investigated either for reference point or to improve the body of knowledge. The world has become individualized, and to eschew corruption in the theory and application of IR, neither precolonial African ideologies nor postcolonial origins should be disregarded or trivialized.

With emerging centers of influence like China, India, Russia, and Turkey, Africa now participates in recurring summit-level meetings. At the same time, Africa continues to take part in summits with the European Union, the United States, France, and Japan. Trade with the East has increased, and so have commercial loans and development aid supporting Africa's large domestic infrastructure development goal (Olukoshi, 2023). This changing dynamics reveals that Africa is central to development in almost all regions and continents of the world. Given its strategic position as the largest voting bloc in the United Nations General Assembly (UNGA), projection of constituting 25% of the world's population by 2050, overwhelming youth population, natural resources, and potential for global power, Africa is a key stakeholder in the global arena that must contribute to the narrative of the IR field.

International Law and Africa's Development

The machinations of IR cannot be defined without international law. Having established the world orders and their unique characteristics, it is expedient to analyze the laws guiding the relations of states particularly within the context of Africa's development. Explicitly, international law is a system of rules and principles governing the conduct of states and other international actors in their relations with one another. These laws are not only the building block for states' interactions but also define how states wield power. Therefore, international law, particularly as it applies to Africa's development, is concerned with issues such as sovereignty, leadership, peace and security, economic agreements, and human rights (Yihdego et al., 2019; Maluwa, 2020). While international law provides a framework for collaboration and the resolution of global challenges, its impact on Africa's development has been complicated. African economies, for instance, are very much restricted to the wonders of free trade, capital flows, trade liberalization, and export orientation, which provide realistic development policy prescriptions (Chime, 2014). Some international laws like the African Growth and Opportunity Act established in 2000 was essentially to establish trade relations between the United States and African states; howbeit, not all African countries are eligible to receive benefits and partnerships.

Africa's abundant natural resources have frequently been used to the benefit of external parties, and international law has played a role in shaping these dynamics. Many African countries have been subjected to exploitative contracts and trading practices, resulting in resource depletion and environmental deterioration. International law, particularly dealing with trade and investment treaties, has at times benefited multinational corporations and foreign interests over African governments. The lack of sufficient legislation and enforcement procedures has allowed these practices to continue, thereby stifling economic development in many African countries.

The international financial system and institutions have a significant influence on Africa's economic growth. African countries have frequently accrued substantial debt burdens, with international financial institutions influencing the terms of these debts. While debt reduction measures have brought some relief, the terms of loans and aid have frequently required African countries to implement specified economic policies. These circumstances, governed by international financial restrictions, have occasionally hampered the development of domestic industry and social programs. While these laws present chances for African countries to gain market access, they also pose difficulties in negotiating advantageous conditions. International trade law and regulations can occasionally impair African countries by limiting their capacity to gain equal access to Western markets.

Similarly, Africa presently has only a weakened type of sovereignty, characterized by the failure of states to have complete authority over the content of their laws. For instance, the UNSC must decide "the existence of a threat to the peace or an act of aggression" and call on the disputing parties "to settle or even authorize the use of force to maintain or restore international peace and security" (Mbaku, 2018, p. 44). Article 34 of the United Nations Charter empowers the UNSC to "investigate any dispute, or any situations that may lead to international friction or give rise to a dispute, in order to determine whether the continuation of the dispute or situation is likely to jeopardize the maintenance of international peace and security" (Mbaku, 2018, p. 44). Nevertheless, as Christian Reus-Smit argues, the extent to which legitimate force can be employed globally to restrain illegitimate power locally is at the heart of world politics' complex interplay between order and justice (Mbaku, 2018). This suggest that international law can be applied negatively to advance alleged order and justice.

In the same vein, the ICC is one initiative that aims to remedy violations of human rights and encourage accountability. The ICC has been criticized for what is believed to be its prejudice against African presidents, which has caused friction and occasionally hampered cooperation. Luis Moreno-Ocampo, the former chief prosecutor for the ICC, announced in July of 2008 that he intended to bring charges against Omar al-Bashir, the President of Sudan, for violating human rights in relation to the country's conflict in the Darfur region. The ICC announced on March 3, 2009, that President Bashir had an arrest warrant issued for him because of accusations of war crimes and crimes against humanity. The Ugandan government brought the court's first case in 2003, and it returned five charges against prominent Lord's Resistance Army (LRA) leaders who are currently at large. In addition, it has jailed a number of rebel commanders from the DRC and the neighboring Central African Republic, among them a former vice president. Inadvertently, four issues stand out as indicative of the role that international law plays in Africa. Hence, decolonization, the use of sanctions to attain racial equality; the incorporation of international human rights norms, including the emerging "right" of good governance in African constitutions; and the increasing acceptance and application of "intervention" in nations that have experienced disintegration remain laws and action by the West to perpetually keep Africa in the brinks.

Conclusion and Recommendations

In the preceding sections, I have established that an analysis of corruption in the IR discipline gives an in-depth understanding of contemporary global relations among states and their effects on Africa. I have also examined the origin and development of IR, the conceptual taxonomies in the discipline, and evidence of corruption in the theoretical underpinnings and application of IR in Africa. In addition, using the three levels of global polarity, I revealed the core issues of corruption in the IR discipline. Utilizing evidence culled from unequal terms of engagement by international institutions and world powers throughout history, I further demonstrated that Africa's global positioning has been a deliberate agenda by the West to keep the continent under perpetual domination. World orders may change from unipolar, bipolar, or multipolar; however, the sustained domination of Africa by the West remains constant.

Despite the fact that African scholars have advanced some narratives, including those against colonialism, racism, and apartheid, and equality for all peoples, Eurocentric ideas such as Westphalianism, civil and political rights, liberal democracy, and the free market economy have gained more attention and credibility in IR. Thus, theories and conceptualizations in IR are conducted and bound by Western perspectives, with Western ideas being reinforced as shared values.

To address this anomaly, first, African ideologies to IR such as *Ubuntu, Ujamaa, Umunna bu ike*, etc., should not only be accommodated but accepted as IR theories, once they meet IR standards. Global collaboration in research is necessary; thus, African scholars should take the initiative, and scholars outside of Africa should not disregard African perspectives. The African thought which predisposes the centrality of African interests, values, and perspectives should place Africa at the center of any IR analysis. IR theories can benefit from African experiences and scholarship, further contributing to the development of the field.

The aforementioned initiatives can be achieved through insights from African scholars, non-African scholars working on Africa, and a close interpretation of African experiences. Also, the focus on Africa should stem from an agent of IR knowledge, rather than an object of IR study.

Second, from the angle of practice, international laws should be obeyed and respected by all states. While the international community has no central policing system like nation-states to enforce international laws, civil society groups and the growing voice of the voiceless through technology should be leveraged to influence compliance by state actors. Similarly, laws binding states in the IR system are not static and, thus, should be assessed from time to time in order to accommodate new realities in global relations. More importantly, Africa must push for laws that will enable development in the continent. To do this, the continent must first strengthen continental and national laws that promote aggressive African theories of development and eschew corruption. Concomitantly, Africa must establish systems and institutions that work internally to boost local products and Africa's capacity that can compete favorably in the global space.

References

Acharya, A., & Buzan, B. (2019). *The making of global international relations*. Cambridge University Press.

Atomic Heritage Foundation. (2018). Proxy wars during the cold war: *Africa*. Retrieved October 29, 2022, from https://www.atomicheritage.org/history/proxy-wars-during-cold-war-africa

Bhalla, N. (2019, April 6). Factbox: Rwanda remembers the 800,000 killed on 25th anniversary of genocide. Reuters. Retrieved October 30, 2022, from https://www.reuters.com/article/us-rwanda-genocide-anniversary-factbox-idUSKCN1RI0FV

Chime, J. (2014). Analysis of the African growth and opportunity act and Nigeria-United States trade relations, 2000–2012. *African Journal of Politics and Administrative Studies, 6*(1), 65–78.

Coate, R. A., Griffin, J. A., & Elliott-Gower, S. (2015). Interdependence in international organization and global governance. In *Oxford Research Encyclopedia of International Studies*. https://doi.org/10.1093/acrefore/9780190846626.013.110

Committee for the Abolition of Illegitimate Debt. (2020, February 11). South/North /Developing Countries/Developed Countries: What is it all about? *CADTM*. Retrieved October 15, 2022, from https://www.cadtm.org/South-North-Developing-Countries-Developed-Countries-What-is-it-all-about

Dolan, L. R. (2018). *The politics of classification in global development (Doctoral thesis, Columbia University)*. Columbia University Libraries. https://doi.org/10.7916/D8NZ9R20

Evans, S. R. (2011, November 22). The scramble for Africa. Gresham College. Retrieved October 29, 2022, from https://www.gresham.ac.uk/watch-now/scramble-africa

Ferencik, J. (2020). What is subaltern realism? (Ayoob Briefly Explained). *The humanists of our generation*. Retrieved October 26, 2022, from https://medium.com/the-humanists-of-our-generation/what-is-subaltern-realism-ayoob-briefly-explained-f904144ccdb8

Gbadamosi, A. (2020). Understanding the developed/developing country taxonomy. *A4ID*. Retrieved October 15, 2022, from https://www.a4id.org/policy/understanding-the-developeddeveloping-country-taxonomy/

Gondwe, G. (2022). Can African scholars speak? Situating African voices in international communication scholarship. *Media, Culture & Society, 44*(4), 848–859.

Haug, S., Braveboy-Wagner, J., & Maihold, G. (2021). The 'Global South' in the study of world politics: Examining a meta category. *Third World Quarterly, 42*(9), 1923–1944.

Heitz, J. A. (2016). The impact of the cold war on African security. *African Security Review, 25*(4), 427–430.

Hickel, J., Sullivan, D., & Zoomkawala, H. (2021). Plunder in the post-colonial era: Quantifying drain from the global south through unequal exchange, 1960–2018. *New Political Economy, 26*(6), 1030–1047.

Ipinyomi, F. (2016). The impact of African philosophy on the realization of international community and the observance of international law. *International Community Law Review, 18*(1), 3–33.

IWM. (2023). What you need to know about pre-first world war alliances. Retrieved October 29, 2022, from https://www.iwm.org.uk/history/what-you-need-to-know-about-pre-first-world-war-alliances

Jackson, A. (2010). The impact of the cold war and new scrambles for Africa. *Journal of Southern African Studies, 36*(1), 229–239.

Jones, B. G. (2005). Africa and the poverty of international relations. *Third World Quarterly, 26*(6), 987–1003.

Jordaan, E. (2003). The concept of a middle power in international relations: Distinguishing between emerging and traditional middle powers. *Politikon, 30*(1), 165–181.

Joseph, K. B. (2011). Effects of the two world wars on the African continent. GRIN. Retrieved October 29, 2022, from https://www.grin.com/document/183276

Kagan, R. (2000). The benevolent empire. In G. P. Hastedt (Ed.), *American foreign policy annual edition*. New York, NY.

Kiely, R., & Marfleet, P. (Eds.). (1998). *Globalization and the third world*. Routledge.

Krauthammer, C. (1991). The unipolar moment. *Foreign Affairs, 70*(1), 23–33.

Lesseraux, M. (2022, July 1). It's the end of the unipolar world as we know it (and I feel …). Pressenza. Retrieved October 30, 2022, from https://www.pressenza.com/2022/07/its-the-end-of-the-unipolar-world-as-we-know-it-and-i-feel/

Lupitu, R. (2014). The collapse of the bipolar world. White house-kremlin relations between 1985–1991 from realism perspective. *Revista de Administratie Publica si Politici Sociale, 12*(1), 61.

Maluwa, T. (2020). Reassessing aspects of the contribution of African states to the development of international law through African regional multilateral treaties. *Michigan Journal of International Law, 41*, 327.

Mbaku, J. M. (2018). International law and limits on the sovereignty of African states. *Florida Journal of International Law, 30*(2), 44–110.

McClelland, C. A., & Pfaltzgraff, R. (2022, August 18). International relations. Encyclopedia Britannica. Retrieved October 10, 2022, from https://www.britannica.com/topic/international-relations

Meldrum, A. (2018, December 1). Africans played key, often unheralded, role in world war I. AP News. Retrieved October 29, 2022, from https://apnews.com/article/e33d9b25471a4f5d9ac94cccce102fb0

Morumbasi, K. (2021). An African worldview on international relations theory and state policy, advances in African economic, social and political development. In A. M. Vasiliev, D. A. Degterev, & T. M. Shaw (Eds.), *Africa and the formation of the new system of international relations* (1st ed.). Springer.

Mvulane-Moloi, T. (2012). Afrikan contribution to international relations theory: An Afrocentric philosophical enquiry. *Africology: The Journal of Pan African Studies, 9*(1), 241–532.
Ngara, C. O. (2017). America's global hegemony since the collapse of the Soviet Union: Implications for Africa's development. *Global Journal of Social Sciences Studies, 3*(2), 113–121.
Niyonkuru, F. (2016). Failure of foreign aid in developing countries: A quest for alternatives. *Business and Economics Journal, 7*(3), 1–9.
Olukoshi, A. (2023, June 12). From rule-taker to rule-maker: Africa in the changing world order. *European Council on Foreign Relations*. Retrieved September 29, 2023, from https://ecfr.eu/article/from-rule-taker-to-rule-maker-africa-in-the-changing-world-order/
Polet, F. (2016). Revisiting the north-south view of the world. *CETRI*. Retrieved October 16, 2022, from https://www.cetri.be/revisiting-the-north-south-view-of?lang=fr
Rourke, J. T. (2007). *International politics on the world stage*. McGraw-Hill.
Russo, A. (2018). Lessons from the past: Analyzing a multipolar world and shifting transatlantic relationships Student Work 1. Retrieved October 29, 2022, from https://pdxscholar.library.pdx.edu/polisci_student/1
Silver, M. (2015, January 4). If you shouldn't call it the Third World, what should you call it? *Goats and Soda*. Retrieved October 16, 2022, from https://www.npr.org/sections/goatsandsoda/2015/01/04/372684438/if-you-shouldnt-call-it-the-third-world-what-should-you-call-it#:~:text=The%20First%20World%20consisted%20of,assigned%20to%20the%20Third%20World
Smith, K. (2018). Reshaping international relations: Theoretical innovations from Africa. *All Azimuth*, 1–12.
Steinmetz, J. (2021). International relations in politics, power, and purpose: An orientation to political science. FHSU Digital Press. Retrieved October 8, 2022, from https://fhsu.pressbooks.pub/orientationpolisci/front-matter/introduction/
Usman, T. (2013, October). African Union accuses International Criminal Court of double standards. *Premium Times*. Retrieved October 30, 2022, from https://www.premiumtimesng.com/news/146497-african-union-accuses-international-criminal-court-double-standards.html
Van Wyk, J. A. (2015). Africa in international relations. In P. H. Bischoff, K. Aning, & A. Acharya (Eds.), *Africa in global international relations: Emerging approaches to theory and practice*. Routledge.
Wohlforth, W. C. (1999). The stability of the unipolar world. *International Security, 24*(1), 5–41.
Yihdego, Z., Desta, M. G., & Hailu, M. B. (2019). In pursuit of peace and prosperity through international law. In *Ethiopian yearbook of international law 2018: In pursuit of peace and prosperity* (pp. 3–8).

Omosefe Oyekanmi holds a PhD in Political Science. She is a post-doctoral fellow at the Pan-African Women Studies Unit, Institute of Pan-African Thought and Conversation, University of Johannesburg, South Africa. She is also a research fellow at the Nigerian Institute of Social and Economic Research in Ibadan, Nigeria. She is a recipient of the British Academy funded program, Writing and Researching the Political Economy of Inequality in Africa, cohorts 2021 and 2023, and a prestigious scholar of CODESRIA College of Mentors (2019). She has over 30 published articles on humanitarianism, development, public policy, gender issues, and international peace building.

Mathematics

Isatu Ramatu Bangura

This chapter examines some ways Africa has been conceptualized vis-à-vis Mathematics, which is generally denoted as the abstract science of number, quantity, and space. Accordingly, the major question probed is this: How has Africa been conceptualized in terms of the academic discipline of Mathematics?

In light of the fact that the major question stated above is a "How?" variety, the *explanatory case study* approach is a suitable method for analyzing the information gathered for this chapter. The approach is denoted as follows: "The Explanatory Case Study method is used to connect ideas to understand cause and effect relating to a particular phenomenon…it has also been used to research complex systems in order to look for explanations of the nature of certain relationships…and should consist of an accurate description of the facts of a case, considerations of alternative explanations, and a conclusion based on credible explanations that are congruent with the facts" (Bangura et al., 2019, pp. 64–65).

Thus, and for the sake of brevity, the following three among the most discussed aspects of the nexus between Africa and the academic discipline of Mathematics are explored in the rest of this chapter: (1) Africa as the birthplace of Mathematics, (2) the state of school Mathematics education in South Africa, and (3) the best mathematics teacher in the world being Sandile Mathebula. Before examining these features, however, I commence with a brief review of how the field of Mathematics is commonly conceptualized. In the end, a conclusion is drawn and recommendations tendered.

I. R. Bangura (✉)
The African Institution, Washington, DC, USA

A. K. Bangura, J. A. Ifedi (eds.), *Conceptualizations of Africa*, African Studies and Research Forum Series, https://doi.org/10.1007/978-3-031-74535-5_12

Mathematics: A Conceptualization

There are two common ways the subject of Mathematics has been conceptualized. One way is in terms of it being studied in its own right—i.e. *pure mathematics*; and, the other way concerns it being explored apropos it being applied to other academic disciplines such as engineering and physics—i.e., *applied mathematics.* I discuss these two facets separately in the remainder of this section for the sake of clarity.

Pure Mathematics

The major focus of Pure Mathematics is on mathematical ideas. The distinction between this branch of Mathematics and Applied Mathematics is not absolute in that while the former is "the most abstract" area of the field, it still has many features that are applicable in everyday life. Also, since it is considered to be a "broad topic," its ideas have therefore been applied to different academic disciplines such as Biology, Chemistry, Engineering, Logic, Physics, and the Social Sciences (StudySmarter, 2023). In the rest of this subsection, I briefly discuss some of the important themes employed by scholars who study Pure Mathematics one by one for simplicity.

First, *Proof* refers to a logical argument which demonstrates whether or not a mathematical statement is true. It is characterized as being "robust" because it takes into account all possibilities, and it must be free of "holes" in the logic. A Proof is built on axioms and is extremely important because without it, mathematicians would not know that their mathematical results are correct. Many different techniques are utilized to prove statements, the discussion of which is beyond the scope of this subsection (StudySmarter, 2023).

Second, *Algebra* deals with the abstract representation of numbers that makes it possible for mathematicians to make general statements consisting of mathematical operations. For instance, should mathematicians want to write a mathematical statement involving an unknown quantity, they could refer to it as x and then see how this variable would change as the statement changes (StudySmarter, 2023).

Third, *Functions* are employed to apply a certain operation or set of operations to an input value in order to yield an output value. Functions are frequently expressed as $f(x)$, denoting that the function has a variable as a value, usually "x" for simpler functions. A basic example is $f(x) = x + 4$, which means that this function simply adds 4 to an input represented by x. Functions are closely connected with graphs, and being able to plot them is an important skill (StudySmarter, 2023).

Fourth, *Coordinate Geometry* is utilized to study Geometry that deals with coordinate systems, frequently dealing with two dimensions with x and y axes. Coordinate Geometry can also be employed for three-dimensional systems. In addition, they can be constituted as graphs on coordinate systems (StudySmarter, 2023).

Fifth, *Sequences and Series* refer to a list of numerical values that follow a pattern or rule, frequently connected by some basic function. Also, closely connected to these sequences and series is the binomial expansion. Accordingly, a mathematician will need to know how to (a) generate terms of a sequence, (b) identify their common function, and (c) find their sums—the sum of a sequence is known as the series (StudySmarter, 2023). I must add here that a "binomial expansion" is a method utilized by mathematicians to expand and simplify algebraic expressions in the form $(x + y)^n$ into a sum of terms of the form $ax^b y^c$. Thus, if n is an integer, then b and c will also be integers, and $b + c = n$.

Sixth, *Trigonometry* deals with angles and the geometric lines of shapes, especially triangles. The subject's applications have been much "wider," as they transcend triangles. It is utilized to study trigonometric functions such as sine, cosine, and tangent and their reciprocals, radians (an alternative form of measuring angles to degrees), and other important rules (StudySmarter, 2023).

Seventh, *Exponentials and Logarithms* are complimentary. The former are functions of the form N^x that increase or decrease quickly as x increases, as number N is raised to a power of x. The latter are the inverse function of an exponential. They can be used to find the power to which a number was raised to get another number. For any exponential, there is a logarithm in the form $\log_a(b)$ (StudySmarter, 2023).

Eighth, *Differentiation* alludes to a technique used to derive rates of change, or gradients of functions. This can also be delineated by drawing the gradient lines of graphs. Since it is not always easy to do or is exact, mathematicians also do it analytically. The result of a differentiation calculation is referred to as the "derivative of a function." The following are several rules that one needs to know in order to solve more complex problems: (a) the "product rule" is used when two functions are multiplied by each other; (b) the "quotient rule" is employed when two functions are divided by each other; and (c) the "chain rule" is utilized for composite functions. A user of the method must also know how to generate trigonometric functions (StudySmarter, 2023).

Ninth, *Integration* is a method used by mathematicians to determine the area under a graph; and, it is also the inverse operation of derivation. The symbol $\int$ is utilized to represent an "indefinite integral." A definite integral, which refers to the area of a given range, is represented as $\int_b$, where a and b indicate a desired range of values (StudySmarter, 2023).

Tenth, *Numerical Methods* refer to techniques mathematicians utilize to estimate mathematical solutions that are difficult to derive. An example of the application of these methods involves estimating the roots of equations and integration. An instance is the use of the Newton–Raphson method, which is an algorithm that is employed repeatedly in order to improve its accuracy each time it is iterated. Underscoring the observation I made earlier that the distinction between Pure and Applied Mathematics is not absolute, numerical methods have been applied extensively and are quite essential not only by mathematicians but also by engineers. Some real-world examples of the utility of Numerical Methods include (a) solving problems in naval engineering, aerospace, and structural mechanics; (b) machine learning algorithms; (c) weather prediction; and (d) price estimations such as the ones done by flight companies (StudySmarter, 2023).

And eleventh, *Vectors* comprise quantities that entail both magnitude and direction, and they can be utilized to indicate the position of a point in relation to another point. Very useful to the representation of vectors are coordinates. Vectors can be expressed using unit vectors i and j, representing the x and y directions, respectively. Also, systems of vectors can be expressed as column vectors when there are two or more vectors. In addition, one needs to know the fundamentals of *3D* vectors at A level, where the z-direction represented by k is introduced (StudySmarter, 2023).

Applied Mathematics

Applied Mathematics is characterized as an "interdisciplinary field of study and research" used to connect the subject of Mathematics with an "extensive scope" of areas of application (University of Waterloo, 2023). Some of these areas include engineering and science, and/or the development of novel or improved methods to meet new real-world challenges. The major goals of the field are (a) explaining observed phenomena; and (b) predicting new, as yet unobserved, phenomena. The emphasis is therefore on both the mathematics—for example, the development of new methods to meet the challenges of new problems—and the real world. Concomitantly, individuals specializing in Applied Mathematics collaborate with experimentalists in the physical and biological sciences, engineering, and the social sciences to see their research results come to life. Also, the generation of the results hinges upon knowledge of various branches of Mathematics, such as analysis, differential equations, and stochastics, utilizing analytical and numerical methods (Northwestern University, 2023).

There are so many subareas of Applied Mathematics that it will require an entire book to cover all of them thoroughly. For the sake of conciseness, I briefly discuss eight of them in this subsection, and individually for perspicuity.

First, *Continuum and Fluid Mechanics* concern the procedures used to study the behavior of materials by disregarding the behavior's distinct nature. To start with, a "continuum" refers to an area that can keep being repeatedly divided infinitely, with no individual particles. It is a simplification that allows mathematicians and scientists to examine the movement of matter on scales larger than the distances between particles. Thus, when investigating the movement of the atmosphere, the fact that it is composed of atoms is ignored. In any case, it would be impossible to predict the motion of each atom. Hence, when addressing questions such as how warm the weather will be tomorrow, mathematicians and scientists are only interested in the average behavior of large numbers of atoms, instead of their individual motion. Accordingly, continuum analysis is employed to investigate a wide array of phenomena such as the flow of air and water, and rock slides (the individual particles being large rocks), snow avalanches, blood flow, and even galaxy evolution. Next, Fluid Mechanics is a subarea of Continuum Mechanics that focuses on the behavior of fluids such as water and gases like air (University of Waterloo, 2023).

Second, *Control Theory* involves using feedback to affect the behavior of a system in order to achieve a desired outcome. An analyst can distinguish the following two classes of systems for which the theory plays an indispensable role: (1) “man-made systems” and (2) “biological systems.” A basic example of a “man-made system” is a “cruise control for a car, whose actual speed is recorded by the speedometer and is ‘fed-back’ and compared to the speed setting on the cruise control, which causes the engine to accelerate if the speed is too low. The cruise control device is referred to as the controller in the system” (University of Waterloo, 2023, p. 1). Indeed, the theory has been closely connected to the fields of engineering and technology, which have been its “traditional sphere of influence, dating back several centuries. For example, in the 18th Century, the invention of the regulator for a steam engine, a type of control mechanism, had a significant impact on industrial development in Europe. The development of the mathematical theory of control, however, began much later and has taken place mainly during the past 60 years” (University of Waterloo, 2023, p. 1).

Third, *Differential Equations* are commonly traced to British mathematician, physicist, astronomer, alchemist, and theologian Isaac Newton’s statement dating back 150 years that “It is useful to solve differential equations” (quoted by University of Waterloo, 2023, p. 1). We are informed that since his pronouncement, researchers in many fields have found the statement to be true, especially in recent times, with the advent of powerful personal computers making it possible to solve complicated differential equations numerically in a routine manner. We are also told that Newton’s enthusiasm was due to his success in using Differential Equations to give the first mathematical description of planetary orbits (University of Waterloo, 2023). For a basic understanding of the method, it behooves me to add a simple definition of “Differential Equation” that it is a statement that the values of two mathematical expressions are equal (indicated by the = sign) involving derivatives (things that are based on other sources) of a function (a relationship or expression involving one or more variables) or functions.

Fourth, *Dynamical Systems* are either physical or biological man-made temporal systems. Examples include “the Space Shuttle in orbit around the earth, an ecosystem with competing species, the nervous system of a simple organism, and the expanding universe” (University of Waterloo, 2023, p. 1). Mathematicians study Dynamical Systems by representing them in terms of Differential Equations. Accordingly, the state of a Dynamical System at an instance of time is delineated by “a point in an n-dimensional space called the state space (the dimension n depends on how complicated the systems is—for a double pendulum, n = 4). As time passes the point moves, sweeping out a curve in the state space, called a trajectory of the system (mathematically, this curve is a solution of the governing differential equations)…A very important aspect of dynamical systems is that they are nonlinear” (University of Waterloo, 2023, p. 1).

Fifth, *Quantum Theory* hinges on the notion that certain effects are subtle and difficult to calculate. Thus, the theory postulates that Classical Physics is incapable of explicating easy-to-observe phenomena that Quantum Theory explains very well. These phenomena include (a) “blackbody radiation,” (b) “the stability of atoms,” (c) “line spectra of atoms,” (d) “radioactive decay,” and (e) “the photoelectric effect.” Stated differently, Classical Physics fails to describe the real world. Therefore, the explication of the aforementioned phenomena called for "the fundamental insight that on the scale of atoms energy is quantised, i.e. it can only be transferred in discrete packets, called *quanta* (the Planck Hypothesis). For example, ordinary light comes in discrete packets of energy called photons" (University of Waterloo, 2023, p. 1).

Sixth, *Relativity and Cosmology* hinge on General Relativity Theory which is the basis for two disciplines. One discipline is "Cosmology," which studies the structure and origin of the Universe on the largest scales. The second discipline is "Relativistic Astrophysics," which investigates the galaxies, quasars, neutron stars, etc. (University of Waterloo, 2023).

Seventh, *Scientific Computing* deals with the "indispensable role" that computer simulations play in the development of mathematical models for technological advancement and scientific research in biomedical research, satellite communication systems, pollution control, etc. In this pursuit, mathematicians develop fast and accurate algorithms for solving a wide variety of problems on computers. As such, algorithm development is most successful when it is grounded in solid mathematics, combined with an understanding of the relevant computer application (University of Waterloo, 2023).

And eighth, *Waves* (i.e., periodic disturbances of the particles of substances which may be propagated without net movement of the particles, such as in the passage of undulating motion, heat, or sound) are studied by mathematicians because there are different forms of them all around us. Waves range from "sound waves, electromagnetic waves, including visible light and radio waves, to large scale high and low pressure systems in the atmosphere, called Rossby waves, that affect our weather. Surface waves are another familiar type of wave which can bring a lot of joy to children and surfers or in large storms can batter boats and shorelines" (University of Waterloo, 2023, p. 1). Since Waves also have nonlinear behaviors and can manifest themselves in different ways, they therefore affect us in many ways as well. An oft-cited example is "surface water waves for which the wave crests can propagate faster than the troughs. This can been easily seen at the beach where shoaling waves break and topple over as the wave crest moves ahead of the base of the wave" (University of Waterloo, 2023, p. 1). In addition, "nonlinearity" has been observed in "waves of different amplitude propagating at different speeds and interacting in other strange ways" (University of Waterloo, 2023, p. 1).

Africa as the Birthplace of Mathematics

There are many topics that can be discussed when it comes to Africa as the place for the genesis of Mathematics. I will discuss three of these topics in this section. The first topic is about most discussions concerning early Mathematics in Africa are about Kemet/Ancient Egypt. The second topic is how Africa South of the Sahara has been written out of Mathematics history. And the third topic deals with Europeans thought the African people they captured and enslaved were not intelligent.

First, vis-à-vis the history of African Mathematics being mostly about Egypt, this orientation marginalizes the much earlier Mathematics in other parts of Africa. For instance, about 35,000 years ago in the Lebombo Mountains of Swaziland, the Lebombo bone was found. It is made of a baboon fibula and was most likely used as a measuring device. It could have been used for menstrual cycles or lunar cycles as well (TaNeter.org, 2023).

Another baboon fibula was found in what is known as the Democratic Republic of Congo and dates to about 20,000 BC. It is known as the Ishango bone and has inscriptions that represent various quantities. On the left are odd numbers with prime numbers between 10 and 20. The right side has added and subtracted numbers. Both columns add up to 60, which is double the lunar or menstrual cycle (TaNeter.org, 2023).

Also, Gebet'a or Mancala from 700 BC in Ethiopia was used many years before in Central Africa. The goal of the game is to get more pieces than your opponent. In the past, the holes were carved into stone, clay, or mud (TaNeter.org, 2023).

Second, as it concerns the sophisticated inventions in ancient Africa South of the Sahara, Sankore, which is the oldest university in the world and located in Mali, was home to a lot of manuscripts mostly focusing on mathematics and astronomy (Brooks, 2021). Also, large-scale money-pooling for mutual benefit is known as *susu* in Sierra Leone, Ghana, Trinidad, etc., and *tontines* in Senegal and Benin, but originally began in Nigeria in the 1700s and is called *esusu* (Brooks, 2021). In addition, the Akan people who lived in modern day Ghana and Côte d'Ivoire had their own number system. It was not influenced by Arab or Persian systems as some people thought. This is shown by the weights that were used to measure gold powder, the preferred currency at the time (Brooks, 2021).

Third, apropos the European thought that the African people they captured and enslaved were not intelligent, many European captains of slave-trading ships were thoroughly impressed by the mathematical skills that the African traders had. They could easily convert currencies and exchange rates. For example, a 14-year-old named Thomas Fuller who was stolen from Africa was considered to be a human calculator for which they called him the Virginia Calculator (Brooks, 2021).

The State of School Mathematics Education in South Africa

Among the many characterizations of the state of Mathematics education in South African schools are the following three prominent ones to which I limit my examination for the sake of brevity: (1) "complex equation," (2) "shocking state," and (3) "need of daring solutions." These characterizations are reviewed in sequential order in the ensuing subsections for lucidity.

Complex Equation

First, we learn from Nick Dall (2022) that the Mathematics results of South African schools are quite disturbing. The reasons stated for this outcome are (a) the lack of qualified Mathematics teachers and (b) the effects of past segregation policies. It is therefore suggested that in order to reverse this negative trend, Mathematics education in South Africa's schools should be reinforced from the very first grade.

Second, we are apprised that, according to the most up-to-date Trends in International Mathematics and Science Study (TIMSS), which compares scores of students in various countries, published in 2019, it has been common knowledge for a long time that South African school students are "bad" at Mathematics (Dall, 2022). The following evidence is culled from the study to support the assertion:

> At primary school level, South Africa had the third lowest score out of the 64 countries. Things are no better at high school, where South Africa's Grade 9 learners received the second lowest score out of 39 countries. Moreover, less than a third of all students in the final year of high school take maths—and only half of them pass their exams, according to data from the South African Institute of Professional Accountants. (Dall, 2022, p. 1)

Third, we are informed that the problem cannot be understood without comprehending the history of South Africa. This is because the Bantu Education Act of 1953 that operated during the apartheid system led to Blacks being poorly educated. Approximately seven decades later, the country's education system still suffers from the ills of Bantu Education, even though the policy was abolished when apartheid was ended in the early 1990s in a series of steps that led to the formation of a democratic government in 1994. To this day, children at former Blacks-only schools continue to deliver dreadful Mathematics results, while those at former Whites-only schools perform on the same level with their contemporaries in Europe (Dall, 2022).

Fourth, the "shortage of qualified teachers" is cited as a major reason for the poor Mathematics results in South African schools. For many students, the "unpleasant working conditions" of the teaching profession discourage them from pursuing a teaching track. In order to address the shortage of qualified teachers, 1-year courses were introduced to train graduates as teachers. Also, low levels of engagement between students and lecturers led to many trainee teachers being quite underprepared at the end of the year-long courses. In addition, the biggest problem was the lack of continuous professional development following completion of the courses. As a result, the general level of Mathematics teachers remains quite inadequate (Dall, 2022).

Fifth and finally, it is conceded that the legacy of apartheid will not be easy to overcome, but that it is not a reason to give up the struggle to remedy the problem of poor Mathematics performance by South Africa's pupils. Giving up is not considered to be a prudent option because the stakes are high as Mathematics helps learners to "develop their cognitive skills which are part of 21st-Century learning." In addition to counting, mathematical skills are noted to "include the ability to think critically, communicate, collaborate and be creative." By acting now, it is believed that "it will help prevent the situation from recurring and affecting the next generation" (Dall, 2022, p. 1).

Shocking State

For starters, the Government Staff Writer (2020) informs us that the South African Department of Basic Education (DBE) TIMSS study mentioned earlier basically paid attention to Grades 4 and 8 students, albeit some countries administered TIMSS to different grades. Nonetheless, it is noted that South Africa, employing its benchmarking systems, assessed Grades 5 and 9 pupils to better match their curricula and in order to maintain trend measurements. Thus, South African students were on average older than many of their other international counterparts who were assessed by the use of the TIMSS instrument. Despite the grade advantage, however, the data reveal that South African pupils consistently scored in the bottom three countries on a range of tests. Based on the TIMMS scale, learners who achieve 400 TIMSS points are considered as having acquired the basic mathematical or science knowledge for that grade.

Next, we are apprised that for South Africa's Grade 5 pupils, among the 64 countries and regions that took part in the Grade 4 TIMSS, the South African pupils scored an average of 374 for Mathematics and 324 for Science—both scores being well below the 400 "basic" threshold. These measures are important because (a) "higher achievements mean that learners possess the ability to apply knowledge in simple or complex solutions and to communicate understandings"; (b) "just over a third (37%) of South African learners demonstrated that they had acquired basic mathematical knowledge, and 28% had acquired basic science knowledge"; and (c) "this means that 63% of learners had not acquired basic mathematical knowledge and 72% had not acquired basic science knowledge" (Government Staff Writer, 2020, p. 1).

Thereafter, we are enlightened that for South Africa's Grade 9 pupils, among the 39 countries that participated in the Grade 8 TIMSS, South African pupils continued to attain lower scores in Mathematics and Science. These pupils' Mathematics score of 389 and the Science score of 370 represent an increase of 17 points for Mathematics and 12 points for Science compared to the 2015 TIMSS scores. The results also indicate that 41% of Mathematics learners demonstrated that they had acquired basic mathematical knowledge and 36% of Science learners had acquired basic Science knowledge (Government Staff Writer, 2020).

Also, it is pointed out that the percentage of South African students with achievements scores was "too low for estimation." This determination was based on whether students' performance on the assessment was no better than could be achieved by simply guessing on the multiple-choice assessment items. The following are the results: "Grade 4 Mathematics: 6% scored too low (average correct was 36%); Grade 4 Science: 28% scored too low (average correct was 25%); Grade 8 Mathematics: 26% scored too low (average correct was 19%); Grade 8 Science:

17% scored too low (average correct was 25%)" (Government Staff Writer, 2020, p. 1).

In addition, several factors are mentioned for the state of affairs of Mathematics education in South Africa's schools. They are as follows: (a) unequal status of students and their differing backgrounds, (b) home conditions continue to be unequal, and (c) disconnection between teacher qualifications and learner achievements (Government Staff Writer, 2020).

Need of Daring Solutions

First, the "need of daring solutions" to address the current appalling state of Mathematics education in South Africa's schools, according to Michael Cosser (2023), is imperative because the aforementioned Mathematics results of South Africa's pupils constitute a "national catastrophe." The situation is perceived to have a very direct impact on South Africa's economic growth. To buttress this assertion, evidence from a Harvard University study is mentioned indicating that a country's economic growth is more significantly correlated with the mathematical proficiency of its high school learners than to their proficiency in other subjects. It is therefore deemed encouraging that the National Education Collaboration Trust (NECT) in South Africa is paying significant attention to supporting the DBE's effort on improving the quality of learner outcomes in Mathematics, in addition to languages and science, with "its motto, taken from the National Development Plan (NDP), being committed to ensuring a South Africa where 90% of learners pass mathematics, science and languages with at least 50% by 2030" (quoted by Cosser, 2023, p. 1).

Second, how close South Africa is in achieving the preceding goal is discussed. Based on the most recently available Grade 12 results reported by the DBE in 2022, it is stated that South African students once more "performed poorly" in Mathematics (Cosser, 2023). According to Cosser,

> The DBE's diagnostic report on Grade 12 learner performance in content subjects in 2021 showed that 77% of learners achieved less than 50% in Mathematics in 2021, only a one percentage point improvement since 2017. (There is no point in looking at performance below 40% or 30% when a pass for any subject should be, and is at university, 50%.) Expressed differently, in 2021 only a quarter of learners achieved above 50% in (that is, "passed") Mathematics. The perennial focus on Grade 12 pass rates at the expense of pass rates in the preceding 11 grades points up the continuing myopia of the education authorities in ignoring the bigger picture—the number of learners who start Grade 1 and drop out of school before Grade 12. (2023, p. 1)

Third, the "Research on Socio-Economic Policy Group at Stellenbosch University" is cited as having delineated "major inefficiencies in the schooling system," with repetition being quite common across the grades and many learners dropping out of the system before reaching Grade 12. It is shown that in terms of Mathematical outcomes in matric, performance in pre-Grade 12 Mathematics is considered to be "a harbinger." It is also revealed that while pupils' performance improved over the period of 2016–2018, performance from Grade 3 to Grade 6 to Grade 9 decreased significantly. The average pass rate in Grade 9 being well below 40% is a reflection of the Grade 12 Mathematics "outcomes profile" (Cosser, 2023).

Fourth, the solutions tendered to deal with the problem are dubbed as "out-of-the-box" and must be "collaboratively daring." To begin with, it is noted that while the NDP is characterized as being extensively focused on the need for collaboration among all education stakeholders if its ambitious targets are to be realized, it is nonetheless believed that based on research conducted in 2020, the target of 90% of pupils passing Mathematics, Science, and languages with at least 50% by 2030 is unachievable. It is posited that "even with a healthier rate of improvement than currently observed, it would be difficult to exceed 60% by 2030" (Cosser, 2023, p. 1).

Next, it is suggested that not only should the number of Mathematics teachers be increased, but also the quality of their teaching should be improved. The following five actions are therefore called for, not sequentially, but simultaneously, if the quality of Mathematics learner outcomes is to improve, and that this is where the "daring" comes in: (1) "conduct a skills audit of all current Mathematics teachers, paying those who achieve above-average scores on a specially designed test (pitched at Grade 12-level) handsomely—above average teacher pay"; (2) "attract competent Mathematics teachers to non-fee-paying schools with offers of subsidized accommodation and above-average remuneration"; (3) "recruit school-leavers with high matric Mathematics marks into teacher training programs in high-performance universities, offering them free tuition and signing contracts with them for post-degree service (notionally for four years) of one year's support for every year for which they receive a bursary"; (4) "as a short-term measure, recruit competent foreign nationals to teach Mathematics on a contract basis, relaxing immigration processes and paying them above-average teacher salaries"; and (5) "engage with teacher unions on the need to drastically increase the number of Mathematics school-leavers with marks good enough to get them into universities to study teaching…" (Cosser, 2023, p. 1).

The Best Mathematics Teacher in the World: Sandile Mathebula

The following two basic questions are addressed in this section: (1) Who is Sandile Mathebula? (2) Why is he considered to be "The Best Mathematics Teacher in the World?" In order to provide clear answers to these questions, they are discussed sequentially in the ensuing subsections.

Who Mathebula Is

Mathebula, who is popularly referred to as "Maths-Son," was born in 1993 in Ncotshane, a small village in Pongola, north of KwaZulu-Natal in South Africa. He was awarded the Best Maths Teacher prize during the Global Teachers' Awards ceremony convened in India in 2022. The award is a significant accomplishment for the then 29-year-old teacher. In addition to having taught Mathematics for 5 years at the time of the award, he also has a passion for Physical Science. He currently teaches Mathematics to Grades 10 to 12 pupils at Siphumelele Secondary School in Mzingazi, located outside Richards Bay (Naile, 2022; Zungu, 2022; Phungula, 2022).

Emerging from meek origins in Pongola's dusty streets, Mathebula beat the odds on his way to becoming the winner of the prestigious teaching award. He is said to describe the environment in which he grew up as follows: "a village that had no running water (and) our schools were of poor quality" (Zungu, 2022, p. 1). He is also quoted as saying that the award is just the beginning for him and that he knows he has a long way to go in order to do many things, especially for "the impoverished learners in rural schools." He is further noted to state that "the award still feels surreal" (Zungu, 2022, p. 1).

Mathebula has begun writing a Mathematics book that is aimed at "simplifying the challenging subject." His main objective for writing the book is to allow all pupils, in his school and others, to benefit from it. According to him, it is imperative for him to write a book that will help the next generation to understand Mathematics better, even after he is dead. He has also started talking with publishers so that when the book is ready it would be distributed widely across South Africa. He further plans to engage the South African Department of Education curriculum developers to consider his book for use in schools (Phungula, 2022). Mathebula is quoted to make the case as follows:

> I was encouraged by being chosen as the world's best maths teacher, so my focus now is writing the book to simplify the subject which everyone regards as difficult. For me, it is not difficult, but the authors of the curriculum did not put much effort into simplifying it for pupils…As we all know that at one stage we are all going to die, it is important that I do not die with the knowledge that would be required in my absence. So I am now focusing on writing the book so that pupils will continue to benefit from it even after my death… (Phungula, 2022, p. 1)

Indeed, Mathebula exemplifies the adage that "Putting Students First Should Never Be a Mere Slogan!"

Why Mathebula Is Considered to Be "The Best Mathematics Teacher in the World"

The answer to the question about why Mathebula is considered to be "The Best Mathematics Teacher in the World" hinges on at least two aspects. The first aspect is what the award means to him. To commence with, he mentions his passion for teaching as what propelled him to walk on the global stage. Next, he indicates that he started teaching right after finishing matric and how he longed to see learners acing Mathematics and Science, two subjects often regarded as the hardest in high school. Thereafter, he tells about how after he completed high school he enrolled for a Bachelor of Education degree that he obtained with ease and high distinction; and, with that degree, his formal teaching career began. Also, he expresses his gratitude for the international recognition which motivated him to continue "changing more lives through chalk and a textbook" (Zungu, 2022, p. 1).

The second aspect is Mathebula's greater intention to improve Mathematics across South Africa. To begin with, he has developed various Internet platforms to assist learners struggling with Mathematics and Science. Next, he believes that everything falls into place when he sees joy and love in the faces of those he assists as they ace the two subjects. This motivates him to do all that he can to simply the subjects and make them enjoyable. In addition, the award reminds him that anything is possible once one set his/her mind to doing it. Moreover, writing the simplified Mathematics book, he believes, is a "higher dream" for instilling the love for the subjects in learners (Zungu, 2022).

Mathebula's love and passion for Mathematics is traced back to when he was a Grade 11 pupil as his teacher of the subject called Masango inspired him to love subjects such as Mathematics and Physical Sciences, and the way she taught Mathematics was awe-inspiring. The following year, Mathebula was already tutoring other Grade 12 pupils in Mathematics. The pupils used to tell him that he taught the subject better than many teachers in the school. The inundation of praises motivated him to pursue a qualification in teaching, first at the University of KwaZulu-Natal and later at the University of South Africa. Due to lack of funds, he had to leave the former university for the latter where he completed his degree. From there, he continued with his schooling by enrolling for the Bachelor of Education which he passed easily (Zungu, 2022), as mentioned earlier.

Today, Mathebula offers online courses in Mathematics. A learner can subscribe to his online classes as well as to his YouTube Channel to get free recorded lessons. For online homework, a learner can book a spot at his website. In addition, a learner in and around Richards Bay can attend in-person lessons and home work (Mathebula, 2023).

Conclusion and Recommendations

It is flabbergasting to see that such a huge number of the descendants of progenitors of a continent that invented Mathematics, and can still manage to produce a "Best Mathematics Teacher in the World," are not proficient in the subject. This deficiency is critical because Mathematics (a) promotes healthy brain function, (b) improves problem-solving skills, (c) supports logical reasoning and analytical thinking, (d) develops flexible thinking and creativity, (e) opens up many different career paths, (f) may boost emotional health, (g) improves financial literacy, (h) sharpens one's memory (Prodigy, 2022), etc.

The question that emerges here then is the following: What can be done to remedy the dilemma? Obviously, the five actions suggested by Cosser (2023) in the third section of this chapter constitute a good place to start. To be added to the recommended policy actions are the following five practical ones: (1) build learners' confidence, (2) encourage questioning and make space for curiosity, (3) emphasize conceptual understanding over procedure, (4) provide authentic problems that increase students' drive to engage with Mathematics, and (5) share positive attitudes about the subject (Levy, 2018).

References

Bangura, A. K., Obando, J., Munene, I. I., & Shisanya, C. (2019). *Conducting research and mentoring students in Africa: CODESRIA College of mentors handbook*. CODESRIA Publications.

Brooks, M. (2021, October 24). Mathematics in Africa has been written out of history books—it's time we reminded the world of its rich past. Independent. Retrieved September 27, 2023, from https://www.independent.co.uk/voices/african-mathematics-black-history-b1944288.html

Cosser, M. (2023, January 23). Daring solutions are needed to solve South Africa's maths teaching crisis. Daily Maverick. Retrieved September 21, 2023, from https://www.dailymaverick.co.za/article/2023-01-22-daring-solutions-are-needed-to-solve-south-africas-maths-teaching-crisis/

Dall, N. (2022, December 15). Complex equation of maths education in South Africa. *The UNESCO Courier*. Retrieved September 21, 2023, from https://courier.unesco.org/en/articles/complex-equation-maths-education-south-africa

Government Staff Writer. (2020, December 8). The shocking state of maths and science education in South Africa. Business Tech. Retrieved September 21, 2023, from https://businesstech.co.za/news/government/455406/the-shocking-state-of-maths-and-science-education-in-south-africa/

Levy, R. (2018, July 6). 5 tips for improving students' success in math. *Edutopia*. Retrieved September 23, 2023, from https://www.edutopia.org/article/5-tips-improving-students-success-math/

Mathebula, S. (2023). Grade 4–7 maths and science lessons. *Maths-Son*. Retrieved August 26, 2023, from http://mathson.co.za/

Naile, S. (2022, November 19). Richards Bay maths teacher scoops global teacher award. The South African. Retrieved August 26, 2023, from https://www.thesouthafrican.com/education/richards-bay-maths-teacher-global-award-19-november-2022/

Northwestern University. (2023). What is applied mathematics. Engineering Sciences & Applied Mathematics. Retrieved July 28, 2023, from https://www.mccormick.northwestern.edu/applied-math/about/what-is-applied-mathematics.html

Phungula, W. (2022, November 17). World's best maths teacher from KZN to write a 'simplified' book on subject. *Independent Online* (IOL). Retrieved August 26, 2023, from https://www.iol.co.za/dailynews/news/worlds-best-maths-teacher-from-kzn-to-write-a-simplified-book-on-subject-a7e73c97-b710-47cf-96f4-38494f6b14f0

Prodigy. (2022, September 23). Why is math important? 9 reasons why math skills improve quality of life. Retrieved September 23, 2023, from https://www.prodigygame.com/main-en/blog/why-is-math-important/

StudySmarter. (2023). Pure maths. Retrieved July 26, 2023, from https://www.studysmarter.us/explanations/math/pure-maths/

TaNeter.org. (2023). Ancient African mathematics. *Ancient African* History Retrieved September 27, 2023, from http://www.taneter.org/math.html

University of Waterloo. (2023). What you can learn in applied mathematics. Applied Mathematics Retrieved July 28, 2023, from https://uwaterloo.ca/applied-mathematics/future-undergraduates/what-you-can-learn-applied-mathematics

Zungu, L. (2022, November 18). Young KZN teacher scoops international maths award. Scrolla. Retrieved August 26, 2023, from https://scrolla.africa/young-kzn-teacher-scoops-international-maths-award/

Isatu Ramatu Bangura's first degree is in Computer Graphics Design, her second degree is in Mathematics, and she is working on her PhD in Mathematics. She is the author of several book chapters and articles in prestigious referred journals. During the past summers, she worked at various United States government agencies designing mathematical models for their operations. Many of her writings have won major national awards. She has designed many book covers, and some of her artworks have been displayed for public viewing and won prestigious awards. She also is the lead trumpet player for her school and community concert, marching and jazz bands.

Sociology

Isaac Akintoyese Oyekola

This chapter conceptualizes what Africa is in the field of Sociology, the field that is concerned with the science of the activities and behaviors of human society and group relations. To achieve this, the assessment of the scope and nature of relationships between and among cultures, societies, countries, and continents, both historically and geographically, is required. Considering the broad, dynamic, and complex nature of human relationships, both within Africa and between Africa and the rest of the world, it is expected that many conceptualizations will emerge. Nonetheless, dealing with all these conceptualizations in a single chapter is apparently not feasible. Hence, three important conceptualizations that explain what Africa is in the current sociological discourse are examined, and these include (1) Africa as the cradle of mankind and of sociological knowledge, (2) Africa as the source of human capital to the world, and (3) Africa as the home of pluralism and collectivism.

Narrative review of existing literature on the conceptualization of Africa in Sociology was conducted to develop an overview of what Africa is in the field particularly and in academic discourse generally for the avoidance of the negative distortion and relegation of African good image/heritage (Green et al., 2006). In the process, key quotations are provided to emphasize or oppose certain points of view, and these are analyzed in terms of descriptive case studies. This is important considering the nature of the general question guiding the analysis: What is the conceptualization of Africa in the field of Sociology?

The essence of investigating how Africa is conceptualized in the field of Sociology is to rejig the seemingly relegated or debated unique values and cultures of African people and to demonstrate the vital importance of these virtues not only to Africa/Africans but also to the world at large. Since the genesis of modern

I. A. Oyekola (✉)
Department of Sociology, Criminology and Security Studies, Achievers University, Owo, Nigeria
e-mail: oyekola.ia@achievers.edu.ng

A. K. Bangura, J. A. Ifedi (eds.), *Conceptualizations of Africa*, African Studies and Research Forum Series, https://doi.org/10.1007/978-3-031-74535-5_13

globalization, Africa has been playing a seemingly concealed but central role in global social development. Hitherto, the continent has been the source of global development and the hope of future development lies with the continent and the people of the continent, although contentions about this may continue until the reality is revealed. With this background, the next sections examine the conceptualization of Sociology as a field of study, discuss three conceptualizations of what Africa is in Sociology, as well as provide conclusions and recommendations on how Africa is and should be conceptualized in the field of Sociology.

Sociology: A Conceptualization

Some scholars in Sociology have analyzed various conceptualizations of the discipline and these have shaped the discipline in very broader terms. While many of these conceptualizations have been agreed upon, some of them are still being debated. Among these conceptualizations are the ontology or the very subject matter of Sociology, methodology (or more broadly, epistemology) of the discipline, history of sociological thought, levels of sociological analysis, future direction of Sociology, as well as the usefulness of sociology in addressing global challenges. In this chapter, three generally agreed levels of sociological analysis are discussed, and these include micro, meso, and macro levels of sociological analyses. The ensuing subsections discuss these one after the other for clarity.

Micro Level Sociological Analysis

Sociologists seem to have established common ground about the value of investigating and understanding social phenomena. Nonetheless, the level at which such investigations and analyses are carried out varies. Consequently, three levels of sociological investigation and analysis have been established. Each of these levels of analysis also reflects the three central concepts in sociology: (1) social interaction, (2) social structure, and (3) social change.

The micro level analysis of social interaction focuses on a one-on-one interaction between individuals. Here, sociologists are not interested in studying the individual (one type of social personality) which Brown referred to as the position occupied by a human being in a social structure or the 'I' (one type of the self) which Meads referred to as the immediate response of an individual to others. Rather, sociological analysis at the micro level examines person (the second type of social personality) which Brown referred to as a complex of social relationships, or me (the second type of self) which Meads referred to as the organized set of attitudes of others which one himself assumes. Thus, sociologists cannot study person or me except in terms of social structure, neither can they study social structure except in terms of the person(s) or me(s), who is (are) the units of which it is composed (recounted by Shankar-Rao, 2006). At the micro level, therefore, sociologists study people's behavior during everyday interactions such as negotiation between customer and seller, confrontations between citizens and law enforcement agencies, as well as conversation between husband and wife, among many other forms of micro social interactions. Sociologists who study micro level interactions examine social exchange (either positive or negative) between two or more individuals, with emphasis on their actions and reactions. During social interactions, individuals share certain forms of internalized norms, rules, and expectations. When these non-material social facts are breached, sanctions are imposed in form of social control based on how deviant or deviation a behavior is from societal norms. In contrast, when these social facts are followed, society or social structure rewards such behaviors based on shared norms and understanding. It is these punishment and reward systems that help maintain social order and sustain social structure.

Social structure is the result of all forms of social interaction in any given society, and it is referred to as an organized pattern of relationships and social institutions. Therefore, micro level sociological analysis of social structure examines how individual behaviors are organized or structured in interpersonal relationships. It entails examination of roles, social class, social status, culture, groups, and social institutions such as media, politics, family, and religion. It studies, for instance, individual socioeconomic status (SES) as a combined measure of economic and social rankings based on an individual's education, occupation, income, and wealth. Importantly, the social structure and the individual's place within the structure shape the person's attitude, perception, and behavior toward others in an organized pattern of relationship.

Micro level sociological analysis of social change examines the shifts in the patterns that characterize individual place in a society. That is, it examines social change at the smallest levels of interaction, even in some cases, the change in 'self' perception since self itself is a social process (see Mead's analysis of the self in Ritzer, 2011). In other words, social change can occur between couples or friends. For instance, the constitution of kinship and friendship has altered social relations in the contemporary world. It should however be noted that the micro level of social change often engenders higher levels of social change. In fact, in most cases, change begins at the micro level before it affects the meso and macro levels.

Meso Level Sociological Analysis

At the meso level sociological analysis of social interaction, a detailed assessment of interactions in a group, community, or organization is provided. Groups, communities, or organizations have individual members who continue to interact on a daily basis; and by virtue of these interactions, social networks are formed. These networks of relationships continue to shape individual perception and behavior in a group, community, and organizations, and these in turn affect the overall group behavior. It is the belief of sociologists that an individual's perceptions and behavior are the results of such individual interactions in groups, communities, and organizations to which the person belongs. Hence, sociologists are much interested in investigating a whole group, community, or even continent, believing that the understanding of the whole can help in the understanding of the parts.

Meso level sociological analysis of social structure assesses the experiences and patterns of relationships in a group or geography. Principally, the organized patterns of associations and social institutions that make up a social entity are the results of all social interactions in such entity. Meso level sociological analysts are therefore interested in the organization and reorganization of these patterns of relationships in social institutions such as families, religion, and education. Sociologists who conduct meso level research might be interested in studying how norms and values of community behaviors vary across cultures or how farming systems in a particular African culture is organized and reorganized, to mention two examples.

Meso level sociological analysis of social change studies the modifications or alterations in the social structures and social relationships that occur in a group and not at the societal or macro level. In order words, transformation in social relations or modification in the accepted social customs within a group that does not affect the entire social system is said to be meso level social change. Changes in social structures in a group determine and influence individual actions, interactions, and reactions within a group. For example, the analysis of changes in social relations among prisoners is said to be a meso level sociological analysis. Nevertheless, when such changes affect all prisoners across correctional centers, then we can begin to think of social change at the macro level.

Macro Level Sociological Analysis

Macro level sociological analysis of social interactions deals with social exchanges between two or among more societies, countries, or continents, with emphasis on how they act, react, and interact toward one another. While interactions between or among these social entities may be motivated by trade, politics, governance, security, education, or arts, such interactions are often macro in nature: that is, they concern or affect virtually all members of societies in one way or the other. Thus, macro level sociological analysis of social institutions examines interactions between or among societies as a whole by considering the broad systems of institutions, hierarchies, and patterns that shape and are shaped by society as a whole. For instance, the interactions among European, African, and American countries during the Triangular Slave Trade were macro in nature, and sociologists have continued to examine the negative impact of such interaction on Third World countries.

Macro level sociological analysis of social structures examines the network(s) of relationships between or among societies, nations, or continents. Every society, nation, or continent has its own structures or an arrangement of persons in institutionally controlled or defined relationships (such as the relationship between brother and sister, master and slave, or that of colonizer and the colonized, European Union and African Union, or global capitalist and global proletariat). In these structures is a body of principles underlying social relations which are often most beneficial to the part that sets the principles. Thus, the sociological analysis of the patterns, principles, groups, and institutions that guide social relationships among societies of the world is said to be macro in nature. As a matter of fact, the structure that defines patterns of relationships between the global North and the global South has been 'sociologicalized' to be exploitative in nature. For example, the social, political, and economic structures that define the relationships between Europe with the United States and China, on the one hand, and with Africa, on the other hand, have always favored one side at the detriment of the other part. Accordingly, scholars are always much more interested in analyzing these structures in order to reveal hidden defects in them, with the aim of changing those structures and achieve balance/equilibrium.

Macro level sociological analysis of social change examines the alteration in the patterns of relationship that define societies. Here, sociologists understand the trends and patterns that relate to change in behaviors, norms, and practices, analyze the forces that influence such changes, and then discover the ways by which such changes have shaped the social behaviors of individuals, groups, and societies. Generally, a key determinant of social exchange between individuals, groups, and societies in any given social entity is social structure as it defines recurring pattern of behavior. Therefore, social change occurs as social exchange/interaction and social structure shift. When social change happens at the macro level, it affects the entire social structure and institutions. In recent times, sociologists have become increasingly interested in studying social change at the global level. Good examples were the capitalist system that heavily overturned European society in the nineteenth Century and the colonial experience of the Third World countries in the twentieth Century that transformed their societies.

Africa as the Cradle of Mankind and of Sociological Knowledge

During the twentieth Century, criticisms against Africa as the cradle of mankind were heavy in the mouths and hands of especially the European desperado scholars, along few European-nurtured and -encultured Africans. Nonetheless, those criticisms no longer hold much substance by reason of many evidences that emerged before the end of the last century and at the wake of the twenty-first Century. Before Charles Darwin's *Origin of Species* (1859), evolutionists believed that humans originated in Central Asia. Nevertheless, fossil evidence was found to later show that it was in the continent of Africa that the basic stock which eventually gave rise to apes as well as humans emerged. According to evolutionists, the pre-humans who had tools were the Australopithecus Africanus and Arubustus discovered by Raymond Dart near Kimberly in South Africa. More recent findings affirm the complexity of the origin of modern human (or Homo sapiens). Nonetheless, evidence still abounds that all modern humans are descendants of Africa but spread out of Africa about 60,000 years ago (Busia, 1960).

The "Out of Africa" model, as opposed to the "multiregional" model, was the most widely accepted explanation on the origin of modern humans. It suggested that modern humans originated in Africa about 200,000 years ago from a single group of ancestors. Modern humans continued to evolve in Africa and had spread to the Middle East by 100,000 years ago and possibly as early as 160,000 years ago. Modern humans only became well established elsewhere in the last 50,000 years. The different physical features now found in modern humans from different geographical areas around the world are believed to have evolved over only the last 60,000 years or so as a result of adaptations to different environments (Dorey, 2020).

Based on these and emerging evidences, Africa has been considered to be the cradle of humankind. Every year, fresh archaeological evidence continues to show that the first home of humans from the dawn of history is Africa. It is claimed that Mary Leakey's Zinjanthropus (also known as Zinj), or the 1.8 million-year-old East African Man found in the Olduvai Gorge, Tanzania, was the world's earliest human, and lived more than 600,000 years ago.

Different races have thus lived and interacted in Africa for thousands or even millions of years, and survivals of extremely old cultural inventions and ways of life appear alongside much more recent cultural developments. Through Egypt, Ethiopia, and North Africa came influences of the ancient cultures of the Mediterranean; through Madagascar, the ancient cultures of Asia; and in modern times, the violent impact of European cultures has been felt everywhere in Africa.

In terms of the source of sociological knowledge, Africa has been considered to be the genesis of sociological theorizing. Since time immemorial, people have shown interest in the understanding of the relationship between individuals and their place in society. Many of these ancient thinkers were inspired by their strong aspiration to describe what an ideal society entails. Many of their classical descriptions of society later laid the foundation for modern sociological topics, theories, and concepts.

In a widely read international text on sociological theory, George Ritzer identified Ibn-Khaldun to be a significant figure in sociological theorizing. According to Ritzer, "There is a tendency to think of sociology as exclusively a comparative modern, Western phenomenon. In fact, however, scholars were developing sociological ideas and theories long ago and in other parts of the world. One example is Abdel Rahman Ibn-Khaldun" (Ritzer, 2011, p. 4). Importantly, the fourteenth century saw the emergence of the world's first sociologists: Ibn-Khaldun (1332–1406). The African-born scholar wrote about sociological and economic topics that are of interest to contemporary scholars such as the theory of social conflict, a description of political economy, a comparison between nomadic and sedentary life, as well as a study connecting ethnic groups' social cohesion to their capacity for power (Hannoum, 2003). George Ritzer expatiated on Ibn-Khaldun by stating the following: "By the time he died in 1406, Ibn-Khaldun had produced a corpus of work that had many ideas in common with contemporary sociology. He was committed to the scientific study of society, empirical research, and the search for causes of social phenomenon. He devoted considerable attention to various social institutions (for example, politics, economy) and their interrelations. He was interested in comparing primitive and modern societies" (Ritzer, 2011, p. 4).

There has been an impressive documentation of the contributions of Africans to sociological theorizing (Oyekola, 2022). It is a commonly shared desire of African people to make much more and greater contributions to the ever increasing sociological knowledge. African sociological theorizing is exciting, and it is of historical interest and geographical relevance. It is valuable in providing a strong base for the understanding of more recent events and ongoing trends of postmodern societies and challenges. Nevertheless, the hegemonic influence of Western sociology in particular and Western knowledge as a whole has siphoned African sociological theorizing from developing beyond infancy. In his *Civilization on Trial*, Toynbee states the following:

> Future historians will say, I think, that the great event of the twentieth century was the impact of the Western civilization upon all the other living societies of the world of that day. They will say of this impact that it was so powerful and so pervasive that it turned the lives of all its victims upside down and inside out—affecting the behaviour, outlook, feelings, and beliefs of individual men, women, and children in an intimate way, touching chords in human souls that are not touched by mere external material forces – however ponderous and terrifying (1948, p. 214).

The influence of Westerners on sociological theorizing best describes Toynbee's illustration: that is, "it has turned lives upside down and inside out," and this probably instigated many African sociologists to investigate various sociological issues such as the impact of Western relationship with Africa and to urgently strive to revive African sociological knowledge. Today, African sociologists, along with other sociologists who are interested in the study of Africa, have been tasked with enormous sociological issues such as the social problems of industrialization and urbanization; the impact of technology, education, population, democratic government, intellectual dependency; as well as the problem of social disorganization (or what Akinsola Akiwowo referred to as breakdown of a variation ('*ajobi*') on the theme of "sociation." According to Akiwowo (1983), sociologists require wisdom to remake the world by applying sociological imagination to address contemporary and future social problems (see also Oyekola, 2022).

Africa as the Source of Human Capital to the World

This section provides an answer to this question: Why is Africa the source of human capital to the world? Before providing an explanation for this fundamental question, human capital as a concept is first discussed. *Human capital* refers to the abilities, knowledge, skills, and experience that human beings possess and that can be used to generate value. In other words, it refers to individual attributes that are considered useful in the production process. Here, *production* means the generation of utility while *utility* refers to as whatsoever is considered useful for mankind or humanity. Generating utility for the eventual benefit of humanity has been going on since time immemorial, and it is crucial for the survival of humankind. While many factors such as money, location, and assets have been considered relevant in production processes, the vital importance of human beings has been recognized. In other words, people have been at the forefront of development in terms of social, economic, political, cultural, and even geographical growth. Human attributes such as strength and vigor, health, resilience, determination, intelligence, and more recently (formal) education, skills and training, social network along with other qualities that are useful in production are the most valuable resources in any developmental project.

Many scholars agree that the history of human capital dates back to the eighteenth Century when Adam Smith wrote on the importance of education and training in championing economic growth. In his book titled *An Inquiry into the Nature and Causes of the Wealth of Nations*, Adam Smith (1776) examined the vital importance of human capital when he explored the knowledge, talent, experiences, training, and wealth of a nation. According to him, human capital development and maximum utilization increased the collective wealth of society. Afterward, many economists and sociologists expanded this idea and developed more sophisticated human capital theories. More recently, human capital was used to capture the required labor for the production of goods as well as the value of human capacities.

Generally, human capital is very vital for social and economic development. When human capital is developed and utilized in a geography or society, it increases the productive capacity or development of that society; but when it is not developed or utilized in a society, it decreases the development of the society (Rodney, 1972). In other words, a positive relationship between human capital utilization and socio-economic development has been established. In turn, an increase in social and economic development tends to enhance the quality of life of people. Nonetheless, human capital theories have been criticized basically on two grounds. First, they legitimized bourgeois individualism which was considered selfish and exploitative. That is, the bourgeoisie considered human capital as a tool for their business growth and development, and not necessarily for the enhancement of human or workers' well-being. Second, human capital theories are criticized because they blame people (and not other factors) when any defects are seen during the production process. By so doing, they make and sustain the capitalists' strengths by placing them in a hegemonic position at the expense of workers or the original owners of human capital.

Why then is Africa the source of human capital to the world? Let me iterate my position that was well elaborated in Walter Rodney's book titled *How Europe Underdeveloped Africa* (1972): Africa made Europe what is it today and it continues to be making other parts of the world including North America and vast parts of Asia. This will be elaborated in three key historical phases: (1) Trans-Atlantic Slave Trade, (2) colonization, and (3) twenty-first Century globalization.

The opening speech of the Secretary General of the United Nations when the Security Council voted to send United Nations military aid to the Congo in July of 1960 is relevant to this discourse. The then Secretary General was reported to have said the following: "We are at a turn of the road where our attitude will be of decisive significance, I believe, not only for the future of this organization, but also for the future of Africa. And Africa may well in present circumstances mean the world" (quoted in Busia, 1960, p. 3). The last sentence in the report, "And Africa may well in present circumstances mean the world" is of utmost importance to the current discussion because it represents the prominent place that Africa has been occupying in international development both in the past and in the present. Today, it is not only the worldwide interest in Africa that is of utmost importance to global leaders, but also the worldwide concern for the future of Africa. Interest in Africa became very evident during the Trans-Atlantic Slave Trade when Europe needed manpower to work on the vast plantations of the Americas, which increased during colonization when Europe wanted raw materials for its booming industries, and heightened in this current world system when the rest of the world requires Africa for its sustained prosperity.

To start with, Africa was the major source of human capital for European capitalists during the Trans-Atlantic Slave Trade. The trade was a segment of the so-called Triangular Slave Trade that transported millions of forcefully enslaved Africans across the Atlantic Ocean to the Americas between the sixteenth and nineteenth Centuries. The Triangular Slave Trade comprises first, the shipment of firearms, textiles, mirrors, and wine, among other petty consumer goods to Africa in exchange for enslaved people of Africa. The second was the shipment of enslaved Africans to the Americas for maximum work on plantations. The third was the shipment of sugar and coffee from the Americas to Europe. According to Rodney (1972), the exportation of African human capital between the seventeenth and nineteenth Centuries was a good source of capital accumulation for the Europeans to be reinvested in Europe. For instance, the emergence of manufacturing centers which gave rise to the Industrial Revolutions were connected (either directly or indirectly) to the seaport towns, notably Nantes, Bordeaux, Seville, Bristol, and Liverpool where enslaved Africans were traded (Rodney, 1972). Summarily, the exportation of human capital out of the continent of Africa contributed significantly to the development of Europe and the impact of such contributions cannot be forgotten in European history (for the benefits derived) and in African history (for the losses recorded).

After the Industrial Revolution in Europe, the American Revolution (1775–1783), and particularly Great Britain's anti-slavery law (1833), trade in human capital diminished rapidly and another product (not directly humans this time) soon caught the attention of the world (again, Europe in particular). This marked the genesis of a new interest in Africa. Since new technologies or machines were being used for production in Europe, there was less demand for human labor but more demand for raw materials such as gold, silver, diamond, coal, iron, copper, bauxite, and cocoa, to mention some. This made European desperadoes to see Africa as their hope for raw materials to service their growing industries. Nevertheless, the generation of these raw materials would not have been made possible without interacting with humans who own the raw materials and using them to extract the raw materials. To achieve this, the Europeans established very solid but exploitative relationships with the people of Africa. The relationships today define colonial masters positively on the one hand and colonized people negatively on the other hand.

During colonialization, African "leaders" and people became great sources of human capital to Europe in particular and to the rest of the world at large (because we must not forget the contributions of the colonized Africans to the First and Second World Wars). Various policies in maximizing the use of human capital were enacted. For example, the French policy of assimilation allowed for the control of the people of Africa (or more specifically, French colonies) directly from France, while the British policy of association permitted the control of African people (or the British colonies) through African leaders/representatives indirectly (from Britain through African leaders/representatives). Again, without these human resources, colonial administration would not have been made easy, if at all possible.

During the colonial administration, African people were paid less than their worth (wherever or whenever the colonial masters deemed it fit to reward African labors). In other words, despite the invaluable contributions of Africa's human capital to global development during the nineteenth and twentieth Centuries, the Westerners did not consider it worthy to reward Africans accordingly and appropriately. In fact, the cheap labor that was found (and possibly established) during the colonial era aggravated the current dispensation. Today, Africans are considered to be indispensable human capital to the world, but the cheapest labor on the continent (until possibly they find their feet on the soil of another continent such as Europe and North America). This, among many other factors, has continued to trigger the exodus of Africans out of Africa (in the form of "brain drain") to serve as a source of human capital to other continents of the world.

Africans are the major source of human capital to other continents across the globe both in terms of their spread and population constitution. Statistics has shown that more than 60% of Africa's population is under the age of 25 years, thereby providing the continent with the greatest asset of human potential. By 2030, young (15–24) Africans are projected to account for 75% of those under age 35 years in Africa and expected to constitute 42% of the global youth (15–24 years) (African Union Commission, 2019). Despite this potential asset, Africa remains the home of cheap laborers as the majority of African youths are victims of the cheap labor syndrome. As noted by Ritzer, "Today we observe firms from across the world looking for cheap labour [Africa in particular] and lucrative niche markets, not as Marx depicted as revolutionaries, but as adaptive players hoping to turn the short-term profit or meet their quarterly projections" (2007, p. 87).

Today, Africa remains the source of human capital and the center for world development. If found on their own soil, the people of Africa serve as cheap laborers for the development of multinational corporations owned by non-Africans; and if found outside of Africa, they serve as expatriates to promote the fame of non-African countries or continents. Either way, the African human capital does not seem to directly benefit Africans.

Africa as the Home of Pluralism and Collectivism

This section describes Africa as a domain of pluralistic societies but with a high spirit of collectivism. A discussion on the pluralistic nature of Africa is provided before delving into the spirit of collectivism that characterized precolonial African people. It is important to emphasize from the onset that African pluralism and collectivism are never to be construed in a negative manner; rather, they are to be recognized as African strengths that the world has not probably openly affirmed. Before turning to this discussion, explanations on the meanings of *pluralism* and *collectivism* will be appropriate at this juncture.

On the one hand, *pluralism* means diversity. It describes people with diverse or varying ethnic groups, governments, and cultures (including their languages, arts, values, and norms). It emphasizes the coming and living together of culturally diverse people in terms of religion, politics, kinship system, ethnicities, and economic systems in a harmonious manner. The nature of pluralism in Africa has never been found in another continent of the world, and its success has never been achieved elsewhere. On the other hand, *collectivism* simply means the practice of prioritizing a group over and above each individual in the group. Collectivism gives priority to group harmony, well-being, and coherence as opposed to personal rights, freedoms, and self-interest. Again, the nature of collectivism in Africa before contact with the external world was not found elsewhere, and this was evident in the way of life of African people before the introduction of individualism (Diop, 1988). The next paragraphs turn to the description of the pluralistic and collectivistic nature of African society.

A look at the size of Africa shows that the continent is indeed very large, covering approximately 11.7 million square miles (5000 miles from north to south and about 4600 miles from east to west), more than 300% larger than the whole continent of Europe and more than three times the size of the United States. The current population of Africa is approximately 1.47 billion (representing 18% of global population), with projection of becoming 2.5 billion (representing a quarter of the total world population) by the year 2050. Of course, this statistic represents an important figure in global population and it shows the increasing population density on the continent. Besides Africa's size in terms of geography and demography, Africa also claims more diverse peoples and ethnicities than any other continent in the world.

An *ethnic group* or *ethnicity* has been defined as a group that regards itself or is regarded by others as a distinct community by virtue of certain characteristics that will help to distinguish the group from the surrounding community. An ethnic group is a category of people who identify with one another based on similarities, such as common ancestry, language, religion, and social and cultural experiences. These people share a common historical background. There are differences among *race*, *tribe,* and *ethnicity*. *Race* is associated with biology and *ethnicity* is associated with culture. *Tribe*, however, is a term that is referred to people perceived to be primitive and may have negative connotations. Based on this, Africa has four distinct ethnolinguistic groupings, and these include (1) Afroasiatic, (2) Khoisan, (3) Niger-Congo, and (4) Nilo-Saharan. The number of ethnic groups in Africa is in the thousands, thereby showcasing the more pluralistic nature of the continent. Despite these cultural diversities or multiculturalism, the people of Africa have been recorded to be living harmoniously, while giving special acknowledgment to the ethnicities and cultures of the minority within the dominant groups. For example, the amalgamation of Northern and Southern protectorates in Nigeria (comprising more than 370 ethnic groups, including the three major ones—(1) Hausa, (2) Igbo, and (3) Yoruba—by the British during the colonial epoch in the year 1914 has not been divided till today. Both minority and majority ethnic groups continue to live together, although not without common challenges.

Multiculturalism in the continent enabled African people in particular and the world at large to recognize the existence of the large number of cultures, and this has helped to improve the values that every culture has to contribute to the development of the continent in particular and the world at large. It has also helped to strengthen the bond among diverse cultures, thereby encouraging respect for each culture's differences. Furthermore, cultural diversities have helped Africans to celebrate differences, and not just tolerating them. In fact, many developed monoculture countries of the world are possibly envious of African cultural diversities.

In addition to ethnic diversity in Africa, the continent also witnessed varying types and systems of governments before the invasion of the Europeans and the eventual imposition of modern democracy. According to Ayittey (1991), the Igbo, Fulani, Somali, Gikuyu, Yoruba, and !Kung governments among others, existed on the continent of Africa with varying forms of government such as federation and confederation but considered a unitary system of government unsuitable for African societies. Again, the existence of political diversities in Africa allowed the choice of the political system considered best or suited for each peculiar African society. As such, every society decided a suitable political system that is appropriate in ensuring consensus and African traditions of participatory democracy (Ayittey, 1991).

It is important to reemphasize at this point that despite Africa's pluralistic nature, the spirit of collectivism was highly entrenched among African people before the introduction of Western individualist nature. African societies were considered communal societies whereby property was collectively owned; goods and services were shared equally after due consideration for age, sex, and position, among others; and work was done in common. Collective responsibility was prevalent among African people, and higher importance was placed on a group's survival over an individual member's interest. In Africa, personal interdependence is valued and people tend to see themselves as connected to one another and define themselves in terms of their relationships with one another. This arguably always makes the majority of African people to always have a link to the continent wherever they might have gone across the globe.

Discussion on the religious point of view regarding the collective nature of Africa has been provided by John Mbiti and Kwame Gyekye. Also, the political perspective on African collectivism has been well discussed by Leopold Senghor, Julius Nyerere, Kwame Nkruma, and Obafemi Awolowo. A popular maxim of Mbiti well describes the collective nature of Africa: "I am, because we are; and since we are, therefore I am." (Mbiti, 1970, p. 141).

As rightly said by Leopold Senghor, "We may be influenced by Europe, but our realities are not identical" (quoted in Oladipupo, 2022, p. 1). Contact with Western societies and their individualistic culture began to impact African collectivisms negatively. The consequence was the manifestation of self-centeredness in varying forms such as favoritism, nepotism, marginalization and ethnic chauvinism. (Oladipupo, 2022).

Importantly, colonial education brought an individualistic tendency to Africa and wiped away the good spirit of collectivism among African people. Walter Rodney rightly puts it as follows:

> In the final analysis, perhaps the most important principle of colonial education was that of capitalist individualism…The European bourgeoisie were progressive when they defended the individual from the excessive control of the father in the family and against the collective regulations of the church and feudal society. However, the capitalist system then went on to champion and protect the rights of the individual property owners against the rights of the mass of exploited workers and peasants (Rodney, 1972, pp. 402–3).

Although individualism may be considered suitable to European society, it has destructive effects on the African people and societies. Walter Rodney goes on to say the following:

> When capitalism had its impact on Africa in the colonial period, the idea of individualism was already in its reactionary phase. It was no longer serving to liberate the majority but rather to enslave the majority for the benefit of a few. When individualism was applied to land, it meant that the notions of private ownership and the transfer of land through sale became prevalent in some parts of the continent. Much more widespread was the new understanding that individual labour should benefit the person concerned and not some wider collective, such as the clan or ethnic group. Thus, the practice of collective labor and egalitarian social distribution gave way to accumulative tendencies (Rodney, 1972, p. 403).

The communal spirit among African people is still evident today, although fading away little by little as Western culture remains strong in the continent and globalization continue to take its effect (Oyekola, 2018). One of the lasting characteristics of Africa is collectivism. It is their rod of emancipation and development and, as such, it needs to be guided jealously.

Conclusion and Recommendations

Sociological conceptualizations of Africa reveal that the continent has maintained strong interactions with the external context and established a durable structure to sustain such interactions, but it requires intentional change for its emancipation. Specifically, contact or interaction with Western culture eroded or dragged away sociological knowledge in Africa, chattered away African human capital, and disrupted the spirit of collectivism among African people. In the process, the Westerners did not fail to entrench solid structures on the continent of Africa in order to preserve their hegemonic position and encourage dependency of all forms. Therefore, social change at the macro or continental level is required to break from the shackles of the Westerners. This requires the three tasks discussed in the following paragraphs.

First, Africans from all works of life such as leaders (political, religious, etc.), scholars, traditionalists, among others, should rejig those almost-forgotten promising knowledge on the continent for the betterment of Africa. For example, knowledge of Africans that has been discovered should be championed more among the global league of scholars, emphasized in the ears of young scholars, and taught everywhere for the benefit of African generations to come. This will allow epistemic freedom and disentangle Africans from intellectual dependency. Also, African culture in terms of languages, dressings, morals and virtues, etc., should be emphasized among younger generations in order to avoid cultural erosion predicted to erode a majority of the African languages by the year 2100 and to avoid the loss of morals that is now evident in Western culture.

Second, African leaders should invest heavily in human capital lying waste in the continent. Human capital development should be taken most seriously in order to be able to annex the enormous human capital that is residing in the young people of Africa. The youths are the backbone of society, a fundamental human capital for development and key agent of social change. With the growing recognition that African youths hold the key to future global development, social engineers and political leaders in the continent should therefore adapt their models to catalyze the strength of the young population for the benefit of the continent before other continents entice them for their own (selfish) gains.

Third and finally, Africans as a whole should get back to the past (although not necessarily return) and select some aspects of the African cultural heritage such as the spirit of collectivism that could improve African empowerment and development. As noted by Moses Oke,

> Given that in the context of our historical past things have not worked out favourably, the rational thing to do is to step back from routine activities and try to fashion out a genuinely African blueprint of social, political and economic life. Such a blueprint will be largely analytical of our experiences. It will also have to be sufficiently comprehensive to take cognizance of the various cultural influences that have now become integral parts of the African life (Oke, 2006, p. 339).

Collectivism is not a cultural heritage that should be jettisoned; it is an enduring African attribute required for the emancipation and advancement of Africa as a whole.

References

African Union Commission—AUC. (2019). Africa's future: Youth and the data defining their lives. *Policy Brief*. Retrieved September 20, 2023, from https://www.prb.org/wp-content/uploads/2019/10/Status-of-African-Youth-SPEC.pdf

Akiwowo, A. A. (1983). *Ajobi and Ajogbe: Variations on the theme of sociation* (Inaugural lecture series 46). Obafemi Awolowo University Press.

Ayittey, G. (1991). *Indigenous African institutions*. Transnational Publishers.

Busia, K. A. (1960). *The sociology and culture of Africa: Its nature and scope*. Universitaire Pers Leuven.

Darwin, C. (1859). *The origin of species*. J. Murray.

Diop, C. A. (1988). *Precolonial black Africa: A comparative study of the political and social systems of Europe and Black Africa, from antiquity to the formation of modern states*. Lawrence Hill & Company.

Dorey, F. (2020). *When and where did our species originate?* Retrieved September 20, 2023, from https://australian.museum/learn/science/human-evolution/when-and-where-did-our-species-originate/
Green, B. N., Johnson, C. D., & Adams, A. (2006). Writing narrative literature reviews for peer-reviewed journals: Secrets of the trade. *Journal of Chiropractic Medicine, 5*(3), 101–117.
Hannoum, A. (2003). *Translation and the colonial imaginary: Ibn Khaldun orientalist.* Wesleyan University Press.
Mbiti, J. S. (1970). *African religions and philosophy* (1st edn republished). Anchor Books Doubleday & Company.
Oke, M. (2006). Cultural nostalgia: A philosophical critique of appeals to the past in theories of re-making Africa. *Nordic Journal of African Studies, 5*(3), 339.
Oladipupo, S. L. (2022). Rethinking the African spirit of collectivism as a tool for African empowerment. *Humanus Discourse, 2*(1), 1–17.
Oyekola, I. A. (2018). Culture and globalisation. In O. A. Ogunbameru, A. L. Adisa, & D. S. Adekeye (Eds.), *Cross-cultural management: A multidisciplinary approach.* Obafemi Awolowo University Press.
Oyekola, I. A. (2022). Sociology. In E. D. Babatunde & A. K. Bangura (Eds.), *Great books written by Africans across the academic disciplines.* Cambridge Scholars Publishing.
Ritzer, G. (Ed.). (2007). *The Blackwell companion to globalization.* Blackwell Publishing.
Ritzer, G. (2011). *Sociological theory* (8th ed.). McGraw Hill.
Rodney, W. (1972). *How Europe underdeveloped Africa.* Bogle-L'Ouverture Publications.
Shankar-Rao, C. N. (2006). *Sociology: Principles of sociology with an introduction to social thought* (6th ed.). S. Chand & Company.
Smith, A. (1776). *An inquiry into the nature and causes of the wealth of nations*, Cannan edn. Online Library of Liberty.
Toynbee, A. (1948). *Civilisation on trial.* Oxford University Press.

Isaac Akintoyese Oyekola obtained his PhD (Sociology and Anthropology) from Obafemi Awolowo University, Ile-Ife. He has keen research interests in Sociology, social change and development studies, reliable health care financing, healthy ageing, reduced inequalities, social welfare and justice, informal and public sectors. He has served in various academic and leadership positions within and outside the University environments; participated in local, national and international conferences; authored a good number of reputable publications; and received some awards, sponsorships and grant. He is a member of local, national, and international organizations, a Lecturer/Researcher at Achievers University, and a Servant in the House of God.

Women's Studies

Fatima K. Babih

In this chapter, I explore the conceptualization of Africa in Women's Studies as an academic discipline, with the aim of developing an understanding about Africa's representation in the field. There is generally a wealth of knowledge about Women's Studies as an academic field in institutions of higher education in the Western world; however, this knowledge as it pertains to Africa is scanty. It is therefore critical to gather knowledge about Africa within this field as such knowledge may contribute to well-informed policies and decisions that are pertinent to the advancement of women in the continent. Accordingly, the key question explored in this chapter is as follows: How is Africa positioned in the discipline of Women's Studies?

In answering the preceding question, I argue that it is not how others position Africa but how African institutions of higher education position the continent in this discipline that matters the most. To explore this answer, I employ a descriptive research approach as an instrument to gain knowledge that can provide descriptions of Women's Studies generally as a discipline and specifically in the context of Africa. Lans and van der Voordt (2002) provided a fitting definition germane to answering my research question, proposing that *descriptive research* emphasizes factual information gathering and not intended to explain why things are the way they are; and that this approach does not aim to develop theory or hypotheses. In this regard, this chapter describes some general features of Women's Studies as an academic discipline, aiming to reveal its historical underpinnings, theoretical frameworks, and evolving discourse. These descriptions are followed by the presentation of Women's Studies in Africa and the discipline's evolution in the continent. Thereafter, conceptualizations of Africa in the field of Women's Studies are presented based on the preceding sections as context. The chapter ends with a conclusion and recommendations.

F. K. Babih (✉)
Women's Studies, African Women's Research Initiative for Social Empowerment, Baltimore, MD, USA

A. K. Bangura, J. A. Ifedi (eds.), *Conceptualizations of Africa*, African Studies and Research Forum Series, https://doi.org/10.1007/978-3-031-74535-5_14

Historical Foundations of Women's Studies

Women's Studies as an academic discipline defies a single definition, but Brown and Moorer summed it well when they proposed that "Women's Studies, also referred to as Gender Studies or Feminist Studies, is the interdisciplinary study of how intersectionality of gender, race, age, class, nationality, ethnicity, ability, sexuality, and other differences impact almost every facet of the social, political, and cultural experience" (2015, p. 736). This definition suggests that Women's Studies is not just focused on issues that impact women's lives and their views of the world, but is also a discipline that studies how various social constructs interact to impact the experiences and perceptions of women in various societies.

The field of Women's Studies as a distinct academic discipline emerged during the second wave of the feminist movement in the 1960s and 1970s in response to the historical negligence of women in academic disciplines (hooks, 1984). Employing feminist and interdisciplinary methods, Women's Studies emphasizes the lives and experiences of women, while examining how societal constructs of gender intersect with other social constructs like race, sexuality, disability, socioeconomic class, privilege, power, and oppression (Smith, 1979). In justifying the need for the establishment of Women's Studies as an academic discipline, Spender (1980) suggested that feminist scholars argued that women's experiences and perspectives had historically been neglected in academia and other institutions. Men who were generally at the forefront of constructing formalized knowledge about the world dismissed women's perspectives and primarily focused on their own perspectives to explain the world. Therefore, a fundamental feature of the Women's Studies discipline is to have women at the center of knowledge gathering and analysis in order to gain a more in-depth understanding about gender dynamics in their diversity of cultural and socioeconomic contexts.

Spender's suggestion echoed an earlier assertion by Robin Morgan, the editor of *Sisterhood is Powerful: An Anthology of Writings from the Women's Liberation Movement*. In this work, Morgan (1970) argued that the Women's Movement emerged from the struggles of women in the Civil Rights Movement in the United States, which supposedly fought for the rights of all Americans. Nonetheless, Morgan points out, women's perspectives were consistently dismissed, which led women to form caucuses within their respective organizations as a strategy for addressing their own issues. These caucuses eventually morphed into independent groups, culminating in the formation of the National Organization for Women (NOW) in 1966. Morgan further wrote that at NOW's founding, its membership consisted mostly of middle and upper class women and men.

African American women were fully involved in the1960s and 1970s era of political movements which helped the feminist movement gain strong footing with demands for societal recognition of women's experiences and perspectives. But because of the racial discrimination that dominated American society at that time, non-White and women from the lower socioeconomic class were not represented in the feminist movement. Since the field of Women's Studies has its origin in that era, the discipline's foundation did not include the perspectives and experiences of non-White women and women from lower socioeconomic backgrounds.

Also, according to Brown and Moorer (2015), the foundation of Women's Studies in academia was rooted in the Civil Rights and women's movements of the 1960s and 1970s. As feminist activism and scholarship grew, women boldly contested traditional academic establishments and pressed for changes in academic disciplines with demands for inclusion of women's experiences and perspectives across disciplines; these demands became a force that contributed to the foundation of the field of Women's Studies.

Emphasizing this historical background of the influence of the political atmosphere on the formation of Women's Studies in academia, Crouch asserted that "...The political climate of the late 1960s had a profound effect on female faculty and students in the academy, which formed the basis for the introduction of Women's Studies into the curriculum..." (2012, p. 17). Having been founded on this political backdrop, Women's Studies essentially introduced feminist activism in the academic arena. Therefore, most Women's Studies programs are equally focused on political action and scholarship (Crouch, 2012).

But the establishment of Women's Studies as an academic discipline was not an achievement for all women, because the main actors and subjects of the discipline at the early stages were middle and upper class, White women. As Collins (2000) argued, "...Traditionally, many United States White feminist scholars have resisted having Black women as full colleagues. Moreover, this historical suppression of Black women's ideas has had a pronounced influence on feminist theory. Theories advanced as being universally applicable to women as a group upon closer examination appear greatly limited by the White, middle-class, and Western origins of their proponents..." (2000, p. 80). This resistance by White feminist scholars toward Black women as colleagues highlights the predisposition of Women's Studies to have a narrow focus on one segment of women, the experiences and perspectives of non-White women, and women from non-Western societies being excluded.

Women's Studies began to expand beyond its narrow focus on middle-class White women in the 1980s and 1990s when it started embracing a more diverse and wider perspective (hooks, 1984; Mohanty, 1988). This shift in the trajectory of Women's Studies came about because of challenges posed to the hegemony of Western feminist theories in feminist scholarship. As the non-Western feminist movement gained traction, feminist scholars from Africa, Latin America, Asia, and Indigenous cultures insisted on the recognition of the value of regionalized feminist strategies (Mohanty, 1988; Spivak, 1988; Braidotti, 2019).

The accompanying changes in Feminist Theory led to the recognition of the diversity of social factors that influence women's perspectives, such as socioeconomic class, sexuality, disability, race, and ethnicity (Collins, 2000), which has led to feminist scholars' embrace of an intersectional approach to feminist studies (Crenshaw, 1997). Intersectionality describes how social constructs such as race, class, and gender are interconnected and interact to produce differences in experiences of privilege and discrimination in society (Crenshaw, 1992). Understanding intersectionality is critical in the field of Women's Studies, as it helps to reveal nuances in women's experiences, the multifaceted nature of women's identities, and the varying injustices they face in their respective contexts.

The changes in approach in Women's Studies led feminist scholars to become more conscious of the wider range of women's experiences and challenges, while acknowledging the relationships among gender and inequality and many other types of social injustices (Crenshaw, 1997; Davis, 2008). With this consciousness among feminist scholars, in the latter part of the twentieth Century, we began to see an emergence of global feminism and transnational perspectives that emphasize the need to understand gender issues on a global level (Mohanty, 2003; Kabeer, 2004). The awareness of the interconnections of challenges and achievements of global feminism motivated scholars to explore the experiences of women from various parts of the world and from diverse cultural backgrounds (Narayan, 1997). This broader outlook adopted by feminist researchers expanded their global reach and deepened understanding of gender dynamics through the inclusion of diverse societal and cultural contexts (Afshar, 2012; Yuval-Davis, 2006).

The field of Women's Studies continues to evolve with a focus on feminist methodologies that embrace inclusivity and challenge established unequal power structures in societies. These feminist approaches highlight the diversity of women's perspectives and experiences to ensure that voices of historically neglected communities of women are taken into account as they work to end gender biases in their respective societies (Harding, 1987). Employing feminist approaches, Women's Studies continues to move toward the postcolonial and decolonization frameworks, while recognizing the effects of colonialism on gender relationships, with a push for undoing the inheritance of colonial ideas that impact women's lives (Mohanty, 2003; Anzaldua, 1987).

In its current iteration, the discipline of Women's Studies is characterized by interdisciplinary and more inclusive approaches to research, drawing from various academic fields to deepen its body of knowledge (Nash, 2008). The discipline relies on techniques that incorporate knowledge from a variety of academic fields. These techniques help feminist researchers to develop a comprehensive knowledge base on gender dynamics by building on knowledge from a wide range of other fields, including Sociology, Anthropology, Literature, and History (Bryant & Charmaz, 2007). Therefore, Women's Studies in its current form can be described as an interdisciplinary academic field that is focused on research that highlights the impact of the interactions among gender and culture, politics, economy, and other social realities on the experiences of women around the world.

Through its interdisciplinary approach, the discipline endeavors to advance greater understanding of the interactions among gender and other social constructs like socioeconomic class, race, and cultural background (Collins, 2000; hooks, 2000). In these ways, the field of Women's Studies helps to bring recognition to the diversity of women's voices and experiences around the world. The discipline also helps to develop a global perspective and better understanding of the experiences of historically marginalized communities of women (Lorde, 2007).

The discipline of Women's Studies is an ever-evolving phenomenon. It has come a long way from its beginning as a discipline that emphasized the experiences and voices of White, middle-class, and Western women to one that is now a more inclusive, with an intersectional research approach and global perspective on women's experiences. The discipline continues to focus on scholarship and activism with the aim of transforming societies into equal and just entities by challenging hierarchies in power structures and, more accurately, reflecting the diversity and depth of knowledge about women's lives around the world. As this shift in the trajectory of Women's Studies continues, it is important to examine its evolution as a disciple in the context of Africa.

The Evolution of Women's Studies in Africa

Exploring multiple viewpoints and synthesizing those ideas are essential in analyzing how Africa is represented in the field of Women's Studies. In this section, I provide three ideologies that have impacted the evolution of Women's Studies in the African context. Exploring these ideologies can help us to develop a better understanding about how Africa is positioned in this discipline. The section consists of the following three themes: (1) colonial feminism and Eurocentrism, (2) Afrocentric feminism, and (3) postcolonial and de-colonial feminism.

Colonial Feminism and Eurocentrism

Colonial feminism and Eurocentrism were foundational ideologies that underpinned the initial conceptualization of Africa in the field of Women's Studies. Scholars who subscribed to these ideologies promoted the idea that the challenges African women faced were no different from those faced by women in the Western world (Mohanty, 1988). As a result of the prevalence of these viewpoints among scholars, the discipline frequently ignored African women's varied and unique cultural, historical, and sociopolitical realities (Mama, 1995).

These colonial and Eurocentric perspectives promoted a distorted understanding of African women's experiences, which led to the neglect of the diversity of African women's identities and the challenges they faced across the continent. According to Smith, colonial feminism also ingrained the ideas of superiority and inferiority by promoting the "Eurocentric notion that African women needed to be saved by Western values and system" (1999, p. 72). In the purview of Eurocentrism, the diversity of African women's identities and agency in their respective local contexts were disregarded, and the interpretation of their experiences was limited in scope (Oyewumi, 1997).

Eurocentric perspectives also dismissed the value and depth of African women's cultural and historical backgrounds, which hindered the availability of complete knowledge about African women's unique experiences in the field of Women's Studies (Spender, 1980). This exclusion of African women's varied backgrounds influenced the perspectives of early scholars in the field of Women's Studies, leading to their failure to account for the diversity of African women's experiences and the unique challenges they encountered in their respective local contexts (Afshar, 2012). In these and many other ways, colonial feminism and Eurocentrism portrayed African women as passive recipients of Western feminists' charity and reducing African women to a level of that portrayed them as weak, lack of agency, and unable to address the unique challenges they faced in their respective societies (Kabeer, 2004).

As its founding was grounded in the political era of the Civil Rights and feminist movements of the United States, Women's Studies in the United States and other Western countries continue to be focused on scholarship and activism. But in the context of Africa, Amina Mama sees it differently, arguing that "...Gender and Women's Studies has emerged through the nexus between feminism and development, and this has been responsible for as many constraints as opportunities, as can be seen from the myths and fables currently circulating under the variously named rubrics of women in development, women and development, gender in development, gender and development and even feminist visions of development" (2009, p. 124).

Mama's assertion suggests relationships among colonial feminism, Eurocentrism, and the perception of African women in Women's Studies and Feminist Theory. Her suggestion also highlights the challenges African feminist scholars face in their efforts to change the trajectory of Women's Studies in Africa. Without an alignment between the discipline and the agenda set by African scholars to develop their intellectual capacities in the discipline, this development agenda in feminism will continue to prevail in Africa.

Postcolonial African feminist scholars have been working to promote a more nuanced knowledge about women by challenging the colonial feminism and Eurocentrism narrative propagated about African women's experiences (Oyewumi, 1997). There is a growing interest in the necessity for decolonizing Women's Studies and adopting intersectional and culturally responsive approaches (Yuval-Davis, 2006). In this respect, most scholars, including African scholars, emphasize the incorporation of Afrocentric feminism; applying multiple perspectives and the intersectionality of gender with various social constructs, to produce a more inclusive and complete representation Africa in the discipline.

Afrocentric Feminism

Afrocentric feminism is a type of feminist activism that places particular emphasis on the experiences, challenges, and viewpoints of Africans and women of African descent. It aims to combat and dismantle racist, sexist, colonial, and other prejudices that negatively impact Black women. Afrocentric feminist scholars emphasize the importance of understanding and highlighting African women's contextual experiences and perspectives. Black women's different identities and social positions should be acknowledged and celebrated, according to Afrocentric feminism. Additionally, this type of feminist activism emphasizes the value of cultural legacy and the need to question Eurocentric standards and norms (hooks, 1984; Lorde, 1984; Collins, 1991; Davis, 1998).

Scholars and activists like bell hooks, Audre Lorde, Angela Davis, and Patricia Hill Collins have significantly contributed to developing and articulating Afrocentric feminism. Their works often critique mainstream feminism's historical negligence of Black women's experiences and advocate for a more inclusive and intersectional feminist movement.

Afrocentric feminism has strong roots in the cultures, histories, and identities of Africa and the African Diaspora. The experiences of Black women cannot be understood in isolation from their racial and cultural surroundings. Therefore, it acknowledges the interconnectedness of race, gender, and other social issues. The idea emerged as a response to the hegemony of Eurocentric ideas about African women, and it takes into account the interaction between gender and other social constructs like socioeconomic class and ethnicity. Afrocentric feminism, which emphasizes the significance of understanding and prioritizing African women's experiences and viewpoints, evolved in contrast to the Eurocentric approach. This perspective promotes the idea that gender, race, ethnicity, class, and other social constructs are interwoven with African women's identities. According to Oyewumi, "…Afrocentric feminism calls for a reevaluation of feminist theory, challenging the universal assumptions made by Eurocentric feminism and stressing the need to integrate African contexts and realities…" (1997, p. 14).

In other words, this perspective suggests that African women's cultural and historical contexts are essential for understanding their experiences and perspectives. Hill Collins (2000) suggested that the emergence of Afrocentric feminism helped redefine and expand mainstream feminism and made it more inclusive to reflect the perspectives and experiences of Black women. This suggestion highlights the idea that feminism is not universal and that women across the world have different experiences and perspectives based on their geographic locations, socioeconomic class, race, and other social constructs.

With the development of Afrocentric feminist theories and disciplinary approaches, the conceptualization of Africa in the field of Women's Studies has gradually and progressively developed. The realities of African women's experiences are gradually becoming more visible through the works of African feminist scholars who have focused mainly on the intersections of various social constructs and gender (Collins, 2000; Anzaldua, 1987). The approach of Afrocentric feminist scholars emphasizes the uniqueness of the challenges faced by non-White and non-Western women; challenges that are based on the many forms of marginalization they experienced. Furthermore, Afrocentric feminist scholars oppose the dominance of Western feminist theories that historically focused on Eurocentric viewpoints (Mohanty, 2003). They suggest the need to decolonize feminist theories and practices to make them more applicable and relevant to women in a global context.

Postcolonial and De-colonial Feminism

Feminist perspectives that are grounded in decolonization ideologies often explore the effects of colonization on the experiences of African Women. As Narayan suggested, "...Postcolonial feminist theory aims to interrogate the dominance of Western feminist perspectives and foster an understanding of the complexities of non-Western women's lives..." (1997, p. 219). In other words, Postcolonial Feminist Theory is focused on evaluating dominant Western feminist theories as a tool to build knowledge about non-Western women's lives. This theory incorporates in its analysis the colonial histories and power dynamics that impacted African nations and their populations. These viewpoints also criticize Western-centric feminist frameworks and propose the decolonization of feminist discourse (Spivak, 1988).

According to the postcolonial and de-colonial feminist perspectives, we can build a just and equitable world by assessing power relations and encouraging collaborations across diverse feminist movements. It is obvious from the synthesis of these perspectives that the conceptualization of Africa in the field of Women's Studies has come a long way, from the Eurocentric foundation to a move toward more intersectional and contextually sensitive frameworks.

Intersectionality in the African Context

Multiple intersecting social constructs like gender, ethnicity, social class, religion, and others significantly impact the lives of African women (Collins, 2000). The interconnections among these constructs contribute to the worsening of women's experiences of discrimination and other social injustices (Crenshaw, 1992). Employing an intersectional approach to research can help scholars better understand the complexity of the dynamics involved and lead them toward more inclusive and effective strategies for knowledge development that target the unique contexts of African women (Davis, 2008).

By embracing intersectionality and working to understand the effects of colonial legacies on African women's experiences, feminist scholars are empowered to develop a more comprehensive base about African women's experiences. Such knowledge can help scholars contribute to the production of context-specific knowledge. Understanding intersectionality in the Women's Studies discipline also allows for a better understanding of the interconnections among various social constructs and their influences on the experiences and perspectives of African women in their respective localities.

Culture and African Women's Experiences

Culture has a significant function in the lives of African women, and it is a major influence on the experiences and perspectives of women in their respective societies. The roles and responsibilities, as well as the status of women in their communities, are mostly determined by cultural practices, beliefs, and traditions (Adepoju, 2001). Therefore, understanding how gender and culture interact is crucial for understanding how to produce authentic and inclusive knowledge about African women.

In African societies, women's lives are generally regulated by deeply rooted gender roles and conventions. Customary gender roles help maintain unequal power dynamics between men and women in African societies; certain expectations and actions are imposed on individuals based on their gender (Amadiume, 2015). These roles and constructs impact the lives of African women in multiple ways, including their abilities to access education, employment, family relationships, property, and civic leadership.

Another area of intersection between gender and African culture is power dynamics. The historical, cultural, and economic systems determine power dynamics between men and women in African societies. Patriarchy is common in most African societies where men often assumed absolute power and authority in the decision-making processes (Oyewumi, 1997). As a system built on domination, colonialism helped to strengthen patriarchal norms, further marginalizing the roles and contributions of women, which further worsened existing gendered power disparities (Mama, 1995). These power relations continue to exist and impact African women's engagement in public discourse, access to resources, and representation in leadership positions. Furthermore, the intersection of power dynamics with other social constructs intensifies inequalities for women in African societies.

Oppression and privilege are another set of factors that impact the lives of women in African societies. Privilege can occur in many different forms: for instance, male superiority, economic privilege, and educational privilege. Men are usually more privileged than women, even those who share the same socioeconomic backgrounds, in their abilities to easily access political space, professional opportunities, and educational attainment (Wyrod, 2008).

Likewise, oppression against disadvantaged groups like women takes many different forms in Africa. Women in Africa frequently experience gender discrimination, which is worsened by factors such as class, ethnicity, religion, and geographic location (Oyewumi, 2003). Limited opportunities to participate in decision-making processes, gender-based violence, and unequal pay for equal work are all examples of how oppression manifests for women in Africa. Creating a just and equitable society requires that we address privilege and oppression by fighting against systemic inequities, promoting inclusive legislation, and raising the voices of disadvantaged groups in society.

The conceptualization of Africa in the field of Women's Studies entails several problems. One major problem that has been cited in literature is the tendency of Western feminist's discourse to privilege Western ideas and experiences over others, and frequently overshadow the distinctive realities of African women (Moghadam, 2005). As a result, there is a knowledge gap about the distinctive sociocultural, economic, and political structures that influence the lives of African women.

Women's Studies Discipline in United States Higher Education

The development of Women's Studies as a discipline started in the United States; it is therefore best to first explore the American experience with this process before exploring it for Africa. In the United States, the first Women's Studies department was established in the 1970s at San Diego State University in the State of California. According to the department's website,

> ...In 1969, students from SDSU's Women's Liberation Group, in cooperation with faculty and community members, formed an Ad Hoc Committee for Women's Studies. They collected signatures from over 600 students in support of establishing a Women's Studies Program at SDSU which the university started in of Spring 1970. By the Fall of 1970, SDSU had formally established the first Women's Studies program in the United States which offered 11 courses....

This story of the establishment of SDSU's Department of Women's Studies may not tell the story of the establishment of the discipline within university systems in the rest of the country; as Crouch (2012) suggested, every institution went about it differently. Nonetheless, there is a common thread that runs through almost all the Women's Studies programs in the country. As Crouch also argued, "...Although each Women's Studies program had unique beginnings and components, several key characteristics defined the programs as they developed throughout the 1970s. The most important distinctive feature of Women's Studies programs was the equal focus on scholarship and political action..." (2012, p. 17).

Since the establishment of SDSU's Women's Studies in the 1970s, there has been a proliferation of the discipline in United States higher education; albeit with challenges and criticisms, which are not relevant for this chapter. Suffice it to say there are currently a large number of Women's Studies programs in several university systems in the United States. Many higher education institutions have realized the value of incorporating Women's Studies as a distinctive interdisciplinary program within their institutions. For instance, the following distinguished universities are among the many United States institutions that have established Women's Studies as distinct departments within their respective institutions: (a) San Diego State University, Department of Women's Studies; (b) University of California, Berkeley, Department of Gender and Women's Studies; (c) Stanford University, Feminist, Gender, and Sexuality Studies; (d) Yale University, Women's, Gender, and Sexuality Studies; (e) University of Michigan, Ann Arbor, Women's and Gender Studies; and (f) University of California, Los Angeles, Department of Gender Studies.

Given their foci on scholarship and political action, Women Studies programs in the United States generally combine gender and sexuality studies. And, the focus of most of the programs' scholarship is the intersection of the combination of race, socioeconomic class, ethnicity, and many other social constructs.

Women's Studies Discipline in African Higher Education

African higher education institutions, like their counterparts in the United States, have gradually realized the value of the interdisciplinary approach promoted by Women's Studies. Therefore, several African universities have embraced Women's Studies as a discipline, intending to address the distinctive contributions, experiences, and challenges of women on the continent.

African higher education institutions began paying attention to Women's Studies at the same time as the global women's movement. African women who had participated actively in the decolonization movement joined the global women's movement to fight for recognition of their contributions as well as for their rights in their societies (Mama, 2004). These movements brought women's issues into the consciousness of societies. Therefore, the fight for women's rights and gender equality in Africa aligned with the decolonization movement during that period.

Mama (2004) also suggested the incorporation of gender perspectives into existing academic disciplines and establishing programs devoted to studying women's experiences and issues in African universities was parallel to the continent's independence movement. And according to Pereira (2004), Women's Studies "...emerged as a field of teaching, research and scholarship in Nigerian universities since the 1980s" (p. 1). Since then, universities in many African countries have established Women's Studies departments.

The following are some of the African higher education institutions that have established Women's Studies disciplines: (a) University of Cape Town (South Africa), African Gender Institute; (b) University of Zambia (Zambia), Women and Gender Studies Program; (c) Makerere University (Uganda), Department of Women and Gender Studies; (d) University of Nairobi (Kenya), Institute of Anthropology, Gender and African Studies; (e) Addis Ababa University (Ethiopia), Center for Gender Studies; (f) University of Dar es Salaam (Tanzania), Centre for Communication Studies—Gender Studies; (g) University of Ghana (Ghana), Centre for Gender Studies and Advocacy; (h) University of Ibadan (Nigeria), Centre for Gender and Policy Studies; (i) University of Nigeria, Nsukka (Nigeria), Gender Studies Programme; and (k) University of Cape Coast (Ghana), Centre for Gender, Research, Advocacy and Documentation.

The effort of these African countries to establish space for Women's Studies at their respective higher education institutions catalyzed a framework for women-focused scholarship in Africa. This effort has led to the formation of regional and global networks like the Association of African Women for Research and Development (AAWORD) and the African Gender Institute (AGI, 1999) in South Africa. These networks were vital in fostering African scholars' focus on an interdisciplinary research approach while encouraging scholarly collaborations throughout the continent (Gaidzanwa, 2009).

African higher education institutions, like their counterparts in the United States, have demonstrated recognition for the value of gender-sensitive research to address the unique socioeconomic and political disparities that influence gender dynamics in African societies (Awumbila, 2007). Therefore, African universities' embrace of

Women's Studies makes it possible for scholars to address the distinctive contributions, experiences, and challenges women face on the continent. African higher education systems' adoption of Women's Studies did not happen in isolation but around the same time as the global women's and the decolonization movements. These movements brought women's issues into the consciousness of societies. The fight for women's rights and gender equality spread to Africa, where it resonated with the decolonization movement for independence during that period.

Conceptualizations of Africa in Women's Studies

Given the discussions in the preceding sections, the underlying question in this section then is the following: How has Africa been conceptualized in the field of Women's Studies? The simple answer to this query is that there are many ways this has been done. In the rest of this section, however, I briefly discuss five of these ways for brevity and one at a time for the sake of clarity.

Source of Africana Womanism

Based on the ways of life of the inhabitants of the African continent and delineated in "Afrocentricity" (i.e., an intellectual philosophy and methodology that pays particular attention to or shaped by Africa or cultures of African origin), *Africana womanism* is an ideal that applies to every woman of African descent. It is rooted in and centers attention on the expectations, occurrences, requisites, and strivings of women in Africa and the African Diaspora (Hudson-Weems, 2004).

Africana womanism is therefore different from "feminism" (i.e., the advocacy of women's rights on the basis of the equality of the sexes) and "Alice Walker's womanism" (i.e., the notion that a "womanist is bold, brassy and universalist") in that the focal point of *Africana womanism* is on the realities and the injustices in society as they pertain to race. With this focus, the ideology separates African women's achievements from those of feminists, Black feminists, and African males (Hudson-Weems, 2004).

Source of Women's Authority

There was no need for a metamorphosis from matriarchy to patriarchy in precolonial Africa because the social structure was basically matriarchal as women held power, passed down property and lineage, and were the flexible party in marriage and sexual unions. Women's authority was altered substantially with the advent of colonialism.

The authority of women in Africa was abraded as colonialists trampled the traditions and rights that had made it possible for women to approbation and equality. As colonialists instituted new forms of gender inequality, many of the cultural foundations of African societies were eroded, and the impairment has been very difficult to eliminate. Thus, to this day, gender inequalities, including women's political underrepresentation, continue to be major challenges for Africa to redress (Klein & Vinson III, 2007; Boris, 2018; Heinrich-Böll-Stiftung, 2024).

Source of Afrocentric Woman

Many African women in the continent and the Diaspora have established Afrocentric organizations by drawing from the cultural and historical essentialities of Africa. For example, they manifest the development in Afrocentric fashion such as the head wraps (Cambridge Dictionary, 2024).

Many other examples of the phenomenon have been noted. The following is a small sample of them: (1) the province of Bahia in Brazil holds most of the Afrocentric carnivals in the world, and women of African descent are quite prominent as organizers and performers in them; (b) literary festivals in the United States include a stage focusing on Afrocentric women authors; (c) schools with an Afrocentric curriculum have been founded by women in the United States; (d) women teachers regularly discuss Afrocentric books, images themes, and values to provide children a sense of self; (e) women singers have shown a shift from gangsta rap to politically conscious Afrocentric rap; and (f) African women speak of the need for a longer term Western engagement with Africa from an Afrocentric point of view (Cambridge Dictionary, 2024).

Source of African Feminism

Employing African history and diversity, some African women scholars developed African feminism. Their primary focus is on the realities of the challenges with which African women contend in their everyday lives traced to historical injustices. Several perspectives of African feminism have been tendered. For instance, some proponents equate equality with men, although they seek inclusion of women in nation-building and participation in society. Other advocates point to feminism in Africa as a stigma. Still others do not perceive African feminism as universal, since they believe that African feminism in the Diaspora differs from African feminism in the continent because of the different historical experiences (Stuhlhofer, 2021).

African feminism is contextually shaped. North African women, for instance, tend to identify with issues from the Arab cultures of their origin instead of matters of Black women in Africa. By the same token, White South African women feminists would identify with Western feminism instead of African feminism. Meanwhile, African feminism focuses on the needs of Black women in Africa. The differences in the perceptions of the three groups hinge upon their realities shaped by their cultural and racial dissimilarities (Stuhlhofer, 2021).

Source of Stiwanism

Advocates of *Stiwanism*, an acronym for "Social Transformation Including Women in Africa," cull from the institutional structures that subjugate women and the way women react to them in order for these scholars to explicate their perspective. These scholars' underlying postulate is that the struggle for African women is a result of colonial and neocolonial structures that frequently place African males at the vertex of social stratification. The scholars also posit that the challenges African women encounter on a daily basis are also pertinent to the way they have internalized the patriarchy and have come to uphold the system (see Ogundipẹ-Leslie, 1994).

Stiwanism originated from acknowledging the enduring influence of colonial and neocolonial systems on African civilizations. These societies have established systems of male dominance that position African men at the highest level of the social strata, which frequently disadvantage women. Ogundipe-Leslie and other proponents of Stiwanism contend that comprehending and attaining the freedom and empowerment of African women necessitates addressing the wider sociopolitical and economic circumstances.

Institutional structures and subjugation refer to the systems and hierarchies within institutions that result in the oppression and domination of certain individuals or groups. Supporters of Stiwanism examine how institutional frameworks, including legal, educational, and economic institutions, sustain the oppression of women. These systems frequently exist as remnants of colonial governance, intentionally established to uphold a societal hierarchy that grants advantages to men. Many African Countries' legal systems still have legislation from the colonial era that imposes limitations on women's rights and freedoms. Likewise, educational systems can restrict opportunities for women and girls, thereby strengthening conventional gender norms.

Internalized patriarchy refers to the subconscious acceptance and adoption of patriarchal beliefs, values, and norms by individuals, regardless of their gender. It is the internalization of societal expectations and gender roles. An essential element of Stiwanism is its emphasis on the manner in which African women have assimilated patriarchal principles and, in certain instances, actively contribute to the perpetuation of these systems. Women may demonstrate this internalization through actions such as endorsing discriminatory policies or opposing feminist causes. Ogundipe-Leslie (1994) highlights the importance of tackling these internalized beliefs as a crucial aspect of the wider fight for gender equality. She contends that genuine societal development necessitates alterations in the underlying systems and modifications in the awareness of individuals and communities as a whole.

Stiwanism proposes ways that can facilitate social transformation by ensuring the inclusion of women in all spheres of societal progress, as a response to these issues. This activism includes endeavors to revise legislation, enhance access to education and health care, and bolster activities aimed at promoting economic empowerment. Furthermore, Stiwanism places great emphasis on the significance of cultural transformation, urging individuals of all genders to actively question and confront conventional gender norms in their societies, with the aim of fostering justice and fairness in communities.

Stiwanism offers a sophisticated and situation-specific paradigm for understanding and dealing with the difficulties encountered by African women. An in-depth examination of the relationship between institutional structures and individual agency provides a complete strategy for accomplishing social transformation. Ogundipe-Leslie's work, along with that of other experts in this field, serves as a source of motivation and knowledge base for feminist activism in Africa.

Conclusion and Recommendations

In this chapter, I embarked on a comprehensive exploration of the conceptualization of Africa in the discipline of Women's Studies, highlighting the essential role of feminist theories and methodologies. I began by providing an overview of Women's Studies as an academic discipline, underlining its historical evolution and emphasizing the significance of incorporating African perspectives within this academic domain. I also examined the relevance of feminist theories in the African context, advocating for more inclusive feminist discourses that account for diverse experiences. The discussion expanded to encompass the methodologies employed in Women's Studies, particularly focusing on feminist methodologies and the interdisciplinary approach by emphasizing their applications in understanding African women's experiences.

Intersectionality emerged as a critical lens for generating knowledge about African women's lives, recognizing the intricate relationships between gender, ethnicity, class, and other social constructs. Additionally, I analyzed societal constructs of gender and the role of culture in shaping the experiences of African women. I further scrutinized power dynamics, privilege, and oppression in the African context, revealing the complex effects of systemic inequalities.

I also recognized the unique challenges that African women face, such as limited access to resources and representation, and emphasized the need to dismantle these entrenched power structures. Understanding power dynamics, privilege, and oppression within African societies is crucial for advancing the transformation of Women's Studies as a discipline. Despite current challenges, embracing inclusive feminist approaches and encouraging context-based research will pave the way for a more representative and empowering knowledge base about African women in the academic sphere. By implementing the following recommendations, researchers and policymakers can contribute to a more inclusive and accurate understanding of African women in the Women's Studies discipline and ultimately foster gender equity and societal progress.

First, I recommend diversification of research representation of African women. To achieve this, researchers must be encouraged to ensure that their study samples include a wide range of African women. African women come from diverse ethnicities, socioeconomic backgrounds, and geographic locations. These factors must be represented in studies to ensure inclusivity.

Second, I propose that Women's Studies faculty and African researchers endeavor to foster collaborations and partnerships with international academic institutions. Such collaborations must be based on mutually beneficial terms, with exchange of knowledge as the main goal. International collaborations in studies about African women could help promote knowledge sharing and ensure accurate and complete representations of African perspectives in Women's Studies.

Third, I advocate for Women's Studies institutions to promote the inclusion of indigenous knowledge and traditional practices in Women's Studies research. By acknowledging the wisdom entailed in African cultures and integrating such wisdom can be enriching and will bring African perspectives into the global academic discourse on African women.

Fourth, I recommend that Women's Studies researchers endeavor to actively engage with policymakers and practitioners in Africa. Engaging these key stakeholders in the research process and educating them on findings would help them make informed decisions. Keeping stakeholders abreast of issues affecting women could help translate research findings into actionable policies and practices in the continent.

Fifth and finally, I propose developing a pipeline for a pool of African Women's Studies scholars across the continent. This can be done by establishing Women's Studies mentorship programs and capacity-building initiatives at institutions across the continent. Such programs could help empower emerging African scholars with relevant skills and resources and help capacitate a new generation of scholars who are equipped to contribute effectively to the discipline.

References

Adepoju, A. (2001). Regional organizations and intra-regional migration in sub-Saharan Africa: Challenges and prospects. *International Migration, 39*(6), 43–60.

African Gender Institute. (1999). Activism and the academy. *AGI Newsletter, 4*, 1–23.

Afshar, H. (Ed.). (2012). *Women and fluid identities: Strategic and practical pathways selected by women*. Springer.

Amadiume, I. (2015). *Male daughters, female husbands: Gender and sex in an African Society*. Zed Books.

Anzaldua, G. (1987). *Borderlands/la Frontera: The new mestiza*. Aunt Lute Books.

Awumbila, M. (2007). Gender and geography in Africa: Developments, challenges, and trajectories for the future. *Documents d'analisi Geografica, 49*, 44–56.

Boris, E. (2018). *Making the woman worker: Precarious labor and the fight for global standards, 1919-2019*. Oxford University Press.

Braidotti, R. (2019). *Posthuman knowledge* (Vol. 2). Polity Press.

Brown, M., & Moorer, R. (2015). Gender and women's studies: Applied research. In J. D. Wright (Ed.), *International encyclopedia of the social & behavioral sciences* (2nd ed.). Elsevier.

Bryant, A., & Charmaz, K. (Eds.). (2007). *The Sage handbook of grounded theory*. Sage.

Cambridge Dictionary. (2024). *Afrocentric*. Retrieved July 1, 2024, from https://dictionary.cambridge.org/us/dictionary/english/afrocentric

Collins, P. H. (1991). *Black feminist thought: Knowledge, consciousness, and the politics of empowerment*. Routledge.

Collins, P. H. (2000). *Black feminist thought: Knowledge, consciousness, and the politics of empowerment*. Routledge.
Crenshaw, K. (1992). *Race, gender, and sexual harassment*. Columbia Law School Scholarship Archive. Retrieved September 25, 2023, from https://scholarship.law.columbia.edu/faculty_scholarship/2867
Crenshaw, K. (1997). Mapping the margins: Intersectionality, identity politics, and violence against women of color. *The Legal Response to Violence Against Women, 43*(8), 1241–1299.
Crouch, B. (2012). Finding a voice in the academy: The history of women's studies in higher education. *The Vermont Connection, 33*(1). Retrieved September 25, 2023, from https://scholarworks.uvm.edu/tvc/vol33/iss1/3
Davis, A. Y. (1998). *Blues legacies and Black feminism: Gertrude "Ma" Rainey, Bessie Smith, and Billie Holiday*. Pantheon Books.
Davis, K. (2008). Intersectionality as buzzword: A sociology of science perspective on what makes a feminist theory successful. *Feminist Theory, 9*(1), 67–85.
Gaidzanwa, R. (2009). The development of women's studies in Africa. In The European Union (Ed.), *Gender mainstreaming in higher education*. Springer.
Harding, S. (1987). Introduction: Is there a feminist methodology? In S. Harding (Ed.), *Feminism and methodology*. Indiana University Press.
Heinrich-Böll-Stiftung (2024). A critique of Africa's post-colonial freedoms through a feminist lens: Challenging patriarchy and assessing the gains. *International Dialogue & African Perspectives*. Retrieved July 1, 2024, from https://za.boell.org/en/2021/07/07/critique-africas-post-colonial-freedoms-through-feminist-lens-challenging-patriarchy
hooks, b. (1984). *Feminist theory: From margin to Center*. South End Press.
hooks, b. (2000). *Feminism is for everybody: Passionate politics*. South End Press.
Hudson-Weems, C. (2004). *Africana womanist literary theory*. Africa World Press.
Kabeer, N. (2004). Globalization, labor standards, and women's rights: Dilemmas of collective (in) action in an interdependent world. *Feminist Economics, 10*(1), 3–35.
Klein, H. S., & Vinson, B., III. (2007). *African slavery in Latin America and the Caribbean*. Oxford University Press.
Lans, W., & van der Voordt, D. J. M. (2002). Descriptive research. In T. M. de Jong & D. J. M. van der Voordt (Eds.), *Ways to study and research urban, architectural and technical design*. DUP Science.
Lorde, A. (1984). *Sister outsider: Essays and speeches*. Crossing Press.
Lorde, A. (2007). *Sister outsider: Essays and speeches*. Crossing Press.
Mama, A. (1995). Feminism or femocracy? State feminism and democratisation in Nigeria. *Africa Development/Afrique et Développement, 20*(1), 37–58.
Mama, A. (2004). Critical capacities: Facing the challenges of intellectual development in Africa. *African Development, 29*(1), 1–23.
Mama, A. (2009). Demythologising gender in development: Feminist studies in African contexts. *IDS Bulletin, 35*(4), 121–124.
Moghadam, V. M. (2005). *Globalizing women: Transnational feminist networks*. Johns Hopkins University Press.
Mohanty, C. T. (1988). Under western eyes: Feminist scholarship and colonial discourses. *Feminist Review, 30*(1), 61–88.
Mohanty, C. T. (2003). "Under western eyes" revisited: Feminist solidarity through anti-capitalist struggles. *Signs: Journal of Women in Culture and Society, 28*(2), 499–535.
Morgan, R. (Ed.). (1970). *Sisterhood is powerful: An anthology of writings from the women's liberation movement*. Random House.
Narayan, U. (1997). *Dislocating cultures: Identities, traditions, and third world feminism*. Routledge.
Nash, J. C. (2008). Re-thinking intersectionality. *Feminist Review, 89*(1), 1–15.
Ogundipẹ-Leslie, M. (1994). *Re-creating ourselves: African women & critical transformations*. Africa World Press.

Oyewumi, O. (1997). *The invention of women: Making an African sense of Western gender discourses*. University of Minnesota Press.

Oyewumi, O. (2003). *African women and feminism: Reflecting on the politics of sisterhood*. Africa World Press.

Pereira, C. (2004). Locating gender and women's studies in Nigeria: What trajectories for the future? In A. A. Ampofo, J. Beoku-Betts, W. N. Njambi, & M. J. Osirim (Eds.), *Women's and gender studies in English-speaking sub-Saharan Africa: A review of research in the social sciences* (pp. 1–23). Routledge.

Smith, B. (1979). Toward a black feminist criticism. *The Massachusetts Review, 20*(1/2), 81–100.

Smith, L. T. (1999). *Decolonizing methodologies: Research and indigenous peoples*. Zed Books.

Spender, D. (1980). *Man-made language*. Routledge & Kegan Paul.

Spivak, G. C. (1988). Can the subaltern speak? In C. Nelson & L. Grossberg (Eds.), *Marxism and the interpretation of culture*. University of Illinois Press.

Stuhlhofer, E. W. (2021). *Navigating African feminisms: Wangari Maathai as a portrait. Draft paper for the Africa knows! Conference; panel G42*. Retrieved July 1, 2024, from https://nomadit.co.uk/conference/africaknows/paper/58023

Wyrod, R. (2008). Between women's rights and men's authority: Masculinity and shifting discourses of gender difference in urban Uganda. *Gender and Society, 22*(6), 799–823.

Yuval-Davis, N. (2006). Intersectionality and feminist politics. *European Journal of Women's Studies, 13*(3), 193–209.

Fatima K. Babih holds a doctorate in education. She is a distinguished educator and researcher in the United States and is passionate about empowering girls and women. She is an accomplished author, visionary founder, and chief executive officer of a nonprofit organization. Her organization is dedicated to advancing research, education, advocacy, and publications on African girls and women. Her dedication to this cause shines through her two published books, making her a prominent voice in the field. Her work inspires and uplifts individuals, significantly improving the lives of disadvantaged girls through education and gender-focused initiatives.

Part II

Humanities

African Religion

Simon Gisege Omare

This chapter is about conceptualizations of what being an African means in the field of African Religion. By African Religion I mean the African ways of sacred engagement with what is taken to be a spiritual reality, perceptions, thinking, feelings, and actions with respect to understanding and interpreting human existence. This chapter reveals that African Religion plays a significant role in the shaping of African identity. I focus on African Religion and identity because the religion shapes the African worldview which provides a framework for understanding the world, one's place in it, and the relationships among individuals, communities, and the divine. Thus, the major research question investigated in this chapter is the following: How does African Religion contribute to conceptualizations of the identity of Africans about being an African? The immediate answer to this question is that many conceptualizations have been offered regarding what being an African is in the arena of African Religion. This chapter is guided by the Afrocentricity Theory; an academic approach to scholarship that seeks to center the experiences and peoples of Africa within their own historical, cultural, and sociological context to bring out multiple conceptualizations.

This chapter employs the qualitative approach which emphasizes words as opposed to numerical values to delineate the conceptualization of being an African. The chapter utilizes secondary data which are analyzed descriptively. Based on the foregoing, what is the essence of investigating how Africa is conceptualized in the field of African Religion? The answer to this question is that African identity is deeply intertwined with the cultural, social, and historical fabric of African communities that is strengthened by African Religion. This religion, as aforementioned, shapes the African worldview on identity by providing a framework for understanding the world, one's place in it, and the relationships among individuals, communities, and the divine.

S. G. Omare (✉)
Philosophy, Religion and Theology, Moi University, Eldoret, Kenya
e-mail: omarexg@mu.ac.ke

A. K. Bangura, J. A. Ifedi (eds.), *Conceptualizations of Africa*, African Studies and Research Forum Series, https://doi.org/10.1007/978-3-031-74535-5_15

The chapter sets out to explain (a) conceptualization of African Religion, (b) the theoretical framework guiding the chapter, (c) wrong perceptions of being an African, (d) how Africans identify themselves, (e) the relations of Africans with other people of the world, (f) African Religion and African identity, and (g) challenges facing African identity in the twenty-first century. In the end, conclusions are drawn and recommendations for the future of African identity provided.

Conceptualization of African Religion

The term *African* refers to people who are native to or have ancestry from the continent of Africa. Africa is a vast and diverse continent with 54 sovereign states, each with its unique history, culture, and traditions. Before European colonization, Africa was a home to a diverse array of cultures, kingdoms, and civilizations with their own unique identities and names for their respective territories. Generally, today, *Africa* is a globally recognized name for the continent, encompassing sovereign states with defined territories. In all, the term *Africa* serves as a unifying term used to refer to the diverse peoples, cultures, and landscapes found across the continent.

Africa is the world's second largest and second most populous continent in terms of land area and population, respectively, and is located primarily in the Eastern and Northern Hemispheres (Newsela, 2017). The continent is bordered by the Mediterranean Sea to the north, the Atlantic Ocean to the west, and the Indian Ocean to the east. Africa is also known for its diverse geography, including deserts, savannas, tropical rainforests, and mountain ranges. It is in addition home to a wide range of plant and animal species, many of which are found nowhere else on the earth. The people of Africa are equally diverse, with over 3000 different ethnic groups and more than 2000 languages spoken throughout the continent. African cultures have a rich and complex history, with traditions and customs that date back thousands of years. Due to its vastness and diversity, Africa is challenging to generalize vis-à-vis the religious conceptualizations across the entire continent.

Before the introduction of foreign religions such as Christianity and Islam, indigenous African Religion was widely practiced throughout the continent (Mbiti, 1975). This religion varied from region to region and involves the veneration of ancestral spirits, nature deities, and a belief in a Supreme Being or Creator, thereby giving a variety of African religious practices. Ancestor veneration, rituals, divination, and communal ceremonies are common elements in African Religion. Ancestor veneration involves honoring and seeking guidance from deceased ancestors who are believed to have the power to influence the lives of their living descendants. Ancestors are seen as intermediaries between the living and the divine, and their spirits are invoked for protection, blessings, and wisdom.

Therefore, African Religion means people's beliefs and opinions concerning the existence, nature, and worship of a deity or deities, and divine involvement in the universe and human life. It is the belief in supernatural beings by Africans. African Religion acknowledges the existence of a Supreme Being or Creator whose names vary among different ethnic groups in Africa (Mbiti, 2012). Additionally, various divinities and spirits are recognized for their representation of different aspects of nature such as water, land, fertility, and animals. Divination practices are integral in African Religion. Diviners, who are considered to possess spiritual insight, use various methods such as interpreting dreams, reading signs in nature, or casting oracles to communicate with the spirit realm and gain insight into the past, present, or future. Divination is often sought for guidance, problem-solving, and decision-making.

African Religion is a revealed religion (Awolalu & Dopamu, 1979, p. 27) that does not have any founder. It is a traditional religion of Africans that does not have written scriptures but transmitted orally from one generation to another through oral traditions such as songs, liturgies, proverbs, short sayings, myths, and other means; hence, the religion is written in people's hearts, minds, or oral history. Apart from the belief in a Supreme Being, spirits, divinities, and ancestors, the religion also involves the use of magic and charms. Generally, the religion does not convert people and it is a way of life of Africans; thus, Africans cannot detach themselves from the religion no matter where they migrate to. The adherents of the religion believe in a cyclic life that involves one's reincarnation after death through a series of rebirth, re-death, *rerebirth,* and *reredeath*—an endless cycle of death and being reborn. Members of the religion do not believe in hell, paradise, end of the world, or messianic hope, and it does not have missionaries.

Over time, African Religion has experienced syncretism with other belief systems (Ike, 2022). This syncretism has resulted from interactions with other religions such as Christianity and Islam. As a result, some African religious practices may blend their elements of traditional beliefs with aspects of foreign religions. It is important to note that Africa is a vast continent with numerous ethnic groups which have their specific religions and cultural traditions. The religious practices and beliefs vary slightly from one region to another; however, most beliefs and practices are almost the same, thereby, necessitating the use of the term African Religion in singular form throughout this chapter.

Theoretical Framework

This chapter is guided by the Afrocentricity Theory, an academic approach to scholarship that seeks to center the experiences and peoples of Africa within their own historical, cultural, and sociological context (Milofsky & Rinke, 2006). It is a theoretical framework and cultural ideology that emerged in the late twentieth century, primarily within African American and other African diasporic communities. It aims to challenge the Eurocentric perspectives that have dominated academic and cultural discourses. Afrocentricity seeks to foster a positive and empowered sense of identity among individuals of African heritage.

The key principles of Afrocentricity focus on the centrality of Africa, reclaiming African identity, critique of Eurocentrism, validation of African knowledge systems, empowerment, social change, and Pan-Africanism (Natchaba, 2023). Afrocentricity emphasizes the significance of African civilizations, knowledge systems, and cultural achievements in shaping world history and human civilization. In addition, Afrocentricity seeks to counter historical and contemporary narratives that have marginalized or misrepresented African culture and experiences. It encourages individuals of African descent to embrace their heritage, history, and cultural practices as sources of pride and strength and further critiques the Eurocentric biases that have been pervasive in academic disciplines, media, and cultural representations. It further challenges the dominant narratives that have perpetuated negative stereotypes and distorted views of Africa and its people.

Afrocentricity acknowledges the value of African knowledge systems, including oral traditions, artistic expressions, and spiritual beliefs. It seeks to integrate and validate these forms of knowledge within academic and cultural contexts. In addition, Afrocentricity advocates for social, political, and economic empowerment within African communities and promotes efforts to challenge systemic racism, inequality, and injustice. This means that Afrocentricity aligns with the principles of Pan-Africanism, which emphasizes the unity and solidarity of people of African descent worldwide. It calls for collaboration and cooperation among African nations and communities to address shared challenges and aspirations. It is essential to understand that Afrocentricity is not about promoting a form of racial superiority or exclusion. Instead, it seeks to redress historical imbalances and contribute to a more inclusive and equitable world where all cultures and peoples are valued and respected. Afrocentricity has been influential in academia, cultural studies, and identity politics, and it has played a role in challenging dominant discourses and fostering a deeper appreciation of African heritage and contributions to human civilization.

Like any other theoretical framework, Afrocentricity has been subjected to criticism and debates, particularly concerning its applications and potential limitations. Critiques of Afrocentricity have emerged from various perspectives and scholarly debates (Brown, 2001). Nonetheless, the theory's critics do not dismiss the entire concept of Afrocentricity but rather engage in a critical analysis of its postulates and practices. Afrocentricity continues to evolve and respond to these critics, with ongoing scholarly debates and refinements aimed at furthering our understanding of African history, culture, and identity. Some of the critics argue that Afrocentricity essentializes African identity and culture through a monolithic and static view of Africa, failing to acknowledge the vast diversity and complexities within African societies and the African Diaspora.

Some scholars have raised concerns about the historical accuracy of Afrocentricity's claims, particularly regarding assertions about ancient African civilizations and their contributions to world history which are sometimes pegged on speculative or insufficiently supported evidence, which undermines its academic credibility. Other critics argue that Afrocentricity, in its opposition to Eurocentrism, risks perpetuating a binary thinking that frames African and European cultures as inherently opposing or mutually exclusive. Still some critics argue that Afrocentricity focuses primarily on historical narratives and cultural heritage, while neglecting contemporary social, economic, and political challenges faced by African communities such as poverty, inequality, governance, and human rights. In addition, there are critics who raise concerns about the methodological rigor of Afrocentricity's scholarship that relies heavily on selective evidence, biased interpretations, or lack of peer review, which can undermine the scholarly validity of the claims made. But, as Abdul Karim Bangura (2013, 2019) and Yoshitaka Miike (2008), a leading scholar of Asiacentricity, have demonstrated, these critics' renderings are based on perfunctory and/or limited reading of the exorbitant amount of work by scholars of Afrocentricity.

This chapter is guided by the Afrocentricity Theory to seek answers to these questions: How is Africa and being an African perceived by non-Africans? How do Africans identify themselves? How do Africans relate themselves with other people in the world? How does African Religion perceive African identity? What are the challenges of African identity in the twenty-first century? These questions are broached individually in the ensuing sections.

Wrong Perceptions of Africa and Being African

Have you ever wondered what it means to be an African? In 2014, I attended the Conference of Young African Scholars in Cambridge, United Kingdom. While in a company of some young African scholars, we interacted with some young men of European origin who inquired about where we came from. I told them that I came from Kenya. Having read some books about Kenya, one of the young men inquired how we managed to live peacefully with wild animals. It took a lot of energy to explain that Africans do not live in the wilderness with wild animals. Although offended, I inquired why they thought Africans live in the wilderness. It seemed like much of their thoughts had been generated from earlier Western scholars' opinions that portrayed Africa and being African in a negative way.

The earlier European scholars were biased in their interpretation of being African, some scholars such as Henry Stanely Morton (1841–1904) regarded Africa as a "Dark Continent" where people had no idea of God and where the Devil in all his abysmal, grotesque and forbidden features, armed to the teeth and with horns complete, held sway (Idowu, 1973). It seems that these theorists fabricated fantastic tales about Africa with unknown intentions which later influenced the attitudes of Europeans about Africa and being African.

When Edward W. Ludwig got to know that Edwin Smith was in Africa as a missionary, he was surprised and asked: "How can the untutored Africans comprehend God? Deity is a philosophical concept which savages are incapable of framing" (Smith, 1966, p. 1). The foregoing excerpt implies that Africans are savages. Ludwig's quote shows the ignorance, prejudice, and pride of these theorists. One may ask the following question: Was Smith serving a personalized God or a universal God? It is an indication that these scholars did not have an understanding of Africa and being African. They portrayed Africa as a continent devoid of culture and religion, especially with particular reference to the knowledge of "their" God bringing in a new perceived identity which ranked the God of Africans as a lesser

God compared to their God. Prominent among such people were Andrew Lang, Archbishop N. Soderblom, and Father Schmidt of Vienna (Smith, 1966).

In the preface of his book titled *African Religions in Western Scholarship*, Okot p'Bitek (1971) describes his experience with Western scholars at Oxford University in 1960. He felt frustrated while in the Institute of Social Anthropology where most teachers referred to and identified Africans as barbarians, savages, primitives, and tribes. He identified early scholars of Anthropology who used derogatory words to refer to Africans in their titles of books and articles in journals such *Primitive Culture, Primitive Religion, The Savage Mind, Primitive Government, The Position of Women in Savage Societies, Institution of Primitive Societies,* and *Primitive Mentality.* Such titles influenced the identity of Africans since the European nations adopted the same words and influenced a clique of "educated" Africans into adopting Westernization.

Notably, the opinions of most classical scholars were biased as they ranked their own religions at a higher status, better and advanced compared to African Religion. For example, the Greek Herodotus (c. 484–c. 425 BC) thought that the religion of Egypt originated from Greece (Ward, 2006). Seemingly, most of the early Western scholars described African religion in abusive terminologies and negative imageries. Further, Herodotus described inhabitants of the Great Sahara as "creatures without heads" in reference to Libyans who he claimed had eyes on their breasts. In addition, George identified the Sicilian historian Diodorus Siculus (c. 90–c. 30 BC) who derided Ethiopians in terms of both body and soul. He noted that Diodorus described them as people who were black in color, with flat noses and woolly hair. According to Diodorus (1935), their spirit was entirely savage and displayed the nature of a wild beast, and practiced uncivilized life in comparison to the rest of mankind.

As Okot p'Bitek (1971) notes, classical scholars painted Africans as a people characterized by anarchy, promiscuity, and cruelty. They described Africans as strange and miserable folk who exist in hunger and fear. This means that they defined Africans in terms of what they were presumably not in the form of inhumanity, wilderness, and lack of proper law. They used arrogant labels such as "primitive." p'Bitek discusses the superstitions of the Westerners during the Middle Ages since they had effects of their nineteenth-century thinking in terms of the relationships between inhabitants of Africa and the invaders. The Superstitions include the description of Herodotus of Harlicarnassus (484–428) that the country and inhabitants of the land to the east of Libya had huge serpents, lions, elephants, creatures without heads and have eyes in their breasts, and also with *wild men* and *wild women* (Rawlinson, 1956, p. 146). Further, Okot notes in his book *Decolonizing African Religions. A Short History of Western Scholarship* (2011) that Frobisher wrote that the American Indians pluck and eat grass like brute beasts and live in caves of the earth. In addition, Okoth (2011) also identifies William den Rhyle who described Hottentots as lawless barbarians and immortal pagans who practiced only those habits to which the blind impulse of nature irresistibly impels them. The foregoing creatures were taken as the identity of Africans. In regard to the foregoing, the superstitions of the Westerners provided a justification to dehumanize Africans, turn them into slaves, and write wrong things about being an African.

One of the most prevalent misconceptions in the Western world is that Africa is a homogeneous entity or a single country. In reality, as mentioned earlier, Africa is a vast and diverse continent with 54 recognized countries, each with its own distinct cultural practices, languages, histories, and traditions. In fact, as also earlier noted, there are over 2000 languages spoken across the African continent and "African" is not one of them. Some Westerners have a wrong assumption that "African" is a language (Kelland & Sánchez, 2018). Ideally, this is the equivalent of presuming that people who live in Europe speak "European." Notably, English is an official language in 24 African nations and it is taught in high level in schools across the continent.

While Africa does face its share of economic and social challenges, it is not solely defined by poverty and underdevelopment as perceived by some people living outside Africa. Some scholars see Africans as helpless and dependent on Western aid for decades (Kwemo, 2017). Therefore, some portray Africa as a place bombarded by images of sad, dirty children with eyes that call you to urgently donate money. The foregoing seems to be in line with the Luganda proverb that says, "He who hasn't travelled or had exposure, thinks that their mother is the best chef or cook." In reality, however, Africa has a growing middle class, booming economies, vibrant cultural scenes, and a wealth of natural resources. It is important to recognize the economic progress and wealth diversity that exist across the continent.

Africans are portrayed as being backward in technology and innovation by most people who live outside Africa and never visited the continent. Contrary to popular belief, Africa has significant growth in technology and innovation. Many African countries have leapfrogged traditional infrastructure and embraced mobile technology, leading to advancements in mobile banking, E-commerce, and other technological sectors (Heifer International, 2019). Africa is home to numerous technology hubs, startups, and innovators making contributions to various industries. Technology in Africa is actually an incredibly fast-growing market, with many global technology giants making big investments in the continent. Research has revealed that people in Kenya, for instance, are four times more likely to own a mobile phone than to have access to a toilet or latrine. By 2013, 80% of African people had access to mobile phones. This means that mobile technology is being used in various places across Africa (Kelland & Sánchez, 2018).

In 2014, Delta Airlines, a major United States carrier, on congratulating the United States World Cup team on a victory over Ghana used a photo of a giraffe to represent the African nation (Kelland & Sánchez, 2018). Unfortunately, there are no wild giraffes in Ghana. While Africa is known for its diverse wildlife and stunning landscapes, it is not solely defined by Safaris and wildlife reserves. Africa is a home to bustling cities, modern infrastructure, cultural heritage sites, and vibrant urban centers, alongside its natural wonders.

Africa has experienced its share of conflicts and challenges, but it is inaccurate to portray the entire continent as a place perpetually engulfed in violence. Today, if one speaks of Africa what comes to the minds of many Europeans and Americans are images of famine and hunger, civil wars, and military coups (Cohen, 2014). Many African countries have stable political systems and are peaceful and safe for residents and visitors alike. It is important to avoid generalizations and understand that each country has its unique context.

As stated earlier, Africans are referred to as backward or primitive and the African continent is often portrayed as a backward or primitive place (Heifer International, 2019). Nevertheless, as I also pointed out, African societies have a rich history and advanced civilizations, and have also made significant contributions to science, art, and philosophy. Therefore, it is crucial to recognize Africa's historical achievements and its modern-day contributions to various fields. In addition, there is a misconception that Africans lack education or intelligence. Africa has a rich intellectual and educational history, with renowned scholars, universities, and research institutions. Many Africans have made significant contributions to various fields, including science, literature, arts, and academia. In relation to the foregoing, another misconception is that all Africans share the same cultural practices, traditions, and languages. Africa is home to a rich tapestry of diverse cultures, ethnic groups, and languages. There is immense cultural, linguistic, and ethnic diversity across the continent, with each region and country having its own unique characteristics.

Some people perceive and identify Africans as "a cursed people" (Fenton, 1996). Fenton explains that the story of the curse is connected to the Biblical Noah and his sons. In the Bible, Noah had three sons: (1) Shem, (2) Ham, and (3) Japheth. This information can be found in the Bible in the Book of Genesis, specifically in Genesis 5:32, which mentions Noah's three sons, and in Genesis 6:10, which also lists their names. Shem, Ham, and Japheth played significant roles in the biblical account of the Great Flood and the subsequent repopulation of the Earth according to the Bible's narrative. After the floods subsided, Noah planted a vineyard and harvested grapes. He made wine from the grapes, got drunk, and fell asleep carelessly exposing his manhood. While Ham was passing inside the tent, he saw his father's nakedness and told his two brothers, Shem and Japheth. Shem and Japheth took a piece of cloth, walked in reverse, and covered their father's nakedness. When Noah got sober, he woke up and sensed what had happened, got annoyed, and cursed Ham (his youngest son), together with his son Canaan, and their generations to be slaves. Shem and Japheth received Noah's blessing because they had covered their father's drunken nakedness, while Ham, on the other hand, violated their father by looking at his nakedness. As a result, the descendants of Ham were cursed. Whizzing forward to the medieval versions, we learn more about the nature of Ham's misdeeds. It is said that Ham mocked Noah's nakedness and invited his brothers to do the same (which they refused). Nonetheless, this is not the first of Ham's transgressions. It is also explained that when they had all been on the Ark together, Noah had insisted that everyone be sexually continent, but Ham, with the aid of a magic demon, slept with his wife. The next day, Noah saw his foot prints, and there grew up an enmity between Noah and his son. Some myths explain that Ham's descendants were punished by being given black skin. Much later, when the world came to be divided up, Japheth received Europe, Shem got Asia, and Ham was awarded Africa.

I conclude this section with Abagusii of east Africa's proverb that goes, "Until the lions have their own historians, the history of the hunt will always glorify the hunter." The foregoing proverb recognizes the importance of having a voice in telling one's own story and history. It speaks to the idea that African identity and history should be conveyed from the perspective of Africans themselves, rather than being defined solely by external influences. The following subsection explains how Africans identify themselves.

How Africans Identify Themselves

It is common to hear people telling one another that "this is African." Surprisingly, there is no universal standard for classifying something as being "African" or not. Nevertheless, there are commonalities in the identities across Africa. Generally, according to Africans, "being African" means acting according to the demands of African Religion; it means being a part of the diverse and rich continent of Africa. Being an African also means observing taboos and totems of African communities. For instance, among the religious beliefs of Abagusii of Kenya, it is a taboo for cousins to intermarry; intermarriage between relatives in African is anti-African. Anything propagated by Europeans but unacceptable in Africa is seen as "anti-African." Most indigenous Africans see Eurocentric actions as those aimed at corrupting their indigenous ways of life (Samir, 1989). To Africans, Eurocentrism can lead to the suppression of diverse cultures, languages, and traditions by enforcing Eurocentric norms and values as a standard, which can be harmful to global cultural diversity. What therefore maintains life, peace, and harmony in the African community is the moral imperative; it is the right thing to do. Therefore, anything that does not maintain or is contrary to life, communal peace, and harmony is immoral or not right; it is the wrong thing to avoid in Africa. African ethics are in forms of laws, rules, customs, traditions, and taboos. Consequently, African morality is governed by unwritten laws that deal mostly with what destroys or promotes humanness, and this gives an identity based on African ethics on morality.

As an African, one may identify himself/herself with a specific country of origin and its unique history, culture, religion, and language, while also recognizing the broader connection to the African continent as a whole. This connection is often expressed through a shared history of colonialism and struggle for independence, as well as a common commitment to promoting African unity, development, and progress. Africans share a rich history and heritage that includes ancient civilizations, kingdoms, and empires which are supported by the region's religion. This history encompasses contributions to art, science, philosophy, and trade, such as the kingdoms of Egypt, Mali, Ghana, and Zimbabwe. Understanding and acknowledging this shared historical legacy is an important aspect of African identity.

There is also a strong sense of pride in African religious cultures and traditions, and many Africans view their cultural heritage as a source of strength and resilience. Nonetheless, this pride is not exclusionary, and many Africans are open to learning from and embracing the cultures of others. Being African means embracing and celebrating the continent's cultural heritage, which includes a rich diversity of music, art, literature, cuisine, and traditional practices. There is a particular mode of attire associated with Africans. Textiles such as *kente* cloth (West Africa), *kanga* (East Africa), and *bogolanfini* (Mali) are renowned for their intricate designs and vibrant colors. This means that there are forms of African attire associated with different regions in Africa such as Nigerian attire, Ghanian attire, and South African attire, among others. Textiles are often used for clothing, decorative purposes, and as a means of cultural expression. Adornments like jewelry, body paint, scarification, and hairstyles are also integral to African art, reflecting personal and cultural identities.

African music is diverse and encompasses a wide range of styles, genres, and traditions that vary across the continent's regions and traditions. It is identified with its complex rhythms and vibrant percussion, and drumming is a fundamental element. The use of vocal techniques such as yodeling, ululation, and vocal ornamentation is common in different African musical styles. Africa has a rich variety of traditional musical instruments such as xylophones, *mbiras* (thumb pianos), *koras* (harp-lutes), *balafons* (wooden xylophones), *ngonis* (lutes), talking drums, and a wide array of wind instruments such as flutes, trumpets, and horns.

Africans identify themselves with traditional African art which reflects the cultural and spiritual beliefs of various African societies. It encompasses a wide range of art forms, including sculpture, masks, textiles, pottery, beadwork, metalwork, and body adornment. Traditional African art often serves ceremonial, religious, or ritualistic purposes, embodying the cultural values and identities of specific communities. In other contexts, Africans identify themselves through sculpture which holds a prominent place in African art. Wood, stone, metal, and clay are commonly used materials. Sculptures can depict human figures, animals, or abstract forms, showcasing the technical skills and aesthetic sensibilities of African artists. Masks are another important form of artistic expression, often used in religious ceremonies, rituals, and performances. Masks can represent spirits, ancestors, or mythological beings and serve as a bridge between the physical and spiritual realms.

It is common for Africans to identify themselves with their traditional cuisines where most of them have religious significance to the specific community. Generally, one cannot miss an African eatery in all major cities globally. Nonetheless, Africans do not have a common African meal for identity since each African region, country, or ethnic group has its own unique culinary traditions, ingredients, and cooking techniques. North African cuisine, for example, is heavily influenced by Arab, Berber (a European misnomer for Amazigh), and Mediterranean flavors and often features dishes like *couscous, tagines,* and *shawarma*. West African cuisine is known for its use of bold flavors, spicy stews, and dishes like *jollof* rice, *fufu,* and *egusi* soup. East African cuisine is characterized by its use of grains, legumes, and vegetables, with popular dishes like *injera*, *pilau* rice, and *ugali*. Southern African cuisine includes dishes like *bobotie, biltong*, and *braai* (barbecue). Africa is known for its vibrant street food culture whereby street vendors and markets offer a wide variety of snacks and street foods, including grilled meats, samosas, roasted plantains, kebabs, fried dough balls, and various fried or grilled snacks.

Being African is to respect the indigenous African religious traditions. African culture is characterized by a deep respect for community, family, and ancestral traditions, as well as a vibrant sense of creativity, innovation, and resilience in the face of challenges. African culture places a strong emphasis on the importance of collective well-being. It is common to refer to people who are individualistic as "not being Africans." This implies that respect for community is deeply ingrained in the social fabric of African societies. Also, Africans identify themselves with their extended families and kinship systems. This means that African societies often have strong extended family and kinship networks that extend beyond immediate relatives to include a wider circle of aunts, uncles, cousins, and even other community members. These networks provide social support, guidance, and a sense of belonging. In Africa, individuals are expected to prioritize the needs of their families and contribute to the well-being of the community as a whole. African identity is closely intertwined with communities. The concept of community plays a vital role in shaping and defining individual and collective identities. This is because African communities often share a common cultural heritage which includes traditions, customs, languages, and historical narratives in the name of *Ubuntu*. Through participation in community activities, individuals engage with their cultural heritage, learn traditional practices, and develop a sense of belonging and pride in their shared identity.

Being African is to have an identity of *Ubuntu* which, as mentioned earlier, is a common philosophy applied across Africa that emphasizes the interconnectedness of individuals and the belief that one's humanity is tied to the well-being of others. The philosophy of *Ubuntu* underscores the idea that individuals are a part of a larger community and that their actions should contribute positively to the collective. *Ubuntu* promotes African religious values associated with Africanness such as compassion, empathy, and communal harmony. Those not having the identified values are commonly referred not to be African. The continent's cultural practices often place a high value on hospitality and generosity, and there is a tradition of sharing resources and supporting one another. It is common to hear people emphasizing the need of being African in reference to good character depicted in taboos. In many African societies, there is a strong emphasis on social harmony and the common good. This means that individuals are expected to act in ways that benefit the community as a whole, rather than just their own individual interests.

Language is a powerful aspect of African identity. Communities often have their own languages or dialects that serve as a means of communication and cultural expression (Eegunlusi, 2017). Through the use of language within the community, individuals develop a sense of belonging and connection to their African heritage. In addition, African communities engage in various religious rituals and celebrations that reinforce their shared identity. These rituals can include rites of passage, religious ceremonies, festivals, and cultural events. Participation in these communal activities helps to reinforce cultural values, transmit knowledge and traditions, and strengthen a sense of African identity.

Alexander Keese (2019) notes that African communities often have a collective historical narrative that informs their identity which connects with the Divine Being through myths. By sharing stories, oral traditions, and historical knowledge, communities preserve and pass down their collective memory to younger generations. This historical continuity contributes to a sense of African identity and a shared connection to the past. It is also good to note that African communities often come together to address common challenges and work toward shared goals.

Africans are known for their resilience and resourcefulness, having overcome many challenges throughout their history, including colonization, slavery, and political instability (Moller & Roberts, 2021). There is also a strong sense of pride in African traditions, and many Africans are committed to preserving and promoting their cultural heritage. It means being resilient, resourceful, and optimistic in the face of adversity, and striving to build a better future for oneself, one's community, and the continent. Most Africans consider themselves hardy because of their relation with the hardy environments they must endure. It is common for Africans to consider people from other ethnic groups to be "weak" since they are considered "soft"—"they do not have the potential to persevere through the hardships." The foregoing is based on the vast challenges associated with the African continent such as hunger, diseases, harsh climatic conditions, attack from wild animals, poor transport, and communication facilities among others.

African culture places a strong emphasis on the role of ancestors and spirits in the natural world which also form part of their identity (Mbiti, 1969). Many African societies believe that the spirits of ancestors are present in nature and that these spirits can help to guide and protect the living. In some African cultures, certain natural features such as rivers or mountains are believed to be inhabited by ancestral spirits (Omare, 2010). Circumstances have valorized religious affiliations so that we think of a person in terms of religion and, as a result, that person thinks of him/herself in terms of religion. Our subjectivities are constructed not by what we think but by how society has constructed how we should think; religion plays a holistic role in determining a person's understanding of his/her origin and purpose. Mbiti maintains that the African worldview on being African is shaped by a rich and diverse cultural heritage that emphasizes community, spirituality, and interconnectedness. African culture often places a strong emphasis on communal living, whereby the needs of the community are prioritized over individual desires. Many Africans place a strong emphasis on community and family, and there is a sense of interconnectedness and interdependence among individuals. For Mbiti, community is a central aspect of African culture and plays a significant role in the daily lives of most Africans. The African concept of community extends beyond just the immediate family to encompass extended family, neighbors, and even the larger society. The concept of community in African culture is often reflected in communal living arrangements, where several families may live together in a compound or village. This allows for the sharing of resources, as well as the pooling of knowledge and skills. The foregoing is considered as the call to *Ubuntu*.

In the African worldview, being Black is not just a physical characteristic but also a cultural identity that is deeply tied to a rich and diverse religious heritage (Mwikamba, 1991). African culture places a strong emphasis on ancestry and lineage, and there is a sense of pride in one's cultural heritage and traditions. Blackness is often associated with a strong connection to the land and the natural world, as well as a deep respect for spirituality and the ancestors. African culture views the world holistically, with the physical and spiritual realms interconnected. In some African communities, the color black is associated with power and strength. Blackness is seen as a symbol of resilience and endurance, with many African societies having overcome various forms of oppression throughout their histories. Nevertheless, it is important to note that there is not a single African worldview on being Black, as Africa is a diverse continent with many different customs and traditions. While many Africans may share similar perspectives on blackness, there are also many variations and nuances depending on geographic location, cultural background, and individual experiences.

Africans also identify themselves through Pan-Africanism, which is an influential ideology that shapes African identity and promotes a sense of African unity (Tunde, 1998). Pan-Africanism is a movement that advocates for the unity, solidarity, and empowerment of African people worldwide. It emphasizes the common history, struggles, and aspirations of Africans and promotes cooperation and collaboration among African nations. Pan-Africanism is the idea that peoples of African descent have common interests and should be unified in pursuing them. Tunde (1998) posits that the objective is to instill in Blacks an awareness of their African identity and culture as a defensive weapon against a pervasive and domineering Eurocentric worldview. Furthermore, Afrocentricity, as hinted earlier, involves re-education and re-socialization designed to rid Blacks' consciousness of the "tragic conception" of their history, culture, and heritage (Asante, 1993). It is supposed to bring Blacks in the Diaspora closer to Africa as they develop their knowledge of Africa.

Many African societies have a deep connection with the land, nature, and the environment (Mbiti, 1969). African identity often incorporates a reverence for the natural world, recognizing the importance of sustainable practices and harmonious relationships with the environment. This connection to the land is often expressed through spiritual beliefs, agricultural practices, and conservation efforts. Have you ever wondered why Africans insist on burying their own in their motherlands in Africa even if they die in far places? There is an attachment to their motherlands. It is a religious belief that in case one is buried far away from home, his/her spirit may never rest and may even haunt the living. We derive an example of what happened to the spirit of the late Vice President of Kenya Michael Wamalwa Kijana (Murimi, 2015). It is said that after his death, his spirit was not "brought home" to Kitale, Kenya, from London, 12 years after his death, in line with the Bukusu traditional beliefs. A team, led by his brother and former Water Cabinet Secretary Eugene Wamalwa, traveled to London on August 14, 2015, to "fetch" the spirit from the Royal Free hospital where Wamalwa died. The foregoing indicates the religious attachment of Africans to their homeland.

In all, I stick to a Luo proverb that says, "however far the stream flows, it never forgets its source." This Luo proverb notes the importance of acknowledging and embracing one's roots and identity, emphasizing that no matter how far individuals may go in life, they should never forget where they come from and take pride in their cultural heritage. I acknowledge that African identity is not static but continuously evolving. It encompasses both traditional cultural elements and contemporary influences, reflecting the realities of modern Africa. African identity recognizes the intersections with other aspects of identity such as gender, religion, and language, and recognizes the diversity within the African Diaspora. Nonetheless, it is important to remember that African identity is also personal and subjective. Individuals may have different interpretations and expressions of their African identity based on their own experiences, cultural backgrounds, and personal beliefs. It is a vibrant and ever-evolving concept that embraces the richness of Africa's past and present. African identity is a complex and multifaceted concept that encompasses the diverse histories, traditions, and experiences of the people who identify as African. It is important to iterate that Africa is a vast continent with numerous ethnic groups, languages, religions, and distinct cultural practices. Therefore, African identity can vary greatly depending on the specific region, country, or ethnic group being discussed.

Relations of Africans with Non-Africans Through Identity

The relationships between Africans and people of other races have been shaped by a complex history that includes colonization, slavery, globalization, migration, and cultural exchange. Africa has experienced the effects of European colonialism, which involved the subjugation and exploitation of African nations and peoples. The Trans-Atlantic Slave Trade, a dark chapter in world history, resulted in the forced migration and enslavement of millions of Africans, thereby impacting their relationships with people of other races, particularly in the Americas and Europe.

Following the independence movements of the mid-twentieth century, African countries established their own governments and began to redefine their relationships with former colonizers. This period birthed various dynamics, including political, economic, and cultural ties, as well as occasional tensions and conflicts. Globalization has facilitated increased mobility and interaction between Africans and individuals from different races and nationalities. Africans have migrated to other countries for various reasons such as seeking economic opportunities, pursuing education, or escaping conflict. These migrations have led to multicultural societies and the blending of different racial and ethnic backgrounds, leading to newer structured identities.

Africans have engaged in cultural exchanges with people of other races through art, music, literature, sports, and other forms of cultural expression. African cultural influences can be found worldwide, and there has been a growing appreciation for African music, fashion, cuisine, and traditions among people of various racial backgrounds. For instance, some sports are always associated with Africans such as long-distance races which are associated with Kenyans and Ethiopians.

The African Diaspora, resulting from historical forced migrations and voluntary movements, has established lasting connections between Africans and individuals of African descent living in other parts of the world. This includes people of African heritage in the Americas, Europe, the Caribbean, and other regions. These connections have shaped cultural and religious identities and fostered a sense of solidarity among people of African descent across the globe. In all, while there have been instances of racism, discrimination, and prejudice, it is also important to recognize the countless examples of cooperation, understanding, and solidarity between Africans and individuals of other races. Building positive relationships and promoting mutual respect, equality, and inclusivity are essential for fostering harmonious and equitable interactions among people of all racial backgrounds.

African Religion and African Identity

Can African identity exist without African Religion? This section reveals that African Religion plays a significant role in the shaping of African identity. It unveils that African identity is deeply intertwined with the cultural, social, and historical fabric of African communities that is strengthened by African Religion. The proposition advanced in this section is that African Religion is closely linked to cultural identity. This is because the religion serves as a repository of cultural values, traditions, and practices that are passed down from generation to generation. It is also important to point out that Africa's religious rituals, ceremonies, and festivals are important cultural expressions that strengthen a sense of identity and belonging within a particular community in Africa. The religion provides opportunities for communal bonding, storytelling, and the preservation of cultural heritage.

In Africa, ancestors are regarded as the guardians of norms that safeguard African identity; thus, ancestors are considered to be a source of guidance, protection, and wisdom. Therefore, the belief in ancestral connections reinforces a sense of continuity, lineage, and a connection to one's roots in Africa. Accordingly, everything revolves around ancestors; they are often invoked during important life events, rituals, and ceremonies, thereby reaffirming the importance of ancestral ties in African identity. Concomitantly, African Religion provides a moral and ethical framework for the identity of individuals in their communities and with other communities in Africa. It offers guidelines for behavior, social norms, and values such as honesty, respect, hospitality, and communal responsibility with which Africans proudly identify themselves. Generally, African religious teachings shape individuals' understanding of right and wrong, and emphasize the importance of harmonious relationships and social cohesion within a community.

African Religion always played a significant role in the resistance against colonialism and external domination. The religion provides a means of preserving cultural identity, resisting cultural assimilation, and asserting African agency. An example of a liberation religious practice connected to African Religion is Rastafarianism, which is a religio-political movement that commenced in Jamaica in the 1930s to disseminate a Pan-African political consciousness across the globe. Through such movements, African religious practices and beliefs serve as a source of strength, resilience, and cultural resistance in the face of historical challenges and marginalization with regard to identity. While there has been an influence of other religious traditions such as Islam and Christianity, many Africans still maintain elements of their traditional religious practices alongside these newer faiths. It is good to note that African Religion contributes to a multilayered, complex identity that encompasses both traditional and contemporary beliefs and practices.

African religious identity emphasizes communal aspects of spirituality; many African religious practices are communal and involve participation of the entire community. Rituals, ceremonies, and festivals are communal events that bring people together to celebrate, seek blessings, or mark important life events. African religious identity reflects a deep connection to both the natural and metaphysical world. Generally, African Religion views nature as sacred by recognizing the spiritual presence in natural elements such as trees, rivers, mountains, and animals with which Africans identify themselves. In turn, African communities often practice rituals and ceremonies that celebrate and honor natural environmental phenomena (Omare, 2010).

How do African communities spread the message of identity to younger generations? Wise men of Nigeria have a proverb that says, "The child who is not embraced by the village will burn it down to feel its warmth." This proverb from Nigeria emphasizes the importance of community and the idea that individuals are shaped by their cultural surroundings hence necessitating educating children on communal values on identity. In Africa, despite having almost homogeneous patterns of identity, there are no written records on African identity. Knowledge on African identity is often passed down through oral traditions, including myths, stories, legends, and rituals. These oral traditions transmit religious knowledge, cultural values, and spiritual practices regarding identity from one generation to another, thereby providing a means of connecting with the divine, seeking blessings, and fostering a sense of community.

African Religion teaches the principle of *Utu*, meaning "personhood." One who has *Utu* is expected to love others without discrimination and respect the lives of others at all costs. The term *Utu* is derived from the Swahili word *mtu*, which means not just "a person" but a "person in relationships." Eunice Kamaara observes that it is without contradiction that indigenous Africans appreciate *Utu* as the essence of individual human persons but only in community (Kamaara, 2012). Kamaara was echoing Mbiti's (1982) words that in traditional African life, an individual does not and cannot exist alone except corporately. Kamaara explains that an individual owes his/her essence to other people, thereby making him/her a part of a whole. Whatever happens to an individual happens to a whole group and whatever happens to the whole group happens to the individual. I agree with the notion that an individual can say "I am because we are and since we are therefore I am" (Mbiti, 1969), and this is the universal spirit of *Ubuntu* which the whole world should embrace. *Ubuntu* infers that all humans are crucial in the society, regardless of age, sex, and race. It calls for togetherness and showing one another love. Any behavior that goes against what could promote love is considered a vice. Each member of the African society is supposed to be an eye of another member. It is common knowledge that an individual's misbehavior can lead to communal curses. For instance, if one mistreats another person in secrecy, the ancestors will revenge on behalf of the person. African brotherhood and sisterhood go beyond human boundaries to embrace the entire creation, including non-Africans, animals, and natural environmental resources. Since non-Africans have red blood just like Africans, Africans identify them as brothers and sisters—thus, equal partners.

We conclude this section with a Zulu proverb that articulates "Until the lion learns to speak, the tales of hunting will be weak." This Zulu proverb connotes the importance of preserving and expressing one's cultural identity. It presages that, unless individuals within a culture actively participate in sharing and preserving their stories and beliefs, the richness of their cultural heritage may get lost or diminished. The lion symbolizes the strength and uniqueness of African identity, and speaking represents the act of communicating and passing down cultural knowledge.

Challenges Facing African Identity in the Twenty-First Century

The legacy of colonialism has a profound impact on African identity (Anyaehie, 2013). Colonial authorities imposed their cultures, languages, and political systems on African societies, leading to a disintegration of traditional identities and the expurgation of local languages and customs. The European colonizers embarked upon the dominion and destruction of African culture. Chinua Achebe in his book titled *Things Fall Apart* writes the following: "The white man is very clever. He came quietly and peaceably with his religion. We were amused at his foolishness and allowed him to stay. Now he has won our brothers, and our clan can no longer act like one. He has put a knife on the things that held us together and we have fallen apart" (Achebe, 2006, p. 124).

Achebe's novel is set in precolonial Nigeria and tells the story of Okonkwo, a respected Igbo leader and warrior, as he grapples with the impact of British colonialism and Christian missionaries on his community and culture. This exchange occurs in a conversation between Obierika and Okonkwo in the novel. In the discussion, which centers on various events that had come to pass since the arrival of the colonialists in Nigeria, Obierika seems to voice Achebe's own thoughts on colonialism that the arrival of White colonizers who brought their religion (Christianity) and other aspects of European culture disrupted the identity of the traditional Igbo society. He writes that the Igbo initially underestimated the colonizers but now realize that their unity and traditional way of life and identity were being eroded, leading to division and conflict within the Igbo community. Achebe's thoughts happened too across the whole of Africa during colonization since there were no exertions to dialogue with African culture. The colonialists termed African culture as backward, primitive, and valueless. African gods were declared evil and the African race was classified as inferior to the European, thereby disrupted and destabilized African values, beliefs, and perceptions which define the people and leading to the loss of their identity.

With the Eurocentric mentality, the colonizers embarked upon the reorientation of Africa to perceive the world from the Eurocentric angle. The Europeans, driven by the spirit of modernism, aimed at subjugating the world by the use of sophisticated culture and technology. Many European writers of this time interpreted the history of Europe as a supermodel for the rest of the world (Eurocentrism, 2012). Such instruments of ranking and racist alignment were used to rationalize slavery, genocide, and other forms of political and economic manipulation. In response, Europe introduced a program they termed "civilization of African brutes"—a characterization that is derogatory. How do you judge another person's identity using your own parameters? We consider the foregoing as subjective and inconsiderate. Apart from Europeans, the French embarked on the assimilation of Africans into French culture because they believed that Africans had an inferior culture.

Religious groups especially Christians and Muslims also embarked on reorienting the African worldview by introducing their own, a matter that affected African identity. Therefore, the European mission disoriented African values and beliefs which promoted African identity. I commend literary African writers such as Chinua Achebe (1960), Ngũgĩ wa Thiong'o (1964), and Chimamanda Ngozi Adichie (2013) who have explored themes on the effects of European colonialism on African identity and culture in their works. Their works offer insightful perspectives on the complexities of postcolonial African identity and the ongoing quest for cultural and political identity. Through their works, readers can gain a deeper understanding of the challenges and resilience of African societies in the face of colonial disorientation.

The increasing influence of globalization and Western media has led to the dilution of indigenous cultures and values. Western media often encourages the use of English or other dominant languages, which normally overshadows the use of indigenous languages. This erodes linguistic diversity and the cultural identity tied to indigenous languages. This means that in such a situation, African societies are confronted with a dominant global culture that often undermines local traditions and tends to instill a sense of cultural homogenization. In addition, indigenous cultures and peoples are sometimes portrayed in a stereotypical or superficial manner when Western media perpetuate misconceptions and biases. Similarly, Western media tend to appropriate elements of African indigenous cultural practices without proper understanding or respect, thereby leading to the dilution of their authenticity.

Africa's diverse population consists of numerous ethnic groups. The competition for some resources has always led to tension, which can lead to conflicts. Africa is rich in natural resources, including minerals, oil, and arable land. The competition for access to and control over these resources can lead to conflicts within and among African nations and hinder efforts to foster unity. The competition for same resources, political power, and historical grievances is a challenge to the formation of a unified African identity. Persistent economic disparities among different African countries and regions lead to feelings of marginalization and division. In her novel titled *Half of a Yellow Sun* (2010), Chimamanda Ngozi Adichie depicts what took place during the Nigerian Civil War and explores the competition for resources and power between different ethnic groups in Nigeria. Generally, economic inequalities can hinder the development of a collective African identity that transcends national boundaries. Promoting cultural exchange and celebrating Africa's diverse cultures can bond Africans and build a shared sense of identity.

The movement of African people to other continents, often due to economic or political reasons, has resulted in the development of significant African Diaspora communities (Magidimisha et al., 2018). Most migrations are caused by factors such as conflict, political instability, and economic disparities that have contributed to both internal and international migration within the continent. Maintaining a strong sense of African identity among these populations while adapting to new cultural contexts can be challenging. In addition, African migration has been occurring for centuries, driven by factors such as the slave trade, colonialism, and economic opportunities. These migrations have played a crucial role in shaping the identities of Africans and their descendants in different parts of the world. The African Diaspora has led to the development of diverse identities among African communities outside of Africa, often influenced by their unique experiences and the cultures of their host countries.

European slavery and colonialism devastated African psyche, rubbished its culture and values, and left it empty of any coherent worldview of reality (Anyaehie, 2013). The travails and backwardness of Africa in social, economic, and political development have been blamed on European colonialism and neocolonialism. The dominance of colonial languages in education and governance can marginalize local languages and cultural practices, making it difficult for African youths to connect with their heritage and history. The digital division between rural and urban areas, as well as disparities in access to technology, can hinder the exchange of ideas and cultural expressions within Africa.

Furthermore, climate change and environmental degradation disproportionately affect African communities, posing threats to traditional ways of life, identity, and cultural practices tied to the land. Climate change can lead to reduced agricultural productivity due to changing weather patterns, leading to food shortages and increased food prices. This affects both rural and urban populations. Environmental degradation and climate change can lead to displacement and resource conflicts (Omare, 2010). Competition for limited resources like water and arable land can exacerbate tensions and lead to conflicts within and between communities.

Conclusions and Recommendations: The Future of African Identity

Based on the discussions in the preceding sections, I conclude that our African identity is the strength and the source of pride of Africans. Embracing our African identity will help us to find our true selves and our place in the cosmos. Therefore, to know Africa is to know the world; and, to know our African identity is to know ourselves. We cannot have African identity without African Religion because African identity is a tapestry plaited from the threads of our ancestors. We must acknowledge that the future of African identity through African Religion is characterized by a mix of challenges and opportunities. I hope that, through Afrocentricity, embracing cultural diversity, promoting unity and solidarity, leveraging technology, and engaging the youth will be essential in shaping a dynamic and inclusive African identity that embraces its rich heritage while looking forward to a brighter future through the principles of *Ubuntu*. This requires a collective effort, commitment, and a deep understanding of the interconnectedness of our shared humanity that can be regarded as *Utu* through the perspective that *I am because we are, since we are, therefore I am.*

Guided by the Afrocentricity Theory, I also conclude that the future of African identity is both dynamic and multifaceted. While the early scholars portrayed a negative image, Africans through African Religion have multiple ways of identity. Despite the challenges which African identity holds, there is a great potential for growth, resilience, and positive transformation. This can be depicted by the growing interest in Afrocentricity, a movement aimed to rediscover, celebrate, and preserve African culture and traditions. Generally, many young Africans are showing a renewed interest in their heritage, languages, and customs, leading to a cultural renaissance that seeks to reclaim and promote African identity on local, national, and global levels. This implies that Pan-Africanism, the idea of unity and solidarity among African people across the globe, is gaining momentum. As Africans recognize the shared history, struggles, and aspirations across the continent, there is an increasing drive to foster a sense of common African identity that transcends national boundaries.

I look at expansion in technology and Internet connectivity as two sides of the coin of African identity. As much as the two affect African identity negatively, I can say they are aspects of promoting African identity. The future is bright because of the rapid expansion of technology and Internet connectivity in Africa which is allowing a greater exchange of ideas and cultural expressions. Digital platforms enable Africans to connect with their peers across the continent and the Diaspora, thereby contributing to a sense of a shared identity. There is great hope that Africa has a youthful population, and the aspirations and values of its youth will shape the continent's identity in the future. Young Africans are increasingly involved in social and political movements, advocating for social justice, environmental sustainability, and cultural preservation. African identity is not monolithic but rather encompasses a rich diversity of cultural practices, languages, and traditions. Embracing this diversity and fostering intercultural dialogue will contribute to a more inclusive and dynamic African identity. African artists, writers, and filmmakers are gaining international recognition and using their platforms to explore and express African identity in all its complexity. These creative expressions play a crucial role in shaping perceptions and challenging stereotypes about Africa and its people.

As Africa experiences economic growth and regional integration, there is an opportunity for greater cooperation and collaboration among African countries. This can lead to a sense of a collective identity that transcends national borders and fosters a shared vision for the continent's development. Efforts to promote indigenous languages and integrate African history and culture into education curricula are gaining traction. Education plays a vital role in nurturing a sense of pride and belonging among African youths. Africa's growing economic and cultural influence on the global stage provides an opportunity to reshape perceptions and narratives about the continent.

African identity through African Religion can be positively impacted by increased representation and recognition in global arenas. Promotion of African Religion will generate more opportunities for the promotion of African identity. The essence of the promotion of African Religion lies in its basic doctrine of *Ubuntu*, which invites all to confront and challenge discriminatory practices, norms, and structures that perpetuate inequality in order to promote a universal identity of brotherhood and sisterhood anchored on the basis of humanity and a global common good. *Ubuntu* can be expressed through a Zulu proverb: "*Umuntu ngumuntu ngabantu*," which translates to "A person is a person through other persons." This encapsulates the essence of *Ubuntu*, highlighting the belief that our humanity is intertwined with the well-being of others; a broader philosophy that is deeply rooted across all African cultures, emphasizing community, compassion, and shared humanity. It calls for the dismantling of barriers that prevent humanity from realizing its full potential and advocates for establishing inclusive and equitable societies with a common identity.

References

Achebe, C. (1960). *No longer at ease*. Heinemann.
Achebe, C. (2006). *Things fall apart*. Penguin Classics.
Adichie, C. N. (2010). *Half of a yellow sun*. Knopf.
Adichie, C. N. (2013). *Americana*. Fourth Estate.
Anyaehie, M. C. (2013). Appraisal of African identity for sustainable development. *Open Journal of Philosophy, 3*(1A), 150–154.
Asante, M. (1993). The Afrocentric idea in education. *The Journal of Negro Education, 60*(2).
Awolalu, J. O., & Dopamu, P. A. (1979). *West African traditional religion*. Onibonoje Press and Book Industries.
Bangura, A. K. (2013). Yosef Alfredo Antonio ben-Jochannan's African origins of the major "western religions". In A. K. Bangura (Ed.), *Fractal complexity in the works of major black thinkers* (Vol. 2). Cognella.
Bangura, A. K. (2019). *Branches of Asanteism*. Rowman and Littlefield Publishing Group.
Brown, C. (2001). Critiques of Afrocentricity, comments on multiculturalism. *Counterpoints, 94*, 539–548.
Cohen, T. (2014, August 7). *African leaders use summit to fight negative perceptions*. Retrieved September 17, 2022, from https://www.cnn.com/2014/08/06/us/africa-summit-perceptions/index.html
Diodorus, S. (1935). *Library of history: Loeb classical library*. Translated by C. H. Oldfather. Harvard University Press.
Eegunlusi, T. (2017). Mental alienation and African identity: Exploring historical perspectives in response to the crises of African societies. *Open Journal of Philosophy, 7*, 1–24.
Eurocentrism. (2012). *Wikipedia*, Retrieved August 1, 2023, from http://en.wikipedia.org/wiki/Eurocentrism
Fenton, J. (1996). *A short history of anti-Hamitism*. New York Review of Books.
Heifer International. (2019). *Africa is not a country and other things you need to know about the continent*. Retrieved August 5, 2023, from https://www.heifer.org/blog/africa-is-not-a-country-and-other-things-you-need-to-know-about-the-continent.html
Idowu, E. B. (1973). *African traditional religion*. S.C.M. Press.
Ike, G. O. S. J. (2022). Religious syncretism in Africa: Toward an enduring solution. *New Horizons, 6*(1), 6. Retrieved July 20, 2023, from https://scholarcommons.scu.edu/newhorizons/vol.6/iss1/6

Kamaara, E. (2012). *(Re)constructing gender: A holistic strategy to controlling HIV/AIDS in Kenya* (Moi university inaugural lecture 15 series no. 2012). Moi University Press.
Keese, A. (2019). *Group identifications: African and global categories*. Retrieved August 6, 2023, from https://doi.org/10.1163/9789004307353_003
Kelland, Z., & Sánchez, E. (2018). *Debunking 15 common myths and misconceptions about Africa*. Retrieved August 1, 2023, from https://www.globalcitizen.org/en/content/africans-are-all-poor-and-15-other-myths/
Kwemo, A. (2017, April 20). *Making Africa great again: Reducing aid dependency*. Retrieved December 3, 2023, from https://www.brookings.edu/articles/making-africa-great-again-reducing-aid-dependency/
Magidimisha, H., et al. (2018). *Crisis, identity and migration in post-colonial southern Africa*. Springer International.
Mbiti, J. S. (1969). *African religions and philosophy*. Heinemann.
Mbiti, J. S. (1975). *Introduction to African religion*. East African Educational Publishers.
Mbiti, J. S. (1982). *Introduction to African religion*. Heinemann.
Mbiti, J. S. (2012). *Concepts of god in African religion*. Acton Publishers.
Miike, Y. (2008). Advancing centricity for non-western scholarship: Lessons from Molefi Kete Asante's legacy of Afrocentricity. In A. Mazama (Ed.), *Essays in honor of an intellectual warrior, Molefi Kete Asante*. MENAIBUC, Imprime per SIA.
Milofsky, A., & Rinke, C. (2006). *Book review: Afrocentricity: A theory of social change*. Urban Education. Retrieved April 6, 2023, from https://doi.org/10.1177/0042085905284322
Moller, V., & Roberts, B. (2021). The unfinished story: African resilience, religion, and hope for the future. In *Quality of life and human well-being in sub-Saharan Africa*. Retrieved April 6, 2023, from https://doi.org/10.1007/978-3-030-65788-8_11
Murimi, M. (2015, August 20). *Kijana Wamalwa's spirit 'brought' home*. Retrieved August 1, 2023, from https://www.citizen.digital/news/kijana-wamalwas-spirit-brought-home-98502
Mwikamba, M. C. (1991). Search for an African identity. *Wajibu, 6*(4) Retrieved May 20, 2023, from https://www.africabib.org/rec.php?RID=Q00003347
Natchaba, N. (2023). *Using the 7 principles of Afrocentricity to frame S: US programs and services*. Retrieved September 26, 2023, from https://sus.org/using-the-7-principles-of-afrocentricity-to-frame-sus-programs-and-services/
Newsela. (2017). *Africa: Physical geography*. National Geographic Society. Retrieved May 20, 2023, from https://newsela.com
Omare, S. (2010). *Religion and environment conservation: The role of Isukha religious beliefs and practices in the conservation of Kakamega Forest*. Lambert Academic Publishing Company.
p'Bitek, O. (1971). *African religions in Western scholarship*. Kenya Literature Bureau.
p'Bitek, O. (2011). *Decolonizing African religions: A short history of African religions in Western scholarship*. Diasporic Africa Press.
Rawlinson, G. (1956). *The histories: Herodotus* (translated by George Rawlinson). Roman Roads Media.
Samir, A. (1989). *Eurocentrism* (translated by Russell Moore). Monthly Review.
Smith, E. W. (Ed.). (1966). *African ideas of god*. Edinburgh House Press.
Tunde, A. (1998). Black Americans and Africa: A critique of the pan-African and identity paradigms. *The International Journal of African Historical Studies, 31*(3), 505–536.
wa Thiong'o, N. (1964). *Weep not, child*. Heinemann.
Ward, A. (2006). Self-reflection, Egyptian beliefs, Scythians and "Greek ideas": Reconsidering Greeks and Barbarians in Herodotus. *The European Legacy, 11*(1), 1–19.

Simon Gisege Omare holds a PhD in Religious Studies. His area of interest is Sociology of Religion. He is a senior lecturer at Moi University in Kenya. Omare is the author of 2 books, over 12 articles in journals, and 12 chapters in books. He has presented several public lectures on religion and intelligent design.

Community Development

Cecy Edijala Balogun

This chapter situates Africa as the origin of community development, given that traditional African communities have addressed their socioeconomic concerns through their indigenous practices. The African experience and practice of community development emphasize indigenous knowledge, culture, identity, interconnectedness, and interdependence of the *Ubuntu* philosophy (an African cultural concept that emphasizes the interconnectedness and interdependence of individuals within a community) is the bedrock of community development in Africa. Nonetheless, this traditional way of community interconnectedness and interdependence was truncated following the colonial presence in Africa, with the introduction of new approaches to community development. These external influences in community development in Africa, especially in the emerging global society that emphasizes collaboration with other societies, have hardly worked in addressing the local concerns of Africa's development.

While a global community that exports development opportunities to undeveloped areas, which is characteristic of most of Africa, the activities of international development agencies in Africa for several decades have yet to translate to meaningful and widespread development. This might not be entirely blamed on the donor agencies, as the leadership of African countries has also played a role in the slow development of African communities. Either way, efforts of community development pursued in most African countries lack the indigenous component which has continued to undermine efforts over the years.

Narratives of African communities as being underdeveloped are not necessarily because Africa lacks what is required for development; rather, models of development that have been used either by African leaders or the international agencies that

C. E. Balogun (✉)
Social Policy Department, Nigerian Institute of Social and Economic Research, Ibadan, Nigeria
e-mail: ce.balogun@niser.gov.ng

A. K. Bangura, J. A. Ifedi (eds.), *Conceptualizations of Africa*, African Studies and Research Forum Series, https://doi.org/10.1007/978-3-031-74535-5_16

engage in community development programs in Africa have failed to understand processes of community development in Africa within the African context to tailor their methods accordingly. Community development, when considered in the African practice, shows some uniqueness that has been successful in the past and in contemporary times in countries and communities that have used indigenous models of community development in addressing the problems of such communities.

In order to distinguish community development in Africa from what is obtainable in the rest of the world, this chapter situates community development in Africa from three perspectives: (1) Africa as the foundation of community development, (2) African models of community development, and (3) lessons learned from the African models of community development.

The chapter argues that in practice, community development that works in the African context differs from what is practiced in other parts of the world. This is because the cultural, social, economic, and historical contexts of African societies form the foundation of any efforts that are targeted at the community. A cultural angle of community development in Africa anchors on the *Ubuntu* philosophy, communalism, and indigenous knowledge that reflect collective well-being and inclusivity that ensures the voices of the community members are at the center of the development intervention. Also, community development in Africa works to remove the ambiguities that were brought about by colonialism that led to the exploitation of African resources, displacement of indigenous communities, and unequal power dynamics in many African communities. Where a partnership is involved in community development in Africa, such partnerships are for the purpose of technical and financial support and capacity building as the emphasis remains on the centrality of the community members in the community development effort.

The chapter uses qualitative documentary analysis that underscores words rather than numerical values, and, where numerical values are used, they are retrieved from secondary sources to buttress the "What if" question (Bangura, 2019), which in this study is presented from empirical case studies to highlight some arguments made in the study.

This chapter is important because it provides insights into what it means to engage in community development in Africa that will truly reflect the African culture that is based on the collective "doing" by members of the community rather than a system that imports development that has persistently failed to address the consistently growing rates of social and economic deprivations that characterize most of the continent. While African governments and their international collaborators have made several efforts to address these problems, two critical social challenges that are widespread and have persisted in Africa are (1) poverty and (2) insecurity. The seriousness of the poverty problem in Africa is reflected in the World Population Review (2023), which indicated that Africa accounted for nine of the ten countries with the highest poverty rates in 2023. In a similar report, the Global Peace Index (2023) indicated that most African countries fall within the low or very low ratings of peace globally. This is understandable given the spate of insecurity that permeates many African countries, including terrorism, armed conflicts, intercommunal clashes, kidnappings and, very recently, the reemergence of military coups in many African countries. Presenting the community development models that can work in Africa is expected in order to inform African governments of processes that work within the African context for development that will address these two important social problems that are threatening the livelihoods and peaceful coexistence of many African societies.

The remainder of this chapter focuses on the conceptualization of community development, the practice of community development in Africa, African models of community development, and lessons from what has worked in the African model that will help to address the social challenges in the continent and other regions of the world with similar experiences in order to provide the context for what follows. That is, how the discipline of Community Development has conceptualized Africa is broached in order to ensure that a coherent conclusion and recommendations are presented at the end.

Community Development: A Conceptualization

Community Development as a concept is not necessarily a discipline, but a development practice that targets changing geographical, social, economic, political, and societal expectations. In this regard, community development in this chapter is conceptualized from a practical perspective.

Two important but interrelated concepts that distinguish community development in Africa from what is practiced in the rest of the world are, as mentioned earlier, (1) the *Ubuntu* philosophy and (2) communalism. The *Ubuntu* philosophy is an African cultural concept that places emphasis on the interconnectedness and interdependence of individuals within a community. The notion of *Ubuntu* stresses the being of an individual in the light of the being of the community. This implies that the community thrives on solidarity, empathy, and collective well-being. Taking the communal notion of African society further, how decisions are made that favor all members of the community and their inclusiveness in such decisions is the point of emphasis of communalism in African society.

Conceptualizing these concepts, Kimmerle (2006) argues that the principles of *Ubuntu* and communalism in Africa emphasize the community rather than the individual, without necessarily undermining the importance of the individual in the community. In their conceptualization of communalism, Nsengiyumva et al. (2019) note that the "being" of the individual is dependent on the "being" of other members of the community, implying that members in a community depend on one another to get things done. Decision-making is an important aspect in community development; and, in African communalism, this is based on a generalized system whereby community members are given a chance to make decisions that affect their development. In this regard, Etta et al. (2016) define communalism in Africa as a decision-making process that is based on consensus achieved through dialogue with the active participation of everyone who is affected by an issue given the opportunity to speak. Communalism for Africans means that their socialization is centered on their culture which promotes the ideologies of community, collectivism, and human unity (Nsengiyumva et al., 2019).

Another important definer of community development in Africa is the use of indigenous knowledge and practices. Indigenous knowledge implies local ownership in development and is seen as a cultural capital that presents an alternative to the imposition of development ideas (Ewane & Ajagbe, 2018). This, in the view of Ewane and Ajagbe (2018), is in contrast to what is obtained in other places where development options are driven by the elites and based on a top-down approach that relies on the use of modern technology and expert knowledge generated from outside the community. Viewed from a human rights perspective, the authors also point out that the use of local ownership in community development implies the utilization of the indigenous knowledge of the community members in the development of projects in their communities.

In the African context, what is emphasized in conceptualizing community development is not the roles of the government and nongovernmental organizations (NGOs) that provide either direction and financial or technical support to the communities, but the indigenous knowledge, or ideas of the people that reflect their culture, identity, values and beliefs. In this way, Ramsey and Blessings (2021) defines community development as the advancement of a group that involves a common sense of identity, values, beliefs, capability, and rationale. From the views of this author, community development in Africa is driven by an effort to empower disadvantaged and marginalized groups such as the rural poor, children, the youth, the elderly, and people with disabilities.

Considering this conceptualization of Africa argues in favor of community development in a continent marked by geographical boundaries, though diverse yet with closely related cultures, identities, and belief systems that are different from other continents, Africa in this context fits into one of the earliest definitions of community development denoted by MacQueen et al. (2001). They conceptualize community development as a group of people with diverse characteristics who are linked by social ties, share common views, and engage in joint actions within a geographical location or setting. This means that from a geographical standpoint, what constitutes community development in Africa may vary from those in Europe or Asia because the social, economic, and political realities that affect communities in these regions vary.

Nevertheless, Bhattacharyya (2004) argues that using geographical location does not provide a sufficient conceptualization of community development. Three reasons are provided for this argument. First, Bhattacharyya (2004) notes that conceptualizing community development based on location implies a neighborhood, small town, or village; this may not necessarily have any form of cohesion in it. Bhattacharyya (2004) also notes that such a conceptualization leaves out the differences and shared interests that go beyond the boundaries of place to unite people and that a conceptualization of a community based on location does not consider the radical social change that modernity provides. Nonetheless, when this argument is considered in the African context, it does not fully describe the African community which, in a way, falls more or less outside the conceptualization of community by Bhattacharyya (2004).

Firstly, the notion that when a community is conceptualized as a small village or town that may lack cohesion is far from the experience of what the African calls or knows as a community. This is because in the African context, what makes a community is social cohesion, mostly described as the shared culture, identity, and common experiences or interests that bind people together. In other words, you cannot describe an African community without talking about social cohesion, which is believed to be a strong cultural tie that binds the people together.

Second, the notion that when a community is limited to a geographical location excludes other people with different or common interests outside the immediate boundaries of the said community also does not align with the African concept of a community. That people share similar interests in a wider community enclave is not sufficient to describe them as a community. This is because in such broader enclaves of the modern community, the interest in most cases is based on economic or political gains or affiliations, and not necessarily based on cultural or ethnic ties. On the contrary, for Africans, sharing similar economic or political interests is not sufficient to describe the affiliations as a community; such relationships or interactions are mainly defined based on the interests they serve and not necessarily in relation to the cultural or ethnic identity that is the bedrock of the concept of a community in Africa. One example of the relevance the African places on culture is in the area of child upbringing whereby it is believed that bringing up a child in a responsible manner is the responsibility of the community and not only that of the immediate family. In such a case, an erring child can be chastised or rebuked by any member of the community and the parents take such in good faith. In most Western societies, the upbringing of children is mainly the responsibility of the parents and, in the worst case scenario, which is becoming trendy, parents cannot even rebuke their children due to restrictive civil laws that almost empower the child above the parents.

Third, the notion that a localized conceptualization of a community could deny one the social change that modernity offers would depend on the context of consideration. When modernity is considered in terms of urbanization and technological advancements, one sure explanation that also challenges this argument is the African experience that is different from the Western notion of modernity. This is because the modernization of a community in the Western idea implies a system whereby the government institutions are at the forefront of the development, providing all that is required for a better life. On the contrary, the notion of modernity does not necessarily have to be engineered by the government which, in the African experience, is more of a joint communal effort to get things done for the betterment of all members of the community. For most of Africa, the problem at the community level is not a lack of ideas of what to do to achieve their expectations of what a modern society should look like, but rather the economic deprivations that almost make it impossible for them to put their indigenous knowledge for their common good.

In another argument, Goel (2014) points out that conceptualizing community development should not only be location-based but also interest-based and at the same time take into cognizance emerging communities like web, social media, and other online groups that transcend physical boundaries in order to interact with unknown people in various locations. This argument appears relevant in this debate of the practice of community development, given that through these new media networks, the world has been reduced to a global community.

Nevertheless, the interactions or communities built through these networks are not primarily defined by a shared culture or identity that is the hallmark of the African community. This does not mean that these "emerging communities" do not share some identities or commonalities, but not in the African sense. In the African sense, this is more established whereby people from the same culture or identity form social connectedness through these new social groupings as a way of enhancing their shared identity. It is in this regard that people with similar cultures have formed WhatsApp groups either as immediate, extended, or communal groups that are scattered in different climes around the world, can be said to be a community in the African sense of the word, albeit not necessarily a group of people with common interests that may be social, economic, or political, yet without a shared culture or identity.

Community Development Conceptualizations of Africa

To discuss all of the conceptualizations of Africa in the field of Community Development would require an entire book, which is unnecessary here. To give the reader a flavor of these conceptualizations, I briefly talk about a very small sample of four of them individually in the subsections that follow for perspicuity. The conceptualizations were selected indiscriminately.

The African Concept of a Community

The way of conceptualizing "community" in Africa in the Community Development discipline is based on concepts such as that of the Akan language of Ghana *abusua*, meaning "community" in English, of all those who share the same blood. *Abusua* is a matrilineal exogamous clan among the Ashanti people of Ghana governed by seven major ancient *abosom*—i.e., female deities. Also, the natural environment is part of the people's concept of *community* and must always be venerated.

Accordingly, the African concept of community emphasizes moral responsibility for the injuries various entities cause to others. This is based on the belief that during conception, "the woman transmits her blood," "the man transmits the spirit," and "God gives the soul." These three components concomitantly make up the "individual" person as follows: (1) "the spiritual from God," (2) "the community from the woman," and (3) "individuality from the man." Thus, the individual is "ontologically" logical. It is the intrusion of Western institutions in Africa that is said to have led to elemental apprehensions in this cultural perspective at all levels: national, local community, and individual person (Asante, 2014, p. 202).

The African Concept for Development

The concept of "development" is employed to conceptualize Africa in the field of Community Development as the type of evolution that accepts approaches, models, and policies aimed at dealing with the socioeconomic hurdles encountered by Africans in the continent. Accordingly, the traditional leadership system with its working in promoting and/or eroding development in Africa is explored. The major focus is on the history of the dynamics of traditional leadership from the precolonial to the colonial and postcolonial epochs (Tshishonga, 2022).

In addition, the core postulate of the advocates of the African concept of "development" in the field of Community Development is that squabbles emerge between traditional and democratic leaders over how political validity, opportunity to use resources, and reformation of traditional institutions can play a more democratic and developmental role. Using case studies of diverse African countries, these proponents broach the essence and dynamics of the traditional leadership system, paying special attention to its reformation (Tshishonga, 2022).

Ubuntu as an African Term for Community Development

The *Ubuntu* term is used to conceptualize Africa in the Community Development discipline as a continent with the well-known term that translates to "I am because we are." As a community development approach, the term is employed to emphasize the perspective in a ubiquitous fellowship of working together and sharing that links all humanity, thereby accentuating the essence of community, caring, and reverence for others (Nomads Den, 2024). Various expressions of the concept, albeit with the same denotation, exist across the African continent.

It must further be noted here that in the Community Development field, the term *Ubuntu* is also translated as "I am because you are" or "humanity towards others," which in isiZulu is *umuntu ngumuntu ngabantu*. This second expression is used in isiXhosa to mean more philosophically as "the belief in a universal bond of sharing that connects all humanity."

Community Values as a Source for Development in Africa

The use of "community values" as a way of conceptualizing Africa in the discipline of Community Development is a vital way of highlighting the essence of values such as (a) "a sense of community life," (b) "the sacredness of life," (c) "respect for authority and elders," and (d) "the conservation of the environment" in the African culture. These cultural values are perceived as critical for the maintenance and welfare of African societies (SciSpace, 2024, p. 1).

The aforementioned African cultural values are anchored on other morals like "unity," "patriotism," and "social cohesion." Also promoted in African culture vis-à-vis development are "the sanctity of life," "decent dressing," "honesty and integrity," "peaceful coexistence," and "communalism." Add to these, the following African traditional values that stress "the importance of wisdom, which is transmitted through proverbs, adages, and folktales with moral lessons. These values are seen as guiding human action towards a common good and contribute to the promotion of peace and unity in modern times. African communities are known for their sense of communal living and concern for others, which fosters solidarity and inclusion. Overall, African cultural values play a significant role in shaping African societies and promoting positive social behaviors" (SciSpace, 2024, p. 1).

Africa as the Foundation of Community Development

The practice of community development is not new in Africa. This is because traditional African communities live in clusters of individuals or families who are related by blood, culture, and identity. In this closely-knit community of people with a shared culture, addressing problems as they arise was always seen as a communal responsibility. For example, community members pool their resources together to provide basic facilities like market structures, the construction and/or maintenance of community roads and bridges, or the building of community halls. Similarly, where disputes arise, they have community courts where they are resolved; and, in cases of insecurity and criminal activities that threaten individuals or their collective existence, culprits are punished based on the community laws. Additionally, where intercommunal conflicts exist, traditional African communities have emissaries who represent their conflicting communities for intercommunal conflict resolutions.

For traditional African communities, the practice of community development is basically community-driven in line with the indigenous culture and identity of the people. In the indigenous African community, community development is seen as an activity that involves all members of the community who participate in different aspects of community projects based on some unwritten cultural rules. For instance, some roles are based on age group, some for women and older men constituting the elders' council to oversee the smooth running of the community. In the traditional African model, the community identifies its problems, proffers solutions, and mobilizes local resources to implement the desired solution. In essence, community development in the traditional African perspective is based on some unique practices that distinguish the African perspective from what is practiced elsewhere in the world. I discuss only four of these practices in the following subsections for the sake of brevity.

Community Development as Inclusive Participation

Inclusive community development in Africa implies the active involvement and empowerment of community members in decision-making and ensuring equitable access to resources, services, and opportunities in the community. Access in this sense implies equitably gaining education, health care, infrastructure, employment, and participation in decision-making processes. Inclusive community development considers the diversities, cultures, languages, and religions of the community members such that their diversities are maximized without excluding or marginalizing any individual or group from benefitting. Inclusiveness is achieved in Africa through a participatory approach such that community members partake in decisions on the identification of their needs, prioritization of such needs based on available resources, and designing and implementing community projects.

In this way, the aspirations and expectations of community members are built into targeted programs designed to address their social and economic needs. Where adequately utilized, inclusive community development in Africa has engendered equitable and sustained benefits to several communities in different parts of the continent. Sebele (2010) points out that inclusive community development contributes to the successful development of the community. Communities maximize development opportunities when they take part in decision-making (Odoom et al., 2021).

Community Development as Self-determination and Empowerment

In Africa, addressing community development issues has also been anchored on a self-determination approach whereby community members take responsibility for their problems and utilize the local resources to address the problems based on their empowered capacities. The traditional African community members believe that they have what it takes to develop their communities in terms of skills, indigenous knowledge, and resources to drive their development. In the African practice of community development, a sense of agency and ownership is established, since the initiatives embarked upon by the community members are rooted in their local realities, cultural practices, and identities, such that the underlying result represents their aspirations for their collective living. A sense of responsibility is also assured which is not only seen in their willingness to support the common good, but also in their drive to protect, maintain, and sustain their implemented projects.

In this way, social cohesion is enhanced among the community members as a sense of inclusiveness, especially for marginalized members of the community such as women and youths who feel a sense of belonging due to their active involvement. As a self-help initiative, self-determination and empowerment programs benefit all members of the community (Nitzberg, 2005), and as noted by Fogel (2004) such programs make community members to be self-reliant and less dependent on external support institutions. Self-determination efforts increase collective access to social resources, including housing, health care, employment, and education, while at the same time reducing inequality and poverty in Africa (Abdulkarim & Ali, 2012; Saliu, 2014).

Community Development as Social Justice

From the colonial invasion of Africa and the poor leadership style of several African communities, social injustice persists. To address this, community development in Africa pursues a social justice system that ensures fair and equitable distribution of opportunities and resources, with equal treatment of all members of society, which is believed to be capable of removing the disparities that have persisted in African communities over time. Social justice in Africa therefore targets interventions in education, health care, infrastructure, employment, and access to other basic services that can lift the disadvantaged communities and bridge the gaps between the rich and poor in African societies.

In principle, social justice in Africa is anchored on the diversity and the cultural background of the community members, and ensures that the voices of the marginalized are considered in development activities while at the same time restoring agency and power to the community. Issues of discrimination are also removed whereby social justice is practiced in community development in Africa, as all members of the community are perceived as one. As indicated by Hlalele (2012), social justice thrives on respect, care, recognition, and empathy.

Community Development as Collective Action

African practice of collective action in community development has involved the working together of community members to achieve a common goal. The process ensures the collaborative and active participation of community members and is believed to contribute to program sustainability in Africa. In collective action, African communities mobilize their resources and harness them to address their common needs. While collective community action is as old as the African communities, it has been used to address poverty through joint processes of contributing to the well-being of the community, addressing infrastructural problems like community halls, markets, and other public facilities, and through collective actions, crime and security challenges have also been addressed in Africa. Dutilly-Daine (2014) point out that collective action among smallholders in Burkina Faso contributes to their overall income.

Meinzen-Dick et al. (2004) posit that measuring the benefits of collective action is usually difficult, since people may not be equally impacted. In their argument, they indicate that for measurable and tangible benefits like access to irrigation water, it is easier to know the benefits that accrue to members of a group, whereas in programs like membership of self-help groups like the provision of labor or cash to group members, measuring the benefits of households that suffer shocks from floods, as an example, may not be easily measured.

African Models of Community Development

The traditional model of community development as discussed in the previous section shows that the resources of the community are used to meet community developmental needs based on the cultural practices of particular communities. Today, the modernity component has affected the traditional African communities. Nevertheless, while the influence of Western societies and other development players in African communities reflects some Western models of community development, some models reflect the uniqueness of the African approaches tailored in line with the indigenous and cultural practices of the communities.

In describing the models of community development that are peculiar to Africa, models that are generally tailored toward empowering community members against poverty outcomes and addressing insecurity are examined in this chapter. This is because as mentioned earlier, two of the major challenges in most parts of Africa are (1) widespread social deprivations that drive poverty and (2) increasing spates of insecurity that threaten lives and livelihoods to the point of regional concerns.

Livelihood Improvement Models of Community Development

Some of the African models of community development that have been used in different parts of the continent are mainly based on the *Ubuntu* philosophy which, as stated earlier, emphasizes community interconnectedness and interdependence. The collective contribution, participation in decision-making processes, design, and implementation of programs that empower members of the community for the collective good of all are reflected in all the programs described from different African countries' practices.

In Rwanda, for example, community development models emphasize community involvement, social cohesion, and sustainable development; and some of the models that have been practiced in the country include the Community-Based Health Insurance (CBHI) through which members make contributions based on their financial capacity for inclusive access to health care (Woldemichael et al., 2019). The scheme is reported to promote equity in access to health care through pooled resources that make the care easily accessible to the community (Nyinawankunsi et al., 2015). To address livelihood challenges in the country, a community empowerment program called *Girinka*, which is translated as "one cow per poor family," is also implemented to generate wealth through a solidarity approach of passing cows as wealth from one family to another (Nilsson et al., 2017).

Kenya has also implemented several models of community development that target community participation, empowerment, and sustainability. The Harambee model of community development in Kenya is particularly interesting as the program is anchored on the collective efforts of mobilizing community resources, especially through fundraising, to fund development projects that include schools, health care facilities, and socioeconomic activities of community members (Chieni, 1999).

Keying into the uniqueness of the indigenous and culturally knitted nature of the African communities, the World Bank has collaborated with several African countries to implement the community-driven development model and this has also proved very successful, given that the programs placed the communities at the center of the operations. Nonetheless, different approaches are used in different countries.

An important example of community-driven development (CDD) in Africa is the Village Savings and Loans Association (VSLAs) which is dominant in countries like Nigeria, Uganda, Malawi, and Kenya. The model has contributed to improving the financial inclusion and entrepreneurship of rural communities as members of the associations make decisions about their savings and loans which are invested in small businesses, education, and health care of their family members (Allen, 2006; Tukundane, 2018; Okello & Mwesigwa, 2022). The Farmer Field School (FSS) is another CDD model that thrives on the indigenous and cultural uniqueness of African countries and is widely implemented in countries like Mali, Ethiopia, Tanzania, and Nigeria to improve farmers' capacity through learning and sharing experiences of agricultural techniques, environmental conservation, and marketing strategies. This has also led to improvements in crop yield, income generation, and resilience to climate change in the countries where the model is used (Bello-Bravo et al., 2011; Oguntade et al., 2012).

The community and social development project (CSDP) is another variant of the CDD that is also based on exploring the indigenous and cultural identities of communities to improve the livelihoods and social infrastructures of rural communities in Nigeria. Olusa (2021) indicates that the CSDP model of community development in Nigeria has contributed to increased participation of community members in development projects and employment generation through the provision of income-generating activities. The successful implementation of the CSDP in Nigeria is operational in 29 of the 36 states and the Federal Capital Territory in Nigeria with an estimated 23 million people as beneficiaries (World Bank, 2021). In Nigeria, community efforts to address people's collective problems are directed to projects like the construction of community markets, schools, recreation centers, health centers, community halls, and roads (Acha, 2014). Rwigema (2022) asserts that CDD as a model of community development has the potential to reduce rural poverty and provide a more inclusive, sustainable, and cost-effective approach than approaches that are managed centrally.

Community Policing as a Model of Community Development

In the formal processes of community policing in Africa, emphasis is placed on partnerships between law enforcement agencies and communities as practiced in other parts of the world. In principle, however, some variations exist in the African context of community policing. These include (a) the principle of *Ubuntu* or interconnectedness and collective responsibility within the community; (b) customary justice approaches that recognize the importance of traditional leaders and community authorities in curbing communal crimes and security challenges; (c) engagement of community members to boost ownership of the process through practices like community watches and neighborhood committees; (d) principles of restorative justice that aim to repair harm, healing of relationships, and reintegration of offenders into the community, rather than depending solely on punitive measures, such that reconciliation and trust are restored among the offenders, victims, and community.

One of the most important foundations of community policing in Africa is the reliance on indigenous knowledge and practice. In this regard, indigenous methods of the community are employed in conflict resolution, community mobilization, and social control. Like community development that targets improving the lives and livelihoods of communities through the provision of access to social infrastructures and income-generating activities, operating on different models across the world with context specificity emphasized in the African practice, similarly, unique models of community policing also abound.

In line with global practices of ensuring peace and security in societies, policing measures around communities in formal processes are patterned after processes that are practiced around the world with variations. These processes have the police at the center of the policing models, rather than the community members. For example, in South Africa, community policing forums (CPFs) are practiced; they are comprised of community members, representatives of the police, and other stakeholders in crime control in the community. Models like the Joint Task Force (JTF) that is practiced in Nigeria, in which there is collaboration among the police, military, and other security agencies in the fight against terrorism, insurgency, and communal violence, is also tailored after the Western models and seen as oppressive and a political instrument against some segments of the society in Nigeria. Hence, it does not reflect the African model of community policing. Similarly, the community policing advisory committee entails collaboration among the police, community organizations, traditional leaders, and other stakeholders for the identification of security needs. It is also tailored after the Western models, since the community members are not central in the process, with several external influences on decision-making and practice. Nevertheless, in contrast to the community policing models that are practiced in other parts of the world with variants practiced in Africa, Africa has some unique models that are built around the indigenous cultural practices in the continent.

In Kenya, *Nyumba Kumi*, translated into English as "ten households" is a community policing model that involves dividing communities into small units of about ten households that are led by a community leader; it is a process that fosters ownership of policing in the community. Nevertheless, the leader of a group works in partnership with the police to share information that is important for the safety of the community. A similar model is practiced in Uganda. It is called the *Bunjako* model of community policing whereby community members are divided into smaller groups and led by a leader who liaises with the police to facilitate communication, information sharing, and community patrols. Community efforts in crime control are emphasized in these models of community policing.

Vigilante groups are also widely utilized in Africa whereby they are involved in patrols of a community, report suspicious activities to the police, and also assist the police in investigations. Community members are encouraged to take responsibility for their own safety and security. This is practiced in countries like Nigeria and South Africa. The vigilante model of community development is also effectively used in crime control in Nigeria. In areas that are crime-prone and in almost all indigenous Nigerian communities, vigilante groups exist. They are also involved in local dispute resolutions.

The growing trends of insecurity with traces of the sectionalization, culturalization, and politicization of approaches to curb crimes in different regions in Nigeria birthed two unique approaches to community policing that are completely indigenous in composition and practice. Severally, the government has been accused of neglect in its approaches to addressing some very life and livelihood security challenges.

One of the unique approaches is the *Amotekun*, which is translated into English as "one that looks like a leopard." It is a regional community policing model that was established by the collaboration of the six southwestern state governments in Nigeria to address the growing insecurity in the region. Although the security outfit was established by the six states, it operates on the principles of indigenous community participation in policing the communities, since the police personnel are completely community members who are empowered to curb crimes like kidnappings, robbery, banditry, and other crimes in the communities within the region. Given the elaborate setup upon which the *Amotekun* operates, the collaborative efforts of the governments ensure a pooled resource base that provides the necessary mobility and equipment for patrol, intelligence gathering, and crime control in the communities, especially rural areas where these crimes are prevalent in Nigeria.

Similar to the *Amotekun*, the *Ebube Agu*, which was established in the southeastern region of Nigeria to address the prevalence of insecurity in the region, is the second unique approach. This security model is also a collaboration of the five governments in the southeastern part of the country and is based on using community resources rather than formal policing instruments to curb crime. What makes the *Amotekun* and *Ebube Agu* community policing models in Nigeria stand out is the institutionalization of the models since they are backed by laws in the respective regions, compared to other community models in Africa.

The discussed models of community policing in this section are based on indigenous African traditions and cultural practices, since the community members, who are familiar with the people and the environment, are at the center of crime control and the police as collaborators, rather than the police operating in the communities and only engaging the community members for intelligence gathering as practiced in the rest of the world. This also reflects the self-help approach of community development that distinguishes Africa from the rest of the world in crime control.

Lessons Learned: What Has Worked in the African Models of Community Development

A number of lessons are provided from the potential of community development in Africa that can be scaled in areas where they are not practiced in the continent and replicated in other continents given the bedrock of collective action, self-determination, and social justice that are based on indigenous cultural connectedness and interdependence. The following are the five lessons learned based on the preceding analyses:

1. When people contribute to their own development, it not only creates a sense of ownership but also a reservoir of community leadership (Nitzberg, 2005).
2. African CDD has contributed to promoting inclusiveness through the involvement of marginalized groups such as women, youth, and ethnic minorities in the development of their communities.
3. One of the gains of the CSDP is that the community members have a sense of ownership of executed projects because they see themselves as stakeholders who have not only benefitted from an implemented project but have contributed to the process of choosing the particular project needed in the community and the funds used for the implementation and various aspects of the planning and implementation process of the projects. Highlighting the gains of the CSDP is reflected in the World Bank's report that the CSDP has benefitted 23 million Nigerians most of whom are vulnerable people in rural communities, and that 16,167 microprojects have been implemented that targeted education, water, electricity, health, environment, transport, and social inclusion (World Bank, 2021). It is also reported that through the model, the CSDP has been implemented in 5728 communities in 29 states in the country and also supported the establishment of an estimated 70,000 new businesses (World Bank, 2021).
4. In as much as the restorative justice model of community policing as practiced in Africa is laudable and encouraged, a problem observed in its practice in Nigeria, especially in managing the spates of insecurity for Boko Haram, bandits, and victims from communities that have been bartered through these criminal activities, a gap is observed in practice. For example, while the Nigerian government has consistently made several efforts to integrate repentant members of the Boko Haram and bandits, not many efforts have been put into the restoration of trust for victims and the associated reconciliation where needed. This means that community policing efforts that target reconciliatory processes must also be inclusive, especially by ensuring that the integration of the victims who are the most affected are adequately addressed.
5. That there is widespread poverty and growing spates of insecurity is not because Africans lack models that can sufficiently address these problems, rather, it is because, first, in terms of population, African communities have grown larger than what their indigenous resources can accommodate; and, second, African governments and development partners have failed to harness the huge potentials that abound within the African communities, especially the indigenous col-

lective approaches, due to their exploration of methods that have worked elsewhere yet failing in Africa.

Conclusion and Recommendations

Narratives about community development cannot be complete without the uniqueness of the African models and practices. This is because from time immemorial, Africans have lived communal lives, whereby they depend on one another with shared values, cultural practices, and identities. They have also addressed their communal problems in a collective way by using their local resources to meet their livelihood and security needs. Community development in Africa is rooted in indigenous values, cultural practices, and a sense of community belonging through utilizing their strengths, traditions, and indigenous knowledge, key social, economic, and political challenges can be addressed.

Thus, four important recommendations are tendered in this chapter. First, African leaders need to look inward to the unique opportunities that the African models of community development offer to drive the development of Africa. Second, development partners who engage in community development programs in Africa also need to pay attention to the indigenous potential in Africa to make their programs work. Third, African leaders should set up better community policing models that indicate community ownership like the *Amotekun and Ebube Agu* models in Nigeria, ensuring that such models are institutionalized for better community safety. Fourth and finally, countries outside Africa should also localize some of these African models in their community development efforts for result-oriented interventions given the success stories from Africa.

References

Abdulkarim, I., & Ali, M. (2012). Vocational education and poverty reduction: A tool for sustainable community development in Nigeria. *Journal of Developing Countries Studies, 2*(2), 67–73.

Acha, J. O. (2014). Community self-help projects as a catalyst for sustainable community development projects in Bekwarra, Nigeria. *International Journal of Continuing Education and Development Studies, 2*(3), 40–49.

Allen, H. (2006). Village savings and loans associations-sustainable and cost-effective rural finance. *Small Enterprise Development, 17*(1), 61.

Asante, P. A. H. (2014). The African concept of community and individual in the context of the market get access arrow. In D. Finn (Ed.), *Distant markets, distant harms: Economic complicity and Christian ethics*. Oxford University (Academic) Press.

Bangura, A. K. (2019). Revisiting the basics. In A. K. Bangura, J. A. Obando, I. I. Munene, & C. Shisanya (Eds.), *Conducting research and mentoring students in Africa: CODESRIA College of mentors handbook*. CODESRIA Publications.

Bello-Bravo, J., Seufferheld, F., & Agunbiade, T. A. (2011). Gender and farmer field schools in agricultural production systems in West Africa. *International Journal of Science in Society, 2*(4).

Bhattacharyya, J. (2004). Theorizing community development. *Community Development, 34*(2), 5–34.

Chieni, S. N. (1999). *The Harambee movement in Kenya: The role played by Kenyans and the government in the provision of education and other social services*. IDE, Moi University.
Dutilly-Daine, C. (2014). Collective action and natural resource management in Northeastern Burkina Faso. In F. Wanyama, C. Poulton, H. Markelova, C. Dutilly-Diane, G. Hendrikse, J. Bijman, & F. S. Wouterse (Eds.), *Collective action among African smallholders: Trends and lessons for future development strategies 5*. International Food Policy Research Institute.
Etta, E. E., Esowe, D. D., & Asukwo, O. O. (2016). African communalism and globalization. *African Research Review, 10*(3), 302–316.
Ewane, F., & Ajagbe, S. (2018). Indigenous knowledge and the development debate in Africa. *International Journal of African Development, 5*(1), 7.
Fogel, S. J. (2004). Risks and opportunities for success: Perceptions of urban youths in a distressed community and lessons for adults. *Families in Society, 85*(3), 335–344.
Goel, K. (2014). *Understanding community and community development*. Doctoral dissertation, Niruta Publications.
Hlalele, D. (2012). Social justice and rural education in South Africa. *Perspectives in Education, 30*(1), 111–118.
Kimmerle, H. (2006). Ubuntu and communalism in African philosophy and art. In H. van den Heuvel, M. Mangaliso, & L. van de Bunt (Eds.), *Prophecies and protests: Ubuntu in Glocal management* (pp. 79–92). Rozenburg Publishers.
MacQueen, K. M., McLellan, E., Metzger, D. S., Kegeles, S., Strauss, R. P., Scotti, R., & Trotter, R. T. (2001). What is community? An evidence-based definition for participatory public health. *American Journal of Public Health, 91*(12), 1929–1938.
Meinzen-Dick, R., DiGregorio, M., & McCarthy, N. (2004). Methods for studying collective action in rural development. *Agricultural Systems, 82*(3), 197–214.
Nilsson, P., Backman, M., Bjerke, L., & Maniriho, A. (2017). *One cow per poor family: Effects on consumption and crop production in Rwanda*. The Royal Institute of Technology, Centre of Excellence for Science and Innovation Studies (CESIS). Retrieved August 20, 2023, from https://www.diva-portal.org/smash/get/diva2:1173747/fulltext01.pdf
Nitzberg, J. (2005). The meshing of youth development and community building. *New Directions for Youth Development, 106*, 7–16.
Nomads Den. (2024). *What is the meaning of Ubuntu?* Retrieved July 1, 2024, from https://www.nomads-den.com/hoedspruit/unembeza-ubuntu-and-other-african-words-explained/
Nsengiyumva, J. C., Muhenda, J., Njuguna, S., & Nyabul, P. O. (2019). Ubuntu philosophy: A contemporary version of the traditional African communalism. *International Journal of Sciences and Applied Research, 6*(9), 16–21.
Nyinawankunsi, J., Kunda, T., Ndizeye, C., & Saya, U. (2015). Increasing equity among community-based health insurance members in Rwanda. *African Health Monitor, 20*, 58–72.
Odoom, D., Annor-Frempong, F., Akaba, S., Agyepong, L., Obeng-Mensah, A., & Obeng-Baah, J. (2021). The challenge of participation in community development activities in rural Ghana: Implications for effective development communication. *Tanzania Journal of Development Studies, 19*(1).
Oguntade, A., Fatunmbi, T., & Okafor, C. (2012). Effects of farmers' field school on the technical efficiency of cocoa farmers in Nigeria. *Journal of Biology and Life Science, 4*(1), 135–144.
Okello, T., & Mwesigwa, D. (2022). *Analyzing the significance of village savings and loan association (VSLA) to community development in Uganda*. Retrieved September 22, 2023, from https://ijiset.com/vol9/v9s6/IJISET_V9_I06_34.pdf
Olusa, A. O. (2021). Impact of community social development projects on community improvement: Case of Ibule-Soro community, Ondo State, Nigeria. *Journal of Infrastructure Development, 13*(1), 7–20.
Ramsey, S., & Blessings, N. (2021). Community development in Nigeria: history, current strategies and its future as a social work method. *The Journal of Developmental Administration, 6*(4), 133–141.
Reliefweb. (2023). *Global Peace Index 2023*. Retrieved June 18, 2023, from https://reliefweb.int/report/world/global-peace-index-2023

Rwigema, P. C. (2022). Community development programs: Conceptions and practices with emphasis on East Africa community. *The Strategic Journal of Business & Change Management, 9*(4), 1447–1486.

Saliu, S. I. (2014). Evaluation of self-help community development projects in Zungeru in Niger state, Nigeria. *Greener Journal of Social Sciences, 4*(3), 093–107.

Sebele, L. S. (2010). Community-based tourism ventures, benefits and challenges: Khama rhino sanctuary trust, central district, Botswana. *Tourism Management, 31*(1), 136–146.

SciSpace. (2024). *What are the values that are considered important in African culture?* PubGenius. Retrieved July 1, 2024, from https://typeset.io/questions/what-are-the-values-that-are-considered-important-in-african-3apuoff4m1

Tshishonga, N. S. (2022). Traditional governance systems and reform: Dynamics and opportunities for Africa's development. In I. Tshabangu (Ed.), *Interdisciplinary approaches to the future of Africa and policy development*. IGI Global (Idea Group).

Tukundane, N. (2018). *Village saving and loan associations transform youth in Uganda*. CTA Experience Capitalization Series.

Woldemichael, A., Gurara, D. & Shimeles, A. (2019). *The impact of community-based health insurance schemes on out-of-pocket healthcare spending: Evidence from Rwanda*. International Monetary Fund. Retrieved September 2, 2023, from https://www.imf.org/-/media/Files/Publications/WP/2019/WPIEA2019038.ashx

World Bank. (2021). *Nigeria: The community-led approach that is helping inclusive development*. Retrieved September 17, 2023, from https://www.worldbank.org/en/news/feature/2021/10/27/nigeria-the-community-led-approach-that-is-helping-inclusive-development

World Population Review. (2023). *Poverty rates by countries*. Retrieved August 14, 2023, from https://worldpopulationreview.com/country-rankings/poverty-rate-by-country

Cecy Edijala Balogun is a research fellow at the Nigerian Institute of Social and Economic Research in Nigeria. She holds PhD in Rural Sociology at the University of Ibadan, Nigeria. She is a prestigious scholar of the CODESRIA College of Mentors and Mentees (2019), a laureate of the CODESRIA Gender Institute (2021) and the CODESRIA Governance Institute (2021), and a fellow of WARIA (2021–2024), the Ife Summer Institute (2021) and the University of Bergen Summer Research School (BSRS, 2024). Her research interests span Rural livelihood, public policy, rural sociology, and women and youth development studies.

History

Hadizat Audu Salihu

In this chapter, I discuss the conceptualizations of Africa in the field of History, an academic discipline which many scholars have defined as the study of past events, people, and societies. It is the exploration of the past through the examination of written and non-written sources, artifacts, and other forms of evidence (Carr, 1961). The goal of history is to understand the past and to explain how and why things happened the way they did. The concept of History has evolved, with different approaches and perspectives. Traditional approaches to History focused on political and military events, while more recent approaches have expanded to include social, cultural, and economic aspects (Burke, 2008).

Historians use a variety of sources to reconstruct the past, including primary sources such as letters, diaries, pictures, drawings, songs, chants, and official documents, as well as secondary sources such as textbooks and scholarly articles. They also use a range of methods, including qualitative and sometimes quantitative approaches, to interpret the evidence and draw conclusions to narratives (Gaddis, 2004). History has important practical applications in all fields of life, such as informing policy decisions, preserving cultural heritage, and promoting social cohesion. It also has intrinsic value as a way to understand and appreciate the diversity of human experience and the complexity of human societies (Bauer, 1948).

Africa has been studied by many Western historians since the 1900s with misconceptions about Africa, such scholars are Hugh Trevor-Roper, Johann Friedrich Blumenbach, David Hume, Hegel, E. D. Morel, and many other European scholars and colonial powers viewed African societies as primitive and uncivilized, with a culture and history that were inferior to their own. This view was used to justify the colonization and exploitation of Africa, with Europeans believing that they were bringing progress and development to a backward continent and in need of outside

H. A. Salihu (✉)
History and Diplomatic Studies, Kwara State University Malete, Ilorin, Nigeria
e-mail: hadizat.salihu@kwasu.edu.ng

A. K. Bangura, J. A. Ifedi (eds.), *Conceptualizations of Africa*, African Studies and Research Forum Series, https://doi.org/10.1007/978-3-031-74535-5_17

intervention. Nonetheless, since 1940, there has been a growing recognition among European scholars of the richness and complexity of African history and culture due to the role played by African scholars in redefining the way African history is studied and understood, with a focus on the contributions and agency of Africans themselves.

The major research question probed in the chapter is the following: What conceptualizations have been offered about Africa in the academic discipline of History? The basic answer to this question is that many conceptualizations have been tendered concerning what Africa is in the field of History which range from the positive to the negative; sadly, the latter are more preponderant. Nevertheless, it is beyond the scope of this chapter to deal with all of these conceptualizations. Therefore, the following three major conceptualizations are examined here: (1) African perspective of its history, (2) European view of Africa, and (3) Africa in the eyes of Arabs.

Since the focus of the chapter is on historical conceptualizations, the ensuing analyses are qualitative: i.e., words are emphasized as opposed to numerical values. Before engaging in the review of the three aforementioned conceptualizations, History is first provided as a backdrop, as it is the discipline upon which the investigation here is hinged. The timeframes covered by the information provided are in line with the nature of the conceptualizations.

The foremost question, therefore, is this: Why is it necessary to investigate how Africa is conceptualized in the field of History? The answer to this is that It helps correct historical biases and misinterpretations of Africa, stops stereotypes, and broadens Africa's history, showcasing the continent's diversity, complexity and the role played by Africa in global history, from the earliest to the 21st Century. Any investigation in the History discipline allows for a thorough examination of primary and secondary sources of information focusing on the events that took place in other to determine how, why, and when such events took place before drawing a conclusion. In essence, the discussion in this chapter makes it possible to expatiate how these factors are relevant in the analyses of what Africa is in the field of History. Accordingly, I begin the examination in this chapter on how the field of History itself is conceptualized.

History: A Conceptualization

The academic discipline of History has been conceptualized in several ways which include (a) History as a narrative, (b) History as a social science, (c) History as a critical analysis of the past, and (d) History as a way of understanding the present. In this chapter, I focus on two concepts of history: i.e., (1) History as a study of the past and (2) History and the present. These two will be discussed one at a time in the following subsection for clarity.

History as a Study of the Past

History is a discipline that critically analyzes the past to understand the present and inform the future. History as a field is also constantly evolving, with different conceptualizations reflecting changing social, cultural, and intellectual trends. At its core, however, history remains a critical analysis of the past, aimed at understanding the present and shaping the future. As noted by Beverley Southgate, History is "the process of investigation and explanation of change over time" (2010, p. 1). It involves the systematic examination of primary sources, secondary sources, and other evidence to construct an interpretation of past events and trends. According to Hayden White, History is a form of narrative discourse, where events are arranged and interpreted to establish meaning and coherence (White, 1978). This approach emphasizes the importance of storytelling and the role of the historian as an interpreter of the past. White's ideas have been influential in the development of postmodernist approaches to the field of History, which emphasize the constructed nature of historical narratives and challenge the idea of a fixed, objective reality.

Another conceptualization of History is provided by E. H. Carr (1961), who posits that history is an ongoing dialogue between the present and the past. According to Carr, historians are not detached observers but are engaged in interpreting the past in light of present concerns and values. This approach emphasizes the importance of context and the need for historians to be aware of their own biases and assumptions. In recent years, there has been a growing recognition of the importance of social and cultural history, which emphasizes the experiences of ordinary people and marginalized groups, especially in underdeveloped countries. Furthermore, rather than focusing solely on political or economic elites, this approach emphasizes the need to understand historical events from multiple perspectives and to recognize the diversity of human experiences.

The study of history can be contentious and controversial, and, in a postmodern age, historical matters are of the greatest importance as they infiltrate every nook and cranny of public and private life in the past, present, and future (Berg, 2019). History may be regarded as actuality, record, knowledge, and thought of past events. It differs from systematic social sciences, such as politics, sociology, and economics, in the time depth with which it deals. As a record, history consists of the signs, symbols, monuments, documents, and papers that convey to posterity the information respecting the actuality of the past which has been preserved or survived the ravages of the time (Bauer, 1948).

Historians use a range of methodologies to analyze historical evidence and construct narratives about the past. These methods can include archival research, statistical analysis, oral history interviews, and comparative analysis of different societies and cultures. The study of history has played a vital role in shaping our understanding of the world and ourselves. It has helped analysts understand the origins and evolution of human societies, as well as the causes and consequences of major historical events such as wars, revolutions, and economic transformations.

History and the Present

The study of history is essential for understanding the present and shaping the future. By examining the historical roots of contemporary issues and trends, historians can gain insight into the complex and interconnected forces that shape lives. Some examples of how historical events and trends continue to influence contemporary society are examined in the ensuing paragraphs.

Colonialism and Its Legacy: Since the twentieth century, the history of colonialism continues to shape contemporary global relations, particularly in terms of economic inequality, political instability, and cultural tensions of former colonies. The exploitation of resources and labor by colonial powers has contributed to the underdevelopment of many countries in Africa, Asia, and Latin America (Gobo, 2020). The legacy of colonialism has had a profound impact on the world in which we live today. Edward Said (1978) argues that the West's construction of "the Orient" as an inferior region helped to justify colonialism and continues to shape our understanding of the world today. Similarly, Walter Rodney (1973) posits that colonialism not only exploited resources but also destroyed local economies, which has contributed to the underdevelopment of many countries today. In addition, the legacy of colonialism has resulted in ongoing conflicts and tensions, such as the Israeli-Palestinian conflict which is rooted in the displacement of Palestinian people during the establishment of the state of Israel (Khalidi, 2019).

Civil Rights Movements are another contemporary issue as the struggle for civil rights and equality, which gained momentum in the twentieth century, continues to influence contemporary social and political movements. The Black Lives Matter movement, for instance, is a direct response to ongoing racial inequality and police brutality in the United States (Keeanga-Yamahtta, 2016). Similarly, the #MeToo movement has been described as a continuation of the feminist movements of the past seeking to address ongoing issues of gender inequality and sexual harassment (Dunn, 2023).

The Forces of Globalization, which have shaped the modern world in numerous ways, have deep roots in historical events such as the Industrial Revolution, the rise of European colonialism, and the expansion of international trade (Bairoch, 1993). The contemporary world economy, characterized by the dominance of multinational corporations and the integration of national economies, is the result of long-term historical processes that continue to evolve (Steger, 2017).

Environmentalism: The contemporary environmental movement has roots in historical events, such as the Industrial Revolution, which led to the widespread pollution and destruction of natural resources. The conservation movement, which emerged in the late nineteenth century in response to the destruction of wilderness areas, has evolved into a global movement to address climate change and protect the planet.

The Roots of Inequality: The study of history provides an understanding of the roots of social and economic inequalities, which continue to be major issues in many societies today. For example, historian Howard Zinn in his famous book titled *A People's History of the United States* (1980) argues that the history of the United

States has been marked by the oppression of marginalized groups such as indigenous peoples, African Americans, and working-class people. Similarly in Africa, there are numerous cases of inequality and marginalization of smaller groups which have constantly resulted in conflict.

The Causes and Consequences of Conflict: The study of contemporary history provides insights into the causes and consequences of conflict, which remain major global issues today. For example, historian Niall Ferguson (1998) points out that the First World War was a result of the breakdown of the European balance of power and the rise of nationalism, which continues to be a factor in contemporary conflicts. Similarly, the ongoing conflict in the Middle East can be traced back to the legacy of European colonialism and the arbitrary borders drawn by colonial powers (Anderson, 2018).

Overall, the study of historical phenomena is essential for understanding the past and the present. It is also important for comprehending the forces that shape the world today for the future.

African Perspective of Its History

The African perspective of its history is multifaceted and diverse, as the continent has over 3000 distinct ethnic groups, each with its own unique history and cultural practices. Nonetheless, a common thread that ran throughout African history is the impact of colonialism and the struggle for independence (Ki-Zerbo & Hama, 1981).

As mentioned earlier, African history has traditionally been written by Western scholars, often with a Eurocentric perspective that perpetuates stereotypes and overlooks the agency and diversity of Africans. As also noted, since the 1940s, there has been a growing movement of African scholars reclaiming the writing of their history and developing new approaches that challenge the dominant narratives. Africa's history during the precolonial era was mainly documented in Arabic written texts; these texts have survived a thousand years and can be found in places like Mali, Ghana, Bornu, Sokoto, Egypt, Ethiopia, and many other African countries. The continent's history was also documented and preserved through cave drawings and paintings, folktales, songs, stories, legends, and myths. Most of this information was passed on to the next generation orally; hence, there was the use of oral tradition as part of African history.

With the use of oral tradition and Arabic texts, some African writers and scholars have written African history in an attempt to change the European misconception of African history through their narratives. One notable perspective on African history comes from the Ghanaian scholar, Kwame Nkrumah, who was a leading figure in the Pan-African Movement and played a key role in Ghana's independence from British colonial rule in 1957. In his very famous book titled *Africa Must Unite*, Nkrumah argues that the history of Africa is one of exploitation and oppression by European powers. He emphasizes the importance of African unity and self-determination as a means of overcoming the legacy of colonialism (Ki-Zerbo & Hama, 1981).

Other notable African historians include Achille Mbembe, who has written extensively on the politics of postcolonial Africa, and Toyin Falola, who has published numerous works on the social and cultural history of West Africa. Similarly, the *African Studies Review* and the *Journal of African History* are two important academic journals that feature articles and book reviews written by African scholars on a range of African historical topics (Appiah & Gates, 2010).

Another important African perspective on history comes from the Senegalese scholar, Cheikh Anta Diop, who was a historian, anthropologist, and linguist specializing in the study of Kemet/Ancient Egypt and its connections to Africa South of the Sahara. In his book titled *The African Origin of Civilization: Myth or Reality*, Diop argues that Egypt was a Black African civilization and that African cultures have made significant contributions to world history. He also emphasizes the need for Africans to reclaim their own history and cultural heritage (Appiah & Gates, 2010). In the book, Diop also posits that African civilization predates that of Europe and that the roots of Western civilization can be traced back to ancient Africa. Diop's work has been influential in the study of African history and has helped other writers to challenge many of the prevailing Eurocentric views of African history (Appiah & Gates, 2010).

Adu Boahen's works discuss African history using the primary sources made available to him. His book titled *African Perspectives on Colonialism* (2020) provides a critical analysis of the impact of colonialism on Africa and examines how colonialism shaped African politics, economics, and culture.

With the efforts of African writers, historians, and other scholars, many works in this vein became popular with European writers embracing oral traditions and other primary sources in the writing of African History. For example, *Africa's Peasant Revolutions* written by Thandika Mkandawire and Peter Wanyande provides a detailed analysis of the rural struggles and social movements that shaped African history (Ngugi, 1986). Another significant contribution is *African History: A Very Short Introduction* by John Parker and Richard Rathbone which offers a concise overview of the major themes and debates in African history from precolonial times to the present (Barbosa, 2012).

The preceding perspectives are just a few examples of the diverse range of views on African history. Other important scholars and thinkers include Chinua Achebe, Wole Soyinka, and Ngũgĩ wa Thiong'o, among others. Many books provide a comprehensive overview of African history from an African perspective. One such book is *Africa: A Biography of the Continent* by John Reader. This book provides a detailed account of the continent's history from prehistoric times to the present, and also offers insights into the social, cultural, and political developments that have shaped Africa over the centuries (Barbosa, 2012).

Between 1965 and 1979, the General History of Africa project originated at the International Congress of Africanists held in Accra, the capital of Ghana, from December 11 to 18, 1962. This was a large event that, with the support of the United Nations Educational, Scientific and Cultural Organization (UNESCO), involved around 500 African specialists from all over the world to develop historical research in Africa (Barbosa, 2012). Over 200 international experts under the auspices of

UNESCO carried out a project of the analysis of internal conflicts involved in the construction of the African perspective of its history. Theoretical and methodological parameters were also constructed in addition to eight volumes of materials published in the 1980s (Appiah and Gates, 2010).

In addition, there were two reasons for UNESCO's participation in the project from its conception. First, at this time UNESCO was concerned with intensifying its work in Africa. This intention was evident, for example, in the decision of UNESCO's 15th General Conference in 1960 to make greater efforts for education in the African continent. UNESCO's support of the Africanist Congress was part of this greater purpose. This new direction was, in turn, a response to the large number of African countries becoming members of UNESCO at the beginning of the 1960s, especially new independent states. It should be noted that in 1960, UNESCO only had nine African member states, while in 1963 this number had risen to 32. Furthermore, UNESCO was able to provide the institutional and financial support that the project demanded. After all, since its very beginning, it has been seen as a scientific project with great scope (Barbosa, 2012, pp. 195–214).

With the aid of UNESCO and the GHA project, Africa has been represented in various ways by African writers and scholars, reflecting diverse perspectives and experiences. Some writers celebrated Africa's rich cultural heritage and its contributions to human civilization, while others have critiqued its legacies of colonialism, slavery, and underdevelopment (Appiah & Gates, 2010). These works told African histories using African perspectives to counter the view that Africa has no history. Many prominent writers leveraged the work and methods adopted by early Africanist writers and then continued to write the narratives which became a major source of documents for African history.

One notable example of these writers is Chinua Achebe, a Nigerian novelist and scholar who wrote extensively on the history of Nigeria in particular and the African continent as a whole. His works show the challenges of postcolonial Africa, including issues of identity, nationalism, and cultural imperialism. In his seminal work, *Things Fall Apart*, Achebe portrays the complexity of Igbo society and its encounters with European colonialism in Nigeria. He also wrote *No Longer at Ease* and *Arrow of God* which further highlight the impact of colonialism on African societies (Achebe, 2012). Also in his book titled *There Was a Country: A Personal History of Biafra*, Achebe offers a personal account of the Nigerian Civil War while also providing a broader historical context for the conflict and its aftermath (Achebe, 2012).

Ali Al'Amin Mazrui, a Kenyan academic who was renowned for his work on African history and politics, worked extensively to showcase the continent to the world using an African perspective. One of Mazrui's very famous books titled *The Africans: A Triple Heritage* entails a comprehensive overview of African history, tracing the continent's past from precolonial times through to the present (Mazrui, 1999). Other notable African historians include Toyin Falola, who has written extensively on the history of Nigeria and West Africa, and John Iliffe, who focused on the history of East Africa. These scholars, and many others like them, have made significant contributions to the field of African history, challenging misconceptions and offering new insights into the continent's rich and complex past. Similarly,

Ngũgĩ wa Thiong'o, a Kenyan writer and activist, emphasized the importance of decolonizing African literature and reclaiming African languages and cultures. In his book titled *Decolonising the Mind: The Politics of Language in African Literature*, he asserts that the use of European languages in African literature perpetuates colonial power structures and marginalizes African voices. He advocates for the use of African languages and the promotion of indigenous knowledge systems (Thiong'o, 1986).

Other African scholars in various disciplines, including History, Anthropology, Political Science, Linguistics, Sociology, Psychology, Mathematics, and Economics, have also contributed to the understanding of Africa's past and present through the methods employed in gathering sources. Examples of such scholars are Wole Soyinka, Chimamanda Ngozi Adichie, Achille Mbembe, Terence Ranger, and Binyavanga Wainaina; all of them have explored various dimensions of African experiences, including the legacies of colonialism, the politics of gender and sexuality, and the challenges of globalization and neoliberalism. Their works have challenged Eurocentric narratives and offered alternative interpretations of African histories.

In recent years, African scholars have been increasingly contributing to the study of African history and, in addition to their books, several online resources offering insights into African history from an African perspective. The website of the African Studies Center at the University of Pennsylvania, for example, offers a range of resources on African history and culture, including articles, research papers, and bibliographies. The website of the African Union also provides information on African history and current events, as well as links to a range of African news sources (Barbosa, 2012).

Overall, African writers and scholars have played a crucial role in shaping the narratives of Africa and challenging dominant discourses that have often misrepresented or silenced African perspectives. Through their works, they continue to contribute to the ongoing project of reimagining Africa and envisioning a more just and equitable future for the continent.

European View of Africa

This section looks at the European view of Africa by focusing on the perceptions, attitudes, and narratives that shaped the European understanding of the continent. From ancient Greek and Roman accounts to the era of colonization, European perspectives on Africa were shaped by a variety of factors, including cultural biases, economic interests, scientific discoveries, and missionary activities. This narrative provides a comprehensive overview of the European view of Africa, highlighting key periods, influential figures, and the evolution of attitudes over time.

The European view of Africa during the precolonial period was shaped by a combination of limited knowledge, prevailing stereotypes, and cultural biases. European encounters with Africa were sporadic, primarily driven by trade and exploration. During the precolonial era, Europe's knowledge of Africa was limited due to geographical distance and the lack of extensive exploration. Europeans had little direct contact with the African continent, relying mostly on second-hand accounts from travelers, merchants, and scholars. This limited knowledge contributed to the formation of misconceptions and stereotypes. For example, the Greek philosopher Aristotle described Africa as a land of extremes and inhabited by monstrous creatures, due to his understanding of the continent based on second-hand information (Boahen, 1985). Similarly, the Roman geographer Ptolemy's influential work titled *Geographia* perpetuated misconceptions about Africa's geography, thereby further shaping European views of the continent (Boahen, 1985).

European perceptions of Africa during the precolonial period were also influenced by stereotypes and preconceived notions that were deeply rooted in cultural biases. These stereotypes depicted Africans as exotic, primitive, and inferior to Europeans. For instance, the medieval European imagination often associated Africa with fantastical creatures and mythical lands. Travel accounts such as the fourteenth-century text, *The Travels of Sir John Mandeville*, portrayed Africa as a place of bizarre and extraordinary phenomena, reinforcing the notion of African otherness (Greenblatt, 2009).

Religious biases also played a significant role in shaping European views of Africa. The Christian religious context characterized Africa as a land of heathens and idolaters, requiring conversion and salvation. This religious lens further accentuated the perception of African culture as inferior (Boahen, 1985).

Despite the prevailing stereotypes, European interest in Africa during the precolonial era was primarily driven by trade and economic factors. Europeans sought to establish trade routes to Africa, particularly for valuable commodities such as gold, ivory, and spices. The Italian merchant republics of Venice and Genoa, for example, established trade links with North African ports, fostering cultural exchange and economic cooperation (Hodges, 1982). Nevertheless, these commercial interactions did not necessarily lead to a deeper understanding of African societies, as Europeans often approached Africa from a transactional standpoint rather than a desire to comprehend its complexities.

The prevailing European view of Africa during the colonial period was influenced by notions of racial superiority, cultural hierarchies, and the "civilizing mission." Europeans often portrayed Africans as primitive, uncivilized, and in need of European intervention and control. This perspective was grounded in social Darwinism, which posited that European societies were more advanced and racially superior to African societies. Prominent figures such as explorer David Livingstone, missionary organizations, and colonial administrators played significant roles in shaping and disseminating this European view of Africa. Their writings, speeches, and actions reinforced stereotypes and narratives that portrayed Africa as a dark and mysterious continent inhabited by "savages" or "backward people."

Europe's historical engagement with Africa was predominantly shaped by the era of colonialism, during which European powers exerted control over and exploited African resources. The European view of Africa during this period was often rooted in Eurocentrism, which perpetuated stereotypes and prejudices about Africans as inferior to Europeans (Rodney, 1973). During the colonial period,

European views of Africa were heavily influenced by racial discourse and scientific racism, which proffered that Africans were biologically and culturally inferior to Europeans. These ideas justified colonization and the exploitation of African resources (Banton, 1998). During the nineteenth and early twentieth centuries, European powers such as Britain, France, Germany, Belgium, and Portugal sought to establish colonial control over various parts of Africa. These colonial endeavors were often motivated by economic interests, including the exploitation of natural resources, expansion of trade, and the desire for geopolitical dominance. Nonetheless, it is important to note that this view was not universally held among Europeans.

During the colonial era, European powers exerted control over vast regions of Africa, shaping not only the continent's political landscape but also the European view of Africa itself. European views of Africa during colonial rule were heavily influenced by Eurocentrism. Walter Rodney's seminal work titled *How Europe Underdeveloped Africa* (1973) sheds light on how European powers justified their colonial projects by characterizing Africans as inferior beings. This Eurocentric perspective established a power imbalance, leading to the exploitation of African resources and the suppression of African agency.

Scientific racism also played a crucial role in shaping the European view of Africa during the colonial period. Prominent European thinkers such as Carl Linnaeus and Georges Cuvier proposed racial classifications that placed Africans at the bottom of a hierarchy (Banton, 1998). These racial theories provided a pseudo-scientific justification for the subjugation of Africans and reinforced negative stereotypes about their intellectual, physical, and cultural capabilities. Such views influenced European policies and practices, resulting in the marginalization and devaluation of African societies.

The European view of Africa during colonial rule perpetuated stereotypes that reinforced the notion of African inferiority. Africans were often depicted as primitive and savage in European literature, art, and media. These stereotypes served to justify European domination and control over Africa. The works of European explorers such as Henry Morton Stanley and David Livingstone further perpetuated these stereotypes, painting a one-dimensional and dehumanizing image of the African continent. These perceptions of Africa had a direct impact on colonial policies such as the belief in European superiority which led to the imposition of European cultural, economic, and political systems on African societies. The Berlin Conference of 1884–1885, where European powers partitioned Africa, exemplified the European perspective that Africa was a land to be divided and exploited, rather than a diverse continent with complex civilizations.

It is important to mention that European views of Africa during colonial rule were not universally accepted. Some European intellectuals, missionaries, and activists challenged prevailing notions of African inferiority and advocated for a more nuanced understanding of the continent. These alternative narratives, although often marginalized, contributed to the eventual demise of colonialism and the emergence of postcolonial perspectives on Africa.

In the twenty-first century, Europe's view of Africa has undergone significant transformations, reflecting the changing dynamics in global politics, economics, and social discourses. While remnants of colonial attitudes persist, European perspectives on Africa have become more diverse, encompassing issues such as development, migration, and cooperation. Since the turn of the century, European views of Africa have increasingly focused on development and cooperation. The European Union (EU), as a collective entity, has emphasized partnerships with African countries, aiming to promote sustainable development, good governance, and poverty reduction. The EU's Africa Strategy, launched in 2020, underscores the importance of cooperation based on mutual interests and shared responsibilities (European Union, 2020).

Another significant aspect of the European view of Africa in the twenty-first century relates to security concerns, particularly in the context of counterterrorism efforts. European countries have acknowledged Africa's strategic importance in combating transnational threats such as terrorism, piracy, and organized crime. This has led to increased military cooperation, intelligence sharing, and capacity-building initiatives between Europe and African nations (Bueger & Stockbruegger, 2020). Also, migration from Africa to Europe has been a key issue shaping European views of Africa in the twenty-first century. The influx of migrants and refugees has sparked debates around border control, immigration policies, and integration. While some European countries have adopted more inclusive approaches, emphasizing the humanitarian aspects of migration, others have espoused more restrictive measures, driven by concerns over national security and socioeconomic impacts (Arne & Zaun, 2023).

In recent years, there has been a growing recognition among European nations of the historical injustices perpetuated during the colonial era. Some European countries have acknowledged the need for reconciliation, reparations, and dialogue with African nations to address the lasting impacts of colonization. Initiatives like the French government's restitution of cultural artifacts to their countries of origin signal a shift toward acknowledging and redressing historical wrongs (Sarr & Savoy, 2018).

Africa in the Eyes of Arabs

Arab-African relations stretch back before the nineteenth century, with a long history of trade, knowledge exchange, and cultural interactions. Arab perceptions of Africa were shaped by these interactions, and their views of the continent were multifaceted and dynamic.

Many medieval Arabic texts categorize people phenotypically into three types of skin color: (1) white, *a'l-bīḍān*, "the white ones" associated particularly with Arabs; (2) red, associated particularly with Romans, or Europeans more generally; and (3) black, *al-sūdān*, "the black ones" associated particularly with darker complexioned Africans (El Hamel, 2002). In pre-Islamic Arabia, Blacks were referred to as *ḥabashī* (related to the term *Abyssinian*); this word's precise meaning is unclear, but it probably denoted people living under Aksumite rule, particularly people from the Horn of Africa. The East African coastal region corresponding to the littoral of what is currently Kenya and Tanzania was called *Zanj*, and the people from there (or imagined to be from there) were called by the same term (John, 2005). Also, during the pre-Islamic period, significant numbers of Africans were present in the Arabian Peninsula, and the image of the Abyssinian and African as a warrior is thought to have been significant in the Arab imaginary, both because of the power and presence of Aksumite forces and Arabs' employment of African mercenaries.

During the Islamic period, dark-skinned Africans in the Arabian Peninsula and elsewhere in the Caliphate were enslaved people captured and sold as properties to work on their masters' lands. For example, al-Ṭabarī estimated that in Southern Basra alone, there were around 15,000 enslaved Africans in the 870s. This situation encouraged Arabs to view themselves as superior to Africans, not the least as a mechanism for Arabs to justify the enslavement of others. For example, Ibn Buṭlān composed a noted stereotyping description of the qualities of enslaved people of different races, which is relatively positive about Nubians, but otherwise particularly negative about the characteristics of Africans (John, 2005).

In the fifth and sixth centuries, Arabia and Ethiopia had very close ties because Prophet Muhammad (Peace Be Upon Him—PBUH) advised his most trustworthy followers whom he wanted to protect to take refuge in Ethiopia in order to escape persecution from the pagans in Mecca. One of the earliest and most energetic reverts to Islam was an Ethiopian named Bilal, whom the prophet made his muezzin ("caller to prayer"). Nonetheless, the spread of the Arabs into Africa had to await the death of Prophet Muhammad (PBUH) in 632. Ten years after the death of the Prophet, the Arabs had conquered the most important cities in the Middle East. Damascus was taken in 636, Jerusalem in 638, and Alexandria in 642. By 679, the Arabs had moved into Libya and Tunisia, and by the eleventh century, the Arabization of the Maghreb had considerably advanced. Then a general push began southward from Egypt, Libya, and the Maghreb. By the twelfth century, the Muslim Kingdom of Kanem was founded. Colonies left by the Berbers (more correctly, Amazighs) on the Senegal and Niger rivers and Lake Chad, in alliance with the local population that had reverted to Islam, played important roles in the formation of the empires of Ghana, Mali, and Goa from the twelfth to the sixteenth centuries and of Kanem-Bornu from the twelfth to the nineteenth century (Jalloh, 1984).

The first five centuries after the emergence of Islam, spanning from the seventh to the twelfth centuries of the current era, was the age when the great Islamic empires dominated world affairs. Arabs had an international presence stretching from Iraq and Arabia to Spain and Sicily. The era of early Islam is a source of pride to all Arabs; however, some Islamists argue that the Arabs were greatest when they adhered most closely to their Muslim faith and, accordingly, the second era of Arab greatness began in the nineteenth century (Eugene, 2010). Nonetheless, the progress of Islam and, therefore, of Arab influence in the Savannah regions of Africa was rather slow. It was resisted by the Mossi and the Bambara and for a long time also by the Fulani and the Hausa. It was only in the nineteenth century that Islam made rapid advances under Alhaji Umar in western Sudan, Uthman Dan Fodio in northern

Nigeria, and the Mahdi Mohammed Ahmad in The Sudan. Thus, when Western colonialists arrived in the nineteenth century they found Islam already dominant in the Savannah regions of West Africa from Senegal to Northern Cameroon (Jalloh, 1984).

The Arabs engaged in extensive trade with Africa, dating back to the early centuries of the Common Era. The trade routes of the Indian Ocean and the trans-Saharan trade facilitated the exchange of goods, including gold, ivory, enslaved people, spices, and textiles, while Arab traders brought in items like pottery, glassware, and luxury goods from the Middle East and Asia. This trade played a crucial role in fostering economic ties between Arab merchants and African communities, thereby contributing to mutual prosperity and cultural interactions (Jalloh, 1984). The Arab traders' fascination with Africa's abundant natural resources and diverse commodities contributed to a positive view of the continent as a valuable economic partner (Horton & Middleton, 2000). The Arab trade with Africa intensified during the nineteenth century as coastal Arab cities like Zanzibar, Lamu, and Mombasa served as vital hubs for maritime trade along the East African coast. These traders established thriving commercial networks that spanned the Indian Ocean, connecting Africa to the Arabian Peninsula, Persia, and India. Arab scholars, explorers, and travelers made significant contributions to the study and understanding of Africa's geography, culture, and history.

Renowned explorers like Ibn Battuta and Al-Masudi extensively documented their journeys across Africa, portraying the continent as a land of marvels, diverse cultures, and rich knowledge. Their accounts painted a vivid picture of Africa's beauty and complexity, thereby challenging simplistic stereotypes and fostering a more nuanced view among Arabs (Jalloh, 1984).

The spread of Islam was one of the most influential aspects of Arab-African interactions before the nineteenth century. Arab merchants, scholars, and Sufi mystics played a crucial role in disseminating Islamic teachings throughout North and East Africa. The peaceful nature of this cultural exchange often resulted in the integration of Islamic values into African traditions, giving rise to unique African-Islamic cultural expressions and architectural styles (Trimingham, 1996). Historical records suggest that Arab interactions with African kingdoms and empires were often characterized by mutual respect and diplomacy. Arab merchants and explorers recognized the advanced civilizations in regions like West Africa such as the Mali Empire, the Ghana Empire, and the Songhai Empire. These exchanges of knowledge and diplomacy contributed to a more positive view of Africa as a land of sophisticated societies and cultural achievements (Diriye, 2001).

Unfortunately, the nineteenth century also witnessed the continuation of the Trans-Saharan Slave Trade, with Arab traders actively participating in the commerce of enslaved Africans. Slavery had a long history in parts of North and East Africa, and Arab traders were instrumental in facilitating the movement of enslaved people from the interior of Africa to markets in the Arab world. Arab-African relations in the context of the trade of enslaved people were fraught with exploitation and suffering for countless Africans who were subjected to forced labor and inhumane treatment. However, it is essential to acknowledge that not all Arab communities were involved in this trade, and there were also instances of resistance and abolitionist movements within Arab societies (Lovejoy, 2012).

According to Ali Al'Amin Mazrui, the majority of the Arab people are now in the African continent as the bulk of Arab lands are located in Africa. He states the situation as follows:

> There are more Muslims in Nigeria than there are Muslims in any Arab country, including Egypt. In other words, the Muslim population of Nigeria is larger than the Muslim population of Egypt. The African continent as a whole is in the process of becoming the first continent in the world with an absolute Muslim majority. The language with the largest number of individual speakers in the African continent is still Arabic. The most influential indigenous African languages are Swahili (Kiswahili) in East Africa and Hausa in West Africa of them profoundly influenced by both Arabic and Islam (1993, p. 163).

Arab views of Africa in the twenty-first century are influenced by a complex interplay of historical, economic, political, and cultural factors. It is important to point out that Arab perspectives on Africa are not uniform; they can vary based on individual experiences, regional dynamics, and geopolitical considerations because many Arab countries have been actively engaging with African nations in trade and economic partnerships. Countries like Saudi Arabia, the United Arab Emirates, and Qatar have invested in various sectors across Africa, including infrastructure, energy, and agriculture. These economic interactions have often been seen as mutually beneficial and reflective of a positive Arab view of Africa's economic potential (Tom, 2014). In addition, Arab nations have been involved in diplomatic efforts and peacekeeping initiatives in conflict-stricken regions of Africa such as Sudan and Somalia. These actions can be seen as an expression of solidarity and a desire to contribute to regional stability (Ifeoma, 2011).

It is important to also note that historical and cultural connections between the Arab world and Africa, particularly through Islam, continue to influence perceptions. The spread of Islam and the presence of significant Arab Diaspora communities in North and East Africa have fostered cultural and religious ties, thereby contributing to a sense of shared identity (Dima, 2008). Since 2000, Arab nations have sometimes been both destinations and transit points for African migrants and refugees. This has led to complex discussions and policies related to immigration, labor markets, and social integration, which can impact Arab views of Africa (Dima, 2008).

Nevertheless, media representation and public discourse can shape Arab views of Africa. Positive stories about African achievements, development, and cultural richness can enhance understanding and appreciation, while negative portrayals can reinforce stereotypes (Ifeoma, 2011).

Conclusion and Recommendations

The general conclusion in this chapter is that Africa as a continent and its people have been looked at from different perspectives by various people with varying continental differences and experiences. These perspectives of Africa by different people revealed that African history and her economy have greatly attracted foreigners from the earliest period. Although some of the perspectives reveal many challenges for the continent, they also show some positive attributes as discussed in the preceding sections. It is also significant to indicate that even among Africans, there are varying perspectives of the continent, as sociocultural experiences and geographical distinctions affect each view and narrative of the continent. It is also important to point out that colonial and postcolonial experiences have a great influence on the way Africans view themselves and the continent at large. Thus, the ultimate question of the chapter is the following: How can the negative perspective of Africa be addressed and what are the implications of this view on the development of the continent? I end here by making some policy recommendations in response to the question and a suggestion for future research on the subject matter.

First, while the African continent is still trying to find a way out of neocolonialism which has been touted by Western powers, and the negative portrayal of Africa by the mainstream media as a cesspool of disease, poverty, conflict, and "backwardness," this perception is intentional because it has more shock value and gets more attention from those who do not know the continent. A lot of people outside Africa and even many people in the continent do not understand the size, scale, history, and diversity of the continent. For example, a lot of people do not realize that Africa is a very massive continent in geographic terms, and it is therefore naive to make sweeping generalizations about the continent. Thus, a close analysis of education and awareness is imperative to changing perceptions as education is a powerful tool. Educational institutions can incorporate curricula that provide accurate and nuanced information about Africa, its history, culture, and contemporary issues. This can help dispel stereotypes and foster a more informed understanding of the continent.

Second, the governments in the continent and Africans in the Diaspora can improve the perspective of Africa through the following means: (1) encourage travel and cultural exchange programs between Westerners and Africans can lead to greater understanding; when people have direct experiences with different cultures, it often leads to more open and positive perceptions; (2) elevate diverse voices and perspectives by encouraging Africans living in the Diaspora to share their stories and experiences, thereby helping to humanize and personalize the African experience for Westerners; (3) governments can play a role in changing perceptions by implementing policies that promote diversity, inclusion, and multiculturalism; this can include anti-discrimination laws, support for cultural festivals and events, and initiatives to promote diversity in workplaces and educational institutions; (4) nongovernmental organizations (NGOs) and civil society groups can work to raise awareness about Africa's challenges and successes; they can also advocate for policies that promote positive engagement with Africa; (5) promote economic ties between the West and Africa; this economic cooperation can foster a deeper understanding of each other's cultures and values; ethical business practices such as fair trade can also help build positive perceptions; (6) art, literature, music, and film can be powerful tools for changing perceptions; the governments should continue to encourage African art and culture in the West and support cultural exchanges that showcase the diversity and richness of African creativity; (7) encourage dialogues and discussions about the sociocultural, economic, and political conditions of Africa in schools, communities, and workplaces; engaging in open and respectful conversations can help challenge stereotypes and broaden perspectives; and (8) political leaders can set a tone for changing perceptions through their statements and foreign affairs policies to promote tolerance, diversity, and respect for all cultures can have a positive impact.

Third, the African Union can project a positive and authentic African image both within the continent and on the global stage through various means such as social activities which include sports, education, cultural awareness, and gender equity. Doing so will help to promote unity, development, and a better understanding of Africa's diverse cultural practices and potentials. It is worth emphasizing that projecting an African image requires a multifaceted approach that involves promoting African identity, culture, and achievements, as well as addressing challenges and fostering unity. The African Union can therefore play a central role in coordinating these efforts and working collaboratively with member states and other stakeholders to project an authentic and positive image of Africa.

Fourth and finally, I suggest that future research on the African perspective is vital for understanding the diverse cultures, histories, challenges, and opportunities of the continent. It can also contribute to more accurate and nuanced narratives about Africa while helping to inform policies and interventions. Research in this area should adopt interdisciplinary approaches that draw on fields such as History, Anthropology, Sociology, Economics, Political Science, and Cultural Studies. This multidisciplinary perspective can provide a holistic understanding of African perspectives which should aim to provide a comprehensive understanding of the complex and evolving viewpoints within Africa, thereby contributing to more informed policies and a more accurate portrayal of the continent.

References

Achebe, C. (2012). *There was a country: A personal history of Biafra*. Penguin Books.

Anderson, P. (2018, May 15). The roots of the Middle East conflict. *The Guardian*. Retrieved January 3, 2023, from https://www.theguardian.com/world/2018/may/15/the-roots-of-the-middle-east-conflict-100-years-of-war

Appiah, K. A., & Gates, H. L. (Eds.). (2010). *Africana: The Encyclopedia of the African and African American experience*. Basic Civitas Books.

Arne, N., & Zaun, N. (2023). Introduction: EU external migration policy and EU migration governance: Introduction. *Journal of Ethnic and Migration Studies, 49*(12), 2965–2985.

Bairoch, P. (1993). *Economics and world history: Myths and paradoxes*. The University of Chicago Press.

Banton, M. (1998). *Racial theories*. Cambridge University Press.

Barbosa, S. M. (2012). The construction of the African perspective: A history of the *General History of Africa* (UNESCO). *Revista Brasileira de História, 32*(64), 195–214.

Bauer, H. R. (1948). The study of history. *The Social Studies Journal, 38*(4), 150–158.

Berg, C. W. (2019). Why study history? An examination of undergraduate students' notions and perceptions about history. *Historical Encounters: A Journal of Historical Consciousness, Historical Cultures, and History Education, 6*(1), 54–71.

Boahen, A. A. (Ed.). (1985). *General history of Africa: Africa under colonial domination 1880-1935* (Vol. 7). UNESCO.

Boahen, A. A. (2020). *African perspectives on colonialism*. Johns Hopkins University Press.

Bueger, C., & Stockbruegger, J. (2020). Beyond security in the global south: Crisis, identity, and the securitization of terrorism. *European Journal of International Security, 5*(2), 211–230.

Burke, P. (2008). *What is cultural history?* MPG Books.

Carr, E. H. (1961). *What is history?* Knopf.

Dima, S. J. (2008). Afro-Arab relations: Romantic or real? In K. Mchombu & B. F. Bankie (Eds.), *African nationalism, strengthening the unity of Africa and its diaspora*. The Red Sea Press.

Diriye, A. M. (2001). *Culture and customs of Somalia*. Greenwood Press.

Dunn, K. R. (2023). Lessons from #Metoo and #Blacklivesmatter: Changing narratives in the courtroom. *Boston University Law Review, 100*, 2367–2410.

El Hamel, C. (2002). Race, slavery and Islam in Maghribi Mediterranean thought: The question of the Haratin in Morocco. *The Journal of North African Studies, 7*(3), 29–52.

Eugene, R. (2010). *The Arabs: A history*. Penguin Books.

European Union. (2020, March 9). *The EU comprehensive strategy with Africa*. Retrieved August 23, 2023, from https://plan-international.org/uploads/sites/28/2022/03/2020_05_18_plan_international_comprehensive_strategy_with_africa_5.pdf

Ferguson, N. (1998). *The pity of war: Explaining World War I*. Basic Books.

Gaddis, J. L. (2004). *The landscape of history: How historians map the past*. Oxford University Press.

Gobo, P. A. (2020). Legacies of colonialism in Africa. *International Journal of Innovative Science and Research Technology, 5*(8), 241–249.

Greenblatt, S. (2009). *Marvelous possessions: The wonder of the new world*. University of Chicago Press.

Hodges, R. (1982). *Dark age economics: The origins of towns and trade, A.D. 600-1000*. Duckworth.

Horton, M., & Middleton, J. (2000). *The Swahili: The social landscape of a mercantile society*. Blackwell Publishers.

Ifeoma, E. E. (2011). The nature of conflict in Africa and its impact on African international relations: The case of Darfur. *World Affairs: The Journal of International Issues, 15*(3), 88–112.

Jalloh, A. (1984). The policies of black African states towards the Arab world: An overview. In *Historical and socio-cultural relations between black Africa and the Arab world from 1935 to the present (report and papers of the symposium organized by UNESCO in Paris from 25 to 27 May 1979)*. UNESCO. Retrieved August 18, 2023, from https://unesdoc.unesco.org/in/documentViewer.xhtml?v=2.1.196&id=p::usmarcdef_0000059309&file=/in/rest/annotationSVC/DownloadWatermarkedAtt

John, O. H. (2005). A region of the mind: Medieval Arab views of African geography and ethnography and their legacy. *Sudanic Africa, 16*, 103–136.

Keeanga-Yamahtta, T. (2016). *From #BlackLivesMatter to black liberation*. Haymarket.

Khalidi, R. (2019). *The hundred years' war on Palestine: A history of settler colonialism and resistance, 1917-2017*. Metropolitan Books.

Ki-Zerbo, J., & Hama, B. (1981). The place of history in African society. In J. Ki-Zerbo (Ed.), *General history of Africa: Volume 1, Methodology and African prehistory*. Heinemann.

Lovejoy, P. E. (2012). *Transformations in slavery: A history of slavery in Africa*. Cambridge University Press.

Mazrui, A. A. (1999). *The Africans: A triple heritage*. BBC Books.

Rodney, W. (1973). *How Europe underdeveloped Africa*. Heinemann Educational Books.

Said, E. W. (1978). *Orientalism*. Vintage Books.

Sarr, F., & Savoy, B. (2018). *The restitution of African cultural heritage: Toward a new relational ethics*. Ministère de la Culture. Retrieved September 22, 2023, from https://www.about-africa.de/images/sonstiges/2018/sarr_savoy_en.pdf
Steger, M. B. (2017). *Globalization : A very short introduction* (Fourth ed.). Oxford University Press.
Southgate, B. (2010). *What is history for?* Routledge.
Thiong'o, N. W. (1986). *Decolonizing the mind: The politics of language in African literature*. East African Educational Publishers.
Tom, W. (Ed.). (2014). *Middle Eastern and African perspectives on the development of public relations: Other voices*. Palgrave Macmillan.
Trimingham, J. S. (1996). *Islam in Ethiopia*. Routledge.
White, H. (1978). *Tropics of discourse: Essays in cultural criticism*. Johns Hopkins University Press.
Zinn, H. (1980). *A people's history of the United States*. Harper & Row.

Hadizat Audu Salihu holds a PhD in History and International Studies from the University of Ilorin in Nigeria. She has been Lecturer of History in the Department of History and Diplomatic Studies at Kwara State University, Malete, Ilorin, from 2013 to the present. She has over 20 scholarly articles, and she is a member of prominent academic bodies such as CODESRIA, Lagos Studies Association, and Historical Society of Nigeria. She was one of the doctoral mentees in the CODESRIA Mentorship Training Program for doctoral students.

Human Rights

Tinashe Gumbo

As demonstrated in the other chapters of this book, Africa can be understood from different academic disciplines. This chapter seeks to contribute to the discussion on the conceptualizations of Africa from the perspective of the evolving Human Rights discipline. It specifically looks at Africa employing particular examples drawn from Zimbabwe and South Africa in particular and Africa in general. Today's international relations are dominated by human rights discourse, of which the African continent is part of the global village which is affected by such discussions. Political discussions in regional and international blocs have been framed in terms of human rights. Clearly, world leaders generally accept the idea of human rights, albeit from different angles. While the focus has always been on civil and political rights, social and economic rights have not been given much space; yet, Africa can best be understood through the latter. Africa as a continent has its own way of respecting and protecting human dignity, which largely hinges on collectivity, brotherhood, sisterhood, togetherness, *Ubuntu* (more on this concept later), and community life.

A lot has already been written about Africa and human rights in general. Nevertheless, this chapter addresses the matter in the context of a comprehensive book that looks at the concept of "Africa" from various disciplines. This makes the chapter different from previous works on Africa and human rights. The chapter is directly informed by already existing literature on human rights as well as my direct involvement in practical processes that are aimed at the promotion, protection, and defense of human rights in the Zimbabwean context. Thus, an insider perspective is applied with regard to Zimbabwe as a representative of the continent in the discussion of human rights, while data on South Africa are largely drawn from existing literature.

The main questions that the chapter interrogates are the following: How is Africa viewed with regard to human rights promotion, protection, and defense? Are there

T. Gumbo (✉)
Programs, All Africa Conference of Churches, Nairobi, Kenya

A. K. Bangura, J. A. Ifedi (eds.), *Conceptualizations of Africa*, African Studies and Research Forum Series, https://doi.org/10.1007/978-3-031-74535-5_18

any specific human rights with which Africa resonates well at the expense of others? What practical steps has Africa taken to show its commitment to social and economic rights? Is Africa a willing violator of human rights? The immediate answers to these questions are clear: Africa is viewed as a part of the global village, and, thus, is expected to fulfill the world's aspirations with regard to human rights protection and enjoyment; Africa views itself as a sovereign continent that determines how its people live; Africa is committed to the enjoyment of social and economic rights but is constrained by economic limitations.

The chapter begins by discussing the concept of Human Rights in general. It then contributes to the perennial discussion on whether human rights are universal or culturally relative. Thus, the chapter indirectly contributes to the debates on the theories of universalism and cultural relativism of human rights. It then zeroes in on specific Zimbabwean and South African examples, mainly the constitutional steps taken by the two countries in protecting social and economic rights. The chapter therefore conceptualizes Africa: as a continent with specific views with regard to human rights and as an unwilling violator of human rights because of poverty. This aspect is further concretized with a presentation of specific ways Africa has been conceptualized in the Human Rights academic discipline. While the concept of Human Rights is sometimes presented in more general terms, the chapter is focused on social and economic rights. This stance is informed by the discussion on Africa being a place where social and economic rights are more relevant than the other categories of rights that are normally emphasized in the literature. A conclusion is then drawn regarding Africa and the discipline of Human Rights before recommendations are proffered for future academic interventions.

Conceptualization of Human Rights

Human Rights can be described as an academic discipline that deals with the distinctive legal, moral, and political concepts of the decades after World War II (Cruft et al., 2015). They can be traced back to the writings of Grotius, Pufendorf, and Locke. Cruft, Liao, and Renzo indicate that human rights are those that all "human beings possess simply by virtue of their humanity and which can be identified simply by the use of ordinary moral reasoning ("natural reason"), as opposed to the sort of conventional reasons created within particular social or institutional contexts" (2015, p. 4). Thus, all human beings possess human rights at all times and in all places simply by virtue of being humans. The corresponding duty bearers and society at large are expected to fulfill them through protection, promotion, and defense of the same.

The Universal Declaration of Human Rights (UDHR) was adopted by the Third United Nations General Assembly in December of 1948. It emerged since then as the model for the constitutions of many countries and domestic and international civil society organizations (Cruft et al., 2015). The declaration triggered many other frameworks that are related to the discourse of human rights and international law. These include the European (1950) and American (1969) Conventions, the

International Covenants (1966), the Convention on the Elimination of all Forms of Racial Discrimination (1969), the International Covenant on Civil and Political Rights (1976), the International Covenant on Economic, Social and Cultural Rights (1976), the Convention on the Elimination of all forms of Discrimination Against Women (1981), and the Convention on Rights of the Child (1990). The question that immediately arose among scholars of international relations is whether these declarations are binding on every country in the world or if there is a need to leave room for local cultures, and thus the ongoing debate on human rights as culturally relative or universal.

The UDHR was made in direct response to the horrific abuses of prisoners, civilians, and minority groups before and during World War II. It can also be argued that it was intended to usher in a new era of international peace and harmony going forward. Central to the UDHR is its Article 1 which speaks to the equality of all human beings. It shows that "All human beings are born free and equal in dignity and rights. They are endowed with reason and conscience and should act towards one another in a spirit of brotherhood" (United Nations, 1948, p. 1).

Nevertheless, the UDHR and the other covenants remained simply declarative statements. They were sets of assertions made by the United Nations delegates on what they believed to be human rights at that given time and in that context. Many values and behaviors have been asserted to be universal human rights, or at least worthy of being protected by universal human rights law (Kulikovsky, 2018). Many issues were listed as human rights, including women's rights, abortion, contraception, workers' rights, children's rights, indigenous peoples' rights, rights for homosexual people, and rights pertaining to religious freedom. Yet, the problem is that all these issues are highly controversial in all cultural traditions (Kulikovsky) thereby evoking the possibility of human rights being culturally relative. Attempting to locate the origin and nature of human rights, Cruft et al. have the following to say:

> Of course, the idea of rights held by all in virtue of their humanity can be found long before 1948, for example in the 1776 American Declaration of Independence and the 1789 French Declaration of the Rights of Man and the Citizen. In the guise of 'natural rights'—rights held by people as a matter of natural law—the idea can be found in the influential seventeenth and eighteenth-century work of Grotius, Pufendorf, Locke, and Kant. Indeed, recent scholarship claims that this idea of natural rights first originated much earlier, either in early medieval thought or before. However, it is worth noticing that whether contemporary human rights are the same as, or are at least a modernized, secularized form of natural rights, is highly controversial (2015, p. 1).

Nickel and Reidy (2009) argue that when people today talk of human rights, they usually have in mind the sorts of rights as found in the UDHR and subsequent treaties. Yet, for Nickel and Reidy, these are "not rights in the sense that they are directed mainly to states and prescribe what their institutions should and should not do" (2009, p. 40). The rights are not primarily interpersonal rights, although they include some of those that persons and other non-state actors can violate such as torture, slavery, discrimination, and others.

Arguing for the ontological basis of human rights, Kulikovsky (2018) holds that human rights law, despite claims to the contrary, is not universally accepted. He says that the subject of human rights has become intensely political as different people are operating opposing moral and cultural understandings of human beings and human nature. Kulikovsky further argues that those involved in the debate neither offer any justification for the rights they proclaim, nor any comprehensive exposition of their definition and scope. What is clear from Kulikovsky's argument is that these instruments indirectly claim to have a "higher authority to stand above all other traditions, religions, cultures, and political ideologies in the world, but this higher authority is never identified" (2018, p. 189). Therefore, who is that higher authority? The question has never been satisfactorily answered. Of course, those arguing from a theological perspective regard God as the authority in question.

In Marxism, human rights are mere by-products of social relations rather than universal, moral, and ethical standards. In other words, a discussion about human rights is simply an expression of a set of conventions associated with a particular period of human history. For Marxists, individual rights are simply a part of the moral, legal, and political framework that underpins the capitalist system (Kulikovsky, 2018). The concept of a higher being is critical in the discussion on human rights in Africa and elsewhere. Indeed, even Christianity in particular is hinged on the firm belief that there is a higher being whose creature called humanity occupies a special place in society. Kulikovsky argues that Christianity teaches that the human is a special creation of God and has been blessed with certain natural (or human) rights. Thus, humanity has a certain dignity that is God-given as it was created in the image of God (Genesis 1:27). This makes human beings special moral, physical and spiritual creatures before God.

The theological basis of human rights is also further discussed by Villa-Vice (2004). He argues that the theological contribution to human rights knows no distinction among the various categories of human rights. The theological contributions to the human rights debate recognize the interrelationships among political rights, social and economic rights, and cultural, ecological, and national rights (Villa-Vice, 2004). Thus, in such instances, the biblical focus on human rights is in tandem with the African Charter on Human and People's Rights (1981). In the case of Africa, any focus on individual rights needs to be realized within the context of community and communal rights (Villa-Vice, 2004). For example, the right to assemble and the freedom of speech can only be fully realized when certain basic social and economic rights have been enjoyed. These include the right to health care, education, and others. This argument resonates well with Ake's (1987) conceptualization of African human rights where he holds that Africa is not interested in all other types of human rights except social and economic rights. Yet, social and economic rights, in turn, can only gain full meaning when a particular person's or group of people's culture is fully recognized within the public debate, argues Villa-Vice (2004).

Africa as Part of the Globe: Universalism Argument

The concept of *universalism* holds that humanity possesses certain inalienable rights simply because s/he is human. His/her national background, religious or political affiliation, gender, or age does not matter. Those who subscribe to this concept claim that international human rights like rights to equal protection, freedom of religion and of association, physical security, and free speech must be the same everywhere in the world. The fact that human beings are different from other creatures places them in a special position in society. Human beings have the agency to choose what is good and bad for themselves, a characteristic that is absent in other creatures everywhere in the world.

Cruft et al. (2015) argue that human beings have the capacity to form a conception of a good life and to pursue the conception of the good life they have chosen for themselves. Citing Griffin, Cruft et al. also indicate that it is from that capacity of humanity that one should understand the notion of *human dignity*, which empowers human beings to choose a plan of life for themselves to pursue without interference. Indeed, humans have the capacity to protect human dignity. When the rights are violated, humanity's dignity is compromised and humanity in general will be under serious threat without any consideration for geographical location, age, race, or political affiliation. Yet, humanity is found everywhere in the world; thus, the universalism of human rights.

In principle, therefore, human rights are universal and inalienable, indivisible, interdependent, and interrelated (Mubangizi, 2006). They are universal because people are born with and possess the same rights, regardless of where they live, their gender or race, or their religious, cultural, or ethnic background. From the "universalist" perspective, human rights guarantee equal citizenship and equality before the law and in society. Yet, there is a category of rights (social rights) that guarantees subsistence, basic health care, and education. While, generally, human rights emphasize the "individual," there are also minority and group rights that protect individuals and groups against genocide, persecution, discrimination, equality, and deprivation. This confirms that human rights are universal because they need to be enjoyed in a similar fashion everywhere, by everyone, including Africans.

In questioning the universality of human rights, Hinz (2009) argues that the majority of the members of the United Nations as known today did not participate in the drafting, debate, and adoption of the UDHR in 1948. Indeed, some of the countries were yet to be politically independent from colonial rule while some of the members at the time actually expressed their disapproval of the declaration. These included South Africa, Saudi Arabia, and the Soviet Union which were driven by different reasons. Hinz further argues that the UDHR was not an immediate panacea to "human rights" violations in different corners of the world. For instance, the legitimacy of colonialism was not questioned; fascism in Greece, Portugal, and Spain was never prevented; war in Vietnam was not prevented; and internal conflicts in newly independent countries were not prevented by the declaration, among other realities of the time. As its title suggests, the UDHR remained a declaration without any internationally binding powers. Socially and politically, the UDHR expressed a *vision of cosmopolitanism*, which is a plea for a world with more dignity and respect for human beings (Hinz, 2009). This perspective supports the concept of the universalism of human rights of which Africa is a part.

Horn (2013) highlights that in the beginning, the human rights movement was mainly confined to the rights of life and freedom with their political implications (free elections, freedom of the press, free exercise of religion, and protection against unlawful acts by the government). He further indicates that citizens' political rights were confined to males only with female voting rights and legal equality of females with males being gained in the twentieth century in the Western world. Yet, social rights for the working class and the socially weak were established and were only achieved later.

Africa as Home to Some Human Rights: Cultural Relativism Argument

Interestingly, there have been equally strong arguments against the notion of the universality of human rights. Africa can also be partly understood within such conceptualization of human rights. The cultural and social diversities and particularities in different countries show that human rights are culturally sensitive; hence, the concept of *cultural relativism*, which is the assertion that human values, far from being universal, vary a great deal according to different cultural perspectives. This theory recognizes the existence of unique cultural practices in individual countries that cannot be confined to the dictates of international law.

One of the major limitations of the theory of cultural relativism is the perception of "culture" as a phenomenon that is stable (unchanging). It ignores the flexibility of culture for social changes and ideological innovations. It can also be argued that cultural relativism can be dangerous as it can allow human rights violations in the name of cultural practices. There are cases when African political leaders have defended their "violation" of some human rights on the basis that they are sovereign countries that cannot be lectured on how to run their countries.

Thus, human rights in Africa can be understood from cultural, theological, and universal perspectives. Culturally, Africa has had its own ways of respecting humanity. This has basically been explained through the *Ubuntu* philosophy. The continent has also been largely influenced by Christianity, among other religions such as Islam, in how it views human beings. Thus, human rights can now also be explained theologically. The third way of explaining human rights in Africa has been through its connectedness to the global village as already noted earlier. Therefore, Africa now views human rights from an international perspective but still maintains its traditional ways of respecting humanity. This further explains Africa's strive for constitutionalism whereby human rights protection, promotion, and defense become a constitutional obligation that is also complimented by local cultures.

From time immemorial, the cultural value that epitomizes togetherness and "caring for one another" in a community has been a way of life in various African communities, including that of Zimbabwe and South Africa (Kamga, 2018). This means that one is his/her brother's or sister's keeper according to the *Ubuntu* philosophy. The philosophy developed into a way of African life, even before the period of Enlightenment in Europe. It is believed to be the basis for respecting human rights discourse in the continent, especially social and economic rights. Thus, a human rights discourse in the form of caring for one another was a lived reality and experience in Africa in terms of this philosophy (Kamga, 2018) before the UDHR. The concept of human rights in the period of the Enlightenment (in Europe and America) was characterized by individualism and the application of rights to abstract subjects (Kamga, 2018) while *Ubuntu* focuses on community or group connectedness, which confirms Africa as a home to social, economic, and cultural rights.

In the philosophy of *Ubuntu* in the Sotho and Zulu languages, the following are notable: *motho ke motho ka batho ba bang* (Sesotho intonation) and *umuntu ngumuntu ngabantu* (Isi-Zulu intonation), which literally mean that a person is a person only through others. It is an expression of a harmonious African community's way of life in which one's happiness is linked to the group's happiness, which basically is the central element of human rights even from the Western perspective. This is a philosophy that is clearly embedded in the African human rights systems such as the African Charter on Human and Peoples' Rights, which provides for peoples' rights as well as ensuring that duty bearers save the interest of the community and its individual members.

Metz (2014) holds that community is probably the most salient feature of ethical-political-legal thought among the indigenous people of Africa South of the Saharan. Metz cites Tutu who maintains that community is itself to be valued for its own sake. Yet, others such as Magesa and Gyekye (cited in Metz, 2014) hold that living communally has the effect of enhancing some other more basic values such as people's vitality or well-being. Both positions still reinforce the idea that Africans do value a communitarian way of life which, in itself, promotes and protects human rights in many ways.

Bience (2009) indirectly raises concerns regarding the concept of cultural relativism when he notes that African cultures seem to disrespect women and gender equality. He cites issues of genital "mutilation" (cutting or circumcision), early marriages, and others as cultural practices that violate human rights in Africa. Certainly, these are the issues that proponents of the universalism concept point to in their arguments as they work to dismantle Cultural Relativism Theory. The positive thing is that African national governments have enacted specific laws against such practices in line with the universal theorists' aspirations. Nevertheless, the practices continue as the tradition is deeply rooted in African society. Bience also argues that culture cannot be legislated away and will continue to have a place in African human rights discourse. He further points out that Africa's struggle for independence was a war for its identity and cultural heritage since the goal was to dismantle colonialism that undermined African cultures and the indigenous people's rights. This explains the adoption of the African Cultural Charter of 1976 by the Organization of African Unity (OAU), the African Union (AU) adopting the Cultural Renaissance of Africa (2006), and many other instruments.

Africa as a Poor Continent

Ake (1987) holds that the Western conceptualization of human rights is not helpful to Africa. He describes Africa as a society that is characterized by hunger, poverty, fascism, and collective opinion regarding life. Ake thus contends that individualistic human rights such as freedom of speech, association, and others are not attractive to African societies. The same view has been largely held by African civil society and individual activists. They often argue that there is a need for a focus on social and economic rights which have been relegated to the periphery by governments and other continental bodies (Khoza, 2004). Khoza points out that in 2004, the African Commission on Human and People's Rights had already faced criticism from civil society based on the widespread prevalence of poverty in the continent with regards to non-prioritization of social and economic rights. It should however be acknowledged that individual governments have visibly been putting efforts into the realization of social, economic, and cultural rights as will be noted in the case of South Africa and Zimbabwe. Yet, many of the countries have captured social and economic rights in their national constitutions but still implementation is lagging behind due to a lack of resources. Thus, the issue remains nothing more than symbolic gestures of progressive protection, promotion, and defense of this category of human rights (Khoza, 2004).

African civil society continues to advocate for the inclusion of social and economic rights in the countries' national constitutions as well as the incorporation of key instruments such as the African Charter and the International Covenant on Economic, Social, and Cultural Rights into national laws to give them effect. The chief argument has been that Africans will actually be deprived of dignity if one emphasizes protection, promotion, and defense of individual human rights at the expense of collective rights that include the right to education, food, health, and others.

Ake (1987) pushed his arguments for the realization of social and economic rights in Africa in the context of the Cold War; hence, his emphasis was on socialism rather than what he calls "procedural liberalism." Thus, for Ake, the best conception of human rights in Africa should be one that effectively addresses the immediate needs of the continent, especially that of poverty. In this case, targeting the disadvantaged groups of society should be enhanced. One is hesitant to allow the argument for prioritizing marginalized groups to go unchallenged. Such a proposal in Africa assumes that the poor and marginalized would choose social and economic rights over civil and political rights. The proposal further presents Africa as a nonpolitical continent that is not sensitive to civil and political violations of people's individual rights.

The principle of equality in the African context is seen within the framework of community or society where each member is regarded as a critical player deserving the attention of others under the *Ubuntu* philosophy. The UDHR clearly places the same principle at the top of its list. The significance of equality for the realization of social and economic rights is also visible in the African Charter. Its conceptual relationship with that of nondiscrimination is also clear. When a community or country advances the principle of equality and nondiscrimination among the people, social and economic rights are automatically enjoyed (Khoza, 2004) and poverty is addressed.

The UDHR focuses on various articles relating to human beings. While many of the articles seem to reinforce individual human rights, collective rights are emphasized in the African context. Individual rights which are mainly civic and political in nature can only be enjoyed if one has food, health care, and education. Articles 25 (1) and 26 (1) focus on health care and education rights, respectively, which can be enjoyed by a community or group, and this resonates well with the African context.

Access to primary health care, education, treatment, and land rights, with all sectors including women playing specific roles in the community, should be the focus for Africa. This explains why the Zimbabwean civil society in particular has continued to advocate for more spending by the government on social sectors such as health care and education over defense. This, however, presents challenges for Khoza (2004) who argues that such advocacy is dangerous as it presents a picture of some human rights standing out as more important than others. For him, this is against the universal principle of indivisibility and interdependence of human rights. This resonates well with Mubangizi (2006) who observes that there is growing international recognition of the universality, interdependence, and indivisibility of human rights. He further notes that the 1993 United Nations World Conference on Human Rights held in Vienna, Austria, clearly proclaimed the same principles. Thus, pushing for the prioritization of one category of human rights at the expense of another will violate the principles.

Mubangizi (2006) notes that in the African context, the African Charter places special focus on the principle of universality of human rights. In its preamble, the Charter links social and economic rights to civil and political rights. It shows that the "satisfaction of economic, social and cultural rights is a guarantee for the enjoyment of civil and political rights." Yet, despite that emphasis, human rights violations in Africa tend to be more focused on civil and political rights while social and economic rights are the perennial concern of the majority of the people.

Africa as Home to Model Constitutions: The South African Case

The debate on how Africa views social and economic rights has ranged in different countries. This has forced some countries to incorporate social and economic rights into their national constitutions. Thus, the constitutional inclusion of social and economic rights in South Africa should be understood in that context. The justiciability of this category of rights is the main issue for discussion. South Africa put to an end the debate by including a comprehensive bill of rights in Chapter 2 of its constitution, although the same move was heavily challenged by some groups of citizens who argued that such rights are not inherently justiciable. Such lines of argument assume that social and economic rights are not suitable for judicial enforcement

(Mubangizi, 2006). Writing in the context of the same debate in Zimbabwe, Kondo has this to say:

> These arguments are couched within the liberal consensus on universal human rights, namely, that there is a hierarchy of rights, with civil and political rights at the top of this hierarchy…This argument stems from the fact that civil and political rights impose a 'negative obligation' (demanding forbearance), while socio-economic rights impose a 'positive obligation' (demanding a redistribution of resources). Therefore, it would seem that civil and political rights would take the apex position in the hierarchy as they are 'an easy way out' because they are easier to guarantee. This is unlike socio-economic rights that demand the mobilization and rearrangement of national resources to assist those who cannot provide the material means for a decent life for themselves. In this case, socio-economic rights remain aspirational rather than judicially enforceable rights (2017, p. 167).

Judicial enforcement of social and economic rights is paramount to the realization and protection of social and economic rights (Ndhlovu, 2023). Ndhlovu (2023) observes that a proactive judiciary that is independent and impartial is a key institutional actor in the domestic framework for protecting social and economic rights.

Later on, such arguments characterized similar debates in Zimbabwe during the Inclusive government when the same had been tasked through the Global Political Agreement (GPA) to come up with a new constitution (GPA, 2008). The GPA was an agreement brokered by the Southern African Development Community (SADC) between the Zimbabwe African National Union-Patriotic Front (ZANU PF) and the two factions of the Movement for Democratic Change (MDC) following the highly disputed elections of 2008. Zimbabwe ended up being governed by the Government of National Unity (GNU).

Critics of the inclusion of social and economic rights in the constitution in Zimbabwe, South Africa, and elsewhere argued that the protection and promotion of such rights should be the duty of the legislature and the executive and not the judiciary. Once included in the constitution, the judiciary will be expected to enforce their protection and promotion. Yet, "transferring" this duty to the judiciary will miss the point according to Mubangizi (2006) who argues that the judiciary lacks the democratic legitimacy that is necessary to make key decisions about the resource allocations for the protection and promotion of social and economic rights. Indeed, to fulfill the social and economic aspirations of citizens, the government should have enough resources that can be channeled through the respective governance infrastructure.

Nevertheless, against all the counter challenges, South Africa can come up with a constitution that captures the social and economic rights comprehensively. The South African constitution has generally been regarded as a model in Africa. This constitution has also confirmed Africa as a place where progressive and model tools for the protection and promotion of human rights are available. Chapter 2 of the Constitution comprehensively captures all categories of human rights including social and economic rights. Chapter 2 Sections 7 (1) and (2) confirm the following: "This Bill of Rights is a cornerstone of democracy in South Africa. It enshrines the rights of all people in our country and affirms the democratic values of human dignity, equality, and freedom. (2) The state must respect, protect, promote, and fulfill the rights in the Bill of Rights" (The Constitution of the Republic of South Africa, 1996, p. 1).

Chapter 1 of the constitution's key founding provisions section indicates that South Africa is a "Sovereign State founded on human dignity, the achievement of equality, and achievement of human rights and freedoms," among others (The Constitution of the Republic of South Africa, 1996, p. 1). One can see that, indeed, the issues of human dignity and equality which are key elements of human rights enjoyment are well captured in the Constitution. It further shows that South Africa is a country that values respect and protection of human rights.

On citizenship, the constitution also reiterates the importance of equality for all. Equality is directly linked to entitlement to the rights, privileges, and benefits of citizens. Certainly, these are central issues in the human rights discourse. Thus, the founding principles of South Africa conform to its seriousness with regard to human rights enjoyment by the citizens. Section 9 in Chapter 2 of the constitution further notes the principle of equality being emphasized where it includes "enjoyment of all rights and freedoms for everyone including people with disabilities" (The Constitution of the Republic of South Africa, 1996, p. 1) and other marginalized groups. In Section 10, human dignity is also elaborated on where the Constitution indicates that "everyone has inherent dignity and right to have their dignity respected and protected" (The Constitution of the Republic of South Africa, 1996, p. 1). The weight of human dignity is also amplified in Section 11where the right to life is captured. Yet, Ilyayambwa (2012) raises reservations regarding the principle of equality. Discussing the South African constitution in the context of the debate on homosexual rights, Ilyayambwa has this to say:

> Equality is a deeply controversial social idea. At its most basic abstract, the formal idea of equality is that people who are similarly situated in relevant ways should be treated similarly. Its logical correlative is the idea that people who are not similarly situated should not be treated alike. In all the above-mentioned provisions, the Constitution gives the reader a prima facie view that persons cannot be discriminated against, regardless of their circumstances (2012, p. 51).

While it is outside the scope of this chapter, it is important to mention that the issue of homosexual rights presents Africa as a heterogeneous continent. The South African constitution gives room for homosexuality while Zimbabwe, Uganda, and others do not recognize the rights of such minority groups. Muparamoto (2020, p. 1) notes that the former president of Zimbabwe Robert Mugabe attracted global media headlines after describing individuals engaging in homosexual behavior as "worse than dogs and pigs," which seemingly popularized official intolerance for homosexual identities in postcolonial Zimbabwe. A similar stance was also noted in Uganda where the issue was formally legislated against. This shows that while equality is central in many African countries, its application with regard to certain rights is not uniform; hence, Africa is heterogeneous in nature when it comes to human rights enjoyment.

South Africa is often commended for the comprehensive inclusion of social and economic rights, despite the counter challenges noted earlier in this chapter. Section 27 captures social and economic rights that should be respected, promoted, and protected within the key social sectors of society. These include health care, food, water, and social security. Section 29 on education further amplifies South Africa's aspirations with regard enjoyment of social and economic rights by citizens (The Constitution of the Republic of South Africa, 1996, p. 1).

Therefore, Africa, represented by countries such as South Africa, should be viewed as a model continent that respects human rights. South Africa in particular stands above all others in terms of the enjoyment of all types of human rights. It is obliged by its constitution to promote, protect, and defend social and economic rights as aforementioned, and also the civil and political rights as captured in the rest of the sections in Chapter 2. It was not within the scope of this chapter to elaborate on civil and political rights.

Africa as an Unwilling Human Rights Violator: The Case of Zimbabwe

Zimbabwe gained its political independence in 1980 from British rule. Since then until 2013, it had been operating under the 1979 Constitution, commonly known as the Lancaster House Constitutions (it was a negotiated constitution at Lancaster in Britain). The 1979 Constitution did not recognize the social and economic rights of the citizens in clear terms. This made it difficult for civil society and other players to raise issues related to the violation of social and economic rights since this was not constitutionally recognized. While activists continued to raise concerns regarding the protection, promotion, and defense of social and economic rights, the matter could not be heard in courts of law. Yet, Zimbabwe was a full and active member of the United Nations that subscribed to the UDHR.

In 2013, Zimbabwe finally adopted a new constitution (Constitution of Zimbabwe), providing for social and economic rights (Kondo, 2017). The country adopted a constitution that fully captures all the human rights in Chapter 4. For the first time in the history of Zimbabwe, citizens' social and economic rights were constitutionally included. Sections 75 to 77 of the constitution elaborate on the social and economic rights of the people of Zimbabwe. These include the right to education, and health care, as well as the right to food and water.

Like in the South African case, there were serious debates about the inclusion of social and economic rights in Zimbabwe's constitution. Arguments for the inclusion of social and economic rights were so compelling that they could not be ignored. Kondo (2017) notes that one of the arguments for the protection of social and economic rights in the constitution concerns Zimbabwe being a state in transition after the repression that reached its climax in 2008. For Kondo, this argument was based on a moral foundation that it was going to be dangerous to marginalize social and economic imperatives. Thus, this moral prerogative that is found in the theory of social justice compelled Zimbabweans to consider social and economic rights. This would further be a major step in the direction of the adoption of a rights-based approach to social policy. Kondo summarizes this argument as follows:

> Herein, the inclusion of socio-economic rights would ensure that the underpinning rights in regional and international human rights instruments, such as the Universal Declaration of Human Rights (Universal Declaration), the International Covenant on Economic, Social and Cultural Rights (ICESCR), and the African Charter on Human and Peoples' Rights (African Charter), were respected and promoted. The inclusion of socio-economic rights in the Constitution of Zimbabwe would merely ensure the domestic accountability of Zimbabwe's obligations to already-accepted and ratified human rights treaties, rather than the extension of existing commitments, in addition to those already in existence. In terms of these human rights instruments, socio-economic rights are the indispensable and inalienable rights of all human beings (2017, p. 166).

Related to the preceding argument, Zimbabwe needed constitutional safeguards against the potential repeat of the 2008 social and economic challenges when people's rights were violated. The hyperinflation in which many citizens were subjected to deplorable living conditions, food insecurity, chronic malnutrition., effects of malaria, and the deaths of thousands because of cholera, all pushed for serious consideration of social and economic rights (Kondo, 2017). Linking the argument to the debate on the universalism-cultural relativism of human rights, Kondo states the following:

> One of the most significant arguments in favor of constitutional socio-economic rights was that they were indivisible, interdependent, and interrelated to civil and political rights. Those in favor of this argument were of the view that socio-economic rights formed part of a larger network of rights that were symbiotic and mutually reinforcing. The substance of their argument was based on the fact that, without socio-economic rights, civil and political rights would have been of a purely nominal character. Conversely, without civil and political rights, socio-economic rights would not be sustainable. Therefore, the standalone civil and political rights in the Lancaster House Constitution were purely nominal and had to be pursued in synergy with socio-economic rights (2017, p. 167).

The postulate that Africa is too poor to fully protect social and economic rights is therefore examined in the ensuing section.

Is Africa too Poor to Fully Protect Social and Economic Rights?

The inclusion of social and economic rights under the national African constitutions is meant to fulfill the legislative obligation imposed by the International Covenant of Economic Social and Cultural Rights and the African Charter on countries as a state party (Ndhlovu, 2023). South Africa and Zimbabwe, among other African countries, sought to set up a framework to ensure social and economic rights in their constitutions are promoted and protected, and where necessary proper redress is provided. This framework includes a proactive judiciary that is independent (Ndhlovu, 2023). While it is outside the scope of this chapter to examine the independence of the judiciary in executing cases related to social and economic rights, one can say that Zimbabwe has been found wanting in this regard.

The South African Constitution Chapter 2 (Section 27) is comprehensive about social and economic rights. For example,

> Health care, food, water, and social security 27: (1) Everyone has the right to have access to—(a) health care services, including reproductive health care; (b) sufficient food and water; and (c) social security, including, if they are unable to support themselves and their dependents, appropriate social assistance. (2) The state must take reasonable legislative and other measures, within its available resources, to achieve the progressive realization of each of these rights. (3) No one may be refused emergency medical treatment (The Constitution of the Republic of South Africa, 1996, p. 1).

Nevertheless, enjoyment of these rights is dependent on the availability of resources as indicated in Section 27(2).

The same limitation is noted in the Zimbabwean constitution whereby the comprehensive rights to education and health care given to the citizens are "not guaranteed" because of the constitutional inclusion of the "clawback" clause. For instance, Section 75 (4) on education and 76 (4) on health care gives room to the executive to argue that it could not fulfill these rights due to lack of resources. The two sections indicate that "The State must take reasonable legislative and other measures, within the limits of the resources available to it, to achieve the progressive realization of the rights set in this section" (Constitution of Zimbabwe, 1979, p. 1). This is a serious limitation of the constitution. The economic situation in most African countries will not allow the executive to avail enough resources for the protection and promotion of social and economic rights. The continent has remained economically constrained with huge public debts, illicit financial flows, and other challenges such as their economies not being able to sustain social and economic development to the satisfaction of the citizens. As of October 2022, Zimbabwe had a huge public debt amounting to USD17.5 Billion (ZIMCODD and AFRODAD, 2022), thereby making it difficult for the country to focus on the enjoyment of social and economic rights as debt servicing does not allow that. This is the reality in most of the African countries. For example, an analysis of the 2018 national budget of Zambia indicates that the combined external and domestic debt repayment amounted to 27% of the national budget (Ngambi, 2022). The debt servicing total was equivalent to the combined amount allocated for health, education, and social protection.

Specificity in the Human Rights Conceptualizations of Africa

In this section, for the sake of brevity, five conceptualizations of Africa in the Human Rights discipline are presented because there are many of them. These conceptualizations, which were chosen randomly, are discussed one at a time in the ensuing subsections for clarity.

Basic African Human Rights

The notion of Africa as a place of "basic human rights" in the field of Human Rights is predicated on the identification of the continent's cultural, economic, and social rights and "the right to development to have equal legitimacy and legal status with civil and political rights, which are traditionally prioritized in the discourse and practice of human rights. Accordingly, it is noted that there is a demand for respect for human rights, constitutional order and democratization," albeit these aspects are in short supply (Ighobor, 2023, p. 1).

Apropos the preceding postulation, it is noted that about 46 national human rights institutions have been established in African countries, and African youths are demanding attentiveness to their rights. It is the reason protest movements have proliferated across the continent. For instance, the #EndSARS protest movement in Nigeria was a result of the demand for human rights. These activities, especially the increase in the representation of women in decision-making processes in some countries, are considered to be positive developments (Ighobor, 2023).

Components of the African Human Rights System

The conceptualization that Africa is has "components of a human rights system" is an idea that reflects the web of treaties and protocols that make up the African Charter, its protocols and associate institutions, including the AU and its constituent parts comprising the quasi-judicial African Commission and the judicial assembly African Court. This conceptualization renders obsolete the proposition that Africa, including its human rights system, is not an inventor, producer, and disseminator of ideas in the human rights domain (Okafor & Dzah, 2021).

The major postulate of some purveyors of the conceptualization is that while "the African human rights system clearly is not a state, the critical but globally under-appreciated roles it has played regarding the globalized socialization of certain human rights ideas fits within, and helps in extending, social constructivist human rights theory and praxis" (Okafor & Dzah, 2021, p. 1). These scholars therefore posit that special attention should be paid to "some key limitations that are observable as to how far the system has been able to travel in the direction of norm leadership in human rights law" (Okafor & Dzah, 2021, p. 1).

Human and Peoples' Rights Charter

Africa is conceptualized as the home of the "Charter on Human and Peoples' Rights" as a throwback to when all of the member states of the OAU reached "Decision 115 (XVI) of the Assembly of Heads of State and Government at its Sixteenth Ordinary Session" convened in Monrovia, Liberia from July 17 to 20, 1979 on the preparation of "a preliminary draft on an African Charter on Human and Peoples' Rights, providing inter alia for the establishment of bodies to promote and protect human and peoples' rights." The decision stipulated that "freedom, equality, justice and dignity are essential objectives for the achievement of the legitimate aspirations of the African peoples" (African Commission on Human and Peoples' Rights, 1981, p. 1).

Those who advance Africa as home of the Charter on Human and Peoples' Rights conceptualization also cite the confirmation of the promise the OAU member states made in Article 2 of the Charter to eliminate "all forms of colonialism from Africa, to coordinate and intensify their cooperation and efforts to achieve a better life for the peoples of Africa, and to promote international cooperation having due regard to the Charter of the United Nations and the Universal Declaration of Human Rights" as pivotal for the promotion of human rights in the continent. These advocates therefore tout the development as a major requirement for Africa's peace and security (African Commission on Human and Peoples' Rights, 1981, p. 1).

Second and Third Generation Rights

The conceptualization of Africa as a venue of "second and third generation rights" hinges on the notion that human rights and human well-being are regarded as "universal" ideas which the continent has embraced. These rights, which are outlined in the 1946 UDHR, are said to have been accepted by Africans as the embodiment of fundamental international standards for human well-being. The human rights guaranteed under the UDHR include (a) "absence of cruel punishment and freedom from torture," (b) "freedom of movement," (c) "right to marriage," (d) "property ownership," (e) "freedom of religion," and (f) "right to education" (Stanford University Freeman Spogli Institute, 2024, p. 1).

The preceding rights have been named by scholars in the field of Human Rights vis-à-vis "generations," with each ensuing generation extending human rights into more areas of human pursuit and involvement. The prevailing generations of human rights are described as follows:

> First generation rights include civil and political rights such as free speech and conscience and freedom from torture and arbitrary detention…Second generation rights are social, economic and cultural and include the rights to reasonable levels of education, healthcare, and housing and minority language rights…Most recently third generation rights have shifted focus from the individual person (first generation rights) and the communities in which they live (social, economic and cultural rights) to the natural world, such as the right to a clean and healthy environment, and the right to species biodiversity (Stanford University Freeman Spogli Institute, 2024, p. 1).

It behooves me to add here that there is now conversation about "fourth generation" human rights which are "epistemic rights in digital lifeworlds." Yet, as of this writing, Africa is not mentioned in the discussion.

Violations of Human Rights

An inimical conceptualization in the field of Human Rights, Africa as a place of rampant "violations of human rights" is based on the numerous compelling accounts of "unlawful or arbitrary killings; torture or cruel, inhuman, or degrading treatment or punishment by African governments; harsh and life-threatening prison conditions; arbitrary arrest or detention; serious government corruption; trafficking in persons; and crimes involving violence or threats of violence targeting lesbian, gay, bisexual, transgender, queer, or intersex persons" (United States Department of State, 2022, p. 1). While it is acknowledged that many governments do investigate, prosecute, and punish some violators of human rights, there are still many accounts of indemnity (United States Department of State, 2022).

In every African country, police officers are assigned the "primary responsibility for internal security," and police commissioners have "operational authority over the police." The heads of state appoint the police commissioner, but ministers of police supervise the commissioners. National defense forces also have domestic security responsibilities. There are numerous accounts of members of the security forces committing many human rights abuses (United States Department of State, 2022).

Conclusion and Recommendations

This chapter has discussed the concept of Africa from a Human Rights disciplinary perspective. The concept of Human Rights was also discussed based on the existing literature and my practical involvement with human rights work in Zimbabwe. The debate on the universality or cultural relativism of human rights was engaged with particular reference to Zimbabwe and South Africa. While the chapter noted the general Human Rights discourse, specific examples were given with regard to social and economic rights. The chapter argued that Africa is actually home to some of the Human Rights concepts, especially those that have a bearing on social and economic rights enjoyment which directly hinge upon togetherness, community, *Ubuntu,* and group identities as opposed to individual rights. Based on the discussion in this chapter, Africa can be viewed as a continent that is sensitive to human rights, albeit from its own perspective. It is a continent that strives to fully respect, promote, and protect social and economic rights, but its economic status lets it down. Constitutionally, Africa has done well to capture comprehensive human rights; yet, its economy does not allow for full enjoyment of the same.

The chapter therefore recommends, to begin with, further research with regard to social and economic rights in Africa. The focus should be on how individual countries have incorporated this category of human rights and the extent of operationalization of the respective constitutions. Next, Africa should also continue to interrogate the principle of equality in order to develop a common understanding with regard to the issue of homosexuality. Furthermore, a common position will amplify Africa's voice at the international level when human rights issues are discussed. In addition, with regard to the debate on universalism-cultural relativism of human rights, scholarly work should now resolve that Africa is a member of the global village, but it should be allowed and supported to ensure that social and economic rights that resonate well with local culture are enjoyed.

References

Africa (Banjul). (1981). *Charter on Human and People's Rights, 1981*. Retrieved November 27, 2023, from https://www.african-court.org/wpafc/wp-content/uploads/2020/04/AFRICAN-BANJUL-CHARTER-ON-HUMAN-RIGHTS-AND-PEOPLES-RIGHTS.pdf

African Commission on Human and Peoples' Rights. (1981, June 27). *African charter on human and peoples' rights*. African Union. Retrieved July 3, 2024, from https://achpr.au.int/en/charter/african-charter-human-and-peoples-rights

Ake, C. (1987). The African context of human rights. *Africa Today, 34*, 5–12.

Bience, G. (2009). The African Union: Concepts and implementation mechanisms relating to human rights. In A. Bosl & J. Diescho (Eds.), *Human rights in Africa: Legal perspectives on their protection and promotion*. Namibia Macmillan Education.

Constitution of Zimbabwe. (1979). Retrieved November 27, 2023, from https://constitutionnet.org/sites/default/files/zimbabwe_constitution_1980.pdf

Constitution of Zimbabwe Amendment (No. 20) Act. (2013). Retrieved November 27, 2023, from https://veritaszim.net/sites/veritas_d/files/Constitution%20of%Zimbabwe%20Amendment%20%No.%2020%29.pdf

Cruft, R., Liao, S. M., & Renzo, M. (2015). The philosophical foundations of human rights: An overview. In R. Cruft, S. M. Liao, & M. Renzo (Eds.), *Philosophical foundations of human rights*. Oxford University Press.

Hinz, M. O. (2009). Human rights between universalism and cultural relativism? The need for anthropological jurisprudence in the globalizing world. In A. Bosl & J. Diescho (Eds.), *Human rights in Africa, legal perspectives on their protection and promotion*. Namibia Macmillan Education.

Horn, N. (2013). *Human rights: Philosophical foundations and legal dimensions, keynote speech, XXV1 world congress of philosophy of law and social philosophy, human rights, rule of law and the contemporary challenges in complex societies, Brazi*l.

Ighobor, K. (2023, March 23). Prioritising human rights in Africa. *Africa Renewal*. Retrieved July 3, 2024, from https://www.un.org/africarenewal/magazine/april-2023/prioritising-human-rights-africa

Ilyayambwa, M. (2012). Homosexual rights and the law: A South African constitutional metamorphosis. *International Journal of Humanities and Social Science, 2*(4), 50–58.

Kamga, S. D. (2018). Cultural values as a source of law: Emerging trends of Ubuntu jurisprudence in South Africa. *African Human Rights Law Journal, 18*, 625–649.

Khoza, S. (2004). Promoting economic, social, and cultural rights in Africa: The African Commission holds a seminar in Pretoria. *African Human Rights Law Journal*, 334–343.

Kondo, T. (2017). Socio-economic rights in Zimbabwe: Trends and emerging jurisprudence. *African Human Rights Law Journal*, 163–193.

Kulikovsky, A. (2018). Christianity and human rights. *The Western Australian Jurist, 9*, 185–207.

Metz, T. (2014). African values, human rights and group rights: A philosophical foundation for Banjul Charter. In O. Onaz (Ed.), *African theory and contemporary problems, critical essays* (Ius Gentium: Comparative perspectives on law and justice) (Vol. 29). Springer.

Ministry of Constitutional and Parliamentary Affairs, Harare. (2008). *Global political agreement*. Retrieved November 27, 2023, from https://constitutionnet.org/sites/deault/files/global_political_agreement_2008.pdf

Mubangizi, J. C. (2006). The constitutional protection of socio-economic rights in selected African countries: A comparative evaluation. *African Journal of Legal Studies, 2006*, 1–19.
Muparamoto, N. (2020). LGBT individuals and the struggle against Robert Mugabe's extirpation in Zimbabwe. *Africa Review, 13*(2), 1–16.
Ndhlovu, N. (2023). The role of courts in the enforcement of socio-economic rights under the 2013 Constitution of Zimbabwe. *Africa's Public Service Delivery and Performance Review, 3*, 29–56.
Ngambi, P. S. (2022). Sovereign debt restructuring in Zambia: A United Nations principles-based approach. In D. D. Bradlow & M. L. Masamba (Eds.), *COVID-19 and sovereign debt: The case of SADC*. Pretoria University Law Press.
Nickel, J. W., & Reidy, D. A. (2009). *Philosophical foundations of human rights*. Oxford University Press.
Okafor, O. C., & Dzah, G. E. K. (2021). The African human rights system as 'norm leader': Three case studies *African Human Rights Law Journal, 21*(2). Retrieved July 3, 2024, from https://scielo.org.za/scielo.php?script=sci_arttext&pid=S1996-20962021000200003
Stanford University Freeman Spogli Institute. (2024). *Second and third generation rights in Africa*. Center on Democracy, Development and the Rule of Law. Retrieved July 3, 2024, from https://cddrl.fsi.stanford.edu/research/second_and_third_generation_rights_in_africa
The Constitution of the Republic of South Africa. (1996). Retrieved November 27, 2023, from https://www.justice.gov.za.29/legislation/constitution/saconstitution-web-eng.pdf
United Nations. (1948). *The Universal Declaration of Human Rights*. Retrieved November 27, 2023, from https://www.un.org/en/about-us/universal-declaration-of-human-rights
United States Department of State. (2022). 2022 *country reports on human rights practices: South Africa*. Retrieved July 3, 2024, from https://www.state.gov/reports/2022-country-reports-on-human-rights-practices/south-africa/
Villa-Vice, C. (2004). Christianity and human rights. *Journal of Lutheran Ethics*. Retrieved September 20, 2023, from https://www.elca.org/JLE/Articles/776?g=fb28378cb89778ad84321e7cab90422a
ZIMCODD and AFRODAD. (2022, October 2022). *Annual debt management report for Zimbabwe*. Retrieved November 27, 2023, from https://afrodad.org/wp-content/uploads/2023/03/2022-Annual-Debt-Management-Report-for-Zimbabwe.pdf

Tinashe Gumbo holds a PhD in Development Studies, Master's in International Relations, Master's in Religious Studies, and an Honor's Degree in Economic History. He is the Programme Executive, Economic and Ecological Justice for All Africa Conference of Churches based in Nairobi, Kenya. He lectured at the Great Zimbabwe University for six years. He is the author of eight book chapters and four scholarly articles, and is currently writing two books on elections and politics. He has also authored more than 80 articles for his blog and more than 20 conference papers on many topics, including mining, elections, and climate change.

International Law

JP Afamefuna Ifedi

This chapter focuses on the conceptualization of Africa relative to the academic discipline of International Law, which is understood as the body of rules, norms, and principles of action which are binding on civilized nation-states in their relationship with one another (Brierly, (1963). The chapter traces the three major trends regarding Africa's role in the development of International Law: (1) European perspective, which is dismissive of Africa's role, (2) contributionists who emphasize Africa's contributions to international law, and (3) critical theorists who posit that Africa is subordinated in its international relations as a legacy that is traceable to International Law.

In this regard, it is pertinent to query whether International Law is, in the main, a set of norms, principles, understandings, protocols, agreements, etc., meant to govern the relationships among states and how it can be that there was no International Law among precolonial African states. Europeans reached an Africa that had established Kingdoms and many independent self-governing nations that had relations with one another, not so different from what was obtained in various parts of Europe. Examples such as the Kingdoms of Benin, Dahomey, Ghana, Kanem-Bornu, Nri, Songhai, etc., had ongoing social and commercial relations with other Kingdoms (states). The continent was governed, and interstate relations were thriving; hence, international relations were established, and International Law was, in essence, being practiced as customary law and practices. It is important to note at the outset that this chapter is not about legal relations between and among African indigenous states, kingdoms, and empires prior to the arrival of Europeans but about the role Africa has played in the development of international law. Essentially, the relevance and contributions of Africa to International Law are simply and squarely a matter of deliberate disposition of the nonrecognition of Africa's

J. A. Ifedi (✉)
Department of Political Science, Howard University, Washington, DC, USA
e-mail: Jifedi@howard.edu

A. K. Bangura, J. A. Ifedi (eds.), *Conceptualizations of Africa*, African Studies and Research Forum Series, https://doi.org/10.1007/978-3-031-74535-5_19

role by Europe's eminent jurists and writers of International Law. This position will be elucidated further later in this chapter.

In the interim, Europeans disregarded any semblance of international relations and International Law in Africa, giving it no credence. Contributionists take an opposite view and emphasize Africa's role as a generator and innovator of international legal norms going well into antiquity. The critical approach, by contrast, emphasizes the ways in which International Law has legitimized Africa's marginality in the world. This difference in emphasis reflects the fact that Africa's historical engagement with International Law cannot be rendered in singular or consensual terms.

The analysis in this chapter is grounded by using the qualitative approach which would be descriptive and narrative. This involves interpretations of literary texts that examine the conceptualizations and how they establish themselves in the discipline of International Law. Having given a brief and general introduction to what I intend to do in this chapter and before an in-depth analysis of the three perspectives of International Law that are identified, I will in the relevant paragraphs examine the general method to be applied to the study.

Robert K. Yin proposes five features of qualitative research: (1) "studying the meaning of people's lives under real-world conditions," (2) "representing the views and perspectives of the people in a study," (3) "covering the contextual conditions within which people live," (4) "contributing insights into existing or emerging concepts that may help to explain human social behavior," and (5) "striving to use multiple sources of evidence rather than relying on a single source alone" (2010, p. 8). The qualitative approach's analytical attributes are the best fit for this study apropos identifying, teasing out, describing and evaluating Africa's role in International Law.

Furthermore, the qualitative approach identifies and attempts to determine associations among phenomena. It also enables a researcher to employ the elucidation of a problem in terms of its components. It, in addition, enables the explanation of phenomena and findings in a structured way to effectively answer the question posed by a researcher. In other words, it allows one to apply information drawn from already available sources to render an evaluation of the material to explain complex issues or find answers to phenomena. According to Maxwell, qualitative researchers "work with a universe of meanings, motives, aspirations, beliefs, values and attitudes, which corresponds to a deeper space of relationships, processes and phenomena that cannot be reduced to the operationalization of variables; and, in spite of its limitations, the qualitative research method is commonly used to produce very compelling research and contribution to social science" (2013, p. 8). The qualitative method is essentially utilized in this chapter for gathering, collating, and evaluating relevant scholarly essays that address the issue of International Law and Africa's role in its development and practice. This includes materials that have to do with a systematic review of other issues related to and useful for the explanation of the subject matter of this chapter.

International Law: A Conceptualization

International Law is established by international regimes and institutions, and it constitutes the customary rules and codified treaties under which international organizations and nation-states function. International Law covers political, economic, and social rights. From a historical standpoint, it developed to protect the interests of states and their right to sovereignty and self-defense. Instantly, however, it also addresses the rights of individual human beings; if nations abuse their citizens, international institutions set up under International Law have the "responsibility to protect" those citizens and intervene in a state's affairs regardless of its sovereignty. This is done to prevent genocide, starvation, etc. Central to International Law is multilateralism in order to include all state actors and often non-state participants as well and to encourage compromise regardless of the ideologies or beliefs participants hold. In present times, substantially all countries and points of view are respected. Tolerance and coexistence are the most important virtues.

Also, International Law consists of a system of customary laws of various nations, treaties, agreements, and other consensus-based understandings among nations that govern the way that they interact and interrelate with one another in the international system. International Law generally falls into the following two different categories: (1) private International Law addresses the controversies among private entities such as people or corporations, which are multinational or transnational, having a significant relationship with more than one country; and (2) public International Law, on which this chapter focuses, concerns the relationships among countries. Some principles of Public International Law are written, or "codified," in a series of treaties, especially since the inception of the United Nations and other qualifying international intergovernmental organizations are accorded limited international juridical personality; but many other rules and understandings that govern the international commons are not generally documented. These are known as "customary" laws, and nations consent to them by simply adhering to long-trusted and time-tested practices by many nations.

Since most of International Law is governed by treaties rather than customary laws, especially in the years following World War II and the formation of the United Nations, it is usually up to the individual nations to enforce the law. Nonetheless, there are a few international organizations that enforce certain specific treaties. The most notable example is the United Nations, which has essentially to date about 192 member states, which has no legislative, executive, or judicial institutions and depends on the community of nations to uphold international rules wherever and whenever it can as a collective responsibility for international norms, practices, consensus, and security. To narrow the focus on this investigation, the critical question of this chapter is the following: What are some of the ways Africa has been conceptualized by the academic discipline of International Law?

Indeed, the nature of International Law has been an issue for a long time relative to its reality; in other words, "experts, writers and other authorities have often debated about whether it is really law in the general and commonly understood sense of the word, especially in comparison with municipal law. In this regard, it is most glaring that "the absence of an international legislature, of courts with compulsory jurisdiction, and of centrally organized sanctions as the main reason for doubting the legal quality of international law" (Payandeh, 2011, p. 974). Also, according to Hart, "these differences make international law to resemble the 'simple form of social structure' which can be found in primitive societies…international law consists mainly of primary rules" (1994, p. 217). No such secondary rules or sanctions exist in International Law. However, it is worth noting that the mere absence of sanctions or the institutional structures of coercion that can be found in a municipal environment in International Law is not to be construed to mean that there is a strong absence of obligations therein. In addition, Hart opines that "it may be argued that the existence of primary rules prohibiting the free use of force and rules providing for the official use of force as a sanction are a necessary condition for every municipal legal system. Since communities of individuals consist of human beings approximately equal in strength and with lots of opportunities to injure each other, natural deterrents alone would not be enough to guarantee observation of the rules" (1994, pp. 218–219). This line of thought is pursued further by Hart, as he observes that it is evident that the international milieu, which is governed by international law, is generally different from the municipal milieu; hence, on the international level, the circumstances are different, and tend to present themselves in a different way. Incidentally, conflict among states can be much more evident in the public sphere than can be the case with conflicts among individuals and likely involve third states. Furthermore, the international milieu is characterized by an unequal distribution of power among states. The existence of sanctions would, therefore, not guarantee that powerful states would always obey the rules, and sanctions would add little deterrent effect (Hart, 1994).

Moreover, sanctions against violations of relevant international systems of rules play a role within the municipal and international legal systems. Sanctions are often weak or difficult to apply in International Law, but their absence at the international level is not a reason to deny its legal quality. Essentially, regardless of the obvious and indicated weaknesses of International Law when compared to municipal laws, the former still represents, in large measure, the reason for the general workability of cooperation in many spheres—social, political, economic, scientific, cultural—of international cooperation and activities among nation-states. Also, as Hart puts it, "The second obstacle to recognizing international law as law is the sovereignty of states. The conception of a state, which is at the same time sovereign and bound by law, is deemed to be radically inconsistent" (1994, p. 220). This inconsistency assumes that the sovereign state, coupled with the absence of central enforcement mechanisms and sovereign equality of states, appears to locate states above the law, thereby making the concept of sovereignty and lack of central enforcement mechanisms the defining characteristics of International Law.

European Conceptualization of Africa's Role in International Law

In this section, the European view of Africa apropos International Law is examined. This view fastens on and is shaped by Europeans' understanding of the continent. From ancient Greek and Roman accounts to the era of colonization, European perspectives on Africa were based on a variety of factors, including cultural biases, economic interests, scientific discoveries, and missionary activities. A staunch opponent of Africa relative to consigning it to the status of irrelevance in the development of International Law and even history was the philosopher G.W. F. Hegel due to his damning verdict on Africa's exclusion from universal history and, thus, reason (Camara, 2005).

European encounters with Africa were compelled prominently by trade and exploration. During the precolonial era, Europe's knowledge of Africa was bounded by geographical distance and the dearth of general knowledge of the continent and exploration. Europeans had limited direct contact with the people in the African continent, relying mostly on second-hand accounts from wayfarers, traders, travelers, merchants, and scholars. This dearth of information and knowledge contributed to the formation of the European view of Africa, which is generally nonflattering, negative, misconceived, and stereotypical. For example, the Greek philosopher Aristotle described Africa as a land of extremes, inhabited by monstrous creatures, due to his understanding of the continent based on second-hand information (Boahen, 1985). Similarly, the Roman geographer Ptolemy's influential work titled *Geographia* perpetuated misconceptions about Africa's geography, further shaping European views of the continent (Boahen, 1985). Europeans generally viewed Africans as uncivilized, primitive, and inferior to Europeans. And, this perception also conditioned their view of Africa's role in the development and practice of International Law.

The dominant European view of Africa was established during the colonial era by the ideas of racial supremacy and Eurocentrism, which perpetuated stereotypes and prejudices about Africans as inferior to Europeans (Rodney, 1973). Hence, in a derisive manner, Europeans tend to think about the history of International Law in Africa as minor local histories, which did not extend beyond Africa and, therefore, not international in scope. International Law is generally viewed from the European perspective as the domestic laws of European nations writ large and made international with a superior army and navy in reference to the advent of colonialism and its implications for Africa. Specifically, the European world did not consider Africa worthy of being included in the ranks of civilized states. Thus, according to Gerhard von Glahn and Larry Taulbee,

> An irony infuses the development of international law during the nineteenth century. On the one hand, it spread through the imperial activities of the European powers; on the other, it became more parochial because it reflected European values and applied in full only to those states admitted to the very exclusive club of 'civilized' nations, determined off course by the current members of the club. Publicists often referred to international law as the public law of Europe...Most areas in Africa...became colonial possessions or dependen-

> cies that in turn had no rights under international law because the members of the club refused to acknowledge that the territories enjoyed any independent legal status juridical personality (2017, p. 38).

Also, the European view of the inception of International Law, which they posit is based on the customary laws of European nations writ large, indicates that the emanation of the community and family of nations and the foundations of modern international relations was laid after the conclusion of the peace treaties concluded at the towns of Munster and Osnabruck, collectively known as the Peace of Westphalia of 1648. The cardinal tenets of the Peace of Westphalia, which established the Westphalian model of modern international relations, rested on the concepts of the sovereignty of nation-states, the horizontal structures of states that succeeded the hierarchical structure that existed before the collapse of the Holy Roman Empire, as well as the idea of the independence and equality of all nation-states. Accordingly, modern international law was set up initially to govern the relations among the new sovereign states, the process of which Africans were not a part. As Von Glahn and Taulbee point out,

> …upon European contact with Africa, the continent came under the control of European nations as subordinates and part and parcel of European nations; hence, the African nations were not sovereign and independent and could not claim to be a part of the formations of international law *ab initio* until after the end of the period of colonialism. Basically, they were of the view that Africans were not contributors to the international law perhaps until after their decolonization and independence. They were, prior to independence, therefore, objects not subject of international law. Presently, to Europeans, although the elements of legal relations could be found between and among African nations in antiquity or even between African nations and European nations, such relations which can take the form of trade and treaties does not qualify African nations to be members of the founders of international law in the modern sense of the concept… (2017, p. 38).

Africa and International Law Prior to European Intervention

Emphasis on Africa's participation in "the formation of international law amounts to contributionism" (Onuma, 2000, p. 2). Scholars of the contributionists school, also referred to as an "inter-civilizational approach" by some, do not reject the Christian or Western origins of International Law. Instead, they argue that Africans participated in shaping it. Regarding International Law prior to the arrival of Europeans in Africa, the contributionists posit that "inter-civilizational participation in the process of crafting genuinely universal norms of international law has historically involved Africa as a central player" (Dieng, 2008, p. 2). In addition, the contributionists "regard international law as the product of several civilizations rather than the sole product of European civilization. Contributionism emphasizes that Africa is an innovator and generator of norms of international law" (Dieng, 2008, p. 2). They have sought to rewrite International Law from an African perspective. This perspective also discusses the distinguishing characteristics of contributionism and essentially assailing Eurocentrism to accommodate and situate Africa relative to its role in the establishment of International Law.

Although the European commentators indicate otherwise, there is copious evidence to evince that there are

> other arenas of 'internationality' concerning international law in Africa's precolonial past. These contacts reach back very far in African history. Three arenas are generally mentioned: the Red Sea area and Ethiopian-Arab relations; the Indian Ocean rim; and finally, the case of nineteenth-century Ethiopia. The dynamics and contact activities between Africa and other peoples are a poignant indicator of Africa's participation in international law, and the qualifying legal activities in Africa mirrors events in Europe during the same period. As Mark Toufayan explains that " ... both [Africa and Europe] shared similar legal ideas. This, in turn, was testimony to 'the unity of all human knowledge and experience,' and [both Africa and Europe] were accordingly brought together under law's 'yoke' (Toufayan, 2014, p. 31).

Evidently, Africa's international legal history goes back deep into antiquity and the colonial period was a small part of it. Colonialism was, as succinctly and famously put by Jacob Ade Ajayi, an episode in African history. Buttressing this point, legal scholar Charles H. Alexandrowicz (1973) confirms that the colonial period in Africa, if considered against the background of African history as a whole, is of negligible duration. So, it is obvious that African international legal histories deserve a larger spectrum and explanatory latitude.

Wider attention has been paid well beyond the African-European "contacts" and to ask for other "contacts" relative to other arenas of "internationality" in Africa's past. For example, the Pharaonic international treaties of alliance with Middle Eastern partners count among the oldest international law documents. A prime example is the international correspondence of Amenophis III and Akhenaten dating from 1400 BC, detailing individual provisions and their acceptance by Egypt's alliance partners (Westbrook, 2000). And, according to Alexandrowicz,

> ...the African regions considered most important in the historiography of international law so far have been: the 'Barbary Coast' region along the middle and western coastal regions of North Africa due to questions of piracy and slave trade; the African west coast for its relevance to the Atlantic slave trade; the Congo basin for its relation to the 'scramble for Africa' and the 'Congo Act' of 1885; and finally, those regions along the coast and further inland whose rulers entered into treaties with European powers, mostly in the decades from 1870 to 1890 (1973, p. 32).

Also, as can be gleaned from the following observation, "...the universality of international law is not solely constituted by Europeans in Europe, but also by Africans. The idea was to end the persistent prejudice that Africans had no history, a view which in turn laid a substantial basis for external slavery of Africans and colonial subjugation of Africa by European countries and stereotypes of African inferiority and backwardness" (Gathii, 2011–2012, p. 532). This racist notion of Africa has been the subject of a staunchly opposing view by the contributionist school of thought about the role that Africa has been playing in the development of international law from time immemorial. They are of the view that Africa should not be subjected to such racist views as is prevalent in Europe. In this sense, the following assertions by Elias and Akinjide are relevant:

> Asserting that the African identity was however not only an assault on but also on notions of Western and white supremacy as represented by colonial rule and other forms of Western subjugation and power over Africa. Contributionists scholars, therefore, seek to jettison the notion of Africans in international law as backward, uncivilized and Barbaric. Contributionist seek to correct this historical record as a major purpose of re-writing the history of international law; thereby, rescuing Africa from their assigned place in history by glorifying a bygone past where the African, much like the European, was a member of ancient kingdoms or political units equivalent to the 'modern' and 'civilized' western states. It was in this sense, that the scholar in the contributionist tradition challenged the myths of black inferiority, servitude, backwardness (1988, p. 3).

This position was further elucidated by Davidson (1973) in his remark that by reinterpreting tropes of the African as uncivilized, barbaric, and backward, these African scholars realigned colonial categories, thereby producing a postcolonial International Law that made the racist and imperial connotations of the colonial discourse speak with race-blind meanings. In addition, recounting international legal history, Elias and Akinjide (1988) argue that prior to the colonial conquest, Africa was and has always been a participant in the international community. Concomitantly, they reject the period of colonization as they move from a people without history to global incorporation. According to them, " if we are to grasp something of the significance of Africa in current international affairs, we must begin with a brief account of the role which different parts of the so-called dark continent played since recorded history in their internal as well as their external relations" (Elias & Akinjide, 1988, p. 3). Furthermore, contributionists, generally conclude, exuberantly, that this "outline should serve as an interesting background to the account now being given of how the Sahara may be said to have dominated the history of the north no less than it has done that of the south" (Elias & Akinjide, 1988, p. 3).

Furthermore, according to contributionist scholars, the conclusion of agreements, treaties between colonialists and international traders, as well as the treaties between African chiefs and European trading companies/powers supposedly ceding African land to colonialists, are considered as additional evidence of the participation of African precolonial kingdoms in the international sphere. As Gathii states, "These treaties reflected the freedom of African chiefs to enter into relationships with European countries. Which, unfortunately, is the logic that British colonial courts used to find that African communities had sovereignty to cede their land to colonial authorities at a time when these communities were under the complete control and jurisdiction of colonial powers" (2007, pp. 1013–1033). This is the basis for the position that there were "problematic origins of unequal treaties and the hesitation of some of the newly independent states to be freed of obligations under such treaties" (Jewa, 1976, p. 7).

Moreover, regarding the issue of Africa's role in International law, the idea of sovereignty is crucial. It is a necessary condition for contribution to International

Law since a non-independent and non-sovereign state is not an international juridical entity and, as such, is not able to act and participate in any activity or process within the family of nations. And, to the extent that the sovereignty of Africa was truncated by the advent of colonialism, it relegated Africa to the margins of the history of the development of International Law, which the postindependence membership in international organizations such as the United Nations commenced to restore; therefore, colonialism interrupted the way African states and/or kingdoms interacted with European states in the precolonial period. Essentially, colonialism led to an abrupt interruption of African sovereignty, which manifested important impulses that left Africa out of its hitherto participation in the development of International Law since only sovereign states can contribute to and are the subject of International Law.

Hence, contributionism is primarily based on a repudiation of the Eurocentric framework of references, perspective, and analysis, which underrates and understates Africa's involvement and participation in the making of International Law. Contributionists posit that Africa is and has been a coequal participant and shaper of international legal principles and norms. The contributionist school also seeks to denounce and remove the Eurocentric cultural or ethnocentric bias in International Law, resist the perspective that the discipline was a cultural achievement by Europeans only, rather than one shared by African states and/or kingdoms. Also, contributionists proffer that although European writers tended to exclude Africa from the development and growth of International Law, this can only be attributed to deliberate neglect, exclusion, not due to lack of evidence of Africa's contributions. In this instance, there is the documentation of African regions in the historiography of International Law (Ginther, 1983).

There is, therefore, a need to bridge a crucial gap in the teaching and writing of International Law, which would bring a new "wholeness" in the approach to the field. In this context, it is important to account for or take into consideration new regions where Africa and Europe intersected in political and commercial activities. One of the most salient examples of an African country participating and contributing to the development of International Law would be the role of Ethiopia, which rightly sought to be admitted to the Family of Nations. The contacts between Ethiopian and European rulers reach back at least to the European Middle Ages. The Vatican, Portugal, and Russia count among the states having the oldest ties with this African state (Zollmann, 2018). In addition, there is indeed no dearth of sources about international relations between European and Ethiopian governments; still, in the late nineteenth century, Europeans and Americans were hesitant to recognize Ethiopia as a sovereign member of the family of civilized nations, and this is the case regardless of the fact that during a period when Africans were generally relegated by "European politicians and academics to the place of 'the 'uncivilized' Ethiopian rulers, despite their Christian faith, found it challenging for their country to be given a place among the tables of the 'civilized' states. Still, in 1884, Ethiopia's Emperor Menelik II signed a treaty with the British over their respective spheres of influence. In 1889, a similar treaty was concluded with the Italians" (Elliesie, 2014, p. 537). Despite this evidence of Ethiopia's international prominence, its diplomatic relations with European powers, and even its proven mettle at defeating Italy, a European state, in order to avoid colonization, it was still not viewed as an equal in the community of nations, prompting the following observation by Zollman:

> Britain, France, Italy, Belgium, Russia, the United States, Germany, and later Turkey set up legations in the new capital Addis Ababa and extended their consular jurisdiction over Ethiopia. From now on, Ethiopia was indisputably on the map of international politics. The victory over the Italians was its *billet d'entrée* into the family of 'civilized nations'—where the 'chief standard of civilization was, of course, power.' Or, as an often-quoted Japanese diplomat put it cynically after his country's victory over Russia in 1905, 'We show ourselves at least your equal in scientific butchery, and at once we are admitted to your council tables as civilized men,' stating that when Ethiopia defeated the [Italians in 1896], she became at once a civilized country (2018, pp. 912–913).

Although a persuasive argument for equality and eligibility for consideration and acceptance as a "civilized" nation that is deserving of a seat at the table as an international juridical entity, Ethiopiana remained denied of this status until the onset of independence emancipated them to that status along with other African countries in the 1950s to the 1970s.

The Critical Tradition on Conceptualization of Africa in International Law

For critical theorists, "a central question is how to defang international law of its imperialist and exploitative biases…in general, and in Africa in particular" (Mutua, 2011–2012, p. 532). The critical school also posits that International Law not only denigrated Africa and denied it participation, it was also used to exploit it, even to date. Adherents "like Makau Wa Mutua, Siba Grovogui, Kamari Clark, Ibironke Odumosu, and Obiora Okafor, among others, by contrast to contributionists, focus on the way modern international law has continued the legacy of colonial disempowerment while providing spaces for resistance and reform. For critical theorists, a central question is how to 'defang' international law of its imperialist and exploitative biases" (Mutua, 2001, p. 201). A primary project of scholars of the critical subscription is a critical examination of the imperial and colonial character of the International Law discipline.

Critics of Africa's role in International Law take exception to the contributionists' evasion of analytical accountability relative to the historical connection of International Law with European colonialism and domination of Africa. So, critical theorists, unlike constructionists, peg their analysis on the structural and economic foundations of African states in the world as their point of departure in evaluating Africa's role in International Law. They also pin their focus on questions of comparative state power and wealth inequities between African countries and the rest of the world as grounds to be wary of the likelihood of meaningful reform within international law. Thus, according to Gutto, "International law is simply transforming itself into [a] public and private law of neocolonialism and imperialism, with some facade of progressiveness due to the narrow and nominal inclusion of human rights principles and de-recognition of the rightfulness of formal colonialism…and overt forms of racial discrimination" (1987, p. 275). In this tradition, the end of colonialism, independence, and self-determination was the beginning of a new era of Africa's subordination and subjugation to Europe through a statehood system modeled closely to the European sociopolitical formations. Hence, as opposed to the contributionists, critical theorists view independence and self-determination not as a moment to return Africa to a glorious past of equal and reciprocal relationship with Europe; but, instead, it portends a regrettable moment of betrayal. As Gathii asserts, "In line with the critical tradition, customary international law is viewed as not to have originated during commercial and diplomatic links between Africa and Europe, but rather as having arisen because of industrial capitalism in the West and the territorial ambitions of western powers…international law was a handmaiden of the expansion of the economic interests of colonizing countries" (2011, p. 15).

Critics of Africa's role in International Law point to slave trade and colonialism as two of the foremost African experiences from their contact with Europeans. Umozurike, an ardent member of the critical school, contends that International Law was used to facilitate the imposition of slave trade and colonialism. He then argues that "while international law helped the establishment of slave trade and colonialism, it was also used in their eradication" (1979, p. 9). The underlying thesis in Umozurike's account is that "an evil system" such as that embodied in International Law cannot alter its essential nature. Umozurike however opined that "in the present age of international law, self-determination remains an important factor in securing rights [that are] internationally recognized" (1979, p. 10). The critics go even further by calling for a withdrawal from the exploitative international relations that characterize colonial relationships carried forward in the postindependence period. Rather than embrace the view that Africa has everything to gain through contact with Europeans, the critical tradition condemns the international system as inhumane and immoral. The critics, therefore, repudiate International Law due to its role in Africa's subjugation historically. In the words of Gathii,

> In the critical tradition, the role of international law is not merely that of regulating relations between states, thereby reducing frictions and promoting cooperation and development. Instead, international law is regarded as the law that governed relations of the civilized and Christian Europe *inter se*. By contrast, international law which governed relations between European States was unknown to 'primitive people' and it therefore did not protect them from European conquest; and it was also used to promote the trade in Africans for the economic benefit of Europeans (2012, p. 17).

Furthermore, Umozurike (1979) identifies the dichotomy of International Law in the sense of the "old" and the "new." In the sense of the "new" and "old" International Law, the essential basis for the relegation of Africa in International Law was founded on the emanation of the modern state system in Europe, prior to which there were identifiable states and kingdoms in Africa. Nonetheless, the end of the 30-year war in Europe and the Peace of Westphalia of 1648 yielded the modern state system based on sovereignty, independence, and equality of states. The emanation of a multiplicity of states necessitated the founding of International Law and the birth of the concept of "international juridical personality" as a new dispensation for managing the new international system. This new system of states and law replaced the old system of contending kingdoms and empires in Europe, much as it was in Africa. The new international system was also founded upon a Christian order and considered by its founders to be "civilized" to the exclusion of all non-Europeans and non-Christians. Thus, Europeans considered Africa to be "uncivilized," ungoverned, and unequal to the Europeans and, therefore, up for the taking through conquest and colonization, justified by International Law.

Regarding the question of the violation of sovereignty of African states and their subsequent occupation and colonization, while in the contributionist tradition, the denial of sovereignty on the part of Africans within colonial international law is considered somewhat inadvertent, in the critical tradition, the denial of sovereignty to Africans is regarded as a "major legal technique for the imposition of colonialism" (Umozurike, 1979, p. 10). Essentially, it is posited that Europeans were in violation of International Law by their colonization of Africa and declaration of Africa as a *terra nullis* or no one's land, open for the taking regardless of their clear understanding of the fallacy of their position. In sum, the critics urge the establishment of a new international order founded on international political, economic, and social spheres under an equitable International Law. It should be noted that violations of international sovereignty of African states, and that of any other state for that matter, through military interventions and other means should not be construed to mean that international law does not apply to African states; it is in the nature of both international law and municipal law that laws and agreements would be violated, but the mere fact that we recognize that laws are violated is in of itself and implicitly indicative that such laws exist for the entity that is being violated, for the matter of violation would not arise if there is nothing to be violated.

Conclusion and Recommendations

The general conclusion in this chapter centers on perspectives concerning the conceptualization of Africa's role in International Law. Also, some policy recommendations would be made relative to the direction of studies and discourses regarding the subject matter.

There are varying but salient perspectives by different schools of thought about Africa's role in International Law. In this regard, Africa is reeling from condemnation, vilification, and marginalization relative to its role in the practice and development of International Law. Essentially, the field, relative to its conceptualization of Africa, fastens upon three salient areas of consideration: (1) perception by European scholars who attribute no recognizable or creditable role to Africa, regardless of the obvious contacts between European nations and parts of Africa, especially the glaring case of Ethiopia; (2) the contributionists who posit that Africa contributed significantly to International Law since antiquity but are merely disregarded by the Europeans; and (3) the critics who insist that Africa may have contributed to

International Law but that the field was and is used to justify the slave trade and subsequent colonization, as well as the continued marginalization of Africa in the international sphere. Europeans leveraged and weaponized International Law to declare Africa a *terra nullis* and open for the taking and control rather than integrate and recognize Africa's contributions. The three perspectives elucidated herein are persistent and dominant features in the analysis of the role of Africa in the development and practice of the discipline of International Law. The contributionist school evinces copious instances of Africa's involvement in the development of International Law, and the critical school acknowledges that Africa was also relevant regarding the field and insists that Europeans simply and squarely brushed aside any such contributions and employed International Law as a tool for the conquest, colonization and continued subjugation of Africa. The European strain argues that not only did Africa not participate in the development and practice of International Law, it also was not even qualified to do so on account of not being Christian and civilized. Proponents of this school also attribute the emergence of International Law to being a corollary to the emergence of the modern state system in which Africa was not a participant.

By way of a recommendation, scholars of International Law should focus on addressing global rules and norms in the interest of all nations vis-à-vis equity rather than using it as an implement in the toolkit of great powers. Next, in order to set aside the persistent and erroneous perspective that Africa did not contribute to International Law, an effort should be made to document and reinforce the contributions of Africa to the field to bring about an inclusive and holistic understanding of the field where no contribution is ignored, denied, or denigrated.

Also, more attention should be devoted to the African perspective on International Law, which is vital for understanding and presenting a more accurate and nuanced narrative about Africa's contribution to the field while informing the way that it is conceptualized. Thus, multidisciplinary approaches should be emphasized over disciplinary exclusionism in the study of the subject. In other words, research in this area should adopt more of a multidisciplinary approach that draws from fields such as History, Anthropology, Sociology, Economics, Political Science, and Cultural Studies. A multidisciplinary approach can provide a holistic understanding of African perspectives, which should aim to present a comprehensive understanding of the complex and evolving viewpoints within Africa, thereby contributing to a more informed and accurate portrayal of the continent and its role in the development of International Law.

In addition, the analysis of the conceptualization of International Law apropos Africa should go beyond the somewhat parochial paradigm of Africa's contribution to the global and general history of the field. Hence, it should not be limited to projecting European customary law into Africa, past and present, but ought to go beyond the confines of European perceptions as set by colonialism and the modern world system. Moreover, other strands of ideas and issues relative to this chapter, which are beyond its present scope but worth further investigation, are the customs, traditions, and perhaps laws that governed the relations between and among indigenous states in Africa prior to the arrival of Europeans. This chapter focuses on the conceptualization of Africa's role in the discipline of international law, and three perspectives have been explained: (1) the European perspective, (2) the contributionists' perspective, and (3) the critics' perspective, not Africa's international legal relations; hence, the limits and scope of this essay put it beyond the purview of the writer and left for further studies by others.

References

Alexandrowicz, C. H. (1973). The European-African confrontation: A study in treaty making. *Leiden Journal of International Law, 31*(4), 1–32.

Boahen, A. A., & UNESCO. (1985). *General history of Africa, Vol. 7: Africa under colonial domination 1880-1935*. University of California Press.

Brierly, J. L. (1963). *The law of nations* (6th ed.). Oxford University Press.

Camara, B. (2005). The falsity of Hegel's thesis on Africa. *Journal of Black Studies, 36*(1), 82–96.

Davidson, B. (1973). *Black Star. A view of life and times of Kwame Nkrumah*. James Curry.

Dieng, A. (2008). Foreword. In J. Levitt (Ed.), *Mapping new boundaries in African international law*. Hart Publishing.

Elias, T. O., & Akinjide, R. (1988). *Africa and the development of international law*. Martinus Nijhoff Publishers.

Elliesie, H. (2014). Treaties and multilateral conventions. *Encyclopaedia Aethiopica, 537*.

Gathii, J. (2007). Imperialism, colonialism and international law. *Buffalo Law Review, 54*, 1013–1066.

Gathii, J. (2011). *African regional trade agreements as legal regimes*. Oxford University Press.

Gathii, J. T. (2011–2012). Africa and the history of international law. In *Oxford handbook of the history of international law* (Legal studies research paper series, no. 48). Oxford University Press.

Ginther, K. (1983). The teaching of international law under a developmental aspect: The relevance of African cases and materials. In K. Ginther & W. Benedek (Eds.), *New perspectives and conceptions of international law: An Afro-European dialogue*. Springer.

Gutto, S. B. O. (1987). Violation of human rights in the third world: Responsibility of states and TNCs. In F. Snyder & S. Sathirathai (Eds.), *Third world attitudes toward international law*. Brill Publishers.

Hart, H. L. A. (1994). *The concept of law* (3rd ed.). Oxford University Press.

Jewa, M. T. S. (1976). *The third world and international law*. PhD Thesis, University of Miami.

Maxwell, J. A. (2013). *Qualitative research design: An interactive approach*. Sage.

Mutua, M. W. (2001). Savages, victims and saviors: The metaphor of human rights. *Harvard Journal of International Law, 42*, 201–245.

Mutua, M. W. (2011–2012). Book review of *Africa: Mapping new boundaries in international law*. In J. I. Levitt & J. T. Gathii (Eds.), *Oxford handbook of the history of international law* (Legal studies research paper series, no. 48). Oxford University Press.

Onuma, Y. (2000). When was international society born?—An inquiry of the history of international law from an inter-civilizational perspective. *Journal of the History of International Law, 2*, 1–66.

Payandeh, M. (2011). The concept of international law in the jurisprudence of H.L.A. Hart. *The European Journal of International Law, 21*(4), 967–955.

Rodney, W. (1973). *How Europe underdeveloped Africa*. Heinemann Educational Books.

Toufayan, M. (2014). When British justice (in African colonies) points two ways: On dualism, hybridity, and the genealogy of juridical negritude. *Leiden Journal of International Law, 31*(4), 31–70.

Umozurike, U. O. (1979). *International law and colonialism in Africa*. Nwamife Publishers.

von Glahn, G., & Taulbee, L. (2017). *Law among nations: An introduction to public international law* (11th ed.). Routledge.

Westbrook, R. (2000). International law in the Amarna age. In R. Cohen & R. Westbrook (Eds.), *Amarna diplomacy: The beginning of international relations*. Johns Hopkins University Press.
Yin, R. K. (2010). *Qualitative research methods from start to finish*. The Guilford Press.
Zollmann, J. (2018). African international legal histories—International law in Africa: Perspectives and possibilities. *Leiden Journal of International Law, 31*(4), 897–914.

JP Afamefuna Ifedi Lectures in Political Science at Howard University in Washington, DC. Ifedi has published in various scholarly peer-reviewed journals and participated in election monitoring and democracy development in Bosnia-i-Herzegovina under the auspices of the Organization for Security and Cooperation in Europe and the United States Department of State. He directs the Council on African World Affairs, an organization dedicated to educating the public on African world issues. His PhD is from Howard University, and he completed a post-doctoral in Political Economy as an Institute for British and Irish Studies Summer Fellow at St. Anthony's College, Oxford and Trinity College, Dublin.

Libraries

Collence Takaingenhamo Chisita
and Tlou Maggie Masenya

In this chapter, we explore the critical role of Africa in developing/decolonizing libraries and world civilization. Africa has contributed significantly to world civilization through ancient and modern/smart libraries. This chapter looks at the multi-layered aspects of how Africa has contributed to the decolonization of libraries by developing modern libraries that resonate with the aspirations of its people. This chapter also examines African libraries before and after the onset of colonialism regarding the production, processing, dissemination, and archiving of knowledge. It in addition investigates the challenges of African libraries in the era of "decoloniality." The chapter further analyzes the ancient African libraries, focusing on their contribution to modern library and information science. Moreover, and more importantly, with the preceding aspects as backdrop, the chapter discusses how Africa has been specifically conceptualized by scholars in the field of Library Studies, also referred to as Library Science and Library and Information Science. In the end, a conclusion is drawn and recommendations are tendered. Accordingly, the following research question guides the chapter: How has ancient African librarianship contributed to modern libraries? In Zulu's argument (2023), the Africans should not be astonished by the knowledge of knowledge and its acquisition since historical evidence confirms that their ancestors, the ancient people of Kemet/Ancient Egypt, referred to as "the black land," were the first to establish and operate libraries and higher education institutions in the world.

Similarly, James (1992) claims that Greek philosophy was stolen from Kemetic philosophy by the early colonial adventures. When the Greeks finally came to Kemet for their education from the sixth century to 322 BC, the invaders used

C. T. Chisita (✉)
Information Science, University of South Africa, Pretoria, South Africa

T. M. Masenya
Information Technology, Durban University of Technology, Durban, South Africa
e-mail: TlouM@dut.ac.za

A. K. Bangura, J. A. Ifedi (eds.), *Conceptualizations of Africa*, African Studies and Research Forum Series, https://doi.org/10.1007/978-3-031-74535-5_20

everything they could learn about Kemet to kill Aristotle (322 BC). It is an anomaly and misnomer that numerous studies on librarianship among library schools focus more on the colonial and postcolonial development of libraries, as evidenced by a lack of studies that explore Africa's role in the development of librarianship as an indicator of polished civilization before the colonial onslaught. Overall, the chapter broaches the establishment, development, and function of libraries in Africa.

There are myriads of conceptualizations concerning ancient Africa's contributions to modern civilization, and this chapter therefore focuses on the following three significant conceptualizations for brevity: (1) ancient African librarianship as a bedrock of modernity, (2) African librarianship challenges and opportunities, and (3) African librarianship as a head cornerstone of human progress.

The chapter's main thrust is ancient African librarianship's contributions to modern librarianship. An interpretive approach encompasses theoretical and philosophical perspectives that interpret reality as a product of social construction (Sibiya & Ngulube, 2023). The theories and philosophies underpinning "interpretivism" are qualitative, since they produce descriptive and analytical data expressed in words (Leavy, 2022). We collected data from secondary sources using thematic analysis. The first conceptualization of "ancient African librarianship as a bedrock of modern librarianship" is used as a contextual background to the chapter.

It is vital to justify why studying ancient African librarianship's contributions to modern librarianship's theory and praxis is critical. The justification and motivation arise from ancient Africa, which colonial ethnographers depicted as a dark continent devoid of any meaningful civilization and unworthy of studying (Trevor-Roper, 1969). Nonetheless, Williams (2020) represents ancient African civilization as a glorious past worth exploring as it provides valuable lessons for restoring the continent as a citadel of human civilization. As cited in Nhemachena (2023), Goody (2006) asserts that colonialists stole African history, including the African past, which led to the establishment of the African status quo ante. Nhemachena (2023) points out that reclaiming ancient African glory should not be mistaken for trying to return Africans to the past but rather for returning Africans to *their* history and past. African history as illstrated in the book "UNESCO General History of Africa", Volume 11, (1980) provides an insightful overview of socio-economic and political developments prior to the dawn of colonialism. Africans do not need to travel back in time to become familiar with the past of modernity, including ownership and control of their resources. The critical question that requires an answer is this: What is the crux of exploring the contributions of ancient African civilization to modern librarianship? The answer to such an epistemological question underpins the current chapter because it will guide the analysis to delve into the basal of African librarianship from antiquity to modernity. The interpretive approach sustaining the present research makes it conceivable to elucidate the contributions of ancient librarianship to modern Library and Information science.

A Conceptualization of Ancient African Librarianship as a Bedrock of Modernity

According to Davis (2015), Africa has indeed been considered the "Dark Continent" (as specified in Joseph Conrad's novel titled *Heart of Darkness* (1899)), backward, and hopeless. Such a racist and myopic view of ancient or precolonial Africa became the justification for colonialism. Contrary to Conrad's (1899) racially misinformed perspective, Tise and Raju argue that "libraries and reading were alien to communities that had powerful oral communication networks for the sharing of information and knowledge" (2015, p. 1). As a consequence of the deliberate distortion of ancient African history, Western writers associate Kemet with the "Middle East" or anywhere else but Africa because of the great past of Kemet that contrasts with all the savage and jungle images that white racism has proffered about African people (Zulu, 2023). Africa has a rich tapestry of civilization; for example, the North-east African cultures include Kemet and Ethiopia, the Western Sudanese Empires (Ghana, Mali, and Songhai), the Kongo Kingdom in Central Africa, the Swahili civilization in East Africa, and the Shona civilization (Zimbabwe), as well as the Buganda and Bunyoro civilizations (Uganda), the Sotho civilization (South Africa), the Zulu Empire (South Africa), and the Tswana civilization in Botswana. Besides Amadi (1981), Mchombu et al. (2004), Ocholla (2003), Mchombu and Cadbury (2006), and Zulu (2023), many other scholars have attempted to reposition Africa as a legitimate participant in librarianship. Ancient African librarianship before colonialism is well documented by scholars, as evidenced by the Library of Ashurbanipal and the Alexandrian Library with its famous editors, who were also known for their work on Homeric texts (Davis, 2015). Libraries as repositories of human knowledge have existed since antiquity. Archeological evidence confirms their presence in ancient biblical places such as Nineveh and Ashurbanipal in Syría, Mali, Mauritania, Senegal, Egypt, Mesopotamia, and Jerusalem, among other places (Harrison, 1999). Tise and Raju (2015) argue that while libraries of printed materials existed before colonialism in the African continent, for example, the famous desert libraries of Timbuktu in Mali, oral tradition and the arts were generally more responsible for transmitting knowledge and cultural values. Human memory, speech, and collective activity served as most African communities' "libraries" and learning centers, as explained by Zulu as follows: "…the crux of the issue of race and the Egyptians is part of an attempt to take Egypt and Egyptian (Kemetian) history out of Africa intellectually and culturally thus substitute the Eurocentric politicization of history that confirms the notion that Africa has no record of importance and that the civilization of Egypt is not part of the African experience but rather is part of the Arab, Asian and European experience (2023, p. 247).

Indeed, African librarianship is a unique branch of global librarianship conceptualized in different ways, namely (a) ancient African librarianship, (b) the colonial library, and (c) the postcolonial library and "decoloniality." The current chapter focuses on x-raying the following critical issues: (a) Ancient African librarianship and its significance, (b) the colonial library, and (c) decolonizing the library.

Ancient African Librarianship: A Conceptualization

Notwithstanding the massive losses of texts written on perishable organic material such as papyrus, wooden tablets, or leather rolls, the progressively large amount of written data emanating from Kemet and the diversity of the text genres, vacillating from administrative to religious, including literary and scientific texts, authenticate the presence of some system for administering all this material (Haikal, 2008; Zulu, 2017). It was a preordained ancient ritual that an invading army should loot libraries and temples for books, manuscripts, and other paraphernalia that were classified as treasures, as was the case with the Roman invasion of Greece in 84 BC and Alexander the Great's invasion of Egypt in 334 BC (James, 2013). Overbey and Folk (2022) note that Kemetic rulers contributed to scholarship by building libraries; for example, the Great Ramses II built several libraries, including the Hypostyle Hall of Karnak, the Abu Simbel, the Abydos Temple Library, and the Temple Library of Luxor. Kemet's libraries of Alexandria, Heliopolis, and Memphis became the target of raids by invading armies. Sroka (2003) indicates that destroying library collections is as old as history; for example, Alexander the Great invaded Egypt in 334 BC. He and his team of invaders looted royal temples and libraries during the war. The ancient city of Alexandria was a Greek invasion force storehouse for contraband, including religious and intellectual artifacts pirated from temples along the Nile and old Nubia.

The pillagers later translated the stolen ancient Kemetic documents into Greek, Latin, Arabic, and English languages. Previously, Alexandria was known as Rakue, being part of Kemet. After its plunder and conquest by the Greeks, its scientific artifacts were transferred and transmitted to the Europeans and Arabs. According to Davids (1999), Alexander the Great conquered Kemet in 332 BC. A line of Macedonian Greeks who ruled the country descended from Alexander's general Ptolemy (King Ptolemy I). Cleopatra VII (the last dynasty ruler) surrendered Kemet to Roman rule, and the land became part of the Roman Empire in 30 BC. Davids (1999) distinguishes between Kemet's private and temple libraries. As Haikal (2008) argues that temples and tombs qualify as libraries because they preserved the oldest and longest religious books in Kemet and perhaps throughout the world; they ranged from the Pyramid Texts from the third millennium BC to the last inscriptions on the Temple of Philae from the fifth century AD. It is important to mention that papyri were also placed in tombs, which included magico-religious "books" meant to protect the owner's progress to the next world and documents related to his day-to-day activities (El-Abbadi et al. 2008; Davids, 1999). In an earlier royal workmen's town, Kahun (Middle Kingdom), the town's archive has revealed documents associated with the local administration, legal, medical, and veterinary matters, conditions relating to the royal workforce, and religious and educational texts (Haikal, 2008).

James (1954) and Zulu (2023) contend that Kemet was the land of temples and libraries, challenging a prevailing misconception that ancient Africa was a "dark continent." Zulu (2023) argues that ancient Africans were familiar with literature and art for many years before their contact with the Western world. According to

Zulu (2023), Kemetic librarianship has a 6000-year continuous history. Timbuktu, a West African city with social stratification, flourished as a center for Islamic scholarship between the fourteenth and sixteenth centuries, as discussed by Singleton (2004). He adds that over 50,000 volumes have been discovered in Timbuktu libraries, thereby providing sufficient evidence of written sources dating back to approximately 1100 AD.

Another documented library was that of Ahmad Umar, who took great pride in copying and annotating the works. He left behind nearly 700 volumes after his death (Singleton, 2004). Ahmad ibn And-Agh-Muhammad produced a work on grammar entitled *al-Futuh al-Qayumiya* in which he cited no fewer than 40 grammatical works throughout his treatise. Ahmad Baba and And-Agh-Muhammad's remarkable works are a testament to the depth and diversity of the book collections to which they had access in Timbuktu. The city grew into a well-regarded Islamic learning center in West Africa from humble beginnings. Its reputation flourished during the Golden Age of the fifteenth century which fostered the emergence of renowned scholars such as Ahmad Baba and Muhammad Baghayogho (Singleton, 2004). Trade, commerce, and a scholarship community thrived in Timbuktu, ruled by Islamic judges and scholars whose books and pens wielded supreme power. Only the most learned could lead, and libraries provided the scholars with the erudition they sought since faith came through intellect, not vice versa.

The Colonial Library

The decolonial agenda demands a reflection on every aspect of libraries as institutions and librarianship, and as a profession and discipline (Jimenez et al., 2022). Matthews (2020) and Wai (2015) argue that the concept of a colonial library transcends a physical library or a single set of texts; it is an abstraction of the immense bodies of readers and symbolic systems that have, over the centuries, collectively invented and continue to invent Africa as a paradigm of difference and alterity. Colonialism justified imperial rule by privileging written knowledge over other forms of knowing, particularly oral knowledge (Nyamnjoh, 2012), and subordinating and even destroying indigenous knowledge. Bob-Milliar (2022) posits that the colonialists pursued Western colonialism in Africa with the so-called 3Cs, namely, "Christianity, Civilization, and Commerce"; thus, the European colonizers superimposed their cultural superiority on their colonies. Chisita (2011) laments how the cantankerous vituperation of everything indigenous by the colonial administrators led to a state of cultural disorientation among the indigenous people, especially regarding identity, health, knowledge, food production, and conflict resolution, among other aspects of culture. For an anti-colonial project, indigenous knowledge recovery is born of anguish over what has been lost and from hope for what will be, so it emerges from the rejection of the centuries of colonialism that attempted to methodically transform African ways of seeing, being, and interacting. Chong and Edwards (2022) emphasised the need for indigenising education and libraries to realise cognitive justice. While the aforementioned authors made the recommendation in the context of Canada, the sugesstion is applicable to all colonised people grappling with deneocololity and decoloniality. Libraries as educational and cultural institutions can contribute towards epistemic justice through adapting a praxis-oriented approaches that will help to leverage the marginalised to a stateof cognitive empowerment as a collective.

Similarly, Williams and Muchena (1991) and Chisita (2011) proffer that nineteenth-century social sciences contributed through ethnic stereotyping and prejudice to current negative attitudes toward indigenous knowledge systems; for example, colonialism and Western educational systems led to the denigration of everything indigenous. A library's primary purpose is to access and preserve published works, implicitly valuing text as a form of knowledge. A vital aspect of propagating scientific knowledge in Global South contexts is undermining traditional knowledge (Cox et al., 2020). There are assumptions about how knowledge should be methodically embedded in the ideologies that shaped colonialism, reflected in the distinction between library, archive, and museum (Jimenez et al., 2022).

The epistemological ties of wounded attachments to the colonial library demonstrate the impact of colonial dominance on wounded accessories (Kaur & Kehal, 2023). According to Kaur and Kehal (2023), the colonial library is an integral partner in reorganizing the targeted geography for the colonizing project to achieve its economic and capitalistic goals. Similarly to colonial archives with specific orientations, colonial libraries provide pathways for meaning-making because they offer a colonial epistemic lens through which to interpret social life (Kaur & Kehal, 2023). The colonial library can be understood by examining the epistemological relationships among the library, the archive, and knowledge production. Kaur and Kehal (2023) contend that the colonial library was established through episteme so that archives were produced by the elites which, in turn, helped actors determine what should be collected. Kaur and Kehal (2023) further proffer that the colonialists instituted the colonial library through a controlling episteme (practicing epistemology) to produce archives which, in turn, actors use to determine what should be collected—i.e., defining relevance and significance.

The University of Al-Karaouine in Fez, Morocco, is the world's oldest higher learning institution. It was founded in 859 AD and served as a religious centre for Muslims as well as a seat of learning that encompassed the study of linguistics, grammar, law, music, Sufism, medicine, and astronomy. Islamic history is replete with ancient manuscripts. Founded in 1300, it has become a center for Muslim studies. As well as serving as a center of higher learning under Mansa Musa I, Timbuktu (now in Mali) was a center of religious study and higher education during the twelfth century. Like Al-Karaouine, Timbuktu (or Sankore) was also a place of higher learning and religious study (Overbey & Folk, 2022). In addition to Islamic theology, scholars in Timbuktu studied "law, grammar, rhetoric, logic, history, geography, astronomy…astrology," and medicine (Cartwright, 2019, p. 1).

A pioneer in written literature, the people of Kemet wrote on papyrus and stone tablets because their language (ciKam or hieroglyphics) is among the oldest written languages in the world. As a result of these early intellectual contributions, libraries were established in Kemet by the elite to collect, house, and organize literature, meaning that "Egyptian librarianship has been active for more than 6,000 years".

Impact of Colonialism on African Knowledge Production in Neocolonial Era

African communities expressed their knowledge through other media instead of the Western standard of paper and ink, such as scrolls, hieroglyphs, petroglyphs, and pictographs. Libraries operated as places where colonizers could preserve their narratives, Eurocentric ideologies, and knowledge and became the epicenters of colonialist thought, thereby excluding African knowledge. Colonial libraries became institutions of knowledge organized in a way that perpetuates colonialism. The historical books or articles written by White authors were shelved or stored in the nonfiction section. On the other hand, librarians designated many books written by African authors who collaborated with their African communities as fiction. The colonial library disregarded the epistemological needs of the colonial subjects, leading to the use of alternative methods of accessing and acquiring information by the colonial subjects. As Boadi (2006) points out that African libraries have become donor-dependent institutions surviving on book donations, which do not engender sustainable growth and development but perpetuate dependency and coloniality of knowledge.

Demeter (2019) illustrates the typical core-like and periphery-like features and processes in the world system of the social sciences by arguing that countries in the core benefit from high representation in terms of publications, overrepresentation in editorial boards and ownership of publishing houses, while those in the periphery are underrepresented in terms of research output and appointments to editorial boards, and have no control over international publishing houses. This observation confirms a dialectical relationship regarding knowledge production between the core and the periphery. It can be a fertile ground for the Global South to rethink and reset its priorities if it is to shape the dynamic knowledge landscape in the twenty-first century amid the growing calls to challenge the coloniality of knowledge. The asymmetric nature of global knowledge production has a spiral effect on libraries of all types as they have to develop collections from an unjust global knowledge system.

Library collections and knowledge production are influenced by systems designed by those from privileged backgrounds (Blume & Roylance, 2020). Western systems perpetuated colonialism and the miseducation, misattribution, and harmful stereotypes about African knowledge. As Brook et al. (2015) note, only the white perspective has been considered and translated into a narrowed perspective within research, literature, and history, while the structure of institutions has led to workflows, policies, and procedures that best serve the White majority. Western hegemony has destroyed other knowledge systems. Many libraries have used the same knowledge systems to gather more knowledge from underrepresented groups. Using decolonial thinking, scholars have critiqued the colonial-modern assumptions and knowledge forms deeply embedded in Western social science (Seth, 2013).

Under colonialism, knowledge production disregarded the internal dynamic of communities, so African knowledge production, for example, was excluded as a means of knowledge production (Dei, 2002). Despite the importance of knowledge in determining people's destinies, Western-centered modernity negated alternative ways of knowing Western ways of seeing, imagining, and understanding (Ndlovu, 2018). For example, academics and scientists have disregarded Indigenous knowledge systems, so the value of primary knowledge was strategically rejected among Western academics (Mji, 2019). The non-European-centered forms of knowledge, such as those of Indigenous peoples from Asia, America, and the Pacific, their classification systems, technologies, and codes of social life, were first preserved by Western science in the eighteenth century and were referred to as "discoveries" of Western society (Tabares, 2022). According to Tabares (2022), Western knowledge has its foundations in non-Western knowledge, albeit denying their contribution. The assertions made by James (1992, 2013) and Tabares (2022) provide evidence that the colonial adventurers from Africa and Pacific lands of the oppressed privileged Western civilization.

Consequently, African countries have adopted Western education, knowledge production methodologies and epistemologies, thereby preventing knowledge from spreading beyond national borders. As a result, African libraries relied on books and journals published in Europe and North America in European languages (Blume & Roylance, 2020). Book shortages at university libraries are common since academic books are primarily published outside Africa (UNESCO, 2005). Africa exports less than 1% of the books published. It imports only 2.3% of the global book market, as the United Nations Educational, Scientific and Cultural Organization (UNESCO) Institute for Statistics (2005) reported. The level of Africa's knowledge production and Africa's share of global cultural goods trade, including heritage goods, recorded media, and visual arts, therefore remained very low in neocolonialism.

Nonetheless, excellent research centers emerged in African countries in the 1960s and 1970s. These included the Institute of African Studies at the University of Ghana, the Makerere Institute of Social Research in Uganda, the Department of Humanities and Ethnography of Cheikh Anta Diop in Dakar, and the historical schools of Ibadan University in Nigeria (Sawyer, 2004). Also, the library resources in most African universities were no longer meeting users' basic needs in the 1980s and the 1990s. Smart (2005) informs readers that African universities had difficulty accessing scholarly research from neighboring countries. African studies published in international journals and books were not available to African authors and researchers, as these journals are not readily accessible within Africa. Therefore, the research findings might not be available to those seeking them and have little impact where needed (Okunoye & Karsten, 2003).

Decolonizing the Library

The concept of a colonial library transcends the actual physical library or only to a particular set of texts; for example, Wai (2015) interprets the term as an abstraction for the immense body of texts and system of representations that have over the centuries collectively invented and continue to invent Africa as a paradigm of difference and alterity. Mudimbe (2020) puts forth the concept of the "colonial library" to designate the body of texts and representations that began to emerge from the writings of travelers and explorers by the end of the nineteenth century and came to encompass the Africanist knowledge produced during and after the colonial period, including that of the social sciences, especially Anthropology. The idea of Mudimbe (2020) was to designate the body of texts and representations that emerged by the end of the nineteenth century from the writings and accounts of travelers and explorers as the colonial library. Matthews (2020) highlights the challenges of escaping the colonial library to produce decolonized knowledge. In the author's view, it is more important to think about resistance than escape from the colonial library and to recognize that resistance is still possible even without it. Arguing from the South African context, Matthews (2020) calls for the following two actions:

1. There is a need to rethink the coloniality of knowledge regarding how a researcher produces knowledge, who is considered capable of producing knowledge, and how, and whether, different stakeholders contest knowledge claims.
2. In addition, there is a need to recognize the possibility of emancipatory re-appropriation through which elements of the colonial library can be used by the colonized in ways that resist the colonial tradition.

Modern African librarianship is anchored on Western ideologies, as evidenced by numerous studies that concur that the colonial empires established Western-model libraries to serve their interests. According to Strand and Britz (2018) and Young (2021), the local people are a subservient class even though it is unclear if they ever considered it. Using decolonization as a strategy to escape the colonial library, Grosz-Ngaté (2020) considers it a method of breaking the colonial contract with the colonial library that transcends the academy and conventional boundaries between inside and outside; hence, there is a need for an alternative way of seeing, decentering, and a re-centering of knowledge as well. African universities must own this process and be more combative in producing knowledge and education while relying on local and endogenous resources as much as possible (Grosz-Ngaté, 2020). In the library or archive, decoloniality involves an active undoing, deconstruction, or delinking from coloniality, and this differs from the process of diversifying collections or ensuring a range of narratives represented in a multimedia format (Crilly, 2019). In reflecting on university curriculum discussions, Quijano (2000) highlight the frequent calls for academic libraries to be less Eurocentric, and they describe "euro-centricity" as follows:

> …a perspective of knowledge whose systematic formation began in Western Europe before the middle of the seventeenth century, although its roots are without doubt much older…It does not refer to all the modes of knowledge or all Europeans and all epochs. It is instead a specific rationality or perspective of knowledge that was made globally hegemonic, colonizing and overcoming other previous or different conceptual formations as much in Europe as the rest of the world (Quijano 2000, p. 549). Instead of decoloniality being reformist, it is radical rather than reformist, focusing less on the struggle to include and represent difference and marginality within colonial forms than on the destabilization and unsettlement of structures—diffused, naturalized, and habitual—that instill colonial power relations (Shultz et al., 2018, p. 1).

As a result of their support of open systems and academic practices, libraries play a crucial role in facilitating access to research and scholarship (Crilly, 2019). In addition, libraries can challenge the high costs of commercially produced journals, providing a level playing field for knowledge production and circulation (Crilly, 2019). Neocolonial onslaughts will severely hamper our capacity to make systematic ventures beyond our current knowledge horizons if we, as Africans, rely exclusively on those aspects of the Western archive that disregard other epistemic traditions (Mbembe, 2015).

The beauty and joy of storytelling is that it allows the listener to take the meaning as stories prepare us for our future; in other words, stories must touch us where we are today, here in our bodies and hearts, to challenge us to think, examine our emotional reactions, and reflect on a story's connection to our lives and spirit as well as extend that connection to all creation (Penak, 2018).

Digitization of Library Collections as a Decolonial Strategy

Ancient libraries are meaningful for projecting knowledge that will be relevant for the future as they hold a wealth of information for communities, including their stories, ceremonies, dirges, and merges culture (classical art of African conversation), medicines, rare book collections (Egyptian and Malian incunabula), and the sacred places (cultural heritage). The San and Khoikhoi people (first nations of Southern Africa) captured their history as cultural heritage through rock paintings. Lessons can be drawn from them for preserving hunter-gatherer communities and developing a historical and cultural collage of images for posterity. The degree of socioeconomic organization of the San and Khoi people based on the communal mode of production provides evidence to counter the Eurocentric assertions that Europeans brought civilization to them.

The Indigenous archive of the First Nations of Southern Africa in rock art provides evidence regarding the division of labor and the existence of vibrant social systems regarding work and economic livelihood. Such cultural heritage helps dispel the lies and myths of African history as one of darkness and blankness as peddled by Trevor-Roper (1965).

These libraries should therefore be used to leverage emerging technologies in digitizing their collections and develop institutional or digital repositories to ingest, store, manage, preserve, and provide access to digital content (Masenya & Chisita, 2022). Digital technologies have been a game changer, enabling access to information and knowledge. Epistemic diversity and social justice are not necessarily brought about by digitization unless used to accelerate decolonization (Turner, 2023). The emergence of digital libraries has also changed the paradigms of libraries by transforming traditional libraries' operations services, aiding space-saving through alternative digital spatial reconfigurations, and promoting access to knowledge.

Concern over limited access and loss of African knowledge and library collections due to colonization and globalization and that African communities may lose control and rights over their knowledge has also raised a need to digitize this knowledge in order to decolonize it. According to Turner (2023), digitization is the binary coding of information, knowledge, and social practices to diversify and enhance access. As Innerhofer et al. (2020) note, digitization exceeds the mere establishment of a symbolic machine-readable representation from the analog sign by encompassing the migration and transformation of social structures to digital logic and technology. African indigenous knowledge, history, libraries, and archives exist in the minds of the departed (living dead, ancestors), the living, and the dreams (intuition), artifacts, rituals, symbols, and oral traditions. Decolonization through digitization can play a role in the dissemination and accessibility of library collections and knowledge by the public. Decolonization aims to productively and justly remedy colonial structures evidenced by the widespread dominance, institutionalization, and normativity of Western scientific paradigms, practices, and lines of descent (Turner, 2023). Unsettling epistemic and coloniality of knowledge through digitization is the common ground within the decolonial impetus. First, decolonization entails territorial decolonization, achieved by the dissolution of colonial relations; and second, structural decolonization, which entails undoing colonial mechanisms of power, economics, language, culture, and thought governing contemporary society, as well as interrogating dominant forms of knowledge, values, norms, and assumptions about their legitimacy and provenance (Mohamed et al., 2020). Other decolonial strategies should include centralizing non-European narratives and autobiographies, emphasizing positionality in producing knowledge, and dismantling dominant power systems.

Critical Points from the Literature

Africa's role in contributing to human civilization is an undeniable scientific fact as evidenced by studies conducted by leading researchers, including James (1954, 1992), Amadi (1981), Ocholla (2003), Mchombu et al. (2004), Mchombu and Cadbury (2006), Goody (2006), James (2013), Cartwright (2019), Zulu (2023), Williams (2020), and Nhemachena (2023), whose writings provide substantive evidence of an ancient African history worthy of serious recognition. These authors' findings invalidate the assertion of Trevor-Roper (1965) and Conrad' (1899) that the African past is not worthy of study because of reports of void coupled with gross barbarism. Trevor-Roper, for instance, puts it as follows: "…to begin with, the black people have no historic pasts. Never having evolved civilizations of their own, they are practically devoid of that accumulated mass of beliefs, thoughts, and experiences that are impenetrable and so hostile" (Trevor-Roper 1965, p. 9), His claim is echoed by the *Patriot Newspaper* (2017) as follows:

> The British historian Trevor-Roper (1965) expressed as well as any this idea: Undergraduates, seduced, as always, by the changing breath of journalistic fashion, demand that they should be taught the history of black Africa. Perhaps, in the future, there will be some African history to teach. But at present, there is none, or very little: there is only the history of the Europeans in Africa. The rest is largely darkness, like the history of pre-European, pre-Columbian America. And darkness is not a subject of history (Tribute to Pioneer of African History, *The Patriot*, February 16, 2017, p. 1)

In his assertions, Trevor-Roper (1965) provides a myopic perspective that reflects racial intonations, considering the findings of the great scholars who have highlighted and exalted African civilization as the basis of modern culture in libraries, knowledge production, and academia (James, 1954, 1992, 2013; Amadi, 1981; Ocholla, 2003; Mchombu et al., 2004; Mchombu & Cadbury, 2006; Goody, 2006; Cartwright, 2019; Zulu, 2023; Williams, 2020; Nhemachena, 2023). Other critical issues raised in this chapter relate to the coloniality of knowledge as articulated by Quijano (2000), Kaur and Kehal (2023), Mbembe (2015), Mudimbe (2020), and Ndlovu (2018). The combative decolonial approach by Quijano (2000) has a significant impact on advocates for a radical approach to decolonization that calls for the destabilization and unsettlement of all forms of colonialism that instill colonial power relations. The library is no exception to the struggle for decolonization because colonial ideas are embedded in the mind; hence, there is a need for new mental costumes (Durodolu et al., 2021).

Conceptualizations of Africa in the Field of Library Studies

Discussed in this section is how Africa has been conceptualized in the discipline of Library Studies, also referred to as Library Science and Library and Information Science. There are many of these conceptualizations; but, for the sake of conciseness, four of them were selected at random and reviewed here. Also, for perspicuity, the conceptualizations are presented individually in the subsections that follow.

Afrocentric Library

The conceptualization of "Afrocentric library" in the field of Library Studies is in reference to libraries in Africa in their current context with a slight turn to the past, in light of their heavier emphasis on publications in the last century. Scholars using this perspective postulate a small number of questions related to Library Studies in Africa and deal with these questions through an analysis of publications from Africa or about Africa. They focus on information, its dynamics and utility at the individual, organizational, and societal levels apropos its rapid growth (Bitso, 2013).

These scholars seek to achieve two major objectives in their work. The first objective is to delineate a broad sphere that would allow them to critically investigate and analyze research in information-centered disciplines such as Computer Science, Information Science, and Library Science since they are rudimentary to the utilization of information either from the system or the human orientation. The second objective is to furnish tenets for the analysis of a variety of topics as they relate to the theoretical, empirical and technical developments of information-centered disciplines (Bitso, 2013).

Colonial Library Africa

In the academic discipline of Library Studies, the concept of "colonial library Africa" concerns the texts on Africa produced within a colonial substructure and the wider system of knowledge and denotation established by these texts. The conceptualization is characterized as notional and geared toward describing the extensive body of texts and systems of representation that for many centuries has functioned to produce Africa as a concept of contrast and otherness (Wai, 2015).

Colonial Library Africa has also been described in two other ways. First, it is said to be a product of a "transdisciplinary space of the huge knowledge capital which constitutes and is constitutive of the epistemological locus of Africa's invention." Second, it is denoted as an "incarnation of a paradox: i.e. while its knowledge capital serves to justify monstrosities such as Atlantic slavery and colonialism, it has also been from within the foundations of its power knowledge regimes that Africans themselves have sought to interrogate Western discourses on Africa, as well as produce their own notions of self-identity, discourses of otherness and ideologies of alterity" (Wai, 2015, p. 263).

The Famous Ancient Library

Africa was the home of the "famous ancient library" as a conceptualization in the field of Library Studies is in relation to the ancient al-Qarawiyyin Library in Fez (also spelled Fes) in Morocco. Established in 859 AD, the library is both the oldest in Africa and the oldest working library in the world, and endowed with ancient manuscripts that date as far back as twelfth century (Eng, 2016). The following are some of the great attributes of the library that are touted by scholars of Library Studies:

> The al-Qarawiyyin Library was created by a woman, challenging commonly held assumptions about the contribution of women in Muslim civilization. The al-Qarawiyyin, which includes a mosque, library, and university, was founded by Fatima El-Fihriya, the daughter of a rich immigrant from al-Qayrawan (Tunisia today). Well educated and devout, she vowed to spend her entire inheritance on building a mosque and knowledge center for her

> community. According to UNESCO, the result is the oldest operational educational institution in the world, with a high-profile role call of alumni. Mystic poet and philosopher Ibn Al-'Arabi studied there in the 12th Century, historian and economist Ibn Khaldun attended in the 14th Century, while in medieval times, Al-Qarawiyyin played a leading role in the transfer of knowledge between Muslims and Europeans (Eng, 2016, p. 1).

The preceding excerpt is particularly important because it highlights the fact that women have played significant roles in the development of Africa that date back many centuries.

The City of Famous Libraries and Scholars

Scholars in the discipline of Library Studies conceptualize Africa as the home of the "city of famous libraries and scholars" to describe the long-lasting and famous scholarly contributions to Islamic and world civilizations in the books that were written by Islamic scholars and copied there beginning from at least the fourteenth century. As scholars in the field of Library Studies are quick to point out, the legendary city of Timbuktu was founded as a commercial center in West Africa 900 years ago, albeit it is regarded today as being utterly remote. Nonetheless, these scholars add, this was not always the case, in that for over 600 years, Timbuktu was a significant commercial, cultural, and religious center whose residents traveled north across the Sahara through Morocco and Algeria to other parts of Africa, Asia, and Europe. These scholars also point out that Timbuktu's location on the edge of the Sahara Desert made it famous among the merchants of the Mediterranean basin as a market for obtaining the goods and products of Africa south of the desert. Accordingly, many people traveled to Timbuktu to acquire wealth and political power (Library of Congress, 2024).

In addition, Library Studies scholars note that many budding scholars went to Timbuktu to study. Concomitantly, the city became revered for the education of leading scholars whose standing was "Pan-Islamic." Furthermore, the geniuses of Sankoré or the University of Timbuktu were unmatched in all of Africa South of the Sahara and were well-known across the Islamic world (Library of Congress, 2024).

Conclusion and Recommendations

Conclusively, this chapter argues that African librarianship has come a long way from the ancient era (6500 BC) to the twenty-first century. The conceptualization of African libraries cannot be complete without connecting them to ancient libraries and ancient ways of generating, processing, representing, sharing, and archiving knowledge for posterity. The definitive question of the chapter is the following: "What lessons can be drawn by the present generation of African librarians from the groundwork and legacy of scholarship that characterized the precolonial African past? This chapter concludes the discourse by making a conclusive statement and suggesting policy recommendations and the way forward. First, when knowledge from different communities is available in libraries for everyone to read, it helps to foster a better understanding of others and how the phenomenon of libraries is connected. It encourages people to appreciate those unique attributes instead of using them as disparities to increase the gap between individuals and their heritages. Nonetheless, most African countries are still underdeveloped due to neocolonialism as these countries are brutally subjugated and exploited by Western governments that overtly and covetously use soft power to manipulate and perpetuate intellectual imperialism.

Second, the project to decolonize libraries may be a long and arduous process; nevertheless, it is imperative to comprehend and apprehend its importance; therefore, there is a need to approach decolonization with mental costumes or lenses that are grounded in the aspirations of African people to realize their potential as a people with a globalizing civilizing mindset.

Third, African countries and their citizens have endured centuries of ideological bamboozlement due to colonialism and neocolonialism to believe that the colonial way was the better way and must therefore be willing to admit that policies and protocols (i.e., knowledge production and accessing policy) to which they adhered were wrong and should acknowledge their ignorance and stereotypes in their societies passed down across generations (Durodolu et al., 2021).

Fourth, the Oriental and Occidental world must respect African people's beliefs, values, and concerns of different communities. China has become a big imperial power considering its investment in Africa and may wonder whether it is the new imperialist disguised as a savior? The time is nigh for Africa to rethink, reset, and re-strategize regarding alternative development pathways that do not undermine its sovereignty as a sovereign continent.

Fifth, in collaboration with communities, policymakers, university libraries, and higher education facilities should unite to effectively decolonize libraries and make African knowledge accessible to all knowledge-seekers. Such initiatives are important because libraries exist for people to enable them to realize their potential as equals in democratic spaces.

Sixth, time has dawned to jettison colonial thinking hallucinations and the need to demolish colonial and neocolonial structures, including edifices and the superstructure, if Africa is to move forward and reclaim its place as a continent among other continents.

Indeed, libraries are the sine qua non-*institutions* in the current battle of the mental universe. Libraries are growing organizations; as such, change is the only persistent factor as we move toward establishing African "*truebraries*" that will serve as an ark to provide for our beloved continent's diverse, dynamic, and growing epistemological and axiological needs as Africans imbued with the spirit of genuine Africanism and combative decoloniality.

References

Amadi, A. O. (1981). *African libraries: Western tradition and colonial brainwashing*. Scarecrow Press.

Bitso, C. (2013, October). Afro-centric library and information science discourse analysis. *Revue de l'Enssib*, 1. Retrieved July 3, 2024, from https://www.enssib.fr/bibliotheque-numerique/documents/66399-afro-centric-library-and-information-science-discourse-analysis.pdf

Blume, R., & Roylance, A. (2020). Decolonization in collection development: Developing an authentic authorship workflow. *Journal of Academic Librarianship, 46*(5), 102175.

Boadi, B. Y. (2006). Income-generating activities: A viable financial source for African academic libraries? *The Bottom Line, 19*(2), 64–77.

Bob-Milliar, G. M. (2022). Africa's contributions to world civilization. In *The Palgrave handbook of Africa and the changing global order* (pp. 25–42). Palgrave.

Brook, F., Ellenwood, D., & Lazzaro, A. E. (2015). In pursuit of antiracist social justice: Denaturalizing whiteness in the academic library. *Library Trends, 64*(2), 246–284.

Cartwright, M. (2019). *Libraries in the ancient world*. World History Encyclopedia. Retrieved September 18, 2023, from https://www.worldhistory.org/article/1428/libraries-in-the-ancient-world/

Chisita, C. T. (2011). *Role of libraries in promoting the dissemination and documentation of indigenous agricultural information: Case study of Zimbabwe* (pp. 10–11). IFLA WLIC.

Chong, R., & Edwards, A. (2022). *Indigenizing Canadian academic libraries: Two librarians' experiences*. Facet.

Conrad, J. (1899). The heart of darkness. *Blackwood's Edinburgh Magazine*.

Cox, A. M., Tiago Martins, J., & Rivera Gonzalez, G. (2020). Reassessing the LIS approach to traditional knowledge: Learning from Xochimilco, Mexico City. *Journal of Documentation, 76*(5), 981–997.

Crilly, J. (2019). Decolonizing the library: A theoretical exploration. *Spark: UAL Creative Teaching and Learning Journal, 4*(1), 6–15.

David, A. R. (1999). *Handbook to life in ancient Egypt*. Oxford University Press.

Davis, G. R. (2015). New imperatives for librarianship in Africa. *Library Trends, 64*(1), 125–135.

Dei, G. J. S. (2002). Spirituality in African education: Issues, contentions, and contestations from a Ghanaian case study. *International Journal of Children Spirituality, 7*(1), 37–56.

Demeter, M. (2019). The world-systemic dynamics of knowledge production: The distribution of transnational academic capital in the social sciences. *Journal of World-Systems Research, 25*(1), 112–144.

Durodolu, O. O., Ibenne, S. K., & Dube, T. V. (2021). New mental costumes: Leveraging ACRL's value of information frame in dealing with infodemics in a post-truth era. *College and Research Libraries News, 82*(4), 175.

El-Abbadi, M., Fathallah, O., & Serageldin, I. (Eds.). (2008). *What happened to the ancient library of Alexandria?* Brill.

Eng, K. F. (2016, March 1). *Restoring the world's oldest library*. Ideas.Ted.Com. Retrieved July 3, 2024, from https://ideas.ted.com/restoring-the-worlds-oldest-library/

Goody, J. (2006). *The theft of history*. Cambridge University Press.

Grosz-Ngaté, M. (2020). Knowledge and power: Perspectives on the production and decolonization of African/ist knowledge. *African Studies Review, 63*(4), 689–718.

Haikal, F. M. (2008). Private collections and temple libraries in ancient Egypt. In M. El-Abbadi, O. Fathallah, & I. Serageldin (Eds.), *What happened to the ancient library of Alexandria?* Brill.

Harrison, F. V. (1999). Decolonizing anthrolopology: Moving further toward an anthropology for liberation 2nd edition. *Anthropology News, 40*(2), 31–31.

Innerhofer, E., et al. (2020). Introduction. In G. Isetti, E. Innerhofer, H. Pechlaner, & M. de Rachewiltz (Eds.), *Religion in the age of digitalization: From new media to spiritual machines*. Routledge.

James, G. G. (1954). *Stolen legacy: The reeks were not the authors of Greek philosophy, but the people of North Africa commonly called the Egyptians*. Philosophical Library.

James, G. G. (1992). *Stolen legacy: Greek philosophy is stolen Egyptian philosophy*, later edn. Africa Research and Publications.

James, G. G. (2013). *Stolen legacy*. Simon & Schuster.

Jimenez, A., Vannini, S., & Cox, A. (2022). A holistic decolonial lens for library and information studies. *Journal of Documentation, 79*(1), 224–244.

Kaur, H., & Kehal, P. S. (2023). Epistemic wounded attachments: Recovering definitional subjectivity through colonial libraries. *History and Theory, 62*(2), 203–224.

Leavy, P. (2022). *Research design: Quantitative, qualitative, mixed methods, arts-based, and community-based participatory research approaches*. Guilford Publications.

Library of Congress. (2024). *Timbuktu: An Islamic cultural center. Collection: Islamic manuscripts from Mali*. Retrieved July 3, 2024, from https://www.loc.gov/collections/islamic-manuscripts-from-mali/articles-and-essays/timbuktu-an-islamic-cultural-center/

Masenya, T. M., & Chisita, C. T. (2022). Futurizing library services in a technology-driven dispensation: Reflections on selected academic libraries in Zimbabwe and South Africa. In T. M. Masenya (Ed.), *Innovative technologies for enhancing knowledge access in academic libraries*. IGI Global.

Matthews, S. (2020). Confronting the colonial library: Teaching political studies amidst calls for a decolonized curriculum. In L. Piper (Ed.), *Decolonization after democracy*. Routledge.

Mbembe, A. J. (2015) *Decolonizing knowledge and the question of the archive*. Public lectures given at the Wits Institute for Social and Economic Research (WISER), University of Witwatersrand, Johannesburg, University of Cape Town and University of Stellenbosch. Retrieved September 18, 2023, from https://wiser.wits.ac.za/system/files/Achille%20Mbembe%20%20Decolonizing%20Knowledge%20and%20the%20Question%20of%20the%20Archive.pdf

Mchombu, K., & Cadbury, N. (2006). *Libraries, literacy and poverty reduction: A key to African development*. Retrieved December 7, 2023, from https://repository.unam.edu.na/bitstream/handle/11070/1325/Mchombu_libraries_2006.pdf?sequence=1&isAllowed=y/

Mchombu, K., Evans, G., Bruton, K., & Cocks, A. (2004). *Sharing knowledge for community development and transformation: A handbook*. Retrieved September, 7, 2023, from https://repository.unam.edu.na/bitstream/handle/11070/1286/Mchombu_sharing_2004.pdf?sequence=1&isAllowed=y/

Mji, G. (2019). *Opting for a walk without limbs: The avoidance of Stellenbosch University to be an African University*. Stellenbosch University Library Auditorium. Retrieved December, 7, 2023, from http://www.sun.ac.za/english/Documents/2019/G%20Mji%20-%20Symposium%20on%20Restructuring%20SU%20Research.pdf/

Mohamed, S., Png, M. T., & Isaac, W. (2020). Decolonial AI: Decolonial theory as sociotechnical foresight in artificial intelligence. *Philosophy and Technology, 33*, 659–684.

Mokhtar, G. (Ed.). (1980). *UNESCO general history of Africa (Vol. II: Abridged edition: Ancient Africa)*. James Currey and UNESCO.

Mudimbe, V. Y. (2020). *The invention of Africa: Gnosis, philosophy, and the order of knowledge (reprint)*. Lulu Press.

Ndlovu, M. (2018). Coloniality of knowledge and the challenge of creating African futures. *Ufahamu: A Journal of African Studies, 40*(2), 95–112.

Nhemachena, A. (2023). Chisi Chako Masimba Mashoma/Kunzi Pakata Sandi Kunzi Ridza: Anthropological musings on the coloniality of dispossession in Africa. *Journal of Black Studies, 54*(2), 87–110.

Nyamnjoh, F. B. (2012). 'Potted plants in greenhouses': A critical reflection on the resilience of colonial education in Africa. *Journal of Asian and African studies, 47*(2), 129–154.

Ocholla, D. N. (2003). An overview of information and communication technologies (ICT) in the LIS schools of eastern and southern Africa. *Education for Information, 21*(2–3), 181–194.

Okunoye, A., & Karsten, H. (2003). Global access to knowledge in research: Findings from organizations in sub-Saharan Africa. *Information Technology and People, 16*(3), 353–373.

Overbey, T., & Folk, A. L. (2022). *Narratives of (dis)enfranchisement: Reckoning with the history of libraries and the Black and African American experience*. American Library Association. Retrieved September 16, 2023, from https://books.google.co.za/books?hl=en&lr=&id=NtTFEAAAQBAJ&oi=fnd&pg=PP1&dq=ancient+african+librarianship&ots=bQxq5LLU75&sig=Hn2gf08UPJgy4KiGOQBP4T5_IOY&redir_esc=y#v=onepage&q=ancient%20african%20librarianship&f=false/

Penak, N. (2018). A story pathway: Restoring wholeness in the research process. In D. McGregor, J. Restoule, & R. Johnstone (Eds.), *Indigenous research: Theories, practices, and relationships*. Canadian Scholars Press.

Quijano, A. (2000). Coloniality of power and Eurocentrism in Latin America. *International Sociology, 15*(2), 215–232.

Sawyer, R. K. (2004). Creative teaching: Collaborative discussion as disciplined improvisation. *Educational Researcher, 33*(2), 12–20.

Seth, S. (2013). Once was blind but now can see: Modernity and the social sciences. *International Political Sociology, 7*(2), 136–151.

Shultz, T., et al. (2018). Editor's introduction: Decolonizing design. *Design and Culture, 10*(1), 1–6.

Sibiya, P. T., & Ngulube, P. (2023). Perceptions of employers in South Africa on library and information science graduates' skills, knowledge and competencies on digital scholarship. *Heliyon, 9*(2).

Singleton, B. D. (2004). African bibliophiles: Books and libraries in medieval Timbuktu. *Libraries and Culture, 39*(1), 1–12.

Smart, P. (2005). Increasing the visibility of published research: African journals online. *Africa Today, 52*(2), 39–53.

Sroka, M. (2003). The destruction of Jewish libraries and archives in Cracow during World War II. *Libraries & Culture*, 147–165.

Strand, K. J., & Britz, J. (2018). The evolving role of public libraries in South Africa in addressing information poverty: a historical context. *Library Management, 39*(6-7), 364–374.

Tabares, J. (2022). The Coloniality of knowledge and situated knowledge. *En-Contexto, 10*(17), 41–44.

Tise, E. R., & Raju, R. (2015). African librarianship: A relic, a fallacy, or an imperative? *Library Trends, 64*(1), 3–18.

Trevor-Roper, H. R. (1965). *The rise of Christian Europe*. Thames & Hudson.

Trevor-Roper, H. R. (1969). The past and the present. History and sociology. *Past and Present, 42*, 3–17.

Tribute to the pioneer of African history. (2017, February 16). Retrieved September 29, 2023, from https://www.thepatriot.co.zw/old_posts/tribute-to-pioneer-of-african-history/

Turner, I. (2023). Decolonization through digitalization? African languages at South African Universities. *Curriculum Perspectives*, 1–10.

UNESCO Institute for Statistics and Sector of Culture. (2005). *International Flows of Selected Cultural Goods and Services, 1994–2003: Defining and Capturing the Flow of Global Cultural Trade*. UNESCO.

Wai, Z. (2015). On the predicament of Africanist knowledge: Mudimbe, gnosis and the challenge of the colonial library. *International Journal of Francophone Studies, 18*(2–3), 263–290.

Williams, D. L., & Muchena, O. N. (1991). Utilizing indigenous knowledge systems in agricultural education to promote sustainable agriculture. *Journal of Agricultural Education, 32*(4), 52–57.

Williams, C. (2020). *The destruction of Black civilization: Great issues of a race from 4500 BC to 2000 AD*. Lulu.com.

Young, J. C. (2021). Environmental colonialism, digital indigeneity, and the politicization of resilience. *Environment and Planning E: Nature and Space, 4*(2), 230–251.

Zulu, I. M. (2017). Synergizing culture: African American cultural recovery through African name acquisition and usage. *Africology: The Journal of Pan African Studies, 10*(5), 128–154.

Zulu, I. M. (2023). The ancient Kemetic roots of library and information science. *Journal of Pan-African Studies, 5*(1), 1–26.

Collence Takaingenhamo Chisita holds a PhD in Library and Information Science. He is a Research Fellow at the University of South Africa (UNISA) in the Department of Information Science in Pretoria, South Africa. He has authored five books, over 20 book chapters, and more than 25 scholarly articles. He is the legatee of the National Research Foundation of South Africa C2 rating for research excellence. He has navigated the globe as a presenter and contributed to Library Information Science through webinars and physical contibutions. He is also a mentor for LIS students at the University of Pretoria in South Africa. He is fluent in Shona, Creole, and English languages, and enjoys researching the tremorous alterations in the information ambiance in the context of world history and how events in one place are connected to the rest of the world.

Tlou Maggie Masenya holds a PhD in Information Science from the University of South Africa and a Master's in Information Technology from the University of Pretoria. She has nine years of experience as a senior lecturer in Information Science, Information Systems and Technology. She is currently heading the Information Technology Department at the Durban University of Technology. She has published two books with numerous book chapters and journal articles focusing on emerging technologies. She is a guest editor for two special issues in IEEE International Journal of Biomedical and Health Informatics and *New Pedagogies and Technology Driven Innovations in Improving the Quality of Learning and Teaching*.

Literature

Somtochukwu J. Metu

The focus of this chapter is on the conceptualization of Africa in the discipline of Literature; a field that dedicates itself to the curation of written and spoken words and works. African Literature dedicates itself to issues that concern the African continent, issues that span across her countries, regions, and provinces. To make clear the objectives of this chapter, the crucial question that is brought to the fore is the following: In what ways have Africa been conceptualized in the field of Literature? Given the broadness of Literature, it will be quite difficult for the answer to this question to cover its multitudinous tentacles. For the task before me, I will examine the conceptualization of Africa in the academic discipline of Literature through three lenses: (1) African Literature and the Negritude Movement, (2) Re-examination of Gender Roles in African Literature, and (3) Identity and Identity Reconstruction in African Literature.

The methodology applied to the analysis of this work is a qualitative research methodology that is descriptive and narrative in approach. This methodology involves textual interpretation of literary texts that examine the aforementioned conceptualizations and how they foreground themselves in the discipline of Literature and, in narrowed form, African Literature. Having given a brief and general introduction to what I intend to do in this chapter and before an in-depth analysis of the three frameworks, I will, in the ensuing section, examine the general principles of Literature.

S. J. Metu (✉)
English and Literary Studies, University of Nigeria, Nsukka, Nsukka, Nigeria
e-mail: somtochukwu.metu@unn.edu.ng; somtochukwu.metu.pg80722@unn.edu.ng

A. K. Bangura, J. A. Ifedi (eds.), *Conceptualizations of Africa*, African Studies and Research Forum Series, https://doi.org/10.1007/978-3-031-74535-5_21

Literature: A Conceptualization

Literature as an academic field and, despite its broadness, has generally been grouped into three genres: (1) Prose, (2) Drama, and (3) Poetry. Each of these genres also engenders subgenres. For better understanding of the academic discipline referred to as Literature, I will discuss its genres and their elements one at a time in the following subsections.

Prose

Prose is a genre of Literature that describes forms of writings that abhor rigid rules of writings. It mostly manifests itself in narrative form. Prose as a genre is further divided into fiction and nonfiction. Fiction, which is the aspect of prose that concerns this chapter, is further divided into (a) short story, (b) novella, and (c) novel. Despite these divisions of fiction as an aspect of prose, all three forms function under five tenets. These tenets are discussed in the ensuing paragraphs.

First, there is an element referred to as *Plot* which constitutes the dynamic whole to which the other parts of a work relate to. It is the distilling center of the choices available to the author; having determined a medium and a mode. For a coherent plot, an author must also choose other essential principles like theme and setting which are the other elements that will be examined after the discussion on plot. Plot must "have a shape; it must have a sequence or order determining the kind and degree of effort at particular points, it must have a size which will help determine that shape and sequence. It must have agents and a society: there must be a language, appropriate not only to them but also to the other elements of the structure" (Childs, 2006, p. 177). Plot is the house that engenders other elements of fiction. In its simplified form, it means sequences of events and incidents that make up a story. A fictitious work in a prosaic form cannot live up to its name and definition without a plot.

Second, there is an element referred to as *Theme.* It is a general concept or doctrine, whether implicit or asserted, which an imaginative work is designed to involve and make persuasive to the reader. Theme is a branch of a subject matter which is indirectly expressed through the recurrence of certain events, images or symbols. It is seen as a thread running through a work, linking features which are related or unrelated. The theme of a fictitious work is the crux of the work. Just like plot, it influences other elements of prosaic work.

Conflict is the third element in the conceptualization of prose as a genre of Literature. A conflict is "a literary device characterized by a struggle between two opposing forces. Conflict provides crucial tension in any story and is used to drive the narrative forward. It is often used to reveal a deeper meaning in a narrative while highlighting characters' motivations, values, and weaknesses" (MasterClass, 2021, p. 1). Conflict as conceptualized in Literature can be internal, external, against nature, environment, and the supernatural. It basically refers to when a character wants something but fate thwarts this plan and gets in the way.

Fourth is *Characterization*, which is a literary device that is used in Literature to highlight and explain the details about a character in a story. It is in the initial stage of a prosaic work that a writer introduces certain characters with noticeable emergence. After introducing these characters, the writer often talks about their behavior; then, as the story progresses, the thought processes of the characters. In characterization, "ideas of the place of the human in the social order, of human individuality and self-determination, clearly shift historically; and this is often mimed in literature by the relation of characters to actions or webs of story. The idea of character often attaches, therefore, to the personalizing or humanizing dimension of literature" (Childs, 2006, p. 23).

Fifth, there is the element of *Setting*. The overall setting of a narrative or dramatic work is "the general locale, historical time, and social circumstances in which its action occurs; the setting of a single episode or scene within the work is the particular physical location in which it takes place" (Abrams, 2009, p. 360). The makeup and behavior of fictional characters often depend on their environment quite as much as on their personal characteristics. It sometimes happens that the main locale of a novel assumes an importance in the reader's imagination comparable to that of the characters (Britannica, 2016). The setting of a novel may be an actual city or region made greater than life. It may also be completely the work of an author's imagination.

Drama

Drama is the genre of Literature that concerns itself with the performance of incidents on stage. These incidents and events may be written or quickly composed by dramatists, but the crux of the existence of drama is performance. The conceptualization of this genre of Literature is viewed through these elements. First is a *Stage*, which refers to a platform in a theater for the performance of drama. A dramatic performance cannot be possible without a stage where dramatis personas act and bring to life the written and oral forms of drama. An important aspect of drama that helps with the smooth communication of actions from personas to the audience is stage direction. In a drama,

> stage directions communicate information for the dramatists, director, and designers. This information is communicated in two ways. First, the scene often begins with a paragraph setting the scene. This typically describes where and when the scene is set, what the stage looks like including important information like props and scenic items, and which characters are there when the scene opens. These stage directions take the form of short paragraphs or full sentences and are often italicized. They are used to relay information about the play's action that are not captured in the dialogue (Study.com, 2021, p. 1).

The second elements are *Monologue* and *Dialogue*. These two go hand in hand because they are used for effective communication between a dramatis persona and himself/herself and a dramatis persona and other personas and audience. A monologue is a speech that may be in an extended form delivered by a dramatis persona on stage. It may be in the form of a *soliloquy* or an *aside*. A soliloquy refers to a speech by a dramatis persona intended for only his/her ears and that of the audience. The speech reveals the inner thoughts and ideas of a character. It is conspiratory in nature as other personas are on stage when it is delivered and it is also meant for only the hearing of the audience. A dialogue is a written line spoken aloud and performed by more than one dramatis persona for effective communication on stage.

The third element is *Chorus*. This represents the voice of a personality commenting on events and interpreting the moral and religious wisdom of the play. The chorus, in its plurality "served mainly as commentators on the dramatic actions and events who expressed traditional moral, religious, and social attitudes. They were presented as attendants and witnesses of the suffering, death, and self-transformation of their master, the god Dionysus" (Abrams, 2009, p. 46). In Greek mythology, Dionysus is a god of pleasure, fertility, wine, and, in extension, theater; the theater being a presentation of all things pleasurable and gory.

Acts and *Scenes* are the fourth twin elements of drama. Acts and scenes refer to the structural foundations of a dramatic work, which is a written form and also referred to as a play made up of acts and scenes. Acts in drama denote the partition of different actions and sequences of events in a drama. Often, this partition takes into consideration themes and actions, especially as they affect the lives of the dramatis personas. The further division of acts is referred to as scenes. In drama, the end of a scene and the introduction of a new one are marked by blackouts and curtain draws.

Poetry

Poetry is the genre of Literature marked by its distinction in structure and arrangement. It portrays stories, ideas and thoughts in couplets, sonnets, stanzas and verses which are sometimes made up of rhyme schemes. Sabarno Sinha brings to mind the encompassing definition of poetry by one of the greatest English Romantic poets William Wordsworth. He defines poetry as "the spontaneous overflow of powerful feelings: it takes its origin from emotion recollected in tranquillity" (Sinha, 2020, p. 1). The paragraphs that follow will further examine the conceptualization of poetry as a genre of Literature.

The first element I look at is *Imagery*, which suggests the way objects, ideas, and patterns of thoughts are formed in our heads and in our minds' eyes. It is used to signify all the objects and qualities of sense perception referred to in a poem or other works of Literature, whether by literal description, by allusion, or in the vehicles of its similes and metaphors. Imagery should not be taken to imply a visual reproduction of the object denoted; some readers of a passage experience visual images and some do not; and among those who do, the explicitness and details of the pictures vary greatly. Also, imagery in this usage includes not only visual sense qualities but also qualities that are auditory, tactile (touch), thermal (heat and cold), olfactory (smell), gustatory (taste), and kinesthetic (sensations of movement) (Childs, 2006).

The twin elements of *Tone* and *Mood* are the second forms examined here. The tone of a piece of poetry is dependent on the stance of the poet. His/her general attitude toward a subject matter is reflected in his/her writing. It is his/her response that engenders the response of readers toward his poetry which in turn is defined as the mood of a piece of poetry. Tone and mood go hand in hand as they give off the point of view and attitude of a poet toward his work and the response such attitude will generate.

Poetic Devices are the next elements that are conceptualized under poetry as a genre of Literature. Poetic devices are literary devices that outline and transform words, sounds, and phrases in poetry to convey meaning. Poetic devices "empower speakers and writers to enhance the literal meaning of words by drawing attention to the sound, form, and function of words. This includes devices that are also classified as literary or rhetorical devices, such as many figures of speech" (Study.com, 2021, p. 1). Some common and reoccurring poetic devices are explained in the next paragraph because of their importance to the understanding of poetry.

Simile is an important and common poetic device. It involves the comparison of two distinct objects with the use of the words "as" or "like." This is opposed to the poetic device *metaphor*, which means "a word or expression that in literal usage denotes one kind of thing is applied to a distinctly different kind of thing, without asserting a comparison" (Abrams, 2009, p. 130). In the application of *personification*, an inanimate object or an abstract concept is spoken of as though it were endowed with life or with human attributes or feelings (Abrams, 2009). A *rhetorical question* is a device employed by a speaker or persona that does not require an answer. The asker of this question is already aware of the answer to his/her question and just wonders aloud. Rhetorical questions are demonstrated in poetry for emphasis, not for examination of the questions posed or for solutions to be proffered. *Metonymy* is a device that examines when one thing is applied to another with which it has become closely associated because of a frequent relation in common experience. Metonymy is closely associated with *Synecdoche*, which is a device whereby a part of something is used to signify the whole, or the whole is used to signify a part (Abrams, 2009). I will now go ahead and examine how Africa is conceptualized in the field of Literature in the next three sections.

African Literature and the Negritude Movement

This section attempts to answer the following question: How is Africa conceptualized in African Literature via the Negritude Movement? Answers to this question will be better understood with the examination of the idea of Negritude and the Negritude Movement.

Quoting Leopold Senghor, Sylvia Ba defines Negritude as "the sum of the cultural values of the black world as they are expressed in the life, the institutions, and the works of black men" (2016, p. 12). The Negritude Movement is today most closely identified with two great writers and poets: (1) Aimé Césaire and (2) Leopold Senghor. They met as students in Paris in the 1930s and in response to the racism they encountered, began to formulate and disseminate ideas that celebrated Black culture and personalities. This was in opposition to the dominant colonial discourses that perceived Africa as lacking in civilization and culture and of Africans as primitive savages (Britannica, 2023). At the heart of Negritude is a concern with "race," but its distinctiveness lies in the ways in which this racial foundation was developed and extended and to encompass an entire "way of life," intellectual, cultural, emotional, physical attributes that all Black people shared. This is the essentialist aspect of Negritude (Childs, 2006). Childs observes that

> The mystic warmth of African life, gaining strength from its closeness to nature and its constant contact with ancestors, should be continually placed in proper perspective against the soullessness and materialism of Western culture; that Africans must look to their own cultural heritage to determine the values and traditions that are most useful in the modern world; that committed writers should use African subject matter and poetic traditions and should excite a desire for political freedom; that Negritude itself encompasses the whole of African cultural, economic, social, and political values; and that, above all, the value and dignity of African traditions and peoples must be asserted (2006, p. 154).

Also, Alexander Onwumere and Florence Egbulonu note that the general ideas behind Negritude are summarized in five ways. First, the mystic warmth of African life, gaining strength from its closeness to nature and its constant contact with ancestors, should be constantly placed in proper perspective against the materialism of Western culture. Second, Africans must look to their own cultural heritage to determine the values and traditions that are most useful in the modern world. Third, committed writers should use African subject matter and poetic traditions and should excite a desire for political freedom. Fourth, Negritude itself encompasses the whole of African cultural, economic, social, and political values. Fifth, the values and dignity of African traditions and peoples must be asserted (Onwumere & Egbulonu, 2014).

The literature of Negritude is dominated by the collective unconscious of the Black writer as a member of a minority group which is subordinated to another and more powerful within the total political and social order. The literary themes of Negritude can therefore be seen as "a counter-movement; they constitute a symbolic progression from subordination to independence, from alienation to self-affirmation" (Irele, 1965, p. 512).

As I have established the premise of the Negritude Movement, I will further elaborate on why it is important for the movement to be conceptualized in Literature. The answers to this question are examined in the works of four sources and writers. The first text is Chinua Achebe's *Things Fall Apart*. This text is a response to Joyce Cary's portrayal of Africans as savages and primitive in his work, *Mister Johnson*. Set in Umuohia, *Things Fall Apart* explores the constant struggle of Black people to sustain their culture. For killing Ikefemuna, Okonkwo has been banished from Umuofia. So, he goes to Mbanta, the native village of Okonkwo's mother. While this is happening, missionaries come to Umuofia to preach and convert the natives to Christianity. They (the missionaries) "had built their church there, won a handful of coverts and were already sending evangelists to the surrounding towns and villages…" (Achebe, 1958, p. 101). These missionaries gather a lot of natives and talk to them through an interpreter. They tell the natives that their gods are false gods and also that the real God lives on high. They worshipped false gods, gods of woods and stones; the true God lived on high and that all men when they died went before Him for judgment (Achebe, 1958). The missionaries try to discard the native people's religious value and impose their religious beliefs on them. They set up schools and judiciary systems and expect the natives to attend the schools so they adopt European culture negating their root and originality. The White people also set up their own judiciary system slacking the native one. They brought in their judiciary system to protect their people and agents, and also to punish the natives who oppose them. In the name of preaching Christianity, "they have built an entire governing system. They want to convert all the black cultural entity into the white one. But apart from the church, the white man had also brought a government. They had built a court where the district commissioner judged cases in ignorance." (Onwumere & Egbulonu, 2014, p. 123). Despite these challenges that bedevil the land of Umuofia with the trespassing and invasion of their homes by missionaries, Okonkwo, being the major character in the text, rises above these challenges and chooses to retain the culture and tradition of his people, waging war against all forms of conversion and conversation with the missionaries. The way Achebe puts it, Okonkwo is a character unbent by the importation of new ideologies. Rather, all actions he takes in the text are suggestive of his desire to depict and appreciate everything Black and African.

The second source is Efua T. Sutherland's *Marriage of Anansewa.* In the text, which is set in rural Ghana, a father submits his daughter's suitors to a test so as to find out which one of them can display financial strength and also seek the welfare of his daughter. Aspects of African culture and tradition are still retained even with the numerous attempts to overhaul them. Ananse finally finds his choice and the daughter, Anansewa, is set for a happy marriage. In *The Marriage of Anansewa,* we see the significance of the "head-drink" as an important aspect by which marriage is legally established. It ratifies the marriage because it is considered evidence that attests to the fact that matrimonial union has duly been entered into. Thus, "it is the duty of any man wishing to marry to pay the head-drink before he can claim the woman as a wife" (Sutherland, 1975). The payment of bride price, for example, is typically viewed in the African marital tradition as the true sign of marital union, without which no marriage can be regarded as legal. The "placing of the head-drink (symbolized by a symbolic amount of money and some drinks) is a crucial procedure by which the marriage is legally registered in this drama, which is based on a Ghanaian tradition" (Abakah & Marfo, 2009, p. 37). Typically, members of the bride's family are given it by the suitor's family. Bride price is a sum of money or goods given to the bride's family by the groom. The bride price takes various forms that include the head-drink, pieces of clothes, ornaments, etc., and they vary depending on the ethnic group and clan. Togbe Klu declares his intentions of marriage to Ananse by presenting the head-drink of Anansewaa. Chief-Who-Is Chief also portrays the Ghanaian culture by presenting a ring, a bag of money, Dumas, white kente and velvet to Anansewaa. Traditional African worshippers offer prayers to the Supreme Being and gods by offering libation, which is the ritual pouring of liquid as an offering to gods or ancestors in memory of those who have died. It is common in many religions and continues to be offered in various cultures today. In African society, libation is offered to show appreciation and to seek protection from the ancestors or to curse someone for an offense.

While paying the bride price in some quarters is considered archaic and frowned upon as the exchange of human life in lieu of material wealth, it is in fact a huge part of West African culture and tradition. While the character Okonkwo in *Things Fall Apart* is one who ensures that the missionaries did not wipe away every aspect of his culture by the introduction of new culture which ultimately leads to culture clash and conflict, Ananse in *The Marriage of Anansewa*, is also a custodian of the customs and traditions of his people. Their sticking to their heritage and embracement of their culture and customs lend credence to the principles of the Negritude Movement.

The third source leads me to the exploration of David Diop's "Africa, My Africa." The persona in the poem reflects on the identity and struggles of Africa, invoking imagery of ancestral warriors, the blood and sweat of its people, the toil of slavery, and the resilience of the continent. Diop's "Africa, My Africa" stands as an important expression of Negritude, a literary and cultural movement that celebrates the African identity and resists the legacy of colonialism. Diop speaks of the "beautiful black blood that irrigates the fields," representing the suffering and sacrifices of the African people. He mentions the blood of sweat, signifying the labor and hard work put forth by Africans. He fondly remembers the African continent in these words:Africa of proud warriors in ancestral savannahs

Africa of whom my grandmother sings

…

The bitter taste of liberty (Diop, 1957, lines 2–3, 23).

The persona of "Africa, My Africa" poses a question to Africa, asking if it is "the back that is bent" that "breaks under the weight of humiliation." This imagery suggests the subjugation and oppression faced by Africans. Diop refers to the trembling back stripped red, which may represent the scars of oppression and the endurance of pain. The mention of the whip highlights the violence and brutality faced by African people "under the midday sun." In response to the persona's question, "a solemn voice replies that Africa is like a young and strong tree. This image represents the resilience and strength of the continent. The tree grows splendidly alone, standing among white and faded flowers, symbolizing the contrast between Africa and its colonizers" (Adedeji, 2023, p. 1). Despite the challenges, Africa continues to put forth new shoots, representing its growth and regeneration. With patience and stubbornness, the continent's fruits slowly mature, acquiring the bitter taste of liberty.

The fourth source is the conceptualization of the Negritude Movement in African Literature in Birapo Diop poem titled "Viaticum." In this poem, the persona notes that

Mother has dipped three fingers
three fingers of her left hand:

…

before me advance the breaths of the forefathers (The West African Verse, 1967, lines 7–8, 43).

The poem "Viaticum" narrates how a mother prepares the sacrifice to her ancestors (forefathers) for the purpose of assured protection for her son who wants to embark on a journey. The title of the poem suggests that it is a term used in religion to refer to monetary gift or other valuable things given to a religious officer or priest in the ancient period who wants to embark on a journey for a religious purpose. It is this idea that Diop brought into his artistic or literary writing to portray the cultures of Africa. Mattew Ogundipe opines that "at the opening of the poem, the ingredients of the sacrifice have been provided by the mother to invoke the spirits of the ancestors for a guaranteed safety of her son on his journey…on certain evenings return the tranquil souls, the breaths of the ancestors" (Okune, 2011, p. 129). The preceding lines express the beginning of the invocations. The thematic preoccupation of this poem is centered on three prominent themes: (1) sacrifice, (2) belief in one's god, and (3) ancestral protection. While the poem evokes imagery of ancestors who were formerly men, mothers, the sea, and imageries of the dead who are long gone, this poem is a representation of the sacrifices of Black people who were here before us. It in extension shows the beauty of the fighting and resilient spirit of the Black person.

Re-examination of Gender Roles in African Literature

In this section, I will attempt to answer this question: What are gender roles and why do they need re-examination in African Literature? The answers to this question are given in the subsequent paragraph after providing a brief background to this particular area of study.

African Literature is replete with write-ups that project male dominance. It becomes imperative to trace the genesis of gender inequality in African Literature. Most male writers in the early phase of African Literature encourage the marginalization of women. In this context, female characters are made marginal to the plot of the fiction, while only a few emerge as powerful and credible protagonists. The "ideal female character created by male writers often acts within the framework of her traditional roles as wife and mother. So strong are social values that the respect and love which a woman earns [are] relative to the degree of her adaptations to these roles" (Fonchingong, 2006, p. 135).

The notion of gender roles in society refers to the prescribed behaviors, expectations, and roles that are associated with individuals based on their perceived gender. These roles often dictate how people are expected to behave, what responsibilities they should fulfill, and the social roles they should occupy. Gender roles are often deeply ingrained in cultural and societal norms and can vary across different cultures and historical periods. Gender roles have become a significant topic of discussion in contemporary society as traditional gender roles persist and perpetuate gender inequalities and stereotypes. Societal expectations and assumptions about gender roles have imposed limitations on women, thereby affecting their behaviors, opportunities, and identities. In addition to being limited, these established rules also permit inequality that inhibits human fulfillment. As such, there is a need to re-examine the notion of gender roles as it would contribute to a more inclusive society.

The indoctrination of gender roles in African countries is mostly embedded in patriarchy, which is a system in which men control all aspects of life, from economics to politics. Thus, patriarchy has its roots in male hegemony, which, in a patriarchal society, refers to the fact that men make all the decisions in their families and their society. Male hegemony as embodied in gender roles shows how men and women are expected to act and react to issues in a patriarchal society. From an early age, young boys are already aware of the roles assigned to them; providers and persons defiant to any kind of leadership by females, while young girls, almost from the cradle are taught to adopt a submissive mien in their dealings with men. Females inhabiting an environment that upholds gender roles usually internalize them without giving much thought to it, as females in their families are the major enforcers of these roles. Also, "females raised in this kind of environment see themselves as mothers, wives and, in many cases, as a combination of mothers and wives. Their roles consist mainly of nurturing their children, nurturing their husbands, and picking up after their children and their husbands" (Metu, 2023, p. 130).

The re-examination of gender roles refers to the process of critically examining and reconsidering the traditional and socially constructed expectations, behaviors, and responsibilities associated with individuals based on their genders. It involves questioning and challenging long-held assumptions about how people of different genders should act, relate to one another, and participate in various aspects of life, with the aim of promoting greater equality and breaking down gender-based stereotypes and biases. The rethinking of gender roles acknowledges that individuals' experiences are shaped by a complex interplay of factors beyond just biology, including culture, socialization, and personal choices. The re-examination of gender roles promotes gender justice, human rights, and freedom of choice, as it provides an opportunity to examine and reassess cultural beliefs, social structures, and laws that perpetuate gender-based inequalities. In many societies, gender roles are deeply entrenched and are often reinforced through socialization, cultural practices, laws, and traditions. For example, the traditional African gender roles assign men as breadwinners and women as caretakers of children and the home. These gender roles can put undue pressure on individuals and contribute to gender inequalities, stereotypes, and discrimination. Women rethinking gender roles involves women's active engagement in the process of critically assessing and reconsidering the traditional expectations and limitations imposed upon them based on gender. It involves women challenging and reshaping societal norms to achieve greater equality, empowerment, and freedom of choice. This rethinking often leads to women breaking through traditional boundaries and pursuing diverse roles and opportunities in various aspects of life, thereby contributing to the ongoing transformation of gender roles in society. To further buttress my points, I will explore four sources and writers whose works bring to the fore how the re-examination of gender roles is conceptualized in the field of Literature.

Aiwanose Odafen's *Tomorrow I Become a Woman* is a text that shows how gender roles are conceptualized in twenty-first-century fiction as characters in the text re-examine and rethink the notion of gender roles. Sally, one of the major characters, firmly believes that no matter how eager she may be to find a husband, she will never submit to a man who resorts to physical violence. Despite pressure from her family, Sally refuses to go into a marriage devoid of happiness and freedom of expression. She says to Uju, “I can take anything, but I will not allow any man born of a woman put his hands on me” (Odafen, 2022, p. 292). Sally, unyielding in her determination, refuses to let her gender hinder her pursuit of her passion and desires, even when society dictates otherwise. The character Janie can be compared to Sally in how Janie ultimately confronts and leaves her second husband, Joe Starks when she realizes he is oppressive and abusive. She refuses to tolerate domestic violence and seeks a life free from such constraints. The character Ego has no intention of getting married. During one of her conversations with Uju, she says the following: “I don’t see how it benefits women in any way, you leave the comfort of your father’s house for a man; you give everything, sacrifice yourself, your ambitions and put your body through the pains of childbirth. We’ve been brainwashed to want it more when they benefit from it more” (Odafen, 2022, p. 269). Ego’s ability to recognize her father’s wrongdoing and her decision not to pursue marriage challenge traditional gender roles that expect her to conform to societal norms. Her independence and willingness to break away from these expectations represent a re-evaluation of the roles and choices typically assigned to women in a patriarchal society. Ego strongly disapproves of how Gozie mistreats Uju, another major character in the text, and she often encourages her mother to leave Gozie to avoid further maltreatment. An illustrative instance of this is when Ego courageously confronts Gozie when she can no longer tolerate his violent actions toward her mother. She thunders: “Leave her alone! Ego commanded, pointing at her father, haven’t you done enough? Aren’t you tired of treating her this way? Will you wait until she’s dead before you stop?” (Odafen, 2022, p. 273). Given that all of Uju’s attempts to leave Gozie had proven ineffective, Ego believes it is time to take matters into her own hands and act according to her own will, regardless of the consequences. Societal expectations or not, she firmly believes that her father’s actions have to come to an end. Ego’s actions empower women to stand up against mistreatment and abuse. Traditionally, women are often expected to endure such maltreatment silently, but Ego’s defiance challenges this norm.

The use of contraceptives such as birth control pills grants women greater control over their reproductive choices. With contraceptives, women can make informed decisions about when or if to have children, allowing them to pursue educational and career goals, among other aspirations. Uju’s choice of contraceptive reflects her desire for autonomy and the pursuit of her personal goals and aspirations beyond the traditional roles of motherhood. This challenges the notion that a married woman’s primary role should be limited to childbearing and homemaking.

Examination of my second source will lead to the exploration of Ama Ata Aidoo’s *Anowa*. In this play, Aidoo presents the eponymous character Anowa as an independent girl who loves to do activities of her choice; for example, playing with boys and roaming around her village without doing any household activities. A character in the play named “Old Man” describes Anowa as “a child of several incarnations; she listens to her own tales, laughs at her own jokes and follows her own advice" (Aidoo, 1970, p. 102). In African society, girls are basically expected to concentrate on household activities and they usually marry men their elders have selected for them. Anoma views these customs as ridiculous. Aidoo presents this character as a bold, independent female who represents the strong, repressed mind that every woman basically carries within her. In this play, it is also portrayed that girls are bound to marry a man chosen for them by their parents. The bride's opinion is not given any importance. Aidoo, thus, presents her protagonist in a different light from what is expected of her from her society.

My third source about the re-examination of gender roles in African Literature will be viewed through the lens of poetry. Angela Miri (2006) in her poem titled "Do not stop me" cries out about the limiting nature of being a woman made possible by customs and traditions and her determination not to conform to such notions. She notes:Do not stop me!

I burn

…

like the wild harmattan fire burning uncontrollably (Miri, 2006, lines 3–5)

The persona of this poem is a woman who is forcefully and "uncontrollably" breaking forth, craving for self-expression; a woman who never minds destroying the barriers that have been relegating her to the background for too long. The image of "fire" signifies this burning desire for freedom. This poet subscribes to the radical approach to moving the centrist male hegemony. With this mindset, her thoughts have moved from the manacles holding her still and transcended into this new realm that allows her to flourish.

Miri's "Single Girl" also traces instances where rigid rules are laid down for women as opposed to the freedom that is bequeathed to men to act as they please. The persona of this poem observes that for a single girl,

She is single—they say

It's a sad diagnosis

…

To this spinster (Miri, 2006, lines 1–2, 7).

The persona of this poem reveals disadvantaged position of a woman in a patriarchal and sexist culture. A woman is truly not seen as free in her singleness and also is she in marriage. Here, we are presented with a heartfelt plea of a single woman who "begs you to leave her single/in this lovely world alone" (Miri, 2006, lines 15–16). The choice of words of the persona is carefully marshaled to reveal the pitiable condition of women even in her singleness in a man-centered world. This ill-treatment is also extended to the poem titled "A Woman's Lament":

A woman

In the home, a slave of man

…

But not discovered (Miri, 2006, lines 1–2, 8).

This perception of women accounts for the reason they are treated without dignity; after all, a slave is a sub-human. The second stanza, which is also the last of the poem, comments on the psychological torture to which a woman is exposed because of her ill-treatment at the hands of men. There is no freedom of will, desire, and action. Women have no choice but to break free in order to regain their battered pride and assert their humanity. The battered pride they have regained helps them to examine their roles in society, make informed choices about them, and discard the constructed roles imposed on them.

Identity and Identity Reconstruction in African Literature

In this section, I set out to answer this question: How are identity and identity reconstruction conceptualized in African Literature? I will first of all look at the concept of "identity" and afterward that of "identity reconstruction."

Identity is a "moveable feast" that is formed and transformed continuously in relation to the cultural systems surrounding us. These systems of meaning and cultural representation establish a bewildering diversity of possible identities. Identity is not something that is fixed or given; it is "a regulative ideal enacted in discourse which is never fully achieved but serves as an organizing principle for our actions" (Butler, 1990, p. 121). Identity is a social construct. It is not a fixed entity but rather something that is constantly evolving. Identity is multifaceted. It is not a single, unified entity but instead a complex collection of different aspects. Thus, identity can be seen as the inner acceptance of social labels, rules, and expectations.

Identity reconstruction is a process of redefining oneself in relation to the changing dynamics of society and the self. It is the process of actively re-evaluating, renegotiating, and reshaping one's identity in response to significant life events, social changes, migration, trauma, or personal growth. The quest to redefine and reconstruct self-identity arises when changing social and cultural norms and values challenge the existing sense of who one is and what one believes. On the journey to identity reconstruction, there is scrutiny of existing relations with others, and tension often arises when there is a clash between individual interests and societal or circumstantial expectations.

The first source to be explored for the affirmation of identity reconstruction in African Literature is the work of Chibundu Onuzo's *Sankofa,* in which she portrays the quest to forge a new sense of self in the face of conflicting identities as she traces the journey of two characters, Anna and Kofi who, driven by an unyielding longing to fit in, reclaim their individuality and find solace in a welcoming community. *Sankofa* tells the story of a mixed-race middle-aged woman named Anna, born and bred in London, who amidst divorcing her husband and reeling from her mother's death, finds a diary written by a father she has never known but about whom she is desperately curious. After this discovery, she sets on a journey to find her father and what her identity truly is. Anna's relationship with her mother is tumultuous, and her childhood as the only Black child in a White family is a stark marker of her being "othered" by the society in which she has grown up. Anna must confront a man she has only known through scribbles on a page.

In the rest of this section, I will examine the social and psychological interactions in light of the first stage of the identity reconstruction process, which is disruption. In this stage, there is a collision between what was and an opposing lived experience. There becomes a persistent and noticeably unstable sense of self. Anna encounters this stage in her late forties when she hits the peak of loneliness in her life. Her mother is dead, her husband is an infidel, and her daughter is very distant from her. It is in the middle of this repining loneliness that her incoherent identity becomes noticeable to her. Left with nothing to do, a desire to find her father, and the desire to be independent of her husband Robert, she subconsciously resolves to make sense of her conflicting identities.

Francis's identity disruption occurs when he finds himself in London, a place that makes him aware of his skin color and the inferiority it carries. This opposing experience collides with the freedom and respect he is used to receiving, the many beliefs he holds, and what he thinks is the order of things. He is aware that he feels inferior and unsafe. He is not actively searching at this point, but his mind is open. When Anna finds out that her father is alive, she decides that she must visit Banama to find him. In Bamana, Anna battles with a lot of emotions. The reception she gets from the locals and her father especially is different from what she envisions. She is rejected at first. She is called an *Obroni* by the locals. She struggles to make sense of the father before her. Kofi is different from Francis. Francis is who she comes to look for, not this strict, power-filled, and proud man. Anna encounters an inner integration of her past and current experiences. She sees mixed ancestry as complementary rather than conflicting and she gets a more coherent vision of herself. The most significant part of this transition comes after she partakes in the Bamaniam ritual for daughters who are about to become women. It gives her a new identity and a new name, Nana. She is no longer a tourist. She is where she belongs, where she is accepted: Onuzo narrates the experience as follows:

> Today, Nana, you have become a woman. Your ancestors congratulate you. Greet them. I turned. There was a crowd on the bank stretching as far as the eye could see, a chain of people linked by their hands. My mother held hands with Grandpa Owen as I had never seen him, straight and broad with a full head of black hair, and Grandpa Owen held the hand of my grandmother, Esther, who I knew only from a photograph, and she held the hand of an African woman in a white blouse and blue wrapper, a headscarf covering her hair and a slim gold chain on her neck, tall and powerful, like Kofi—Kofi's mother (2021, p. 439).

This ritual is symbolic in helping her come to terms with her past. It is a rebirth of Anna's identity: Nana Anna Bain-Aggrey. She accepts her father for who he is now. He is Kofi. Not Francis anymore. Francis is a man of the past. She accepts her mother's harmless ignorance while raising her. Onuzo constructively engages the psychosocial conditions of Anna and Kofi. The first thing that strikes a reader's attention is the title. *Sankofa* literally means "to go back and get it." It is a term coined by the *Akan* people, meaning that one should remember the past to make positive progress in the future. It is a symbol of a bird with its head turned backward, carrying an egg in its mouth, representing the idea of looking back at our past to learn from it and move forward.

Alex Asigbo's *The Reign of Pascal Amusu* is the second source examined. Identity reconstruction takes place in this play through the principle of "otherness," which entails an ideology of "us" and "them" where "us" represents our leaders and oppressors and "them" stands for the marginalized. *The Reign of Pascal Amusu* studies the military and civilian officials that run the fictive Naijaland and excludes everyone who is not part of their elitist class as the "other" of the society. Naijaland, as it should be noted, is a metaphor for Nigeria and other Third World countries, particularly African countries, that are bugged by bad leadership, particularly military dictatorship. In the play, the military dictators (Masi, Shasha, and Pascal Amusu) see themselves as the owners of the state, and the citizens are simply the "other" whom they treat disdainfully. The consequences of the exclusion of the "other," particularly the civilian population from power are many. One, the elitist class rules without the rule of law, and citizens are imprisoned or detained without trial. The elite class, in order to perpetuate themselves in power, also carpets the members of the legislature and the judiciary through intimidation and bribery. For instance, the judges who the dramatis persona Odibo claims to have given three hundred million each nullify his governorship election. When such havoc has been consistently done on a nation, it takes a toll on the populace and requires just a reaction to tip and change the tides for the better. Najaland is a nation whose identity has been marred by "corruption, abuse of power, and disillusionment, and every time it is mentioned as a nation, these attributes follow suit. To shed this identity, soldiers and the civilian population joined in the uprising that ousted the despotic government run by an elite class and bedeviled with violence, corruption, and ineptitude" (Asigbo, 2008). By the "other" taking charge, they reconstructed the identity foisted on their nation by the actions of their leaders.

Muhammad Al-Fayturi's "A Message to Khartoum" is the third source explored in order to lend credence to identity reconstruction in African Literature. The persona of this poem notes that he…creeps on my sorrows

and the thorns of my bed

…

the wounded victims of history (Poem Hunter, 2021, lines 4–6).

The persona's feelings of alienation and nostalgia as reflected in the preceding poem can also be attributed to personal factors. As a cultural and interracial hybrid, Al-Fayturi has not been able to reconcile the two parts of his mutilated self. Witnessing the miserable life conditions of the Black people who were recruited from the Sudan to serve Western soldiers during the war further helps his stance to emphasize his identity as a Black African. Removing the cloak he wears to shield his identity and taking a firm stance further helps in his identity reconstruction. Expressing the predicament of the African poet who is divided between his African roots and his Arab culture, Al-Fayturi affirms his identity as a Black African in the poem titled "I am a Negro" as follows:

Say it, do not be a coward
say it in the face of humanity

…

long live Africa (Poem Hunter, 2021, lines 1-2, 7).

The persona of this poem faces the dilemma of bridging the gap between identity and culture. He also confronts the difficulty of writing in a manner that blends his double consciousness as an African and Arab Muslim. Al-Fayturi encounters his feelings of alienation and displacement through an affirmation and embracement of his African identity, celebrating African glories in the past and present. The conflicting realities and possibilities of the poet's interracial background have given rise to intense and agonizing debates about the forces that drive him toward Africa. He is able to resolve this conflict by the reconstruction of his identity.

Conclusion and Recommendations

Conceptualization of Africa in a literary and literature format poses some challenges, given that the exploration and answers to these challenges in this chapter are culled from literary texts. While there may be disagreements about what constitutes literature and its literariness, the general consensus will always be on the side of the three genres of Literature field which always helps to better understand the vast nature of this academic discipline. As I have viewed the conceptualization of Literature through three frameworks, there is always room for more lacunae in knowledge about this topic to be filled.

I will start off my recommendations by suggesting that Africa can also be explored in African Literature from other areas like colonial, postcolonial, psychoanalytic, and Marxist angles. Given the genres of Literature, the conceptualization of the field most times seems to be lacking in certain genres while others receive hundreds of criticisms and reviews. The definition of Africa cannot be fully appreciated if different genres of Literature do not fully express their meaning through their different forms and elements. It has been observed that drama and in its written form, play, is a genre of Literature that is almost dying off and long lost. One may present an argument for this point by looking at the part of this chapter where I presented elements of drama; it is not a literary or linguistic act that presents certain points of view like its sister, prose. It has been observed also that many prosaic and poetic works should have been children of drama but many do not want to deal with the technicalities of it. Thus, the literary genre of drama will grow and benefit from this expansion.

Next, there is a saying that "nobody tells our story better than us," The trueness of these words resonates with the objectives of this chapter. As I have viewed the continent through the frameworks of Negritude, negating the belief of the docility and backwardness of African women and the need to transform and shed the identity that no longer serves us, I ask that further studies be conducted on identity distortions and the great division between White Africa as exemplified by countries in North Africa and part of South Africa and Black Africa represented by the rest of Africa. The significance will add to the number of studies conducted on the conceptualization of Africa in African literature.

References

Abakah, P., & Marfo, C. (2009). Expressing culture through drama: A reading of *anowa* and *the marriage of anansewa*. *African Journals Online, 12*(3).

Abrams, M. (2009). *A glossary of literary terms*. Wadsworth.

Achebe, C. (1958). *Things fall apart*. Heinemann Educational Books.

Adedeji, R. (2023). David Diop's "Africa, My Africa." *Literature Padi*. Retrieved August 9, 2023, from https://www.literaturepadi/daviodiopafrica/

Aidoo, A. (1970). *Anowa*. Longman.

Asigbo, A. (2008). *The reign of Pascal Amusu*. Valid Publishing.

Ba, S. (2016). *The concept of negritude in the poetry of Leopold Sedar Senghor*. Princeton Legacy Library.

Britannica. (2016). *Setting*. Encyclopedia Britannica. Retrieved June 5, 2023, from https://www.britannica.com/art/setting/

Britannica. (2023). *Negritude*. Encyclopedia Britannica. Retrieved June 5, 2023, from https://www.britannica.com/art/Negritude/

Butler, J. (1990). *Gender trouble: Feminism and the subversion of identity*. Routledge.

Childs, P. (2006). *The Routledge handbook of literary terms*. Routledge.

Fonchingong, C. (2006). Unbending gender narratives in African literature. *Journal of International Women's Studies, 8*(1), 135–147.

Irele, A. (1965). Negritude-literature and ideology. *The Journal of Modern African Studies, 3*(4), 499–526. Retrieved June 23, 2023, from http://www.jstor.org/stable/159175/

MasterClass. (2021). *Different types of literary conflict and how to create conflict in writing*. Retrieved July 7, 2023, from https://www.masterclass.com/articles/what-is-conflict-in-literature-6-different-types-of-literary-conflict-and-how-to-create-conflict-in-writing/

Metu, S. (2023). Representation of male hegemony in Cheluchi Onyemelukwe-Onubia's the *son of the house*. *Awka Journal of English Language and Literary Studies, 9*(1), 129–144.

Miri, A. (2006). *Running waters and other poems*. Malthouse Press.

Nwoga, D. (1967). *The west African verse*. Longman.

Odafen, A. (2022). *Tomorrow I become a woman*. Scribner.

Okune, S. (2011). Themes of idealism and nostalgia in negritude poetry. *LWATI: A Journal of Contemporary Research, 8*(2), 127–139.

Onuzo, C. (2021). *Sankofa*. Little Brown Book Group.

Onwumere, A., & Egbulonu, F. (2014). The influence of negritude movement on modern African literature and writers. *African Journal of New Writing, 15*(7), 146–161.

Poem Hunter. (2021). *The poems of Muhammad Al-Fayturi*. Retrieved August 14, 2023, from https://www.poemhunter.com/al-fayturi/

Sinha, S. (2020). *What are the definitions of William Wordsworth poetry?* Retrieved April 11, 2023, from https://www.quora.com/What-are-the-definitions-of-William-Wordsworth-poetry

Study.Com. (2021). *Directions: Definitions and examples*. Retrieved April 11, 2023, from https://study.com/learn/lesson/identifying-stage-directions-in-a-drama.html

Sutherland, E. (1975). *The marriage of Anansewa*. Longman.

Somtochukwu J. Metu is a lecturer in the Department of English and Literary Studies at the University of Nigeria, Nsukka, where she teaches Studies in Fiction, European Theatre Since Ibsen, African-American Literature, Introduction to Drama and Nigerian Literature. She holds a Master of Arts Degree in English Literature and is currently working on her doctoral thesis. She is a 2019 CODESRIA Doctoral Fellow. Her research interests straddle Literary Studies and Queer/Gender and Feminist Studies. Her poems are published in *The Muse: A Journal of Critical and Creative Writing*.

Youth

Jeremiah Oluwadara Omotayo

In this chapter, I delve into the understanding of what Africa is from the perspective of youth. It was not until the early twentieth century, particularly during the colonial period and beyond, that the concept of youth began to gain prominence in Africa. Interestingly, the notion of youth is absent in the traditional vocabulary of African languages, as noted by Peatrik (2020). This stands in sharp contrast to developed countries, especially Western nations, where youth conventionally encompasses children and teenagers. In Africa, the concept of youth can sometimes be considered a social construct beyond age categorizations. Here, older individuals who are or are not actively involved in a profession, skill, business, or means of earning a livelihood, and who may even be married, can still be categorized as youth. Nevertheless, this definition is gradually changing across Africa as more people are achieving these milestones, albeit at a slower pace compared to their peers in other countries. It is important to note that Africa boasts of the world's youngest population, with 70 percent of Africans South of the Sahara under the age of 30 (Mulikita, 2022; El Habti, 2022).

Nonetheless, the narratives of conflicts, violence, corruption, and bad governance have impacted the concept of youth in Africa. Oftentimes, in Africa, youth is often referenced mostly when it comes to conflict, violence, unemployment and other negativity, which are often a fallout of the many decades of bad leadership in the continent. There are, however, emerging narratives of youth productivity in the entertainment industry and technology that could be attributed to the effect of globalization. Nevertheless, this is just a little fraction of the whole youth population in Africa; as in reality, the concept of youth in Africa often signifies struggles and efforts of a generation trying to get out of a position in which it had been trapped for

J. O. Omotayo (✉)
Political and Governance Policy Department, Nigerian Institute of Social and Economic Research, Ibadan, Nigeria
e-mail: jo.omotayo@niser.gov.ng

A. K. Bangura, J. A. Ifedi (eds.), *Conceptualizations of Africa*, African Studies and Research Forum Series, https://doi.org/10.1007/978-3-031-74535-5_22

many years by preceding generations. Moreover, the understanding of youth in Africa has evolved significantly to the extent that the historical literature no longer fully captures the essence of African youth today. As a result, this chapter takes a novel approach by examining Africa through the lens of youth, thereby shifting the perspective from what youth in Africa are to what Africa represents within the context of its youth population.

Today, the term youth in Africa connotes vitality and a disruptive force. This phenomenon is evident across various domains ranging from social issues to scientific advancements, reflecting its ubiquity across all facets of human existence. It is noteworthy to mention that the younger generation also plays a prominent role in matters concerning vices and rebellion. This can be attributed to their vulnerability, which makes them susceptible to both positive and negative influences. Nonetheless, it is important to distinguish this discourse from the negative rhetoric prevalent in literature, which often presents African youth in a demonized light. This argument posits that their actions are in response to the circumstances established by African leadership rather than a deliberate choice. In essence, African youth are a product of societal and generational influences, and their actions reflect the impact of various policies.

In this chapter, I embark on an exploration of the concept of youth in Africa, recognizing the continent and its various youthful attributes as a distinct demographic group that sets it apart from other continents. What follows is an analysis of this concept through three perspectives: Africa as (1) a young democracy, (2) a continent characterized by a youthful demographic, and (3) a continent rich in young talents. Employing a qualitative methodology and drawing upon secondary data sources, this study delves into each dimension to illuminate the multifaceted nature of youth in Africa. The culmination of this research endeavors to assert that Africa is intrinsically characterized by its youth. The chapter draws to a close with a set of recommendations derived from the insights garnered throughout this study. Before doing all this, however, a conceptualization of the term youth is tendered in the ensuing section.

Conceptualization of Youth

The African Youth Charter (2006), initiated by the African Union, defines *youth* as those aged 15–35 years. This categorization has been argued to be demographic and rooted in statistical reality for developmental purposes (Peatrik, 2020). Nonetheless, as mentioned earlier, youth in Africa transcends age groupings. It represents a phenomenon and an ideology (van Dijk et al., 2011). For about two decades, studies on youth have been a center of attraction for academia, policymakers, and the international community. One reason for this special interest is their peculiar needs and importance in society. For instance, across the 54 countries in the African continent, the youth demography going by age categorization alone represents about 60 percent of its population. Moreover, different entities, including governments, religious and political figures, and non-governmental organizations (NGOs), have embraced the idea of youth as a framework for structuring society and handling interests and resources. The youth, in turn, have adopted this concept as a proactive ideology to pursue their own goals, consequently cultivating their own ideological influence (van Dijk et al., 2011).

Young individuals falling within the youth category, as defined by the African Union, constitute the most vibrant, energetic, creative, courageous, risk-taking, problem-solving, and intellectually astute segment of Africa's population (Jega, 2017). African societies have developed various systems for categorizing age and different frameworks for understanding the stages of life. None of these systems directly aligns with the Western concept of youth as commonly understood (Peatrik, 2020). In recent times, African youths have carved out a new path for themselves, making substantial contributions in technology, entertainment, entrepreneurship, and activism, despite facing challenges related to unemployment, education, poverty, insecurity, and HIV/AIDS. Moreover, the youth tend to be notably ambitious, enthusiastic, and full of potential when it comes to setting and pursuing their objectives. Paradoxically, they are also more susceptible, impressionable, and emotionally sensitive, indicating that they possess distinct needs and concerns deserving significant attention to fully harness their potential. This unique characteristic sets them apart from other demographic groups. Hence, borrowing from Vigh (2008), youth is often perceived as existing in a paradoxical state of "constant crisis."

One way to understand the idea of the youth in Africa is to go back in time. Cole (2011) explains that the idea of the youth and their transition into adulthood in the past rested with African patriarchal figures who sought to consolidate their political authority by overseeing the labor of young individuals and ensuring the proper preservation of gender-based and generational hierarchies. This control was maintained by regulating the process of transition from youth into social adulthood. To manage this transition across genders, older men often employed the strategy of granting or withholding the right to marry and have legitimate offspring, while for the women, fathers exercised their authority over their daughters' sexuality, reproductive functions, and labor contributions, as these aspects were crucial to establishing and sustaining local kinship networks (Cole, 2011).

Also, in earlier times, numerous African societies emphasized the cultivation of character and the imparting of positive societal values to young people as part of their indoctrination or socialization process. For instance, many traditional African cultures established demanding age-grade initiation rituals and traditions with the aim of instilling values like honesty, courage, unity, selflessness, and moral integrity in the younger generation.

The acquisition of social worth among youth was heavily dependent on their reproductive, labor, and caring abilities, which in turn led to the attainment of higher social power and adult status as they positioned themselves as benefactors within established systems of exchange. The enduring presence of these cultural beliefs in present-day society has resulted in the significant importance placed on achieving adult status, which is deemed a vital component of attaining full personhood. According to Chabal and Deloz (1999), contrary to the Western viewpoint that regards youth as the most desirable stage of life, African youths aspire to reach an age that will bestow upon them a presently withheld authority. Nevertheless, societal progress and the evolution of modern African nation-states have led to a relaxation in their efforts to educate and socialize the youth with these invaluable principles (Cole, 2011).

From another perspective, some scholars have argued that the categories of age and generation are not innate or intrinsic but rather are constructed through sociocultural processes and power dynamics that establish who can identify and be acknowledged as a child, youth, or adult (Durham, 2007; Cole, 2011). As proposed by Durham (2000), considering youth as a socially constructed category with historical underpinnings, a relational dimension, and a collective of engaged participants provides a highly effective framework for emphasizing the influence of social processes in Africa and various other global regions. This viewpoint enables us to scrutinize how power dynamics and frameworks are flexed, reshaped, and sustained as individuals assert their entitlements and needs, with age as a defining factor—a process marked by mutual interaction but characterized by inherent imbalances. Thus, the youth occupy a central position within this dynamic African context.

Complex cultural dynamics are illuminated by studies conducted in various African societies highlighting the disparity between an individual's chronological age and his/her generational status. In the context of lineal descent groups in Ghana, Fortes (1984) demonstrated that individuals at a very young age could hold senior positions over their older counterparts. This finding challenges the traditional notion of age-based hierarchy within these groups. Fortes' research suggests that factors other than age, such as individual capabilities or qualifications, may influence the assignment of senior positions within lineal descent groups. (Peatrik, 2020). Essentially, an individual's social status within a kinship group, such as being identified as a mother or aunt in relation to her child or niece, bore greater weight than her actual chronological age in determining her seniority (Cole, 2011).

The composition of African youth is frequently confined to the African continent, thereby disregarding the intricate and multidirectional nature of cultural production within the Diaspora. This often prioritizes a specific location rather than the processes and interactions occurring in Africa and globally. Additionally, the concept of youth is already subject to much debate and ambiguity, as it varies depending on geographic, disciplinary, temporal and various other contextual factors. Importantly, due to their marginalized social and economic position, the status of the youth is becoming increasingly flexible, leading to a prolonged transition into adulthood (Ritchie, 2017).

Africa: The Continent with Young Democracies

Africa is a continent that houses many young democracies. In the mid-twentieth century, when the third wave of democratization swept across Africa in the wake of the Cold War (Huntington, 1991; Schraeder, 1995), it witnessed a shift from colonial rule to independence, ushering in the establishment of new African-led governments through democracy. Nevertheless, most African countries inherited democratic political structures that had been quickly established by colonial powers in their preparations to depart. Although many Africans had engaged in discussions about local matters, their primary experience with politics beyond their villages had not been democracy but rather autocratic governance imposed by foreign authorities (Lancaster, 1991). Consequently, in the years following independence, many of these newly formed governments faced challenges, leading to either their collapse or a return to authoritarian rule, which marked a period of clientelist regimes and military coups (Barkan, 2002).

There were a few exceptions to the prevailing trend of personalized rule in post-independence Africa. Notably, Botswana, The Gambia, and Mauritius have upheld open and democratic political systems, even though the ruling party has consistently remained in power in Botswana and The Gambia. Senegal moved toward a more open and competitive political system in the 1970s. Meanwhile, Ghana and Nigeria have experienced shifts between democratic and military rule. Kenya and Tanzania have managed to maintain some degree of electoral choice despite operating under one-party states. Zimbabwe has retained a multiparty democratic system since gaining independence in 1980, despite President Robert Mugabe's efforts to establish a one-party state (Lancaster, 1991). Furthermore, the 1990s brought about a second wave of liberation for Africa, which was characterized by the restoration of democracy and enhanced governance through multiparty elections in many countries (Mozaffar, 2004). The choice of electoral systems in these emerging democracies is shaped by a combination of contextual factors tied to political histories and contingent factors linked to the processes of democratic transitions.

Due to their relatively nascent nature, African democracies have displayed a sense of youthful exuberance that has somewhat hindered their democratic advancement. This has resulted in the weakening of institutional structures; limited political diversity; intolerance toward differing and critical viewpoints; the consolidation of political elites; insufficient involvement of women, youth, and minority groups in politics; corruption; and a lack of transparency, particularly when addressing human rights violations. The repercussions of these challenges include widespread poverty, instability, and conflict, which, paradoxically, disproportionately affect the youth, who are among the most vulnerable segments of society.

For instance, the Democracy Index report for 2022 by Economist Intelligence Unit (2022), which used 60 indicators across five broad categories, namely (1) electoral process and pluralism, (2) political culture, (3) political participation, (4) functioning of government, and (5) civil liberties, revealed that only Mauritius of the 54 countries in Africa enjoyed full democracy with an impressive Democracy Index score of 8.14 percent. And about nine other countries operated a flawed democracy, while other countries fell between a hybrid and authoritarian regimes (Oluwole, 2023).

The EIU report notwithstanding, it is important to recognize that within a young cohort, not every child will exhibit negative behavior; there will be individuals with positive qualities worth imitating. Thus, there are some positive and encouraging developments in democratic governance on the continent. Countries such as Botswana, Ghana, Namibia, Mauritius, Senegal, Benin Republic, and South Africa have served as beacons of hope in the advancement of democracy. They have achieved this through their commitment to political rights, civil liberties, the strengthening of democratic institutions, and the maintenance of cohesive relationships despite facing numerous challenges (Cheeseman, 2019). For instance, consider Botswana, a small landlocked nation situated in a region historically plagued by various threats to sovereignty (Kaufmann, 2023). Since gaining full independence in 1966, Botswana has successfully developed into a thriving, open, and competitive multiparty state, making it the longest-standing uninterrupted democracy in Africa (Gleeman, 2019).

In Zambia, citizens managed to overcome a repressive political environment through the election that was held on August 12, 2021. In this election, they chose the opposition presidential candidate, Hakainde Hichilema, who had previously made five unsuccessful bids for the presidency despite enduring numerous assaults from the then-ruling party (Kasambala, 2022). The inauguration ceremony of Zambia's seventh president sparked significant optimism among Zambians as a crowded stadium in Lusaka celebrated this historic moment. This event also inspired people across Africa, serving as a testament to the possibility of overcoming repressive governments. Hichilema, who was 59 years old at the time, particularly resonated with Zambian youths, who affectionately referred to him as "Bally" (slang for father) due to his focus on addressing issues affecting their demographic, which plays a crucial role in the country (Olewe, 2021).

While it is undeniable that there is a concerning resurgence of military coups and authoritarian regimes in some parts of Africa, particularly Africa South of the Sahara, it is important to recognize that this trend is not solely a consequence of the budding years of democratic rule in Africa. Rather, it is often driven by factors such as corruption and the insatiable thirst for power among political leaders. Even before the outbreak of the Coronavirus Disease (COVID)-2019 pandemic, an increasing number of African leaders had been taking steps to undermine executive term limits or manipulate elections in order to prolong their stay in power (Campbell & Quinn, 2021). Cassani (2020) asserts that leaders in Africa, South of the Sahara, even dating back to the 1990s, displayed a proclivity to exploit executive term limits as a means to propel their countries toward autocracy and to reestablish personal rule. This highlights the reasoning behind the incorporation of term limits, particularly for the president, into constitutions.

Nevertheless, the pandemic presented these leaders with additional opportunities. It provided a pretext for postponing elections in countries like Somalia and Ethiopia, thereby enabling the suppression of opposition figures in Uganda and Tanzania and allowing for restrictions on media outlets across the continent. According to a report by Campbell and Quinn (2021), security forces frequently enforced pandemic-related restrictions with harsh tactics, curtailing freedoms and sparking protests in Kenya and even in more established democracies like South Africa.

Additionally, the resurgence of militarization, reminiscent of the political landscape in post-independence Africa, has raised significant international, continental, and policy concerns. To date, African countries have witnessed a total of 98 coups since 1952, with Sudan experiencing the largest number of coups, totaling 17, including the most recent one in 2021 (Duzor & Williamson, 2023; Mwai, 2023). The frequency of government ousting reached its lowest point in 2017, a period that included events like the "Arab Spring," which led to the removal of long-standing autocrats, notably Hosni Mubarak in Egypt. Nonetheless, more recently, coups have occurred in countries like Chad, Mali, Burkina Faso, Guinea, and the most recent one in Gabon (Duzor & Williamson, 2023).

It is intriguing to observe that the phenomenon of the youth bulge is also evident among coup plotters. In recent times, many coups have been orchestrated by Africans in their 30 s and early 40 s, which stands in contrast to the continent's typical leadership profile where the average leader is in his/her 60s. For example, in Burkina Faso, Captain Ibrahim Traoré, who successfully led a coup on September 30, 2022, was just 34 years old at the time. While this trend of younger coup leaders is not entirely new in Africa's history of militarization, its recent emergence in the current era of democracy is noteworthy.

Furthermore, considering the significant youth demographic in terms of population size (as will be discussed in the next section), it is relevant to highlight recent comments made by former Nigerian President Olusegun Obasanjo regarding the rising number of coups across the African continent. According to him, it is essential to recognize that the youth are seeking liberators beyond the current government because they perceive it as failing to deliver democratic benefits, largely due to issues like corruption and the prolonged stay of leaders in power (Taiwo, 2023).

This aligns with the findings of an Afrobarometer report, which conducted a survey involving nearly 50,000 Africans across 34 countries from 2019 to 2021 to gauge their perspectives on democracy in Africa (Gyimah-Boadi & Asunka, 2021). According to the report, a significant majority of Africans, approximately seven in ten (69 percent), expressed a preference for democracy over any other form of government (Gyimah-Boadi & Asunka, 2021). Also, more specific indicators within the report appear to reinforce this strong commitment to democracy. Substantial and consistent majorities consistently rejected authoritarian alternatives, including military rule (75 percent), one-party rule (77 percent), and one-person rule (82 percent). While the majority of respondents believed that the military should refrain from interfering in politics and allow political parties to compete freely for power, they also strongly agreed that elderly leaders who cling to power should step aside. On average, 76 percent of the respondents expressed support for limiting their presidents to two terms in office (Gyimah-Boadi & Asunka, 2021).

The strong commitment to democracy demonstrated by the African public reflects a growing endorsement of young democracies in the continent. African citizens, more so than their leaders, have come to recognize the inherent advantages of democracy, which ultimately translate into long-term development. In light of the evolving global landscape following the COVID-2019 pandemic, Africans now have more opportunities to demand accountability from their governments, lend their support to robust democratic institutions, and, notably, persist in their legitimate efforts to help young African democracies mature.

The preservation of the democratic landscape in Africa has been significantly influenced by the emergence of social movements that have effectively mobilized

African citizens. It is important to note that various strategies, such as the utilization of social media campaigns, protests, the endorsement of petitions, legal actions, election reruns, increased voter participation, community-led monitoring, active participation of civil society organizations, protest votes, and other forms of engagement, are contributing to an ideological transition process. This process, which is akin to the historical African concept of youth articulated by Cole (2011), depicts the evolution of the youth into adulthood. These movements are exerting a pivotal influence in molding the prospective trajectory of African democracies, which are poised to assume the mantle of democratic leadership in the near future.

Africa: The Continent with a Youthful Population

The demographic composition of Africa is notably youthful. It stands as the world's youngest continent, with a population of nearly 200 million individuals aged between 15 and 24, constituting more than 20 percent of the population in many African nations. Moreover, over 60 percent of Africa's population comprises young men and women under the age of 25 (Appiah et al., 2020; Kariba, 2020). Projections for the near future indicate that by 2030, nearly 1 in 4 young people worldwide will hail from Africa. While these statistics are well-established, the central question revolves around what Africa intends to do with this significant demographic potential, which has captured global attention. The continent is expected to harness a demographic dividend from its youthful population.

For decades, human development specialists, industrialized nations, and policymakers have raised the alarm about the burgeoning youth population in Africa, which could be attributed to high fertility coupled with declining child mortality. Concerns have been about the inability of African leaders to purposefully harness this youth demography to bring about meaningful development in Africa in particular and the world at large. There are fears that illiteracy, poverty, conflict, policy neglect, and disenfranchisement would escalate. More so, the unemployment rate keeps increasing. As reported by the African Development Bank in 2015, of Africa's nearly 420 million youth aged 15–35, one-third are unemployed and discouraged, another third are vulnerably employed, and only one in six is in wage employment (AfDB, 2016).

Certainly, from a policymaker's perspective, Africa's youth employment challenge is undeniably a global issue (Donkor, 2021). This is particularly relevant when considering how to prepare the youth for an ever-evolving knowledge-based economy. It is important to emphasize that African youth, especially the millennials and Generation Z, are far from passive, despite the remarks of a former Nigerian president about his youth. Nonetheless, the fundamental question revolves around the environment in which they find themselves, which, to a significant extent, is not conducive to progress due to political and economic factors that hinder their potential. Consequently, these factors limit their ability to contribute to increased productivity and foster stronger and more inclusive economic growth across the continent. Realizing the potential of a young population requires establishing a supportive environment for the youth to take the initiative (Kariba, 2020). Regrettably, as pointed out by Cheeseman (2019), Africa's gerontocracy shows no signs of yielding to a younger generation despite the pressing need for youthful leaders with fresh ideas to steer the continent forward.

In some ways, it appears that the global community and a portion of the young population are the only ones who truly grasp the gravity of the situation. The unique challenges faced by Africa's youth population set it apart, as it has the potential to become a source of instability rather than a valuable resource, which differs from the more optimistic perspective of youth demographics in other regions of the world (Jega, 2017). The frustration and hopelessness experienced by unemployed young people can, when taken to an extreme, result in serious consequences that have the potential to affect not only Africa but the entire world (Kariba, 2020). Yet, it seems that many African leaders are primarily preoccupied with retaining power. In fact, some scholars tend to concur that these leaders bear significant responsibility for Africa's underdevelopment (Ojo, 2016).

As early as 2005, the Commission for Africa provided a concise summary of the deplorable role played by African leaders as follows: "Africa has suffered from governments that have looted the resources of the state; that could not or would not deliver services to their people; that in many cases were predatory, corruptly extracting their countries' resources, that maintain control through violence and bribery; and that have squandered and stolen aid" (2005, pp. 94–95, cited in Ojo, 2016). It could be argued that the current state of underdevelopment in Africa is not solely the result of external factors. The continent has had ample time to forge a different path, but systemic corruption, a profound disregard for democratic principles, and the entrenched "sit-tight" mentality of the political elite have played significant roles (Ojo, 2016; Agbiboa & Maiangwa, 2012).

African leaders often significantly differ in age from the populations they govern, and, unfortunately, this trend seems unchanging. Interestingly, the continent is experiencing a growing youth population while simultaneously becoming more authoritarian. Nevertheless, a notable development in recent times is the resilience of the African youth and their strong sense of agency in resisting poor governance and corrupt leadership (Makura, 2020). Many of the uprisings that have taken place involve civil disobedience, protests, strikes, and petitions led by young people against their governments. For example, in 2020, during the height of the COVID-2019 pandemic, when lockdown measures and government corruption were exacerbating economic frustration, online movements gained traction across Africa to address various issues hindering young people from realizing their potential and competing effectively with their counterparts in developed countries.

The hashtag revolution, facilitated by digital technologies and social media, has amplified the voices of African youth. This phenomenon began with events like the Arab Spring (#ArabSpring) in 2010 and extended to campaigns such as the #BringBackOurGirls (#BBOG) movement in Nigeria, particularly in response to the abduction of the Chibok schoolgirls in its Northeastern zone. Notably, in 2020, the continent and the world witnessed a series of online protests that subsequently translated into physical demonstrations. For instance, #VidasAngolaNasImportam highlighted concerns about the increasingly authoritarian leadership of the People's Movement for the Liberation of Angola (MPLA) party, which has been in power since 1975 following independence from Portugal. The reported human rights violations escalated, especially during the pandemic, when numerous young Angolans were reportedly arrested, detained, and tragically died while in police custody (Wells, 2021).

The #Congoisbleeding hashtag shed light on the exploitation of children working in the cobalt mines of the Democratic Republic of Congo (DRC). Cobalt is a crucial component used in the production of lithium-ion batteries and magnetic steels for various tech companies and computer hardware manufacturers. The corrupt practices accompanying child labor have resulted in the tragic deaths of many children who toiled for 12 hours a day for a meager wage of two dollars amidst the backdrop of ongoing conflicts in the country (Kara, 2018). Shockingly, it was reported that approximately 40,000 Congolese children were engaged in cobalt mining in East DRC between 2019 and 2020, contributing to around 70 percent of the world's cobalt production (Mutabazi, 2023). Moreover, aside from the issue of child labor, exposure to cobalt fumes is known to be extremely hazardous and can lead to hard metal lung disease (Wahlqvist et al., 2020).

#ShutItAllDown was a powerful protest initiated by young women in Namibia to combat gender-based violence and femicide. This protest, which reverberated through the capital city of Windhoek in October 2020, aimed to draw attention to the horrifying incidents of violence against women and girls in a society largely characterized by male dominance. Despite existing regulations pertaining to gender, abortion, and child support, the actual situation in Namibia paints a different picture (Wells, 2021; Ossenbrink, 2020). For instance, between 2017 and 2018, there were approximately 3500 reported cases of teenage pregnancies in schools in the Northern Region. Moreover, a United Nations Educational, Scientific and Cultural Organization (UNESCO) representative disclosed that almost one-fifth of Namibian teenage girls experienced unintended pregnancies, with 40 percent of these resulting from non-consensual sexual encounters (Melber, 2020). According to a study carried out by female researchers at the Institute for Public Policy Research in 2018, they concluded that the prevailing gender landscape in Namibia requires active challenge, particularly from those who benefit from it, notably heterosexual men who exhibit characteristics typically associated with traditional male gender roles (Alweendo et al., 2018).

#EndSARS was a youth-led protest that erupted across Nigeria in October of 2020, stemming from long-standing grievances against the notorious Special Anti-Robbery Squad (SARS) and encompassing broader issues like police brutality, political corruption, unemployment, and more. It originated on social media in 2017 and gained momentum in 2020, mobilizing young Nigerians who make up a substantial portion of the population. They organized, raised funds, provided medical support, and documented evidence to support their cause. The movement, one of Africa's largest recent protests, pressured the government to disband SARS. Nonetheless, the authorities responded with a military crackdown, including a massacre at the Lekki Toll Gate, and froze the bank accounts of protesters and supporting organizations (Kazeem, 2020a, 2020b; Commodore & Frimpong, 2021).

Recently, young Africans organized the #OccupyJolorbiHouse protest in Ghana. They used the term *Jolorbi* (meaning "thievery" in Ghana) to mock the Presidential villa, Jubilee House, as the "House of Thieves." This three-day protest (September 21–23, 2023) was aimed at denouncing alleged financial mismanagement, government indifference, rising living costs, and persistent governance failures causing hardships for Ghanaians. Young Ghanaians designed posters and displayed billboards featuring government officials, including the president and ministers, along with corruption allegations (#OccupyJolorbiHouse, 2023, September 27).

Furthermore, there is a growing demand for increased youth participation in the decision-making processes across Africa. Initiatives like #NotTooYoungToRun, a global campaign championed in Africa by YIAGA Africa, a civil society group, advocate for aligning the age requirement for running for political office with the official voting age. This movement has led to the emergence of numerous young leaders in parliaments across various African countries, including Nigeria, Ghana, Cote d'Ivoire, Kenya, South Africa, Egypt, Tunisia, Morocco, Cameroon, Zambia, Tanzania, Uganda, and others. As of April 2023, the Inter-Parliamentary Union (IPU) reported that 17.30 percent of parliamentarians worldwide are under the age of 40, with Sub-Saharan Africa having 2.17 percent under the age of 30, ranking third globally after Europe (3.93 percent) and the Americas (2.75 percent). Additionally, 20.25 percent of parliamentarians in Sub-Saharan Africa are under the age of 40, which is the second-highest percentage after Europe (21.67 percent) (Inter-Parliamentary Union, 2023).

Engaging young individuals in the process of decision-making extends beyond the notion of inclusion; rather, it is an imperative element for fostering economic advancement, innovation, peace, and security. The lack of youth participation in governance persists due to disempowerment, alienation, or the perception that their involvement lacks significance, given the prevalence of electoral manipulation and the arbitrary conception and implementation of policies, disregarding input from essential stakeholders. It is crucial to accord African youth greater acknowledgment and perceive them as catalysts of progress, possessing valuable contributions to offer, instead of consistently viewing them as victims or instruments for perpetrating violence due to their vulnerability (Mulikita, 2022).

African youth are currently facing a dilemma, torn between political and economic exclusion on the one hand and the hope for a vibrant, globalized, and prosperous future on the other (Kayizzi-Mugerwa, 2019). Despite not holding political power, the youth have been actively challenging the existing social order, as demonstrated by the widespread protests in October 2020 and similar, though smaller, uprisings and coups in various parts of Africa. While there is a deep sense of discontent among the youth regarding the current state of affairs, their relative marginalization and limited influence have paradoxically fostered greater solidarity and political participation within this demographic. This development has occurred despite the diverse nature of the youth as a collective and the significant variations in their age distribution, social status, upbringing (whether rural or urban, impoverished or affluent), and gender (Kayizzi-Mugerwa, 2019).

The expressions of dissent and public displays of disapproval exhibited by the younger generation in Africa toward their governing authorities can be interpreted as indicative of the underlying and profound social, economic, and political predicaments plaguing the entire continent. These active engagements have, in fact, brought about a significant transformation in the prevailing narratives that previously portrayed African youths as being devoid of agency. According to a report compiled by Africa No Filter (2020), an analysis of no fewer than 29 pertinent sources, encompassing surveys, scholarly articles, and research publications, was conducted with the aim of comprehending the prevailing youth culture in Africa and their perspectives on the future trajectory of the continent. The salient outcome of this investigation was the realization that the global community's most youthful population segment does not primarily align themselves with Pan-Africanism, nor do they exhibit a keen interest in the act of voting; instead, they assert themselves as self-initiators, holding an unwaveringly optimistic outlook on life and harboring ambitious aspirations, all while making effective use of popular culture as a means of expression.

Africa: The Home of Young Talents

The continent is brimming with remarkable talents and untapped potential across various domains. African youth have shown their resilience by embracing challenges and actively promoting African culture. They achieve this by acquiring new skills, embracing new identities, migrating to urban centers in significant numbers (not excluding the massive transnational migration of Africans to developed countries); and, whenever possible, discarding traditional cultural norms that they perceive as restrictive or outdated (Sommers, 2015; Okunade & Awosusi, 2023). Young Africans have emerged as influential forces in shaping global trends, showcasing their creativity in fields such as fashion, comedy, music, dance, visual arts, photography, film, curation, and technology. It is crucial to emphasize that in addition to Africa's youthful and entrepreneurial population, the continent boasts rapidly evolving landscapes characterized by expanding regions and rapid urbanization, abundant natural resources, dynamic economies, diverse ecosystems, and a Diaspora community that provides valuable support. This reinforces the notion that Africa possesses all the essential elements to nurture homegrown talent (African Union Commission and OECD, 2018).

The ninth edition of the Forbes Africa under 30 Summit, which took place in Botswana in April of 2023, acknowledged individuals of African descent under the age of 30 who have achieved entrepreneurial success through their remarkable acumen in establishing enterprises and brands that are entirely focused on providing solutions (Forbes Africa, 2023). Significantly, a number of the youthful honorees hailed from the technology, music, and healthcare sectors. This observation underscores the reality that Africa remains a breeding ground for burgeoning young talents.

In an article by the Economist titled "The Scramble for Africa," it is stated that observers from outside the continent have recognized the increasing significance of Africa, primarily due to its expanding share of the world's population. According to United Nations projections, by 2025, Africa will surpass China in population size. Consequently, governments and businesses worldwide are actively seeking to enhance their diplomatic, strategic, and trade relationships with African nations. This situation presents extensive opportunities, and if Africa manages this global interest astutely, the primary beneficiaries will be the Africans (The Economist, 2019).

In this third segment, I explore the dynamic domains of technology and popular music to underscore the ways in which Africa functions as a fertile terrain for fostering and showcasing its burgeoning talents. Africa has been undergoing a technological revolution that is primarily propelled by its younger generation. Tech-savvy individuals across the continent who are in the prime of their youth are harnessing the capabilities of technology to tackle a multitude of challenges and make valuable contributions to the growth of the economy. Moreover, African music, notably genres such as Afrobeat, Afro-hip-hop, Bongo Flava, etc., has garnered international acclaim and influence, primarily attributable to the inventive prowess and aptitude of young musicians.

Tech Talents

While the global tech talent pool faces shortages, Africa stands out with its enormous workforce. Statistical data indicate that the count of proficient African developers increased from 690,000 to 716,000 between 2020 and 2021, marking a growth of 3.8 percent (Månsson, 2022). Although the majority of these developers are of the male gender, African developers, on average, possess a comparative advantage in terms of youthfulness, being 7 years younger than their counterparts worldwide and additionally possessing up to 3 years of professional experience. Moreover, African developers demonstrate a remarkable level of proficiency in the domains of web and mobile programming, with one out of every two developers specializing in Android application development (Google & Accenture 2021).

At present, the continent of Africa accommodates more than 150 functioning Google Developer Groups and 100 Developer Student Clubs. These collaborative entities interact with a community of more than 200,000 members spread across 40 out of the 48 countries situated within Africa South of the Sahara (Gajria, 2022). The Google report further shows that in the year 2021, the monetary influx of African startups exceeded a staggering $4 billion, which is 2.5 times higher compared to those of the previous year 2020. Remarkably, more than 50 percent of this substantial funding was contributed by fintech startups. Additionally, the transition toward remote work has presented an array of employment opportunities for African developers, transcending geographical and temporal boundaries. Again, this paradigmatic shift has had a notable impact on the remuneration of experienced professionals, particularly in senior positions. Consequently, there has been a surge in the recruitment of African developers by multinational corporations, reaching unprecedented levels (Google & Accenture 2021).

With the projected working-age population of Africa estimated to reach 1.3 billion by 2050, and with the implementation of coding, programming, and robotics into the primary and secondary school curricula of countries like Kenya and South Africa (Dosunmu, 2022; Khumalo, 2022), the neglect of Africa as a key provider of tech-savvy individuals to the global community becomes increasingly difficult to justify. The recruitment of young African talent for remote work has the potential to unlock substantial revenue for international organizations while also fostering the potential and visibility of millions of African youth (Månsson, 2022).

Nigeria functions as a captivating exemplification of the mutually beneficial connection between digital transformation and the expansion of the developer community in Africa. The developer ecosystem in Nigeria is prospering due to substantial backing from major technology companies and startups, attaining the highest cumulative funding in the African continent in the year 2021 (Gajria, 2022). As countries like Nigeria undergo a transformation, they will open up additional avenues for developers, ultimately contributing to economic growth.

Diop (2022) asserts in the inaugural report on Foresight Africa by Brookings that the African continent is currently encountering a unique opportunity that arises only once in a generation. This opportunity has the potential to shape a more advanced, environmentally sustainable, and inclusive future for Africa. The attainment of this objective can be facilitated through the allocation of resources to infrastructure development, support for small enterprises, and the cultivation of human capital. These strategic investments are capable of mitigating the worldwide shortage of technological talent and yielding long-term advantages for future generations.

Music Talents

Once again, Africa stands out as a thriving epicenter for emerging musical talents. The continent has borne witness to the creativity of young African musicians who have propelled African music to attain global recognition, resulting in substantial revenues for the continent from its musical exports. Drawing inspiration from the musical genius Fela Anikulapo Kuti and his pioneering creation of the Afrobeat genre in the 1960s which ingeniously fused African traditional music with Ghanaian high life, funk, and jazz, often accompanied by intricate instrumentation (Stewart, 2013; Oikelome, 2013; Fisher & Idowu, 2023), young African artists, particularly in West Africa during the late 1990s and early 2000s, have further evolved this genre into Afrobeats. This musical landscape encompasses a rich variety of styles, encompassing popular and hip-hop music, often referred to as Afro-fusion or Afro-pop that emanates from this vibrant region (Osiebe, 2020).

In the twenty-first century, Africa has been a witness to the emergence of numerous music artists who have risen to become influential figures in the global music industry. Among these talented individuals is Damini Ebunoluwa Ogulu, widely known by his stage name, Burna Boy, hailing from Nigeria. At the 63rd Grammy Awards in 2021, Burna Boy was honored with the prestigious Best Global Music Album accolade for his remarkable album named "Twice as Tall" (Yglesias, 2021). This achievement further solidifies his significant accomplishments and impact on the international music scene, encompassing his exceptional performances, evocative lyrics, captivating videos, and unwavering determination. It is noteworthy that he recently achieved a significant milestone when one of his album releases debuted at the coveted No.1 position on the Official United Kingdom (UK) Albums chart, thereby establishing himself as the first African artist of international stature to attain such recognition (Anazia, 2023; Brandle, 2023).

Another example is the song "Jerusalema," composed by South African producer and DJ Master KG with vocalist Nomcebo Zikode, which was released in November of 2019 but premiered in December of 2019 as the COVID-2019 pandemic protocols were beginning to take hold across the world (Makura, 2020; Hissong, 2020). The song unexpectedly became a source of solace for the world during the pandemic, topping the digital music playlists in many countries across the world. It enjoyed collaboration in a remix with Nigerian artist Burna Boy and a dance routine performed by a group of Angolan youths whose candid video became a viral sensation. This led to the trending hashtag #jerusalemadancechallenge on social media, with people from various corners of the globe participating, including nuns and monks in France, Italian and German flash mobs, health workers in South Africa, a newly married couple in Zimbabwe, and countless others. On the official YouTube link, the song has amassed an impressive 579,478,122 views, 5,000,000 likes, and 150,179 comments (Master KG, 2019).

In recent years, particularly during and after the COVID-2019 pandemic, young African talents have leveraged digital technologies and the Internet to amplify the captivating sounds of African music on global platforms such as Apple Music, Audiomack, Boomplay, and Spotify (Johnson, 2021). This digitalization of African music has not only expanded the reach of African artists but also unlocked numerous opportunities for the continent's youth and its music industry. The streaming sector is poised for substantial growth, with an estimated 52.8 million users projected by 2025. While this may not lead to immediate revenue spikes, the World Bank Group in its report (2021) indicated that the music streaming and digital music landscape in Africa was anticipated to reach a market value of US$271 million in 2021. It is poised for significant expansion, with an estimated annual growth rate of 16.11%, culminating in a projected market volume of US$493 million by 2025.

Young African talents have been signing substantial deals with some of the biggest labels in the world. For instance, Def Jam Recordings, a multinational American record label owned by Universal Music Group, and famous for launching the careers of big popular artists like Jay Z, Kanye West, DMX, LL Cool J, Rihanna, Justin Bieber, among others, on May 26, 2020 launched a new division in Africa (South Africa and Nigeria) with Nasty C (South Africa), Vector (Nigeria), Tshego (South Africa), etc. (Yglesias, 2020). Similarly, Elaine, a South African young artist, who was the first independent female artist to climb the number one spot on Apple Music for Africa South of the Sahara, got signed on at Columbia Records/Sony Music, the same recording label with Beyoncé and Adele (Thema, 2021). Furthermore, the Universal Music Group, Sony Music, and Warner Music Group, in addition to signing up young African artists have entered the African music market to expand it, giving young talents an opportunity to grow their music. For instance, the Universal Music Group has licensed its music catalog to Boomplay, which is Africa's largest local streaming platform (World Bank Group, 2021).

Young talents have also made significant contributions through the establishment of music-related organizations and brands aimed at promoting their peers and indigenous music platforms to showcase African music. For instance, "Africulturban," a nonprofit organization founded in Dakar, Senegal by rapper Babacar Niang (Matador), is dedicated to supporting Senegalese urban culture and music development. They run the Hip Hop Akademy program, offering free training in music production and creative arts to young professionals. Additionally, companies like Africori, the largest digital music distribution firm in Africa, and Mkito, an online music distribution platform based in Tanzania, have played a crucial role in supporting young music artists and establishing employment opportunities for many youths (World Bank Group, 2021).

Conclusion and Recommendations

The common African paradox revolves around the perplexing situation where, despite the youth constituting a significant majority of the population in demographic terms, they often find themselves marginalized and inadequately represented within the continent's societal framework. This situation frequently leads to their characterization as vulnerable groups, criticized by governments for their perceived "disruptive" tendencies and viewed as potential threats to political stability. Consequently, they are sometimes unfairly labeled as destitute, uneducated, lacking in empowerment, and facing reproductive health challenges, including sexually transmitted diseases and HIV/AIDS. Nonetheless, this perspective fails to fully grasp the productive and transformative potential of the African youth, which has garnered global recognition, as demonstrated by this chapter.

Africa is not merely a continent defined by its Black population or plagued by corrupt leadership. It is a vast land brimming with opportunities, blessed with abundant natural resources, and elevated by its youthful demographics. These untapped young potentials stand poised to bring forth a wealth of economic, cultural, and social benefits, both for their local communities and the global stage. By harnessing the industrious and entrepreneurial spirit of its youth, Africa can effectively address the persistent issues of unemployment and poverty while preserving its rich cultural and traditional heritage. In doing so, it not only transforms its own future but also becomes a beacon of inspiration and progress for the world.

The youth in Africa are the present and future custodians of the continent. Democracy has become a powerful vehicle for their expression and engagement in governance, demonstrating their preference for a system that allows them the freedom to voice their opinions in stark contrast to the authoritarian rule that characterized much of Africa's history. While young democracies in Africa may still be in their "infancy," the globalized world and the exchange of culture and knowledge with developed nations are empowering the continent's youth. There is a growing sense of agency among African youths, fueled by a desire to reject old, repressive, and corrupt leadership in favor of democratic principles that give a voice to the majority—i.e. Africa's youthful population.

Africa's burgeoning population of young individuals should be viewed through an optimistic lens rather than with fear or uncertainty. Although the historical trajectory of Africa has been marred by warfare, conflict, impoverishment, and a plethora of other adversities that have frequently cast it as a troubled continent in need of external intervention, fresh narratives are swiftly emerging. A considerable number of the youth in Africa are resolute in their determination to surmount these obstacles and engender a positive impact, consequently reshaping the perception of Africa. The "warrior mindset" and indomitable spirit are deeply ingrained attributes within numerous Africans, and the younger generation is compellingly showcasing these qualities through their activism, demand for representation in the decision-making process, and their contributions across various domains, as expounded upon in prior discussions within this chapter.

Focusing on Africa as a hub for young talents introduces a fresh narrative on young Africans and their achievements particularly in the fields of technology and popular music as discussed in this chapter. Their recognition by esteemed organizations like Forbes and the Grammy Awards reinforces this point. Interestingly, despite the challenging environment that often hinders these youths from flourishing and developing their talents, they have managed to captivate the attention of the world. In the realm of young tech talents, it is worth noting that even though Africa grapples with the highest Internet service costs globally and deficient infrastructure, young Africans have successfully brought global tech giants into their homes. In the domain of popular music, the innovative work of young musicians in genres like Afrobeats and Amapiano showcases the creativity that Africa embodies. Moreover, it is not just renowned entertainment companies seeking to invest in African young talents; the digital music space has generated significant revenues and employment opportunities for both the youth and the continent.

As a recommendation, African leaders, foreign governments and partners, international and regional bodies should support African youths by investing in human capita development through innovation and training as well as providing an enabling environment for the development to take place. The governments in Africa especially must have the political will to rive this through.

Another recommendation is the promotion of a free and democratic African society in which African youths can exercise their fundamental human rights, including the right to engage in politics through constitutional means such as protests or petitions, or by electing young representatives without the fear of repression or victimization. This will empower the youth to play an active part in the consolidation of young democracies in the continent.

References

#OccupyJolorbiHouse [@occupyjolorbi]. (2023, September 27). *A statement on who we are and what we want to achieve... #OccupyJulorbiHouse [Tweet].* Retrieved on September 29, 2023 from https://x.com/occupyjulorbi/status/1706997856601559122?t=cFZHAxV-PZSBMuMrZ-wvSA&s=08

Africa Development Bank (AfDB). (2016). *Jobs for youths in Africa: Catalyzing youth opportunity across Africa*. Retrieved September 27, 2023, from www.afdb.org

Africa No Filter. (2020). *Literature review: African youth and the impact of narrative*. Retrieved September 28, 2023, from https://africanofilter.org/literature-review-on-african-youth-and-the-impact-of-narrative

African Union Commission and OECD. (2018). *Africa's development dynamics 2018*. Retrieved September 29, 2023, from https://doi.org/10.1787/3290877b-en

African Youth Charter. (2006). *African youth charter*. African Union Commission.

Agbiboa, D. E., & Maiangwa, B. (2012). Corruption in the underdevelopment of the Niger Delta in Nigeria. *The Journal of Pan African Studies, 5*(8), 108–132.

Alweendo, N., Andreas, R., & Rafla-Yuan, D. (2018). *Landscaping gender-based violence in Namibia*. Institute for Public Policy Research, Special Briefing Report, 25. Democracy Report 1.

Anazia, D. (2023, September 30). Burna Boy releases video for fan's favourite, City Boys. *The Guardian*. Retrieved September 30, 2023, from https://guardian.ng/saturday-magazine/weekend-beats/burna-boy-releases-video-for-fans-favourite-city-boys/

Appiah, G. K., Prempeh, K., Benn, S., & Oduro, E. (2020). Panel data analysis of employment and unemployment in sub-Saharan Africa and its impact on annual percentage change in GDP growth. *Open Science Journal, 5*(2), 1–26.

Barkan, J. D. (2002). The many faces of Africa. *Harvard International Review, 24*(2), 72–77.

Brandle, L. (2023, August 29). *Burna Boy bolting to U.K. no. 1 with 'i told them...'*. Billboard. Retrieved September 30, 2023, from https://www.billboard.com/music/chart-beat/burna-boy-uk-no-1-midweek-i-told-them-1235402481/

Campbell, J., & Quinn, N. (2021, May 26). *What's happening to democracy in Africa?* Council on Foreign Relations. Retrieved September 26, 2023, from https://www.cfr.org/article/whats-happening-democracy-africa

Cassani, A. (2020). Law-abiders, lame ducks, and over-stayers: The Africa Executive Term Limits (AETL) dataset. *European Political Science, 20*(3), 543–555.

Chabal, P., & Deloz, J. (1999). *Africa works: Disorder as political instrument*. Indiana University Press.

Cheeseman, N. (2019, July 23). Democracy in Africa: Success stories that have defied the odds. *The Conversation*. Retrieved September 25, 2023, from https://theconversation.com/democracy-in-africa-success-stories-that-have-defied-the-odds-120601

Cole, J. (2011). A cultural dialectics of generational change: The view from contemporary Africa. *Review of Research in Education, 35*, 60–88.

Commodore, R., & Frimpong, O. B. (2021). #EndSARS youth protests in Nigeria: Lessons and opportunities for regional stability. *The Southern Voices Network for Peace Building, Africa Program, Wilson Center, Special Paper Series, 1*, 1–8.

Diop, M. (2022). Africa's pandemic recovery requires investments that build the foundation for the region's future. *Brookings, Foresight Africa, 1*, 8–23.

Donkor, A. (2021, October 19). *Africa's youth unemployment crisis is a global problem*. Foreign Policy. Retrieved September 29, 2023, from https://foreignpolicy.com/2021/10/19/africa-youth-unemployment-crisis-global-problem/

Dosunmu, D. (2022, August 2). *Kenya becomes the first African country to teach coding as subject in schools*. TechCabal. Retrieved September 29, 2023, from https://techcabal.com/2022/08/08/kenya-becomes-the-first-african-country-to-teach-coding-as-subject-in-schools/

Durham, D. (2000). Youth and the social imagination in Africa: Introduction to parts 1 and 2. *Anthropological Quarterly, 73*(3), 113–120.
Durham, D. (2007). Empowering youth: Making youth citizens in Botswana. In J. Cole & D. Durham (Eds.), *Generations and globalization: Youth, age, and family in the new world economy*. Indiana University Press.
Duzor, M., & Williamson, B. (2023, October 3). By the numbers: Coups in Africa. *VOA News*. Retrieved December 5, 2023, from https://projects.voanews.com/african-coups/
Economist Intelligence Unit. (2022). *Democracy Index 2022*. Retrieved September 28, 2023, from https://www.eiu.com/n/campaigns/democracy-index-2022/
El Habti, H. (2022, September 19). *Why Africa's youth hold the key to its development potential*. World Economic Forum. Retrieved September 27, 2023, from https://www.weforum.org/agenda/2022/09/why-africa-youth-key-development-potential/
Fisher, A., & Idowu, S. A. (2023). Music as a tool of political activism in Nigeria: A case study of Fela Anikulapo Kuti. *Eduvest: Journal of Universal Studies, 3*(3), 535–543.
Forbes Africa. (2023, April 19*). Forbes Africa 30 under 30 class of 2023: Tomorrow's titans*. Retrieved September 29, from https://www.forbesafrica.com/under-30/2023/04/19/forbes-africa-30-under-30-class-of-2023-tomorrows-titans/
Fortes, M. (1984). Age, generation and social structure. In D. I. Kertzer & J. Keith (Eds.), *Age and anthropological theory* (pp. 99–122). Cornell University Press.
Gajria, N. (2022, February 21). *African developers: Creating opportunities and building for the future*. Google Blog Post. Retrieved September 28, 2023, from https://blog.google/around-the-globe/google-africa/african-developers-creating-opportunities-and-building-future/
Gleeman, D. (2019, March 28). *The oldest continuous democracy in Africa is reported to be on a negative governance trajectory*. Democratic Erosion. Retrieved September 26, 2023, from https://www.democratic-erosion.com/2019/03/28/the-oldest-continuous-democracy-in-africa-is-reported-to-be-on-a-negative-governance-trajectory-by-dylan-gleeman/
Google & Accenture. (2021). Africa Developer Ecosystem Report 2021. Retrieved from https://www.22onsloane.co/wp-content/uploads/2022/04/Africa_Developer_Ecosystem_Report_2021.pdf
Gyimah-Boadi, E., & Asunka, J. (2021, November 2). *Do Africans want democracy—And do they think they're getting it?* Afrobarometer. Retrieved September 25, 2023, from https://www.afrobarometer.org/articles/do-africans-want-democracy-and-do-they-think-theyre-getting-it/
Hissong, S. (2020, October 16). How South Africa's 'Jerusalema' became a global hit without ever having to be translated. *Rolling Stone*. Retrieved September 30, 2023, from https://www.rollingstone.com/pro/news/jerusalema-global-dance-hit-south-africa-spotify-1076474/
Huntington, S. P. (1991). Democracy's third wave. *Journal of Democracy, 2*(2), 12–34.
Inter-Parliamentary Union. (2023). *Data on age: Global and regional averages*. Retrieved April 7, 2023, from https://data.ipu.org/age-brackets-aggregate/
Jega, A. M. (2017). Youth and the future of Nigeria. In *5th convocation lecture*. Nile University, University Village.
Johnson, J. (2021, December 29). African music industry: An outlook of trends in 2022. *The Guardian*. Retrieved September 30, 2023, from https://guardian.ng/art/c74-arts/african-music-industry-an-outlook-of-trends-in-2022/
Kara, S. (2018, October 12). Is your phone tainted by the misery of the 35,000 children in Congo's mines? *The Guardian*. Retrieved September 28, 2023, from https://www.theguardian.com/global-development/2018/oct/12/phone-misery-children-congo-cobalt-mines-drc
Kariba, F. (2020, July 30). The burgeoning Africa youth population: Potential or challenge? *Cities Alliance*. Retrieved September 24, 2023, from https://www.citiesalliance.org/newsroom/news/cities-alliance-news/%C2%A0burgeoning-africa-youth-population-potential-or-challenge%C2%A0
Kasambala, T. (2022, September 1). *How African democracies can rise and thrive amid instability, militarization, and interference*. Freedom House. Retrieved September 25, 2023, from https://freedomhouse.org/article/how-african-democracies-can-rise-and-thrive-amid-instability

Kaufmann, B. (2023, March 28). *Botswana: Africa's longest uninterrupted democracy goes global.* Swissinfo.ch. Retrieved September 25, 2023, from https://www.swissinfo.ch/eng/politics/botswana%2D%2Dafrica-s-longest-uninterrupted-democracy-goes-global/48395820

Kayizzi-Mugerwa, S. (2019). Youth in Africa: Between marginalisation and demographic dividend. *Southern African Journal of Policy and Development, 4*(2), 15–25.

Kazeem, Y. (2020a, October 26). *How bitcoin powered the largest Nigerian protests in a generation.* Quartz Africa. Retrieved April 12, 2021, from https://qz.com/africa/1922466/how-bitcoin-powered-nigerias-endsars-protests/

Kazeem, Y. (2020b, October 13). *How a youth-led digital movement is driving Nigeria's largest protests in a decade.* Quartz Africa. Retrieved April 12, 2021, from https://qz.com/africa/1916319/how-nigerians-use-social-media-to-organize-endsars-protests/

Khumalo, A. (2022, April 10). *Coding and robotics become school subjects in 2023: These are the careers they open.* News 24. Retrieved September 29, 2023, from https://www.news24.com/news24/bi-archive/coding-robotics-are-subjects-coming-to-schools-in-2023-here-are-the-careers-you-can-go-into-2022-3

Lancaster, C. (1991). Democracy in Africa. *Foreign Policy, 85*, 148–165.

Makura, M. (2020). The 'Jerusalema' phenomenon shows Africa's trendsetting abilities. *Okayafrica.* Retrieved September 30, 2023, from https://www.okayafrica.com/master-kg-jerusalema-africa-trendsetting-potential/

Månsson, C. V. (2022, November 8). *Africa's youths can help solve the global tech talent shortage.* Brookings. Retrieved September 28, 2023, from https://www.brookings.edu/articles/africas-youths-can-help-solve-the-global-tech-talent-shortage/

Master KG. (2019, December 12). *Master KG: Jerusalema [Feat. Nomcebo] (Official Music Video).* YouTube. Retrieved September 30, 2023, from https://www.youtube.com/watch?v=fCZVL_8D048

Melber, H. (2020, October 29). *#ShutItAllDown in Namibia—The fight against gender-based violence.* The Conversation. Retrieved September 28, 2023, from https://theconversation.com/shutitalldown-in-namibia-the-fight-against-gender-based-violence-148809

Mozaffar, S. (2004). Africa: Electoral systems in emerging democracies. In *The handbook of electoral system choice.* Palgrave Macmillan.

Mulikita, J. J. (2022, August). *Young people's potential, the key to Africa's sustainable development.* United Nations. Retrieved September 27, 2023, from https://www.un.org/ohrlls/news/young-people%E2%80%99s-potential-key-africa%E2%80%99s-sustainable-development

Mutabazi, G. (2023, April 12). *Congo is bleeding: The forgotten unrests in the heart of Africa.* TANTV. Retrieved September 28, 2023, from https://www.tantvstudios.com/congo-is-bleeding-the-forgotten-unrests-in-the-heart-of-africa/

Mwai, P. (2023, August 30). *Gabon coup: The latest in a series of military takeovers on the continent.* BBC News. Retrieved September 26, 2023, from https://www.bbc.com/news/world-africa-46783600

Oikelome, A. (2013). Performance practice in Afrobeat music of Fela Anikulapo Kuti. *Journal of Arts and Humanities, 2*(7), 82–94.

Ojo, E. O. (2016). Underdevelopment in Africa: Theories and facts. *The Journal of Social, Political and Economic Studies, 41*(1), 89–103.

Okunade, S. K., & Awosusi, O. E. (2023). The Japa syndrome and the migration of Nigerians to the United Kingdom: An empirical analysis. *Comparative Migration Studies, 11*(27), 1–18.

Olewe, D. (2021, August 24). *Hakainde Hichilema: Zambia's new president inspires African opposition leaders.* BBC News. Retrieved September 26, 2023, from https://www.bbc.com/news/world-africa-58270973

Oluwole, V. (2023, May 25). *Top 10 African nations leading in democracy index rankings.* Business Insider Africa. Retrieved September 25, 2023, from https://africa.businessinsider.com/local/lifestyle/top-10-african-nations-leading-in-democracy-index-rankings/y0p62pd

Osiebe, G. (2020). Methods in performing Fela in contemporary Afrobeats, 2009–2019. *African Studies, 79*(1), 88–109.

Ossenbrink, L. (2020, October 13). *Why are anti-femicide protesters taking to Namibia's streets?* Al Jazeera. Retrieved September 28, 2023, from https://www.aljazeera.com/news/2020/10/13/why-are-anti-femicide-protesters-demonstrating-in-namibia
Peatrik, A. (2020). Towards an anthropology of youth in Africa. *Ateliers d'anthropologie, Revue éditée par le Laboratoire d'ethnologie et de sociologie comparative, 47*, 1–23.
Ritchie, G. (2017). "Youth" as theory, method, and praxis. In S. Carpenter & S. Mojab (Eds.), *Youth as/in crisis* (pp. 13–26). Sense Publishers.
Schraeder, P. J. (1995). Understanding the 'third wave' of democratization in Africa. *The Journal of Politics, 57*(4), 1160–1168.
Sommers, M. (2015). *The outcast majority: War, development, and youth in Africa*. University of Georgia Press.
Stewart, A. (2013). Make it funky: Fela Kuti, James Brown and the invention of Afrobeat. *American Studies, 52*(4), 99–118.
Taiwo, O. (2023, September 20). *Obasanjo blames bad governance for military coups in Africa*. The Punch. Retrieved September 26, 2023, from https://punchng.com/obasanjo-blames-bad-governance-for-military-coups-in-africa/
The Economist. (2019, March 7). *The new scramble for Africa*. Retrieved September 29, 2023, from https://www.economist.com/leaders/2019/03/07/the-new-scramble-for-africa
Thema, L. (2021, June 16). *The is why international labels are rushing to sig African artists*. Medium. Retrieved September 30, 2023, from https://themalesetja.medium.com/the-is-why-international-labels-are-rushing-to-sign-african-artists-917d9f54cf61
van Dijk, R., de Bruijn, M., Cardoso, C., & Butter, I. (2011). Introduction: Ideologies of youth. *Africa Development, 36*(3–4), 1–17.
Vigh, H. (2008). Crisis and chronicity: Anthropological perspectives on continuous conflict and decline. *Ethnos, 73*(1), 5–24.
Wahlqvist, F., Bryngelsson, I. L., Westberg, H., Vihlborg, P., & Andersson, L. (2020). Dermal and inhalable cobalt exposure—Uptake of cobalt for workers at Swedish hard metal plants. *PLoS One, 15*(8), 1–14.
Wells, R. (2021, May 24). *Africa's hashtag activism—2020*. Pan African. Retrieved September 30, 2023, from https://pan-african.net/africas-hashtag-activism-2020/
World Bank Group. (2021). Unlocking opportunities for youth in the orange economy: Music in Africa. *Solutions for Youth Employment, Knowledge Brief Series, 15*, 1–18.
Yglesias, A. N. (2020, May 27). *Def Jam Africa launches with Nadia Nakai, Cassper Nyovest, Nasty C & more African Artists*. Grammys. Retrieved September 30, 2023, from https://www.grammy.com/news/def-jam-africa-launches-nadia-nakai-cassper-nyovest-nasty-c-more-african-artists
Yglesias, A. N. (2021, March 15). *Burna Boy wins best global music album for 'twice as tall' 2021 GRAMMY awards show*. Grammys. Retrieved September 30, 2023, from https://www.grammy.com/news/burna-boy-wins-best-global-music-album-twice-tall-2021-grammy-awards-show

Jeremiah Oluwadara Omotayo is presently pursuing a doctorate in Political Science at the University of Ibadan in Nigeria. In addition, he serves as a Research Fellow II in the Political and Governance Policy Department at the Nigerian Institute of Social and Economic Research. Omotayo has made significant contributions to the field through his work in book chapters, academic papers, and monographs, particularly focusing on areas such as youth politics, federalism, security, legislative studies, and peace and conflict. Furthermore, he has taken on key roles as a principal investigator in various political and social research studies conducted across Nigeria.

Index

A. K. Bangura, J. A. Ifedi (eds.), *Conceptualizations of Africa*, African Studies and Research Forum Series, https://doi.org/10.1007/978-3-031-74535-5

The manufacturer's authorised representative in the EU is Springer Nature Customer Service Centre GmbH, Europaplatz 3, 69115 Heidelberg, Germany. If you have any concerns regarding our products, please contact ProductSafety@springernature.com

Printed and bound by CPI Group (UK) Ltd, Croydon, CR0 4YY

30/09/2026

02225596-0013